BILL WYMAN'S
BLUES ODYSSEY

WRITTEN BY
BILL WYMAN
WITH RICHARD HAVERS

A DORLING KINDERSLEY BOOK

LONDON, NEW YORK, MELBOURNE, MUNICH, DELHI

For Brian, the only cat who got it,
and Stu, who loved them.

Design & Art Direction
Richard Evans

Design
Soo Abram, Thomas Keenes, Debbie Orme

Editors
Peter Doggett, Jake Woodward

Senior Managing Editor
Anna Kruger

Senior Managing Art Editor
Lee Griffiths

Map Artworks
Andrew O'Brien

Picture Research
Emily Hedges

DTP Design
Louise Waller

Production Controller
Heather Hughes

Index
Mike Evans

First published in Great Britain in 2001
by Dorling Kindersley Limited
80 Strand, London WC2R 0RL
A Penguin Company

4 6 8 10 9 7 5 3

A CIP catalogue record for this book is available from the British Library

ISBN 0 7513 3442 1

Colour reproduction by GRB Editrice Slr. Italy
Printed and bound by A. Mondadori Editore, Verona

See our complete catalogue at

www.dk.com

Contents

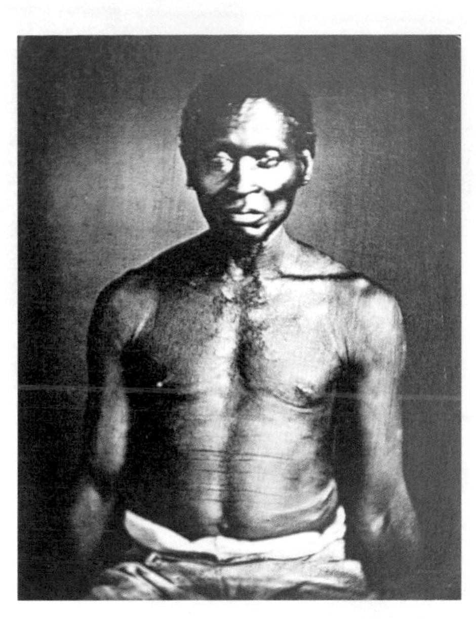

FOREWORD

I WAS BORN IN SOUTH-EAST LONDON just prior to the outbreak of World War II. Although my father worked, we were far from well off; life was a struggle. Years later I found that many black musicians grew up in the Southern States of the USA in difficult circumstances, something of a shared experience. However, I did not share the awfulness of segregation and the problems of being treated as a second-class citizen. When I was eleven years old I experienced one small instance of being on the 'outside'. I did well in my exams and was sent to a school where my cockney accent and my background made me different… I didn't like it.

I discovered music during my teenage years and after I joined the Royal Air Force, I found that I loved music that had its roots in the sound of black people from the Southern States of America. The way I learnt their music seemed to echo the way their forebears had taught them: it was about tradition, a tradition passed on by word of mouth. I learned so much from the Blues, and have come to realise that there is much more to the Blues than people think.

Listening to this wonderful music has been such a rich and rewarding experience for me and along the way I came to recognise the importance of the Blues in the development of 20th century music. Being fortunate enough to have been a member of The Rolling Stones placed me in the position of being involved in a musical family tree with some of the greatest musicians of the last 50 years. Listening to the Blues has taught me so much about history, social issues and even life itself. I wanted the opportunity to tell people more about why I love this music and to share with them its heritage. My *Blues Odyssey* is an opportunity for me to acknowledge my debt to the blues men and women who have not only helped me to understand the music's wonderfully rich tapestry, but who have also given me endless hours of musical pleasure.

In their song from 1929, Tarter and Gay sang "That the Blues that keep you worried are the Blues you can't explain" ; and yet I have done my best to explain what the Blues are all about. I hope that you will find this odyssey to the heart and soul of the Blues as fascinating as I have.

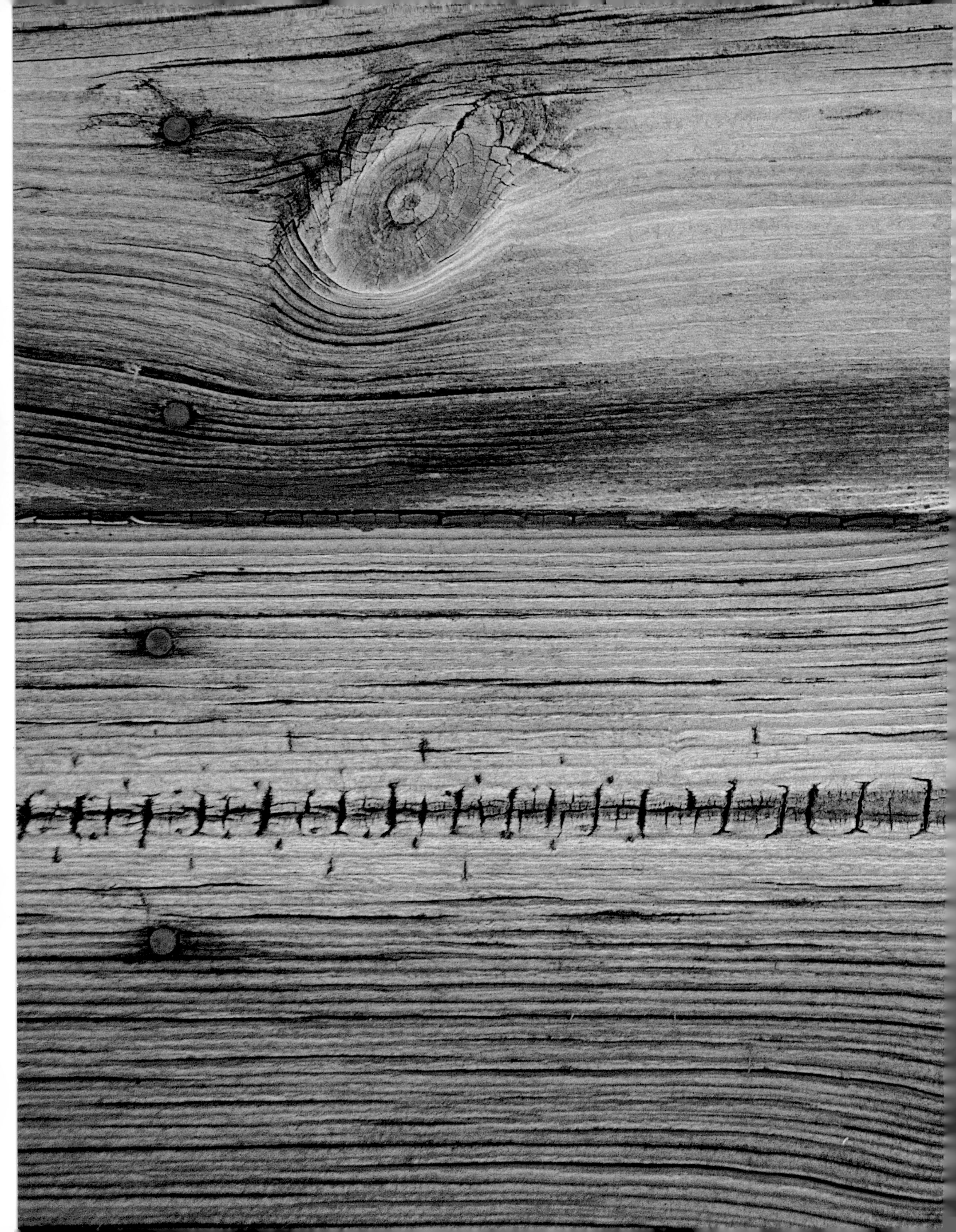

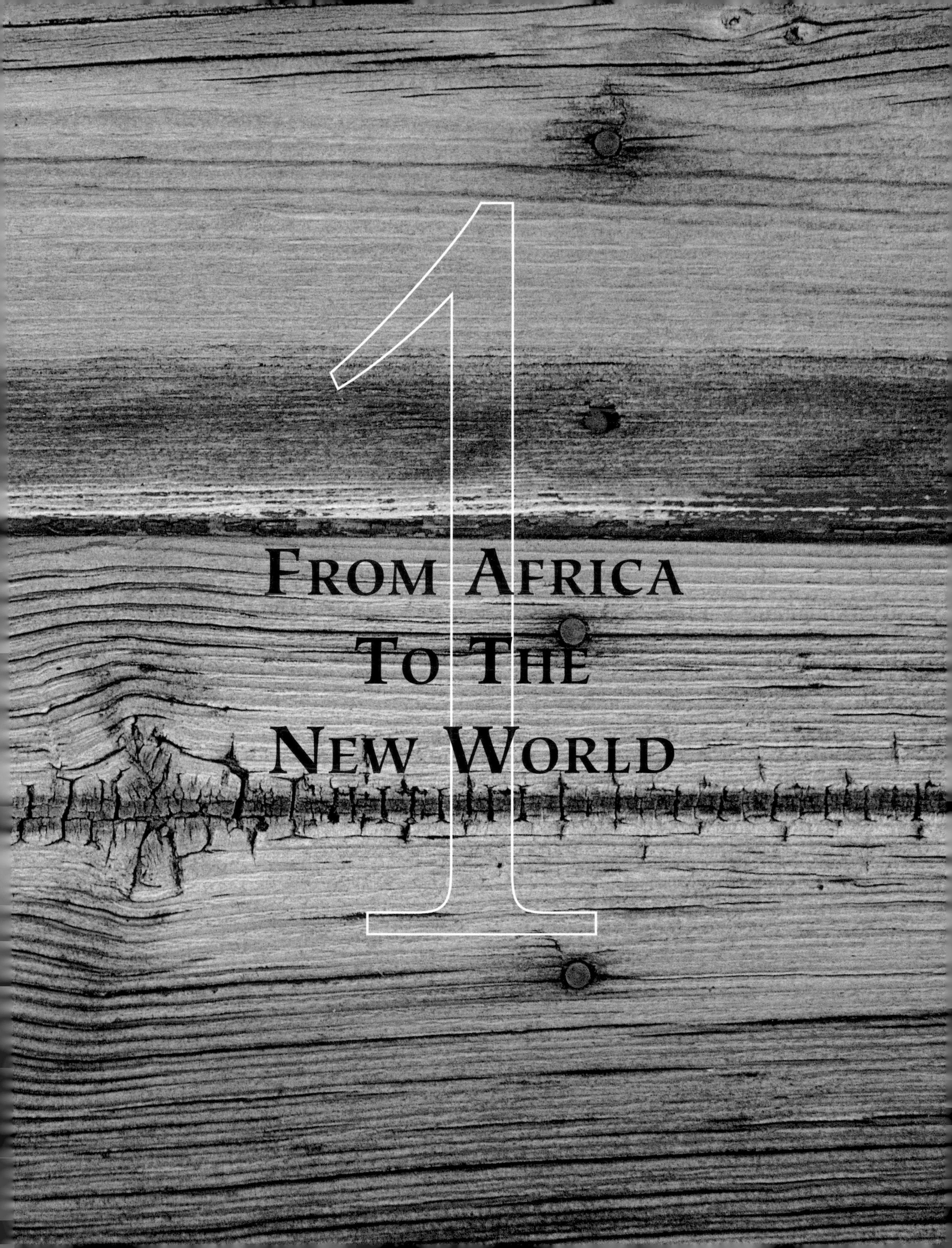

1 From Africa To The New World

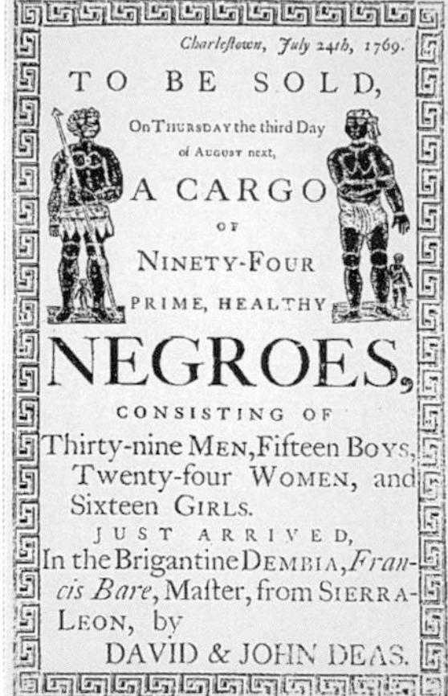
Charlestown, July 24th, 1769.
TO BE SOLD,
On THURSDAY the third Day of AUGUST next,
A CARGO
OF
NINETY-FOUR
PRIME, HEALTHY
NEGROES,
CONSISTING OF
Thirty-nine MEN, Fifteen BOYS,
Twenty-four WOMEN, and
Sixteen GIRLS.
JUST ARRIVED,
In the Brigantine DEMBIA, *Francis Bare*, Master, from SIERRA-LEON, by
DAVID & JOHN DEAS.

SLAVE SALE NOTICE
Published in Charleston, South Carolina, 24th July, 1769. In that same year, Thomas Jefferson began his campaign to outlaw slavery in the state of Virginia.

THE SLAVE TRADE

THE STORY OF THE BLUES begins not with musicians or singers, but with one of the most tragic and far-reaching events in the history of civilization. If any one person can claim to be the Father of the Blues, then it is probably a 17th-century Dutch sea captain. He took part in a brutal sale of human lives, and set in motion the harrowing chain of conflict, struggle and hardship that was to bring the Blues into our lives.

In 1619, *"About the last of August, Came a Dutch man-of-warre that sold us twenty Negars".* This is how Captain John Smith, in his *Generall Historie of Virginia*, described the arrival of the first black Africans to be captured and sent to the English colonies on the east coast of what is now the United States of America. There were three women among this group of 20 who were sold into 'indentured servitude'. This was the forerunner of what was to become full-blown slavery in the colonies.

Given America's position as the single most powerful developed nation in the world, it is little wonder that the slave trade – which took hundreds of thousands of men and women from their homes in Africa to a new life in the New World – is still such an emotive issue, as it has been for the last 200 years.

The 20 Africans who arrived in Virginia in 1619 were far from being the world's first slaves. Ever since man first walked the earth, members of tribes or family groups have captured their enemies in raids and in battles. The 'owners' have then used their new 'possessions' to perform tasks that they regard as unpleasant or beneath them. While almost every 'civilisation' has held slaves, the word (which has its roots in Slav) only entered the language around the 9th century, when the Vikings took slaves from the so-called barbarian kingdoms of Europe, and sold them to rich eastern Mediterranean Muslims.

THE CONCEPT OF SLAVERY

In modern times, the concept of slavery has become synonymous with the transportation of black Africans to America. Between 1619

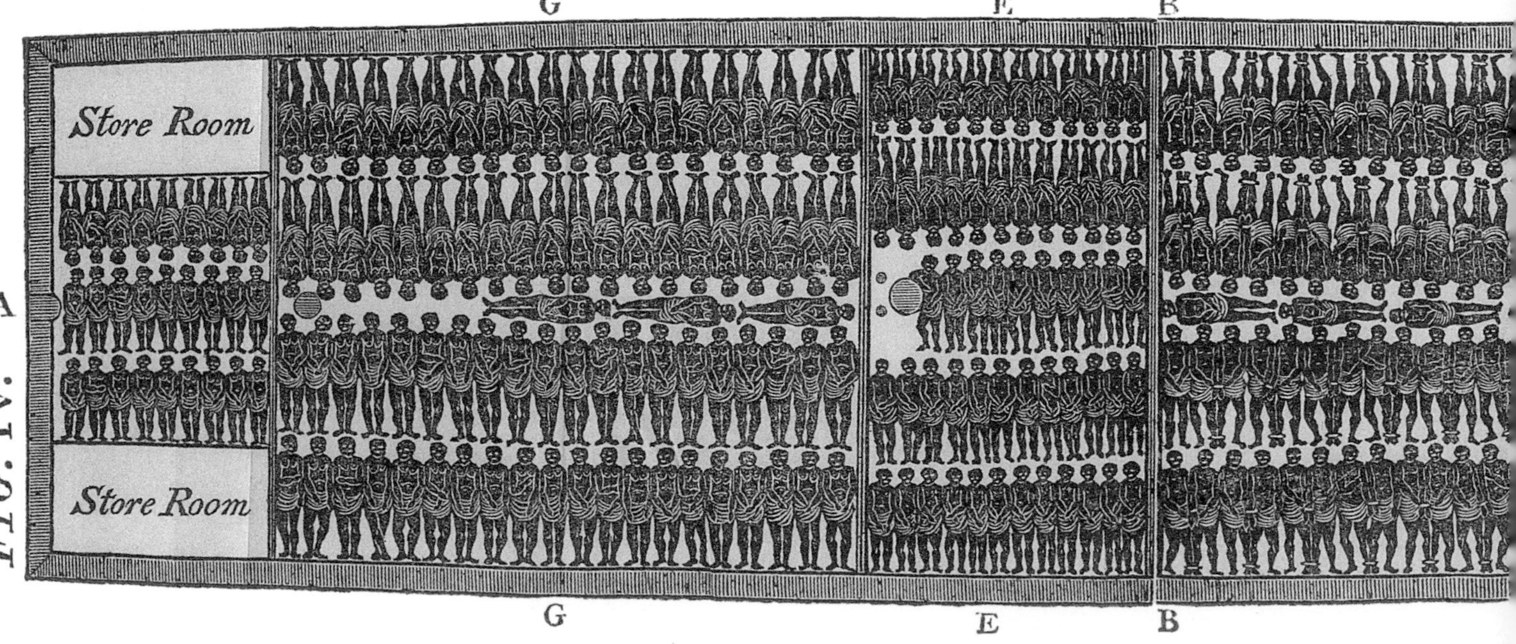

THE STOWAGE OF SLAVES ON THE BROOKES SLAVER OF LIVERPOOL
As reported by Captain Parrey as evidence for the Petitioners for the Abolition of the Slave Trade, 1791.

and 1670, around 5,000 slaves arrived in the colonies. Over the next 25 years, there was a four-fold increase in the slave trade, to the extent that by 1700 there were around 28,000 slaves on the North American mainland. Initially, they arrived in small groups known as 'parcels', but demand was so strong that soon entire shiploads of people were being transported.

The conditions under which the slaves were transported were foul and horrific. We cannot imagine what it must have been like to have made that voyage; neither can we imagine their fear. None of us today really makes a journey into the unknown. We have already seen or been told about everywhere we can envisage visiting, even space. These slaves bound for the colonies had no conept of what awaited them.

Kingdoms and Empires

The Africans came from the countries we now know as Cameroon, Dahomey, Democratic Republic of Congo, Gabon, Gambia, Ghana, Guinea, Ivory Coast, Liberia, Nigeria, Senegal, Sierra Leone and Togo. In the 17th century, this area was made up of a number of kingdoms and empires, such as Kanem-Bornu, Ghana, Hausa, Ashanti, Benin, Oyo and Mali. The first slave traders who visited the 'Slave Coast' found that they were dealing with sophisticated and well organised political organisations.

Then, as now, the most important aspect of African life was the tribal grouping. The colonists largely manufactured political divisions in Africa; lines were drawn on a map to divide a parcel of land into a country. These artificial divisions could be changed as easily as they were created, but it was their descent from common ancestors which divided the people of West Africa into their tribes, such as the Ibo, the Fulani, the Fanti, the Mandingo, the Ashanti and the Jolof.

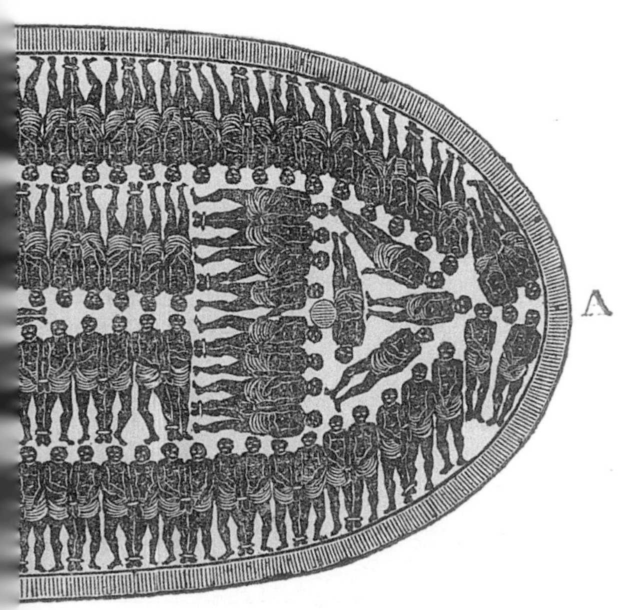

Ill Treatment

In 1630 the State of Massachusetts introduced a law that protected African slaves who fled from their owners because of ill treatment. Ten years later a black man and six white servants who had conspired to escape received their sentences. The whites received extra years of servitude, while the black man was whipped, branded with an 'R' and forced to wear shackles for a year. In 1652, Rhode Island became the first state to pass a law against slavery, limiting it to 10 years. In the same year all blacks and Native Americans living with English settlers were required to undergo military training because of the threat of Indian attack. Just four years later, the same state barred blacks and Native Americans from military service because of the fear that they might instigate an uprising.

Throughout the 17th century there were numerous acts of barbarism against slaves. But at the same time there were signs that some people felt a need to curb the worst excesses of the trade. In 1686, under English law, any master who wilfully killed his servant or slave would be sentenced to death. In 1695, the

A fugitive slave girl

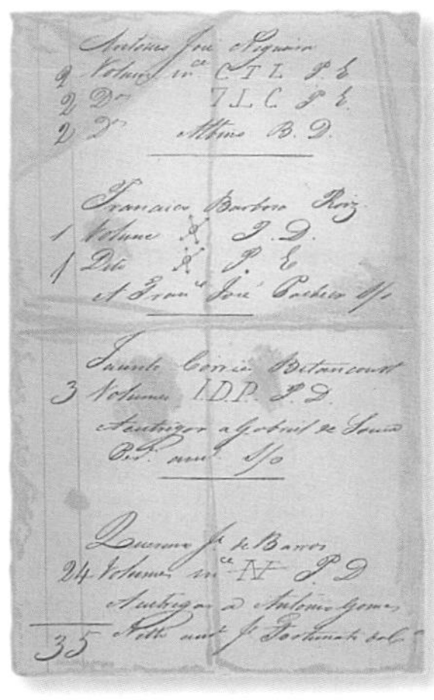

A Bill of Lading

An export document for slaves from Loanda, Cameroon, West Africa.

Racial Identity

In the early years of the American slave trade, there were immediate signs of how difficult it would prove for the colonies to cope with their mixed racial and cultural identity. In 1630, a Virginian named Hugh Davis was sentenced to be whipped, "Before an assembly of negroes and others for abusing himself to the dishonour of God and shame of Christians by defiling his body in lying with a negro".

THOMAS JEFFERSON
In 1806 the US President urged the United States Congress to ban the slave trade following a 20-year restriction clause in the United States constitution of 1787.

FASSENA
A slave who worked as a carpenter on the BF Taylor plantation, South Carolina in the 1840s. This daguerreotype (right) was made in Columbia, South Carolina in 1850.

first school for slave children was started in Goose Creek, Charleston, South Carolina. Then in 1698 the slave trade was opened to any ship carrying the British flag. The tidal wave of slavery was set to begin.

At the beginning of the 18th century, there were many more slaves in the Southern states than in the North – of the 28,000 slaves in the colonies, 23,000 were in the South. By 1708, blacks actually outnumbered whites in the Carolinas. In 1712, Pennsylvania became the first state to pass legislation prohibiting the slave trade. Nine years later, Carolina invoked a statute that limited voting rights to 'free white Christian men' only; the differences between North and South were already becoming apparent. In 1729 this situation crystallized still further when North and South Carolina split into separate states. North Carolina became the Southern state most strongly opposed to slavery.

By 1750, there were around 236,000 slaves in the colonies, of whom 206,000 lived south of Pennsylvania. Over the next 10 years the total number increased to 326,000. Attitudes towards slavery continued to shift, and no state illustrated the changes better than Georgia. In 1735 the state passed a law banning the importation of slaves and prohibiting their use within the colony. In 1750, the law was repealed and slavery was once again recognized. Then five years later Georgia decided to allow an increase in the number of slaves permitted on a plantation, and reduce the penalty for murdering a slave.

Economics was the major factor in these changes, as slavery increased in pace after 1760. In 1765 the price of a 'field slave' was around $200, at a time when there were 90,000 blacks in South Carolina and fewer than half that number of whites.

THE AMERICAN WAR OF INDEPENDENCE

The American War of Independence of 1775 marked a sea-change in the fate of African slaves in North America, not least for the estimated 100,000 who ran away from their masters during the war. South Carolina was reported as being able to provide very little in the way of military manpower, as all the state's soldiers were required at home 'to quell slave rebellions'. When the war came to an end in 1783, several thousand blacks emigrated to Great Britain, while others went north to Canada, and some even preferred to risk a hazardous, if free, life in the humid swamps of Florida rather than continue living in slavery.

It is estimated that by 1800, there were around one million blacks (20% of the population) in North America, most of them slaves. It was just 13 years since the structure set up by the constitution of the United States had been created in Philadelphia, and adopted by the 13 states which had broken away from the British Empire.

The constitution imposed some political unity on the original 13 states: New Hampshire, Massachusetts, Rhode Island, Connecticut, New York, New Jersey, Pennsylvania, Delaware, Maryland, Virginia, North Carolina, South Carolina, and Georgia, but also allowed for new states to be absorbed into the United States. The constitution also provided for some degree of autonomy for individual states – at times, a state's economic or social interests would come into conflict with the supremacy of the Union. In the early 19th century there were periods when this dissent was strong enough for some states to talk of disunion.

> *We hold these Truths to be self-evident, that all Men are created equal, that they are endowed by their Creator with certain unalienable Rights, that among these are Life, Liberty, and the Pursuit of Happiness*

THE AMERICAN DECLARATION OF INDEPENDENCE

The Abolition Issue

In 1807, after heated debate, the British government abolished slavery. The United States Constitution signed in 1787 had included an agreement to a 20-year moratorium on the slave trade. In 1806, President Thomas Jefferson urged the United States Congress to ban the slave trade as soon as the restrictions expired. The principle of human equality had been eloquently set out in the Declaration of Independence.

It had been decided in 1787 to leave out of the Declaration a denunciation of the slave trade, written by Jefferson. As early as 1769, he had attempted to have a bill passed in the Virginia House of Burgesses to emancipate slaves. Five years later he described the abolition of slavery as a goal of the colonists and accused Great Britain of standing in the way of efforts to end the slave trade. The whole question of slavery became a millstone around the neck of the new government. Much of the country's economic lifeblood depended on slave labour, yet many people, particularly in the Northern states, still opposed the whole concept of slavery. The debate was side-stepped temporarily by the decision that three-fifths of slaves should be

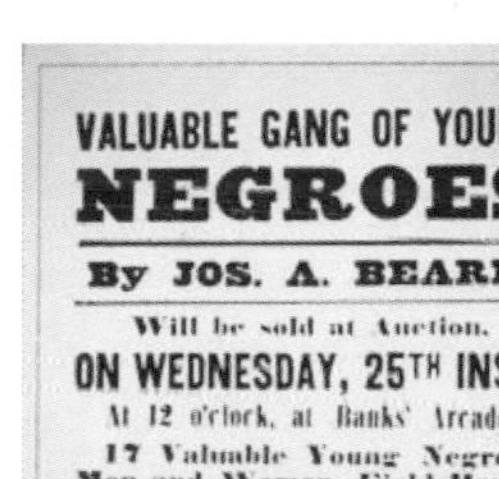

A Valuable Gang
A poster for a slave sale held in New Orleans in March, 1840. Slaves were sold in batches to work as field hands or as domestic staff.

Sold at Auction
A slave sale at Charleston, Virginia, in 1856.

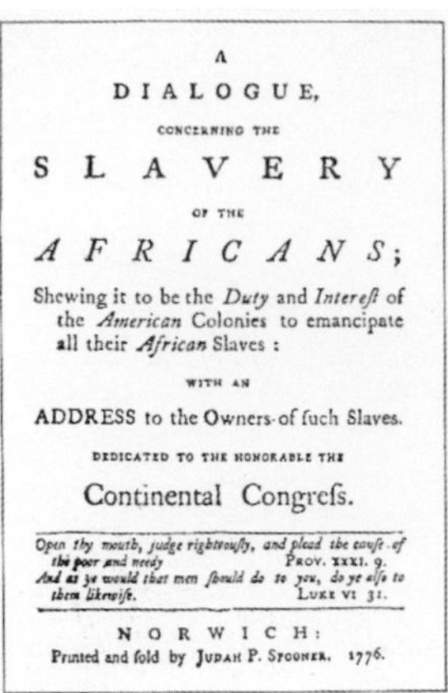

A

DIALOGUE,

CONCERNING THE

SLAVERY

OF THE

AFRICANS;

Shewing it to be the *Duty* and *Intereſt* of the *American* Colonies to emancipate all their *African* Slaves :

WITH AN

ADDRESS to the Owners of ſuch Slaves.

DEDICATED TO THE HONORABLE THE

Continental Congreſs.

Open thy mouth, judge righteouſly, and plead the cauſe of the poor and needy PROV. XXXI. 9.
And as ye would that men ſhould do to you, do ye alſo to them likewiſe. LUKE VI 31.

NORWICH:
Printed and ſold by JUDAH P. SPOONER. 1776.

ABOLITION OF SLAVERY

As early as the 1770s, there had been calls for the abolition of slavery, as the title page of this pamphlet from 1776 illustrates.

counted as people, but that they should also be counted as property for tax purposes. It was further decided that Congress could forbid the African slave trade, but not for another 20 years. On 1st January, 1808, the importation of slaves into the United States was banned by an Act of Congress. Despite this, illegal importation continued for many more years. In fact, anticipation of the ban only helped to increase the traffic in human cargo, and some 39,000 slaves were imported legally into the United States between 1801 and 1808.

By 1810 there were 1.38 million blacks in North America, a number that rose by a further one million over the next 20 years. This increase was, in part, fuelled by the rapid expansion of commerce and agriculture; but it was only made possible by a total failure to uphold the 1808 law. The act abolished the import of slaves, but definitely did not abolish slavery. Children born to slaves were themselves deemed to be slaves, which increased the supply of slave labour. But not all blacks were slaves. The emancipation laws introduced by most of the Northern states meant that there were around 300,000 'free' blacks in North America by 1808.

THE ANVIL OF SLAVERY

Cotton became the anvil of slavery, aided by the invention of the cotton gin (see picture below) in 1793. This invention allowed the widespread growing of cotton across the Southern states, and created a massive need for labour. The demand for cotton from Europe was huge and the potential profits enormous. Cotton became the dominant American export and pricipal source of foreign exchange.

Cotton was not the only trade to benefit from slave labour. In Virginia, which had more slaves than any other state, the principal crop was tobacco. These shifts in demand for labour created a new business: the sale and export of slaves from one state to another. The purchasers were often the frontier territories that had not been accepted as fully-fledged states within the developing

ELI WHITNEY'S COTTON GIN

Invented in 1793, Eli Whitney's cotton gin revolutionized the cotton trade. The gin enabled cotton fibre to be separated from the seeds mechanically.

United States. Often male slaves were sold, but their wives and children left behind.

The economics of this situation helped to drive the politics. New Southern states were admitted to the Union, bolstering the nation's economic and political power. The first state to be admitted was Louisiana, which had been sold to the United States by France in 1803. It was followed by Mississippi in 1817, Alabama in 1819, Missouri in 1821, Arkansas in 1836, Florida in 1845 and Texas in 1845.

THE ANTI-SLAVERY DEBATE

The addition of Southern, slave-owning states to the Union created a potential problem. The 'free' states of the North could see that they might be politically outmanoeuvred. There was an inevitable compromise: in 1821, it was agreed that no further slave states would be allowed into the Union from any area north of Missouri's southern border.

The abolition of the slave trade sharpened the whole anti-slavery debate. The concept of creating colonies of freed slaves. was mooted. Many thought this ridiculous, despite the fact that most whites could not envisage living in an entirely free multi-racial society. In 1827 slavery was abolished in New York State and over 10,000 blacks were freed.

Some newspapers led the way in demanding change. *Freedom's Journal*, the first African-American newspaper in 1827, and *The Liberator*, founded in Boston in 1831, became the leading campaigners for abolition. The latter was supported by contributions from black people, and supported efforts, at both national and state level, for radical change. Meanwhile in the South, opinion was still strongly pro-slavery. In 1829 the Governor of South Carolina, Stephen Miller, said: "Slavery is not a national evil; on the contrary it is a national benefit".

A TIDE OF FEAR

In 1830, there was a rising tide of fear across the white community, brought about by slave insurrections. The major casualties of this situation were children, as there was a cessation of educational opportunities for blacks that lasted until after the Civil War. Throughout the Northern states, the debate intensified. In 1838 the Pennsylvania Hall in Philadelphia was destroyed by a pro-slavery mob after an abolitionists' meeting. The police offered no resistance as rioters lit fires and destroyed sections of the city. In Boston free blacks opposed segregation on trains and steamboats. It was a period of radical change, when tempers ran high, although violent protest was the exception not the rule. The black clergy was the principal force behind the call for abolition, founding the American Anti-Slavery Society. By 1840, with 2.9 million blacks in the United States, some of the more dissident clergy broke away from the AASS to form the American and Foreign Anti-Slavery Society, which sought to apply political pressure for abolition.

The absurdity of segregation was demonstrated in 1841 when South Carolina legislature prohibited black and white mill-workers from looking out of the same window. In Georgia, meanwhile, blacks and whites were required to swear on different Bibles in the same courtroom.

While the illegal import of slaves had started to slow down, slaves were no less important to the nation's economic future. By 1850 there were 3.6 million blacks in North America, the vast majority of them slaves (16% of the population). By 1860 the number was 4.4 million. It has been estimated that from the start of the ban on importing slaves in 1808, around 250,000 were illegally imported into the United States.

SWEAT AND TOIL

Two scenes of slave life in the Southern cotton fields, in the 1860s. The invention of the cotton gin benefited the traders, but merely increased the demand for entire families of slaves, young and old, to work the fields.

VÉRITABLE EXTRAIT DE VIANDE LIEBIG.
La culture du coton-3
Récolte dans l'Amérique du Nord.
Voir l'explication au verso.

FROM AFRICA TO THE NEW WORLD

THE FIRST SLAVES from West Africa were taken to Portugal. In 1619 the first slaves arrived in North America, a year before the Pilgrim Fathers landed at Plymouth, Massachusetts. By 1700 slavery was an accepted fact amongst the thirteen colonies. It is estimated that around nine million Africans were taken from Africa to North America, the West Indies, and South America (notably Brazil).

For the slave ships, the journey began in Europe. From there they carried clothes, hardware and guns, which they traded for slaves in West Africa. Once the slaves were unloaded in North America the ships took on their cargoes of exports from the colonies, especially cotton, sugar, and tobacco.

COTTON PLANTATIONS
In North America it was the plantation system that fuelled the fire of slavery. Initially the slaves were taken to Virginia, Carolina, and Georgia.

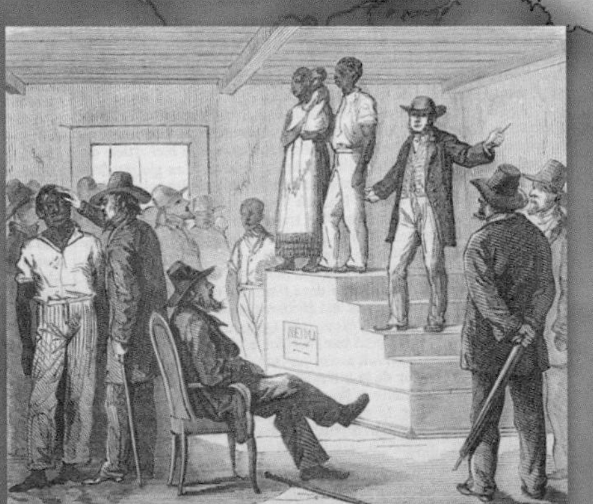

SLAVE SALES
Africans who had been free men within their tribal system were bought and sold – although some were already slaves within the African system.

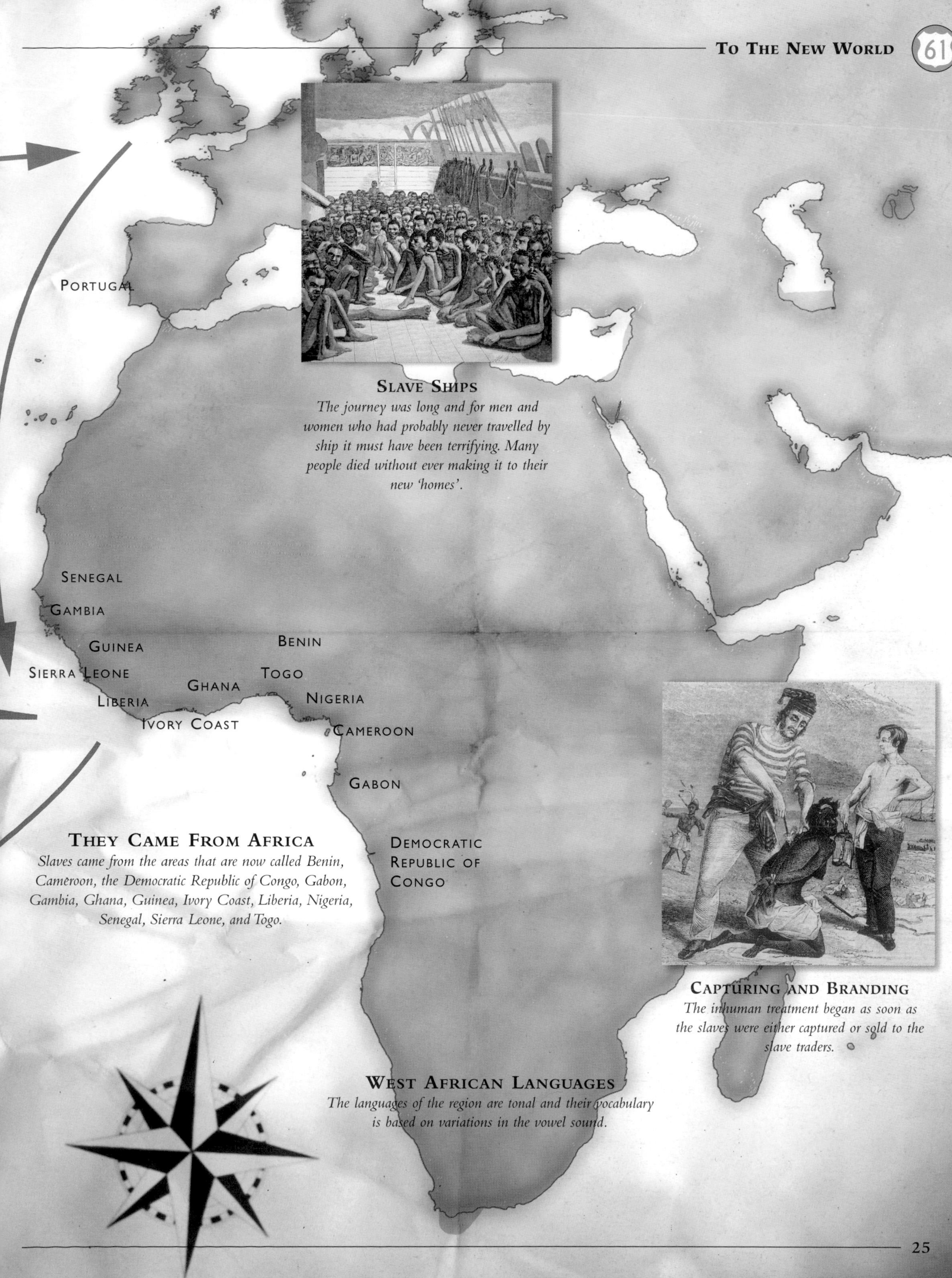

Slave Ships
The journey was long and for men and women who had probably never travelled by ship it must have been terrifying. Many people died without ever making it to their new 'homes'.

They Came From Africa
Slaves came from the areas that are now called Benin, Cameroon, the Democratic Republic of Congo, Gabon, Gambia, Ghana, Guinea, Ivory Coast, Liberia, Nigeria, Senegal, Sierra Leone, and Togo.

Capturing and Branding
The inhuman treatment began as soon as the slaves were either captured or sold to the slave traders.

West African Languages
The languages of the region are tonal and their vocabulary is based on variations in the vowel sound.

THE SOUNDS OF AFRICA

WHEN TOURISTS and television programmes describe the amazing sounds to be heard in Africa they are usually referring to the sounds of nature – animals, birds, insects, and even wind and rain. What they may not realise is that these are the same sounds that have inspired African musicians for centuries.

With the increasing interest in world music in the latter part of the 20th century, we have become a little more familiar with African music, but outside that continent, few people still really understand this dynamic tradition. Many non-African listeners find it hard to make the cultural leap from highly structured European-based music to the free-form dynamic of African music.

Music plays a similar role in Africa to most other societies around the world. There is music for all occasions – work songs, lullabies, religious songs and military anthems. But strangely there is no noun for 'music' in most African languages, probably because the principal aim of an African musician is to reflect everyday life. Music is simply an integral part of every African's existence.

From childhood onwards, many Africans take an active role in music, often making instruments by the age of three or four. These are used in elaborate musical games that they play, which are essentially training for adult activities like farming and hunting. So complex and fundamental to tribal beliefs is music that in some tribes women may not even handle the instruments. Neither is everyone allowed to play any instrument: during ceremonies, only professional musicians, from specific families or castes, may play certain instruments. The combination of music, drumming and dance is a pivotal element within the religious, social and economic life of West Africa.

Strangely there is no noun for 'music' in most African languages.

African music is dominated by the form known as 'call-and-response'. A factor that had an enormous influence on blues and jazz. Another significant tradition within African music is the use of instruments to mimic the human voice, which became another key element of jazz.

RHYTHMICAL SENSE

Attempts to understand African music have baffled many musicologists. In one of the earliest studies of African music, Henry Edward Krehbiel described the African musicians who played at the World's Columbian Exposition, held in Chicago in 1893.

'The players showed the most remarkable rhythmical sense and skill that ever came under my notice. Berlioz in his supremest effort with his army of drummers produced nothing to compare in artistic interest with the harmonious drumming of these savages. The fundamental effect was a combination of double and triple time, the former kept by the singers, the latter by the drummers, but it is impossible to convey the idea of the wealth of detail achieved by the drummers by means of the exchange of the rhythms, syncopations of both simultaneously, and dynamic devices'

DRUMMERS AND DANCERS
A pageant at the Katsina Durbar in Nigeria.

The imitation of the human voice is demonstrated by the *kalangu*, the talking drum of West Africa. Drums were fashioned out of a variety of discarded items.

> *'There wasn't no music instruments… [instead they used] pieces of sheep's rib or cow's jaw or a piece of iron, with an old kettle, or a hollow gourd and some horsehairs'*
>
> WASH WILSON, A FORMER SLAVE

The way in which African music infiltrates everyday life is demonstrated by the range of instruments played, which varies from region to region across the continent. Both flora and culture influence the kind of instruments that are dominant in particular regions. It is not a coincidence, for example, that drums are most prevalent in the forest regions of West Africa.

The brutality and suddenness of their transportation meant that slaves had no opportunities to take their instruments with them, but memory of what they had left behind allowed them to fashion new instruments from everyday items they found around them. The xylophone was one such hybrid, while the banjo was based on the West African gourd guitar.

Researchers for the 1930s Federal Writers' Project who recorded the memoirs of former slaves, demonstrated how African-Americans were able to use these techniques to make music after they arrived in America.

Throughout West Africa, the designated professional musicians are known as the Griot. Their role goes far beyond making music, entering the realms of magic. Like the medieval minstrels they are the tellers of tales and the broadcasters of news, but also the keepers of their tribes' myths and history. The Griot are often feared as well as admired, but in one of those paradoxes so commonly found in Africa, they are often treated with contempt because they come from a lower caste.

Today traditional African music is under threat, as the essential strength that helped it become so significant in the story of the Blues is also its fundamental weakness: it is a purely oral tradition, never written down. Whether or not this rich tradition survives, it is impossible to deny its past importance and its role in the story of the Blues.

WEST AFRICAN STRINGED INSTRUMENTS
Instruments of the Hausa Fulani tribes.

KETTLE DRUMS
A musician from the Democratic Republic of Congo using cooking utensils as drums.

> *'African music is the key that unlocks the secrets of jazz'*
>
> SHINING TRUMPETS – THE HISTORY OF JAZZ BY RUDI BLESH

THE AMERICAN CIVIL WAR

As I would not be a slave, so I would not be a master. This expresses my idea of democracy.

ABRAHAM LINCOLN

THE DEBATE OVER SLAVERY HAD been raging back and forth between North and South for many years. When Abraham Lincoln became the 16th President of the United States on 6th November, 1860, it precipitated action by one of the South's slave states that proved to be one of the most significant acts on the road to the American Civil War. On 20th December, 1860, South Carolina voted to secede from the Union, and in so doing it repealed its 1788 ratification of the US Constitution. This was the catalyst for action by the Southern states, whose economy was wholly based on the use of slave labour.

Lincoln had first entered politics in 1834 when he won a seat in the Illinois legislature. For the next 24 years he combined careers as a lawyer and a politician. The final stage in realising his long held ambition to be president began in June 1858, when the Illinois Republican Party chose him to challenge Senator Douglas for a Senate seat. On a hot humid evening, at the Republican Party meeting, Lincoln took the unprecedented step of publicly stating his position on slavery; politicians at that time normally took a more detached standpoint. Lincoln began his speech with these famous words. "In my opinion, (the current slavery agitation) will not cease, until a crisis shall have been reached, and passed. 'A house divided against itself cannot stand.' I believe this government cannot endure, permanently half slave and half free. I do not expect the Union to be dissolved – I do not expect the house to fall – but I do expect it will cease to be divided. It will become all one thing, or all the other. Either the opponents of slavery will arrest the further spread of it, and place it where the public mind shall rest in the belief that it is in the course of ultimate extinction; or its advocates will push it forward, till it shall become alike lawful in all the States, old as well as new – North as well as South. Have we no tendency to the latter condition?"

Lincoln was criticised for predicting a radical shift in attitudes to the slavery crisis. But at the time it had already been openly mooted that the Supreme Court could force the North to accept some form of slavery. History has shown Lincoln's prognosis to be completely accurate.

Street Banner

Slavery is founded on the selfishness of man's nature – opposition to it on his love of justice

ABRAHAM LINCOLN

The secession of South Carolina was followed by six more states: Mississippi, Florida, Alabama, Georgia, Louisiana, and Texas. Four more states threatened secession: Virginia, Arkansas, Tennessee, and North Carolina. These 11 states eventually formed the Confederate States of America. In February 1861, the original seven seceding states formulated the Confederate Constitution in Montgomery,

EMANCIPATION PROCLAMATION

Lincoln's famous statement of his beliefs, first made on 1st January, 1863.

The Battle of Shiloh

The Union forces won this initial battle in April 1862, but only with a terrible loss of life on both sides.

Alabama. Although similar to the United States Constitution, it allowed for a greater level of autonomy for each state. Jefferson Davis was named provisional President of the Confederacy until elections could take place.

The Conflict Ignites

February also saw the first military act of conflict between North and South, when Confederate forces seized forts in the South. At Fort Sumter in South Carolina, Confederate troops repulsed a supply ship that was trying to reach the Union troops who still held the fort. At this early stage in the conflict both sides felt that all-out war was not necessarily inevitable. They both expected a quick victory – which for neither side would have brought freedom to the million or so slaves in the United States. On 4th March, 1861, Lincoln stated at his inauguration that he had no plans to end slavery in those states where it already existed, but that their secession was unacceptable. However, he still hoped to resolve the crisis without warfare.

Fort Sumter figured again in the early months of the conflict. In April the first shots of the war were fired at the fort, after the commander refused to surrender to Confederate forces. The attack prompted the four remaining states to join the Confederacy, and to name Richmond, Virginia as their capital. Not all the slave states joined the Confederacy, however: Delaware, Kentucky, Maryland, and Missouri were kept from seceding by a mixture of political manoeuvring and Union military pressure.

The first battle of the war was fought at Bull Run, near Manassas in Virginia. The Confederacy won and the Union troops retreated in disarray towards Washington. The South was jubilant and anticipated that a speedy victory to the war would be theirs. Then something of a cold war followed, with the main military efforts concentrated on building a Union Navy to blockade the South's ports. At the same time General George B McClellan, whom Lincoln had appointed to head the army, was slow to take action. This caused Lincoln to issue a War Order on 27th January, 1862, authorising McClellan to take 'aggressive action', an order which the general largely ignored. By March, Lincoln was growing extremely frustrated with his commander's inactivity and he relieved McClellan of overall command of the army, placing him in charge of the army of the Potomac.

Finally, in April 1862, there was action: on the 6th, Confederate forces attacked Union forces under the command of General Ulysses S Grant at Shiloh, Tennessee. At the end of the day it looked like another

Manassas

In 1972, 110 years after the Battle of Bull Run, Bill Wyman played bass on Stephen Stills' third solo album, entitled Manassas. As a keen student of the Civil War, Stills took his band to Manassas railroad station to be photographed for the album cover.

LINCOLN AT ANTIETAM
The president meeting his officers in September 1862.

Confederate victory, but Federal troop reinforcements, arriving during the night, helped to bring the North its first victory of the war. But victory was won at a tremendous cost, for victor and loser alike. Approximately 13,000 of the 63,000 Union soldiers and 11,000 of the 40,000 Confederate troops were killed during the battle. Both sides were so exhausted that when the Confederacy retreated, the Union troops were too tired to follow.

It was a grim foretaste of what was to come. The American Civil War was a story of battles on an unprecedented scale, huge loss of life, and generals who sometimes appeared detached from the consequences of their actions. Both sides regularly recorded, or claimed, victories, but many of them were nothing more than pyrrhic.

CONFEDERATE VICTORIES

July 1861	**First Battle of Bull Run**
May 1862	**Shenandoah Valley**
June 1862	**Seven Pines**
August 1862	**Second Battle of Bull Run**
December 1862	**Fredricksberg**
May 1863	**Chancellorsville**
June 1863	**Winchester**
September 1863	**Chickamauga**
May 1864	**Wilderness** *(inconclusive)*
June 1864	**Cold Harbor**

TO ABOLISH OR NOT TO ABOLISH

Lincoln himself was deeply and openly opposed to slavery, but he did not believe that he wielded the constitutional power to abolish it. He was also not sure that he could hold the North together with a policy that was radically anti-slavery. In August 1862, Horace Greeley, the editor of the *New York Tribune*, appealed in his paper for Lincoln to make the abolition of slavery the focus of the North's war aims. Lincoln felt unable to agree and sent this reply:

Hon. Horace Greeley:

Executive Mansion,
Washington, August 22, 1862

Dear Sir,

If there be those who would not save the Union, unless they could at the same time save slavery, I do not agree with them. If there be those who would not save the Union, unless they could at the same time destroy slavery, I do not agree with them. My paramount object in this struggle is to save the Union, and is not either to save or to destroy slavery. If I could save the Union without freeing any slave I would do it and if I could save it by freeing all the slaves I would do it; and if I could save it by freeing some and leaving others alone I would also do that. What I do about slavery, and the colored race, I do because it helps to save the Union; and what I forbear, I forbear because I do not believe it would help to save the Union.

ABRAHAM LINCOLN

As the war progressed, and the South proved to be a tougher opponent than anticipated, Lincoln's views were slowly to change. He began to believe that if the North adopted a policy of emancipation as a stated aim, that would encourage slaves in the South to revolt. His initial idea was a policy of 'compensated emancipation', whereby slave owners would be financially compensated for their loss. Congress agreed to this plan, but none of the slave states which remained in the Union would accept the proposal. Lincoln knew then that there was only one alternative: compulsory emancipation.

On 1st January, 1863, Lincoln made his Proclamation of Emancipation – which contrary to popular belief did not free the slaves of those owners who had remained loyal to the Union.

Lincoln only made this order in his role as commander-in-chief, which meant that the whole matter was constitutionally flawed. He knew that for the Proclamation to be legally binding, he needed to get Congress to amend the Constitution. His first attempt failed; his second, in January 1865, for which he summoned up all his persuasive powers, was finally passed – by just one vote.

Lincoln was re-elected president in November 1864, having been opposed by the Democratic candidate, his former army commander, General McClellan. War weariness in the North had initially made defeat at the polls for Lincoln a distinct possibility. However, General Sherman's victory at Atlanta, in late summer 1864, helped to ensure that Lincoln won by a wide margin. Sherman's victory also meant that defeat for the South was now almost inevitable. Atlanta was the munitions centre of the Confederacy, and its loss was effectively the beginning of the end.

In 1862, Lincoln had decided to involve blacks in the North's war effort. They made a significant impact on the conflict; indeed, their involvement may have been decisive in the North's victory. One estimate is that around half a million black slaves fled to the North during the war, and many of these were among the 186,000 blacks who served in the North's army by the end of the war.

By the opening months of 1865 the war was as good as over, but diplomatic moves to end the conflict in February came to nothing. The President of the Confederacy, Jefferson Davis, refused to send delegates to a peace conference because Lincoln would not recognise the independence of the South.

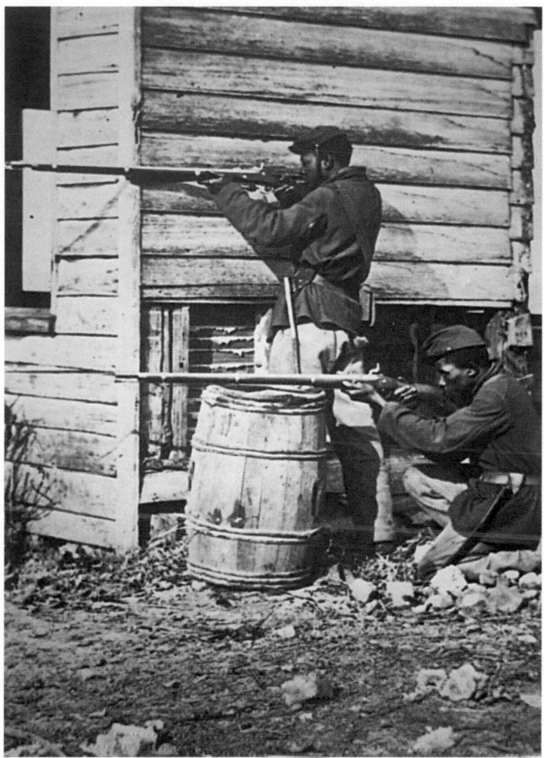

Black Troops

Lincoln first involved black soldiers in the conflict in 1862. 186,000 blacks eventually took part, making a crucial contribution to the outcome of the Civil War.

With the South suffering desertion from its army at an alarming rate, and morale at its lowest ebb, General Robert E Lee was finally defeated after he attacked General Grant's forces near Petersberg on 25th March. By 9th April, General Lee's troops had surrendered at Appomattox Courthouse. They were sent home on parole, soldiers with their horses, and officers with their sidearms.

The remaining Confederate troops were defeated between the end of April and the end of May; Jefferson Davis was captured in Georgia on 10th May.

On 14th April, while President Lincoln watched a performance of *Our American Cousin* at Ford's Theatre in Washington DC, he was shot by John Wilkes Booth; Lincoln died the next morning. Booth, an actor from Maryland, wished to avenge the Confederate defeat. He escaped to Virginia, where 11 days later he was cornered in a burning barn, and inflicted with a fatal bullet wound by a Union soldier. Nine other people were implicated in the assassination: four were hanged, four imprisoned, and one acquitted.

The Proclamation and Europe

The Emancipation Proclamation was also designed to discourage England and France from entering the war on the side of the Confederacy. The South exported cotton and tobacco to Europe, and initially Europe supported the Confederacy's cause. When the war became an argument over slavery, the European nations, opposed to human bondage, then gave their support to the Union.

Union Victories

April 1862	**Shiloh**
September 1862	**Harpers Ferry**
September 1862	**Antietam**
May 1863	**Vicksberg**
July 1863	**Gettysberg**
November 1863	**Chattanooga**
May 1864	**Wilderness** *(inconclusive)*
August 1864	**Atlanta**
December 1864	**Nashville**
April 1865	**Petersberg**

The Civil War in Numbers

- 10,455 military engagements
- 1,094,453 total casualties
- 110,100 Union troops killed in action
- 224,580 Union fatalities from disease
- 164,000 Confederate fatalities from disease
- 94,000 Confederate troops killed in action
- 275,175 Union troops wounded in action
- 194,026 Confederate troops wounded in action
- War cost to the Union: $6,190,000,000
- War cost to the Confederacy: $2,099,808,707

Entertaining the Troops
Black musicians performing on guitar, banjo and tambourine.

Free and Proud
Andrew Scott was a freed slave who served in the Union army between 1861 and 1865. His proud demeanour and fearless expression provide a sharp contrast to the downtrodden, defeated appearance so familiar from pictures of those who were enduring the burden of slavery - like Fassena, who was shown earlier in this chapter. The contribution made to the Union war effort by former slaves undoubtedly helped to alter racial attitudes in the Northern states after the war was over.

PAPA CHARLIE JACKSON

IN THE 1920S, there was no such thing as a'blues singer'; pioneers like Papa Charlie Jackson performed in a variety of styles, depending on the demands of their audience. Using a banjo rather than a guitar, Papa Charlie became one of the first bluesmen to record. His prolific career paved the way for other blues performers.

FACT FILE

BORN: *c.1885*
New Orleans, Louisiana

DIED: *Spring 1938, Chicago, Illinois*

INSTRUMENT: *Banjo, Guitar, Ukulele*

FIRST RECORDED: *1924*

INFLUENCED: *Big Bill Broonzy*

Little is known of William Henry Jackson's early life, and it is not even certain that he was born in New Orleans. He probably toured the South as part of various minstrel and medicine shows in the early 1900s. Sometime around the end of World War I, Jackson settled in Chicago and began playing street corners for small change. He was soon a familiar sight at the Maxwell Street Market where he sang and played his

often bawdy blues tunes, which were later known as 'hokum blues'. Jackson not only sang blues, but also specialised in novelty songs and ragtime.

Jackson was one of the first bluesmen to record. In August 1924 Paramount took him into the studio in Chicago to cut 'Papa's Lawdy Lawdy Blues' and 'Airy Man Blues'. These were the first of more than 70 sides that Jackson was to record, all for Paramount except for his last four sides, which were recorded for OKeh in 1934. It was at Jackson's fifth

MA RAINEY
In 1928 Ma Rainey recorded two songs with Papa Charlie Jackson – the last recordings she ever made.

recording session in May 1925 that he recorded one of his most enduring numbers, the dance song, 'Shake That Thing'.

In mid-1926 Paramount asked him to provide vocals on a recording of 'Salty Dog' by Freddie Keppard's Jazz Cardinals. His 10-year recording career created opportunities for other blues artists to record. He also made records with a number of other artists, including Blind Blake, Hattie McDaniels, Ida Cox, and Lucille Bogan. At the end of 1928, Jackson recorded two sides with Ma Rainey which were destined to become the final recordings of her career.

While details of Jackson's life are sparse, the supposition that he was born in New Orleans is supported by the way in which he played. He was a sophisticated musician, with a talent for chord sequences that was well beyond contemporary country blues players. He played a six-string banjo, but not in conventional style, instead picking, strumming, and tuning it like a guitar. He inspired Big Bill Broonzy, and the two men recorded together in 1935, but none of their three sides were released. The man who was described as 'a sophisticated all round entertainer' died in 1938, but the circumstances of his death, like most of his life, are shrouded in mystery.

ESSENTIAL RECORDINGS

CLASSIC SONGS

'Airy Man Blues' 1924
'All I Want Is A Spoonful' 1925
'Shake That Thing' 1925

THE SOURCE

3 CDs of his complete works on Document Records

2 The Roots Of African-American Music

THE ROOTS OF AFRICAN-AMERICAN MUSIC

THE AFRICAN TRADITION OF passing on music orally, rather than through a recognisable series of annotated notes, was fundamental in the creation of the Blues. When they arrived in their new homeland, the slaves were able to bring their music with them, keeping their traditions alive by the mere act of singing. But in a strange foretaste of what would happen centuries later with the Blues, African music did not always meet with the approval of the European colonists. Some early references talk about the 'unpleasant' nature of African singing. In 1638, less than 20 years after the arrival of the first slaves, John Josselyn, who was travelling in Massachusetts, wrote rather disapprovingly of an African woman's voice: "Mr Maverick's negro woman came to my chamber window and in her own country language and tune sang very loud and shrill." Others spoke of the "strong nasal tones" in which the men sang.

AT HOME
'A Visit From The Parson' is the title of this somewhat patronising and obviously staged photograph from the late 19th century.

In these early days the slaves' music was purely African in form and feeling. But it was not long before the traditional music of Africa, and the ballads, airs, hymns, psalms and musical instruments brought to the colonies by the European settlers, began to leave their mark on each other. In the essentially rural society of the 17th century there were three areas in which music was to be found. Hymns and psalms were sung in churches or meeting houses, principally in a vocal style. But despite the fact that life was hard for everyone in the colonies, their music was not all about work and religion. There were dances, too, and here the violin or fiddle, played by both black and white musicians, provided the entertainment. There was also military music, played on the trumpet, fife, and drum.

MUSICAL SLAVES

The 18th century witnessed the development of cities along the eastern seaboard of North America. From Boston comes one of the earliest references to a black musician, when it was reported that a black trumpeter gave the New Year's Day salute in 1705. With the growth of the cities came a change in the popular musical presentation of the day. Vocal music became more popular, as did concert performances, as well as more refined dancing in ballrooms. The first public concert in the colonies took place in 1731 in Boston, described as a '*Concert of Musick On Sundry Instruments*'.

By 1766 there were even adverts appearing in the newspapers offering slaves for sale who possessed musical talent. Their owners were aware that these skills undoubtedly increased their value:

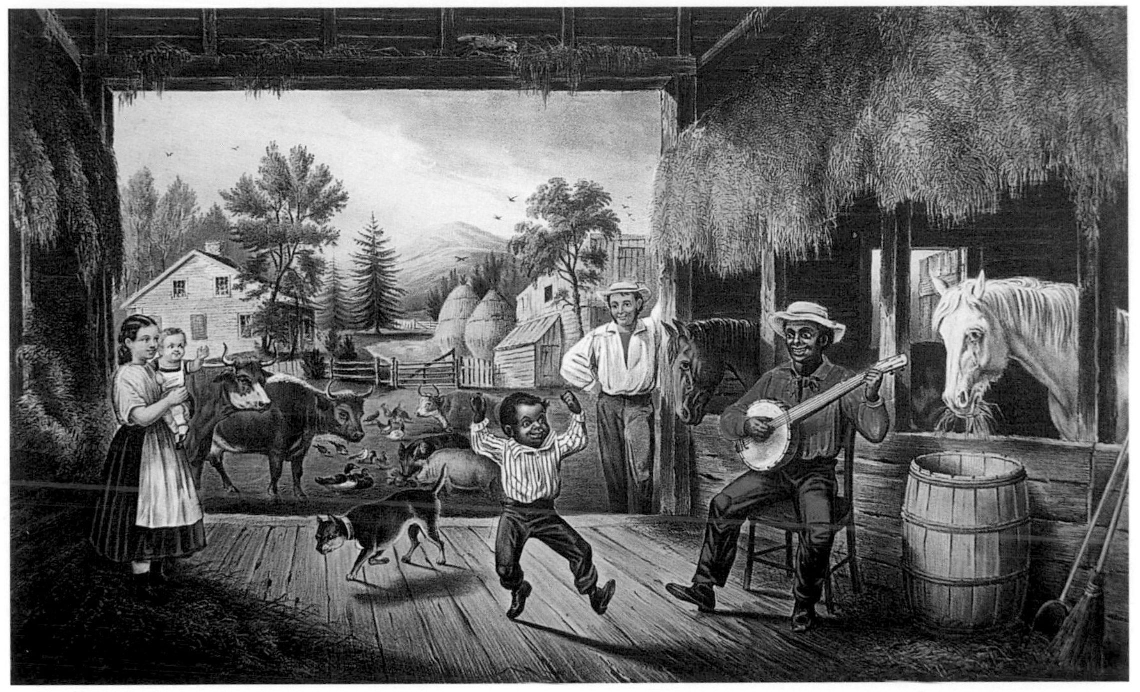

Slave Barn Dance in Kentucky
This Currier and Ives print from 1868 presents a sanitized view of slave life in the old South.

To Be Sold: A young healthy Negro fellow who has been used to waiting on a Gentleman and plays extremely well on the French horn.

Throughout the second half of the 18th century there were numerous references in the newspapers to musical slaves, most often fiddle or violin players. Often slaves were offered for sale with their instruments. Nicholas Cresswell, in his journal of 1774, described slaves in Maryland dancing to a banjo made from a gourd, "something in the imitation of a guitar with only four strings. They would sing in a very satirical manner about the way they were treated, the words and music being rude and uncultivated."

Hymns and Spirituals

The 18th century also brought an increase in the number of slaves singing in church, who could then take their new-found music back to their living quarters. A major priority for each denomination that established itself in the colonies was the conversion of blacks to their particular brand of Christianity. In New England, the white population were primarily Congregationalists of British stock. Elsewhere, Dutch, Swedes, Germans, and Finns were to be found, and with them their religious groupings of Quakers, Catholics, and Methodists. With the exception of the Quakers, who were opposed to singing, all the religious groups used the teaching of psalms to spread the Christian message, and this helped to involve the Africans in European music. As formal education was extended to include some slave children, the singing of psalms was retained as part of the curriculum.

In 1707, Dr Isaac Watts, an English Minister, published a book called *Hymns And Spiritual Songs*. This became very popular throughout the colonies, especially with black people, as it offered a livelier form of music than the more sedate, slow-paced psalms. As the 18th century progressed, more hymnals were published in the

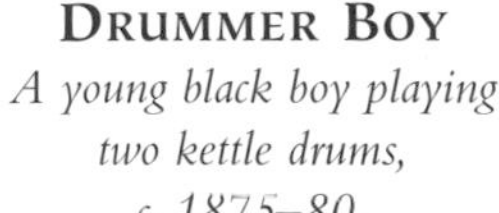

Drummer Boy
A young black boy playing two kettle drums, c. 1875–80.

colonies; some were even produced locally. These took note of local conditions and contained hymns that seemed to be particularly applicable to the colonists.

As people's lives became more settled, their thoughts were less about survival and more about living a life. Social events became more

SOCIETY DANCE
This stylized image was used as an American Christmas greetings card in the 1880s.

popular, and not just those that occurred on high days and holidays. The farming year allowed for a variety of community events that were often followed by a dance. City dwellers had taverns in which music could be heard, and by the end of the 18th century regular concerts were being performed in every city.

The Africans began to embrace some elements of their white owners' music, particularly through the Christian Church. They recognized the Church's power, and the potency of its music, but they wanted and needed to retain elements of their own heritage. And so it was that they began to couple their own heritage with religion, the basis, as they saw it, of their owners' power. The results were some of the earliest building blocks of the Blues.

THE SPIRITUAL
An emotional, sometimes melancholy, religious song, often with a biblical text, that is syncopated – strong beats become weak and vice versa. It is structured around two or more rhythms, and uses five whole tones.

SLAVES AND TEACHERS

The American War of Independence disrupted the everyday lives of vast numbers of the colonists, and slaves were no exception. But concerts and other musical events resumed soon after the war, and dancing and singing schools soon reopened. Music teachers were quite common in the colonies; including some that had emigrated from Europe. One of the first black music teachers was Newport Gardner. He had been a slave who managed to purchase his freedom in 1791 and set up a music school in Newport. He was not alone: in New York, Frank the Negro was identified as a teacher; while in Philadelphia John Cromwell was actively teaching in the early part of the 19th century.

Prior to the War of Independence, black Africans worshipped at the same churches as the white colonists. In most churches the blacks sat in segregated pews, but blacks and whites sang the same hymns and psalms. Even before the war there was a move to create separate black churches, precipitated by blacks who were growing frustrated with discrimination. The first black man to be granted a licence to preach was George Leile, who set up a church in Savannah, Georgia as early as 1782. Over the next 25 years, separate black churches were established in a number of Virginian cities, as well as in Boston, Philadelphia, and New York.

Around 20% of the American Methodist Church's membership was already black, so they were the hardest-hit denomination as blacks began to separate. Under the leadership of Richard Allen, the African Methodist Episcopal Church was established, and it was not long before it separated totally from the Methodist church. In 1816, Richard Allen, himself a former slave, was elected the first black bishop in America. Fifteen years earlier he had published a hymnal entitled *A Collection of Spiritual Songs and Hymns Selected from Various Authors by Richard Allen, African Minister*. It is now widely assumed that Allen, who was self-educated, must have written some of the hymns himself, besides altering existing hymns to make them more appropriate for his black congregation. The first hymn in the collection has a stanza-chorus format, which at the time was frowned upon by the traditional white churches, who favoured the more spartan stanza-only construction. The chorus in the first hymn is clearly relevant to the plight of

CONTRABAND CAMP
An illustration depicting a prayer meeting in a contraband camp, Washington, 1862.

MASTER JUBA
(William Henry Lane 1825 –1853)
The greatest of all dancers in the first half of the 19th century, he learned from Uncle Jim Lowe, a talented black jig and reel dancer. He toured both America and Europe, and unusually he was allowed to perform on stage with members of an all-white minstrel company. Juba was a link between the authentic African material and the blackface minstrel show.

the slaves, and it became a recurring theme throughout black gospel music, and then in amended form within the Blues. It talks of the hope of a better life to come: "*Hallelujah to the Lord who purchas'd our pardon, We'll praise him again when we pass over Jordan...*"

Interestingly these 54 hymns would not have had their own individual tunes, as melodies were often shared. It also seems likely that the tunes of the hymns were taken from folk songs, a practice also popular with some white Christian groups.

CAMP MEETINGS

In the last years of the 18th century and the early years of the 19th, the curious American phenomenon of the camp meeting flourished. It originated under the preaching of James McGready in Kentucky and spread rapidly with the revival movement. These events, embracing both black and white, were essentially day- or even week-long services that mostly took place in the woods and forests. They drew crowds of many thousands

"... they sing for hours together, short scraps of disjointed affirmations, pledges or prayers, lengthened out with long repetition choruses. These are all sung in the merry chorus-manner of the southern harvest field, or husking frolic method, of the slave blacks. This was hardly the way a God-fearing person should behave!"

LATE 18TH-CENTURY REPORT BY A PROMINENT METHODIST

HANDEL'S MESSIAH
Blacks were among the choir that gave the first performance of Handel's Messiah in the colonies in 1770.

and were distinguished by the power of the singing, as massed choirs sang for hours at a time.

Contemporary reports talk of black singers vastly out-performing their white counterparts, both in terms of volume and the duration of their performances. They also said that the blacks would apparently sing in a more free-spirited style.

These reporters were writing about the distinctive spirituals which emerged from these camp meetings. While the spiritual song had been in existence for around 100 years, it now took on an altogether new meaning. The camp meeting spiritual had choruses and melodies reminiscent of folk songs, and lyrical content that referred to everyday occurrences as well as religious concepts. Picking up on the theme of crossing the River Jordan, one of the most popular camp meeting song phrases became 'Roll, Jordan, Roll'.

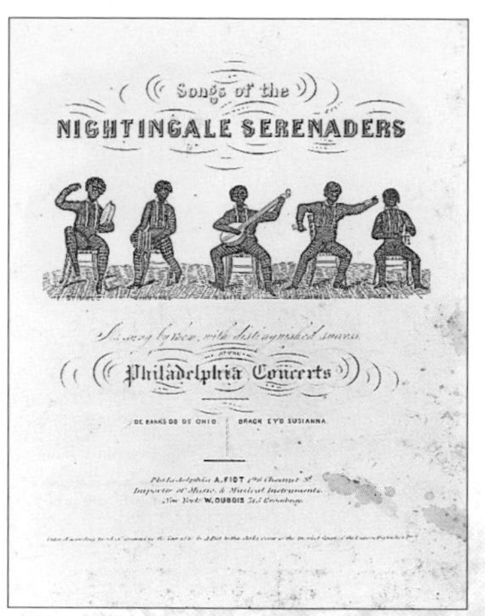

THE NIGHTINGALE SERENADERS
Poster advertising a minstrel show in Philadelphia by the Nightingale Serenaders, c.1847. Among the songs promised for the evening's entertainment are 'De Banks Ob De Ohio', and 'Brack Ey'd Susianna'.

Dancing also formed a major part of the African involvement in camp meetings. They were observed slapping their thighs, as well as performing the traditional shuffle-step dance. The African roots of the congregation were clearly apparent in the melodies, style of service, music, and movement, which had been transported in the slaves' strong memories of their homelands.

The musical taste of the new nation was undoubtedly influenced heavily by European interests. Indeed, the strong influence of the Church guaranteed that this would be the case. However, there was clearly other musical activity at the time that has gone almost completely unrecorded. What went on in the fields and the homes of the slaves was not a matter of interest to most white people, so white chroniclers would have paid scant regard to the work songs and hollers sung by the slaves – an oversight that continued for most of the next century.

THE ANTE-BELLUM PERIOD.

The early part of the 19th century, up to the beginnings of the Civil War, is known as the Ante-Bellum period, which simply means 'before the war'. With the increasing urbanisation of America, the musical scene went through a period of rapid change and development. Traditional European classical music was featured at concerts and recitals throughout the major Northern cities and, not surprisingly, these featured few black musicians. But, overall, there was also an increasing number of black performers, partly attributable to white America's interest in seeing black people perform. Many visitors from Europe were also curious about the musical abilities of black people. It should be remembered that most of this activity took place in the North, or in the major Southern cities.

Philadelphia was America's premier cultural city in this period, and musical events of every type proliferated there. The city boasted an all-black marching band, black musicians in the theatre orchestras, a Colored Choral Society and Frank Johnson's Band. This primarily woodwind band of black musicians toured England in 1838 and even gave a command performance for Queen Victoria. They were also popular at dances, where they usually added a string section. Johnson's ability to rework songs into dance music was an essential part of his popularity. It has been said that Johnson's ability to 'jazz' his music, even before jazz had been invented, was the key to his success. In 1817, Johnson became the first black man to publish sheet music. He was well ahead of his time as, until the final decades of the 20th century, most black performers and especially bluesmen, failed to grasp the importance of publishing their own songs.

BLACK MUSIC IN NEW YORK

Other cities also had thriving musical scenes. New York naturally had its share of black musical stars, and the only all-black theatre, The African Grove. The emancipation of slaves in New York State in 1827 was a cause for celebration, and perhaps the impetus for the city's unique musical character. By 1842, when Charles Dickens visited the country and chronicled his experiences in *Notes On America*, there was a rich diversity in the city's musical scene. One of the many dance halls in New York was Almacks. When Dickens visited he saw a "corpulent black fiddler and his friend who plays the tambourine". The author was also impressed by "a lively young negro, wit of the assembly and the greatest dancer known" – the world-renowned black dancer, Master Juba.

Other dance halls flourished in this period, the antecedents of the famous black cabaret clubs of the 1920s. At these clubs 'hot music' could be heard – so called because the music stirred the dancers into frenzied activity, no doubt making them a little hot! A contemporary reference talks of "a red-faced trumpeter" and "the bass drummer that sweats and deals his blows on every side, in all violation of the laws of rhythm".

BLACK MUSIC ON THE MISSISSIPPI

A print of 1870 by Currier and Ives of a flatboat with a black man dancing to fiddle music. In the background are Mississippi showboats.

THE CRESCENT CITY - MUSICAL CRUCIBLE

If Philadelphia was the city of culture, New Orleans could lay claim to being the most musically and culturally divergent city in America. The city had a strong French feel as the state of Louisiana had only been sold to the Americans by the French in 1803. Twelve thousand blacks made up one-third of the city's population, while many other national groups also flourished there, which all made for a heady mix.

The dancing that took place in the Place Congo was without doubt one of the most exciting and exotic sights in 19th century America. These dances were created in the late 18th century, and by the time architect Benjamin Latrobe wrote about them in 1818-20, they were at the height of their popularity. Each group of dancers was accompanied by its own small band, consisting of drums, banjos and rattles. Latrobe noted: "The music consisted of two drums and a stringed instrument . . . which no doubt was imported from Africa. On the top fingerboard was the rude figure of a man in a sitting posture, and two pegs behind him to which strings were fastened. It was played upon by a very little old man, apparently 80 or 90 years old." Like the dancers at camp meetings, the Place Congo dancers were emulating their African forebears.

Musical talent of all types was to be found in New Orleans, where there were European-style bands, as well as slave orchestras and brass bands. Such was the city's fervour for brass bands that whites even offered to pay for the musical education of blacks. Out of these divergent musical traditions – the black orchestras, brass bands, Creole singing and dance musicians, all allied to the free-spirited dance and rhythms of the Place Congo – was to come jazz. Jazz made New Orleans yet more famous and helped change the whole face of popular music.

By 1834 the rich musical heritage of New Orleans began to spread to the Delta. Black musicians from the city often played on board the showboats that travelled up and down the length of the Mississippi.

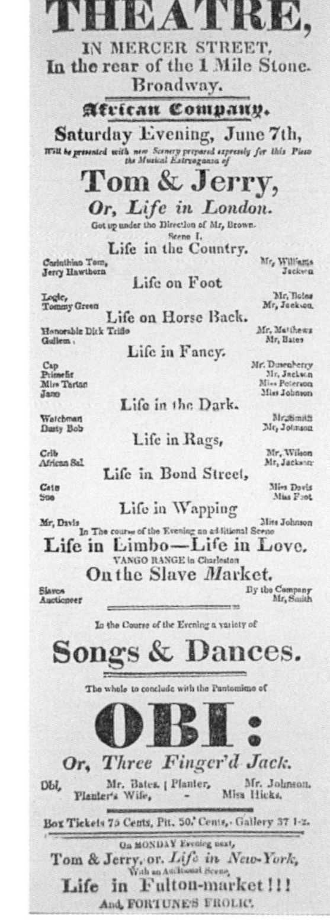

THEATRE,
IN MERCER STREET,
In the rear of the 1 Mile Stone.
Broadway.

African Company.

Saturday Evening, June 7th,
Will be presented with new Scenery prepared expressly for this Piece the Musical Extravaganza of

Tom & Jerry,
Or, Life in London.
Got up under the Direction of Mr, Brown.
Scene I.

Life in the Country.
Corinthian Tom, — Mr, Williams
Jerry Hawthorn — Jackson

Life on Foot
Logic, — Mr, Bates
Tommy Green — Mr, Jackson.

Life on Horse Back.
Honorable Dick Trifle — Mr, Matthews
Gullem, — Mr, Bates

Life in Fancy.
Cap — Mr. Dusenberry
Primefit — Mr, Jackson
Miss Tartar — Miss Peterson
Jane — Miss Johnson

Life in the Dark.
Watchman — Mr, Smith
Dusty Bob — Mr, Johnson

Life in Rags,
Crib — Mr, Wilson
African Sal — Mr, Jackson

Life in Bond Street,
Cate — Miss Davis
Sue — Miss Foot

Life in Wapping
Mr, Davis — Miss Johnson
In The course of the Evening an additional Scene

Life in Limbo—Life in Love.
VANGO RANGE in Charleston
On the Slave *Market.*
Slaves — By the Company
Auctioneer — Mr, Smith

In the Course of the Evening a variety of

Songs & Dances.

The whole to conclude with the Pantomime of

OBI:
Or, Three Finger'd Jack.
Obi, — Mr. Bates. | Planter, — Mr. Johnson.
Planter's Wife, — Miss Hicks.

Box Tickets 75 Cents, Pit. 50 Cents, Gallery 37 1-2.

On MONDAY Evening next,
Tom & Jerry, or. *Life in New-York,*
With an Additional Scene,
Life in Fulton-market!!!
And, FORTUNE'S FROLIC.

THEATRE BILL

'The African Company of Negroes' who played in New York City on Broadway in 1821.

THE MISSISSIPPI DELTA

BIRTHPLACE OF THE BLUES

THE MISSISSIPPI DELTA begins at Vicksburg, 300 miles from the mouth of the river, extending for 250 miles northwards to Memphis. The vast almond-shaped alluvial plain was formed after thousands of years of flooding by the mighty Mississippi River in the west and the smaller Yazoo River in the east. This vast lush plain, 'flat as a griddle', is cotton country.

Until 1820 the Delta was an undeveloped area of hardwood forest, but around 1835 settlers began to clear the Delta so that cotton could be grown. After the Civil War the land was completely cleared and plantations were developed across the Delta's length and breadth. The Delta gave birth to the music – an unrelenting environment from which the only outcome could have been the Blues.

HERNANDO DE SOTO
On 8th May, 1541, Hernando de Soto discovered the Mississippi River.

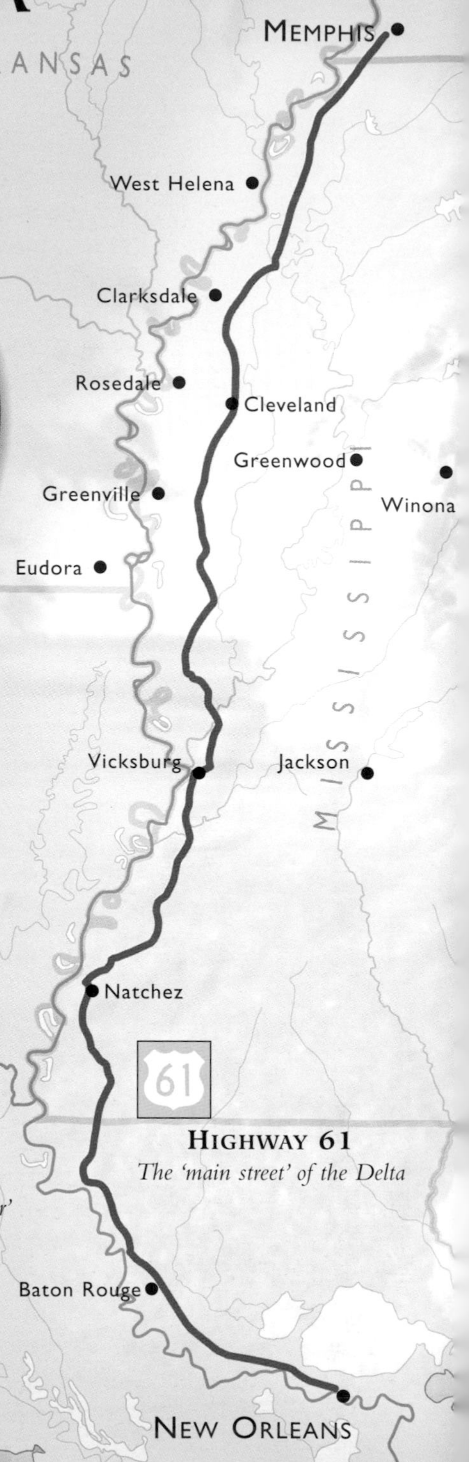

GREAT RIVER
The name 'Mississippi' comes from the Chippewa; mici zibi, *'great river' or 'gathering-in of all the waters'.*

HIGHWAY 61
The 'main street' of the Delta

TENNESSEE

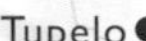

Mississippi Steamboats

The Mississippi is the chief river of the United States, rising in the north of Minnesota and flowing about 2,350 miles to enter the Gulf of Mexico in Louisiana. The main means of transporting cotton and other goods along 'Ol' Man River' in the 19th century was the steamboat.

Cotton Planations of the Delta

If 'cotton is king' then the plantations of the Delta are its castles. For the black population of the region that is just how they must have seemed.

New Orleans

Founded in 1718, most of the original city lies on reclaimed swamp and marshland. The population in 1900, a period that was very important in the development of jazz and the Blues, was around 250,000.

FLORIDA

COTTON AND THE PLANTATIONS

COTTON
Cotton is a shrubby plant (genus Gossypium*) of the Mallow family. Its white or downy fibres, which twist and flatten as they dry, surround each of the seeds, contained in capsules, or bolls. These fibres can be spun and then woven into a cloth. Since prehistoric times cotton has been spun, woven and dyed.*

RURAL LIFE IN EARLY 19TH CENTURY America centred around the plantation. Many think that the South was comprised entirely of white owners and their slaves. In fact, only around 25% of Southern whites actually owned slaves. Another popular misconception is that there were only vast estates employing many hundreds of slaves. In 1800 only around 15% of the owners had more than 20 slaves. The majority of slaves lived on plantations that had no more than 15 slaves, and often as few as two.

Neither was the plantation economy exclusively based on cotton. Rice, sugar cane, and tobacco were also grown, with the choice of crop in part dictated by the nature of the soil. But after the vast plain of the Mississippi Delta was cleared of woodland, it was possible to grow cotton, which triggered a demand for a huge workforce. When Mississippi entered the Union in 1817 there were 70,000 people living in the state, of whom 30,000 were black. By 1860, the population was 791,000, 435,000 of them black, and most of those were slaves.

COTTON IN AMERICA
The American cotton industry as portrayed in an advertisement for J and P Coats' 'best six cord' cotton-sewing thread.

THE CLIMATE OF COTTON

The Southern states of the US are climatically ideal for growing cotton. The combination of warmth and humidity from spring through summer is perfect to maximize the harvest. The cotton is planted in April and shoots are seen within a week. As soon as they appear, the plants need constant attention: they are stripped of unwanted growth and the rows are constantly weeded, a practice known as 'chopping out', to create the ideal growing environment. Between the rows of cotton the earth is ploughed, then banked up around the plants to provide the stand of cotton with support. Fortunately, the plants need less attention when summer is at its hottest in July, so there is a brief respite, before the onslaught of the August harvest.

Picking cotton used to be tough work, as it clings tenaciously to the boll. This intensive work needed a vast labour force until 1948, when International Harvester began producing a mechanical picker which changed the face of the Delta, and inadvertently of America too. Before the Civil War, cotton's vast black enslaved work force lived on the huge plantations that went from Virginia in the east through an arc that swept through Mississippi to Texas in the west.

On the bigger plantations the slaves worked in gangs that were supervised by overseers or a 'driver', but on a smaller plantation the owner very often took on this responsibility himself. Tasks were allocated to slaves, and if they failed to complete them, their fate was in the hands of their owner or driver. Failure to comply with their master's wishes or to work hard enough was usually rewarded with a lashing, even from the more lenient owners, of whom there were plenty. No one was spared the lash, the young or the old, the pregnant woman or the sick. Slaves were sometimes beaten to death: life was cheap, and another slave could always be bought to

'Cotton is King'

James Henry Hammond,
South Carolina cotton planter and politician, 1858

Cotton Picker
International Harvester's 1948 mechanical cotton picker which was to change the face of the Delta and, inadvertently, of America too. The picker above was the first machine to appear in the Delta, on Hopson's Plantation, Clarksdale.

replace the dead one. Although there were some efforts to control the beatings, they met with little success: it was a black man's word against his white superior's. Even if the slave's account sounded plausible, courts did not accept the testimony of a black man.

The Backbone of the South

Between 1795 and 1860 the cotton gin had a huge impact on the South, making it possible to turn vast areas of the region into cotton plantations. The machine for separating the cotton fibres from the seeds was invented by a 26-year-old American, Eli Whitney, in 1793, just eight years after the first bale of cotton was exported from America to Britain. The plantation was the backbone of

Eli Whitney
(1765-1825)
The inventor, in 1793, of the cotton gin. It transformed the economics of the cotton trade in America.

the South's economy; most of them had 50 or fewer slaves, although larger plantations employed several hundred. Besides planting and harvesting, slaves undertook many other types of work. There was land to clear, ditches to be dug, livestock to tend, as well as buildings and tools to maintain; and they also worked as mechanics, blacksmiths, and carpenters. Besides caring for their own families, the women cooked, spun, and sowed. Some slaves worked as domestic servants and were known as 'house servants'. Although their work appeared to be easier than that of the 'field slaves', in some ways it was not, as they were always under the close scrutiny of their masters.

From these plantations came the cotton that was exported to Europe, and Britain in particular. Until 1820, when it was overtaken by Mississippi and Alabama, South Carolina was the largest exporter of cotton from the South. Before the invention of the gin, just over 40% of the population of the South was enslaved; by 1820 it was over 50%; and prior to the Civil War about half of all slaves worked on plantations. The fruits of slave labour made their masters wealthy, and also allowed them to dominate the social, economic, and political life of the Southern states. At its zenith in the 1850s, cotton was truly king.

After the Civil War, the South was forced to abandon slavery, but it did not relinquish the plantation economy. Plantations still existed, and blacks still provided the labour, but now through a system of tenant farming, whereby they were allowed to farm the fields of the white landowners in return for a share of the crop when it was harvested. The landowners also owned the tools, provided their clothing and ran the stores where the workers bought their supplies. Some plantation owners even had their own money, called script, that could only be used at their plantation commissary. This

Cutting Sugar Cane
Plantations grew not just cotton but also sugar cane and tobacco.

BLACK SERVANTS
Latimer's plantation, Belton, South Carolina in 1899.

debt-creating system was known as sharecropping.

In Texas, the cotton industry in the area skirted by Austin, Dallas, and Houston had its own unique organisation of labour. A large and infamous prison farm system operated there, in which gangs of prisoners, predominantly black, were leased to white land-owners.

Long after the Civil War, there was a steady influx of black workers into the South and in particular to the fertile Mississippi Delta. This influx continued right up until World War I, when blacks in the area outnumbered whites by four to one. The feudal sharecropping system operated well into the 20th century, until the automated cotton harvester effectively ended the plantation economy in the 1950s.

The legacy of the plantations and of sharecropping still remains on the American conscience, and the Blues bear eloquent testimony to this dark period in the nation's history.

ESCAPE FROM POVERTY

For those working on a plantation or existing as sharecroppers, life was unimaginably hard, though both slaves and farmers made every attempt to live a normal life. Everyone was allowed Sunday off, but it was also a day for going to church, tending to small vegetable plots, and doing other household chores. That left Saturday night free for fun and enjoyment.

It has been said that no slave quarter was without the sound of a fiddle player, and it was even known for owners to purchase a fiddle for their slaves. While some slaves earned enough money to buy their own instruments, many simply made their own. Across most of the South, however, drums and horns were expressly forbidden. They were seen as a potential method of sending warnings or raising alarm to other slaves, although it is unclear whether any of the slaves had retained the ability to play the African talking drums.

There is no question that this brutal system perpetuated anger, harsh treatment, and inhumanity and that for all those involved it was a dark period in world history. The oppressive owners gave the slaves little opportunity to rebel against the system, although there were occasional uprisings. Control was vested in the men with the guns and the whips, and the slaves had to content themselves with expressing their anger and rebellion through their

A HOME MADE FIDDLE OR BANJO
A slave needed a knife, pine boards, and the gut of a slaughtered cow. The gut would be cut into strips, then dried and treated. Others made theirs from a dried gourd, using horsehair for the strings and bow. A banjo would be made from a gourd with a thin piece of skin or bladder stretched across the gourd. Gut strings would be stretched across a bridge. There are also reports of the tanned hide of a groundhog being stretched across a small wooden box.

The Plantation

Plantation was a term originally used by the English to represent any colony that was established overseas. By the mid-to-late 17th century, the word 'plantation' came to mean a large agricultural venture and labour force that produced crops for export. The word was first found in middle English as 'plantacioun'. The word comes from the Latin 'plantatio', meaning 'propagation of a plant, as from cuttings'. In medieval Latin it grew to include 'planting' and 'nursery', or 'a collection of growing plants that have been planted'.

> *'White Men use whip*
> *White Men use trigger*
> *But the Bible and Jesus*
> *Made a slave of the nigger'*
>
> Verse Fragment from Slavery Times

music, and through their servitude. Often their owners misunderstood the slaves' apparently downtrodden demeanour, seeing them as their 'merry slaves' or 'cheerful flock'. With their songs and their singing, they were simply doing their best to lift their spirits, as one slave said: "If we were to let our spirit weaken, we should die".

Freedom and Confinment

The end to the Civil War did not mean an end to slavery; it merely brought about a period of instability and uncertainty. Some slave owners tried to prevent their slaves from hearing about the Emancipation Proclamation, which led some of the black population to believe that the law was somehow unenforceable. Throughout the South were heard the sentiments expressed by a Mississippi planter: "Not much like the old times, when they were all working quiet like in the fields… Now it's all frolic, I reckon they'll starve. What kin they do alone?" This reinforced the Southern view that slavery was a necessity, and that black people were members of an inferior race who were incapable of working without the compulsion of slavery. This added to the feeling that the whole economic lifeblood of the South was at risk with the breakdown of slavery, and created a truly volatile situation. In many cases, whites did not want to live alongside blacks, and they certainly did not want to talk to them. A planter at the time remarked: "I ain't nothin' against a free nigger, but I don't want him to say a word to me".

Many slaves fled to the North, while some went West. With rumour rife in the South, some slaves clung to the view that they would receive 40 acres and a mule. This never materialized, although some former slaves did receive land under the Southern Homestead Act. In a world where things moved much more slowly than they do today, they were still arguing about the situation in 1873. The *Vicksburg*

Old Runaway Jack

"Then O – I – O
I'm now on freedom's shore
And I guess this black,
Old runaway Jack,
Will never go back no more."

A popular minstrel song from the 1860s sung by Louis Lindsay.

LEAD BELLY

FACT FILE

BORN: *January circa 1888, Mooringsport, Louisiana*

DIED: *6th December, 1949, New York*

INSTRUMENT: *Accordion, Bass, Guitar, Harmonica, Mandolin, Piano*

FIRST RECORDED: *1933*

ACCOLADES: *Inducted into the Blues Hall of Fame, 1986*

INFLUENCES: *Blind Lemon Jefferson*

INFLUENCED: *Woody Guthrie, Lonnie Donegan, John Koerner, Sonny Terry & Brownie McGhee, Pete Seeger, Eric Burdon*

LEAD BELLY, WHAT A NAME! If a man's name is indicative of his personality, then no one could have been more aptly described.

The man who provided the soundtrack for a journey through American musical tradition was christened Huddie William Ledbetter. He was born to sharecropping parents who lived on a Louisiana plantation, and when he was five the family moved to Texas. He left home when he was still very young and little is known of his early life, because Lead Belly himself was reluctant to talk about it. We do know that he met Blind Lemon Jefferson in 1915, but after working with him for a short while he was imprisoned in 1917, having killed a man in Texas. Six years were added to his 33-year sentence after he tried to escape. In 1925 the ever-resourceful Lead Belly earned a pardon from Texas governor Pat Neff after he composed and sang a tune pleading for his freedom.

It was during his brief time with Jefferson that Lead Belly learned to play the 12-string guitar. Its rich tones and volume, which made it ideal for playing in Texas saloons, perfectly complemented his assured and powerful playing.

In 1930 Lead Belly was arrested again, on an assault charge, and this time he was sent to the Angola Prison Farm in Louisiana. In 1933, while he was still in prison, John and Alan Lomax recorded him for the Library of Congress, and petitioned Louisiana governor OK Allen for a pardon. Somewhat surprisingly, Lead Belly soon found himself free for a second time. He became the Lomaxes' chauffeur, but was still able to perform.

> *'Please, Governor Neff, Be good 'n' kind*
> *Have mercy on my great long time...*
> *I don't see to save my soul*
> *If I don't get a pardon,*
> *try me on a parole...*
> *If I had you, Governor Neff,*
> *like you got me*
> *I'd wake up in the mornin'*
> *and I'd set you free'*

THE WORDS OF THE SONG THAT EARNED LEAD BELLY HIS FIRST RELEASE FROM PRISON

Lead Belly was not a traditional blues singer but more of a songster. He performed blues, spirituals, dance tunes and folk ballads – in fact, anything that his audiences demanded. Fortunately, he had a repertoire of 500 songs. In 1934 he moved to New York and recorded for the Library of Congress & Folkways Records, mostly selling to white audiences.

Despite his stature among white folk singers, he made little money. He continually lived on the brink of poverty, and when he died in 1949, he was penniless. Ironically, soon after his death his song 'Goodnight Irene' became a million-selling No.1 single for Pete Seeger's group, The Weavers. In the 50s Lonnie Donegan used Lead Belly's 'Rock Island Line' to launch the skiffle craze in Britain.

ESSENTIAL RECORDINGS

CLASSIC SONGS

'CC Rider' 1935

'Rock Island Line' 1937

'Goodnight Irene' 1938

THE SOURCE

King Of The 12-String Guitar
Columbia Records

Leadbelly's Last Session
Smithsonian Folkways

All Colored People

THAT WANT TO

GO TO KANSAS,

On September 5th, 1877,

Can do so for $5.00

IMMIGRATION.

WHEREAS, We, the colored people of Lexington, Ky., knowing that there is an abundance of choice lands now belonging to the Government, have assembled ourselves together for the purpose of locating on said lands. Therefore,

BE IT RESOLVED, That we do now organize ourselves into a Colony, as follows:— Any person wishing to become a member of this Colony can do so by paying the sum of one dollar ($1.00), and this money is to be paid by the first of September, 1877, in instalments of twenty-five cents at a time, or otherwise as may be desired.

RESOLVED, That this Colony has agreed to consolidate itself with the Nicodemus Towns, Solomon Valley, Graham County, Kansas, and can only do so by entering the vacant lands now in their midst, which costs $5.00.

RESOLVED, That this Colony shall consist of seven officers—President, Vice-President, Secretary, Treasurer, and three Trustees. President—M. M. Bell; Vice-President—Isaac Talbott; Secretary—W. J. Niles; Treasurer—Daniel Clarke; Trustees—Jerry Lee, William Jones, and Abner Webster.

RESOLVED, That this Colony shall have from one to two hundred militia, more or less, as the case may require, to keep peace and order, and any member failing to pay in his dues, as aforesaid, or failing to comply with the above rules in any particular, will not be recognized or protected by the Colony.

SEGREGATION BY BRIBERY

'Colored people' were encouraged to leave Kentucky.

Herald even urged the US government to seize a large part of Mexico and send all the blacks there. The idea of sending the black population elsewhere was plainly ludicrous. It was fuelled by the press, but in the minds of most practical planters it remained an impossibility, as the war had made growing and picking cotton no less difficult. What was required was a system that would harvest cotton without the need for slavery.

THE AFTERMATH OF THE CIVIL WAR

The situation stabilised over the coming decades. Many former slaves were fairly compliant, which perhaps came naturally to them after their long years of oppression. There were few incidents of any violence from ex-slaves towards their former owners, although in 1874, 75 blacks were killed in race riots at Vicksburg. The climate was soothed by the withdrawal of the North from the South - both literally, as occupying troops returned to their homes, and figuratively, as they lost interest in the black cause. Capitalism was also hard at work: the United States needed to rebuild its agricultural and industrial activities to re-establish itself in the pecking order of world economics. The financial panic of 1873 also served to focus white people's minds on their own fortunes rather than the black community. Southern States were gradually readmitted to the Union and given back the power to pass laws re-establishing white supremacy. In 1875 Congress passed a Civil Rights Bill that made all public racial discrimination illegal, but it was the last of the North's efforts to 'control' the South.

The changing political climate was influenced by the power of the Southern Democrats, who actually took control of the House of Representatives after the Civil Rights Bill was passed. It was the State of Mississippi that laid down the procedure, copied by other Southern States, for reinforcing white rule. Its leaders were aided by the close-fought Presidential elections of 1876, which found the Republican Rutherford Hayes and the Democrat Samuel Tilden deadlocked in the popular vote. Hayes eventually triumphed, but at a price. Union troops were removed from South Carolina, while industrial and railroad interests were put before black emancipation. By 1883, the Supreme Court had declared the 1875 Civil Rights Bill to be unconstitutional. Thereafter, formal segregation entered almost every aspect of Southern life, and it stayed that way until after World War II.

RUTHERFORD BIRCHARD HAYES

(1822–1893) 19th President of the US from 1877–81. Hayes won the presidency over his Democrat rival, Samuel Tilden – but at a price.

BLACK PIONEERS

Black homesteaders the Shore family and their sod house in Nebraska, 1887. Blacks were encouraged to exodus from the South after the Civil War.

STOVALL'S PLANTATION

MUDDY WATERS GREW UP on Stovall's plantation, one of thousands spread across the South. The Stovall plantation, around 3,500 acres, is still farmed today by the family with just eight full-time employees. Once it took hundreds to tend to the cotton crop; now the use of aircraft and modern machinery have transformed the operation of the farm. Muddy left Stovall's Plantation and headed for Chicago, not long after Alan Lomax's visit to make recordings of him and other musicians for the Library of Congress in August 1941 and July 1942.

STOVALL FARMS
Stovall's is still a working cotton plantation.

THE STOVALL FAMILY

GEORGE (STOVOLD, STOFFOLDE, STOWFOLD) *was born around 1555 in England. He married Lettice Stone on 15th September, 1583, in Albury, Surrey, England. He died on 15th February, 1609/10, in Cranley, Surrey, England.*

GEORGE STOVOLD II *was born around 1588/90 in Surrey, England. He married Margaret Farley on 11th October, 1612. George, a blacksmith by trade, died 1657/8.*

GEORGE (STOFFOLD, STOBBOLD, STOVELL, STOVAL) *was born around 1623 in Albury. George married Joan Tickner before 15th October, 1653. Joan's father was Bartholomew. George and Joan possibly became Quakers. Despite Quaker beliefs, he was buried in Albury on 8th November, 1665, with all rites of the Church of England. They had only one child.*

TO AMERICA

BARTHOLOMEW STOVALL *was born on 24th August, 1665, in Albury. His birth was recorded four times in the Quaker Records of Guildford as Bartholomew Stowell. He was baptized at the age of 18 on 11th November, 1683, in the Episcopal church (Church of St Peter and St Paul) at Albury. He may have done this in order to emigrate since Quakers were not held in the same regard as the members of the Church of England. On 7th July, 1684, aged 21, he signed an indenture document to serve John Bright; he was Merchant of London for four years on arrival in the colonies. At the end of his indenture, Bartholomew got a marriage license on 6th August, 1693, and married Ann Burton. He purchased 318 acres next to Deep Creek and the James River in what is now Powhatan*

BARTHOLOMEW, JR. *born circa 1707 in Henrico Co., VA, died in 1777 in Powhatan Co., VA.*

JESSE, *born 1760 in Virginia. Married Elizabeth Howard, daughter of William and Jane Howard. Jesse died 1809 in Green Co., Kentucky.*

WILLIAM HOWARD STOVALL *was born 1793 in Powhotan Co., Virginia. Married Martha Jane Minter, and they had several children. Veteran of the war of 1812. Died in Green Co., Kentucky, date unknown.*

GEORGE *1695 – 1786.* WILLIAM *1697 – 1736.* HANNAH *1699 – 1773.* THOMAS *born circa 1700-05, death unknown, but did marry.* JOHN *born circa 1700 - 1781.* MARGARET *born 1701, death unknown, but did marry.*

WILLIAM HOWARD STOVALL II *born 20th February, 1834, in Kentucky. Moved to Memphis and to Coahoma County, Mississippi. Veteran of the American Civil War.* *(See other page.)*

WILLIAM HOWARD STOVALL II
A portrait of the Civil War veteran hangs in the Stovall home; his Confederate Army dog tags hang on the corner of the frame.

WILLIAM JOHN OLDHAM *(21st January, 1793 – 17th May, 1850). Came to the Mississippi Delta from South Carolina to cut timber. Acquired land from the American government pursuant to the 1830 Treaty of Dancing Rabbit Creek with the Choctaw Indian nation and the Treaty of Ponotoc with the Chickasaw nation, which resulted in land being offered for $1.25 per acre, and the two nations being forced to move to Oklahoma. Married Nancy Carver (1790 – 1839).*

JOHN WILLIS FOWLER *(20th March, 1805 – 2nd January, 1870). Married Caroline Oldham 14th May, 1839; she died four months later at age 19. Married Louisa Oldham (5th September, 1817 – 3rd April, 1851) on 12th September, 1840, in Memphis, less than a year after Caroline's death. Louisa died about three weeks after the birth of Caroline Azalia, when Louise Irene was nine years old. Fowler married a third time to Rosa Minter Eagle (unknown – 24th January, 1912) in January 1858, when Louise was 16 and Caroline was seven.*

LOUISE IRENE FOWLER *(5th November, 1842 – 31st July, 1875), in 1866 married* **COLONEL WILLIAM HOWARD STOVALL II** *(20th February, 1834 – 1916) of Memphis, a lawyer and veteran of the Civil War, who served as adjutant to the 154th Tennessee Regiment. They married 10th May, 1866, three years after Stovall had been discharged from the Confederate Army due to bad health (an eye injury). Practiced law in Memphis, but in 1865 moved from Memphis to Coahoma County, MS. Louisa died of consumption in Denver age 32, one month after her baby Caroline died in Alum Springs, Kentucky. On 23rd October, 1888, Stovall, aged 54 and a widower for 13 years with a 17-year-old son, married Louise Goodwin; she died in childbirth. Three years later Stovall married Roberta Lewis Frank in 1892. He was 61 years old when William Howard was born. Stovall, Goodwin, and Franks were, in fact, cousins, as Stovall's mother Martha Jane (née Minter) was sister to both Louise Goodwin's mother (Louise Minter) and Roberts Franks' grandmother (Sarah Ann Minter).*

WILLIAM HOWARD STOVALL III *(18th February, 1895 – 1970), veteran of WW1 in the United States Air Force, achieving 'ace' status with six confirmed kills in a Spad XIII in France. Recipient Distinguished Service Cross. Served in World War II on the senior staff of the 8th Air Force. Received Order of the British Empire and Légion d'Honneur. Retired with rank of Brigadier General. Married Eleanor Doyle Carter.*

MATTHEW CARTER STOVALL *(July 20, 1925 – 1997), married Meriwether Lewis and had two children, Meriwether Stovall McGettigan, (b. 1950), and Matthew Carter Stovall Jr. (1952 – 1968). Divorced, married Nancy Gilmore (b. February 6, 1936) in 1961.*

WILLIAM HOWARD STOVALL IV *(1923 – 1944), KIA, US Air Force. Buried in Margraten, Holland.*

MARIE STOVALL WEBSTER *b. 1926,*

ROBERT LOUIS STOVALL *b.1932,*

WILLIAM HOWARD STOVALL V. *Born 1962, resides in Memphis where he is Executive Director of The Blues Foundation. Married Baylor Ledbetter and has two children, Margaret Carter Stovall (b. 1999) and William Howard Stovall VI (b. 2000).*

LAURENCE GILMORE STOVALL *Born 1964, resides in Stovall, MS where he operates Stovall Farms.*

THE PLANTATION BELL
Gil Stovall stands by the bell, which once served as the plantation's clock. It announced the beginning and the end of the working day.

WILLIAM HOWARD STOVALL III
His official World War II USAF staff portrait hangs next to his WW1 squadron insignia, which he cut off his canvas-covered Spad aircraft and brought home from France.

STOVALL'S PLANTATION TODAY
The view towards the farm HQ from the site where Muddy Waters' childhood home once stood. Muddy's cabin is now on display at the Delta Blues Museum in Clarksdale, MS.

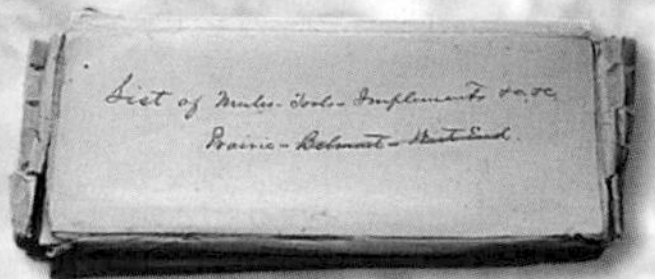

Left: A list of 'Mules, Tools, Implements, etc.', 1872

BLACK MUSIC BEFORE THE BLUES

EVEN A DETAILED HISTORY of black music in America must inevitably be incomplete. The status of slaves before the Civil War was not regarded as important enough for more than a cursory mention of their music. When there was interest in black performers, it was almost always in the context of black men performing white men's music. It was not until after 1840 that any real attempt was made to collect black music.

What is surprising is the fact that black folk music was able to develop in this alien environment and at the same time retain so much of its African identity. In 1867, a book entitled *Slave Songs Of The United States* was published, which was one of the earliest attempts at black song collecting, but given the structure of society at that time it could only provide a snapshot of African-American singing.

In a wonderful book, *On The Trail Of Negro Folk Songs*, written in 1925, Dorothy Scarborough, the daughter of a Texan District Judge, writes: "Folk songs are shy elusive things. If you wish to capture them, you have to steal up behind them, unbeknownst, and sprinkle salt on their tails". Fanciful, yes, but the truth is that many black people, who sang their songs in the country, would have been reluctant, embarrassed and possibly even frightened to sing their songs for 'white folks'. The lack of any recording machinery is another reason for our paucity of knowledge. Also, this was an age when people were not as interested in documenting cultural history as we became in the 20th century. Life then was dominated by thoughts of survival and hard work. The notion that people outside your own area, or even country, would be interested in what you were singing was unimaginable.

PLANTATION MELODIES OLD AND NEW
WORDS BY R. E. Phillips, J. E. Campbell, P. L. Dunbar.
MUSIC COMPOSED, OR TRANSCRIBED AND ADAPTED BY H. T. Burleigh.
Pr. $1.00 net
New York G. Schirmer

HARRY T. BURLEIGH
Burleigh, born in 1866, was one of the earliest composers and arrangers of African-American music. Burleigh was a student of Anton Dvorak, and taught him many black folk songs. Dvorak later used these as the inspiration and basis for his Symphony No. 9 in E minor, From The New World, *which premiered in New York in 1893.*

ANTON DVORAK
(1841-1904)
In 1893, Dvorak told America 'the future music of this country must be founded on the negro melodies'.

BLACK SPIRITUALS OF THE SLAVES

Living in a world where they heard European folk songs and hymns left a major impact on the black population. What resulted was a unique amalgam of African musical idioms with European influences. First came the spirituals, a direct result of black men copying white gospel hymns. One significant difference between black spirituals and gospel hymns lay in the words, probably as a result of the slaves' somewhat more limited vocabulary. They used lyrical concepts borrowed from gospel hymns and simply adapted them to their own ends. This gave the songs a force that allowed some of them to retain their popularity and their emotional resonance throughout the next 150 years.

Although they were popular before the Civil War, black spirituals took on a more recognisable form, and became even more prevalent, in the post-war period. They served both as work songs and songs of social gathering. The strength of the black church was a key element in developing and differentiating pure folk songs from religious songs. Some spirituals gradually took on a more secular form and eventually ceased to

The Fisk Jubilee Singers
Nashville's Fisk University was established in 1866 by Northerners who were keen to educate the newly freed slaves. By 1868, the college's finances had become precarious, so its treasurer, George White, hatched a plan to raise money for the school. He organized the students into a chorus and trained them for a concert tour. The spirituals they sang were presented in a way that was acceptable to the largely white audiences who were unaccustomed to seeing blacks in serious stage roles. They started an American tour in late 1871, and after a faltering start they scored a resounding triumph. They then went to Europe, enjoying unprecedented success and establishing an enduring interest in black spirituals. By the time of their return to America in 1878, they had raised $150,000 for the university funds.

be religious in nature. The Church specifically banned the singing of secular songs as sinful, and many churchgoers refused to sing secular material, but there was clearly no way of enforcing this strict code with everybody. But secular songs were definitely taboo at any activities organised by the Church, even purely social events like picnics.

Some of the most famous spirituals endure today in the same form as they were first sung in the 19th century. These include 'Deep River', 'Nobody Knows The Trouble I Seen', 'Ain't Goin' To Study War No Mo' and perhaps the most famous of them all, 'Swing Low Sweet Chariot'.

Religion and Railroads

During the 19th century the world offered simple choices to the black community. Religion was the starkest choice of all: either you joined the church or you faced eternal damnation. The people most open to the Church's message were those who stayed put and worked on their small plots of land, or who continued to work on the plantations, though not as slaves. Others decided to follow a life that was less virtuous in the eyes of the Church.

Many of the freed slaves sought work on the railroad, on steamboats, mining, at lumber camps, or with the levee gangs, and many of

The Rock Island Line
In 1852, the railroad that became famous as the Rock Island Line ran its first train from Chicago to Joliet, Illinois. In February 1854, the line was extended to Rock Island in Mississippi to give Chicago a rail link to the Mississippi.

"Oh, the Rock Island Line
Is a mighty fine line
Oh, the Rock Island Line
Is the road to ride
If you want to ride
You gotta ride it
Like you're flyin'
Get your ticket at the station
On the Rock Island Line."

SWING LOW SWEET CHARIOT

By the time Eric Clapton performed 'Swing Low Sweet Chariot' on his 1975 album There's One In Every Crowd, *it had already been performed by an incredible range of artists, from BB King to Bing Crosby and Peggy Lee to Fats Waller.*

them eventually found themselves in prison. They were incarcerated on the slightest pretext by a Southern culture that still regarded the former slaves as their property, to do with as they pleased.

Both the railroad and the prison helped to shape the black man's musical future. The first transcontinental railroad was completed in 1869 and throughout this period many former slaves followed the railroad building schemes in search of work. The railway's expansion through the Southern states had been fast, as it was only in 1850 that the train began to threaten the riverboat as a means of carrying freight.

From life on the railways came a whole tradition of both black and white railroad songs, one of the most famous being 'John Henry'. It tells the story of a 220-pound black rail hand who became a folk hero to his people. There are many versions of the song but all essentially tell the same tale of a man who worked himself to death in a vain attempt to beat a mechanised steel drill.

> *'John Henry says to his Cap'n,*
> *Send me a twelve poun' hammer aroun,'*
> *A twelve poun' wid a four-foot handle,*
> *An I beat yo' steam drill down,*
> *An I beat yo' steam drill down.*
> *John Henry went down on de railroad.*
> *Wid a twelve poun' hammer by his side,*
> *He walked down de track but never come back,*
> *'Cause he laid down his hammer an' he died,*
> *Yes, he laid down his hammer an' he died'*
>
> 'JOHN HENRY'

While 'John Henry' is clearly a secular folk song, there are the vestiges of religion in the lyrics. Spirituals such as 'Hammering', which tells of 'Jewsus' crucificion', is a link, as is 'The Hammers Keep Ringing'. Railroad songs were a logical and natural development in the whole saga of work songs, particularly appropriate to many of the black population who saw trains as an escape route from their oppressive lifestyles.

But a train ride was just a dream to most slaves, as they needed a written bond from their owner before they were allowed to travel on a train. Spirituals also came under the influence of the train metaphor, as phrases like 'Getting on board the Gospel Train' began to appear in lyrics.

MUSICAL MELTING POT

For the last 50 years in particular, there has been heated and sometimes vitriolic debate about the influence of European music on African-based music in America. Considerable intellectual muscle has been exercised to 'prove' on the one hand that black folk music is purely a black African invention, and on the other that it is almost entirely the result of European influence. What is clear is that everything in the United States was changing, and that this increasingly mixed society was a huge melting pot of ideas, style and substance.

Music was subject to all these influences, and during the second half of the 19th century it developed at a rapid rate. No doubt this was in part due to the freeing of the slaves, but it must also have been altered as the character of the nation changed too. The development of cities and larger towns, allied to the expansion of the nation in general, which was happening with the help of the railroads, combined to mould the musical map of America.

This, then, was the land in which the Blues began to develop. We can of course never know who wrote the first blues song, and even using the term 'wrote' is a misnomer.

THE UNDERGROUND RAILWAY

The legendary clandestine escape route to the North for slaves was called the 'Underground Railway'. The people who helped en route were called 'conductors', while the places where they hid, in barns or cellars, were known as 'stations'. Spirituals were used as codes to indicate that a journey was to start: 'Steal away, steal away to Jesus'.

In fact, it is absolutely certain that no one actually 'wrote' the earliest songs, as the Blues emerged from the complex oral tradition of African-based music, developing rapidly during the last 40 years of the 19th Century.

The rise of the spiritual is relatively easy to follow, given the organised way in which the Church went about its business. But the passing on of folk music was a more complex process: without TV, radio, CDs, records, tapes, or any other process for hearing recorded music, the population had to spread its songs literally by word of mouth.

It is hardly surprising, then, that songs were changed and 'improved' as they made their journey through America. Naturally this process was nowhere more haphazard than in the countryside. Devoid of theatres or other places to go and hear music, people tended to learn new songs from itinerant musicians and collective singing in family or other groups.

ROUSTABOUTS
New Orleans Levee roustabouts unload barrels from a riverboat.

The debate over the African-American musical heritage has provoked extensive research into its early years, and produced many weighty tomes attempting to categorize the music. These theories and ideas would have baffled the people who actually sang and played their music back in 19th century America. But beyond the division into the religious and the secular, it is possible to be more specific about the music that emerged during the second half of the 19th century.

Work songs, in all their various guises, came on a direct route from Africa, certainly in style if not in lyrical content. Not surprisingly, given the number of people employed on the rivers during the earlier part of the century, many of the work songs and hollers were related to river work.

Similarly, songs sung by people who gathered together outside of church activities would also form a distinct grouping, although spirituals were also sung on these occasions as well. Many of these songs would have derived from ballads of English, Irish, and Scottish origin, or even French in the case of Louisiana; these were songs heard by the former slaves and their parents from the lips of their white owners.

MINSTREL COMPANIES

Although there were some isolated examples before the Civil War, it was only after the war that black minstrel companies really came into their own. There were also white minstrel companies; both black and white minstrels became the first really organised attempts at 'light entertainment'. There were three large black companies: the Hicks and Swayers Minstrels, the McCabe and Young Minstrels, and Richard and Pringle's Famous Georgia Minstrels. There were also several mixed companies, including the Primrose and West Minstrel Company. In addition to these major companies that employed 30 to 70 performers apiece, there were countless small companies that may have had just two or three musicians and not many more singers.

The black minstrel shows favoured the music of black writers such as James Bland, Gussie Davis and Samuel Lucas, but also songs by the white composer Stephen Foster.

THE END WAS JUST THE BEGINNING

The change in working practices after the Civil War meant that the old work gangs who toiled on the plantations largely disappeared. The small farms that formed the basis of sharecropping required different styles

MARK TWAIN
Mark Twain was the nom de plume *of former Mississippi riverboat pilot Samuel Langhorne Clemens. Born in 1835, he adopted the pseudonym when he worked as a Virginia City newspaper reporter, around 1863. The name comes from the cry used by Mississippi riverboat leadsmen to indicate a 12-foot depth of water, usually the lowest depth that is safe for a Mississippi riverboat. A cry could typically go:*

*'No bottom
Mark four
Quarter less four
Quarter less three
Half twain
Quarter twain
Mark twain'*

'SHINING TRUMPETS' BY RUDI BLESH

This book, published in 1949, gives one of the best accounts of the history of jazz and blues. It also does an excellent job of categorising the musical styles that were to be found in 19th century America.

RELIGIOUS

A: Congregational

1. Preaching with Responses
2. Congregational Singing, the Spirituals
3. Singing the Spirituals
4. 'Holy' Dancing
5. Ring Shouts

B: Street Singing

The Revivalist

SECULAR

A: Work Songs

1. Plantation & Rural (Choral)
Cotton Picking
Hoeing & Cotton Chopping
Water Songs
Ploughing
Mule & Ox Driving
Chopping Sugar Cane
Quitting Time Songs
2. Various Occupations (Choral)

PRIMROSE AND WEST MINSTRELS

Poster for a Minstrel show of the 1880s, featuring 40 whites and 30 blacks.

of working; and while people still sang, they did so in a different way. Southern prisons, however, maintained a method of working that was almost identical to the old slave gangs, in conditions that both emulated and rivalled the tradition of slavery. While the white guards stood by, the blacks toiled all day in the fields or on road gangs, all the while singing their songs to create a rhythm to which they could work. As with the railroad songs, the prisoners sang to keep themselves working better and harder; perhaps it also had the consolation of making the time go just a little faster.

Whether they were under the new sharecropping system or as meagrely paid farm workers, fieldworkers now toiled in smaller groups than in the past. As they were often separated by several fields, the practice of 'hollering' replaced the work song. Again, the very act of singing aided the whole work process, making things a little more bearable in the harsh climactic conditions of the Southern states – which were nowhere harsher, of course, than in the Mississippi Delta.

JAMES BLAND – THE WORLD'S GREATEST MINSTREL MAN

Born in 1854, Bland was the heir to Stephen Foster's crown. His songs were performed by black and white minstrel shows, and sung by people everywhere, many of whom probably never realized that he was black. He was a self-taught banjo player who, after working as a performer at parties in Washington, joined Haverly's Colored Minstrels. He travelled to Europe in 1881, and when his troupe returned to America, he remained to tour Europe's music halls, becoming a major star. By the early 1900s, Bland's star had waned, and in true showbiz tradition he died penniless in Philadelphia in 1911. He wrote more than 700 songs, including 'Oh Dem Golden Slippers' and 'Carry Me Back To Old Virginny'. The latter was adopted by the state of Virginia as its official song in 1940; once again, few knew it was a song written by a black minstrel. In 1965, when Jerry Lee Lewis released his final Sun Records single, it was none other than 'Carry Me Back To Old Virginny'.

Four-fifths of the black population lived in rural areas, and so all they knew was the hand-to-mouth existence of farming. If you were black and not engaged in farming, then you were probably doing some other equally menial and exhausting job.

The march towards segregation was now becoming relentless. By 1900, 14 states had segregation laws in place.

One outcome of the new laws was that church worship in the South was no longer shared by blacks and whites. In 1895, a black minister founded the Church of God in Christ in Memphis, Tennessee. This was the start of a fundamental change in black worship, which in turn sparked a revolution in black church music – and the seeds of what has now become known as soul music.

Black men working in fields, in prison gangs, on railroads, or in any lowly job, had no alternative but to make their own entertainment. For them, the idea of being entertained by a radio sitting on the workbench or placed next to them in a field was totally unimaginable.

In the 21st century, we have to rely solely on word of mouth to tell us what these people sang about to relieve the monotony of their daily grind. But their hollering was about to move from the fields and railroads into cities across America, as it was taken up by a New Orleans musician – and soon began to change the world.

Whatever the reason for their singing, the prison gangs helped to maintain an important element of what would become the Blues in later years.

'Shining Trumpets'
(Continued)

Axe Chopping
Sea Shanties
Riverboat Chants
Levee Chants
Railroad Songs
Steel Work
3. Various Solitary Occupations
Hollers for Many Occupations
Street Cries, Vendors' Chants and Songs
River Sounding Calls

B: Dances
Square Dances & Reels
Fiddle Songs
Cake Walks
Jigs and Ragtime Struts

C: Play Songs, Especially Children's
Kissing Games
Hiding Games
Ring Games
Dancing Games
Lullabies

D: Ballads
Narrative
Epic or Legendary

A Prison Road Gang from the 1930s
Not so long ago this was a familiar sight in Texas, Mississippi, and Louisiana.

3

Ragtime, Jazz & The Birth Of The Blues

WAREROOMS
PIANOS
207.

RAGTIME

The left hand maintains a regular bass beat, the right hand a syncopated melody.

RAGTIME'S ROOTS
Ragtime's roots came from plantation life. The 'cakewalk' became a popular form of plantation entertainment, when couples in fancy dress would promenade, and the best walkers would 'take the cake'. Later the cakewalk found its way to American vaudeville theatre and eventually to Europe. Another popular musical form that developed around the same time was the 'coon song', which involved loud whooping and hollering.

As a forerunner of jazz, ragtime was another building block in the story of the Blues, helping to bring the music to a wider audience. As one commentator noted, it marked "the blackening of American musical grammar". While it was initially very much an 'underground' style, ragtime soon took America, and the world, by storm.

Ragtime originated in part as an attempt by black pianists in the brothels of New Orleans's Basin Street to emulate the sound of the city's brass bands, who 'shifted the accent' from the strong to the weak beat.

Piano rags were able to imitate the sound of a banjo – not just one banjo, but three or four. Some maintain that the earliest published rag was 'New Coon In Town', which was published in 1884 as a 'banjo imitation'. The first published piece with 'ragtime' in its title was 'Ma Ragtime Baby' by a Detroit man, Fred Stone, in 1893. Another contender for the prize of the first rag was an 1895 composition by Ben Harney in Louisville which was entitled 'You've Been A Good Old Wagon'. William Krell is credited with composing the first instrumental rag, 'Mississippi Rag', which came out in January 1897.

Regardless of who came first, rags were soon all the rage, and they remained popular for the next two decades. While they had sprung from the heady cosmopolitan atmosphere of New Orleans, they quickly spread across the country, often carried by musicians who left to seek their fortunes in Memphis, St Louis, and the other big cities within striking distance of the Mississippi River. As their inspiration, ragtime composers used cakewalks, European ballads, polkas and waltzes. In the second half of the 20th century, ragtime became synonymous with the piano, but in its heyday it was much broader than that. It was the 'pop' music of the day, as ragtime songs, either in the form of 'coon songs' or vocal group numbers, were just as common as piano rags. One entrepreneur even opened a chain of ragtime instruction schools that included a branch in Hawaii.

St Louis became the spiritual home of ragtime. The city, which numbered 500,000 people in 1895, was a haven of gambling, drinking and pleasure. It has been described as "a sinful city that was the very epitome of the naughty nineties". One of the earliest ragtime composers grew up in St Louis and did much to establish the city's reputation. He was the rather grandly named Thomas Million Turpin, who besides being the composer of the first black instrumental ragtime number, 'Harlem Rag' (1897), and 'St Louis Rag', was also an inspired performer.

Many have mistakenly believed that because white men published the first rags, they also invented the form, but blacks were playing ragtime

Doing the Cakewalk, St. Louis, 1895

Left: St Louis, Missouri, the spiritual home of ragtime, in the early 20th century.

SCOTT JOPLIN
Ragtime composer, musician, 1911.

long before Krell's Orchestra. Most of the black composers and performers of ragtime made enough money in tips, and hardly felt it was worth the effort of seeking out a sympathetic white publisher.

One composer has become inexorably linked with ragtime, and is almost as famous today as he was during his lifetime: Scott Joplin, 'The King of the Ragtime Writers'. He was born in 1868 in Texarkana, which straddles the border between Texas and Arkansas; Joplin was born on the Texas side. Having previously published marches and waltzes, he published his *Original Rags* in 1899.

Joplin was born into a musical family. His father played the violin, his mother sang and played banjo, his three brothers and two sisters also played and sang, and Scott learned the guitar and later the cornet. When his father heard him playing a neighbour's piano, he was persuaded to buy Scott a second-hand instrument of his own. Scott was taught by a German piano teacher, who gave him free lessons. Much later, when he had become rich and famous and his teacher was impoverished, he repaid his mentor by sending him money.

Joplin's mother died in 1882, after which he left Texas and headed for Sedalia, Missouri, where he met John Stark, a music-store owner. Stark was apparently in a club having a drink when he first heard Joplin's music, and he soon became his publisher. By 1899 Joplin and Stark had published the seminal 'Maple Leaf Rag'. Although sales were initially slow, it eventually became a nationwide best-seller. This opened the floodgates for other, much less accomplished ragtime composers and their publishers, who churned out rags to capitalise on the trend.

The first recording of 'Maple Leaf Rag' was made in 1903, in Minneapolis, though sadly no copies are known to have survived. Joplin only made a piano roll of the tune in 1916, and this unique artefact of the era was marred by the fact that Joplin's health was failing and he made many mistakes. Ten years earlier, he had moved to New York, where he composed his most ambitious piece, the opera *Treemonisha*. In the same year, in Paris, the French composer Claude Debussy wrote his rag-style 'Golliwog's Cakewalk'.

Dogged by syphilis, Joplin died in 1917, aged 49. While some argue that he was not the greatest ragtime composer, he is undoubtedly the best known. In 1976 Joplin was posthumously awarded a special Pulitzer Prize for music.

While classic ragtime was on the wane at the time of Joplin's death, it continued to have an important influence on the development of jazz and blues. Jelly Roll Morton saw the opportunities of broadening the appeal of ragtime by providing a more free-flowing style, especially in the bass line. This style became known as 'stomp' piano. James Johnson, the creator of 'stride' piano, moved ragtime further toward jazz and blues, while Charles (Cow-Cow) Davenport, the pioneer of the boogie-woogie style, was also trained in ragtime.

THE RAGTIME REVIVAL

In 1965, Joshua Rifkin, a former member of The Even Dozen Jug Band – a group that included John Sebastian (later to join the Lovin' Spoonful), Steve Katz (later of Blood Sweat & Tears) and Maria Muldaur – made a recording of Joplin rags for the Nonesuch label. Rifkin's elegant and slow performances were quite different to what people had come to think of as ragtime, but the record became a best-seller. A mini ragtime revival was soon underway, and the music even began to be used in TV commercials. In 1973, film director George Roy Hill used Joplin's song 'The Entertainer', first published in 1902, as the theme to his film, *The Sting*. Many who bought the resulting record assumed that the piece was actually called 'The Theme From The Sting' by screen composer Marvin Hamlisch!

THE EARLY HISTORY OF RECORDING

NEWSPAPER ADVERTISEMENT
Edison's perfected Phonograph, which was available to adventurous American listeners for a mere $2 per month.

TODAY, IT IS EASY TO FORGET that it is not much more than 100 years ago that commercial recordings first became available. Nowadays we take it for granted that we can hear a CD or some other form of recording. But as the 19th century ended, the only real way to 'hear' a performer was to see them live. That experience would seem strange to the modern listener, as back then there was no amplification. This inevitably made things more intimate, and solo performers had their work cut out, simply to get their songs heard.

In the last quarter of the 19th century a German, Emile Berliner, and an American, Thomas Edison, set about changing the way that people could listen to music.

1877 *Emile Berliner invents the first microphone and sells the rights to Bell Telephone. Thomas Edison invents a better microphone, which in 1878 becomes the one used by Bell.*

1878 *The world's first phonograph company, The Edison Speaking Phonograph Company, is established in New York. The first phonograph for home use is sold by Edison for $10: it is called 'The Parlour Speaking Phonograph'.*

1878 *Emile Berliner patents the 'gramophone', a talking machine that employs laterally cut discs.*

1887 *The first demonstration of disc recording and reproduction by Berliner takes place in Philadelphia. A 12-year-old pianist makes a two-minute cylinder recording in Edison's laboratory.*

1889 *A toymaker (Kammerer and Reinhardt) starts making Berliner's hand-wound gramophones that play five-inch discs. Frank Goede, a piccolo player, makes the first commercial cylinders, for The North American Phonograph Company, who had purchased the rights from Edison in 1888.*

1890 *Berliner makes recordings which include 'The Lord's Prayer'.*

1891 *Miss Stewart becomes the first vocalist to record a cylinder, 'My Love And I, Pattison's Waltz Song'.*

1892 *The first known recording by a black artist is 'Mama's Black Baby Boy' by the Unique Vocal Quartet. Music's first million-seller is 'After the Ball' by J. Aldrich Libbey.*

1894 *Berliner launches the United States Gramophone Co. from Washington, DC.*

1895 *George C. Gaskin records 'I Don't Want To Play In Your Back-Yard'.*

1897 *The first recording studio opens over a shoe shop in Philadelphia, where Berliner also opens the first record shop. The Sousa Band releases several dance records.*

1898 *Eldridge Johnson perfects the first system of mass duplication of pre-recorded discs. Johnson improves on Berliner's methods by mastering on wax instead of the acid etching method, and by using several metal positives which each make multiple stampers.*

1899 *Johnson presses the first commercial two-sided discs, which are children's records.*

1900 *Columbia starts producing and selling disc records.*

1903 *Victor introduces 12-inch and 14-inch disc records under the Deluxe name. Columbia boasts that it is now producing two million records a month, a claim which is refuted by Edison.*

Background picture: Emile Berliner.

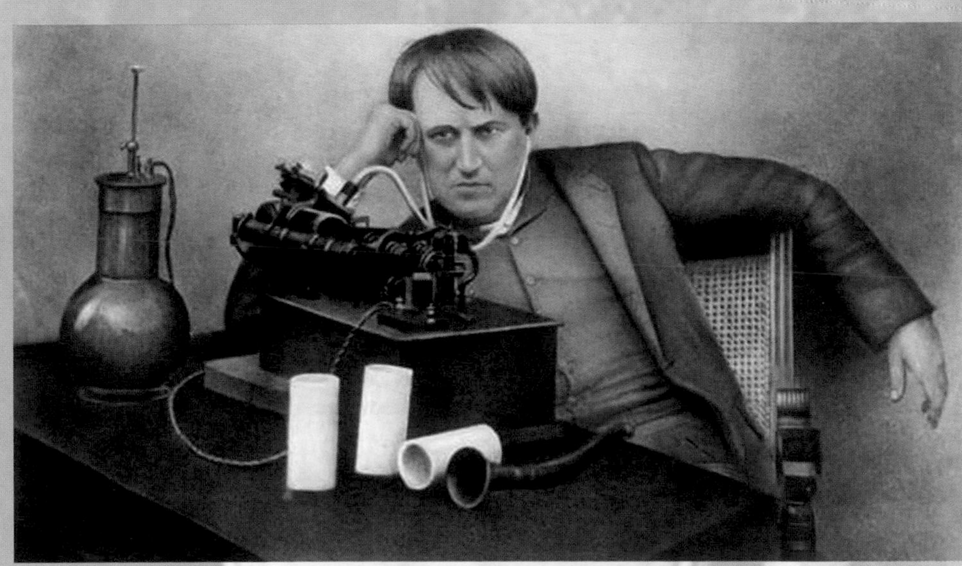

Thomas Edison and his Parlour Speaking Phonograph.

JAZZ

St Charles Street, New Orleans

WHILE THERE IS LITTLE DEBATE about the origins of jazz, there is plenty of disagreement about how it came by its name. One theory is that an itinerant black musician known as Jazbo Brown played in the Mississippi Delta, and his audience would shout 'more Jazbo, more Jaz'; another that the title was a corruption of the name of a New Orleans band, known as Razz. What is clear is that the roots of jazz lay with country people, the former slaves who lived and worked in the predominantly rural areas of the Southern states.

New Orleans, the Crescent City, is widely accepted as the birthplace of jazz, but the reasons why are still hotly debated. Certainly the city was filled with young black men who had few opportunities to find work, but who were inspired to take up music by what they heard all around them – from street parades, and the open windows of dancehalls. With the burden of poverty there was little chance that these young people could buy their own instruments, so they had to make

Jazz has been described as 'a fusion of blues and ragtime with brass band and syncopated dance music'.

'SIX MUSICAL SPILLERS'

Early 20th-century American 'darky jazz variety act'.

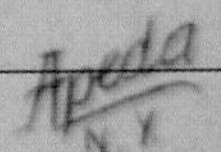

BUDDY BOLDEN BAND c. 1900
Standing, left to right: Jimmy Johnson (double bass), Buddy Bolden (cornet), Willie Cornish (valve trombone), Frank Lewis (clarinet). Seated, left to right: Jeff 'Brock' Munford (guitar), William Warner (clarinet).

their own, or somehow earn enough to buy an ageing instrument from a junk shop.

The musical heart of New Orleans was Storyville. This area, with Canal Street running through its centre, contained streets that have become inexorably associated with jazz: Franklin Street, Rampart Street, Tulane Street and, perhaps most famous of all, Basin Street. This bustling and vibrant area was a mass of saloons, clubs, brothels, theatres, churches, restaurants, shops, and businesses. The music did much to create a heady atmosphere around the turn of the century that is almost unimaginable to modern visitors to New Orleans. In 1897, Storyville was designated as the 'tenderloin' district, a sort of sexual cleansing to cut off its vice from the rest of the city.

Storyville created an inexhaustible demand for musicians, many of them young, many of them black. Few of them could read music, and few needed to, as they concentrated on playing the best-known tunes of the day in their own expressive styles. In 1894 the city had enacted a segregation code that moved the mixed-race Creoles to this uptown area. Creole musicians proved very influential on the younger, less experienced, black musicians.

Among the best bands in the city at that time were the Excelsior Brass Band and The Onward Brass Band, both formed in the 1880s. These were definitely establishment bands, who had little in common with the music and rhythms of Storyville. The best jazz bands in town were to be found in the better 'professional houses' of the quarter, and very soon they were playing a style that became known as 'hot jazz'.

The first noteworthy exponent of this style was Charles 'Buddy' Bolden, who started his own outfit in the early 1890s. By 1895, he was acknowledged as the 'King of the Cornet' and his group was reckoned to be the best of the New Orleans hot bands, a reputation that lasted some 12 years. Bolden, unlike many of his contemporaries, could read music, but he preferred to play by ear as he had a natural flair for jazz phrasing and spontaneity. Bolden primarily played parades and dances, and not surprisingly his band included some of the city's best players. His repertoire of songs included 'Make Me A Pallet On The Floor' and 'Buddy Bolden's Blues'. To modern ears, Bolden's brand of jazz might not seem all that adventurous, but his contemporaries were impressed by his fiery rhythms and the way he freely embellished the melodies. In 'Buddy Bolden's Blues', he was probably interpreting a field holler which he had heard either during his travels, or from former slaves who had moved to New Orleans. His career took a dramatic turn around 1907, when he went mad while playing in a street parade. He was committed to an institution, where he died without ever regaining his sanity, in 1931.

Bolden's contemporaries, all of whom helped to establish New Orleans' reputation for jazz, included cornet player Willie 'Bunk' Johnson (who played with Bolden), clarinettist Frank Lewis, trombonist Buddy

WILLIE 'BUNK' JOHNSON
Cornet player Bunk Johnson started his career playing with Buddy Bolden's Band, but went on to establish a strong reputation of his own in the New Orleans jazz world.

King Oliver
New Orleans, 1918. As a trumpet player and then most famously as a bandleader, Joseph 'King' Oliver helped to put New Orleans jazz on the musical map. It was in Oliver's band that the great Louis Armstrong received his big break.

Johnson, guitarist Charles Galloway and drummer Black Benny Williams. A second wave of equally outstanding performers soon appeared, all of whom had worked their apprenticeships with those pioneers, men like trumpeters Freddie Keppard and Joseph 'King' Oliver, trombonist Frank Dusen, and clarinettists George Baquet, Johnny Dodds, and Sidney Bechet.

Then there was Louis Daniel Armstrong. Born in New Orleans in 1900, he learned to play cornet from Bunk Johnson, later mastering the bugle while he was at a boys' home. By the end of World War I, Armstrong was playing with Kid Ory, before moving to Chicago to join King Oliver's band – and the rest, as they say, is history.

In 1908, 25-year-old Keppard formed a band that became the first from New Orleans to tour throughout the nation. They started out as a seven-piece, but soon reduced to a quintet. By 1913 they were known as the Original Creole Jazz Band and were touring extensively across the whole of North America, from New York to Los Angeles. Their music was steeped in the blues tradition, giving many audiences their first exposure to this exciting new music. Meanwhile, King Oliver, having played with Kid Ory's band, moved to

King Oliver's Creole Jazz Band
From left to right, the personnel in this historic picture are: Baby Dodd, Horpre Dutrey, King Oliver, Bill Johnson, Johnny Dodds, Louis Armstrong and Lil Hardin (who married Armstrong in 1924).

JELLY ROLL MORTON AND THE LIBRARY OF CONGRESS

'I invented jazz'

... is how Jelly Roll Morton often introduced himself. During the 1920s he had a much publicised feud with WC Handy, as Morton disputed Handy's reputation as 'The Father of the Blues', claiming that he was merely a plagiarist. The pinnacle of Morton's career was his recording session for the Library of Congress in 1938. He related his 'highly personal' history of jazz to Alan Lomax, illustrating it with piano solos and songs, which added up to more than one hundred individual compositions.

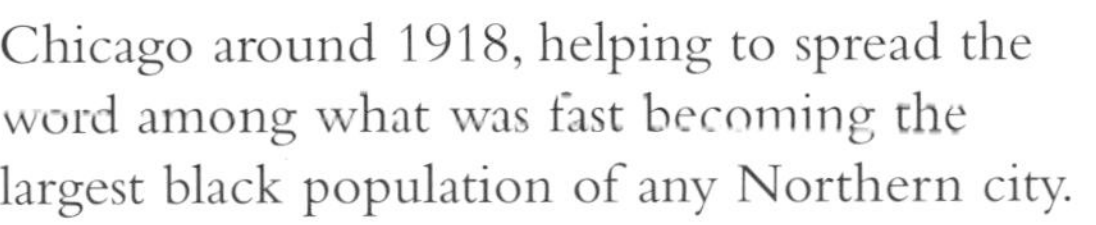

Chicago around 1918, helping to spread the word among what was fast becoming the largest black population of any Northern city.

Ferdinand Joseph Morton, known to the world as 'Jelly Roll', was born in the Crescent City in 1885. While still in his teens, he learned to play rags and stomps from blues pianist Mamie Desdume. To fool his parents he pretended that he had a job in a factory, while all the time playing the piano down in Basin Street. He was another musician who eventually wound up in Chicago, having worked his way across the South as a solo pianist. He died in California in 1941, after a rollercoaster career. His involvement in the Blues was limited but his legend and inspiration live on.

One reason for the 'mass exodus' of musicians from New Orleans was the fact that in 1917 the US Navy demanded that Storyville should be closed down. This symbolic act effectively marked the end of an era, but it also coincided with the dawn of a revolution. The combination of radio and 78rpm records was about to take music to a mass market, and change the face of entertainment forever.

WC HANDY

The legendary composer of 'St Louis Blues' is commemorated by a statue just off Beale Street in his hometown of Memphis. 'St Louis Blues' has been recorded by dozens of different artists, in every conceivable genre from traditional jazz to rowdy rock'n'roll.

THE BIRTH OF THE BLUES

'Goin' where the Southern cross' the dog'

MANY OF THE MOST obvious features of jazz are derived directly from the Blues, but whereas the Blues is primarily a vocal style, jazz usually replaces the voice with an instrument or combination of instruments. Personality exemplifies what makes great jazz, as well as great blues: both styles require a performance of an individualistic nature. Although jazz evolved as an ensemble form, it still requires free expression and charismatic playing to lift performers and performances above and beyond the confines of the style.

The Blues are very much about the individual, so it is fitting that it was an individual who inspired the self-styled 'Father of the Blues', WC Handy. Much later he recalled the incident in his autobiography:

"Then one night in Tutwiler, as I nodded in the railroad station while waiting for a train that had been delayed nine hours, life suddenly took me by the shoulder and wakened me with a start. A lean, loose-jointed negro had commenced plunking a guitar beside me while I slept . . . As he played he pressed a knife on the strings of the guitar in a manner popularized by Hawaiian guitarists. The effect was unforgettable. His song too, struck me instantly. *'Goin' where the Southern cross' the Dog'*. The singer repeated the line three times, accompanying himself on the guitar with the weirdest music I had ever heard."

This was in 1903, when Handy was working in Clarksdale as the director of the nine-man Knights Of Pythias Band. What he clearly found unusual was the fact that he was hearing a vocal refrain; like most of his contemporaries, he was used to hearing the blues form played by bands. When Handy heard 'the Blues', it may well have been in existence in a recognisable form for as long as 30 years. Many scholars believe that the Blues was well established across the Southern states by 1870. Regional variations persisted – indeed, without the wireless or phonograph it would have been surprising if they had not - but there was a cohesion to the overall form. With this knowledge, it is somewhat surprising that Handy's first encounter with the Blues came so late, as the style was undoubtedly popular throughout the vast rural tracts of the South. In fact, the Blues had already reached many Southern cities well before 1903; 'Buddy Bolden's Blues', for example, dates from the mid-1890s. Ten years or so later, musician Harrison Barnes went to New Orleans to play the piano in a brothel, just off Canal Street. The girls would ask him to play their

PLANTATION WORKERS
An evocative picture of working life on a sugar plantation near New Orleans, around 1901.

SAVANNAH STREET SCENE C.1926
Although this is a 20th century picture, it accurately captures life in the rural South. The scene is typical of 19th-century street life.

favourite songs. Many years later he recalled:

> *'They were slow tunes, unhappy. They was what they call the Blues now, only they called them ditties in them days'*

This may explain some of the possible confusion. People in the rural South were not much concerned with what a particular musical style was called. This was just music that they made to entertain, and sometimes even assist themselves while they were going about their everyday lives. Poor Southern blacks and whites never imagined that future generations would be looking at their culture, trying to analyze the subtle nuances of musical form that were, to them, just songs.

Some historians argue that the Blues began in the 1890s, taken by migrants from the plantations and farms to the cities. But it seems inconceivable that in the slow-moving world of the 19th century, the Blues could have travelled to the cities in a matter of just a few years, so circa 1870 seems a much more likely 'birth date' for the Blues.

A few years before Handy came across the Blues at Tutwiler, a white archeologist, Charles Peabody, was excavating at a site near Stovall, Mississippi with a team of black diggers. He noted that his workers sang improvised songs that were blues in form. Between 1905 and 1908, folklorist Howard Odum, who later published a large collection of black folksongs, travelled throughout the Delta and Georgia on a field trip. More than half of the songs he documented were blues, and much of their lyrical content appeared in blues songs that were recorded much later on. What is particularly interesting about Odum is that he tells us how and where these songs were sung: after church, at social gatherings, at dances, on the front porches of shotgun shacks or around the fireside. The Blues had most likely been around for a long time before Odum started his research.

The birthplace of the Blues is the vast arc that runs from Georgia to Texas, and includes the Mississippi Delta, as well as the valley that runs from southern Illinois. This huge area was made up of farms, forests, and plantations, and it was home to a black population attempting to carve out an existence in the aftermath of the Civil War and under the cloud of Southern white attitudes which were often openly hostile. It was the contemporary lack of interest in documenting the songs of this beleaguered

THE SOUTHERN CROSS' THE DOG
The intersection of the Southern Railroad and the Yazoo & Mississippi Valley Railroad (the Dog) at Moorhead, Mississippi, that inspired the unknown singer at Tutwiler. The crossing dates from 1895.

BLACK COMMUNITIES
A typical street in a black district of Atlanta, c. 1925.

people that caused our lack of precise knowledge about when the Blues began.

WHAT IS THE BLUES?

The debate about when the Blues began is somewhat academic. What is more important is to know, and to understand, what it is.

> *"Blues is a natural fact, something that a fellow lives. If you don't live it, you don't have it"*
>
> BIG BILL BROONZY

Writing in 1925 in her book *On The Trail Of Negro Folk Songs*, Dorothy Scarborough said:

"For the last several years the most popular type of negro song has been that peculiar, barbaric sort of melody called 'the Blues', with its irregular rhythm, its lagging briskness, its mournful liveliness of tone. It has a jerky tempo, as of a cripple dancing because of some irresistible impulse. A 'blues' (or does one say a 'blue'? what is the grammar of the thing?) likes to end its stanza abruptly, leaving the listener expectant for more – though, of course, there is no fixed law about the thing."

The use of the word 'blue' to describe a feeling or a mood goes back to the 16th century. During the 19th century, its precise definition became somewhat blurred. It was variously used to describe a fit of depression, boredom or sheer unhappiness, and it was not particularly associated with the black population. By 1912 when Handy published 'Memphis Blues', which ironically is not a blues tune but an instrumental cakewalk, the fad for using the word 'blues' was already several years old. Handy's tune was the third to use the word in its title. Hart Wand's 'Dallas Blues' has the distinction of being the first, while the second was Arthur Seals' 'Baby Seals' Blues'. Ironically, while Seals and Handy were both black, Wand was white, although in form his piece was a black blues tune.

For many the 'vision' offered by Lead Belly sums up what the Blues is all about:

❛When you lay down at night, turning from one side of the bed to the other and can't sleep, what's the matter? Blues got you❜

TEACH YOUR CHILDREN WELL

An African-American mother teaches her two young sons. Formal education wasn't available for most of the blues pioneers: Big Bill Broonzy didn't learn to read until he was around 60.

While this may define the Blues for many people, there are many other forms of the music. They can be difficult to define precisely, but you know they are *the Blues* and you know when you have them.

In form, structure and content, blues songs are fairly standard, although this template is open to variations. The blues stanza tends to consist of eight or 12 bars, although there are many other permutations – even twelve and a half! What is more important to the musician is that the song should sound right. Along with the form of the stanza go the flattened third and seventh notes which give the Blues its sound; not surprisingly these have become known as 'blue notes'.

Idiosyncratic singing styles are another typical aspect of the Blues. Often the last word or syllable is dropped from the end of a line, creating a loose and unfinished sound to the performance. A partial explanation of this could be the fact that many songs have their origins in the call-and-response structure of the work song or spiritual. The chorus would often finish a line that had been started by the caller. One further lyrical trait of the Blues is the use of the entendre or double entendre, often with relation to women trouble:

❛They've been diggin' my potatoes
Tramplin' on my vine
They've been diggin' my potatoes
Tramplin' on my vine
I have a special plan restin' on my mind
Said my vine's all green, potatoes solid red
Never found a bruised one
Till I caught them in my bed
You know they're diggin' my potatoes,
Tramplin' on my vine
I have a special plan restin' on my mind❜

WASHBOARD SAM, 1939

As our story unfolds we shall see that the Blues is not exclusively about complaints and worries. It is just as likely to be about sex or social comment, or the more positive aspects of life. In fact, even in despair, the Blues is often filled with great good humour. But given the situation that most black people found themselves in after the Civil War and during the early years of the 20th century, it is hardly surprising that the style contains an ample dose of the downbeat.

Put on a blues song now and listen to the singer. If you are struck by nothing else, you will be touched by his or her commitment, emotion, passion, the sheer potency of feeling. That is what the Blues is all about.

CHARLEY PATTON

CHARLEY PATTON WAS ONLY in his mid-40s when he died in 1934, and he had been recorded on just four occasions. But he remains one of the giants of the acoustic tradition – a child of the Mississippi Delta who combined spiritual and secular lyrical imagery with an earthy lifestyle that allowed him to create some of the most resonant country blues material ever recorded. A unique performer and instantly recognisable singer, Patton had an enormous influence on his Delta contemporaries. He showed great panache when playing live and has been called the first rock'n'roller.

Patton's father was a preacher and Charley grew up one of 12 children on a farm in the Mississippi Delta. He moved to Will Dockery's plantation when he was still a child, and learned to play the guitar around 1908, when he was 19.

It has been said that Patton was the first great Delta bluesman, that he was the fountainhead from which that distinctive style flowed. He certainly had a very individual style of playing, extremely rampant and raw, yet rhythmic too. His vocal delivery was often hoarse, more of a holler than singing, which made him sometimes difficult to comprehend. He was also one of the first men to establish and develop the slide guitar sound.

Not only did Patton play the blues, he lived it too. He was imprisoned, he drank heavily, he had around eight wives, and he travelled extensively, which may have accounted for the number of wives! Nor did Patton play blues in a sombre and laidback

$25 2-17 Steel-string Martin guitar, 1930

FACT FILE

BORN: *c.1889*
Edwards (Hinds Co.), Mississippi

DIED: *28th April, 1934*
Indianola, Mississippi

INSTRUMENT: *Guitar*

FIRST RECORDED: *1929*

ACCOLADES: *Inducted into the Blues Hall of Fame in 1980*

INFLUENCES: *Henry Sloan, Lem Nichols*

INFLUENCED: *Just about every Delta blues player, especially Son House, Muddy Waters, Robert Johnson and Howlin' Wolf*

WILL DOCKERY'S FARM

Dockery Farms Plantation, where Patton grew up and learned to play guitar in his teens.

fashion. He was a consummate showman: he would often play his guitar behind his neck and between his legs.

What he loved to do was clown with his guitar, just puttin' it all under his legs and back behind him.

SAM CHATMON,
DELTA BLUESMAN
(1897 –1983)

He learned from one of the earliest Delta bluesmen, Henry Sloan, but exactly what he learned isn't certain, as Sloan never recorded. By the time he was in his mid-20s, the five-foot five-inch Patton was known throughout the Delta, playing at picnics, juke joints, house parties, and levee camps. His friend Willie Brown often accompanied him, and the two of them must have put on some first-class entertainment. Despite his size, Patton had a big voice, which could carry more than 500 yards when he performed out of doors.

Patton had time to hone his skills before he began recording – he was around 40 when he was 'discovered'.

A Mississippi music store owner and part-time record company scout, Henry Speir, contacted the Paramount Record Company and arranged for Patton to record in Richmond, Indiana on Friday 14th June, 1929. He recorded 14 sides on that occasion, probably the cream of his extensive repertoire at the time. The first record that Paramount released was 'Pony Blues' coupled with 'Banty Rooster Blues', and it established Patton's reputation. His third Paramount release, 'Mississippi Boweavil Blues', was credited to 'The Masked Marvel' – a case of marketing, 1929 style! What we know now is that it was Patton who originally wrote to Speir, asking if he could arrange for him to record.

About three months later Patton once again headed north, this time to Grafton, Wisconsin. There he recorded another 22 sides for Paramount, this time accompanied by Henry 'Son' Sims on fiddle. At his third recording session in 1930, Willie Brown accompanied him; blues pianist Louise Johnson and Son House took the trip to keep them company. With the onset of the Depression, Patton's recording career took a downturn, like most blues performers of the era.

He did not record again until 1934, when over a three-day period he recorded around 25 more sides, although only about 10 were issued. His last wife, Bertha Lee, sang on some of those sides. Patton was now in poor health and the couple quickly returned to Mississippi, where he died just three months later.

Many of Patton's recordings were personal blues, tales of his own life. But they were songs that many of his Delta audience could relate to, which was clearly a significant factor in his success. He also recorded topical songs that were, in their own way, the newsreel of the Delta - for example, 'High Water Everywhere', about the Mississippi flood of 1927.

If any performer can be said truly to reflect the sound of the birth of the Blues, it was Charley Patton. He was there at the start, absorbing and shaping the Blues, besides creating the opportunities for others to record. He may not haved been the first country blues player to record, but he was definitely the greatest of the early Delta bluesmen.

He was the loudest blues player I ever heard

SLEEPY JOHN ESTES

Charley Patton was amazing, but because his recordings are hard to to listen to today, it detracts from his brilliance. But he was influential to many who followed him

BILL WYMAN

ESSENTIAL RECORDINGS

CLASSIC SONGS

'Pony Blues' 1929
'High Water Everywhere' 1929
'A Spoonful Blues' 1929

THE SOURCE

3 CDs of his complete works on Document Records

CA
LD
LT

4

The Blues . . . When They Were a Girl Thing

THE FIRST BLUES RECORD

On the afternoon of Tuesday 10th August, 1920, the Jazz Hounds – alias clarinettists Johnny Dunn and Ernest Elliott, trombone player Dope Andrews, Leroy Parker on violin and pianist Perry Bradford – were in a New York studio. With singer Mamie Smith, they were there to play a song by Perry Bradford, called 'Crazy Blues'. What Smith and the Jazz Hounds didn't realise was that they were about to make history. 'Crazy Blues' is now regarded as the first blues song ever to be recorded.

> *'She was a very high-class entertainer, as well as being one of the best-looking women in the business'*
>
> PIANIST WILLIE 'THE LION' SMITH, TALKING ABOUT MAMIE SMITH

Mamie was not specifically a blues singer, more of a vaudeville cabaret performer. In fact, at this time, no singer sang only the Blues. The date of her birth, probably in Cincinnati, is still open to question, but it is generally felt to be May 1883. That made her 37 years old, and certainly no youngster, when she left her mark on history. Mamie had left home before she even entered her teens to work as a dancer with a touring company on the Southern circuit. She met Bradford in 1918 while working in his musical revue, *Made in Harlem*, at the Lincoln Theatre in New York. She continued to work there regularly over the next two years. Her first session for OKeh was held in February 1920, but the numbers she recorded that day, 'That Thing Called Love' and 'You Can't Keep A Good Man Down', were not blues songs. It took 'Crazy Blues' to win Mamie her place in history.

'Crazy Blues' certainly sold well; some estimates talk of 75,000 copies in the first month, and a million in the first year. These numbers may well be inflated, but there is no over-estimating the record's importance, nor the fact that it was a sizeable hit.

Over the next three years Mamie recorded some 60 sides for the OKeh label, although much of her material was closer to vaudeville than blues. But by the summer of 1923 her popularity was on the wane and OKeh dropped her. She did record a few sides for other labels over the next three years, and in 1929 she briefly returned to OKeh, but could not replicate her past glories. While Mamie was not a great singer, she deserves recognition as the first of what have been called the 'Classic Blues Singers' – women who were deeply rooted in the vaudeville and tent show circuit of the South and East.

Some of the credit for the success of Mamie Smith, and indirectly those who followed, must go to Perry Bradford. It was he who convinced OKeh executive Fred Hagar that black people wanted to buy records made by black singers. This persistence helped to establish what became known as the 'Race Records' genre. Prior to this time the record business had been largely closed to black performers, and black singers in particular. But when there was a hint of profit, old habits keeled over and died very fast. Other black vaudevillians were quickly signed up when rival companies attempted to emulate OKeh's success.

Arto Records were the first to respond, when Lucille Hegamin recorded 'The Jazz Me Blues' in November 1920, followed by Columbia with Mary Stafford's 'Royal Garden Blues' in January 1921. Meanwhile, Black Swan recorded Ethel Waters' 'Down Home Blues' in May 1921, and four months

CRAZY BLUES
The sheet music for 'Crazy Blues' by Mamie Smith and her Jazz Hounds, recorded in New York, 1920. Willie 'The Lion' Smith played piano on the record.

later Columbia pushed a second artist into the fray when Edith Wilson released 'Nervous Blues'.

New York City, You're a Woman

All these recordings were made in New York, which at this time had a virtual monopoly on the fledgling record business. But sophisticated New York taste did not easily come to terms with the Blues, and most of the sales were 'down South'. In any case, many of the 'blues songs' of the day were somewhat distant cousins of 'real' blues. They were an attempt to cash in on the craze for the style, without necessarily understanding what it was. The same thing had happened with ragtime: call a tune a rag, and people will believe it is! It would be another two years before real blues began to have a significant impact.

There was one exception to this rule: Trixie Smith. She had moved to New York in 1915 aged 20, having (unusually for the time) attended university, and from 1918 onwards she worked on the TOBA circuit (see right).

Ethel Waters

Legendary jazz and blues singer Ethel Waters (1896-1977), in ostrich feather dress and hat, during her heyday with the shimmy in the 1920s, and her recording of 'Down Home Blues' for the Black Swan label.

Like her namesake Mamie, Trixie Smith regularly played the Lincoln Theatre. While she was not as popular as Mamie, she began to build up something of a following for her live work. In 1922, she recorded 'Trixie's Blues' for the Black Swan label, and later that year she won a New York blues contest with the song (beating Lucille Hegamin, amongst others). This success launched a recording career that lasted, initially, until 1926. She is best remembered for 'Railroad Blues', and 'The World Is Jazz Crazy And So Am I', both of which featured Louis Armstrong and highlighted Trixie's excellent voice. She has tended to be somewhat overshadowed by Bessie, Clara, and Mamie Smith, but in the case of the latter two that neglect is undeserved. Trixie was also the first blues singer to incorporate more Southern roots-based material into her repertoire. Songs like 'Mining Camp Blues' (which also featured Armstrong) and 'Freight Train Blues' (with Fletcher Henderson) were indicative of the way the Blues was heading.

Sweet Mama Stringbean

Trixie and her Black Swan labelmate, Ethel Waters, were very much at the forefront of the Blues, and the whole 'race records' movement. The fact that Black Swan was black-owned obviously smoothed their path; but Ethel Waters was another really good singer, who deserved every bit of the acclaim she received. Twenty-three-year-old Ethel arrived in New York in 1919, having been a regular on the Eastern and Southern vaudeville circuits. She was tall, with a willowy figure, and as a result she was billed as 'Sweet Mama Stringbean'. For two years she cut a number of excellent blues records for Black Swan, including 'There'll Be Some Changes Made', 'Spread Yo' Stuff' and 'Georgia Blues'. On these and most of her other Black Swan records she was backed by a band billed as 'Her Jazz Masters', who included the hard-working pianist Fletcher Henderson. After she left Black Swan, she went on to record for both Paramount and

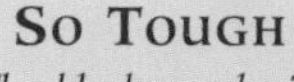

So Tough

The black vaudeville circuit was booked by the "Toby" or TOBA (Theatre Owners Booking Association). Many of the artists who worked the circuit felt that they were somewhat mistreated and as a result the TOBA became known by many in the business as "Tough On Black Asses".

Vocalion, before signing for Columbia in 1925. It was at this juncture that she played the prestigious Plantation Club on New York's Broadway, performing mostly for white audiences.

While her records were still very much 'race' in style, aimed at black listeners, she gradually moved away from the Blues towards more mainstream pop. But she never entirely lost her blues credentials: in 1933, she had a big hit with the blues-influenced 'Stormy Weather', written by Koehler and Arlen. She also enjoyed a successful career in films and on Broadway during the 1940s, while by the late 1950s she was touring with the evangelist Billy Graham.

What is remarkable about Ethel Waters' story is the hardship she overcame to achieve so much. She was born illegitimate, after her 13-year-old mother was raped at knifepoint. Her childhood was spent in squalid conditions; then, at the age of 13, she got married, though the union lasted only briefly and she suffered terribly from her husband's cruelty. She worked in a variety of low-paid menial jobs before she was 'discovered' at a party by a couple of small-time vaudeville showmen. Truly the stuff of the Blues!

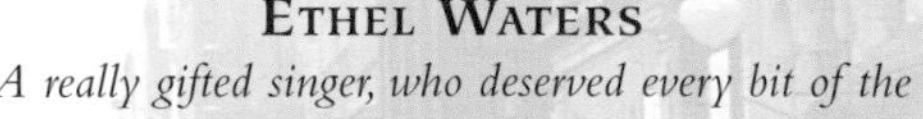

ETHEL WATERS

A really gifted singer, who deserved every bit of the acclaim she received.

In 1998, when I was looking for tracks to record on my second Rhythm Kings album, Anyway The Wind Blows, *I came across an old song that my writing partner Terry Taylor and I re-arranged. It's called 'When Hollywood Goes Black & Tan' and it celebrates black stars in the 1930s leaving Harlem and the East coast and heading for Hollywood. The song contains the line: 'Ethel Waters with a fan dance shakes those feathers off the fan'*

BILL WYMAN

NOBODY KNOWS YOU WHEN YOU'RE DOWN AND OUT

DESCRIBED AS BESSIE SMITH'S 'personal epitaph', this well-loved classic, with its references to bootleg liquor (the car in her fatal accident was driven by her bootleg-running lover), disappearing money (she lost much of her fortune) and being ostracised (many friends from her glory years distanced themselves later), was an uncannily accurate summation of Bessie's life.

DEREK & THE DOMINOS

The recording by Derek (alias Eric Clapton) and the Dominos also features Duane Allman on guitar, Bobby Whitlock, organ, Carl Radle, bass, Jim Gordon, drums, and Albhy Galuten on piano. Made on 31st August, 1970, at Criteria Studios in Miami, it was the second song recorded for the album Layla And Other Assorted Love Songs, *the first being Big Bill Broonzy's 'Key To The Highway'.*

★ Derek & The Dominos' version is:

'But when you finally get back up on your feet again, Everybody wants to be your old long lost friend…'

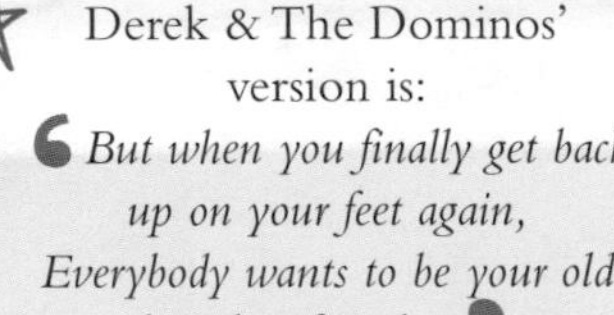

ACOUSTIC ERIC

In 1983 Eric Clapton performed the song live on the first leg of his American tour. By 1997 he was again performing the song as an acoustic number.

NOBODY KNOWS YOU WHEN YOU'RE DOWN AND OUT

Written by Jimmie Cox.
Recorded by Bessie Smith in New York City, Wednesday 15th May, 1929

Once I lived the life of a millionaire
Spending my money, I didn't care
I carried my friends out for a good time
Buying bootleg liquor, champagne and wine

Then I began to fall so low
I didn't have a friend, and no place to go
So if I ever get my hand on a dollar again
I'm gonna hold on to it till them eagles green

Nobody knows you when you down and out
In my pocket not one penny
And my friends I haven't any
But if I ever get on my feet again
★ *Then I'll meet my long lost friend*
It's mighty strange, without a doubt
Nobody knows you when you're down and out
I mean when you're down and out

Mmmmmmmm… when you're down and out
Mmmmmmmm… not one penny
And my friends I haven't any
Mmmmmmmm… Well I felt so low
Nobody wants me round their door
Mmmmmmmm… Without a doubt,
No man can use you when you're down and out
I mean when you're down and out

NOBODY KNOWS YOU…

The first song with this title was by Bobby Leecan, released sometime around June 1927. Recorded on the Paramount label under the name Blind Bobby Baker, the lyrics may have been the basis for Bessie's version two years later. After little over a year, Clarence 'Pine Top' Smith and Alberta Reynolds recorded a version of the song for Vocalion, but it was never released. Four weeks later Pine Top recorded a solo rendition that was released along with 'Big Boy They Can't Do That'.

ALBERTA HUNTER

The fact that Alberta Hunter covered this song adds a certain symmetry to the whole story. In 1923 the young Bessie Smith covered Alberta Hunter's 'Down Hearted Blues' for her first release on the Columbia label.

SELECTED VERSIONS

- 1927 Bobby Leecan
- 1929 Pine Top Smith, Bessie Smith
- 1943 Eddie Condon
- 1945 Josh White
- 1947 Lead Belly
- 1954 Louis Jordan
- 1962 Odetta, Jimmy Witherspoon
- 1964 Sam Cooke
- 1965 Barbra Streisand
- 1968 Otis Redding
- 1970 Derek & The Dominos
- 1973 Tim Hardin
- 1978 Alberta Hunter
- 1988 Rod Stewart
- 1989 Ruth Brown
- 1995 Peter, Paul & Mary
- 1999 BB King

BESSIE SMITH

FACT FILE

BORN: *15th April, 1894 Chattanooga, Tennessee*

DIED: *26th September, 1937 Clarksdale, Mississippi*

INSTRUMENT: *Vocalist*

FIRST RECORDED: *1923*

ACCOLADES: *Inducted into the Blues Hall of Fame in 1980*

INFLUENCES: *Blind Lemon Jefferson, Ma Rainey*

INFLUENCED: *Billie Holiday, Mahalia Jackson, Odetta, Janis Joplin, Victoria Spivey, Big Mama Thornton, Dinah Washington*

THE WOMAN WHO BECAME KNOWN as the 'Empress of the Blues' had a humble birth and upbringing - and a sad one. She was one of seven children born to a part-time Baptist preacher and his wife, but both her parents were dead by the time Bessie was nine years old. Bessie and her brother Andrew were then already singing on the streets of Chattanooga for spare change; meanwhile her brother Clarence joined a travelling vaudeville show, as a comedian and dancer.

In 1912 Clarence arranged an audition for Bessie with the Moses Stokes Company. She joined them as a dancer, and rose through the ranks to be a featured singer. The established star of the company was Ma Rainey, and ever since blues historians have debated whether or not she coached young Bessie's vocal skills. Either way, it is inconceivable that the younger woman could have watched a star like Rainey at work without picking up some tips.

Years of working the vaudeville circuit honed Bessie's skills as a powerful singer and entertainer, and along the way she became an established star with black audiences. By this time she had already been married and widowed. She moved to Philadelphia in 1921, well aware of her namesake Mamie Smith's success with 'Crazy Blues'. Attempting to get her own recording career underway, she auditioned for OKeh Records, but her recording of 'I Wish I Could Shimmy Like My Sister Kate' was not deemed worthy of issue. Auditions for other record companies followed, but each time she was rejected. Finally, on 15th February, 1923, Columbia Records' Frank Walker took Bessie into the company's New York studio,

Bessie Smith in 1924

where she recorded 'Taint Nobody's Bizness If I Do' and 'Down Hearted Blues' – though once again neither side was issued. On the following day, she recorded a cover of Alberta Hunter's two-year-old song 'Down Hearted Blues', plus 'Gulf Coast Blues' and 'Keep On A-Rainin''. The first two sides made up her first release, which sold more than 80,000 copies in 1923 - a figure that probably eclipsed Mamie Smith's success with

'Crazy Blues'. That year she also met and married Jack Gee, an illiterate nightwatchman, although they would divorce in 1929.

Between 1923 and 1933 Bessie recorded more than 150 songs for Columbia, making her one of the most prolific artists of the period. In April 1923, at her third session, she finally recorded a version of 'Taint Nobody's Bizness If I Do' that Columbia felt was worth releasing - and what a release: it became a classic. While many of her earlier recordings featured just Bessie's powerful voice and piano accompaniment, she later worked with small groups that included many of the finest musicians of the period, such as pianists Fletcher Henderson and James P. Johnson, saxophonist Coleman Hawkins, and legendary trumpeter Louis Armstrong. In 1929 Smith recorded what some have referred to as her 'personal epitaph', 'Nobody Knows You When You're Down And Out'. That same year she made her only film appearance, alongside James P Johnson in *St Louis Blues*.

In 1931, Columbia dropped Bessie from their roster, which all but marked the end of her recording career. She held just one further session after that, recording four sides for OKeh on 24th November, 1933, a date that was arranged by John Hammond. In 1934 she worked in a touring show and in 1935 she appeared, to critical acclaim, at the Apollo Theatre in New York. Then, once again, Bessie returned to her musical roots in the South. Her style of singing had become outdated, and the record-buying public now preferred a more sophisticated style, but despite this she remained a good draw on the live circuit. It was while being driven to another gig by her lover Richard Morgan (jazzman Lionel Hampton's uncle), that she suffered a fatal accident – an event that helped to stoke the legend of Bessie Smith.

In the end, Bessie Smith was much more than just a blues singer: she became an icon for her race. She lived her life in the fast lane, with the needle permanently in the red, throwing herself into drinking, fighting, and sex with both men and women. In fact, Bessie Smith lived the life she sang about.

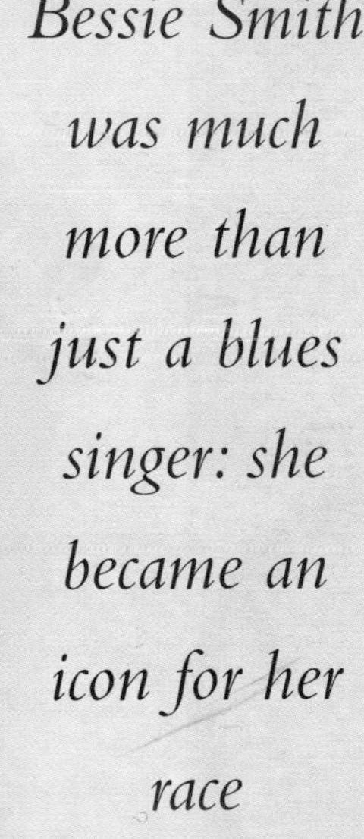

Bessie Smith was much more than just a blues singer: she became an icon for her race

ESSENTIAL RECORDINGS

CLASSIC SONGS

''T'aint Nobody's Business If I Do' 1923
'Mama's Got the Blues' 1923
'Backwater Blues' 1925
'Nobody Knows You When You're Down And Out' 1929

THE SOURCE

Bessie Smith Vols 1-8
Frog Records

LIGHTN
Frank V
Bessie Sn
gin mill in
in 1917
sign a
influenti
later, wh
'discove
legends o
Han

'Crazy Blues'. That year she also met and married Jack Gee, an illiterate nightwatchman, although they would divorce in 1929.

Between 1923 and 1933 Bessie recorded more than 150 songs for Columbia, making her one of the most prolific artists of the period. In April 1923, at her third session, she finally recorded a version of 'Taint Nobody's Bizness If I Do' that Columbia felt was worth releasing - and what a release: it became a classic. While many of her earlier recordings featured just Bessie's powerful voice and piano accompaniment, she later worked with small groups that included many of the finest musicians of the period, such as pianists Fletcher Henderson and James P. Johnson, saxophonist Coleman Hawkins, and legendary trumpeter Louis Armstrong. In 1929 Smith recorded what some have referred to as her 'personal epitaph', 'Nobody Knows You When You're Down And Out'. That same year she made her only film appearance, alongside James P Johnson in *St Louis Blues*.

In 1931, Columbia dropped Bessie from their roster, which all but marked the end of her recording career. She held just one further session after that, recording four sides for OKeh on 24th November, 1933, a date that was arranged by John Hammond. In 1934 she worked in a touring show and in 1935 she appeared, to critical acclaim, at the Apollo Theatre in New York. Then, once again, Bessie returned to her musical roots in the South. Her style of singing had become outdated, and the record-buying public now preferred a more sophisticated style, but despite this she remained a good draw on the live circuit. It was while being driven to another gig by her lover Richard Morgan (jazzman Lionel Hampton's uncle), that she suffered a fatal accident – an event that helped to stoke the legend of Bessie Smith.

In the end, Bessie Smith was much more than just a blues singer: she became an icon for her race. She lived her life in the fast lane, with the needle permanently in the red, throwing herself into drinking, fighting, and sex with both men and women. In fact, Bessie Smith lived the life she sang about.

Bessie Smith was much more than just a blues singer: she became an icon for her race

ESSENTIAL RECORDINGS

CLASSIC SONGS

''T'aint Nobody's Business If I Do' 1923
'Mama's Got the Blues' 1923
'Backwater Blues' 1925
'Nobody Knows You When You're Down And Out' 1929

THE SOURCE

Bessie Smith Vols 1-8
Frog Records

THE GREATEST OF ALL CLASSIC BLUES SINGERS

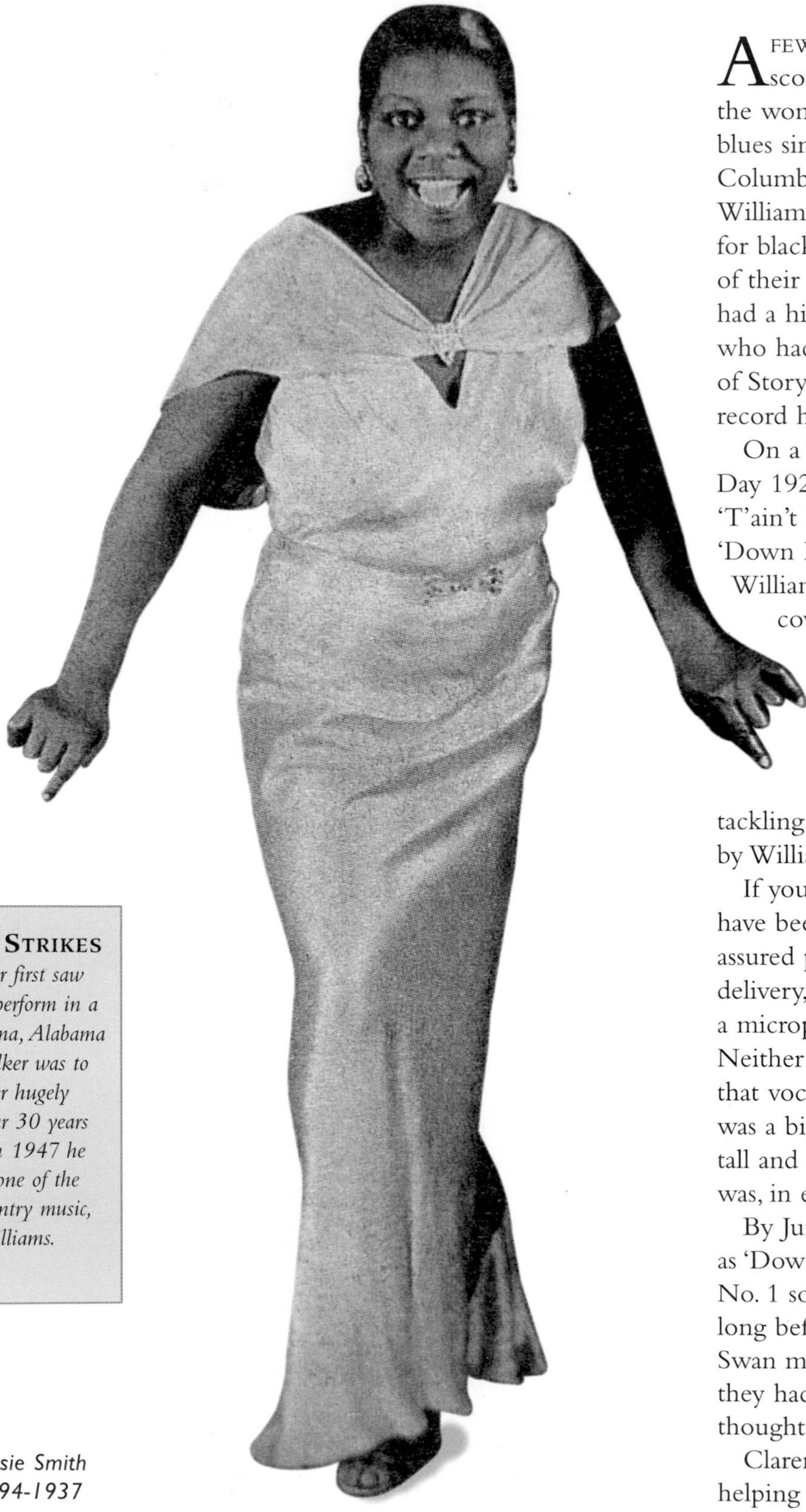

A FEW MONTHS BEFORE Ethel Waters scored her last blues hit, 'Georgia Blues', the woman who was to transform female blues singing made her first record for the Columbia label. Pianist-composer Clarence Williams knew that Columbia was looking for black blues singers to emulate the success of their own Edith Wilson, who had recently had a hit with 'Birmingham Blues'. Williams, who had left New Orleans after the closing of Storyville, arranged for Frank Walker to record his protégée.

On a Thursday, the day after Valentine's Day 1923, 28-year-old Bessie Smith cut 'T'ain't Nobody's Business If I Do' and 'Down Hearted Blues', accompanied by Williams on the piano. The latter song was a cover of a two-year-old hit by Alberta Hunter on which Williams owned the publishing. The session was not quite right, so next day Bessie and Clarence returned, re-recording 'Down Hearted Blues', and also tackling 'Gulf Coast Blues', a song written by Williams.

If you had been at the session, you would have been struck by Bessie Smith's self-assured phrasing and the power of her delivery, honed from years of singing without a microphone on the vaudeville circuit. Neither was it difficult to work out where that vocal power came from: Bessie Smith was a big woman, standing around six feet tall and weighing nearly 200 pounds. She was, in every sense, a remarkable woman.

By June 1923 Bessie Smith was a huge star, as 'Down Hearted Blues' was effectively the No. 1 song in America (although this was long before proper record charts). Black Swan must have been kicking themselves, as they had rejected Bessie, because they thought her voice was 'a little too rough'.

Clarence Williams was instrumental in helping to secure Bessie's Columbia contract,

LIGHTNIN' STRIKES

Frank Walker first saw Bessie Smith perform in a gin mill in Selma, Alabama in 1917. Walker was to sign another hugely influential star 30 years later, when in 1947 he 'discovered' one of the legends of country music, Hank Williams.

Bessie Smith
1894-1937

*There ain't nothin' I can do or nothin' I can say,
That folks don't criticize me;
But I'm going to do just as I want to anyway,
and don't care if they all despise me*

'T'AIN'T NOBODY'S BUSINESS IF I DO'

CLARENCE WILLIAMS
Jazz composer Clarence Williams, who began playing the piano at the age of eight, became a featured entertainer at Storyville's 'Poodle Dog Cabaret'.

but he was not altogether acting out of altruism. Allegedly the contract that Bessie thought she had signed with Columbia actually tied her to an exclusive management deal with Williams, giving him 50% of her record earnings.

When Bessie found out, she and her boyfriend made a surprise visit to Clarence Williams's office. They secured a release from the old deal and Bessie was then able to sign directly with Columbia. The new contract gave Bessie $200 per issued side, against just $125 from the first contract, although she still earned no royalties from her recordings.

Bessie saw her records as a way of promoting her live performances, a strategy that proved very successful. She is reported to have earned around $2,000 per week at the height of her career – although even that was nothing to what she could have earned if she had been on a royalty-based contract – 'Down Hearted Blues' is rumoured to have sold as many as two million copies. Bessie's treatment by the record business was typical of what happened to many blues artists (as well as rock, jazz, country, and pop performers), male and female, for the remainder of the century… and possibly beyond.

VAUDEVILLE
A typical vaudeville theatre in Seattle. Bessie Smith honed her craft in such theatres, singing without a microphone.

THE LEGEND OF BESSIE SMITH

'I've travelled and wandered almost everywhere
To get a little joy from life
Still I've gained but worries and despair
Still struggling in this world of strife
Oh me, oh my
Wonder what will the end be
Oh me, oh my
Wonder what will become of poor me'

'WORRIED LIFE BLUES'

THE TRAGIC CIRCUMSTANCES of Bessie's death added an extra layer of pathos and mystery to what was already a fascinating and monumental career.

Her last New York appearance was on a cold February Sunday afternoon in 1936, at the original Famous Door on 52nd Street. At the time much was made of the fact that Mildred Bailey refused to follow Bessie's performance.

Eighteen months later, on 26th September, 1937, the day before John Hammond was due to leave for Mississippi to take Bessie back to New York to record, she and her lover Richard Morgan were on Route 61 in Coahoma County, just north of Clarksdale, Mississippi.

Morgan was driving when their car was involved in an accident and ran off the road. It is thought that he was following the telegraph poles that were illuminated by the moonlight. Unfortunately he did not realise that the poles carried on but the road turned sharply to the right.

As a result their car fell down a steep embankment created by the Yazoo flood plain. Bessie broke ribs in the crash, and as she was lying by the side of the road being treated for her injuries, a truck ran over her right arm, nearly severing it.

BESSIE SMITH'S ROOM
The room in which Bessie Smith died of internal injuries at the Riverside rooming house is now a shrine to her memory and is kept un-let.

COULD SHE HAVE BEEN SAVED?

For many years a rumour circulated that her life could have been saved, if she had not been refused treatment at a whites-only hospital in Clarksdale, fourteen miles from the crash site.

Much of the responsibility for this erroneous story must be attributed to none other than John Hammond, who wrote an article in *Down Beat* magazine claiming that Bessie died after being denied admission to the hospital because of her skin colour. Hammond later admitted that his article had been based on hearsay. Bessie was in fact treated by a white doctor, Dr Hugh Smith, at Clarksdale's blacks-only hospital on Sunflower Avenue.

The building is now a hotel-cum-rooming house, called The Riverside, and the room in which Bessie died of her internal injuries is kept un-let, as a permanent shrine to her memory.

Residents at The Riverside with a blues connection have been numerous, including Robert Nighthawk, Sonny Boy Williamson and Ike Turner. In more recent times, Levon Helm from The Band stayed there, as did the former president's son John Kennedy Jr in the 1990s.

MA RAINEY MAKES HER MARK

IRONICALLY, THE OLDER Ma Rainey, the woman credited by some as having coached Bessie Smith in her young days, made her own recording debut after Bessie. By the time of Rainey's first session in December 1923, Bessie had already scored five hit records, including a remake of 'T'ain't Nobody's Business If I Do', the Clarence Williams song she had attempted at her first session. Whereas Bessie was recorded by Columbia in its modern New York studios, Ma – who was also known as Madame – signed to Paramount. It may have been the emerging label in the 'race' field, but its studio was based in Chicago, and used technically inferior equipment.

As a result, Ma Rainey's records are definitely not as pleasing to the ear of 21st-century listeners as those by Bessie Smith and some of the other early stars. This has undoubtedly harmed her long-term reputation, but the importance of Ma's work should certainly not be underestimated. What made Rainey such an icon in her prime was that, more than most of her contemporaries with the possible exception of Trixie Smith, she really understood her audience. She was a true veteran of the vaudeville circuit, who was already 37 years old when she made her first recordings, and she was unquestionably a powerhouse talent. Her age and experience gave her a worldliness, cynicism, and outlook that made her a true voice of the Blues.

Ma's first recording session provided both sides of her debut record, 'Bo-Weavil Blues' and 'Last Minute Blues', as well as follow-ups which included 'Bad Luck Blues', 'Walking Blues' and 'Moonshine Blues'. Lovie Austin and Her Blues Serenaders accompanied her at that first session.

Lovie was 26 years old at the time she recorded with Ma; she is now regarded as one of the best blues piano players of the period, along with Lil Hardin Armstrong. Lovie trained in music theory at a university in Tennessee, and her songwriting skills can be heard on 'Down Hearted Blues', which she co-wrote with singer Alberta Hunter.

During her six years with Paramount, Ma Rainey recorded around a hundred songs, including the classic 'See See Rider', 'Ma Rainey's Black Bottom', and one of the earliest recordings of 'Stack O'Lee Blues'. The ever-present Fletcher Henderson played piano on many of her recordings, including 'See See Rider', on which Louis Armstrong also appeared.

GERTRUDE 'MA' RAINEY *and her Georgia Jazz Band, in Chicago, Illinois, 1925. Thomas A Dorsey, the 'Father of Gospel Music', is playing piano.*

Ma Rainey

FACT FILE

Born: *26th April, 1886*
Columbus, Georgia

Died: *22nd December, 1939*
Columbus, Georgia

Instrument: *Vocalist*

First Recorded: *1923*

Accolades: *Inducted into the Blues Hall of Fame in 1983*

Influenced: *Bessie Smith, Big Mama Thornton, Janis Joplin*

Ma Rainey's real name was Gertrude M Pridgett and she was the daughter of two minstrel performers. She first performed on stage in 1900, becoming 'Ma' Rainey four years later when she married the minstrel performer William 'Pa' Rainey. The couple billed themselves as 'Rainey and Rainey, Assassinators of the Blues'. They toured extensively through the South with various tent shows, including the Rabbit Foot Minstrels and it was during this period that Ma is alleged to have 'coached' the young Bessie Smith. She later claimed that she was singing the Blues as early as 1902. This may be debatable but there is no doubt that she was one of the very first blues singers of either sex.

'Ma was loaded with real diamonds – in her ears, around her neck, in a tiara on her head. Both hands were full of rocks, too; her hair was wild and she had gold teeth. What a sight!'

Mary Lou Williams, who saw Rainey as a teenager in early 20s Pittsburgh

In late 1923 she was signed to Paramount Records, who billed her as 'The Mother of The Blues'. Her first recordings were made in December and included her debut, 'Last Minute Blues' and 'Bo-Weevil Blues'. Over the next five years she recorded around 100 sides for Paramount, often backed by her Georgia Band. She was also accompanied by the young Louis Armstrong, Fletcher Henderson, Coleman Hawkins, Blind Blake, and Tampa Red. Her success as a singer, and her ongoing reputation, rests on the fact that she bridged the gap between urban and country blues. She never lost touch with her country fan base, writing songs with which they could identify, and singing them in a style that they loved. Her power as a singer cannot be disguised by the poor quality of her recordings, and she delivered her songs in a rich, earthy, and direct manner. She was first and foremost a performer and then (not necessarily in order) a jazz singer, dancer, a singer of bawdy songs, and a great blues stylist.

Rainey was known to be free with her favours, which is perhaps surprising as she was hardly a looker. But she always dressed the part of a blues queen; she covered her stocky frame with all manner of outrageous costumes, glittery headbands, and feathers too. With the onset of the Depression her career came to a close, but she was already a rich lady. She retired to the town of her birth, and lived there in luxury until she died of a heart attack in 1939.

'Maybe I'm partial. Ma was the greatest of the blues singers'

Georgia Tom Dorsey

Essential Recordings

Classic Songs

'Bo-Weavil Blues' 1923
'See See Rider Blues' 1924
'Stack O'Lee Blues' 1925

The Source

Ma Rainey's Black Bottom
Yazoo

THE UNCROWNED QUEEN

SHORTLY BEFORE PARAMOUNT signed Ma Rainey, the label recorded another of the best singers to come out of the 1920s, an era sometimes dubbed the 'Theatre Blues' period. Ida Cox made her first records, 'Graveyard Dream Blues' and 'Weary Way Blues', in June 1923; whether Ida herself had a morbid outlook, or Paramount simply saw a niche in the market, many of her records had death themes. They included 'Graveyard Bound Blues', 'Black Crêpe Blues', 'Cold Black Ground Blues', 'Bone Orchard Blues', 'Marble Stone Blues', and 'Death Letter Blues'. The last of these songs featured some wonderful electric guitar playing from one of the earliest guitar heroes, Charlie Christian.

Born Ida Prather in Georgia in 1896, Cox was 27 years old when she made her first record. Like many of her contemporaries she left home to work the Southern tent show and vaudeville circuit, where she met and married Jesse 'Tiny' Crump, a Texan pianist. It was her work with Jelly Roll Morton that brought her to Paramount – she recorded 78 songs in seven years. She was always considered a shrewd business-woman, shown by the fact that during her Paramount contract, she also recorded for labels like Silvertone and Broadway, using pseudonyms that included Velma Bradley, Kate Lewis, Julia Powers, and Jane Smith.

THE SEPIA MAE WEST

Paramount, like other record companies, was always on the look-out for a new angle to promote its female stars, and Ida was billed as the 'Uncrowned Queen of the Blues'. In fact, her charismatic performances were as close to vaudeville as they were to blues, and she became known as 'The Sepia Mae West'. Undoubtedly some of her success was due to the ready identification of her black female audience with the subject matter of her songs. These told of the conditions that placed women at the very bottom of the social scale, with little prospect of gaining respect, especially from their men folk. To the poor black women of the South, Ida must have represented the ultimate in urban sophistication. She was a stylish black woman, something that her audience could never aspire to, in a world where necessity took precedence over luxury.

Ida Cox

Ida Cox continued to perform and occasionally record throughout the 1930s, although like many of her contemporaries she was hit by the weight of the Depression. She appeared in John Hammond's celebrated *From Spirituals to Swing* concert at Carnegie Hall in 1939, performing two songs, 'Lowdown Dirty Shame' and 'Fore Day Creep', which amply demonstrated her star quality. She had a strong but not rough voice, great phrasing, and was also a talented writer, penning 'Fore Day Creep' and many of her other records during the 1920s.

THE SEPIA MAE WEST

The singer described as 'the sepia Mae West' was in her prime in the 1920s, but she made a triumphant appearance as late as 1939 at the From Spirituals to Swing *concert.*

While the first phase of 'classic' blues was centred on New York, and slightly later Chicago, by 1923 there were signs that the business was developing beyond the principal Northern cities. In their eternal search for 'The Next Big Thing' – in this case, more performers who would appeal to the Southern black market - record companies started to make field trips to record 'local talent'. A new and vitally important age of blues music was about to begin.

PARAMOUNT AND THE RACE LABELS

PARAMOUNT RECORDS WAS LAUNCHED around 1916 by the New York Recording Laboratory of Port Washington, Wisconsin. The company was a subsidiary of the Wisconsin Chair Company, who made not just chairs but also other furniture, including cabinets for phonographs. The original idea behind Paramount was that it would give away records with its phonograph cabinets.

Paramount's record sleeve

This was not the first specialist label for black music; that honour falls to OKeh, who also coined the 'race' series to describe records by black artists. But Paramount began releasing black records just a year after OKeh, in 1922. The label appointed Mayo Williams, a black college graduate, as its talent scout in 1922 and he immediately signed a number of classic blues singers and began releasing records by Alberta Hunter, Ida Cox, and Ma Rainey.

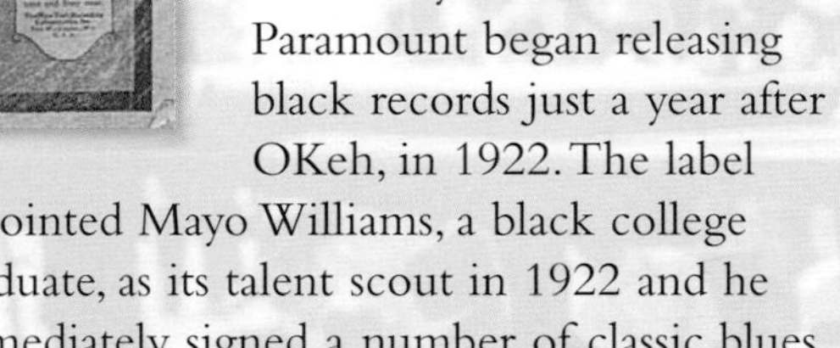

SEARCHING FOR TALENT

Williams wanted to find a male artist for his roster, so he went to Maxwell Street in Chicago and came across Papa Charlie Jackson and his six-string banjo. Jackson's success led the company to look for other male talent and it was not long before Blind Lemon Jefferson and Blind Blake both began their careers with the label.

Paramount used 'field scouts' to seek out new talent, although this is a somewhat grand title for men like HC Speir, who ran a store in the South and kept an eye out for local performers. Through Speir, Paramount 'discovered' Tommy Johnson, Ishman Bracey, and most importantly Charley Patton. It was Patton who took Son House, Willie Brown, and Louise Johnson to Grafton, Wisconsin, to record in Paramount's new studios in 1930.

A Paramount jazz record

Unlike most of its rivals, who went on field recording trips, Paramount preferred to bring its artists to Chicago (where its studio closed in 1929), New York (closed around 1926), and later Grafton. Paramount also used a number of subsidiary labels to issue existing recordings using pseudonyms. Among these subsidiaries were National and Broadway. Similarly, other entrepreneurs ran labels which released Paramount material. For instance, the Herwin brothers in St Louis had the Herwin label.

During its 10 years in business Paramount released more than 1,100 records, many of which are much prized by collectors today (often because they sold in such small numbers). That total also includes some of the greatest pre-war blues recordings.

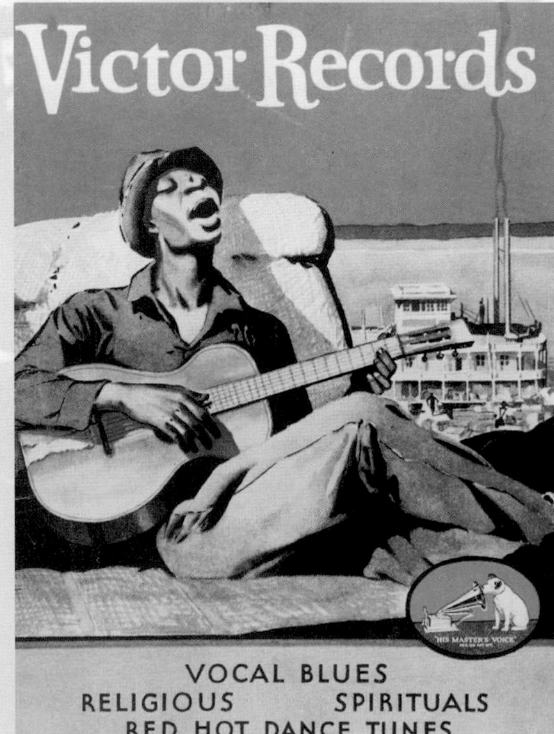

Victor Records 'race records' catalogue, 1929

Ironically, Paramount's records were cheap and their quality was often poor, with lots of intrusive surface noise. The label withdrew from recording in 1932, having fallen victim to the Depression like so many blues artists.

Other artists that recorded for Paramount included Skip James, Elzadie Robinson, Henry Sims, Ramblin' Thomas, Big Bill Broonzy, Gus Cannon, Teddy Darby, and Bumble Bee Slim.

OKeh

The label's name comes from a Native American word, but it was launched by a German immigrant, Otto Heineman. Mamie Smith was its first great success amongst black artists, even before she recorded 'Crazy Blues'. OKeh became one of the first companies to undertake field trips, using Ralph Peer as its field recording manager. It was also the first company to issue a country blues record by a black artist, Ed Andrews.

OKeh merged with Columbia in 1929. While most artists remained with the company that had originally signed them, some did appear on both labels. Blind Willie McTell, for example, recorded as Blind Sammie for Columbia and Georgia Bill for OKeh.

The final issues on OKeh came in 1934 when ownership of the company passed to ARC (American Recording Company). ARC was later bought by the Columbia Broadcasting System (CBS). Another ARC subsidiary, Brunswick, had a race label, Vocalion, which CBS then renamed as OKeh, while Brunswick (confusingly!) became Columbia.

OKeh artists included Bo Carter, Lonnie Johnson, Little Hat Jones, the Mississippi Sheiks, Sylvester Weaver, Memphis Slim, Blind Boy Fuller, and Memphis Minnie.

Columbia

The label's history goes back to the very start of recording. Even by 1891 they had a section in their catalogue called 'Negro Music'. After Mamie Smith's success, Columbia jumped in with Bessie Smith, Mary Stafford, and Clara Smith. There were some financial problems in the early 1920s, but the company reorganised itself and tried to mirror OKeh's success.

It became the first label to release superior quality electrical recordings, at the same time as it began extended field trips in the South. The first country blues singer to be recorded on a Columbia field trip was Peg Leg Howell in Atlanta. A victim of the Depression, the English Columbia label sold off its American subsidiary sometime around 1931–32.

Columbia artists included Barbecue Bob, Blind Willie Johnson, Blind Willie McTell, Oak Cliff T-Bone (T-Bone Walker), Whistlin' Alex Moore, Lewis Black, Curley Weaver, and Washington Phillips.

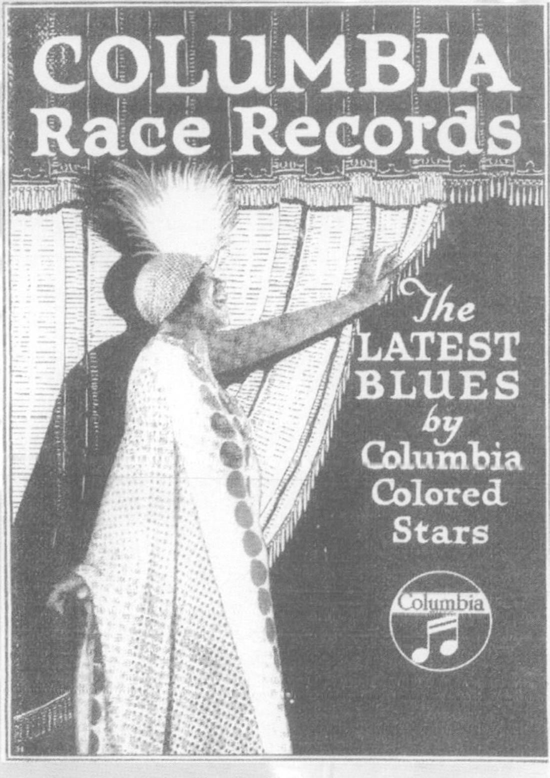

Columbia Race Records catalogue, 1925

Race Records
Left: Record labels for QRS and Bluebird. Below: Mamie Smith does some promotion for Ajax Records of Chicago – the 'Quality Race Record'.

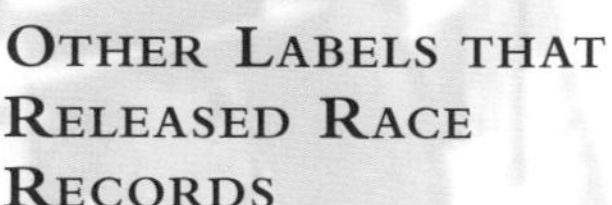

Other Labels that Released Race Records

- Victor and Bluebird
- Gennett and Champion
- Black Patti
- Black Swan
- Meritt
- QRS
- Ajax
- Decca (started as an offshoot of the English company in 1934.)

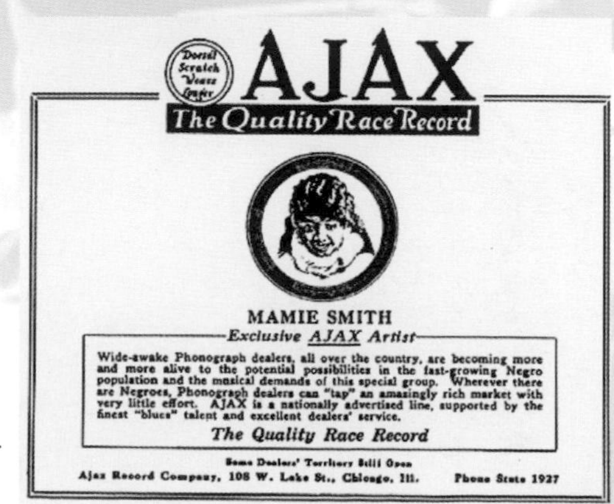

Those Low Down, Dirty Blues

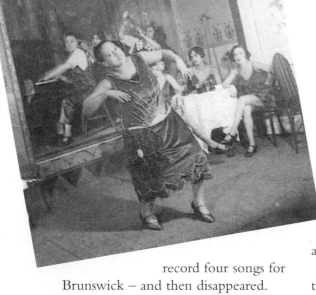

In early June 1923, representatives of OKeh Records took their recording equipment to Atlanta, Georgia, one of the grand cities of the Old South. There they recorded Lucille Bogan singing 'Pawn Shop Blues' and Fannie May Goosby performing 'Grievous Blues'. For Lucille, it was the start of a long, if intermittent, recording career, but Fannie May's moment in the spotlight was much briefer. She cut eight sides for OKeh in 1923, some of them with Clarence Williams on piano, but nothing more was heard of her until 1928, when she went on to record four songs for Brunswick – and then disappeared.

Lucille, on the other hand, proved to be a major find. A week or so after the Atlanta session, she travelled to New York and cut five more songs for OKeh. She was not really at the peak of her powers on these early records and it is easy to see why OKeh did not record her again.

In March 1927, she returned to the studio, this time for Paramount, using Papa Charlie Jackson as her banjo-playing accompanist; her later accompanists included Tampa Red and Cow Cow Davenport. By then, her voice had deepened and her material was stronger.

Lucille Bogan never equalled the popularity of Bessie Smith or Ma Rainey, but her talent and influence were undeniable. As her performance of 'Sloppy Drunk Blues' demonstrates, she was another artist who lived out what she sang. She also helped to bring a new style of raunchy lyrics into the Blues.

> *'I'd rather be sloppy drunk, than anything I know'*
>
> 'Sloppy Drunk Blues'

By 1933 Lucille was recording under the pseudonym Bessie Jackson for the American Record Company, where she cut 'Shave 'Em Dry'. This is without doubt the dirtiest song ever recorded; her delivery makes Janis Joplin sound like an angel! Lucille recorded two versions of the song, one full of double entendres and the other rather more direct.

Needless to say it was the 'clean' version that was released in 1935. After this ARC did not renew her contract and she went back to live in Birmingham, Alabama – where she had spent some of her childhood – leaving behind a legacy, and something of a reputation, which epitomized the output of blueswomen in the 1920s and 1930s.

Sloppy Drunk

'Sloppy drunk' refers to the effects of drinking moonshine liquor; especially what is left after the higher quality liquor is removed.

Those English Blues

In Britain in the 1930s singer Elsie Carlisle from Salford, Manchester, covered the classic 'My Man O' War'. It was quickly withdrawn from sale as it was just a little too much for polite British society. The following year Elsie cut 'My Handy Man'. Her career lasted around 15 years. She was extremely popular on radio and on record.

The Black Bottom

Edith Wilson struttin' her stuff doing the Black Bottom.

Risqué Blues

If 'Shave 'em Dry' was the most outrageous example of raunchy, dirty blues, female blues singers produced plenty of other material in the 1920s and 1930s that would still cause a few raised eyebrows today. An entirely subjective list of the best and most risqué could include the following:

'I'm A Mighty Tight Woman'
Sippie Wallace

'Sissy Man'
Ma Rainey

'Crazy 'Bout My Lollipop'
Ada Brown

'Butcher Shop Blues'
Bernice Edwards
'He cuts my steak in the night-time
He grinds my sausage in the day
And the machine he uses
Will really take your breath away'

'Boy In The Boat (BD's Dream)'
Georgia White

'Prove It To Me Blues'
Ma Rainey

'Women Won't Need No Men'
Lucille Bogan

'Ain't Got Nobody (To Grind My Coffee)'
Clara Smith

'On The Wall'
Louise Johnson

'Black Eye Blues'
Ma Rainey
'You low-down alligator, just watch me sooner or later
Gonna catch you with your breeches down'

'Anybody Here Want To Try My Cabbage'
Maggie Jones

'Can I Get Some Of That'
Leola B Wilson

'Whip It To A Jelly'
Clara Smith
'I wear my skirts up to my knees
And whip that jelly with who I please'

'If It Don't Fit, Don't Force It'
Barrelhouse Annie

'Sam The Hot Dog Man'
Lil Johnson

'My Stove's In Good Condition'
Lil Johnson

'My Handy Man'
recorded by both
Ethel Waters
& Victoria Spivey
'Some times he's up long before dawn
Trimming the edges of my rough lawn'

'New Bumble Bee Blues'
Memphis Minnie

'My Man Of War'
Lizzie Miles
'All night long he's drilling me
He's my man of war
His bayonet makes me cry for aid
Oh, he handles his hand grenades'

'Banjo Papa Stop Picking On Me'
Lizzie Miles

'Elevator Papa, Switchboard Mama'
Butterbeans & Susie

Ladies Sing the Blues

From the earliest days of the Blues, songwriters regularly used place names in their lyrics – possibly instructed by record companies to provide material that would appeal to people in particular areas. More likely, is that performers used these songs in their acts, changing the city name to match the town in where they were performing. Whatever the reason, it was the classic blues singers who pioneered the use of American city and regional names in their songs, establishing a trend that has continued in rock, pop, and the Blues ever since. Strangely, this is not a phenomenon that has been much exploited in Britain; perhaps those 'Dirty Old Scunthorpe Blues' just don't cut it!

These are just some of the many songs that feature cities, mostly in the South, where the blues-buying market was strongest.

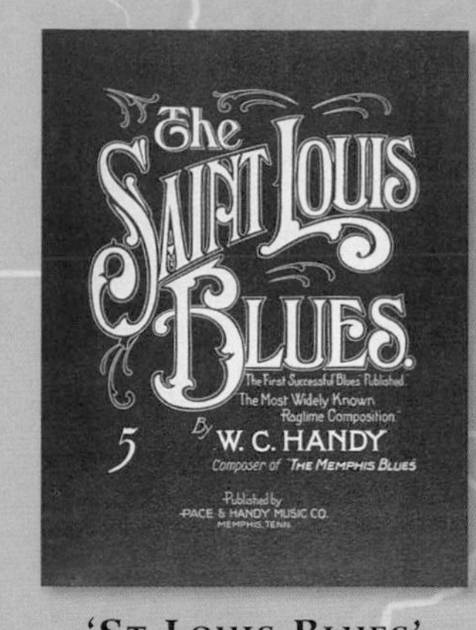

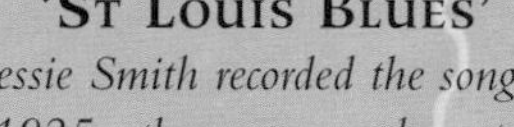

'St Louis Blues'

Bessie Smith recorded the song in 1925; other women who cut it included Ethel Waters, Katherine Henderson, and Virginia Childs.

NEBRASKA

'Nebraska Blues'
Victoria Spivey (1931)

KANSAS

Kansas City

'Kansas City Man Blues'
Clara Smith (1923)

St Louis

'St Louis Blues'
Bessie Smith (1925)

MISSOURI

BLACK SWAN
2010—B Blues Song
DOWN HOME BLUES
(Tom Delaney)
ETHEL WATERS AND THE JAZZ MASTERS
P115—1
Manufactured by Pace Phonograph Corp. New York

'Arkansas Road Blues'
Victoria Spivey (1927),
'Arkansas Blues'
Lucille Hegamin (1921)

ARKANSAS

'Oklahoma Man Blues'
Lucille Bogan (1927)

Memphis

'Jacksonville Blues'
Nellie Florence (1928)

Jacksonville

Little Rock

'Little Rock Blues'
Pearl Dickson (1929)

Fort Worth

'Fort Worth And Denver'
Bessie Tucker (1928)

'Mississippi Blues'
Lucile Hegamin (1921),
'The Mississippi Blues'
Laura Smith (1927),
'Mississippi Delta Blues'
Bessie Brown (1924)

TEXAS

'The West Texas Blues'
Ida Cox (1922)

'Galveston Blues'
Blanche Johnson (1927)

'Louisiana Hoodoo Blues'
Ma Rainey (1925)

Houston

Galveston

New Orleans

'Houston Blues'
Tiny Franklin (1923),
'Houston Bound'
Elzadie Robinson (1926),
'Big Houston Blues'
Victoria Spivey (1926),
Victoria Spivey came from Houston.

'New Orleans'
Mamie Smith (1922),
'New Orleans Hop Scop Blues', Sara Martin (1923),
'New Orleans Hop Scop Blues', Bessie Smith (1930),
'New Orleans Mojo Blues'
Katie Winters (1927)

'Michigan Water Blues'
LENA WILSON (1923)

CHICAGO

'Tight In Chicago'
MOZELLE ANDERSON,
'Chicago Bound Blues'
BESSIE SMITH (1923)

ETHEL WATERS

'Down Home Blues' was recorded in New York City in 1921. Ethel Waters could have been singing about anywhere down South, but did she have her hometown, Chester, Pennsylvania, in mind?

NEW YORK

'Folks In New York City Ain't Like Folks Down South'
MARGARET JOHNSON (1926),
'New York Blues'
VICTORIA SPIVEY (1930)

'Memphis Tennessee'
IDA COX (1922),
'Memphis Tennessee'
LENA WILSON (1923),
'Memphis Bound Blues'
MA RAINEY (1925),
'Memphis Bound'
ROSA HENDERSON (1924)

Knoxville

'Satan Is Busy In Knoxville'
LEOLA MANNING (1930)

Chattanooga

'Chattanooga Man'
LUCILLE HEGAMIN (1923)

Muscle Shoals

'Muscle Shoals Blues'
IDA COX 1924)

ATLANTA

'Atlanta Blues'
SARA MARTIN (1923)

BIRMINGHAM

'Birmingham Blues'
IDA COX (1922)

'Alabama Blues'
MAMIE SMITH (1922)

Macon

'Macon Blues'
DOROTHY EVERETTS (1928)

'Georgia Blues'
CLARA SMITH (1923),
'Georgia Man'
CHIPPIE HILL (1926),
'My Georgia Grind'
LUCILLE BOGAN (1930)

Pensacola

'Pensacola Blues'
IDA COX (1922),
'Pensacola Blues'
TRIXIE SMITH (1922)

MAMIE SMITH

Born in Cincinnati, Ohio, Mamie was not sufficiently inspired by the city to sing about it. Minnie Wallace's 'Cincinnati Blues' from 1935 went unreleased at the time.

'MISSISSIPPI DELTA BLUES'

In 1924, Bessie Brown sang the only known blues song predating World War II to be named after the traditional home of the Blues. Accompanying Bessie on this song are Coleman Hawkins and Fletcher Henderson.

MANY MORE LADIES SING THE BLUES

OKEH'S OTHER MAIN discovery beyond its New York base was Beulah Thomas, born in Houston, Texas, who became much better known as Sippie Wallace. She recorded 'Shorty George Blues' and 'Up The Country Blues' in Chicago during the late autumn of 1923.

A hard-hitting singer, Sippie was another performer who specialised in risqué lyrics, although hers weren't quite as raunchy as Lucille Bogan's.

She was one of a second phase of blues singers who kept closer than their predecessors to their rural roots. Like many of her peers, she benefited from the support of Louis Armstrong, as well as Johnny Dodds and Sidney Bechet. Sippie wrote most of the 40 sides she recorded for OKeh, either alone or with her pianist brother. But she faded from the scene as the Depression set in, moving to Detroit, where her husband and brother George both died in a hotel fire in 1936. As a result Sippie 'found' religion, and for 40 years she played the organ at a Baptist church in Detroit.

In 1966 Sippie's friend Victoria Spivey encouraged her to join the folk blues festival circuit. She also resumed recording with an album called *Sippie Wallace Sings The Blues*, featuring Roosevelt Sykes and Little Brother Montgomery. This is the album that is said to have inspired a 17-year-old from Burbank, California called Bonnie Raitt to play the blues.

Like Wallace, Victoria Spivey hailed from Houston; born in 1906, she was eight years younger than her friend. What Victoria's voice lacked in refinement was more than replaced by her Texas country blues phrasing and her ability to wail with the best of them. Her songs had a realism that struck an immediate chord with her audience.

Her debut for Okeh in 1926 was 'Black Snake Blues', a song Blind Lemon Jefferson would record a year later as 'That Black Snake Moan'. In 1927 Victoria cut the wonderful 'T.B. Blues', dealing with the hardships faced by tuberculosis victims; her delicate voice was strikingly at odds with the powerful subject matter. Later that year she recorded one of the very first songs in any genre to deal with the problems caused by cocaine, the aptly titled 'Dope Head Blues'. Other songs in her repertoire, like 1928's 'Organ Grinder Blues' and 'My Handy Man', came straight out from the risqué blues drawer.

Victoria wrote much of her own material, which, coupled with her head for business, extended the scope of her career well beyond most of her contemporaries. She continued recording throughout the 1930s, although less frequently than in the 1920s. After a period away from the Blues in the 1950s, when somewhat inevitably she sang only in church, she returned in the 1960s, when she formed her own record company and worked with Lucille Hegamin, Sippie Wallace, and the young Bob Dylan, who played harmonica and sang at a session she shared with Big Joe Williams in 1962.

Lucille Hegamin, the second singer ever to record a blues song back in 1920, hailed from Georgia. While she never aspired to the heights of the other classic blues singers, she was very popular in her day. Her best known song was 'He May Be Your Man, But He Comes To See Me Sometimes'. Hegamin also sang with the jazz great Jelly Roll Morton.

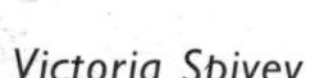

Victoria Spivey

Winding up at the Cameo label, she recorded around 70 sides in all before fading from the scene in the 30s, another victim of the Depression.

Any Woman's Blues

The 'race' labels recorded a whole host of female blues singers in their efforts to find just the right voice for their market. Some of these singers, like Louise Johnson, Flo Johnson, Edna Johnson, Sharlie English, or Dorothy Everetts, were fated to have very short careers, cutting as few as two sides. Others, like Rosa Henderson, were able to record for a number of years but are not well remembered today.

One reason for this neglect is that Henderson used around a dozen pseudonyms on her hundred or so sides, of which 'Can't Be Bothered With No Sheik' is a particular highlight, with very sassy lyrics.

Sara Martin was another woman who enjoyed a lengthy career, though she was 38 before she started recording for OKeh in 1922. Like many of her contemporaries, she was deeply rooted in vaudeville and the tent shows, but she was a more than competent blues singer, every bit as popular as her long list of recordings suggests. Record companies didn't issue records for the sake of it; they had to sell if the artist was going to be kept on the roster.

At Sara Martin's first session she cut 'Sugar Blues', which was later recorded by Bob Wills. She recorded until the end of the decade, and at her last session she cut 'Mean Tight Mama', which proved to be one of her best numbers. It featured the Clarence Williams Orchestra; yes, he was still around! Sara left the business in the early 1930s to return to live in her birthplace, Louisville, where she sang gospel while running a nursing home.

Besides Sara, OKeh signed up another good classic blues singer, Bertha 'Chippie' Hill. She was a veteran of the TOBA circuit and was very popular with Southern black audiences, though if anything she was closer in style to the male country blues singers who were starting to emerge at this time. One of 16 children, she first recorded in 1925, backed by Louis Armstrong. In 1926 she recorded 'Georgia Man' and 'Trouble in Mind', also with Louis. While Chippie faded from the scene in the 1930s, she did work again in 1946 with Lovie Austin's Blues Serenaders, though she was well past her best by this point.

Another star of the late 1920s was Edith North Johnson, who first recorded for QRS in 1928 before switching to Paramount in late 1929. At her first session in Richmond she recorded 'Honey Dripper Blues', accompanied by pianist Roosevelt Sykes (who throughout his early career went by the nickname of 'The Honey Dripper').

The Queen Of The Moaners

Clara Smith was the fourth of the 'big name Smiths' of the period, though there were lots of lesser Smiths too. She was dubbed the

Sara Martin

Fletcher Henderson born in 1897, he was the son of a Georgia school teacher.

Queen of the Moaners (that was a compliment!) and like her namesake Bessie boasted a mighty voice. She first recorded in 1923 for Columbia, in the vaudevillian style that owed little to the Blues' Southern roots. After 1925, however, her delivery notably improved and she even recorded some risqué blues tunes, including 'Whip it To Jelly', as well as titles like 'Shipwrecked Blues' with the legendary Louis Armstrong on cornet and Fletcher Henderson on piano. She recorded for almost 10 years, and continued to perform until 1935, when she suffered a heart attack and died in Detroit.

One female blues singer whose career started in the 1920s really had little connection with this period of classic blues. Lizzie Douglas, or Memphis Minnie as she was known, was born in 1897, but she did not begin her recording career until 1929. Her first husband may have been Will Weldon, who himself began recording in 1927, but by the time Memphis Minnie began her own career she was married to Joe McCoy, who made records under the name Kansas Joe. They accompanied each other at their first recording session on June 18, 1929, as besides being a fine singer, Memphis Minnie was an excellent guitarist. One of the three songs she recorded with Joe at that first session was the superb 'Bumble Bee'. She is one of the most important blues artists of her time, but we shall return to her story later as she was much more influential on the urban scene of the 1930s. Suffice it to say here that her career spanned three decades, and that she was responsible for keeping female blues alive in an increasingly male-dominated era.

Helen Humes' career proved to be equally durable, and she became best known for her work in the 1930s and 1940s with Count Basie. Born in Louisville, Kentucky, she came from a middle-class family, having both piano and singing lessons before being discovered at the age of 14 by guitarist Sylvester Weaver in 1927. Her first session in St. Louis, with Lonnie Johnson on guitar, produced four songs, including 'Stomping Weaver's Blues'. She had two more sessions in New York, at which she recorded mainly blues material. Between then and 1938, Helen worked in cabaret in New York, before joining the Count Basie Band, where she took the place of Billie Holiday. She worked in jazz throughout the 1940s before going back to her blues roots in the 1960s and 1970s, until her death from cancer in 1981.

Louise Johnson is typical of those female artists whose careers didn't reflect the extent of their talent. She recorded for Paramount in 1930, having accompanied Charley Patton, Willie Brown, and Son House to a session in Grafton, Wisconsin. Son House said that she was originally Patton's girlfriend, but on her way to Grafton she took up with Son after she and Charley argued.

Memphis Minnie

Whatever the truth, there is no doubting her talent, as she accompanied herself on piano and sang some strong blues. She was only in her late teens at this point, but she was never heard on record again. She went back to the Clarksdale area where she lived, apparently playing local juke joints. Her performances of 'On The Wall', 'By The Moon and Stars', 'Long Ways From Home', and 'All Night Long Blues' are worth seeking out, not least to hear Son House and Willie Brown encouraging her as she plays.

End Of An Era

The decline of the classic female blues singers is often attributed to the rise of the male blues artists, which began after Papa Charlie Jackson recorded for Paramount in August 1924. That same month, OKeh recorded Sloppy Henry in Atlanta. But the male presence only emerged slowly: it was not until a little over a year later that Blind Lemon Jefferson made his debut, and another year until Willie Jackson was recorded by Columbia on a field trip to New Orleans, while Blind Willie McTell only appeared on the recording scene in 1927. So it's not accurate to say that the men suddenly appeared on the scene and stole the women's popularity. In many ways the heat had already gone out of the female blues flame by the latter years of the Roaring Twenties. For example, Bessie Smith recorded more than 30 sides in 1925, but fewer than 20 in both 1926 and 1927, including significantly more Tin Pan Alley material, such as 'Alexander's Ragtime Band' (1927). Then as now, the changes in the blues scene owed much to the fluctuating tastes of the mass audience.

But whatever the reason, the result was the same: by the late 1920s, the era of the classic female blues icons was on the wane.

Hume and Basie
Helen Hume recording with the Count Basie Band at Columbia Records' studios, New York, 1941.

Helen Hume

51

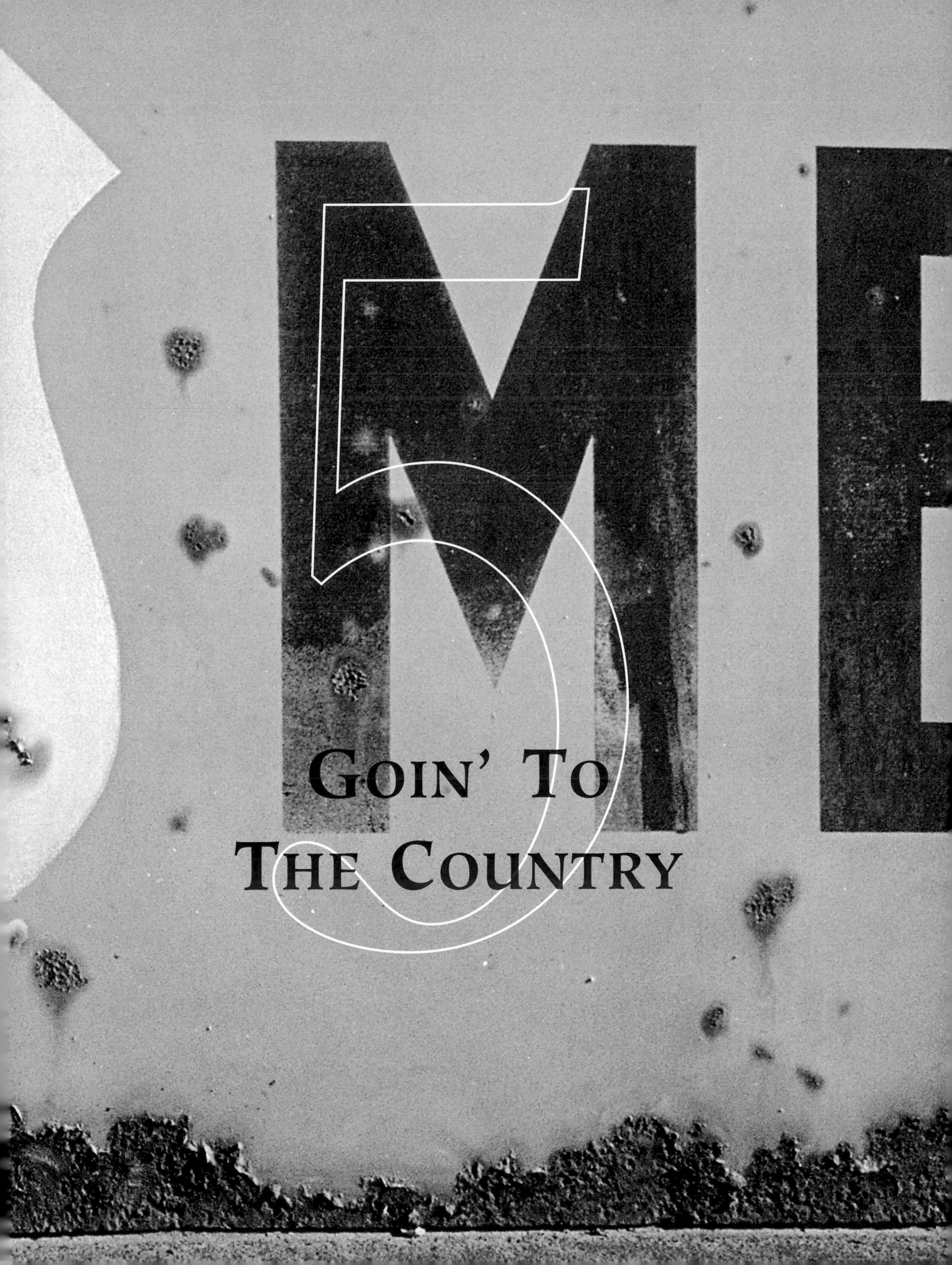

5
Goin' To The Country

Before Men Really Got the Blues

While women dominated the early pages of blues history, men were skirting around the fringes of the music. Four months before Mamie Smith recorded 'Crazy Blues', a male singer recorded another song with blues in the title. 'Unlucky Blues' was not actually a blues tune, but it highlights a key forerunner of the blues: the black vaudeville tradition, in which singers and entertainers drew large crowds to theatres with their expressive singing, dancing, and humour. The creator of 'Unlucky Blues' was Bert Williams, one of the first, and certainly one of the biggest, black stars of the early 20th century.

Bert Williams
Bert Williams hamming it up in the Ziegfield Follies of 1915.

Egbert Williams was born in Antigua in 1875, but his family soon migrated to New York, and then on to San Francisco. After abandoning a career in engineering, Bert used his skills as an entertainer to work San Francisco's cafés for tips. In his well-polished routine, he played a downtrodden man with indefatigable spirit, and his own perceptive philosophy on life. Between 1912 and 1919 he was one of the top stars of the Ziegfield Follies. Along with Eddie Cantor and Al Jolson, Bert Williams has been called "one of the three great minstrel style performers".

When he recorded 'Unlucky Blues' on 18th April, 1920, in New York City for Columbia Records, Bert was already a veteran recording star. He had first recorded in October 1901 with George Walker, and over the next 18 years he released many vaudeville numbers. Bert cut only one other side with a blues title, 'Lonesome Alimony Blues' in May 1920. While this was still somewhat musically removed from the Blues, its subject was certainly acceptable for a blues song!

Bert Williams fell seriously ill in Chicago in early 1922. His last recording session was on 24th February, 1922, and he died just eight days later, on 4th March. While he does not strictly fit into the story of the Blues, he was still a pioneer, who did much to change the public perception of the role a black man could occupy on the stage. Despite being required to wear blackface make-up, he never lost his dignity, and he was living proof that a black man could make it in what was still a white-dominated field. Given the racism still prevalent in American society, there was much bittersweet irony in his success.

Bottleneck Blues

In the wake of Mamie Smith's ground-breaking recording debut, it was women only as far as the Blues were concerned. With their background in the theatre, women singers enjoyed a clear advantage over their male counterparts. In fact, the first black man to record as a country blues musician initially did so as a guitarist, not a singer. Sylvester Weaver from Louisville, Kentucky, visited

OKeh's New York studio in late October 1923, to back Sara Martin on a couple of songs. The following month he did the same again, but this time he was allowed to record two of his own tunes, 'Guitar Blues' and 'Guitar Rag'. He remade 'Guitar Rag' four years later, and the tune was inspirational to black blues players as well as white country musicians. Like the women blues singers, however, Weaver was probably more at home performing a variety of material, from vaudeville to ragtime, rather than concentrating simply on blues. He had a superb sense of timing and played with great verve, skills that ensured his popularity with his tent show audiences. His recording career lasted until 1927, and he also made a number of sides with another guitarist, Walter Beasley. Their 'Bottleneck Blues' is not only a brilliant recording, but one of the few slide guitar duets on record. At that session, Weaver and Beasley also accompanied the 14-year-old Helen Humes, whom Weaver had brought to Okeh from their shared hometown of Louisville. This was Sylvester's penultimate recording session: like many of the country blues artists who recorded in the 20s, he simply faded from the scene.

HELEN HUMES IN THE EARLY 30S
At the age of 14 Helen Humes was recording for OKeh, accompanied on guitar by Sylvester Weaver and Walter Beasley.

Many people quote Papa Charlie Jackson as the first country blues singer to appear on record, but this is not actually the case. The honour of being first should probably go to the enigmatic Ed Andrews – unless, that is, you count Charles Anderson. On 24th October, 1923, in Chicago, Anderson recorded three sides, including 'Sing 'Em Blues', which shared the same tune as 'Baby Seals' Blues', the song written back in 1912 by Arthur Seals. Anderson recorded for OKeh, accompanied by Eddie Heywood on piano, and he recorded a number of other sides in December 1924, including 'Dirty Mistreating Blues' (another of those recurring blues themes). Little else is known about Charles Anderson, other than the fact that he also yodelled, and that he recorded four more unreleased sides in 1928 with pianist Earl Hines.

Equally obscured by history and possibly his own talent is Ed Andrews, who quite probably knew Sylvester Weaver. OKeh recorded Ed during one of the first field recording trips, in Atlanta in late March and early April 1924, which was also when Sara Martin recorded (again with Weaver on guitar and banjo). Against Weaver's comparatively sophisticated style, Ed Andrews sounded like a true country blues player, fresh from a country juke joint or one of Atlanta's many barrelhouses. 'Barrel House Blues' was in fact the title of one of the only two sides he recorded. Nothing more was ever heard from Mr. Andrews, which on the evidence of this recording is not surprising, as his performance was less than inspiring.

THE BATTLE OF RICHMOND

In 1920, Richmond, Indiana, was a prosperous town of around 25,000 people, and its largest business was the Starr Piano Company. By 1915, the owners, Henry Gennett and his three sons, were selling around 15,000 pianos annually; and in the

SARA MARTIN
Vaudeville and medicine show singer Sara Martin made over 130 recordings featuring the likes of King Oliver, Sydney Bechet and Sylvester Weaver. She was later to be responsible for introducing Butterbeans and Susie to the OKeh label.

The Starr Piano Company

King Oliver's Creole Jazz Band

One of the greatest and most influential of all the New Orleans' bands, particularly during the period when Louis Armstrong played trumpet.

same year they began to produce vertical-cut records. By 1919, they had realised that these records were not competitive, and that they should switch to lateral-cut records, which had already been patented by Victor. Undeterred, the Gennetts began to produce their own lateral-cut records, but Victor quickly sued them for patent infringement.

After three years of court battles the Gennett label finally triumphed, thereby creating an opportunity for other small labels to challenge the might of Victor and Columbia. Gennett's timing was immaculate, as radio had not yet reached the mass market and the demand for records was growing at a fantastic rate. Gennett saw the opportunity to record both black and 'hillbilly' entertainers to satisfy a growing demand, especially in the Southern states. It also recognized a potential market for jazz, and quickly signed up some of the big names from Chicago. By April 1923, King Oliver's Creole Jazz Band was in Gennett's studio at the Starr Piano factory in Richmond recording 28 sides that were to make history. Oliver's band included Louis Armstrong, drummer Baby Dodds and clarinettist Johnny Dodds, and their recordings were the first great masterworks of the jazz age. Later that year, Jelly Roll Morton also went to Richmond to record some of his early classics.

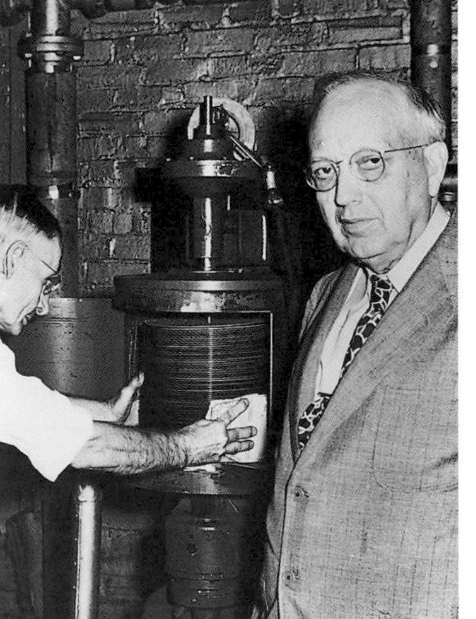

Gennett Records

Harry Gennett, son of founder Henry Gennett, at the pressing plant.

A Gennett record cover

Songsters and Stovepipes

On 10th May, 1924, a 57-year-old Alabaman (bizarrely) named Daddy

Stovepipe was recording in Richmond. His real name was Johnny Watson, and he had gained his nickname from his age, and the top hat that he wore. For recording 'Sundown Blues' and 'Stovepipe Blues', he was probably paid a session fee of around $10. The following Friday, Gennett recorded another 'Stovepipe', this time a man named Samuel Jones who worked as 'Stovepipe No. 1'. This singer got his nickname from playing a length of stovepipe, which produced a booming bass sound. Of the six sides he recorded, three were blues and one was a rag, while the other two were in the songster tradition. In fact, both men were songsters, whose style of playing and performing owed much to an earlier tradition. Their repertoire catered to their street-corner audiences, securing them hefty tips when the hat was passed around; some 20 years later, Lead Belly was cut from the same mould. Daddy Stovepipe recorded with his wife Mississippi Sarah until 1935, although neither they, nor Sam Jones, who ceased recording in 1927, were very successful. Having had its fill of Stovepipes, Gennett went on to record more sensibly named artists – if you think Cow Cow Davenport is more sensible!

WORKINGMAN BLUES
King Oliver and his Creole Jazz Band recorded by Henry Gennett for his own label.

BUTTERBEANS AND SUSIE

Six days after Stovepipe No.1's session, OKeh Records took its latest signing into a New York studio. Jodie and Susie Edwards worked professionally as Butterbeans and Susie, and OKeh, which had launched Mamie Smith's career three years earlier, had high hopes for them. Susie came from Florida and Jody from Georgia and they met in a vaudeville troupe, even marrying on stage when Jodie was 15 and Susie 14. Sara Martin was responsible for getting OKeh to record the duo, whose material was a mix of comedy, dance, and vaudeville songs, as well as a small proportion of blues tunes, which were enhanced by Susie's expressive phrasing. The duo's career with OKeh lasted until 1930, and they were backed between 1924 and 1930 by Atlanta-born pianist Eddie 'Professor' Heywood, who also accompanied Charles Anderson on OKeh. These early recordings demonstrate just how tightly knit the recording world was at this time, with the same accompanists cropping up again and again.

The ubiquitous Heywood provides our link to another artist who was recording before the bluesmen really came into their own. Waymon Henry, or Sloppy Henry as he was known, recorded a couple of blues songs for OKeh in late August 1924. 'Tom Cat Rag' and 'Cannon Ball Blues' were recorded in Atlanta on a field-recording trip that also yielded Annie Summerford's only two sides (this was clearly not OKeh's most productive field trip). Sloppy recorded another 16 sides for OKeh over the next five years, among them the first recording of 'Canned Heat Blues'. Tommy Johnson is the man credited with writing the song, but his rendition was recorded on 31st August, 1928, just 18 days after Sloppy cut his version in Atlanta.

DADDY STOVEPIPE IN 1963
Photographed shortly before he died.

BUTTERBEANS AND SUSIE
Jodie 'Butterbeans' Edwards of Marietta, Georgia and Sue Hawthorn of Pensacola, Florida, were one of the great duos of the black vaudeville stage. They married on stage when Jodie was 15 and Susie was 14.

CHICAGO IN THE 1920s

IN MAY 1917 *The Chicago Defender* announced the Great Northern Drive that effectively urged black people to 'flee the South'. This exodus had already begun, but soon many more were heading for the city. Between 1915 and 1925, 1.5 million blacks migrated to the North, and the 110,000 who moved to Chicago between 1916 and 1918 tripled the city's black population.

NEGROES STILL DEPARTING

The exodus of negroes from the south to the north has not stopped if all communities are having the same experience that Savannah is having. Any one who believes that the negroes have stopped going north is deceived. We imagine that nearly one hundred a week are getting out of Savannah. This may be a slight exaggeration, but it is true, nevertheless, that the departures are many and numerous. And those who are going are the better class of blacks. The worthless ones are remaining here to be cared for. The Negroes who are ... and industrious are ...

THE CHICAGO DEFENDER

'The exodus of negroes' as reported on Saturday 21st April, 1917.

Robert S. Abbott founded *The Chicago Defender* on 5th May, 1905, as "The World's Greatest Weekly". The paper was one of the most influential publications in the history of the black press. Two-thirds of its readership was located outside Chicago, and the paper was read extensively throughout the South. Black porters and entertainers distributed it across the Mason/Dixon line, and at its height around 500,000 people read the paper. For record companies like Paramount, *The Defender* was an ideal vehicle for advertising their artists. On 6th February, 1956, the paper became *The Chicago Daily Defender*, the largest black-owned daily in the world.

The Loop, Chicago

The city changed tremendously during the first half of the twentieth century. Every day, immigrants from across America – and especially black people from the Southern states – arrived in Chicago looking for the bright new future that they had read about in *The Defender*.

Chicago was without doubt the most musically vibrant city in America, home to thriving blues and jazz communities. After World War I, black vaudeville theatres like the Vendome and the Pekin were hugely popular, helping to bring both Ma Rainey and Ida Cox to prominence.

INTO THE LOOP

The Loop was the centre of Chicago's bright-light district in the 20s, boasting hotels, dance halls, theatres, burlesque houses and brothels. The crowds who flocked to the Loop provided an audience for the itinerant blues musicians who found their way to the city. State Street, lined with department stores, ran through the centre of the Loop. Bluesmen worked the street corners, looking for tips from the affluent shoppers.

'On State Street
they used to offer
to give it away
But now you can't get it
if you offer to pay
You can't get the stuff
no more'

'YOU CAN'T GET THE STUFF NO MORE'
TAMPA RED, 1932

On the edge of the Loop was Chicago's skid row, catering almost exclusively for men. This area was primarily working class, as well as inter-racial, and it was where many of the blues players were to be found.

PAPA'S ARCHETYPAL BLUES

'I'll look at this music, sing you this song
The woman on your mind's done broke your heart
Put you out, told you to go'

THESE ARE THE OPENING LINES from 'Airy Man Blues', which Papa Charlie Jackson cut (along with 'Papa's Lawdy Lawdy Blues') in Chicago during August 1924. Certainly Papa Charlie was 'on song' with what many people see as the archetypal blues theme.

Papa Charlie was a tall and, from his publicity shots, extremely well-dressed man. Though his experience and musical tradition harked back to an earlier age, he was the first real star of the male blues genre to make a record. His success was a conduit, which allowed other artists to record. He proved that there was a market for a male blues singer, and he did it while playing the banjo. His choice of the six-string banjo, tuned like a guitar, owed much to his background. Promotional material from the time suggests that he was born in New Orleans, and his sophisticated playing gives credence to this notion. He was a veteran of the medicine and tent show circuit from the early 1900s, and close to 40 years old when he first recorded, which is probably why he was called Papa.

He came to the attention of Paramount when he was playing around Chicago's Maxwell Street for tips. Within a year of his first recording, Charlie duetted with Ida Cox on 'Mister Man', a ploy to exploit the appeal of both these Paramount artists. Charlie also recorded with Hattie McDaniel, Ma Rainey, Lucille Bogan, Lottie Beamon, Amos Eaton, and Teddy Edwards, in a Paramount career that lasted until 1930, during which time he recorded around 70 solo sides. Much of his work has been called 'Hokum blues', and his comedic approach proved inspirational to artists like Tampa Red. He was also one of the first blues artists to concentrate on his own material in the studio, and the first to record up-tempo blues numbers. His biggest hit, 'Shake That Thing', was covered by a number of artists. Its dance rhythms blazed a trail that many others were to follow:

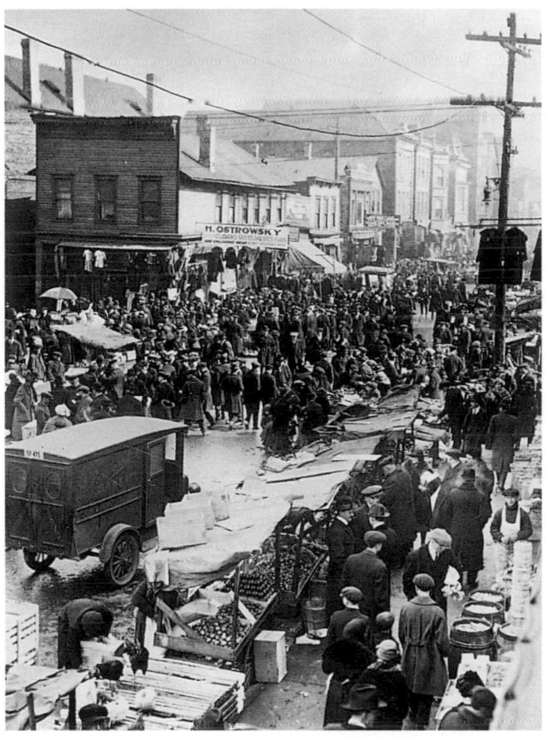

MAXWELL STREET, CHICAGO
The street on which many early blues singers worked for spare change and the chance to record.

'Now down in Georgia
they've got a dance that's new.
There ain't nothin' to it, it's easy to do
They call it shake that thing'

'SHAKE THAT THING'
PAPA CHARLIE JACKSON, 1925

LET'S GET ALONG
A 1926 advertisement for Papa Charlie Jackson's 'Let's Get Along'.

A few months before that session, Charlie recorded the original 'clean' version of 'Shave 'Em Dry'. In the hands of Lucille Bogan in 1935, this song became the ultimate in risqué blues. Jackson may have taught it to her when the two worked together in 1927.

Guitar Swing

That same year, 1925, was one in which another major blues artist came to prominence. This was no country blues player, as we think of them today, but a man who oozed urban sophistication. Lonnie Johnson first recorded as a member of Charles Creath's Jazz O-Maniacs on November 2, 1925. Two days later, he recorded two solo sides with John Arnold on piano, one of which was 'Mr Johnson's Blues'. This was not only a great piece of self-promotion, but also demonstrated Lonnie's superb guitar playing; he was a guitar legend before we knew what they were. You can trace his playing style in a direct line through T-Bone Walker and B.B King to Eric Clapton, and the British skiffle pioneer Lonnie Donegan even borrowed Johnson's name. Lonnie Johnson was both sensitive and sophisticated, but most of all he could swing.

Lonnie was another native of New Orleans, who had even travelled to London and Europe in 1917 as part of a musical group. He returned to Europe some 46 years later as part of the Second American Folk Blues Festival in 1963. Live recordings of that tour from Germany show that he had lost none of his sensitivity. By this time, he was around 70 years of age, though no one is quite sure exactly when he was born. His playing was as elegant as ever and one could only listen in awe as he delicately let his guitar do the talking. The 1963 American Folk Blues Festival included Muddy Waters, Sonny Boy Williamson, and Big Joe Williams, and you can only imagine that they were equally awe-struck.

Lonnie Donegan

Lonnie recorded around 130 blues sides between 1925 and 1932. He was also in demand as a session player, effectively acting as OKeh's in-house guitarist. Among the many people he backed were Chippie Hill, Helen Humes, Clara Smith, and Victoria Spivey. Lonnie's jazz recordings are equally brilliant: he worked with King Oliver, Louis Armstrong and Duke Ellington, as well as Eddie Lang, the white guitarist from Paul Whiteman's Orchestra. Their duets, like their 1929 recording of 'Guitar Blues' are defining moments in the history of the jazz guitar. As Duke Ellington proclaimed, "It don't mean a thing, if it ain't got that swing" – and on 'Guitar Blues', it certainly did.

Lonnie Johnson
A superb guitarist and a sharp dresser who oozed urban sophistication.

STACK O'LEE BLUES

THE FACT THAT MA RAINEY recorded the first version of 'Stack O'Lee Blues' does not mean she was the song's originator. It had been doing the rounds of the South, travelling up and down the Mississippi River, since the turn of the century. There are well over 60 known recorded versions, and countless others that were never recorded. Mississippi John Hurt's is considered the definitive version.

THE ST. LOUIS GLOBE DEMOCRAT, 1895

"William Lyons, 25, a levee hand, was shot in the abdomen yesterday evening at 10 o'clock in the saloon of Bill Curtis, at 11th and Morgan Streets, by Lee Sheldon, a carriage driver. Lyons and Sheldon were friends and were talking together. Both parties, it seems, had been drinking and were feeling in exuberant spirits. The discussion drifted to politics, and an argument was started, the conclusion of which was that Lyons snatched Sheldon's hat from his head. The latter indignantly demanded its return. Lyons refused, and Sheldon withdrew his revolver and shot Lyons in the abdomen. When his victim fell to the floor Sheldon took his hat from the hand of the wounded man and walked away. He was subsequently arrested and locked up at the Chestnut Street Station. Lyons was taken to the Dispensary, where his wounds were pronounced serious. Lee Sheldon is also known as 'Stag' Lee."

Footnote:
Billy Lyons later died from his wounds. Lee Sheldon was convicted and served time.

STACK O'LEE BLUES

Recorded for the OKeh label by Mississippi John Hurt, 28th December, 1928, New York City.

Police officer, how can it be?
You can 'rest everybody but cruel Stack O' Lee
That bad man, oh, cruel Stack O' Lee

Billy de Lyon told Stack O' Lee, "Please don't take my life,
I got two little babies, and a darlin' lovin' wife"
That bad man, oh, cruel Stack O' Lee

"What I care about you little babies, your darlin' lovin' wife?
You done stole my Stetson hat, I'm bound to take your life"
That bad man, cruel Stack O' Lee

...with the forty-four
When I spied Billy de Lyon, he was lyin' down on the floor
That bad man, oh cruel Stack O' Lee

"Gentleman's of the jury, what do you think of that?
Stack O' Lee killed Billy de Lyon about a five-dollar Stetson hat"
That bad man, oh, cruel Stack O' Lee

And all they gathered, hands way up high,
at twelve o'clock they killed him, they's all glad to see him die
That bad man, oh, cruel Stack O' Lee

Frank Hutchison from West Virginia, who played the guitar held on his lap, recorded the song in 1927 for OKeh. He was a white man who learned to play from a black musician neighbour. This early recording illustrates the close links between the music of poor blacks and whites in the South.

'Stack O' Lee Blues' has been released with many variations on the title, including: Stackalee, Stackolee, Stack-A-Lee, Stackerlee, Stagger Lee, Staggerlee, Stag-o-lee, and Stagolee.

The song has made the US Hot 100 three times, getting to No. 1 in 1959 with Lloyd Price (No. 7 in Britain). Wilson Pickett had a hit with it in 1967 and Tommy Roe in 1971. Besides the commercially released versions of the song, 16 versions were recorded by the Library of Congress during its field trips in the 30s and 40s. The first of these was by Ivory Joe Hunter in 1933. Later versions included one by a female convict at a Florida prison in 1936.

The Grateful Dead's version updated the story to 1940:
'1940 Christmas evening
With a full moon over town
Staggerlee met Billy De Lyon
And he blew that poor boy down.'

Bill Wyman's Rhythm Kings do a great version of 'Stagger Lee' on their live shows, sung by ex-Procol Harum vocalist Gary Brooker.

SELECTED VERSIONS

- **1925** Ma Rainey
- **1927** Furry Lewis, Long Clive Reed, Frank Hutchison
- **1928** Mississippi John Hurt
- **1956** Woody Guthrie, Lonnie Donegan
- **1958** Jesse Fuller
- **1961** Memphis Slim
- **1969** Taj Mahal
- **1978** Grateful Dead
- **1986** Merle Travis
- **1993** Bob Dylan

BLIND LEMON JEFFERSON

FACT FILE

BORN: *11th July, 1897 Couchman (Freestone Co.), Texas*

DIED: *December 1929, Chicago, Illinois*

INSTRUMENT: *Guitar*

FIRST RECORDED: *1925*

ACCOLADES: *Inducted into the Blues Hall of Fame, 1980*

INFLUENCED: *T-Bone Walker, BB King, Lightnin' Hopkins, Rev. Gary Davis, Lead Belly*

'When I was a boy, I think the first blues record I ever heard was Blind Lemon Jefferson singing 'Black Snake Moan''

MISSISSIPPI FRED MCDOWELL

BORN BLIND IN EAST TEXAS, Jefferson was one of seven children. He probably learned to play guitar to earn a living, and by 1917 he was performing at house parties. Soon after, he moved to Dallas, where he played on street corners. He was obviously talented, as he was soon earning enough to support both a wife and a child; rumour has it he could earn $150 on a good day. Although he is known as a bluesman, he also sang spirituals and folk tunes, as it was important to play a variety of material with popular appeal to earn a living. There is little doubt that Jefferson travelled extensively before he took up recording, which both accounts for the diversity of his material and also indicates the depth of his talent.

In 1925, a Dallas record storeowner recommended Jefferson to Paramount Records in Chicago. Paramount decided to record his spirituals under the name of Deacon L.J. Bates, and his blues as Blind Lemon Jefferson – though it's not certain whether he had already been using the latter name. Jefferson's almost immediate success encouraged Paramount to seek out other country blues players, including Blind Blake. Between 1926 and 1929 Jefferson cut more than 90 sides, making him the most recorded of the early bluesmen. His massive record sales afforded him the luxury of two cars and a chauffeur.

Jefferson's a unique talent combined a high-pitched voice with great guitar virtuosity. The offbeat phrasing of his playing and free-form vocals marked him out from his contemporaries. He was also one of the first artists regularly to record his own material, which hitherto had not been the case among blues singers. While some of his songs were naturally derivative of earlier folk idioms and tunes, Jefferson gave them a uniqueness that was steeped in Southern black culture.

As with many early bluesmen, Jefferson's death is shrouded in mystery. He may have died of a heart attack, or possibly have frozen to death in a Chicago snowstorm around Christmas 1929.

ESSENTIAL RECORDINGS

CLASSIC SONGS

'Matchbox Blues' 1927
'See That My Grave Is Kept Clean' 1927
'Black Snake Moan' 1927

THE SOURCE

4 CDs of his complete works on Document Records

'One of America's outstanding original musicians'

THE WORDS ON JEFFERSON'S TOMBSTONE

THE REAL COUNTRY BLUES

'I'm goin' to the country, baby do you wanna go?'

'STATESBORO BLUES' BY BLIND WILLIE MCTELL

NO ONE KNOWS FOR SURE if Lemon was his real name, but Blind Lemon Jefferson represents one of the pinnacles of country blues music. He began his career playing for tips on street corners in Dallas, and he must have been very good, as it is reported he could earn as much as $150 a day. He might have stayed on the streets but for the foresight of a Dallas storeowner who sold Paramount's records. R.T. Ashford contacted Art Laibly, Paramount's marketing director, suggesting he should record the blind 27-year-old singer and guitarist.

Ashford's approach to Paramount was not that unusual. Nor was he motivated by kindness, for he simply saw an opportunity to make money for himself. It was obvious that Jefferson was popular around Dallas and Ashford relished the chance of selling records to his local fans. Paramount agreed to record Jefferson, and sometime in December 1925 or January 1926 he was taken to Chicago. For some strange reason, however, Blind Lemon recorded no blues tunes, merely two spirituals, before heading home to Dallas. A couple of months later he was back in Chicago, and this time he did record the Blues. Four sides were cut, including what became his debut release in May, 'Long Lonesome Blues'. Paramount could not have anticipated the consequences: with their help, Blind Lemon changed the face of recorded blues, and arguably the direction of popular music, forever.

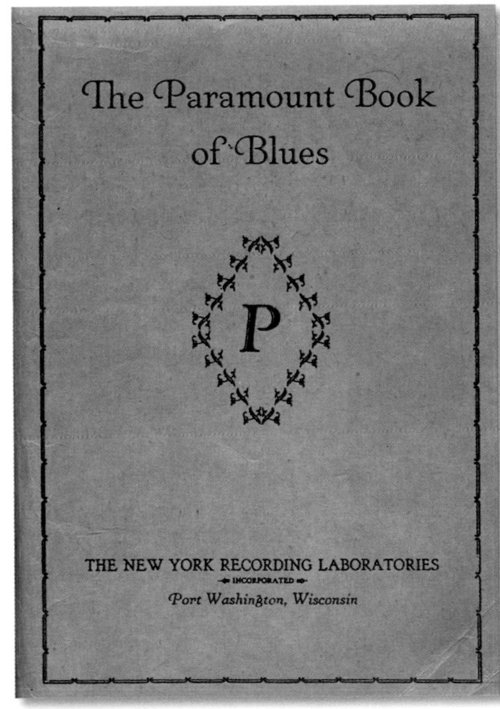

The Paramount Book of Blues
P
THE NEW YORK RECORDING LABORATORIES
INCORPORATED
Port Washington, Wisconsin

What made Blind Lemon unique was his unusual phrasing and the way he combined his guitar and vocals to enhance the melody line. His material was also brilliant, and combined with his unorthodox delivery this made him almost impossible to copy. It was common practice for record companies to produce cover versions, on which one of their own stars replicated a rival's record, allowing them to take a share of the sales. But Blind Lemon produced something that set him apart from other artists. He had a 'sound', not just a song. For the first time, the artist was the star, not the material. In effect, Blind Lemon Jefferson became the first male pop star. And his success meant that men now dominated the Blues.

Jefferson's first spiritual recordings were released a few months later under the name Deacon L.J. Bates; other Deacon Bates recordings followed over the next few years. Jefferson's popularity meant that other record companies suddenly woke up to the opportunities that lay outside their traditional recording bases. It may also have dawned on them that their Southern audiences wanted records by performers who sounded

"Can anyone imagine a fate more horrible than to find that one is blind? Such was the fate of Blind Lemon Jefferson . . . He learned to play a guitar, and for years he entertained his friends freely – moaning his weird songs as a means of forgetting his affliction."

PARAMOUNT'S BOOK OF THE BLUES
A 40-page book containing the words and music to 30 songs and profiles of their six biggest recording artists.

while its own new studio at the company's pressing plant in Grafton, Wisconsin was being finished.

Three months after his Richmond session, this giant of the blues was dead. He had either frozen to death in the snow, or suffered a heart attack after leaving a club in Chicago. He was found dead in the street the next morning, covered in snow; his guitar lay by his side.

He was taken back to Texas and buried in Wortham Negro Cemetery. Someone eventually listened to his plea, and a marker was placed on his grave on 15th October, 1967 – 37 years after his death.

How long Blind Lemon would have continued recording if he had lived has to be a matter of conjecture. Like other artists of the period, his career would have been affected by the Depression, the onset of the radio, and changing fashion. All too often, the man who is first is overtaken by events. In any case, Jefferson's status as a pioneer meant that he lived his life in the white heat of publicity, something for which he was ill-equipped.

After Blind Lemon Jefferson's death, Blind Blake was unrivalled as Paramount's leading blues singer. He was a prolific recording artist, working under pseudonyms such as Blind George Martin, the Hokum Boys, Billy James, and, most unusually of all, Gorgeous Weed and Stinking Socks.

Besides all his other talents Blake should be regarded as one of the foremost guitarists of his generation. He played fantastic ragtime guitar on numbers like 'Southern Rag' and 'Blind Arthur's Breakdown', and his talent led Paramount to use him on a number of sessions for other artists. Blake's individualistic playing can be heard alongside artists such as Ma Rainey and Irene Scruggs, while he also cut a memorable duet, 'Hastings Street', with Charlie Spand. As well as his many solo records, he occasionally appeared with a small band. The precise circumstances of Blake's death are unknown, as is the date, but it is likely that he died soon after the demise of Paramount Records in the early 1930s. His influence lived on in the work of other bluesmen from the East, such as Blind Boy Fuller.

SEE THAT MY GRAVE IS KEPT CLEAN
Blind Lemon Jefferson's grave in Wortham Negro Cemetery, Wortham, Texas.

THE WORLD'S FIRST SAMPLER RECORD

'Hello, folks. We are gathered here to do the Home Town Skiffle. Everybody shake that thing.'

In 1929, Blind Lemon Jefferson and other stars of the Paramount label made what has been described as the first sampler record. Entitled 'Home Town Skiffle' by the Paramount All Stars, the label credits Blind Lemon Jefferson, Blind Blake, Will Ezell, Charlie Spand, Papa Charlie Jackson, and the Hokum Boys. The Hokum Boys were all the other artists plus Alex Hill and Georgia Tom Dorsey. The record features one or two choruses of a number of the artist's best known records, and it marks the first known mention of the word 'skiffle'. In Britain, skiffle had a profound effect on the development of rock music in the late 1950s and early 1960s.

'Chris Barber, the trombone player, was the first person to bring people like Big Bill Broonzy and Muddy Waters to Britain. In the middle of his traditional jazz thing, he had a little skiffle section, named after a record called 'Home Town Skiffle'. Lonnie Donegan played in this little segment, which just took off and skiffle became enormous. Everybody in the 1960s rock bands – the Who, Zeppelin, the Stones, the Beatles – started off playing skiffle. After Donegan went on to greater fame, Chris Barber replaced him with a blues segment, and the guitarist there was Alexis Korner. That's where the British blues thing came from: it all started out of skiffle'

BILL WYMAN

BLIND BLAKE

FACT FILE

BORN: *c. 1890-95*
Probably Jacksonville, Florida

DIED: *c. 1933, Florida*

INSTRUMENT: *Guitar*

FIRST RECORDED: *1926*

ACCOLADES: *Inducted into the Blues Hall of Fame, 1990*

INFLUENCED: *Blind Boy Fuller, Big Bill Broonzy, Josh White*

THE FACTS REGARDING Blake's birth date and early life are hard to unravel; even his real name is cloaked in mystery. He was most likely born Arthur Phelps; the 'Blake' in his nickname denotes an unrelenting and tough character. It is believed that he spent his youth in Georgia, working as a blind street musician.

He later travelled across the Southern states, playing for road gangs, at picnics and fish fries – in fact, anywhere he could be fed and scrape together a meagre wage.

He moved to Chicago in the early 1920s and probably began his recording career as an accompanist; he first recorded as a soloist for Paramount in August 1926.

Blake's first record, 'West Coast Blues', a ragtime number, became a hit. Between this debut and 1932, he recorded more than 80 solo titles. Some of these were released under such names as Blind George Martin, Blind Arthur, Billy James and, somewhat bizarrely, Gorgeous Weed and his Stinking Socks!

Among the other artists whom he is known to have accompanied on record are Ma Rainey, Leola Wilson, Irene Scruggs, and Papa Charlie Jackson; he also recorded a memorable duet, 'Hastings Street', with Charlie Spand. In the 1930s he toured with a small band and also appeared in a show called *Happy Go Lucky*.

Many of Blake's records were characterised by incorporating ragtime and jazz into the Blues. He was one of the most popular blues recording artists of the 1920s. There are some who quibble about his blues credentials, as he also produced old-style ballads and vaudeville numbers, but he did definitely record many straight blues tunes. His success was certainly a factor in persuading record companies to seek out other country blues players to record.

Blake's playing was also responsible for encouraging many other performers to latch onto the idea of playing a riff on their guitars, although for many years few of them could match his masterful technique. Many young blues players in the 1930s learned and were inspired by listening to his records.

'Jackson: *Say Blake!*
Blake: *What is it, boy? What you want?*
Jackson: *What is your right name?*
Blake: *My name is Arthur Blake!*
Jackson: *Where did you get that Arthur at?*
Blake: *Oh, I'm the author of many things*'

1929 PARAMOUNT RECORDING 'BLIND BLAKE AND PAPA CHARLIE JACKSON TALK'

ESSENTIAL RECORDINGS

CLASSIC SONGS

'West Coast Blues' 1926
'Southern Rag' 1927
'Blind Arthur's Breakdown' 1929
'Hastings Street' 1929

THE SOURCE

4 CDs of his complete works on Document Records

DOWN SOUTH BLUES

BARBECUE BOB
Robert Hicks was given his name, surprisingly enough, because he worked at a barbecue. In keeping with his new identity, his first release was called 'Barbecue Blues'.

ATLANTA MUST HAVE BEEN a busy old blues town in March 1927, as Columbia Records based its field recording unit in the city. We can only speculate as to whether any of its artists crossed paths with Blind Lemon Jefferson, who was well known throughout the South, having spent much of his time away from Texas, travelling throughout the Delta and beyond.

The first artist recorded by Columbia in Atlanta was the delightfully named Barbecue Bob, a 25-year-old from Walton County, Georgia. Bob, whose real name was Robert Hicks, was discovered by Dan Hornsby, a local musician and Columbia talent scout. The recording session, in a downtown hotel, was under the supervision of Frank Walker, the man who discovered Bessie Smith. Bob's first record, 'Barbecue Blues' and 'Cloudy Sky Blues', sold around 15,000 copies, which made him the label's best-selling male artist. Encouraged by this, Columbia took Bob to New York for more sessions, and over the next 42 months he recorded around 70 sides for the label, some with his older brother. Charlie Hicks was billed as Laughing Charley, a name, so they say, totally at odds with his character; Bob got his nickname from working at a barbecue. Both Bob and his brother played 12-string guitars. Amongst the sides Bob recorded were 'Goin' Up The Country' and 'Motherless Chile Blues'.

*'There's a big red
headline in the
Chicago Defender News,
There's a big red
headline in the
Chicago Defender News,
Sayin' my gal down South
Got them
Up the country blues'*

'GOIN' UP THE COUNTRY'
BARBECUE BOB,
APRIL 1928

Both men's lives ended tragically. Bob died of pneumonia in 1931, shortly after he had recorded some great sides with Curley Weaver and Buddy Moss as the Georgia Cotton Pickers. Charley never recovered from Bob's early death: he became an alcoholic, murdered a man on Christmas Day 1955, was convicted and sent to prison in 1956, and died there in 1963.

Peg Leg the Bootlegger

In April 1927, another Columbia artist, Peg Leg Howell, recorded his second session for the label; the first had been held in Atlanta the previous November. In all, the former bootlegger, who lost his leg in 1916 as a result of a gunshot wound, recorded nearly 30 sides for Columbia. Peg Leg, whose real name was Joshua Barnes Howell, has the distinction of being the first true country blues artist to record for Columbia.

The other artist whom Columbia recorded during this field trip went on to become something of an anomaly in the country blues field. De Ford Bailey cut two sides, both unissued, before returning just over two weeks later to re-record the amazing 'Pan American Blues', this time for Brunswick. This song, in which he replicated the sounds of trains on the harmonica, became his showpiece. Bailey called his style, which had evolved from the music of the more traditional string bands, black hillbilly music.

What set Bailey apart was the fact that from the late 1920s until 1941, he performed on the *Grand Ole Opry* radio show, the bastion of white country music. Many listeners were unaware that Bailey was even black, but few could have been unimpressed by his playing. He was a major influence on many later exponents of the blues harp.

On Columbia's other field trips in the late 1920s, a number of singers were recorded. Some, such as Billy Bird, never really figured in the story of the blues. Pink Anderson, who recorded four sides with Simmie Dooley in 1928, is better remembered for his name than his music. In 1965 a British rock band led by Syd Barrett, who had started out playing R&B, took the first part of their name from Pink and the second from Floyd Council.

Pan American Blues
De Ford Bailey recorded his trademark 'Pan American Blues' in 1927. He died in Nashville, Tennessee, in 1982.

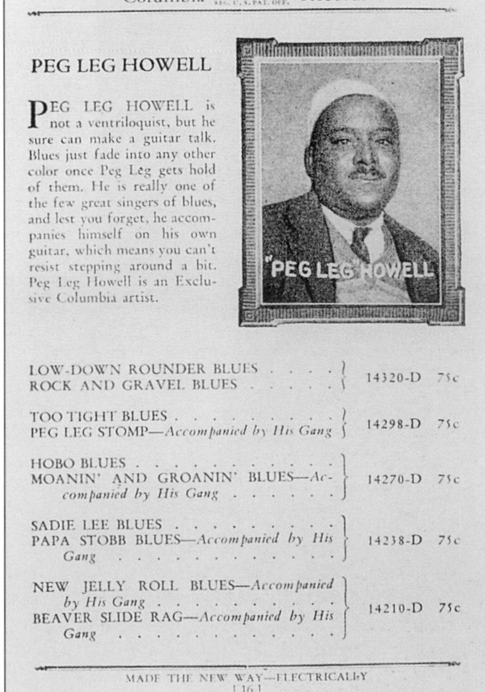

Columbia "New Process" Records

PEG LEG HOWELL

PEG LEG HOWELL is not a ventriloquist, but he sure can make a guitar talk. Blues just fade into any other color once Peg Leg gets hold of them. He is really one of the few great singers of blues, and lest you forget, he accompanies himself on his own guitar, which means you can't resist stepping around a bit. Peg Leg Howell is an Exclusive Columbia artist.

"PEG LEG" HOWELL

Titles	Number	Price
LOW-DOWN ROUNDER BLUES / ROCK AND GRAVEL BLUES	14320-D	75c
TOO TIGHT BLUES / PEG LEG STOMP—*Accompanied by His Gang*	14298-D	75c
HOBO BLUES / MOANIN' AND GROANIN' BLUES—*Accompanied by His Gang*	14270-D	75c
SADIE LEE BLUES / PAPA STOBB BLUES—*Accompanied by His Gang*	14238-D	75c
NEW JELLY ROLL BLUES—*Accompanied by His Gang* / BEAVER SLIDE RAG—*Accompanied by His Gang*	14210-D	75c

MADE THE NEW WAY—ELECTRICALLY
[16]

Peg Leg Howell
A Columbia Records catalogue promoting his recordings of 'Low Down Rounder Blues', 'Too Tight Blues', 'Hobo Blues' and others, all accompanied by His Gang.

VICTOR(Y) AT LAST

Victor Records' dabblings in the Blues had been few and far between before 1926. Lizzie Miles and Rosa Henderson were recorded back in mid-1923 but that was about it. Then in autumn 1926 Victor recorded Bobby Leecan and Robert Cooksey; Leecan was a talented guitarist, while Cooksey played the harmonica. Their output was the usual mix of jazz and vaudeville, but they did record some blues too. It is thought that they came from the North, probably Philadelphia.

In February and March 1927, around the same time as Columbia was in Atlanta, Victor executives were in Memphis searching for blues artists to record. They do not seem to have had much idea of what they were looking for as they recorded mostly spirituals from Sadie McKinney, Ollie Rupert, A.C. Forehand, and Blind Mamie Forehand. Arah 'Baby' Moore did record a couple of blues songs but that was the label's sole excursion into the Blues – except for eight recordings of four different songs by the Memphis Jug Band. These proved to be the start of long, on-and-off careers for the various members of the band. A summer recording trip to Bristol in Tennessee, Charlotte in North Carolina, and Savannah, Georgia provided the label with some more rather uninspired blues singers.

12-STRING STELLA GUITAR
Willie McTell used a 12-string Stella guitar because it was the ideal instrument for playing on the street. Louder than the six-string, it allowed the singer to attract and then entertain a large audience.

THE DEAN OF ATLANTA BLUES

Then, on a recording trip to Atlanta in October 1927, Victor finally struck gold. On Tuesday 18th October, a 27-year-old man who has been called 'The Dean of The Atlanta Blues School' recorded the first of four sides for Victor, accompanied by his own guitar. In his nine-year pre-war career, Blind Willie McTell recorded some 60 sides for Victor, Columbia, OKeh, Vocalion, and Decca under a variety of pseudonyms, including Blind Sammie, Georgia Bill, Hot Shot Willie, and plain Blind Willie.

No one is sure if Willie McTear, as he was born, was blind at birth or whether he became blind as a small child. Whatever the case, he attended several blind schools, and was taught to play the guitar by his mother. Willie played the 12-string guitar and is regarded as one of the great blues exponents of the instrument.

Even before he recorded, he was a well-known figure on the Atlanta blues scene, where he was a good friend of Curley Weaver and Buddy Moss. He was a regular at house rent parties, on street corners, and at fish fries, and he also worked the medicine and tent show circuit. In 1933 he worked street corners with Blind Willie Johnson, and they made a formidable pair. Just imagining the chance to see these two amazing artists working side by side is enough to get the blues juices flowing. Both were masters of their craft, both were blind, and both were brilliant guitar players who inspired future generations.

THE MCTELL LEGACY

McTell was typical of his generation of blues singers, as he sang a variety of material, performing rags, spirituals, and traditional songs nearly as often as he sang the Blues. What set Willie apart from many of his contemporaries was his sensitive vocal delivery. In many ways he was the total antithesis of what people think of as a country blues singer. But this also makes him an ideal artist to play to people who say that they don't like the blues – because after they have listened to Blind Willie McTell, they soon will!

By 1934 he married Kate, who can be heard singing on some of his later records. During his career Willie McTell was not a

FIELD RECORDING

THE MAJOR RECORD companies only started to record the classic women blues singers in the early 1920s in New York, when these artists were appearing in the city's theatres. It was OKeh, an independent label started in 1918, that took the revolutionary step of releasing Mamie Smith's 'Crazy Blues' (OKeh 4169) in November 1920, and not one of the big two, Columbia and Victor.

In 1921 record sales in the US reached 100 million for the first time. By 1923, both Columbia and Victor had become active in the 'race' recording field, although Bessie Smith and Clara Smith gave Columbia a definite edge. Paramount was also in the ascendancy, and the most effective of all the labels in exploiting the vast untapped market for recordings by black performers.

Paramount's artists from the South had to travel to their recording studio in Chicago, while the other labels all maintained studios in New York City. Then, after the initial success of the classic blues singers, the labels had to look further afield for artists to record. The first 'field trips' – when record label representatives actively searched the South for suitable talent – took place in 1923, and more followed in 1924 and 1925. But it was the discovery of Blind Lemon Jefferson in 1926 that spurred all the labels into a frenzy of field recording. Interestingly, although Blind Lemon was discovered in Dallas he was taken to Chicago to record, in true Paramount fashion.

Scouts from the record companies trawled the South in their quest for new artists. They would either arrange for a performer to travel north to a company's home base, or alert the company so that a mobile recording unit could record them the next time they were in the area. These field trips weren't restricted to black artists, or blues singers. They also unearthed gospel and religious performers, as well as hillbilly artists, the forerunners of today's country stars.

The mobile units visited cities for periods ranging from a few days to several weeks, often setting up its recording unit in a hotel. The time taken to alert potential recording artists to their arrival somewhat dictated the length of time the units spent in each city. Some artists would remind themselves of when a company made their annual or bi-annual visit to the town, and make sure they were around. Field recording also inadvertently encouraged the practice of artists adopting pseudonyms in order to record more sides for different labels.

Gennett Records' field recording vehicle.

Sporadic field trips took place late into the 30s, and the Library of Congress was also running its own, more academic, trips in the 30s and 40s. The opening of local recording studios, however, not only helped to put an end to these trips, but also spawned another phenomenon that would have a vital influence on the entire history of blues and rock'n'roll: the local independent label.

Field trips were a very important episode in the history of the Blues and popular music. Without them the story of the Blues would have been very different, as some major artists would never have recorded; history would have passed them by.

St Paul
1927: Gennett
CLARA SMITH

EARLY FIELD RECORDING TRIPS

OKEH AND COLUMBIA made the most frequent and extensive field trips. When Victor, and its Bluebird subsidiary, went into the field it tended to record a more limited number of artists. Once ARC, The American Recording Company, began its own field trips in 1934 they became fairly frequent. ARC was the label that recorded Robert Johnson in San Antonio, Texas, in 1936 and 1937.

GRAFTON, WISCONSI
Paramount's ho studio after 192

All trains goin' to Memphis town,
Shovel the coal, see the wheels go round,
Lord, everybody's goin' down to Memphis town

LEROY CARR, 1931

ILLINO

KANSAS

Kansas City
1929: Brunswick

St Louis
1923–1927: OKeh; 1934: ARC
LONNIE JOHNSON, VICTORIA SPIVEY, HELEN HUMES, LEROY CARR

MEMPHIS, TN

1927 – 1930	*Victor*
1927	*Columbia*
1928	*OKeh, Victor*
1928 – 1930	*Brunswick*
1939	*ARC*

THE MEMPHIS JUG BAND, TOMMY JOHNSON, FURRY LEWIS, JOHN ESTES, RUBE LACY, JOHN HURT, SPECKLED RED, MEMPHIS MINNIE, BLIND BOY FULLER

MISSOURI

ARKANSAS

Memphis

DALLAS, TX

1925 – 1929	*OKeh*
1927 – 1929	*Columbia*
1928 – 1929	*Brunswick*
1929 – 1932	*Victor*
1935 – 1939	*ARC*
1937	*Decca*

BLIND WILLIE JOHNSON, BILLIKEN JOHNSON, DALLAS STRING BAND

Hot Springs
1937: ARC

Dallas

Fort Worth
1934–1936: ARC
FUNNY PAPER SMITH, BLACK ACE

Shreveport
1930 OKeh
MISSISSIPPI SHEIKS

Jackson
1930: OKeh; 1935: AR
MISSISSIPPI SHEIKS, BO CARTER, CHARLIE MCCOY

TEXAS

LOUISIANA

I'm goin' back to Texas,
Sit on easy street

HENRY THOMAS, 1928

San Antonio
1928–1930: OKeh;
1934–1938: Victor; 1935–1936: ARC
BO CARTER, MISSISSIPPI SHEIKS, TEXAS ALEXANDER, LONNIE JOHNSON, LITTLE HAT JONES, ROBERT JOHNSON

NEW ORLEANS, LA

1924 – 1929	*OKeh*
1925 – 1929	*Columbia*
1926 – 1936	*Victor*
1927 – 1929	*Brunswick*
1935	*Decca*

MISSISSIPPI SHEIKS, BO CARTER, LITTLE BROTHER MONTGOMERY, BLIND WILLIE JOHNSON

N
ORLE

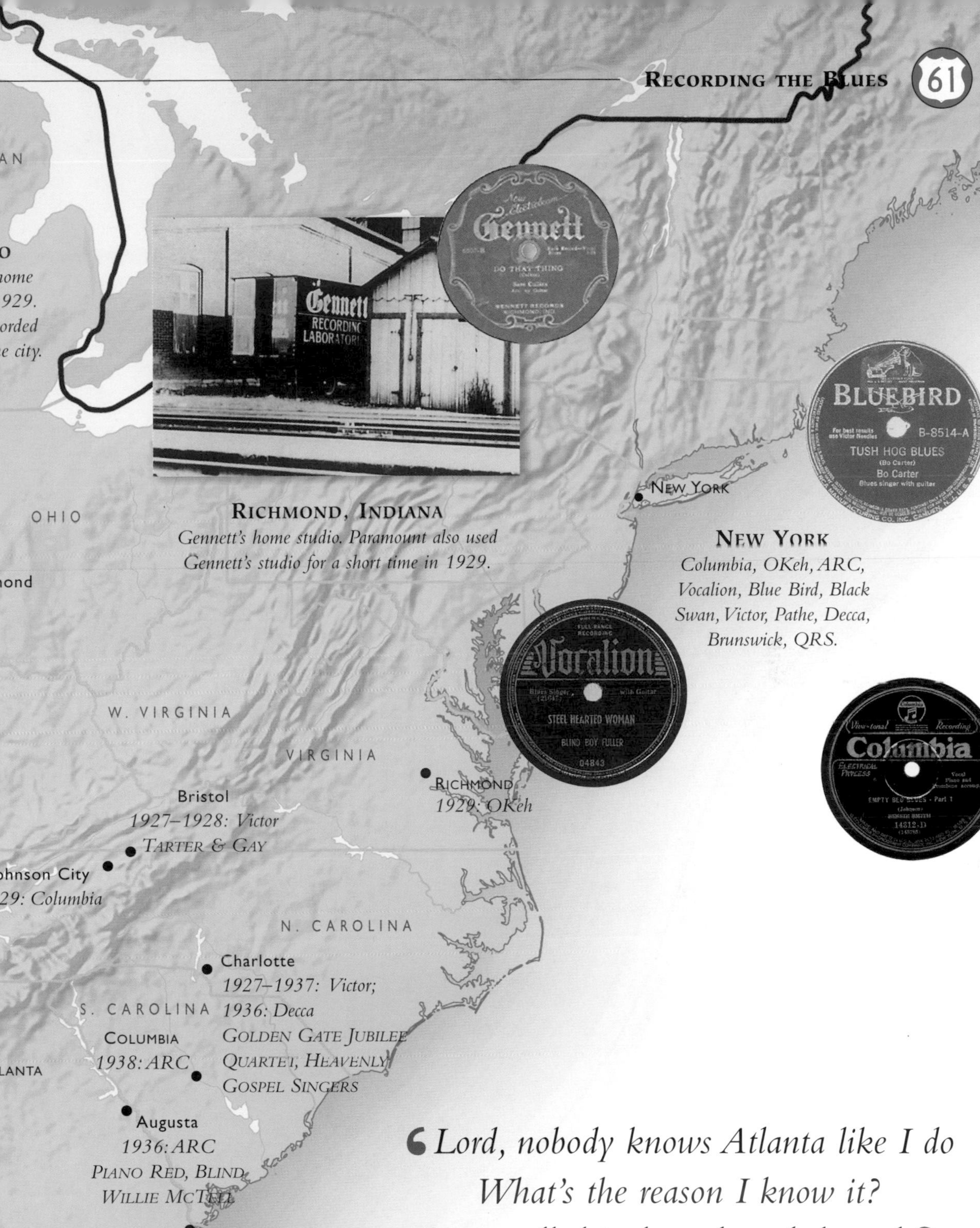

Indianapolis
1928: Brunswick
Leroy Carr

Nashville
1928: Victor

Hattiesburg
1936: ARC

Lord, nobody knows Atlanta like I do
What's the reason I know it?
I've travelled it through and through

Barbecue Bob, 1930

Atlanta, GA

1923 – 1931	*OKeh*
1924 – 1930	*Columbia*
1925 – 1940	*Victor*
1928	*Brunswick*

Blind Willie McTell, The Memphis Jug Band, Barbecue Bob, Curley Weaver, Pink Anderson, Lucille Bogan, Blind Lemon Jefferson, Blind Willie Johnson, Mississippi Sheiks, Bo Carter

Key to Recording Information

Town, State
Recording date(s) *Record Company*
Recorded Artist(s)

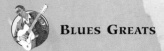

BLIND WILLIE MCTELL

FACT FILE

BORN: *5th May, 1901 Thomson (McDuffie Co.), Georgia*

DIED: *19th August, 1959 Milledgeville, Georgia*

INSTRUMENT: *Guitar, Harmonica*

FIRST RECORDED: *1927*

ACCOLADES: *Inducted into the Blues Hall of Fame in 1981*

INFLUENCES: *Blind Willie Johnson*

INFLUENCED: *The Allman Brothers, Bob Dylan*

NO ONE IS QUITE SURE if William Samuel McTell was totally blind at birth, partially sighted, or became blind in his early youth. But there is no doubt that he was totally blind by the time he ran away from his home, in Statesboro', Georgia, to follow medicine and minstrel shows in his early teens. Having learned the guitar from his mother as a child, he abandoned the instrument for about eight years, only starting again when he attended a Blind School in Macon around 1922. He hoboed around the East Coast, playing at parks and on street corners from around 1925.

On 18th October, 1927 he recorded four sides for Victor Records in Atlanta. Almost a year to the day later, he held another session for Victor, at which he recorded his classic 'Statesboro' Blues' and three other sides, including 'Three Woman Blues'. Another year passed before he recorded again, this time as Blind Sammie for Columbia – the first of many times he used a pseudonym to sidestep his contractual liabilities. More sessions followed for Victor, and then he went back into the studio for Columbia as Blind Sammie in 1930 and 1931. At the latter session he recorded 'Broke Down Engine Blues' and 'Southern Can Is Mine'.

DYLAN'S BLUES

Bob Dylan composed a song entitled 'Blind Willie McTell' which appeared on his 1991 Bootleg Series Vol.1-3.

He continued to record until 1936 for Victor, Vocalion, and Decca, working with Piano Red, Curley Weaver, and his wife Kate, whom he married in 1934. Throughout this period he played for tips down on Atlanta's Decatur Street, as well as hoboing through the South and East.

Many of McTell's recordings were not blues but rags or folk songs, but they all display his deft guitar playing, and the exceptionally warm voice that some have likened to a white man trying to sound black. He was not a major commercial success, but his legacy lives on, in many ways defining the 'South East blues sound'.

On November 4, 1940, folklorist Alan Lomax and his wife were driving through Atlanta when they spotted a guitarist at a food stand, who turned out to be McTell. The next day they recorded him in their hotel room, as he played and talked about his life. This complete Library of Congress recording is now available on Document Records, and it is a remarkable testament to an important artist.

'I'm gazing out the window
Of the St James Hotel
And I know no one can sing the blues
Like Blind Willie McTell'

'BLIND WILLIE MCTELL'
BY BOB DYLAN

ESSENTIAL RECORDINGS

CLASSIC SONGS

'Statesboro' Blues' 1928
'Broke Down Engine Blues' 1931
'Southern Can Is Mine' 1931
'Searching The Desert For The Blues' 1932

CLASSIC ALBUMS

Blind Willie McTell 1940
Recorded in an Atlanta hotel room by Alan Lomax

THE SOURCE

The complete pre-war recordings on Document Records

big seller, but he has come to be regarded as a great performer, someone to whom even the most famous artists are willing to acknowledge a debt.

In 1993, Bob Dylan covered 'Broke Down Engine', one of Blind Willie's best songs originally recorded in 1931. Both the Allman Brothers, the Atlanta blues band of the late 60s and 70s, and Taj Mahal boosted their careers by performing 'Statesboro Blues', a song written and recorded by Willie in 1928.

In 1949 and 1950 Willie recorded again, cutting some spirituals and duets with Curley Weaver, but this wasn't what people wanted to hear at this point, so he went back to singing on the streets of Atlanta. After one more session in 1956, he died of a brain haemorrhage in 1959.

TEXAS FLOOD

Blind Lemon Jefferson's success must have given rise to the notion that there were other blues men in Texas, but given the speed at which things happened in the 1920s, record companies were slow to respond to the idea. The first Texan artist to be recorded after Jefferson's success was Henry Thomas, who was taken to Chicago by Vocalion. Henry was an old-style songster, already over 50 when he first recorded in June 1927. His material, honed for street corner perfection, was the usual songster mix of novelty songs, rags, traditional ballads, and a little smattering of the blues. At his first session he recorded one of the earliest versions of 'John Henry'; over the next couple of years he recorded 25 sides in all.

OKeh took Alger Alexander to its New York studio to record in August 1927, and to ensure people knew where he came from, they even named him Texas Alexander. Twenty-seven years old when he first recorded, he was an older cousin of a future blues legend, Lightnin' Hopkins. His East Texas background was reflected in his songs, but unusually for a male blues performer he could not play an instrument. At his first session he was accompanied by Lonnie Johnson, while later sessions saw him working with Johnson again, Eddie Heywood, King Oliver, Eddie Lang, Little Hat Jones, the Mississippi Sheiks, and Carl Davis; sometimes not playing an instrument could be an advantage! His powerful vocals on songs like 'Levee Camp Moan' and 'Penitentiary Moan Blues' made him a popular artist, particularly in Texas.

He recorded over 60 sides by 1934; he returned to recording after World War II, cutting some records with his cousin, Hopkins. In the late 30s, the guitarist Lowell Fulsom travelled with Alexander and said of him:

> *What he talked about, he lived it*

Lowell was right: Alexander died in the mid-1950s from syphilis.

DECEMBER IN TEXAS

Frank Walker and Columbia Records undertook their first field trip to Texas in 1927. At the end of November, they arrived in Dallas, which had a black population approaching 50,000 out of a total of 250,000. On December 2, they started to record, and during six busy days they cut 21 sides with five different artists: Washington Phillips, Billikin Johnson, Coley Jones, pianist Willie Tyson, and harmonica player William McCoy. These proved to be the only sessions for McCoy and Tyson, who was probably a theatre pit pianist. The others recorded again in December 1928 and 1929 when Columbia made return trips to Texas.

Coley Jones was the leader of the Dallas String Band, although on most of his 1927

THE MISSISSIPPI SHEIKS

'Things About Comin' My Way', recorded for the OKeh record label. The Sheiks backed Texas Alexander on a 1930 session in San Antonio, Texas.

while Lemon was playing on the Texas streets.

All these musicians must surely have known each other, as their paths would undoubtedly have crossed; T-Bone, for example, had been working on medicine shows since the mid-1920s. In 1930, he won a Dallas talent contest, and his prize was the chance to perform with Cab Calloway's band. After that he played with other Texas outfits, including the Lawson Brooks Band & the Count Biloski Band. T-Bone left Texas for California in 1934, but rest assured he looms large in the remainder of our story. T-Bone's friend, Charlie Christian, who took his place in The Brooks Band, is now considered the first great electric guitar player in the field of jazz.

The OKeh and Columbia labels had merged in 1926, but up until 1929 they continued to run separate field trips. On the last OKeh trip to Texas, the label recorded Texas Alexander, Lonesome Charlie Harrison, Jack Ranger, and Little Hat Jones. Little Hat's real name was Dennis Jones and he is best remembered for his booming vocals and unique guitar style. While he displayed elements of the Texan finger-picking style, he also played interesting bass runs, more boogie-like in nature. He recorded just 10 wonderful sides, and then in true country blues fashion was never heard of again.

DEPRESSION AND SURVIVAL

The history of country blues performers is littered with 'nearly' men. The very nature of the recording process mitigated against an

artist building a long-term career, and by the end of the 1920s the Depression had well and truly taken hold. The fact that there was then a hiatus in recording meant that many of the artists who had cut records throughout the 1920s would become inspirational for those who were to follow. Record sales dropped dramatically after the onset of the Depression, with the result that records from the late 1920s had an unexpectedly long shelf life, continuing to resonate years after they might have been expected to be forgotten.

Many of the books that have been written about the Blues try to arrange artists neatly into 'schools', often dependent on where they came from. While we have taken a similar approach, that doesn't necessarily mean that there was a relationship between artists who came from a particular region.

The itinerant nature of these pre-war artists, the places in which they recorded, and the songs that they covered all added up to an intriguing musical mix that helped to create and mould the sound of the Blues.

Paul Oliver, in his 1969 book *Story Of The Blues*, was one of the first to recognize that the whole process was dynamic, rather than strictly geographical or chronological. He argued that there was no pattern to the history of the Blues, just a sequence of subtle influences and changes in emphasis on the performers and their material. It was the performers themselves who were inspirational, and sometimes that inspiration spread far and wide – a theme to which we shall return throughout our odyssey.

THE GREAT DEPRESSION

A free soup kitchen for the unemployed in Chicago at the heart of the Depression, c.1933. The prolonged financial crisis left its mark on every layer of American society.

83
CAPY
LT WT

6

Memphis, Jug Bands & The Delta

DESTINATION MEMPHIS

'That's the Memphis Beat – just far enough behind to be ahead of everyone else'

'MEMPHIS BEAT'
LARRY NAGER

IF YOU WALK AROUND MEMPHIS today, you'll see signs everywhere proclaiming the city as 'The Home of the Blues and 'The Birthplace of Rock'n'Roll'. And you would be hard pressed to disagree with either of these claims. Certainly, no other city has been so pivotal in the history of American music. So what is it about Memphis music that makes it so different? As the first big city north of the Mississippi Delta, it was a magnet for many young black men. An equal split between its black and white populations allowed for cross-cultural exchange between the poorest people from both groups. In Memphis, the traditional met the new, and developed into something totally different. It made Memphis so important, as well as unique.

ANDREW JACKSON
Seventh US president and one of the founders of the city of Memphis.

MEMPHIS

The town of Memphis (named after the Egyptian city on the Nile) was founded in 1819, at which time its population was 364. One of its founders was Andrew Jackson, the 7th US president (1829-1837). The town became a city in 1849, but in 1861, at the start of the Civil War, it was still a fairly small community of around 22,000 people – many of whom earned their living, in many cases a considerable one, from the cotton trade. The city's importance stemmed from its role as a communication centre and its position on the Mississippi River. This significance was enhanced in 1857 when the Memphis & Charleston Railroad was completed, linking the river with the Atlantic Ocean.

Memphis was captured by Union troops in 1862, but as there was little resistance from the Confederacy, the city and its buildings were relatively unscathed. After the end of the war, during the period of reconstruction, Memphis began to re-establish itself as the principal economic location north of the Delta. It suffered its first taste of racial tension in 1866, when there was a riot which left 46 blacks dead.

By 1870 the city's population had grown to around 40,000, though it was estimated that nearly one in eight of them was addicted to opium. By 1880, the population had been reduced to 33,000, after an epidemic of yellow fever in 1878 claimed more than 5,000 lives. This had a significant effect on the city's economy, and Memphis took the unusual step of declaring itself bankrupt in 1879. Things slowly returned to normal, and over the next twenty years Memphis tripled in size to 102,000, again becoming the premier city in Tennessee. By the time WC Handy wrote 'Memphis Blues' in 1912, the population had grown by another 30%. Over half the population was black, many drawn to the city in search of work, and most of them found their way to what later become known as 'the Main Street of Negro America'.

KU KLUX KLAN
The Invisible Empire of the Ku Klux Klan was formed in Pulaski, near Memphis, in 1866. It was founded by wealthy and privileged whites, who feared that their supremacy might be threatened by the North's victory. Initially, the organisation seemed to be relatively harmless; it has even been likened to a group of college students playing pranks, albeit very unpleasant ones. But soon their tactics changed. The Klan's name began to strike terror into the hearts of black people throughout the South – as indeed it still does in some particularly bigoted Southern communities.

Beale Street

‘... owned largely by Jews, policed by the whites, and enjoyed by the negroes... ’

George W Lee

That's how George W Lee, one of the first blacks commissioned as an officer in the US Army during World War I, described Memphis's most famous street in his 1934 book, *Beale Street – Where The Blues Began*. He went on to write: ‘Beale Street is where the blues began. Rising out of the Mississippi River, it runs for one mile straight through the busy heart of Memphis and loses itself in the muddy bottoms of East Street. The echoes of its fantastic music have been heard around the globe, for this colourful little thoroughfare is known the world over; its fame has penetrated into every nook and cranny where sound carries the echoes of the English voice. It has been talked about, written about, sung about so much that sightseers from every quarter are lured there in search of adventure or to gaze upon the scenes and surroundings that represent its vanished glory.’

Beale Street Blues
Beale Street immortalised in song by WC Handy.

In the 1840s, Beale Street was a wealthy suburb of Memphis. The Hunt-Phelan home, which still stands today near the east end of the street, reflects this affluence. After the city's decimation by yellow fever, Beale Street went into something of a decline. It was ‘rescued’ in the 1890s, largely as a result of one man's efforts. Robert Church, the son of a white riverboat captain and a mixed-race woman, had built himself a fortune, becoming the South's first black millionaire. In 1899, he established Church Park on Beale Street, a park for blacks, which immediately became a magnet for the city's black population. Beale Street also became the centre of black business. As the 20th century dawned, Beale was a bustling street, and at night music could be heard in the clubs and bars, as well as the churches. By the 1920s, the area was a heady mix of music, booze, brothels and gambling, peopled by a cast of dubious characters. It was into this vibrant atmosphere that Ralph Peer and the men from Victor entered when they made their first field recording trip to Memphis in February 1927.

Beale Street may not have given birth to the Blues but it certainly helped to define them.

‘... Beale Street was like no other street on the face of the earth... ’

Rufus Thomas, born in Memphis, 1917

The Crossroads

Today Beale Street has become a cornerstone of the city's marketing strategy. *‘Blues music was the music of working people. As they stepped out of the Mississippi Delta, they came to the big city of Memphis, and that's where the blues manifested itself. All roads led to Beale and 2nd Street, better known as Beale and Highway 61, the Crossroads of America's music’*

Kevin Kane, President, The Memphis Convention and Visitors Bureau

You've heard the 40 acres and a mule kind of cliché? That's really what it was. Each family had a little piece of the plantation. A family had 40 acres to mind

GILL STOVALL, JULY 2000
FIFTH-GENERATION PLANTATION FARMER

1931. But neither Whistler nor the Cincinnati Jug Band, which recorded two sides for Paramount in 1929, could match the success or the ability of their Memphis rivals. There was a special feel to the jug bands from Memphis, based on their ability to capture something of the Delta blues sound while also drawing inspiration from older musical traditions. During the early 60s folk revival, a number of jug bands were formed on the East Coast, inspired by this 35-year-old music. Among them were the Even Dozen Jug Band, which featured Steve Katz (who later formed The Blues Project and Blood Sweat & Tears), renowned guitarist Stefan Grossman, mandolin virtuoso David Grisman, Joshua Rifkin (the man who helped popularise Scott Joplin in the 60s), Maria Muldaur, and John Sebastian (who later formed The Lovin' Spoonful). Their rivals included the Jim Kweskin Jug Band from Boston, and Dave Van Ronk's Hudson Dusters who, like The Even Dozens, came from New York.

Hopson's Plantation, Clarksdale, Mississippi

COTTON PLANTATION WORKERS
From the dawn of slavery until well into the 20th century, cotton plantations were a central part of the landscape of the deep South.

Right: Sunflower County, Mississippi

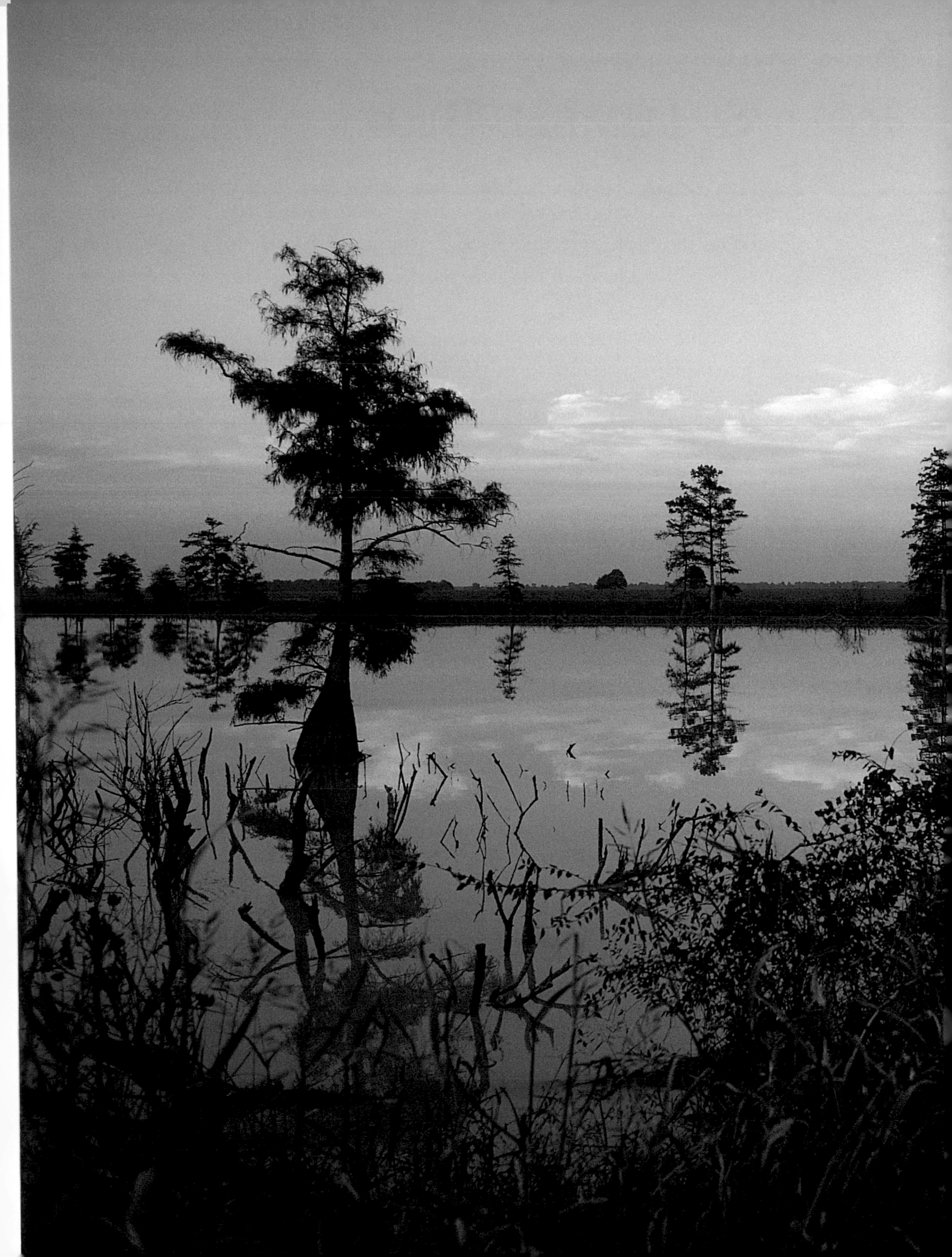

DELTA BLUES LEGENDS

WHILE MANY blues legends began performing at local picnics, house rent parties, and Saturday night fish fries they had to leave the Delta to establish their reputation. Most of those celebrated artists who remained and did not leave the region, were from the pre-war era.

Great blues songs often tell of life in this harshest of landscapes. The singers knew about the Blues, because they lived them. As John Grisham commented in *Visualizing the Blues* 'suffering gave rise to creativity'. Those men and women who grew up in the Delta playing the Blues did so, not to make money but to escape.

JAMES 'SON' THOMAS

Bluesman and sculptor James 'Son' Thomas was born in Eden and grew up around Leland. He lived all his life in the town and died there in 1993. The words on his tombstone (right) are from one his own songs… It should be called a bluesman's prayer.

"Give me beefsteak
When I'm hungry,
Whiskey when I'm dry,
Pretty women when
I'm living, heaven
When I die"

HERMAN 'LITTLE JUNIOR' PARKER

The co-composer with Sam Phillips of 'Mystery Train' was born in Clarksdale.

NEW ORTHOPHONIC VICTOR RECORDS

	Number	Size	List pr
Boogaboo—Slow Blues — Jelly-Roll Morton's Red Hot Peppers / *Kansas City Stomps—Stomp* — *Jelly-Roll Morton's Red Hot Peppers*	V-38010	10	.75
Bootlegging Blues *with Guitar* — Jim Jackson / *Policy Blues* — *Jim Jackson*	21268	10	.75
BRACEY, ISHMAN—with Guitar and Mandolin			
Brown Mamma Blues	21691		
Four Day Blues	V-38560		
Leavin' Town Blues	V-38560		
Left Alone Blues	21349		
Saturday Blues	21349		
Trouble-Hearted Blues	21691		
Breakfast Dance—Fox Trot — Ellington's Cotton Club Orchestra / *March of the Hoodlums—Fox Trot* — *Ellington and His Cotton Club Orch.*	V-38115	10	.75
Bright Boy Blues—Fox Trot — Cecil Scott and His Orchestra / *Springfield Stomp* — *Cecil Scott and His Orchestra*	V-38117	10	.75

Ishman Bracey

ISHMAN BRACEY

Like many of the earlier Delta bluesmen, Ishman was not only born but died there too (Jackson, 1970).

TENNESSEE

MISSISSIPPI

Memphis

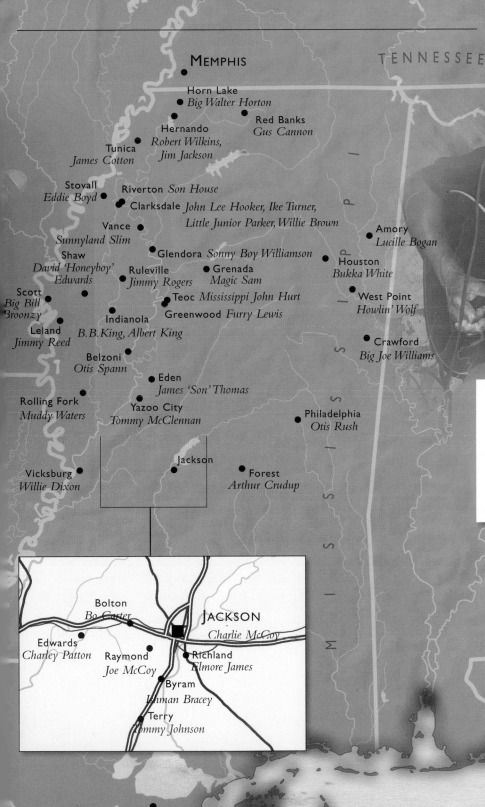

Horn Lake
Big Walter Horton

Red Banks
Gus Cannon

Hernando
Robert Wilkins, Jim Jackson

Tunica
James Cotton

Stovall
Eddie Boyd

Riverton *Son House*

Clarksdale *John Lee Hooker, Ike Turner, Little Junior Parker, Willie Brown*

Vance
Sunnyland Slim

Amory
Lucille Bogan

Shaw
David 'Honeyboy' Edwards

Glendora *Sonny Boy Williamson*

Houston
Bukka White

Ruleville
Jimmy Rogers

Grenada
Magic Sam

Scott
Big Bill Broonzy

Teoc *Mississippi John Hurt*

West Point
Howlin' Wolf

Indianola
B.B. King, Albert King

Greenwood *Furry Lewis*

Leland
Jimmy Reed

Crawford
Big Joe Williams

Belzoni
Otis Spann

Eden
James 'Son' Thomas

Rolling Fork
Muddy Waters

Yazoo City
Tommy McClennan

Philadelphia
Otis Rush

Jackson

Vicksburg
Willie Dixon

Forest
Arthur Crudup

Bolton
Bo Carter

Jackson
Charlie McCoy

Edwards
Charley Patton

Raymond
Joe McCoy

Richland
Elmore James

Byram
Ishman Bracey

Terry
Tommy Johnson

New Orleans
Papa Charlie Jackson
Lonnie Johnson

FLORIDA

Levee Camp Moan	*with Guitar*	Clifford Gibson	V-
Hard-Headed Blues		*Clifford Gibson*	3857
LEWIS, FURRY—with Guitar			
Furry's Blues			V-3851
I Will Turn Your Money			V-3850
Judge Harsh Blues			V-3850
Kassie Jones—Parts 1, 2			2166
Mistreatin' Mamma			V-3851
LEWIS, NOAH—Harmonica Solos			
Chickasaw Special			V-3858
Devil in the Wood Pile			V-3858
Lie Was Told, But God Know'd It		Elder Richard Bryant	2169
Wild Man in Town		*Sermon* Elder Richard Bryant	
Little Orphan Annie—Fox Trot	*with*	Coon-Sanders Orchestra	2189
Bless You! Sister—Fox Trot	*Vocal Refrain*	*Coon-Sanders Orchestra*	

Furry Lewis

Furry Lewis
Born in Greenwood, Mississippi, Furry was 88 when he died in Memphis in 1981.

Sonny Boy Williamson (Rice Miller)
Born in Glendora, Sonny Boy cut some of his best sides for the Trumpet label based in Jackson. His popularity in the Delta was aided by his broadcasts on KFFA radio from Helena, Arkansas.

THE DELTA IS A DARK PLACE

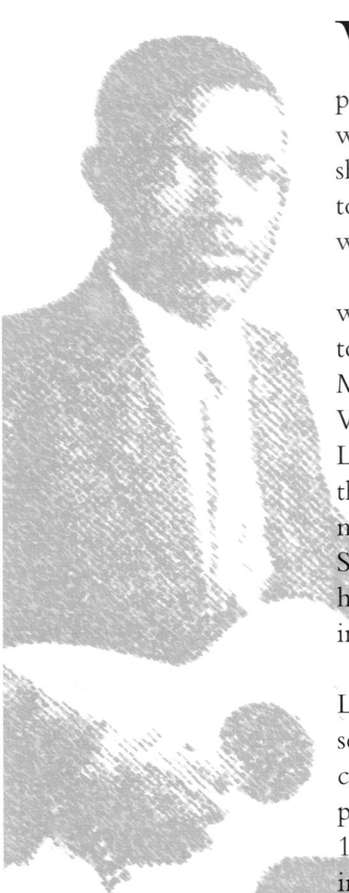

WHY DID THE DELTA BLUES DEVELOP, as distinct from the Blues heard in other parts of the South? A partial answer is that it was spawned by the plantations and the sharecropping economy. The struggle simply to exist, to survive, to hang on to life itself, is what created the Delta blues.

Walter Lewis from Greenwood, Mississippi, was one of the earliest singers from the Delta to record. He travelled to Chicago from his Memphis home to cut some sides for Vocalion in April 1927, just a year after Blind Lemon Jefferson's first releases. Lewis learned the guitar aged six and was given his nickname, Furry, while he was still at school. Shortly after leaving school he started to hobo his way across the South, losing his leg in a train accident around 1917.

Like many of his contemporaries, Furry Lewis was a songster first and a bluesman second. But there is no doubting his credentials as a witty and talented blues performer. When he supported The Stones in 1975, one of his onstage introductions included an aside which was probably typical of the sort of patter he would have used as a young man in the Beale Street saloons: 'Like the time I lost my wife – no, she didn't die, her husband came and got her'. He cut more than 20 sides between 1927 and 1929, some in Chicago and some in Memphis. After his first flush of success, Furry disappeared from the world of music until blues historian and record producer Sam Charters located him in Memphis in 1959. He then returned to the studio, continuing to work until his death in 1981.

Lewis had worked with Jim Jackson, Will Shade and Gus Cannon in medicine and tent shows. In October 1927 he returned to Chicago, this time with Jim Jackson, for a recording session where Jim cut 'Jim Jackson's Kansas City Blues Parts 1 & 2'. It was one of the most successful blues records of the 1920s; some estimates of its sales go as high as one million copies. Debuting with such a big hit record ensured that Jim could enjoy a prolific recording career for the rest of the decade, cutting minstrel tunes, novelty songs, pop songs or rags, but also his fair share of blues tunes – all in an attempt to please the rapidly changing market. Performers like

RONNIE WOOD AND FURRY LEWIS

Backstage after The Stones' concert at the Memorial Stadium, Memphis, 5th July, 1975.

'We landed at Memphis Airport at around 2.00am on the 4th July 1975. We were a month into our tour, which was a typical 70s rock tour – chaotic, in other words. Our aircraft had left Washington hours late, we had encountered storms in flight and we were pretty tired by the time the aircraft parked. The steps were positioned for us to disembark, and you can imagine our surprise as we walked down the steps and there sitting on a couple of whiskey cases was Furry Lewis playing and singing 'Let Me Call You Sweetheart'. The next day we played a show at the Memorial Stadium with The Charlie Daniels Band, The Meters and The J Geils Band, to an audience of 51,500. We were very anxious for Furry to perform, so he did. Rolling Stone magazine wrote at the time: "Bill Wyman treasures his rare Lewis recordings from the Twenties and Richards is a fan. And, as a black entertainer whose repertoire predates the beginning of the Blues, Lewis represents one of the sources of a Memphis musical tradition." When Furry finished, the audience had been there for six hours in 90-degree heat. We went on stage to our usual opening, Copland's 'Fanfare For The Common Man'. But with hindsight it would have been more appropriate for Furry to have had the privilege of using Copland's piece. I took this picture of Woody and Furry backstage at the concert'

BILL WYMAN

Why should I expect that old guy
To give it to me true
Fallin' to hard luck
And time and other thieves
While our limo is shining on his shanty street
Old Furry sings the blues

'FURRY SINGS THE BLUES'
JONI MITCHELL

JONI MITCHELL
In 1976 Joni Mitchell wrote and recorded a song called 'Furry Sings The Blues' for her album Hejira. *It is a lovely tribute to the man, as well as being a pithy comment on the way that some people had treated the rediscovered bluesmen.*

Jackson earned their living from pleasing their audiences, who were often of widely differing ages and tastes. While he continued to work after 1930, his recording career was effectively over, and he died in 1937, aged around 50.

Meanwhile, the field recording trips continued. Columbia, which had been concentrating on Atlanta and New Orleans, switched to Dallas and Memphis in December 1927. Dallas proved more productive than Memphis, but in Tennessee Columbia did find Reubin Lacy, though it deemed his recordings unworthy of being released. Rube, as he was called, did release a record the following year on Paramount. Though he rarely recorded, Lacy was an important member of the Delta blues

Record catelogue ad for 'Billy Lyons and Stack O'Lee'

FURRY LEWIS
Born in Greenwood, Mississippi in 1893, Furry lived to the age of 88.

community, which also included Ishman Bracey, Tommy Johnson and Charlie McCoy. In the early 30s Lacy joined the Church and became a Baptist minister, later moving to California, where he died in 1972.

MEMPHIS WITH TWO MICROPHONES

In early 1928 the Victor engineers set up in the Memphis Auditorium. A field studio was not simply a tape recorder and a microphone: although makeshift, they were complete studios. Victor was ahead of its rivals in one respect, as it used two, albeit temperamental, carbon microphones, while its rivals used just one. This improved the quality of the Victor recordings, though the resonant sound of the jugs created a challenge for the engineers.

The first artists that Ralph Peer recorded on this second trip to Memphis were Gus Cannon's Jug Stompers, the Memphis Jug Band, and Jim Jackson, all established performers. No doubt Peer wanted to get his best sessions done first. On 3rd February he called Tommy Johnson and Charlie McCoy in the auditorium; Charlie was there because Delta guitarists often liked working with a second guitar player. The two men cut Tommy's debut sides, 'Cool Drink Of Water Blues' and 'Big Road Blues', both of which are classic Delta blues. Tommy was born on a plantation a few years before the start of the 20th Century, and grew up in Crystal Springs, Mississippi, a place which was evocative in name only.

Johnson's strong vocals, which drifted into falsetto, were coupled with his simple yet effective guitar style, creating what has been described as the definitive Delta sound. In many ways he was the typical bluesman: a drinker, with no apparent preference between commercially produced liquor and cheap bootleg booze; a ladies' man; and, when he wanted to be, a hellraiser. He was also a great showman, who had learned much of his 'stagecraft' from Charley Patton – he, Tommy, and Willie Brown played together throughout the Delta region in the 1920s.

Tommy Johnson

> *'Tommy Johnson was brilliant and very influential. His playing displayed all that was best about Delta blues. His problem was that he was too Delta to appeal to people in the Northern cities'*
>
> BILL WYMAN

TOO DELTA FOR THE DEPRESSION

Howlin' Wolf later attested to the influence of Tommy Johnson, who but for his alcoholism and itinerant ways might have become a much bigger star. But then his reckless attitude was as much part of him as his blues singing. Johnson released just 12 sides during his lifetime. It is true to say that he was a casualty of the Depression, but he was equally a victim of his own lifestyle. He was also a little bit too Delta: his performances must have been less

JUKE JOINTS

... and my Mama said
Do you know what goes on
In a juke house?
Boy don't you know there's gambling,
And a whole lotta drinking,
And a lotta hot women.
And I don't want no boy of mine
In a juke house

'JUKE'
BY BLIND MISSISSIPPI MORRIS & BRAD WEBB

JUKE IS A WEST AFRICAN WORD meaning wicked or disorderly in one language, or a building without walls in Congolese. It passed into popular usage among Southern blacks as a word with sexual overtones and later came to describe a sort of dance. Like many derivative words its definition has been clouded by the passage of time. Juke joints were generally found in rural areas and it has been suggested that there was a link to the jute fields and the jute workers who frequented makeshift bars. Long before there was a blues industry, there were juke joints. They usually had a bar that fronted the street, often with a dance floor and a back room for gambling or other activities. Some juke joints also doubled as brothels.

The need for music in places like these was obvious. During the 1930s, travelling Delta bluesmen played regular gigs at juke joints, which is how the music was passed from one generation to the next. For example, it was in a juke that Robert Johnson watched Son House, and Tommy Johnson studied Charley Patton.

In the early days a juke joint was sometimes in a person's house, which was a good way of keeping the law at a distance. It was also a place to sell bootleg liquor.

Boss Hall's juke joint, Leland, Mississippi

Saturday night at Red's in Clarksdale

MODERN DELTA JUKE JOINTS

Today juke joints can still be found throughout the Delta, although their number is in decline. There are several in Clarksdale, including Red's, which features regular live music. In Leland, Mississippi, there is a great juke called Boss Hall's, which is owned by WC 'Boss' Hall and is one of the last 'real feeling' places where you can experience the atmosphere that sustained the Blues in the Delta.

We had these little juke joints, little taverns at that time. On a weekend there was this little place in the alley that would stay open all night. We called them Saturday night fish fries, they had two or three names, they called 'em juke houses or suppers.

MUDDY WATERS

HONKY TONKS, BARRELHOUSES & JUKE JOINTS

A honky tonk is the redneck equivalent of a juke joint. The difference between the two is the music you'll find on the jukebox and the colour of the women in the beer adverts.

Barrelhouses are much the same and take their name from the fact that the beer was kept in barrels! More commonly associated with piano players, barrelhouses were usually found in towns.

The biggest thing around Vicksburg was Curley's Barrelhouse. At the time you could hear Little Brother Montgomery

WILLIE DIXON

JUKEBOXES

The naming of the jukebox was no accident, as it was the ideal source of music for such establishments. It was invented in 1927 by the Automatic Music Instrument Company (AMI), who created the world's first electrically amplified multi-selection phonograph. AMI had evolved from the National Piano Manufacturing Co., producers of player pianos. By the end of the 1930s jukeboxes were manufactured by the 'big four' – AMI, Wurlitzer, Seeburg, and Rock-Ola.

A 1937 Wurlitzer Model 316

CANNED HEAT BLUES

Sterno was a cooking fuel based on denatured alcohol, similar to methylated spirits. It was also known as Canned Heat. Tommy Johnson was addicted to it.

popular further away from his blues heartland. Surprisingly, given his lifestyle, Johnson continued to work Delta juke joints well into the 1950s, eventually dying in 1956 after a heart attack.

His influence was not limited to those musicians who saw him. In the 1960s, the band Canned Heat named themselves after his 'Canned Heat Blues', an autobiographical account of drinking Sterno.

BORROWING THE BLUES

On his first recorded side, 'Cool Drink Of Water Blues', Johnson sang the immortal lines:

> *I asked her for water*
> *And she gave me gasoline*

'COOL DRINK OF WATER BLUES'

The following day his friend and juke-playing partner Ishman Bracey took his turn at the microphone, also accompanied by Charlie McCoy, and his first recording was 'Saturday Blues'. The fourth verse went:

> *Now, she's the meanest woman*
> *That I've ever seen.*
> *And when I asked for water,*
> *Gave me gasoline*

'SATURDAY BLUES'

This is a very obvious example of the free flow of lyrics, themes, and melodies that took place between these itinerant Delta artists. It even begs the question of who really sang or composed these lines, Ishman or Tommy. Then again, it might just as easily have been someone who never went near a microphone. This episode illustrates the futility of the 'who did what first' game: just listen, admire, and take the music at face value, in the way that the artists originally presented it.

Ishman Bracey was born in Byram, Mississippi in 1901, and had been working jukes, parties and street corners with Johnson and McCoy for a number of years. It is rumoured that he acted as a guide for Blind Lemon Jefferson when he visited the Delta, though this may well have been one of those boasts designed to boost the teller's standing. Whatever the case, he was a good guitar player, with a nasal tone to his rough sounding Delta vocals. After cutting some more sides for Victor, he recorded for Paramount. In the late 1930s he turned to religion, and in 1951 he became a Baptist minister – as the story goes "he never played the blues no more". He died in 1970.

Two weeks after Victor recorded these sessions, OKeh's executives were in Memphis. On Valentine's Day 1928, they recorded the first sessions by a singer who became one of the most revered of all the Delta players after he was rediscovered in the 60s. Mississippi John Hurt, as he was billed, was born in Teoc, Mississippi in 1893, and was already 35 years old when he first recorded. In latter years Hurt named white country singer Jimmie Rodgers as one of his principal influences, a theme to which we shall return. As he was somewhat older than his recording contemporaries, it is hardly surprising that his style was that of a songster, featuring a potent mix of hand-me-down folk songs, rags, and blues. Of the 13 sides he recorded for OKeh in 1928, only seven were issued at the time, and Hurt quickly faded from view, returning to his day job on a Delta farm.

In 1963, Tom Hoskins, a fan, tracked Hurt down by following the trail of his 1928 recording, 'Avalon Blues':

> *Avalon's my hometown,*
> *Always on my mind*
> *Pretty mama's in Avalon,*
> *Want me there all the time*

'AVALON BLUES'
MISSISSIPPI JOHN HURT

Right: A cotton field near Oxford, Mississippi

BLUES GUITARS

❛ Oh, play it now, everybody get hot
I long to hear that old guitar rag
I long to hear that guitar rag
Whenever I hear it, I do that guitar drag ❜

THE FAMOUS HOKUM BOYS
GEORGIA TOM, VOCALS; BIG BILL BROONZY
AND FRANK BRASSWELL, GUITARS

EVERY GENRE OF MUSIC has its own distinctive guitar sound. In the 60s it was the Fender Stratocaster used by Jimi Hendrix; in the 70s, the Les Paul was the guitar of choice for heavy metal and hard rock bands.

Back in the 20s and 30s, things – and guitars – were very different. Without the benefits of amplified sound, guitar players had one very special requirement: they needed to be LOUD, to cut through the noise of the crowd. For this reason one guitar was more closely associated with the Blues than any other: the National Resonator. The National was at least four times louder than a conventional wooden guitar, which was pretty handy if you wanted to make yourself heard on a street corner, in a tent show, or above the noise of a juke joint.

In the late 20s, three Los Angeles men invented the National Resonator guitar. George Beauchamp had the original idea of creating a Hawaiian guitar which sat on a stand, and had a horn attached to the bottom. That idea failed, but two brothers, John and Rudy Dopyera, experimented with a design that used three very thin, conical, aluminium resonators inside an all-metal body. John Dopyera led the way, and applied to patent his 'tricone' guitar in 1927.

NATIONAL STYLE O, 1930S

The Resonator sounds as if it has a rhythm section built in. This particular model has Hawaiian scenes sandblasted on the front and back.

Beauchamp found the investors, and the National String Instrument Company was formed. Production began in 1927, and by 1928 it was mass-producing guitars. At its peak, the company was able to manufacture nearly 50 instruments a day.

THE SINGLE RESONATOR MODEL

Problems soon emerged when Dopyera rejected Beauchamp's idea of making a guitar with a single resonator. Beauchamp thought that this was the perfect design for a lower cost instrument; and with the Depression just around the corner he was proved right. The single cone model, patented by Beauchamp in 1929, saved

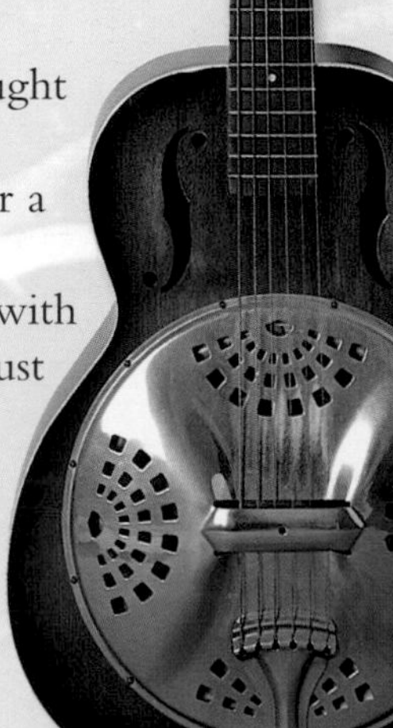

THE WOODEN-BODIED DOBRO

Cliff Carlisle was the first to record with a Dobro.

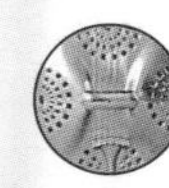

National from bankruptcy.

The National was intended for Hawaiian and jazz players but it became the favoured guitar of the great blues guitar players of the late 20s and 30s. However, Beauchamp's patent caused a rift between the two parties and John Dopyera decided to leave National, to work on a wooden-bodied guitar with a single cone. He called this the 'Dobro' (made up from *(Do)*pyera and *(bro)*thers). Then in 1932 the companies merged and became the National-Dobro Company. The cones of a National were volcano-shaped, while a Dobro was dish-shaped. The wooden-bodied Dobros were marketed as an inexpensive alternative to the metal Nationals, and Dobros became associated with acoustic country music and artists like Jimmie Rodgers and Roy Acuff.

A tricone guitar had a smoother tone with greater, richer sustain (in other words, the notes lasted longer), while a single resonator made a sharper, and clearer sound, with much more attack.

A Stella 503GC (Grand Concert) listed in a 1921 catalogue at $6.00

TAMPA RED

In 1928, Tampa Red was the first blues artist to record with a National steel resonator-type guitar. Tampa played a tricone. Listen to his 1934 side, 'Denver Blues', to appreciate the man they dubbed 'The Guitar Wizard'.

> *Stellas, they played the old cheap Stella guitars – across the board!*
>
> BLUES TALENT SCOUT, HC SPEIR

STELLA GUITARS

Of course, blues players did not only play Nationals. Blind Lemon Jefferson found fame before the invention of the National and he used a 12-string Stella guitar. Lonnie Johnson also used a Stella before taking up the electric guitar. The Oscar Schmidt Company in Jersey City, New Jersey, made Stella guitars between 1900 and 1939. In 1921 a No. 503 Grand Concert size Stella was selling for $6. Lead Belly, Barbecue Bob, and Blind Willie McTell all played 12 strings, while six-string Stellas were preferred by Blind Blake, Charley Patton, Willie Brown and Blind Willie Johnson.

Gibson guitars were popular too. Robert Johnson was photographed playing a Gibson L-1 (see page 214), while Eddie Lang switched from Stella to Gibson prior to his seminal albums with Lonnie Johnson.

BLUE GUITARS

Some of the best guitar playing of the late 20s came from the pairing of two virtuosos, Eddie Lang and Lonnie Johnson. Eddie was white, the son of a fretted instrument-maker, while Lonnie came from a family of 12 in New Orleans, where his father was a musician. Sides like 'Have To Change Keys To Play Those Blues', 'Blue Guitar' and 'Guitar Blues' virtually define their era. Many artists subsequently learned from their unique approach to guitar duets: neither player attempted to upstage the other; they just spurred each other on to greater feats of dexterity.

CHOOSE YOUR INSTRUMENT

TAMPA RED: *Tricone*

SON HOUSE: *Single resonator, either a Triolian or Duolian*

BUKKA WHITE: *Square neck Tricone*

BO CARTER: *Style N*

BLIND BOY FULLER: *Duolian*

PEETIE WHEATSTRAW: *Tricone*

SCRAPPER BLACKWELL: *Triolian*

BUMBLE BEE: *Style O*

BLACK ACE: *Tricone*

REVEREND GARY DAVIS: *Single cone*

OSCAR 'BUDDY' WOOD: *Tri-plate*

The cost of a National in the 30s varied according to the model. A Duolian cost $32-$35, a Triolian $45-$50 and a Style O around $65.

1936 Gibson Super 400

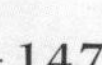

THE PATTON CLAN

CHARLEY PATTON'S LEGEND strides across the Delta like no other bluesman of his generation. He was already over 40 when he first recorded for Paramount in June 1929 in Grafton, Wisconsin. In fact, it wasn't just his legend which crossed the Delta: he travelled extensively, which in many ways helps to account for his influence. Tales of his singing, playing, and life are plentiful and they all point to the fact that he was an original, someone who many younger players looked up to. But above all else Charley was an entertainer. He was popular precisely because he gave his audiences what they wanted: a mix of predominantly blues-based material delivered with the panache of a true showman. In fact, Patton has even been called the first rock'n'roller.

What is important to the story of the Blues, and not just the Delta blues, is Patton's influence on many artists who are held in high esteem today. Willie Brown, Son House, Howlin' Wolf, Tommy Johnson, Robert Johnson, Muddy Waters, Bukka White, Big Joe Williams, Pop Staples, and David 'HoneyBoy' Edwards all came under Patton's influence in some way. They may have played with him, known him as a friend, seen him perform, or quite simply have aspired to be both as good and as well-known as he was. Patton was particularly close to Willie Brown, who travelled with him throughout the 1920s playing rent parties, picnics, juke joints, and workers' camps. They often performed for white audiences, especially in Lula, Mississippi. Their initial base was Dockery Farms, where Patton's father had moved his large family in 1912.

THAT'S *MR* PATTON TO YOU...

Charley was confident in his musical ability, and he raised some people's hackles with his 'uppity' demands to be addressed as 'Mr Patton'. Whether it was arrogance or confidence we can never know, but as blues historian Paul Oliver contends, 'Charley Patton is without question one of the most impressive and important of bluesmen on record'. We can only imagine what it must have been like to have seen him live. Patton has been called a 'clown' for the way he sometimes acted when he played, which might be implied criticism, but was more likely fuelled by a tinge of jealousy on the part of some of his contemporaries. He was a showman, undoubtedly, but that was what was required from an entertainer, and we shouldn't let Patton's tendency not to take himself too seriously undermine our view of his musicianship or status. What is clear from listening to his records is that he was an original, who wrote wonderful songs and interesting lyrics, and then delivered them with a great deal more panache than any of his contemporaries. Despite their comradeship, there was a degree of competition amongst Delta musicians, as they made their living from playing live, not from record sales, which only served to 'spread the word'. A performer had to give the audience a show, and that is what Charley Patton did, better than anyone.

In October 1929, Charley added 24 sides to the 14 he had already recorded in June. Fiddle player Henry Sims went with him on this return trip to Gratfon, and accompanied him on four sides. Some of these early recordings were actually religious, including the powerful two-part 'Prayer Of Death'; on these sides, Patton was credited as Elder JJ Hadley.

For Charley's third release, Paramount's marketing department went into overdrive, and did his career no harm in the process. They released 'Mississippi Boweavil Blues' and 'Screamin' And Hollerin' The Blues' under the name of 'The Masked Marvel' and asked record buyers to guess who the artist was. Their prize was another Paramount record of their choice – for free.

LOVE ON THE ROAD

A little over six months later Patton headed North once again, this time accompanied by

Willie Brown, Son House, and Louise Johnson. Charley and Louise were an item at the start of the trip, but by the end she had switched her favours to Son: that's life on the road! At this session Charley cut just four sides, perhaps because he'd already recorded the cream of his material at an earlier session (the 1920s equivalent of that difficult third album?). The Depression was also underway and Paramount may have been limiting its recording sessions, as it already had a backlog of unreleased Patton sides.

Nearly four years were to pass before Charley was able to record again, this time in New York. He cut 36 sides there for Vocalion over three days, 10 of which were released at the time. These performances were not as strong as Charley's earlier work – not surprisingly, as he had a serious heart condition, and a knife wound in his neck. His last wife Bertha Lee accompanied him on some of these sides; sadly, the masters of the unissued tracks are missing.

Rosetta Patton, Charley's daughter.

Patton and Bertha Lee left New York and went back to Mississippi. Three months later, on 28th April, 1934, the 43-year-old Patton died at Holly Springs, near Indianola. At his last recording session he recorded the prophetic 'Oh Death':

> *Oh, hush, good Lordy, oh hush,*
> *Somebody is callin' me*
> *Lord I know,*
> *Lord, I know my time ain't long*
>
> 'Oh Death'
> Charley Patton

The exact details of the trip that Son House, Willie Brown, and Louise Johnson made to Grafton with Charley Patton are inevitably somewhat sketchy. It is generally thought that Art Laibly of Paramount Records had asked Charley to 'scout' a few artists for the label to record. At this time Patton was the label's biggest star, so they would have been confident that Charley could do the job.

The first person he recruited was Willie, his regular playing partner, who accompanied Charley on guitar, as well as performing his own material. Next came Son House. The three of them were due to drive north together, but Patton stopped first at a plantation near Robinsonville to pick up pianist Louise Johnson, who was his sometime mistress. Another singer, Wheeler Ford, drove the car that took the four musicians north; he was the leader of an acappella group, the Delta Big Four. Wheeler's group took part in a session three days before Son, Willie, and Louise all made their recording debut on 28th May, 1930.

Willie Brown was born in Clarksdale, Mississippi, in 1900. Besides playing in the early 1920s with Patton he also performed with Son House on the usual round of plantation picnics, parties, and dances. He recorded four sides in Grafton, although only the first two, 'M&O Blues' and 'Future Blues', have survived. They are pure Delta, featuring Willie's hard-edged vocals and deft guitar playing, and 'Future Blues' in particular is one of the core examples of Delta blues.

> *You can run, you can run,*
> *Tell my friend Willie Brown*
> *That I got the cross road*
> *blues this mornin',*
> *Lord, babe, I'm sinkin' down*
>
> 'Cross Road Blues'
> Robert Johnson, 1936

A tantalising question: is this *the* Willie Brown that Robert Johnson is referring to? Or one of the other William/Willie Browns who recorded for the Library of Congress, or just a friend of Robert's who happened to have the same name? We will never know...

> *Well, my stepfather came home and told me. I was sitting on the front porch in a rocking chair and he said, "Rosetta, I have something to tell you". He said, "Don't get upset, I have something to tell you". And Momma, she rushed to the door, she said, "What is it? What are you going to tell her?" He said, "Her father's dead". And I know that they say he had asthma and a heart attack. He went out to play that night, a Saturday night, he took a real sick attack and they rushed him home and he died before he got to the doctor back there.*
>
> Rosetta Patton
> Summer 2000

HOUSE OF BLUES

Born in Riverton, Mississippi, Eddie 'Son' House was two years younger than Willie, and just over 28 when he recorded ten songs in Grafton, eight of which were released by Paramount. His vocal style was less hard-edged than Willie's but a whole lot more intense; in fact, intense is the perfect word for Son House and his blues. He was a major influence on Muddy Waters and Robert Johnson, and like both of those legendary performers, when Son sang the Blues you had to believe him.

Son had been a Baptist preacher in his early 20s, and apparently his sermons were as intense as his blues. His second record was the two-part 'Preachin' The Blues', in which he explains how the Blues stole him away from the Church:

Oh I'm gonna get me a religion,
I'm gonna join the Baptist church
Oh I'm gonna get me a religion,
I'm gonna join the Baptist church
I'm gonna be a Baptist preacher
And I sure won't have to work

Oh I'm gonna preach these blues
and then want everybody to shout
Mmmmmm I want everybody just to shout
I'm gonna do like a prisoner,
I'm gonna roll my time on out.

Oh I went to my room, I bowed down to pray
Oh I went to my room, I bowed down to pray
Sayin' the blues come along
And they blowed my spirit away

Oh, I'd have had religion, Lord this very day
Oh, have had religion, Lord this very day
But the womens and whiskey,
Well, they would not let me pray

'PREACHIN' THE BLUES'
SON HOUSE

In 1928, House shot and killed a man, it is said in self-defence, and thereafter spent time in Parchman Farm prison; he was released in

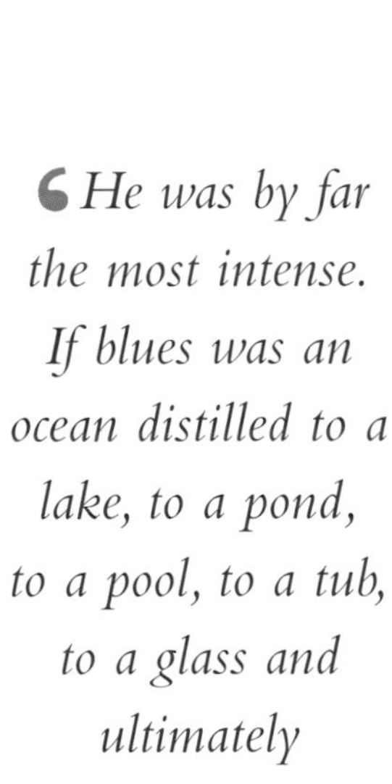

He was by far the most intense. If blues was an ocean distilled to a lake, to a pond, to a pool, to a tub, to a glass and ultimately to a drop, the essence, the very concentrate, this is Son House

DICK WATERMAN

Son House at Pete Welding's house before a concert in 1964.

In June of '65 Mr House and I went into Muddy Waters' dressing room. One of Muddy's sidemen poked somebody with an elbow and pointed to Son, to make fun of him. Now Muddy was not a physical man at all, but Muddy quickly moved across and grabbed that guy and everybody turned around and their jaws dropped. Muddy pushed the man and said, "Don't you be mocking that man". And everybody just went "Wow". And Muddy said, "Don't you be making fun of him. When I was a boy coming up that man was king, you hear me? That man was king. Here you are mocking and making fun of him. If it wasn't for that man you wouldn't be here because you wouldn't have a job because I wouldn't be here. Don't you ever make fun of that man; he was king when I was a boy coming up." Muddy's eyes were flashing fire

DICK WATERMAN, WHO REDISCOVERED SON HOUSE IN 1964

Son House

FACT FILE

Born: *21st March, 1902 Riverton (Coahoma County), Mississippi,*

Died: *19th October, 1988, Detroit, Michigan*

Instrument: *Guitar*

First Recorded: *1930*

Accolades: *Inducted into the Blues Hall of Fame, 1980*

Influenced: *Robert Johnson, Muddy Waters, Howlin' Wolf, Sonny Boy Williamson*

'My dad was a student of Son House, and he learnt a lot of stuff from him, watching him. Son House was a powerful, powerful performer'

Big Bill Morganfield (Muddy Waters' son)

Eddie James House Jr. was named after his father, who played in the family brass band. House grew up on a plantation near Clarksdale. He was preaching in church by the time he was 15, and worked in a variety of jobs. He taught himself to play the guitar around 1923 and was soon playing house rent parties and local picnics. After serving time on Parchman Farm in 1928, he worked with Charley Patton, playing levee camps and country dances around Clarksdale.

In 1930, Patton arranged for him to make his first record for Paramount, in Grafton, Wisconsin. Accompanied by Willie Brown, he cut a total of 10 songs, of which eight were issued. He and Brown soon returned to the Delta, playing at dances, juke joints and picnics throughout the remainder of the 1930s. House's next recordings were for Alan Lomax and the Library of Congress in 1941.

He recorded six songs at Lake Cormorant, Mississippi, during the same few days that Lomax recorded Muddy Waters at Stovall's Plantation. Lomax recorded House again in 1942, soon after the bluesman moved to New York. He was not heard of again musically until 1964, when he was rediscovered living in an apartment, with his wife of 30 years, and in a poor state of health, suffering from a drink problem. After his rediscovery by Dick Waterman, he was asked to perform at the Newport Folk Festival and signed to record for CBS. His subsequent album, *Father Of The Folk Blues*, won him the opportunity to play in America and Europe.

House was one of the creators of the Delta blues sound, and his emotionally intense voice and forthright guitar style influenced many of those who followed, including Robert Johnson and Muddy Waters. His religious leanings, combined with his secular music, created what has been described as the forerunner of soul music. After spending the first few years of the 1970s touring, he retired, spending his last 14 years in Detroit before his death at the age of 86.

'I met Son House when we recorded ABC TV's 'Shindig' in Hollywood. He came with Howlin' Wolf. House spent most of the time backstage trying to win money playing cards.

Listening to Son House's records today is like listening to the Delta of yesterday. He picks you up and puts you down in the 1930s'

Bill Wyman

Essential Recordings

Classic Songs

'My Black Mama' 1930
'Preachin' The Blues' 1930
'Dry Spell Blues' 1930

Classic Albums

Father Of The Delta Blues 1963

The Source

Preachin' The Blues Catfish Records

1929 after a judge re-examined his case. Son fell victim to the Depression, and to the failure of Paramount. He went back to the Delta and the usual round of picnics, parties, and poorly paid gigs. Then in 1941 Alan Lomax recorded both House and Willie Brown for the Library of Congress. Later, Son moved to Rochester, New York, and worked for the railway. Dick Waterman found him in there 1964 – a fascinating story to which we shall return.

'OUTSIDE WOMAN BLUES'
Blind Willie Reynolds' song 'Outside Woman Blues' was covered by Cream on their album Disraeli Gears, *released in 1967.*

WAYSIDE BLUES

We have made the acquaintance of some who came out of the Delta to record as the 1920s rolled into the 1930s. Others artists, such as Bo Carter, the Mississippi Sheiks, Bukka White, Kokomo Arnold, Skip James, and Sleepy John Estes, will appear later in our story. And others' stars flashed only briefly, cutting just a couple of sides before the Depression got them, or stardom's fickle finger passed them by.

One such was Garfield Akers, who cut a couple of sides at the Peabody Hotel in Memphis in September 1929, with Joe Calicott. Calicott released a record of his own in 1930, at a Memphis session where Akers cut two more sides, but this was the final recording date for both of them. Or it would have been had a folklorist not rediscovered Joe and recorded him in 1967. Joe had stopped playing after Garfield's death in the late 1950s, and he himself died around 1969. Others from the Delta who recorded or released just a few records include Kid Bailey, Jim Thompkins, Jed Davenport, Mooch Richardson, and Arthur Pettis.

Then there was Blind Joe Reynolds, or was it Blind Willie Reynolds? He went to Grafton in November 1929 and recorded four sides as Joe. A year later he cut four more sides for Victor in Memphis, this time as Willie. He was a violent man blinded in a 1920s shotgun fight. At his first session he recorded 'Outside Woman Blues'. He performed in the Delta well into the 1960s.

THE PEABODY HOTEL, MEMPHIS, TODAY
It has been said that the Mississippi Delta starts in the lobby of the Peabody Hotel.

Robert Wilkins' Prodigal Sons

The Rolling Stones were named after a 1950 Muddy Waters song, 'Rollin' Stone'. Both the tune and lyrics of Muddy's song were derived from 'Catfish Blues', a traditional Delta blues tune which was first recorded by Robert Petway on 28th March, 1941, just five months before Muddy made his first recordings for the Library of Congress at Stovall's Plantation.

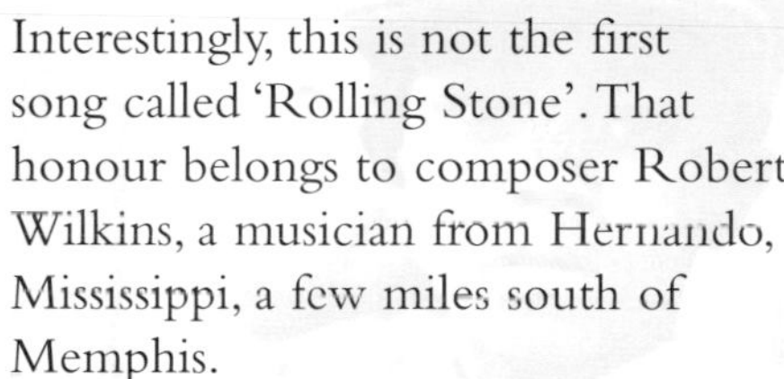

Interestingly, this is not the first song called 'Rolling Stone'. That honour belongs to composer Robert Wilkins, a musician from Hernando, Mississippi, a few miles south of Memphis.

Born in 1896, Wilkins was an idiosyncratic songwriter who was popular on the Memphis blues scene in the 20s. He cut his first sides in September 1928 for Victor, including his first release, 'Rolling Stone'. He recorded a further 18 sides between 1928 and 1935. He was a much better composer than he was a singer, a key factor in his less than scintillating record sales. Late in the 30s Wilkins turned to the Church, becoming an ordained minister for The Church of God in Christ in 1950 – which is ironic when you consider the link that he has with The Rolling Stones.

Return of the Prodigal

At his third session in September 1929, Wilkins recorded four songs, including 'That's No Way To Get Along':

I'm goin' home, friends,
Sit down and tell my, my mama
Friends, sit down and tell my mama
I'm goin' home,
Sit down and tell my mama
I'm goin' home,
Sit down and tell my mama
That that's no way to get along

These low-down women, mama,
They treated your, ah, poor son wrong
Mama, treated me wrong
These low-down women, mama,
Treated your poor son wrong
These low-down women, mama,
Treated your poor son wrong
And that's no way for him to get along.

In 1968 The Rolling Stones recorded this song for their *Beggars Banquet* album, by which time it had been renamed 'Prodigal Son'. The lyrics were made more religious in content, but the tune and lyrical feel of Wilkins' original were retained:

Well, a poor boy took his father's bread
And started down the road
Started down the road
Took all he had and started
Down the road
Going out in this world,
Where God only knows
And that'll be the way to get along

Well, poor boy spent all he had,
Famine come in the land
Famine come in the land
Spent all he had
And famine come in the land
Said, 'I believe I'll go
And hire me to some man'
And that'll be the way I'll get along

Wilkins was yet another veteran who was rediscovered in the great folk/blues revival in 1964. That year, he recorded a gospel album and performed at the Newport Folk Festival. He continued to perform occasionally until his death in 1987, when he was 91 years old.

> *'We recorded 'Prodigal Son' at Olympic Studios in London with producer Jimmy Miller and our old friend Glyn Johns as engineer. We worked on it at various times between March and June 1968. Ry Cooder played acoustic guitar with Keith'*
>
> Bill Wyman

Rolling Stone Songs

- **7th September, 1928** 'Rolling Stone' Robert Wilkins
- **4th May, 1937** 'Rolling Stone Blues' Charley West
- **April 1939** 'Rolling The Stone' Jimmy Yancey
- **11th January, 1940** 'Rolling Stone' Lee Brown
- **3rd April, 1941** 'Rolling Stone Blues' Frank Tannehill
- **1950** 'Rollin' Stone' Muddy Waters

7

The Depression, No Depression & Some Boogie Woogie Too

THE DEPRESSION

PRICES OF STOCKS CRASH IN HEAVY LIQUIDATION.
TOTAL DROP OF BILLIONS.
PAPER LOSS $4,000,000,000.
2,600,000 SHARES SOLD IN THE FINAL HOUR.
MANY ACCOUNTS WIPED OUT.

THE NEW YORK TIMES, 24TH OCTOBER, 1929

HISTORY CREATES ITS OWN punctuation marks, and none was more significant for America than the Wall Street Crash and the Depression that followed. It had an impact on every aspect of life, and the recording business was no exception. Labels that had sprung up in the boom of the 1920s found the going tough, and some, like Paramount, went into liquidation. Others were forced to cut back on their activities as the demand for records slumped. This turbulent era also brought a marked shift in the musical taste of the increasingly urban black population. The change was born out of economics, migration, technology, ambition, and fashion; in effect, it was the beginning of 'pop' music.

The Wall Street Crash came on 24th October, 1929. Its impact can be measured from headlines in the *New York Times* (above).

The US economy had gone into recession some six months before the October crash, yet no one anticipated how severe it would be, or dared to imagine the consequences. In fact the Depression lasted most of the following decade, triggering the most catastrophic economic slump ever experienced in the modern Western world.

HERBERT HOOVER
Underestimated the Depression.

The fall in the value of American stocks was catastrophic: by 1932, they were worth just 20% of their value in 1929. While it was individuals who bore the brunt of the crisis, banks and other financial institutions also went into free-fall. By 1933 nearly half of America's 25,000 banks had collapsed, and almost 30% of the working population was jobless. Chaos on such a grand scale produced a nationwide loss of confidence, which led in turn to drastically reduced spending. It was a case of 'panic not-buying', as people cut their spending on non-essentials to a minimum, and even essential purchases became luxuries. This had an

This great nation will endure as it has endured, will revive and will prosper. So first of all, let me assert my firm belief that the only thing that we have to fear is fear itself – nameless, unreasoning, unjustified terror which paralyses needed efforts to convert retreat into advance

Franklin Roosevelt's inaugural address, 1933

inevitable impact on production; by 1932, output had fallen by 54%. All of this led to industrial, commercial and personal misery on a scale that has never been matched in the developed world in peace-time.

Nothing to Fear But Fear Itself

The American President, Herbert Hoover, publicly underestimated the impact of the Depression. In 1930 he urged Americans to remain confident:

The fundamental business of this country, that is, production and distribution, is on a sound and prosperous basis

Herbert Hoover

He could not have been more wrong. In the eyes of most Americans, it was Hoover's fault – despite the fact that he had personally intervened in the crisis, spending millions of dollars on government projects designed to stimulate the economy.

In the 1932 presidential election, Hoover's opponent was Franklin D Roosevelt. What he offered the electorate was short on specifics, but he had one key advantage: he was not Hoover. What Roosevelt did promise was termed the 'New Deal'. It may not have ended the Depression, but Roosevelt was credited by many with saving their jobs, their homes, and even their lives. He dominated the political landscape in a way that no subsequent president has been able to match. He was re-elected three times, and eventually died in office in April 1945, aged 63.

The Depression affected every level of American society, from the share-owning sophisticates of the big cities to the rural poor. The Southern states were particularly hard-hit, and the black communities at the bottom of the economic heap often suffered more than the whites. But if you were poor at the start of the Depression, you just got poorer – whether you were black or white.

"I hear the Depression is ending."
"Oh, has Hoover died?"

Contemporary Vaudeville Joke

BOLL WEEVIL BLUES

The troubled state of Mississippi finally began to receive some financial relief in 1933. Over the next six years, millions of 'New Deal' dollars were pumped into the Mississippi economy, helping to put planters, merchants and banks back on their feet. But just when people in the Delta thought that things were starting to get better, the state was plagued by a new enemy: the boll weevil.

The boll weevil plague was particularly virulent during 1931–32, causing crop failures that the beleaguered farmers and sharecroppers could ill afford. The beetle first arrived from Mexico in 1899, attacking the cotton in Texas, and reaching the Atlantic coast by 1916. In 1921 the Georgia cotton crop was decimated, which perhaps sparked the beetle's first appearance in a blues song, Ma Rainey's 1924 debut release, 'Bo-Weavil Blues'. Numerous blues singers sang about the notorious beetle, including Joe Callicot, Lead Belly, Blind Willie McTell, Oscar Woods, Kokomo Arnold and, perhaps most famous of all, Charley Patton. Fortunately, this proved to be the last serious boll weevil attack on Delta cotton, although its effects were still being felt as late as 1950.

As the Depression, the boll weevil, and the droughts of 1933 and 1934 took their toll on the poor people of the South, more and more black men and women were prompted to head North, where there was work to be found in the factories of industrial cities like Chicago, Detroit, and Cincinnati and, of course, Memphis. With them went the music that came out of the fields and juke joints of

BOLL WEEVIL
This small, grey, long-snouted beetle punctures cotton buds to lay its larvae, irrevocably damaging the cotton boll. Conservative Southern Democrats in the House of Representatives were often nicknamed Boll Weevils.

> *"There's a little boll weevil she's movin' that thing in, Lordy*
> *You can plant your cotton and you won't get a half a cent, Lordy*
> *Boll weevil, boll weevil where's your native home, Lordy*
> *Around Louisiana, and here, and Texas is*
> *where I was bred and born, Lordy"*

'MISSISSIPPI BOWEAVIL BLUES' CHARLEY PATTON, 1929

Tampa Red and Leroy Carr

They began recording in the late 1920s, and as individuals dominated the Blues at the start of the next decade.

the South. The Blues was going to find a new home among the bright lights of the big cities.

Depression Hits The Blues

The Depression was more of a semicolon than a full stop in the careers of some bluesmen. Nevertheless, many artists found that their recording careers had simply ground to a halt. Even the biggest stars witnessed a decline in their sales, recording activity, and live work. Their audiences barely had enough money to survive; for most people, luxuries were simply not an option.

The shift away from country blues, as epitomised by Charley Patton, Son House, and Tommy Johnson, towards a more sophisticated urban blues style did not happen overnight. As black people relocated from the country to the city, so they preferred a smoother, less earthy sound that reflected their change in status. Artists who produced this more sophisticated sound soon became prime targets for the record company scouts.

Two artists who made their first solo recordings within a couple of weeks of each other in the early summer of 1928 went on to dominate the Blues in the early 1930s. Leroy Carr and Tampa Red both sold large numbers of records, the majority of them recorded in Chicago for the Vocalion label.

The Guitar Wizard

Tampa Red, whose real name was Hudson Woodbridge, came from Florida. He was 24 years old when he cut his first side for the Paramount label in May 1928. By September he had switched to Vocalion, where his debut, 'It's Tight Like That', sold very well and established his reputation. Accompanying Tampa on piano was Georgia Tom Dorsey, and together they invented the 'hokum' style of blues. With its light, almost jazzy melodies and humorous, sometimes risqué lyrics, this new sound soon became the rage. So popular was their debut, and the sound of hokum, that the two men were billed as The Hokum Boys or Tampa Red's Hokum Jug Band.

By 1932, their partnership had come to an end, as Georgia Tom became disillusioned with the Blues and turned to God and gospel music. During their brief career, the pair had cut nearly 75 sides together, including 'The Duck's Yas Yas Yas' (one of the few examples of rhyming slang in the Blues) and the wonderful 'You Can't Get That Stuff No More' (recorded at their last session in February 1932).

Vocalion's 25 Best-sellers

Frankie 'Half Pint' Jaxon

Dubbed the 'Guitar Wizard', Tampa's slide playing and single-string picking were influential on many who followed. His style was the very antithesis of Delta blues: he offered sophistication to newly arrived, city dwelling blacks, and the dream of sophistication to aspiring country dwellers.

Tampa signed to the Victor label in 1934 and stayed with it, and its subsidiary label Bluebird, for the next 20 years. The company cleverly pitched his music to several different markets. For his records in a dance band style, he was billed as Tampa Red & the Chicago Five. When he recorded more straightforward blues songs, usually accompanied by a pianist (often Black Bob) or Willie B James on second guitar, he was simply Tampa Red.

Historians have argued that Bluebird was trying to help Tampa 'cross over' to the white market, and the superficial evidence certainly supports this theory. Some of his records featured white artists on the flip side, notably Bill Boyd's Cowboy Ramblers in 1936. But it is probably more likely that Bluebird, a budget label selling its wares at 35 cents, was using Tampa as its 'race' (or black) entry into the dance band market. Tampa's reputation and success rested firmly on his black audiences in the Northern cities.

ROCK AND ROLL IN THE 1920S

❛After I started collecting blues records I found a great song, recorded in 1929, by Tampa Red's Hokum Jug Band. 'My Daddy Rocks Me (With One Steady Roll)' may be the earliest example of 'rock and roll' appearing in a song title.

My man rocks me with one steady roll
It makes no difference if he's hot or cold
When I looked at the clock,
clock struck one.

I said honey oh let's have some fun
But you rock me with one steady roll

It all sounded a little familiar to me – shades of Chuck Berry. Then I found another song from July 1945: Wynonie Harris, with the Johnny Otis All Stars, singing 'Around The Clock'. Compare his lyrics with Tampa's:

Sometimes I think I will,
Sometimes I think I won't
Sometimes I believe I do,
And then again I believe I won't
Well I looked at the clock,
The clock struck one
She said come on Daddy
Let's have some fun
Yes, we were rolling,
Yes, we rolled a long time.

Was it coincidence, divine inspiration or a great memory? Well, Chuck's memory was obviously working overtime when he cut 'Reelin' And Rockin' in 1957...

Sometimes I will,
Then again I think I won't
Sometimes I do,
Then again I think I don't
Well I looked at my watch it was 9.21
Was at a rock'n'roll dance,
Having nothing but fun
We was reelin' and rockin',
Rollin' 'til the break of dawn.'

Another interesting thing about Tampa's recording was the singer, Frankie 'Half Pint' Jaxon. He was unusual for a blues performer; he was a female impersonator! He had begun working vaudeville when he was 15 years old, in 1910. Little Frankie graduated to working with Freddie Keppard and King Oliver, among others. He later appeared in various touring shows with some of the great theatre blues singers like Bessie Smith and one of my favourites, Ethel Waters. His recording career continued off and on during the 30s, including work with The Harlem Hamfats❜

BILL WYMAN

TAMPA RED

FACT FILE

BORN: *8th January, 1904 Smithville, Georgia*

DIED: *19th March 1981, Chicago, Illinois*

INSTRUMENT: *Guitar, Kazoo, and piano*

FIRST RECORDED: *1928*

ACCOLADES: *Inducted into the Blues Hall of Fame, 1981*

INFLUENCES: *Lonnie Johnson*

INFLUENCED: *Big Bill Broonzy, Robert Nighthawk, Brownie McGhee*

THE MAN WHO GOT HIS nickname from the town of his youth and the colour of his hair was born Hudson Woodbridge, but was soon given his grandfather's surname of Whittaker. Tampa cut his first record in May 1928 for the Paramount label. Four months later he switched to Vocalion – and Paramount lost one of the biggest stars of the 30s. He moved on to the Victor label in 1934 and stayed there for 20 years, in one of the most enduring recording deals of the era.

A bawdy duet with Georgia Tom Dorsey, 'It's Tight Like That', became his first success. It established a pattern to Tampa's early recordings – a regular diet of risqué blues punctuated with regular re-workings of that landmark hit. Dubbed 'the Guitar Wizard', he also displayed his dexterity with a number of solo instrumentals. His partnership with Dorsey came to an end in 1932 after they cut the excellent 'You Can't Get That Stuff No More'. Not that Tampa had only worked with Dorsey. His success created the craze for 'hokum' music that found him releasing records as Tampa Red's Hokum Jug Band, which included Frankie Jaxon on vocals, as well as a variety of other musicians.

By the end of the 30s Tampa was recording with the Chicago Hot Five and in 1941 he worked with pianist Big Maceo. The late 40s saw Tampa continuing to record with pianists Blind John Davis, Big Maceo and Johnnie Jones. In 1953 he cut four sides with Big Walter Horton on harmonica. His final recordings were in 1960, including the wonderfully titled *Don't Tampa With The Blues*, an album on Bluesville Records. This poignant record featured re-workings of his biggest hits, along with some other classic blues tunes, and featured just Tampa, his guitar and kazoo.

> *"Tampa Red's house was a madhouse for old time musicians... Tampa Red's wife would be cooking chicken and we'd be having a ball"*
>
> WILLIE DIXON, IN HIS AUTOBIOGRAPHY, 'I AM THE BLUES'

With his wife Frances, Tampa ran a Chicago boarding house for musicians at 35th and State, which was fondly remembered by those who stayed there – among them Big Bill Broonzy, Memphis Slim, and Big Maceo.

The man whose early career was built on classics of double entendre like 'Let Me Play With Your Poodle', was quoted in 1960 as disapproving of some rock'n'roll songs. "They only have one fairly smutty meaning," said Tampa, who had obviously forgotten his duets with Georgia Tom Dorsey.

ESSENTIAL RECORDINGS

CLASSIC SONGS

'It's Tight Like That' 1928
'The Duck's Yas-Yas' 1929
'You Can't Get That Stuff No More' 1932
'It Hurts Me Too' 1940

THE SOURCE

The Bluebird Recordings 1936–1938
RCA
The Complete Recordings 1928–1934
Document Records

BLUES IN THE CITY

As America's economic woes began to lift slightly after Roosevelt's election, the career of pianist Leroy Carr started to enjoy a similar rise in fortune. He and his partner, guitarist Francis 'Scrapper' Blackwell, developed a wholly urban sound that became the model for many subsequent blues performers during the 1930s and early 1940s.

PROHIBITION
A federal agent closes a saloon during the prohibition.

Leroy was born in 1905 in Nashville, Tennessee. A self-taught pianist, he appeared in a circus, worked as a bootlegger and served time in the army before teaming up with Scrapper to play at parties, tent shows, bars and roadhouses throughout the South and Midwest. The two men had met when Carr, an inveterate drinker, bought some of Scrapper's bootleg corn liquor. Their debut for Vocalion in 1928, 'How Long, How Long Blues', has become a Blues standard, and it set the pattern for the duo's recording career. Carr's relaxed vocal styling and understated piano were perfectly complemented by Scrapper's single-string picking.

Leroy's career flourished with a little help from an Englishman. The man, remembered only as Mr. Guernsey, persuaded Vocalion to capture the duo on its portable recording unit. Carr and Blackwell duly recorded 'How Long, How Long Blues' and 'My Own Lonesome Blues' at radio station WFBM in Indianapolis. The duo had been reluctant to travel to Chicago to record because Scrapper was worried his bootlegging business would suffer. Like so many other performers, he saw recording as a sideline – which given its meagre financial rewards was not surprising.

BOOZING AND BLUESING

Blackwell continued to work as a part-time bootlegger, while Carr became a full-time drinker. Even so it seems that Carr was the more likeable of the pair, as Blackwell

PROHIBITION IN ACTION
Workers dismantle a still, as alcohol is banned across the US in the 1920s.

appears to have been an aggressive character. Guernsey said that they were 'hard to manage'. Almost inevitably there was tension between the two artists, probably triggered by Scrapper's frustration at having to take a back seat. But while Carr achieved most of the recognition, Blackwell's contribution should not be underestimated. Whatever their personalities, the pair forged a musical relationship that made them the most successful duo of the decade. They recorded more than 100 sides during their six years together, setting them amongst the era's most prolific recording artists.

The duo's final sessions for Vocalion were held in December 1934, after which they switched to the Bluebird label. It is rumoured that Tampa Red, who was already a Bluebird recording artist, was behind the move; indeed, it has even been suggested that Tampa was about to replace Scrapper. But any plans for the future proved to be in vain. On 29th April, 1935, two months after Leroy had recorded eight sides for Bluebird, he died in Indianapolis of acute alcoholism. Thousands of mourners visited the funeral home to pay their respects to the 30-year-old singer.

Prohibition and Bootlegging

The alcohol-related death of Leroy Carr, and the bootlegging activities of his duet partner, illustrate one of the primary concerns of everyday American life in the

Scrapper Blackwell and Leroy Carr

> *The man whose combination of bluish notes struck a deep sympathetic response in the souls of thousands of colored people throughout our country*
>
> The Indianapolis Recorder, 1935

> *Everyone in the 30s came under the influence of Leroy Carr. In 1935, at their final session, he and Scrapper recorded 'When The Sun Goes Down'. Two years later Robert Johnson used Leroy's song as the inspiration for one of only two Johnson songs that the Rolling Stones ever released. When you listen to Leroy's song you can clearly hear where Robert Johnson got his inspiration for the melody and feel of 'Love In Vain'. In early summer 1969 we recorded 'Love In Vain' at Olympic Studios in London, Ry Cooder later overdubbed mandolin. We also featured it at our Hyde Park free concert on 5th July, 1969. For a while it was featured in our live shows, and you can hear it on* Get Yer Ya-Ya's Out, *the live album of our 1969 shows at Madison Square Gardens. It was a long, long way from Leroy Carr. It was only later that I discovered the link from Robert Johnson to Leroy Carr...but with the Blues you are always fitting another new piece into the jigsaw*
>
> Bill Wyman

"Prohibition makes you want to cry into your beer and denies you the beer to cry into"

DON MARQUIS, AMERICAN HUMOURIST, IN 1927

1920s and 1930s – drink, or to be more accurate, the prohibition of drink. As the sale of alcohol was forced underground, the leading lights of the Blues reflected this illicit trade in their songs.

Prohibition was as much a part of America between the wars as the Depression, and it will always be linked in our minds with pictures of mobsters, bootleggers, speakeasies, and G-men, the mainstay of Hollywood thrillers in the 1930s. But Prohibition was actually a 19th-century idea, which was advocated by the US Temperance Movement, and then taken up in 1869 by the Prohibition Party.

First proposed in 1917, the 18th amendment to the US Constitution was adopted in 1919 by every state except Connecticut and Rhode Island. The amendment strictly limited the production of liquor, and it was quickly followed by the Volstead Act, which mapped out the details of the new law.

One immediate result of the Volstead Act was that illegal trafficking in alcohol became a huge industry, controlled in the cities by organised crime and in rural areas by small-time crooks who ran their own illicit stills. By 1926 this illegal liquor trade was estimated to be worth $3.6 billion. Bootlegging was at the heart of the criminal underworld, and the spoils were used to branch out into other lucrative criminal and non-criminal activities. Men like Al Capone became synonymous with the Chicago bootlegging industry, 'running' vast amounts of liquor into the city from across the Canadian border.

"The prohibition law, written for weaklings and derelicts, has divided the nation, like Gaul, into three parts – wets, drys, and hypocrites"

FLORENCE SABIN, AN AMERICAN TEACHER, IN A SPEECH ON 9TH FEBRUARY, 1931

AL CAPONE

The most notorious of the Chicago gangsters built his empire on the illicit trade in bootleg liquor.

"I got good corn liquor, I'm the best bootlegger in town. All the other bootleggers get mad when they see me comin' round"

'CORN LIQUOR BLUES' PAPA CHARLIE JACKSON, 1928

Leroy Carr

FACT FILE

Born: *27th March, 1905 Nashville (Davidson Co.), Tennessee*

Died: *29th April, 1935 Indianapolis, Indiana*

Instrument: *Piano*

First Recorded: *1928*

Accolades: *Inducted into the Blues Hall of Fame, 1982*

Influenced: *Eddie Boyd, Champion Jack Dupree, Otis Spann, T-Bone Walker*

> *He was exceptionally varied in his choice of songs and poetic in his blues*
>
> Paul Oliver, 1973

When he was a child, Carr's family moved to Louisville, Kentucky, and then to Indianapolis, where he attended school. Carr taught himself the piano and dropped out of school to join a travelling circus, before enlisting with the army when he was about 16. Later he made a living from playing at house rent parties, accompanying singers and playing at dances, and even tried bootlegging.

In the mid-20s, he met guitarist Scrapper Blackwell (born Frances Hillman Blackwell, 21st February, 1903), and the two of them popularised the piano-guitar blues duet. Their first record was on the Vocalion label. Recorded on 19th June, 1928, in Indianapolis, it featured 'My Own Lonesome Blues' and 'How Long, How Long Blues'. The duo created a sophisticated urban sound which broadened the appeal of the blues, steering it away from its less sophisticated country roots.

Carr and Blackwell became prolific recording artists. Throughout the second half of 1928 and all of 1929 they worked in Chicago, playing clubs and theatres, and recording around 80 sides for Vocalion, about half of which were released. By 1930 the duo were recording a little less, but still working live shows, often around St Louis. Carr did not record much again until 1934, when he cut over 40 sides for Vocalion – like everyone he felt the privations of the Depression. In 1935, just one recording session took place on 25th February, when Carr and Blackwell cut eight sides in Chicago for RCA's Bluebird label. Two months later Carr was dead from acute alcoholism: ironically, the last side that he recorded was 'Six Cold Feet In The Ground'.

Carr's piano style was both relaxed and understated, and Blackwell's single string guitar picking was an ideal accompaniment to Carr's haunting vocals – drifting over the top. Carr's influence was still going strong in the 1990s, when Eric Clapton featured both 'How Long, How Long Blues' and 'Blues Before Sunrise' on his album *From The Cradle*. Blackwell, who got the nickname Scrapper as a child from his grandmother, was shot in the back in Indianapolis on 7th October, 1962.

Essential Recordings

Classic Songs

'How Long, How Long Blues' 1928
'Low Down Dog Blues' 1931
'Mean Mistreater Mama' 1934
'Blues Before Sunrise' 1934

The Source

6 CDs on Document Records, his complete works
The Essential Recordings of Leroy Carr
Indigo Records

Leroy Carr

Eventually politicians realised that prohibition was causing more social problems than the open sale of alcohol. On 5th December, 1933, the 21st amendment to the US constitution repealed prohibition. This had an immediate impact on the blues scene in Chicago and other Northern cities. It meant that liquor could now be served freely in clubs, which allowed them to hire star performers to provide the entertainment. Leroy Carr, Tampa Red, and Big Bill Broonzy were among those

The Shadow of Danger
U.S.
WHISKEY
If you believe that the traffic in Alcohol does more harm than good- help stop it!"
Strengthen America Campaign

Save America from Drink
The brewers' campaigns were countered by moralists preaching the evil of alcohol.

who benefited from this change in the law, and it helped to speed the move away from country blues towards recorded urban blues. But while urban blues flourished in the North, the Delta blues tradition was kept alive in the country by house rent parties and picnics, and its survival proved to be vital in the creation of post-war electric blues.

Leroy's Buddies

The third giant of the urban blues scene outstripped even the achievements of Tampa

Fight for the Right to Drink
Brewery workers calling for the repeal of the 18th Amendment, 1920s.

You gotta dress right for the Blues
Little Bill Gaither, Memphis Slim and Big Bill Broonzy, c.1940.

Red and Leroy Carr. William Lee Conley Broonzy, born in Mississippi and raised in Arkansas, took what he knew from the Delta blues, imbued it with urban sophistication, and, in the process,became the dominant bluesman of the pre-war Chicago scene.

Big Bill Broonzy, as he was dubbed on his first record for the Paramount label in late 1927, was almost universally liked. "Big Bill? That's the nicest guy I ever met in my life", said Muddy Waters, who met him in post-war Chicago. Muddy and his contemporaries grew up listening to Big Bill's recordings, and they always looked up to him - because quite simply he had done it all. Besides being a prodigious solo recording artist, Broonzy was a hard-working accompanist. He worked with Jazz Gillum, Washboard Sam (his cousin), the original Sonny Boy Williamson, Lil Green, Cripple Clarence Lofton, Victoria Spivey, and Amos Easton (alias Bumble Bee Sam), to name just a few. He also enjoyed a simultaneous recording career as part of The Famous Hokum Boys and The Hokum Boys.

Broonzy was a prolific songwriter, too, and his work appealed to the more sophisticated city audience as well as those who shared his Southern country background. The broad sweep of his repertoire helped to establish Bill's reputation. He performed across a wider musical spectrum than almost any other bluesman, before or since. He played ragtime, hokum blues, straight-ahead country blues, sophisticated city blues, jazz-tinged songs, folk songs, and spirituals. On top of all that, he was the founding father of the electric blues from post-war Chicago. His 1945 recordings like 'Where The Blues Began', with Big Maceo on piano and Buster Bennett on sax, or 'Martha Blues', with Memphis Slim on piano, were the bridge that allowed many younger musicians to reach the future of the Blues.

Cut a slice through any year of the 1930s, and you'd find Bill Broonzy, as central as the writing through a stick of seaside rock. He

Big Bill Broonzy

"If I was to stop playing the real old slow blues, I don't know what would become of it," said Big Bill. He was as great a self-publicist as he was a bluesman. Muddy Waters called him "the nicest guy I ever met in my life", and among his contemporaries, Big Bill Broonzy was almost universally liked.

was a mentor, a performer, an inspiration and the man who was responsible, perhaps more than any other, for taking the Blues to Britain and Europe. As the self-proclaimed 'last of his line', he wooed the young Turks of the European jazz scene. Eager to understand and learn about the Blues, they took Bill to their hearts. If Bill played it, it was good, and it was the genuine article.

SCRAPPER BLACKWELL AND LEROY CARR
Leroy Carr's premature death left a gaping chasm in the Blues. His old sideman Scrapper Blackwell was one of many singers who marked his death with a tribute record, 'My Old Pal Blues'.

LEROY'S CLONES

Leroy Carr's premature death created a void in the musical spectrum of the period. Not surprisingly Scrapper Blackwell was not the man to fill this vacuum; only rarely can someone step up from sideman to frontman. Not that he didn't try: the Champion label even put Blackwell in the studio to record a tribute record to Leroy. The result, 'My Old Pal Blues', was prophetic:

> *'The day of his funeral I hated to see Leroy's face Because I know there's no one could ever take his place'*

Decca, which owned Champion, was not content to capitalise on Leroy's death just once. At the same session, Scrapper accompanied Bumble Bee Slim on 'The Death of Leroy Carr'. Obviously someone was unsure of the record's chances of success, as a week later Bumble Bee was back in the studio cutting two more Leroy tributes, a remake of 'My Old Pal Blues' and another called 'Last Respects'. Scrapper wasn't the only singer climbing on the Carr bandwagon: in December 1935, Bill Gaither ('Leroy's Buddy', as Decca called him) recorded 'Leroy Carr's Blues'. Over the course of the next six years, Gaither recorded a large number of sides for Decca, sometimes as Leroy's Buddy or Little Bill Gaither, accompanied by pianist Honey Hill. In 1940 he even cut 'The Life Of Leroy Carr' for the OKeh label. But while he was popular with record buyers, Gaither was rather too imitative to win a lasting reputation.

The day after he recorded 'My Old Pal Blues', Scrapper cut four more sides, which proved to be his last pre-war sessions. Asked later why he stopped recording, Scrapper replied: 'I just had enough'. Most likely he knew life would not be the same for anyone, least of all for him, without Leroy's talent. Instead, he worked as a labourer in an asphalt plant, a sad fate for such a noted talent. Having already influenced such major figures as T-Bone Walker and Muddy Waters, Scrapper did return to the studio in the late 1950s and early 1960s. But before he could benefit from his renewed success, the 59-year-old was shot dead near his Indianapolis home in 1962 – by a 75-year-old neighbour.

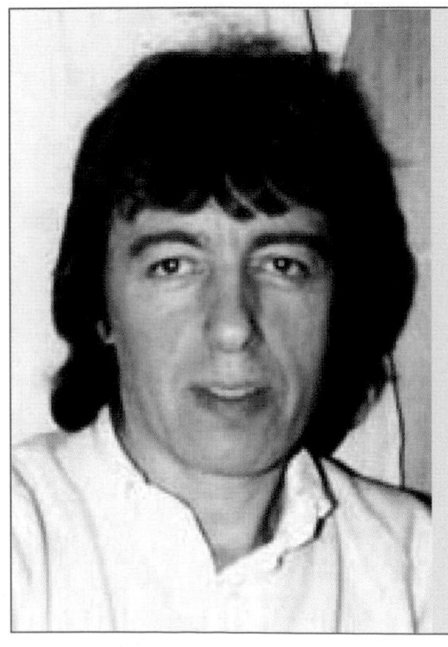

'In 1930 Big Bill Broonzy was billed as Sammy Sampson on some records he cut for the Perfect label. Many years later I came across a song called 'Who Shot Sam' by my favourite country singer George Jones that was a hit on the US country charts in 1959. The lyric says,

'I met Sammy Sampson down in New Orleans
He had a lot of money, and a big limousine.
He took me honky-tonking on Saturday night'

I have always wondered if that was just a coincidence, or whether George Jones did actually meet Big Bill'

BILL WYMAN

HOW LONG, HOW LONG BLUES

LEROY CARR'S FIRST RECORD became a huge hit and set the pattern for his career. It was a remake of 'How Long, Sweet Daddy, How Long', which had been Alberta Hunter's first release in 1921. Leroy's version wasn't actually the first cover of the song, as Ida Cox (accompanied by Papa Charlie Jackson) recorded it in 1925.

HOW MANY VERSIONS?

Six months after Leroy and Scrapper Blackwell cut their original version, they made 'How Long, How Long Blues Part 2' and 'No. 3'. A year later came 'New How Long How Long Blues', while in 1931 there was 'New How Long How Long Blues Part 2'. . . they certainly got their money's worth out of this song. Leroy also cut 'How Long Has That Evening Train Been Gone' in 1932 which was in the same vein. On top of that, at least six cover versions were rushed out in the six months after Leroy's original.

TIM HARDIN

'How Long How Long Blues' appeared on Tim Hardin's 1965 debut album as 'How Long'. John Sebastian of the Lovin' Spoonful played harmonica.

HOW LONG, HOW LONG BLUES

Recorded by Leroy Carr (piano) with Scrapper Blackwell (guitar)
19th June, 1928, Indianapolis, Indiana

**How long, babe how long, has that evening train been gone*
How long, how long baby, how long

Lord and I stood at the station watch my baby leaving town
Blue and disgusted no where could she be found
How long, how long baby, how long

I can hear the whistle blowing, but I cannot see no train
And it's deep in my heart baby that I have an aching pain
How long, how long baby, how long

Sometimes I feel so disgusted and I feel so blue
That I hardly know what in this world, baby, just to do
How long, how long baby, how long

And if I could holler just like a mountain jack
I'd go up on the mountain and I'd call my baby back
How long, how long baby, how long

And if some day you gonna be sorry that you have done me wrong
But it will be too late baby because I'll be gone
How long, how long baby, how long

My mind gets a ramblin' I feel so bad
Thinking about the bad luck that I have had
How long, how long baby, how long

The 1935 and 1936 versions were all recorded in the wake of Leroy Carr's death. In particular, Amos Easton (alias Bumble Bee Slim) and Bill Gaither both specialised in covers of Carr's songs.

LONNIE DONEGAN

Lonnie Donegan recorded the song for his 1956 album *Lonnie Donegan Showcase*. He starts by singing in a laconic manner before building to a jazzy crescendo - totally different from other interpretations. It's a perfect snapshot of skiffle crazy Britain in the 50s, attempting to give pre-war blues a contemporary significance.

* A 1948 version by Sister OM Terrell turned the song into a religious homily on the sin of adultery. The opening changed to:

'How long, Great God, how long, How long you gonna live in your sin, Great God how long?'

ERIC CLAPTON

'How Long' appears on Eric Clapton's 1994 album *From The Cradle*.

SELECTED VERSIONS

- 1921 Alberta Hunter
- 1925 Ida Cox
- 1928 Blind Lemon Jefferson, Gladys Bentley, Willie Jackson, Tampa Red's Hokum Jug Band
- 1929 Tampa Red, Jed Davenport
- 1935 Kokomo Arnold, Amos Easton
- 1936 Bill Gaither (Leroy's Buddy)
- 1940 Joe Turner
- 1943 Lead Belly
- 1946 Chippie Hill
- 1948 Sister OM Terrell
- 1949 John Lee Hooker
- 1956 Lonnie Donegan
- 1965 Tim Hardin
- 1994 Eric Clapton

THE RIPLEY SOUND

While some musicians made their way to Chicago, Memphis continued to be a magnet for bluesmen from the Delta and surrounding areas. Just a month before the Wall Street Crash, John Adam Estes, a native of Ripley, Tennessee, cut his first sides for the Victor label.

By 1919 the 15-year-old was already a precocious talent. That year he first worked with James 'Yank' Rachell, from the nearby town of Brownsville. Yank was just 11 at the time and already a very good mandolin player. The two teenagers worked fish fries, dances, and house rent parties throughout the early 1920s. In 1935, Estes began another long-term partnership, this time with a 17-year-old harmonica player, Hammie Nixon. Hammie learned the instrument from Noah Lewis, one of Cannon's Jug Stompers, and in 1930 the three younger men became Noah Lewis's Jug Band.

By 1929 Estes was performing regularly in Memphis in a small group, the Three Js Jug Band, also featuring Yank and a jug-playing pianist, Jab Jones, who sometimes recorded with the Memphis Jug Band. The Three Js was a rather loose grouping; John Estes's first release actually featured Johnny Hardge on piano plus Rachell on mandolin. 'The Girl I Love, She Got Long Curly Hair' proved to be the biggest seller of Estes' early records. The Three Js earned $300 each for their first recordings; they admitted later that they quickly spent the cash in West Helena, known as the 'vice capital' of Arkansas.

Estes had lost an eye in a baseball game in his teens. With his cast eye, 'Sleepy' seemed the natural choice of nickname.

The name first appeared on a record in 1935 when he signed to the Champion label. That was also when John's songs began to take on a more autobiographical feel. As he said later, "I got to thinking about the people and I figured I could make good hits out of songs about the peoples I known, make it sell good." He sang about the place where he lived ('Brownsville Blues'), his near death ('Floating Bridge Blues') and one of his patrons ('Lawyer Clark Blues'). In 'Down South Blues', recorded in 1935, he vividly explained what the Depression meant to him and many others living in Memphis: 'Down South Blues' was recorded after a five-year lay-off, induced by the changing financial climate of the Depression. By the time Estes returned to recording, his old sidekick Rachell had 'gone solo', signing to the American Record Company in 1934 and recording in New York. By 1938 Yank had switched to Bluebird and was working with

JOHN ADAM ESTES

Sleepy John was born in Ripley, Tennessee; Eric Clapton was born in Ripley, Surrey.

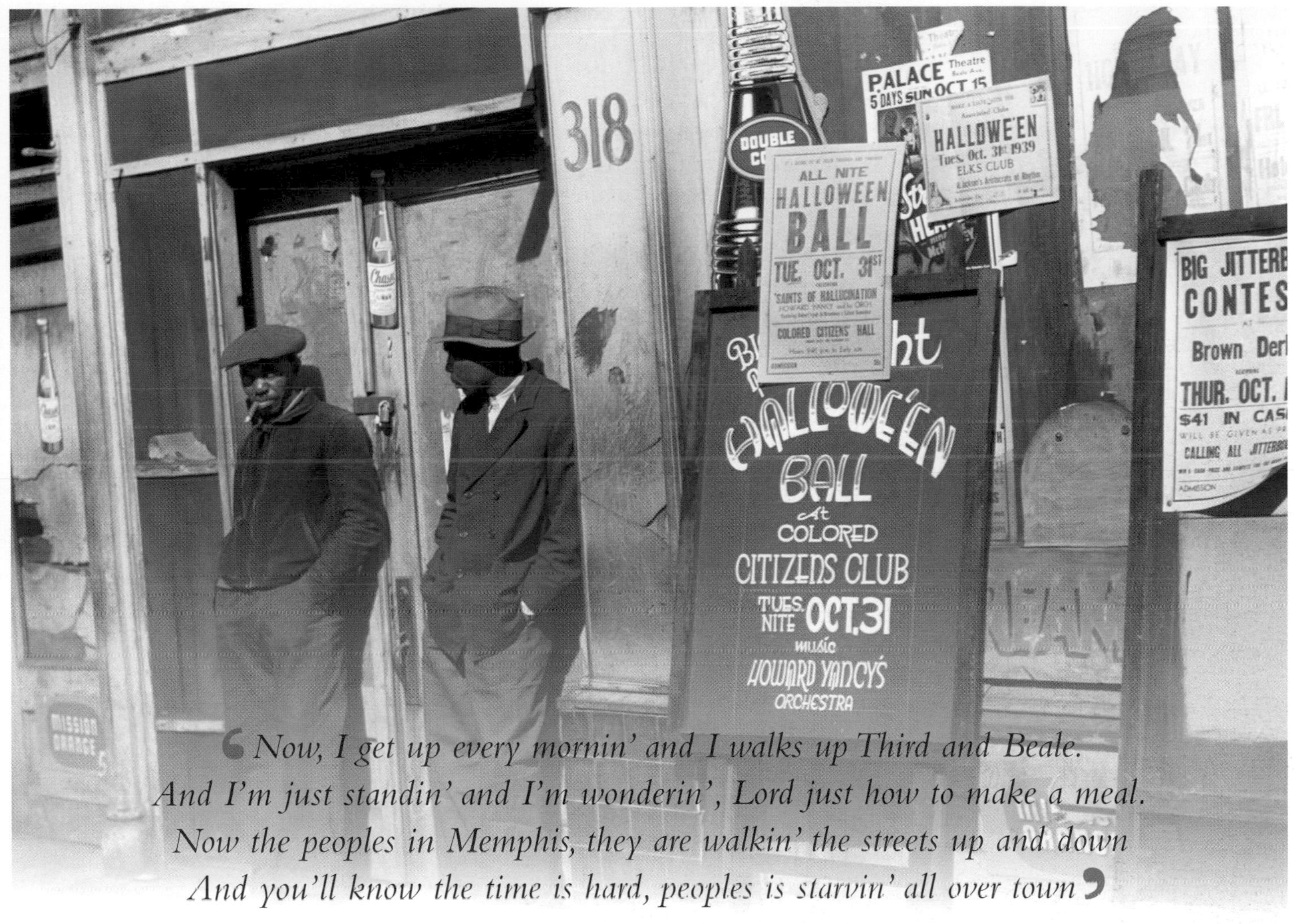

“Now, I get up every mornin' and I walks up Third and Beale.
And I'm just standin' and I'm wonderin', Lord just how to make a meal.
Now the peoples in Memphis, they are walkin' the streets up and down
And you'll know the time is hard, peoples is starvin' all over town”

'Down South Blues' by Sleepy John Estes
Recorded 1935 in Chicago

the original Sonny Boy Williamson. Estes recorded with Decca in 1937, 1938, and 1940 before he too switched to Bluebird; these were his last sessions before he returned to live in Brownsville, in what were fairly desperate circumstances. Sleepy John, Yank, and Hammie occasionally worked together after the war, eventually recording together during the 1960s folk-blues revival.

Son of a Preacher Man

There is one artist who enjoyed only the briefest of recording careers, and yet today is considered to be among the best of the Delta bluesmen. Nehemiah 'Skip' James was born in Bentonia, Mississippi, in 1903, the son of a Baptist minister. He learned to play the piano at school, but dropped out when he was about 15. He began to hobo around Mississippi, meeting up with Henry Stuckey, who was several years his senior, and the two of them worked picnics, parties and barrelhouses across the Delta.

The partnership of Stuckey and James survived throughout the 1920s, but only Skip was offered the opportunity to record in February 1931. Skip auditioned 'Devil Got My Woman' for the Jackson record store owner, and part-time talent scout, HC Speir, who had no hesitation in recommending Skip to the Paramount label. Two days later Skip travelled to Grafton, Wisconsin, where he cut 26 sides, including 'Devil Got My Woman' and '32-20 Blues', both of which were later adapted by Robert Johnson. Skip's first release, 'Hard Time Killin'

FRESH CREAM

Cream's 1966 debut album Fresh Cream, *featured Skip James' song 'I'm So Glad'. It was to be a regular number in the band's live set list throughout their brief two-year career.*

Floor Blues', carried as bleak a view of the Depression as any recording of the era:

> *Hard time here, and everywhere you go.*
> *Times is harder than ever been before*
> *And the people are drifting from door to door*
> *Can't find no heaven, don't care where they go.*
>
> *Let me tell you people just before I go.*
> *These hard times will kill you, just travel on slow.*
>
> *When you hear me singing my blue*
> *lonesome song.*
> *These hard times can last us so very long.*
>
> *If I ever get off this killin' floor*
> *I'll never get down this low no more*

'HARD TIME
KILLIN' FLOOR BLUES', 1931

'Hard Time Killin' Floor Blues' was delivered in James' distinctive falsetto, which somehow made the song even more poignant. His vocal styling, combined with his neat guitar work and subtle lyrics, created a unique slice of Delta blues.

Not long after his trip to Grafton, Skip James left the secular world of the Blues, and took up with his father to work in the ministry; he was following his own advice from one of his 1931 recordings, 'Jesus Is A Mighty Good Leader'. He became a Baptist minister in 1932, though by 1946 he had switched his allegiances, becoming an ordained Methodist minister. Like many Delta veterans, Skip James was 'rediscovered' in the 1960s; he played the Newport Festival in 1964 and undertook small-scale tours. Of the 26 sides that Skip remembers recording, 18 were released on nine records, among them 'I'm So Glad', which was covered by Cream in 1966 on their debut album, *Fresh Cream*. The $6,000 of royalties Skip received from this recording helped with his medical expenses, and, ironically, covered the cost of his funeral in 1969. Maybe it also softened the feelings about his career that he expressed in a 1965 interview with Peter Guralnick:

"I was so disappointed. Wouldn't you be disappointed, man? I cut 26 sides for Paramount in Grafton, Wisconsin. I didn't get paid but $40. That's not doing very good. Wouldn't you be disappointed?"

Skip James articulated what many of his generation felt. You sense that he recognised that he had failed to fulfil his potential, a feeling made stronger by his rediscovery. Happiness can come from the feeling that you have exceeded your expectations; Skip James seemed like an unhappy man.

Skip James in the 1960s

THE MYSTERY OF THE ORIGINAL HOWLING WOLF

There were two styles of Texas blues, and both of them were exemplified by Blind Lemon Jefferson. There was a somewhat sombre sound, reminiscent of the Delta, and a lighter, ragtime style. The old-time songster Henry Thomas was the first man to be recorded in the ragtime style, between 1927 to 1929, and was even dubbed 'Ragtime Texas' on some of his Vocalion sides. Nearly 40 years later, the jug band-influenced rock group, the Lovin' Spoonful, named one of their songs after him, while his sound also inspired another rock-blues outfit, Canned Heat.

In this tradition was the superbly named JT 'Funny Paper' Smith, who recorded for Vocalion in September 1930, aged around 40. His debut was the two-part 'Howling

Wolf Blues'. His unusual nickname actually came from a printing error: Smith actually called himself 'Funny Papa'! By July 1931 he had recorded 20 sides, but then his career came to an abrupt and mysterious halt. Almost four years later, in April 1935, he recorded 18 more solo sides for Vocalion over a three-day spell, but none of them was ever released.

What makes JT's story so intriguing is the fact that we know almost nothing about him, except from the testimony of the Texas bluesman, Thomas Shaw, who claimed to have known Smith. He said that JT was a plantation supervisor, who was convicted of killing a man in an argument in 1931, and sent to jail. Maybe the prison governor allowed him to record in 1935; perhaps he had already been released. Or maybe Shaw got his dates mixed up, and JT was imprisoned after 1935, prompting Vocalion not to release his records. Admittedly, this would have been out of character for a record company, then or now: why would they let a mere murder stand in the way of a sale?

Frustratingly, while a couple of songs he recorded with Bernice Edwards and Black Boy Shines were released, the masters of his 1935 Vocalion sides have never been found: they represent some of the great lost recordings of the era. While JT was not a great guitarist, or a particularly distinguished vocalist, he was a fantastic lyricist - a poet of the Blues.

His 'Fools Blues' is particularly inspired. In the spoken intro, JT conjectures:

‘You know I'm a single handed fool
And getting old too.
Well, they say God takes care of old folks and fools, so I guess he will’

By the end of the song, he has changed his mind.

‘Now I've got TB's, I've got LT's
I've got the third degrees in both diseases.
My health is gone now, left me with those sickness blues.
People it don't seem likely to me that God takes care of old folks and fools’

Other songs, like 'County Jail Blues', 'Hoppin' Toad Frog' and 'Seven Sisters Blues', all feature JT's highly creative lyrical flair and original blues imagery.

The Complete Recordings
Skip James' Complete 1931 Recordings *on Document Records includes 'Hard Time Killin' Floor Blues', 'Jesus Is A Mighty Good Leader' and 'I'm So Glad'.*

Baptist & Methodist
Skip James became a Baptist minister in 1932, though by 1946 he had switched his allegiances, becoming an ordained Methodist minister.

THE LIBRARY OF CONGRESS

Alan Lomax

It added the voice of the common man to the written history of America

ALAN LOMAX

IN 1928 THE LIBRARY OF CONGRESS in Washington DC decided to establish the Archive of Folk Song, to document the music of rural America. Its first archivist was Robert W Gordon, who became one of the first people to undertake field-recording trips to capture ethnic folk music. Using somewhat fragile, but portable, cylinder recording equipment, he visited both Georgia and North Carolina between 1926 and 1938. The recordings he and his successors made, many of which featured black men and woman, inaugurated what has become the greatest repository of a nation's folk music anywhere in the world.

As early as 1932, the initial funding for the project ran out and the prospects for the archive looked bleak, as Gordon could no longer be employed. Around the same time, John Avery Lomax suggested to his New York publisher that he should produce an *Anthology of American Ballads And Folk Songs*. The enthused Lomax arranged a field-recording trip to add to his collection of folk material, using recording equipment provided by the Library of Congress. In June 1933, accompanied by his son Alan, he made his first trip across Texas.

John was born in Goodman, Mississippi in 1867, and grew up on the Texas frontier, just north of Meridian. After teaching at a local university, John attended Harvard as a graduate student, before returning to Texas in 1909, around the same time that he co-founded the Texas Folklore Society. In 1910 he published his first book, *Cowboy Songs And Frontier Ballads*. When he returned to teaching, he continued to pursue his hobby. By the early 30s, however, his fortunes were at a low ebb. His wife had died in 1930, and he had been bedridden in 1932 and lost his job as a result. His son Alan was about to enter his first year of college, when at the age of 17 he set off with his father on their first field trip.

In his book, *Adventures Of A Ballad Hunter*, John wrote:

Stored in the rear of the car were two cots and bedding, a cooking outfit, provisions, a change of clothing, an infinite number of 'etceteras' which will manage to encumber any traveller. Later, as a crown to our discomfort, we also carried a 350-pound recording machine – a cumbersome pile of wire and iron and steel – built into the rear of the Ford, two batteries weighing 75 pounds each, a microphone, a complicated machine of delicate adjustments, coils of wire, numerous gadgets, besides scores of blank aluminium and celluloid disks, and finally, a multitude of extra parts

In 1933, father and son covered 16,000 miles collecting songs that were integral to the lives of Americans, whether black or white. John had managed to convince the academic establishment that they should not just be collecting folk songs of European origin. He wanted to collect vernacular material from every ethnic background, and in particular from black people. Many of their recordings were made in State

LEAD BELLY
The Lomaxs met Lead Belly in Angola Prison, and assisted in obtaining his release. The recordings that Alan Lomax made for the Library of Congress can be heard on the album The Titanic *which includes songs such as 'Shreveport Jail' and 'Angola Blues (So Doggone Soon)'.*

BLIND WILLIE McTELL
John Lomax recorded Blind Willie McTell in the St James Hotel in Atlanta, Georgia, sometime around 1940. On the recording McTell sings and plays guitar and talks about his life as a blind musician.

MUDDY WATERS AT STOVALL'S

In 1941, while searching for Robert Johnson, Alan Lomax went to Stovall's plantation in Clarksdale, Mississippi and recorded 26-year-old McKinley Morganfield (Muddy Waters), a tractor driver on the plantation.

MUDDY WATERS

The recordings that Alan Lomax made of Muddy Waters can be heard on Muddy Waters: The Complete Plantation Recordings. *Waters' classic 'I Can't Be Satisfied' appears as 'I Be's Troubled', and there are two takes of 'Country Blues', the predecessor to 'I Feel Like Going Home'. Five sides are of the Son Simms Four, a string band in which Muddy plays guitar with Henry 'Son' Simms on vocal and violin, Percy Thomas on guitar, and Louis Ford on mandolin.*

Penitentiaries and on prison farms, and these have proved invaluable in furthering our knowledge of slave songs, and in particular gang worksongs. The prison work gangs used these as a method of keeping time and alleviating the back-breaking work, just as slaves working in the fields had done in earlier centuries.

That same year the Lomaxs met Lead Belly in Angola Prison, and assisted in obtaining his release. Lead Belly wound up chauffeuring them, as well as helping to persuade prisoners to record, visiting various correctional establishments to demonstrate what the father and son song-hunters were looking for. When John remarried in 1934, his new wife became involved in the song collecting, while the Library employed Alan to work on the project. Field trips were made in the remainder of the 30s across the Southern states, while specific events and artists were recorded in some northern cities.

By 1939 Alan had his own radio show, and when his father retired in early 1940, he took over as curator of the collection, funding for which was now provided by the Carnegie Foundation. After serving in the army during the war, Alan worked for Decca Records, while continuing to collect songs. John died aged 80 in 1948, but Alan continued to collect throughout the 50s and early 60s.

The work of the Lomax family has been pivotal in furthering our knowledge of the Blues and its offshoots and antecedents. Through their work for the Library of Congress, the Lomaxs and their comrades gave:

> *'A voice to the voiceless'*
>
> ALAN LOMAX

LIBRARY OF CONGRESS ARCHIVISTS

Other archivists who recorded for the Library of Congress included:
Mary Elizabeth Barnicle
Harold Spivacke
Charles Seeger
Sidney Robertson
Stetson Kennedy
Robert Cook
Carita Dogget Corse
Robert Cornwell
John W Work
John Henry Faulk
Lewis Jones.

LIBRARY OF CONGRESS
FIELD RECORDING TRIPS

THE FIELD TRIPS WERE MADE NOT just to record blues singers or black performers. They covered the whole gamut of ethnic folk, secular and religious material including sermons, as well as interviews. Neither were the trips focused on obscure musicians; they also recorded some of the key figures from 20th-century musical history. WC Handy told of his life, while Jelly Roll Morton made 51 recordings on which he talked and played. Musicians such as Son House, who had recorded commercially, were also captured. Others who would go on to have successful careers also recorded for the Library, including Muddy Waters who first recorded in 1941 at Stovall's Plantation.

LOMAX & HOLLY

In January 1937, John A Lomax recorded in Lubbock, Texas, just five months after the birth there of Charles Hardin Holley (Buddy Holly) on 7th September, 1936.

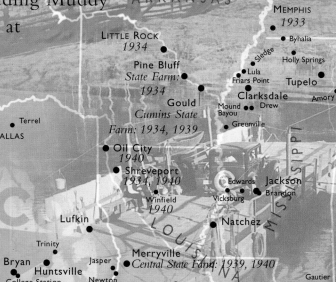

FIELD RECORDINGS IN TEXAS

Egypt, 1933
Terril, 1933
Trinity, 1933
Wiergate, 1933
Huntsville, 1933; State Penitentiary 1934, 1939
Sugarland, 1934; State farm, 1933, 1942
Sandy Point, Darrington State Farm 1933, 1934
Luling, 1936
Lubbock, 1937
Brazoria, Clemen's State Farm, 1939
Burkeville, 1939
Burkeville, 1939
Otey, Ramsey State Farm, 1939
Newton, 1939
Austin, 1941
Bryan, 1941
College Station, 1941
Comache, 1941
Dallas, 1936
Garfield, 1941
Jasper, 1940,
Littig, 1941
Lufkin, 1940
Manor, 1941
Navasota, 1941
Plantersville, 1941
Praire View, 1933
San Marcos, 1941
Stamford, 1942
Walter County, 1941

RICH PICKINGS

Plantations were fertile ground for the song hunters, who visited the Moorehead Plantation in Lula, the Alma Plantation near Baton Rouge, and Hopsons near Clarksdale.

FIELD RECORDINGS IN MISSISSIPPI

Parchman Farm, 1933, 1936, 1937, 1939
Brandon, 1937, 1939
Jackson, 1937
Tupelo, 1939
Vicksburg, 1939
Amory, 1939
Byhalia, 1939
Cockrum, 1939
Edwards, 1939
Gautier, 1939
Greenville, 1939
Holly Springs, 1939
Clarksdale, 1940, 1942
Drew, 1940
Natchez, 1940
Coahoma, 1941, 1942
Lake Cormorant, 1941
Lula, 1941, 1942
Mound Bayou, 1941
Stovall, 1941, 1942
Friars Point, 1942
Robinsonville, 1942
Sherord, 1942
Sledge, Reed State Farm, 1942

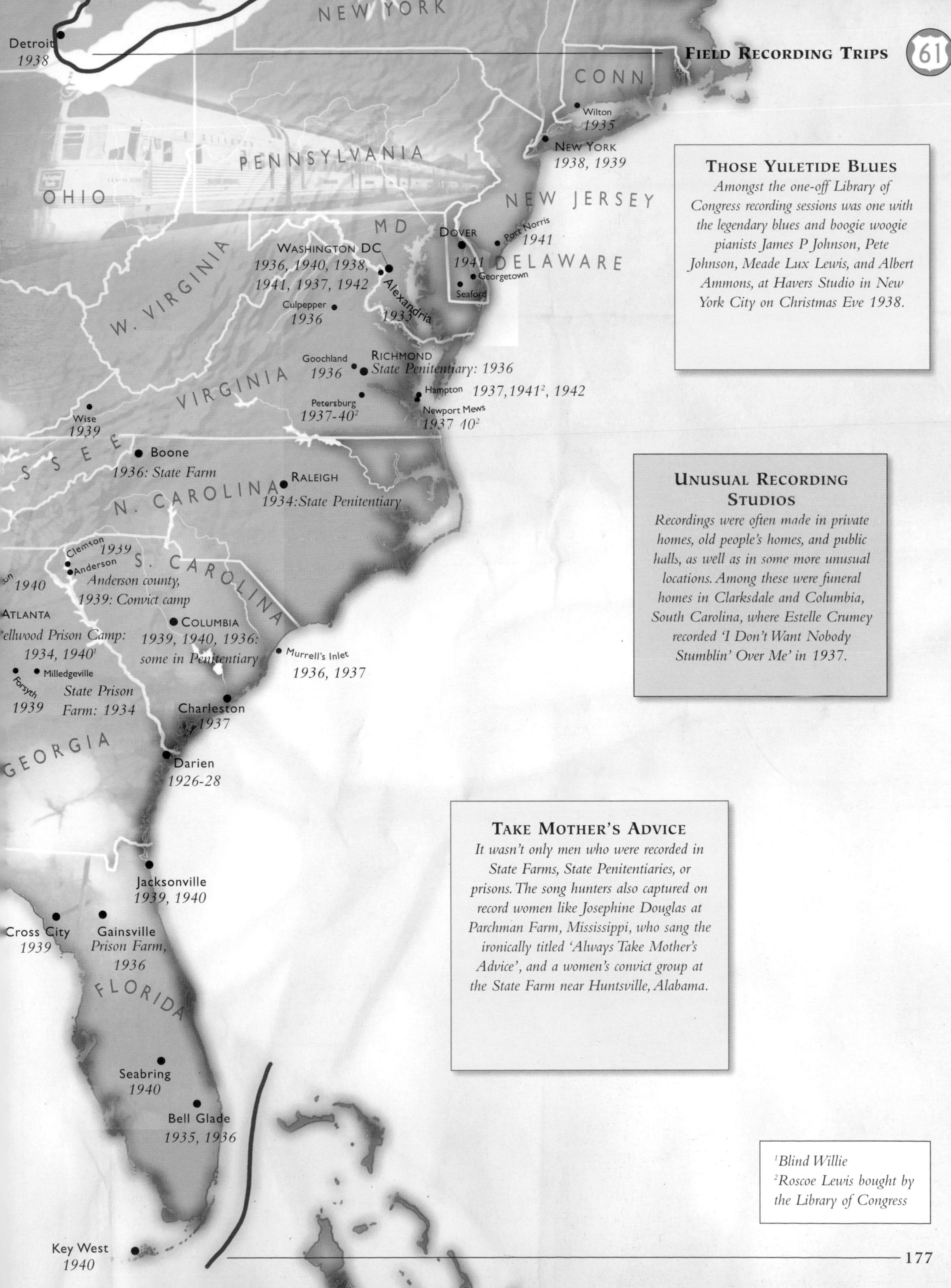

THOSE YULETIDE BLUES

Amongst the one-off Library of Congress recording sessions was one with the legendary blues and boogie woogie pianists James P Johnson, Pete Johnson, Meade Lux Lewis, and Albert Ammons, at Havers Studio in New York City on Christmas Eve 1938.

UNUSUAL RECORDING STUDIOS

Recordings were often made in private homes, old people's homes, and public halls, as well as in some more unusual locations. Among these were funeral homes in Clarksdale and Columbia, South Carolina, where Estelle Crumey recorded 'I Don't Want Nobody Stumblin' Over Me' in 1937.

TAKE MOTHER'S ADVICE

It wasn't only men who were recorded in State Farms, State Penitentiaries, or prisons. The song hunters also captured on record women like Josephine Douglas at Parchman Farm, Mississippi, who sang the ironically titled 'Always Take Mother's Advice', and a women's convict group at the State Farm near Huntsville, Alabama.

[1] *Blind Willie*
[2] *Roscoe Lewis bought by the Library of Congress*

Train Songs, Pain Songs, and Texas Swing

The Governor in Memphis

A few days before Victor recorded Sleepy John Estes and the Memphis Jug Band at the Memphis Auditorium in May 1930, the label cut some sides with Oscar 'Buddy' Woods and Ed Schaffer. The two men were dubbed the Shreveport Homewreckers, after the town where Buddy worked as a street singer – noted for playing his guitar flat across his lap and using a bottleneck to slide the notes. Woods and Schaffer cut one song with a country blues singer from Louisiana called Jimmie Davis – who, unlike the other leading players in this story so far, was white.

James Houston Davis

James Houston Davis was born in Quitman, Louisiana in 1899, one of 11 children of a sharecropping family. He gained an MA in education and psychology at Louisiana State University, and briefly became a teacher in Shreveport. In 1928 he was working in the city as a clerk when his interest in music blossomed into a part-time career, via both songwriting and performing. He began to appear on a Shreveport radio station, which led to Victor signing him in 1929.

Shreveport, Louisiana

Among his first recordings was the ground-breaking 'She's A Hum Dum Dinger (From Dingersville)', performed with Woods and Schaffer. At the same session he also recorded some country numbers, including 'My Louisiana Girl'. Six months later Davis and the Homewreckers were back to cut three more blues sides together, including 'Bear Cat Mama From Horner's Corner'. Jimmie recorded another 10 blues songs over the next 15 months; in total he recorded 68 sides for Victor. Many of them were openly sexual, including 'Tom Cat And Pussy Blues', 'Red Nightgown Blues', and 'The Organ Grinder Blues'.

Jimmie Davis would have been no more than a footnote in blues history, except for one thing – he became the only blues singer ever to live in a governor's mansion. Before he got there, he broadened his writing and singing career, scoring hits for Decca like 'Nobody's Darlin' But Mine' in 1935, which was covered by artists such as Bing Crosby.

In 1940 Jimmie, who by this time was a crooner, wrote one of the best-known tunes of the 20th century, 'You Are My Sunshine', which King George VI claimed was his favourite song.

Whatever the story behind his most famous number, Jimmie Davis wrote more than 100 songs in his long career. He died in November 2000, aged 101, although his birth date is shrouded in mystery. No one, even Davis himself, was quite sure of it, but he held his 100th birthday party in September 1999. He served his first term as Governor of

Louisiana in 1944, played himself in a Hollywood biopic in 1947, and returned to the Governor's mansion in 1960 (though a third attempt in 1972 failed). From the 1950s onwards, Jimmie turned his back on the blues, recording only religious songs.

Buddy Woods continued to record in the late 1930s, and did some sessions for the Library of Congress in 1940. It is interesting to speculate whether this excellent lap guitar player ever ran into Jimmie during his term as governor, and what might have passed between them. Jimmie's electorate had probably forgotten about his early career as a master of the double entendre, or more likely they didn't care!

Hill-Billy 'Round-Up'

Included in this booklet, given away free with the Wild West Weekly *in 1938, is Jimmie Davis's 'Nobody's Darlin' But Mine'. The introduction to the 18 songs states that they "all have one thing in common – their sad haunting melody. There is a good reason for this. The hill-billy folk are poor and primitive. For long stretches when riding the range they never see a human face… the words have in them all the loneliness of the lonely prairies." Marketing, 30s style: the concept of hillbilly music was built on the premise of 'old timey' tunes, played by 'old timey' people.*

White Country Blues

Jimmie Davis was far from the only white country musician who had roots in the black country blues tradition. Segregation may have been a painful fact of life between the World Wars, but there were definitely not six degrees of separation between black and white country musicians. In fact, the lineage of white country music is interwoven with the music of Southern black people. Poor whites and poor blacks grew up sharing the same dirt, the same hardships and the same chords.

One of the earliest – maybe even the first – country music acts to record was Fiddlin' Bob Haines & his Four Aces, who made an Edison cylinder of 'Arkansas Traveler' in the early 1900s. Like many of their black counterparts, they performed in tent shows, vaudeville and country dances. Fiddlin' Bob and the artists who followed him were labelled 'hillbilly' musicians, which in the minds of the record companies neatly differentiated them from 'race' artists.

In 1922, Eck Robertson from North

> *I was born in 1923 and grew up on the farm in Florence, Alabama, which is 150 miles east of Memphis. That's when I became so interested in the Blues. I sensed and felt things from being around black people, country people and desperate people in that repressed age. There was nothing I heard that was more entertaining, more attractive to me as a child, aged six or seven years old, than hearing black people singing, whether it be in the corn patch or cotton field*
>
> Sam Phillips (Sun Records)

Eck Robertson
Recorded the first 'country' instrumental tune.

Who really wrote 'You Are My Sunshine'?

It was a multi-million seller, recorded in more than 30 languages by 350 artists, among them Bing Crosby and Gene Autry. But more recently it has been claimed that Jimmie Davis did not actually write the song at all. Part of the mystery is that Jimmie claims to have written and recorded the song in 1931, but prevented its release because he was unhappy with the performance. Research has suggested that Paul Rice of the Georgia-based Rice Brothers Gang actually wrote the melody of the song, while the words were penned by a woman who listened to the Brothers' radio show. When the Rice Brothers recorded it in September 1939, they could not remember her name, so Paul Rice was listed as the song's writer.

It seems that Davis then bought the song for around $100 from Rice, and interestingly there was no composer credit on Jimmie's original 1940 recording. In any event, Jimmie Davis claimed to his dying day that *he* wrote the song: given the size of the royalty cheques, he would have been stupid to have done otherwise.

WHITE NO RICHER THAN BLACK

Many black artists failed to make much money from their recordings, but it was not simply a matter of colour prejudice. Vernon Dalhart benefited little from his recording career, although estimates put his sales in excess of 10 million. He wound up working as a hotel clerk in Connecticut.

Georgia recorded 'Arkansas Traveler' for the Victor label, which is considered the first 'country' instrumental record. Soon afterwards, Fiddlin' John Carson cut 'Little Old Log Cabin In The Lane', the first country vocal record. But before these recordings were made, another country artist had recorded 'Lonesome Road Blues', though it was not released until after Fiddlin' John had enjoyed some success. The singer was Henry Whitter, from Galex, Virginia, who belatedly achieved a sizeable hit with his record, which was in a standard blues form. It is believed that this song had long been in the repertoire of both black and white performers.

Like many blues performers, Whitter performed on street corners, even handing out photos of himself. It seems that his approach may have been a little more direct than that of his black counterparts:

> *'Howdy do? I guess you've heard tell of me. I'm the celebrated Mr Henry Whitter of OKeh recording fame. I made 'The Wreck Of The 97' what it is today. They's been millions of copies of it sold. OKeh gave me a good contract and that record made me barrel o' money. I got money to burn, by God!'*

FIDDLIN' JOHN CARSON
Despite his name, Fiddlin' John has passed into the history of country music as the first man to release a vocal record in the style.

The record Henry was referring to was the B-side of his hit, actually called 'The Wreck Of The Southern Old 97', which was also extremely popular with Southern audiences. It was covered by the Texan singer Vernon Dalhart on both the Edison and Victor labels, coupled with 'The Prisoner's Song', and became the biggest selling hillbilly recording to date.

HILLBILLY BLUES

These men were the pioneers of country music, who recorded what were known at the time as 'hick songs'. Soon this trickle of white country artists became a flood, as regular releases appeared by Riley Puckett, a blind guitarist, Roba Stanley, the first woman to record a country song, Carl Sprauge, who was the first to record 'cowboy music' rather than folk-based songs, and Uncle Dave Macon who first recorded in 1924. Macon

Henry Whitter

came from Tennessee, and learned many of his songs from black vaudevillians, as well as country people, both performers and amateurs. He recorded 'Hill Billie Blues', a reworking of WC Handy's 'Hesitation Blues', and other titles such as 'Backwater Blues'. Whereas many of Macon's contemporaries merely used the word 'blues' to spice up their repertoire, much as earlier performers had used 'rag', Uncle Dave was true to the tradition of the Blues.

The field recording trips made by the major labels documented both black and white artists, so by 1927 a number of white blues players had emerged. Doc Boggs, for instance, a banjo player from Virginia, recorded 12 sides in 1927 and 1928. Then there were Darby and Tarlton: Darby was a singer who learned from black performers in Columbus, Georgia, while Tarlton was an excellent slide guitar player. Both Jimmie Davis in the 1940s and Willie Nelson in the 1960s covered their biggest hit, 'Columbus Stockade Blues'. When they recorded the original, Darby and Tarlton opted to take a session fee of $75 rather than a royalty on the sales – just another case of the record company winning out over the artist.

A year before Darby and Tarlton made their first record, a miner and part-time slide guitar player from West Virginia emerged on the OKeh label. Twenty-nine-year-old Frank Hutchinson had learned much of his material from a local black singer, Bill Hunt, and honed his slide guitar skills (using a penknife as a slide) from black guitarist Henry Vaughn, neither of whom ever recorded. Hutchison's debut was 'Worried Blues', which he learned

Frank Hutchinson

No Depression in Heaven

Amazingly, Jimmie Rodgers was not the only bona fide future legend who auditioned for Ralph Peer in Bristol, Tennessee. Two women and a man, who lived a 'secluded lifestyle' in Maces Springs, Virginia, also answered his advertisement. As Peer recalled, "He's dressed in overalls and the women are country people from 'way back there.' But as soon as I heard Sara's voice, that was it, I knew it was going to be wonderful." The three backwoods singers were the Carter Family: AP, his wife Sara, and their sister-in-law, Maybelle. They recorded six sides at Bristol – the beginning of a 25-year, off-and-on career which produced more than 300 recordings, and spawned a

The Carter Family

country music dynasty.

The Carter Family's influence is almost incalculable. Without their example, it is doubtful if musicians like Bill Monroe would have been able to invent bluegrass, for instance. The Carters inspired Bob Dylan, Woody Guthrie, Doc Watson, and just about everyone in country and folk music. Their recording of 'Worried Man Blues' became a country standard. Maybelle's daughters Anita and June both recorded, taking over the mantle of the Carter Family in the 1960s, which was also when June married country star Johnny Cash. June's daughter Carlene and Cash's daughter Rosanne began by singing with their parents, but both women then launched highly successful solo careers in country music.

The great Depression now is spreading.
God's word declared it would be so.
I'm going where there's no depression.
I'll leave this world of toil and trouble.
My homes in heaven, I'm going there.

'No Depression in Heaven'

JIMMIE RODGERS

"Rodgers crystallized the white blues form and ensured its future in country music." (*Tony Russell,* Blacks, Whites And Blues, *1970).*

MARKETING RODGERS

So popular was Rodgers at the height of his fame that when people went shopping at their local general store, they were said to ask for: "A pound of butter, a dozen eggs, and the latest Jimmie Rodgers record."

from Hunt. Over the next few years he cut some brilliant sides, that ranged from folk songs and rags to comedy songs and more blues sides – a total of 30 songs, which included 'Stackalee', 'John Henry', 'Miners Blues' and 'Logan County Blues'.

THE FATHER OF COUNTRY MUSIC

Alhough Hutchison was the first white country player to perform a blues-dominated repertoire, it was a Mississipian who was second to none in establishing the popularity of the Blues with white audiences. Jimmie Rodgers, who has passed into legend as the 'Father of Country Music', was living in Asheville, North Carolina, in 1927 when he came to the attention of Ralph Peer, the man who recorded Mamie Smith's 'Crazy Blues'. Now working for Victor, Peer decided to undertake field trips to Atlanta, Savannah, Bristol, and Memphis. He advertised for artists in the local Bristol newspaper and received an encouraging response.

Amongst the applicants was Jimmie Rodgers, who telephoned to say that he sang with a string band. Peer offered him an audition at the old furniture store he was using as a studio, and was immediately struck with one aspect of Jimmie's sound: "I thought that his yodel alone might spell success", he said later. They cut two sides in Bristol, and then Peer asked Jimmie to come to Camden, New Jersey. There they recorded 'Blue Yodel No. 1', also known as 'T For Texas', which became the first of Jimmie's many hit records. His falsetto yodel was similar in style to Tommy Johnson's vocals, and some historians have claimed that Rodgers actually saw Johnson perform.

WHITE MAN GONE BLACK

As a young man, Jimmie Rodgers had worked with his father on the railroad. Rodgers senior was a foreman in charge of a black gang, known as 'Gandy Dancers', who were responsible for repairing the track. Jimmie learned many of his blues songs from the crew, and was inspired by their work songs and hollers. Later he found work as a brakeman, which earned him the nickname 'The Singing Brakeman', although he only worked on the railroad for a few months, as his health was somewhat fragile.

Described at the time as a 'white man gone black', Jimmie was an inspiration for both black and white country performers. 'Blue Yodel No. 1' was followed by a string of

"Jimmie Rodgers connected with you. He came from the same place as the black folks that were singing the Blues"

SAM PHILLIPS

other 'Blue Yodels', each with a number and an alternate title. 1931's 'Blue Yodel No. 8' was 'Mule Skinner Blues', while on 'Blue Yodel No. 9' Jimmie was accompanied by jazz legend Louis Armstrong. By the time of his death from a tubercular haemorrhage in May 1933, Rodgers had cut 110 sides, around a third of which were blues-based. Such was his dedication to his music that, just two days before his death, Jimmie was in a New York studio, cutting his final 12 sides.

The Steel Guitar Wizard

Jimmie Rodgers had many imitators, including Cliff Carlisle, who was the first man to be recorded playing a Dobro guitar. Cliff was more than just an imitator, he was also a brilliant slide guitar player. But many of his recordings either had a direct link to Jimmie or were strongly derivative, like 'Memphis Yodel', a cover of a Rodgers 1928 record. Songs like 'Hobo Blues' were so similar to Jimmie Rodgers' train songs that you would be forgiven for thinking they were covers. Cliff and his long-time partner Wilbur Ball, who played Spanish guitar and sang harmony, also covered the Darby and Tarleton hit, 'Columbus Stockade Blues'. In 1931 Cliff accompanied Rodgers on a yodelling blues track, 'Looking For A New Mama', and later that year they teamed up to tour Kentucky, Illinois and Michigan. By 1934 Cliff's brother Bill had replaced Wilbur; they cut 'That Nasty Swing' in 1936, five months before Robert Johnson's 'Phonograph Blues', which is very similar in feel. 'That Nasty Swing' was another of those songs with thinly veiled sexual imagery, as Cliff sang about 'winding the motor' and 'putting his needle in the hole'; white country and black country blues had more in common than just 12 shared bars. In 1937 Cliff cut 'Trouble Minded Blues', a remake of Chippie Hill's 1926 recording, 'Trouble In Mind'. Cliff eventually recording more than 300 sides in the 1930s and 1940s, and besides his records he was able to promote the sale of his songbooks via his radio appearances. By the 1950s Cliff had retired, but he did make a brief comeback in the 1960s, even recording once again with Wilbur Ball. The man billed as the 'Yodelling Hobo' died in Kentucky in 1983, aged 79.

Left: 'The Carter Family and Jimmie Rodgers In Texas' sung by . . . The Carter Family and Jimmie Rodgers.

Jimmie Rodgers
He was elected one of the first members of the Country Music Hall Of Fame in 1961.

It Don't Mean a Thang if it Ain't Got That Swing

Jimmie's Blue Yodels influenced another genre of white country music. Known as Western swing, this exciting new style originated in Texas, and its first big stars were Milton Brown and Bob Wills. Both started out as members of the Aladdin Laddies and the Light Crust Doughboys, performing on

"Our second British No. 1 was 'Little Red Rooster', which we recorded on 2nd September, 1964, at Regent Sound in London. It was written by Willie Dixon and had originally been recorded by Howlin' Wolf in 1961. It followed in a tradition of songs in both white and black country blues that celebrated the cockerel. As I became more interested in the Blues and discovered Charley Patton, I found that he had cut 'Banty Rooster Blues' at his first session in 1929. Cliff Carlisle cut 'Shanghai Rooster Yodel', 'Chicken Roost Blues' and 'It Takes An Old Hen To Deliver The Goods', and Casey Bill Weldon made 'Rooster Blues' in 1937. Brian Jones really liked our recording of 'Little Red Rooster' and I loved his very simple slide guitar solo"

Bill Wyman

RIDE WITH BOB

'Brain Cloudy Blues' was derivative of Kokomo Arnold's 'Milk Cow Blues' from 1934. Texan legends Asleep At The Wheel recorded two albums in the 1990s with star guests, as a tribute to Bob Wills. On the second album was 'Milk Cow Blues' featuring Tim McGraw, and WC Handy's 'St. Louis Blues' with Merle Haggard. The album also included covers of Emmett Miller's 'I Ain't Got Nobody' and 'Right Or Wrong'.

their sponsor's radio programmes. They later recorded with the Fort Worth Doughboys, and by 1934 each had his own band: Milton his Musical Brownies and Bob his Texas Playboys.

Western swing drew influences from a broad musical palette. In his book *Lone Star Swing*, Duncan McLean describes the music as "a chilli-pot of New Orleans jazz, old country fiddling, big-band swing, ragtime, blues, pop and mariachi . . . it dominated Texas, Oklahoma, Louisiana, and beyond - all the way from San Francisco in the west, Memphis in the east - from the mid-Thirties till mid-Elvis. This was Western swing."

Milton Brown and his Musical Brownies

Recording for Bluebird between 1934 and 1936, Milton Brown produced some brilliant sides before he died of pneumonia, as a result of a punctured lung sustained in a 1936 car accident. Milton's lasting legacy was that he introduced Bob Dunn into his Brownies. Dunn played amplified steel guitar - revolutionary back in 1934.

A-HA, IT'S BOB WILLS

Bob Wills worked on radio station KVOO in Tulsa, Oklahoma, besides being the resident band in a Tulsa ballroom. Signing the band to the Brunswick label, Bob established his Playboys as the premier Western Swing outfit after Milton's untimely death. Fiddle-playing Bob always employed the very best musicians, including singer Tommy Duncan. He was very open to black music, reworking many blues songs including 'Sitting On Top Of The World', 'Corrine Corrina' and 'Brain Cloudy Blues'. It is said that he once even rode 20 miles on a mule to see Bessie Smith perform.

By the late 1930s, Western Swing had been adopted by Hollywood, the result being an inevitable 'smoothing' of both its subject

matter and style. This took the genre further away from its blues influences, but Bob Wills himself never lost touch with the Blues. In the early 1940s he starred in a number of movies, and even after the war he still dominated the genre. His last big hit, 'Faded Love', came in 1950, but he continued making records through the 1950s, though Western swing was in terminal decline, both commercially and artistically. Two heart attacks and a massive stroke in the 1960s confined Wills to a wheelchair, effectively signalling the end of an era. Inducted into the County and Western Hall of Fame in 1968, Wills has been an influence on just about every Texan country musician since, from Willie Nelson to Asleep At The Wheel and George Strait to Waylon Jennings. Waylon paid his tribute with 'Bob Wills Is Still The King' in 1975, the year that Wills died.

While Bob Wills was certainly the greatest exponent of Western swing, he was not the only one who sought inspiration from the Blues. The Tune Wranglers covered Tampa Red's 'Tight Like That' in 1936, Jimmie Revard & his Oklahoma Playboys cut 'Big Daddy Blues' the same year, the Nite Owls recorded 'Married Man Blues' in 1937, and Buddy Jones, who had recorded with Jimmie Davis, cut 'Mean Old Lonesome Blues' also in 1937. In 1939, Buddy cut 'Rockin' Rollin' Mama', which may not have had a backbeat but was definitely heading in the right direction. Those Western swingers loved their blues, and there were plenty of blues people who loved Western swing.

'Emmett Miller is one of the most intriguing and profoundly important men in the history of country music'

NICK TOSCHES,
THE TWISTED ROOTS OF ROCK AND ROLL

LOVESICK BLUES

As Willie Nelson said, 'Until Hank Williams came along, it was just Bob Wills. But Hank could not have emerged without the example of a white country performer who performed in blackface make-up, sang the Blues. . . and yodelled, too.

'I Ain't Got Nobody', the song that Bob Wills cut in 1935, was a yodelling blues reminiscent of Jimmie Rodgers, but it was originally recorded in 1928 by Emmett Miller. Miller had first recorded for Okeh in 1924 and remained with them throughout

EMMETT MILLER
Hardly a household name, but arguably one of the most influential men in country music.

the decade. He later recorded four sides for Bluebird in 1936, before disappearing from the recording scene, while continuing to perform in vaudeville until the early 1950s.

Born in Georgia, Emmett was performing on the vaudeville circuit by 1919 as a blackface performer. In 1925 he moved to Asheville, the town from which Jimmie Rodgers would emerge. Some historians have speculated that Emmett might even have taught Jimmie to yodel. While in Asheville, he recorded what became his theme song, 'Lovesick Blues'. He later cut 'Right Or Wrong', which became a Western swing standard in the hands of Bob Wills - who later quoted Emmett Miller as one of his major influences.

THE FIRST COUNTRY SUPERSTAR

In 1949, the young Hank Williams also cut 'Lovesick Blues', the record that made him a country superstar. He was 25 years old and hailed from Alabama, the son of a World War I veteran who had been in hospital for most of Hank's early life. To add to his woes, the young Hiram King Williams suffered from spina bifida as a child, he could not read or write, and he had a limited vocabulary . . . but he was immensely talented. As a child he learned music from a black man, Rufe Payne, in Greenville, where he grew up.

By eighteen Hank had formed the Drifting Cowboys and was playing regularly

The young Hank Williams.

on local radio in Montgomery, where he and his mother now lived. Two years later he met and married a woman named Audrey, who

> ❛ *Without a doubt my father learned 'Lovesick Blues' somehow from Emmett Miller. It was either by record or he heard him perform it in person at a minstrel show* ❜
>
> Hank Williams, Jr

played bass in his band and took over as his manager, though this mixture of romance and business was destined to end in conflict. Hank cut his first records in 1946, and a year later 'Move It On Over' became his first country hit. Then at a time when 'Lovesick Blues' stayed at No. 1 on the hillbilly chart for 16 weeks, Hank played the legendary *Grand Ole Opry* radio show and was given six encores. He rapidly became the biggest star in country music history.

There was a string of hits thereafter, including the No. 1 'Long Gone Lonesome Blues'. Like some of the pre-war blues singers, Hank had a parallel career singing religious material, calling himself Luke The Drifter. But despite his religious faith, Hank was ill-equipped for stardom, and he was soon dependent on drink to see him through. By 1952 he and Audrey had separated, and Hank had discovered drugs. With his career in disarray, Hank Williams died on New Year's Day 1953, his body exhausted by drugs and alcohol. His funeral became a national event, drawing enormous crowds, while a string of country stars turned out to honour the man dubbed the 'Father of Contemporary Country Music'.

All of these country pioneers and legends drew much of their inspiration from the Blues. While the Blues went to the city, white country music somehow stayed put in the country. It soon came under the control of the rhinestone mafia. Nashville was home to the Holy Grail, and the Blues was written out of the official history of country music. And that's the way it remained until country music's outlaws rode into town in the late 60s. As outlaw pioneer Waylon Jennings sang in 1974:

> ❛ *I don't think Hank done it this way* ❜

Low Down Blues
Hank certainly did it his way. The very antithesis of Nashville's sanitised country music image, he was the Father of Outlaw Blues.

Hank Williams, the father of Outlaw Blues.

THE BOOGIE BOYS AND THE SWINGING LEFT HAND

THE BLUES IS USUALLY ASSOCIATED with the guitar, but it was the piano which was responsible for giving the music a more sophisticated, urban sound. Leroy Carr and Scrapper Blackwell had already used the instrument to create a distinctive style, which was very definitely not country blues. Most blues pianists learned to play in the country, or in small towns where pianos were a standard feature of barrelhouses and other places of ill repute. The obvious problem was that you could not take a piano with you on the road; a guitar was much more portable if you wanted to hobo on the railroads. That's why the guitar became the trademark of country blues.

In the very early days, the piano acted as an accompaniment to the theatre blues singers. For example, Perry Bradford played with Mamie Smith on 'Crazy Blues', and later she was accompanied by a whole string of pianists. Bessie Smith worked with the ubiquitous Clarence Williams for a while, and then Fletcher Henderson. Ma Rainey used Lovie Austin and later Tampa Red's pianist Georgia Tom Dorsey. A whole slew of piano players made a comfortable living out of the Blues during the 1920s, either as solo accompanists or as part of a small backing band.

These early piano players tended to be rooted firmly in a 'city' style, and in the early days there was little evidence of what a purely 'Southern piano' style sounded like. But Hersal Thomas, Sippie Wallace's brother, did record a piano roll in 1924 on his seminal piece, 'The Fives', when he was just 14! Two years later he was dead from food poisoning, having left a tragically small legacy. Another pianist, Will Ezell from Shreveport, recorded just 17 sides from 1927 to 1929. He was the first to use 'boogie' in the title of a record; September 1929's 'Pitchin' Boogie'. What happened to him isn't known, but he backed Lucille Bogan, and Bertha Henderson amongst others. Paramount Records obviously thought enough of him to include him as one of the Paramount All Stars who recorded in October 1929.

WHAT EXACTLY IS BOOGIE WOOGIE?

Boogie woogie is typically 12-bar blues with a consistent bass pattern that is played with the left hand, while the right hand carries the melody. The greatest boogie pianists were wonderful improvisers. Most of all, boogie woogie is music that makes it impossible not to tap your feet or hands. It's about as infectious as piano music can get. Jazz, rock'n'roll and everything in between were influenced by boogie woogie.

COW COW BLUES

The first piano player to achieve something of a breakthrough in his own right was Cow Cow Davenport, although he too started out as an accompanist, to Dora Carr in 1924. Back then he was calling himself Charles, but he acquired his nickname from a seminal boogie woogie piece in which his piano imitated a train. 'Cow Cow Blues', recorded in 1928, evolved from ragtime, which Davenport had played in New Orleans and Atlanta brothels, as well as barrelhouses and dances. With its walking bass style, 'Cow Cow Blues' has become one of the most enduring boogie woogie records of all time.

Davenport recorded extensively during 1928 and 1929, and as if Cow Cow wasn't a strange enough name, he also called himself Bat The Hummingbird on some releases, as well as the slightly less unusual Georgia Grinder. Silenced by the Depression, he did briefly record again in 1938, although he had suffered an apoplexy attack and could no longer play the piano. He returned to the studio in the 1940s and died in 1956. A prolific songwriter, he (like many fellow performers) sold his publishing rights for a fee and received no royalties, with the result that his breakthrough recording and talents brought him scant reward in his old age.

PINETOP'S BOOGIE

Five months after the recording of 'Cow Cow Blues', the 24-year-old Clarence Smith entered Vocalion's studio in Chicago. Over the course of three weeks he cut eight sides before, on December 29th, recording

Cow Cow Davenport

Charles Edward Davenport was 30 years old when he accompanied Dora Carr.

something they deemed worthy of release…and what a release! 'Pinetop's Boogie Woogie' is considered one of the most important boogie woogie pieces to emerge from the 1920s, and it has influenced every boogie pianist who has followed since.

It was Cow Cow who suggested that Pinetop should move to Chicago from Pittsburgh, where he had worked with Ma Rainey. A native of Alabama, Smith was self-taught and like 'Cow Cow' had worked his way around the circuit. Besides writing and performing a classic, Pinetop also takes the credit as the first person to use the term 'boogie woogie'.

Two weeks after his first session, Pinetop was back in the studio to cut some more sides. There was one more session on 13th March, but two days later tragedy struck. He was playing piano in a Chicago night spot when he was hit in the chest by a stray bullet, the innocent victim of someone else's argument. He was just 25 years old.

When Pinetop moved to Chicago, he lived in an apartment house with Meade Lux Lewis and Albert Ammons, both of whom would redefine boogie woogie in the mid-1930s. Lewis did record for Paramount in December 1927, but inexplicably they did not release his recording of 'Honky Tonk Train Blues' until 1929. Recession-hit America was not receptive, and it was almost six years before Lewis got another shot at stardom. He recorded 'Honky Tonk Train Blues' again in 1935; it is actually very similar to 'Pinetop's Boogie Woogie', perhaps because the two men had regularly jammed together.

Big City Boogie

In the second half of the 1930s Lewis, Albert Ammons, and Pete Johnson became the rage. Ammons first recorded in January 1936 with his Rhythm Kings. Pete Johnson's first sides were made for the Library of Congress, along with Ammons and Lewis, in December 1938. This was five days after the three pianists had played together at John Hammond's ground breaking *From Spirituals To Swing* concerts in New York City's Carnegie Hall. On stage the three boogie masters performed 'Cavalcade Of Boogie' together, and quickly brought people out of their seats. It was the beginning of boogie woogie's golden era, which lasted into the early 1940s. For the next three years, all three men recorded regularly, sometimes together. Ammons' signature piece was 'Boogie Woogie Stomp', while Pete's was 'Roll 'Em Pete'. Pete also backed Big Joe Turner at Carnegie Hall, and on some of his recordings. They got their break after

Pete Johnson

Born in Kansas City, he learned drums before piano.

Albert Ammons (far left) and Elliot Paul (right)

At Cafe Society, sophisticated New Yorkers admire that boogie woogie beat.

FATS WALLER

FACT FILE

BORN: *21st May, 1904 New York City*

DIED: *15th December, 1943, Kansas City*

INSTRUMENT: *Piano, Organ, Harmonium, Celeste*

FIRST RECORDED: *1922*

INFLUENCED: *Every piano player*

THOMAS WRIGHT WALLER, the King of the Harlem stride pianists, was born the son of a preacher in New York City. His first musical experiences were playing the harmonium for his father's services. It was not long before he was entertaining his classmates with his piano playing, accompanied by his trademark 'eye rolling' and funny faces.

After leaving school he began to earn a living playing the organ to accompany silent films. It was at this time that he met James P Johnson, the writer of the 'Charleston'. Johnson began to coach young Thomas and he was soon playing Harlem house rent parties and in 1922 he recorded his first piano roll. Soon Waller was writing songs with Andy Razaf and their partnership produced such gems as 'Honeysuckle Rose' and 'Ain't Misbehavin''. The latter was written for the 1929 Broadway show *Hot Chocolates*, which featured Louis Armstrong.

> *"I love Fats Waller. His playing is brilliant and his humour added so much without ever taking anything away from his musical genius. Like many others, I have found him an inspiration. If you ever get the chance to see one of the films in which he appeared... don't miss it!"*
>
> BILL WYMAN

While his piano playing become an inspiration to many, it was not until Fats began singing in 1930 that he found real fame. In 1932, he joined radio station WLW at Cincinnati, where he broadcast the *'Fats' Waller Rhythm Club*, which did much to further his reputation. It was in 1934 at a party given by the composer George Gershwin that Fats got his biggest break. Fats entertained the party with his singing, playing, and clowning and a Victor Records executive offered Fats a lucrative recording contract. Most of Fats' records for Victor were released as Fats Waller and his Rhythm... and what a rhythm. It was his phrasing and piano style that secured him his place in the story of the Blues. Virtually every one of his piano-playing contemporaries, and those that followed, owed something to Fats' style. In all he made over 500 recordings, often recording as many as ten sides in a single day.

In 1935 Fats made his movie debut in *Hooray For Love*, followed in 1936 by *King of Burlesque* and in 1943, the year of his death, he co starred in *Stormy Weather* with Lena Horne and Cab Calloway. Fats was a renowned drinker and certainly this contributed to his death, aged just 39, on board a train at Union Station, Kansas City, in 1943.

ESSENTIAL RECORDINGS

CLASSIC SONGS

'Ain't Misbehavin'' 1929
'Honeysuckle Rose' 1935
'It's A Sin To Tell A Lie' 1936

THE SOURCE

The Very Best of Fats Waller BMG

appearing on Benny Goodman's radio programme.

Johnson stayed in New York, where he teamed up with Ammons and Lewis on a more formal basis as the Boogie Woogie Trio. The three of them became the house act at the Cafe Society Club, New York's premier jazz and blues venue throughout 1939 and 1940. Johnson and Ammons often performed as a duo in the 1940s, but in 1952 Pete lost a finger in an accident, which effectively ended his career. He died in 1967. Ammons also performed with Benny Goodman, Harry James, and Lionel Hampton, joining Hamp's band in 1949. It was a tragically short stay, as he died in December that year. After the boogie craze waned for a second time at the end of 1941, Lewis moved to Los Angeles, playing clubs as well as recording. He performed at low-key venues throughout the 1950s and died in a car crash in 1964.

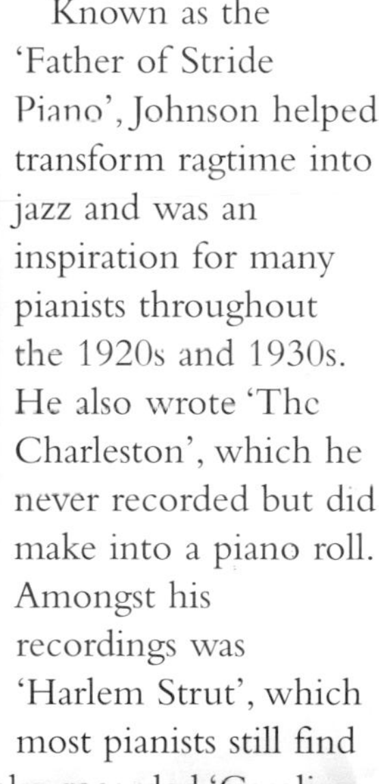

James P Johnson
'The Father of Stride Piano'

A fourth pianist starred in *From Spirituals To Swing* in 1938: James P Johnson. He was a decade-and-a-half older than the three boogie boys, and his playing owed something to another age. Johnson came from Harlem and by 1915 was already regarded as one of the greatest piano players in the land. The master of the stride piano cut his first piano rolls in 1916 and first recorded in 1921. Most of Johnson's records were jazz or ragtime but he also backed Bessie Smith and Ethel Waters.

Known as the 'Father of Stride Piano', Johnson helped transform ragtime into jazz and was an inspiration for many pianists throughout the 1920s and 1930s. He also wrote 'The Charleston', which he never recorded but did make into a piano roll. Amongst his recordings was 'Harlem Strut', which most pianists still find very difficult, and he also recorded 'Carolina Shout', from which the young Duke Ellington learned to play. Johnson also performed for the Library of Congress on Christmas Eve 1938, and one of the tunes he cut, 'Ethel Waters Blues', was a tribute to the Blues lady who was by then appearing with Duke Ellington's Orchestra. James P Johnson was also a mentor for young Thomas Waller, who would become better known to the world as 'Fats'.

Parlor Piano
Albums of great piano playing are regularly reissued

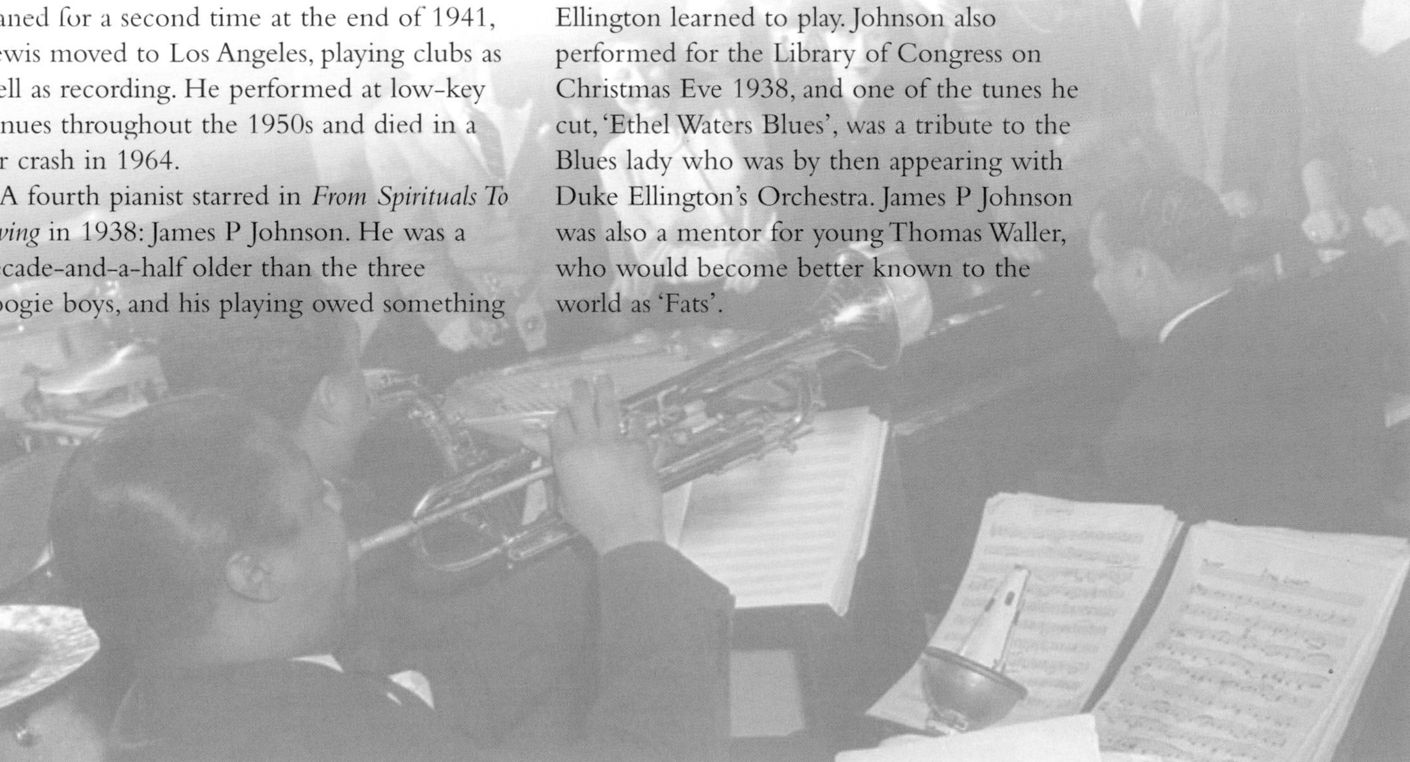

ROOSEVELT SYKES

Sykes was nicknamed the Honey Dripper when he was a young man because he had a reputation as a ladies' man!

STUMP AND THE HONEY DRIPPER

The third piano-playing Johnson to make an impact on the scene was James 'Stump' Johnson. Given his nickname because he was both short and stocky, this man from Elmer, Arkansas, was more typical of the blues piano players, as he was as much a singer as a pianist. He was the first man to have a hit with 'Duck's Yas Yas Yas' in early 1929. Recorded in New York when he was 23 it was his biggest-selling number. He also recorded a couple of sides in 1932, singing with Roosevelt Sykes on piano. Besides Leroy Carr, Sykes was the major piano-playing blues star to emerge from this era.

Sykes was the epitome of the urban blues pianist, equally comfortable as an accompanist and a solo artist. He was always neat in his playing, with a style that included jazzy fills. He learned his trade in the barrelhouses of Helena, Arkansas, and honed them to perfection when he moved to St. Louis in the mid-1920s. His first release, '44 Blues', did much to establish his reputation, although he often recorded for different labels under the inevitable pseudonyms. Unlike Cow Cow, he stuck to more traditional names like Dobby Bragg, Willie Kelly, or Easy Papa Johnson; fortunately he dropped the over-familiar Johnson name after just one session.

Sykes was still able to record, albeit sporadically, during the depths of the Depression, which is a testament to his popularity. He returned to the limelight in 1936, with another pseudonym - The Honey Dripper. That was the name of a song he recorded in New York in February 1936, with Kokomo Arnold playing alongside him, and it became one of his biggest hits. The

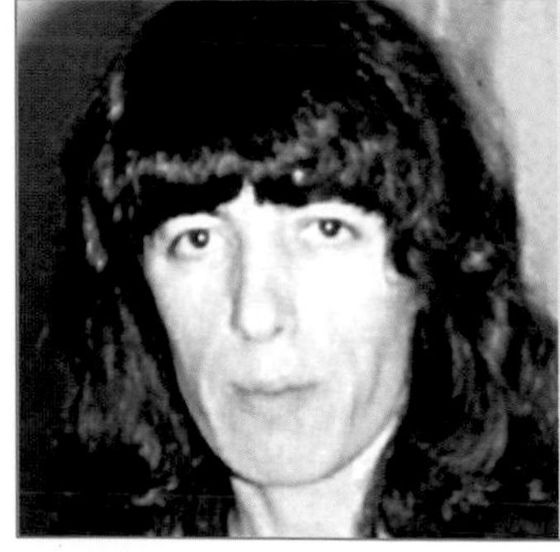

'On 26th June, 1972, while we were on tour in the USA, I went out to dinner with Charlie Watts, Mick Taylor, Ahmet Ertegun and Truman Capote. We had an excellent meal and then went to an old barn-like recording studio. Mick and Keith were already there, along with the rest of our tour entourage. Ahmet had arranged a wonderful party for us, where Snooks Eaglin, Professor Longhair, and a New Orleans Street Marching Band performed. Best of all, though, was Roosevelt Sykes, who played brilliantly and reminded me of Ian Stewart our piano player. You would never have thought he was 66! I finally got back to the hotel around 2.30am, having had a great evening and the chance to see one of the legends of pre-war blues.'

BILL WYMAN

following year he cut 'The Night Time Is The Right Time', which has become a blues standard. In the 1940s he moved to Chicago, where he continued to record solo, in addition to working as a first-rate accompanist. By 1954 he was living in New Orleans, still recording and playing live, and the following year he cut a wonderful (and influential) version of Robert Johnson's 'Sweet Home Chicago' with Dave Bartholomew, Fats Domino's producer. He enjoyed something of a renaissance in the 1960s, visiting Britain in 1961 to play with Chris Barber's Jazz Band, and appearing in the American Folk Blues Festivals of 1965 and 1966. He offered the audience the opportunity of seeing one of the few pre-war legends still active on the blues scene. While his powers began to decline, he was still an inspiration until his death in 1984.

Sykes' skills as an accompanist were always in demand. In June 1930, at the Hotel Sinton in Cincinnati, Ohio, Roosevelt Sykes played on a session by Walter Davis, whom he had brought in from St Louis, in his capacity as a part-time talent scout. The four sides they cut were the first of more than 100 that Davis would record for Victor and Bluebird over the next decade. By 1935 Walter was accompanying himself on piano, in a straightforward but effective style. He could put across good lyrics in a melancholic voice, and this was the basis for his not inconsiderable success in the 1930s. Songs like 'Ashes In My Whiskey', on which he was accompanied by Henry Townsend's excellent guitar playing, exemplified his approach. Maybe it was a 'sign of the times', but melancholia was very definitely 'in'. After the war, Davis's career never really picked up, despite some sporadic recording. He turned to the church and worked as a hotel receptionist in St Louis, where he died in 1963.

Walter Davis

He often accompanied Big Joe Williams and Henry Townsend.

How Come the Devil has All the Good Music?

Few people would disagree that the Blues were the definitive soundtrack to an era which almost brought America to its knees. Gradually during the 1930s, economic conditions began to improve, although the Depression would not truly end until America entered World War II.

This period of economic and social turmoil was vital in the development of the Blues, which was about to undergo a marked change of direction, and emerge as a much more recognisable forerunner of the music we know today. After the Depression, the Blues became more varied in style, while the foundations for its electrification were also being laid down.

But while things were changing in the cities there was a man in the Delta, that dark place, who was making a deal with the devil - or so people said. A man who would become an inspiration and a legend, as well as a conduit for others to make untold fortunes from the Blues. But before he came along, there was the little question of the devil's son-in-law.

Barrelhouse Blues

Bill Wyman has collected many blues piano albums down the years.

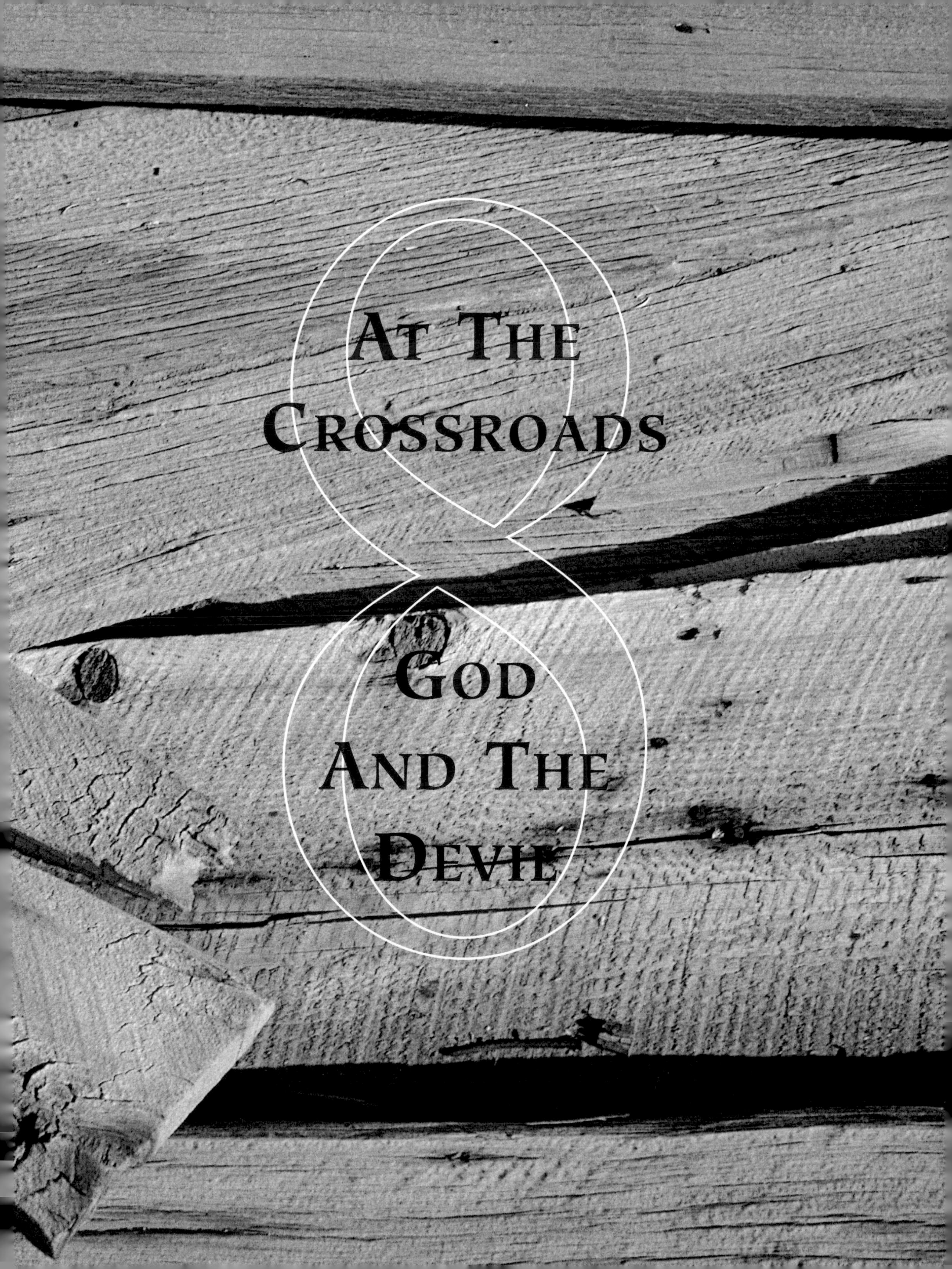

8

At The Crossroads

God And The Devil

Life is A Dirty Deal

As America's economy strengthened in the wake of Roosevelt's 'New Deal', certain blues artists found they had a new deal of their own. For some of those who maintained a recording career through the depths of the Depression, it was a matter of luck; while for others, it was down to their unstoppable talent.

There was a change, too, in the way that the business of the Blues was conducted. New record labels entered the fray. The English-owned company, Decca Records, introduced the 35-cent record in September 1934, helping to stimulate the market. Of more significance was the introduction by Victor of its cheaper, Bluebird label in January 1933. Lester Melrose, talent scout and record producer, was to the Blues what Phil Spector, Sam Phillips, and Berry Gordy have been to their musical genres. He made things happen. He controlled the musical output of Bluebird in the pre-war years, creating the 'Bluebird Beat', the sound of the label. He decided who was recorded, what was recorded, and in many respects how it was recorded. He dictated the sessions and the musicians who played on them, which is one reason why musicians in the 1930s had such interwoven careers. Melrose had an even tighter grip on the financial aspects of the record business than most that followed him, as he also acted as a music publisher.

While Lester Melrose and his ilk grew rich on the Blues, the artists hardly seemed to benefit from their success. The fact that black artists were poorly paid was, in part, a reflection of the social status of the black community. While it was true that some white artists did not receive what was due to them, it was likely that if you were black, you *never* would. Segregation in the record industry was no subtler than in life.

Politics began to take, a small, but significant role in the Blues. While political lyrics had featured in the Blues they were, in the main, restricted to blacks singing to and about blacks. In the latter half of the 1930s, white liberal Americans began to come under the influence, as well as to influence the Blues.

This period of change would see an accelerating shift away from country blues to the urban big city blues. In this period of transition the Blues would, for the first time, sound like the ancestor of rock'n'roll. There was also the little matter of religion, the Devil, and the crossroads – a battle between

Rex Billiard hall
As black culture shifted from the county to the city, black people established their own network of clubs and bars.

the secular and the sacred that was never far from the heart of the Blues.

Dealing with the Devil

The myth of Satan, a man's soul, and the midnight meeting at a deserted Delta crossroads had not yet been invented when Peetie Wheatstraw staked his claim to the Devil's patronage. Peetie was a great singer, and an able pianist, who had only a limited repertoire of melodic ideas and lyrical topics. But he was one of the biggest stars of the late 1930s, recording more than 160 titles in the eleven years between September 1930 and his death. Peetie was popular because his lyrics were especially appealing to contemporary audiences, and his songs were enhanced by his exuberant delivery. Moaning, mumbling, and slurring, he certainly knew how to sell a song.

Little is known of Peetie's early life: his real name was William Bunch but no one is quite sure where he was born. Most likely it was four days before Christmas 1902 in Ripley, Tennessee, hometown of Hambone Willie and Sleepy John Estes. Early on he relocated to Arkansas, before moving to East St. Louis around 1929. He was a better guitarist than pianist, which is surprising given that he would later accompany a number of singers, including Kokomo Arnold, Jimmie Gordon, and Casey Bill Weldon, on the piano. From the outset, Peetie was canny in his choice of accompanying guitarists, beginning with Charlie Jordan (who had to walk with crutches, after being shot in the spine) and later Lonnie Johnson, while both Kokomo Arnold and Casey Bill also returned the favour.

Peetie's first recording was a duet with a mysterious man known only as Neckbones. A week after this one-off session, he began a five-year association by recording four songs with Charlie Jordan, which were credited to 'Peetie Wheatstraw'. Written underneath his name on the label was 'The Devil's Son-in-Law'.

Here and gone

By 1931 Peetie set about establishing his own legend when he switched to Bluebird to record four sides. His first cut, 'Devil's Son-in-Law', was backed with 'Peetie Wheatstraw', perhaps the most blatant piece of self-promotion in the history of the blues.

> *Now, if anybody asks you, baby, honey,*
> *now, who composed this song*
> *Now, now, will you please tell them*
> *it was Peetie Wheatstraw, mama,*
> *now, he's been here and gone*
>
> 'Peetie Wheatstraw'

Although the Depression had limited his opportunities to record, from March 1934 his career went into overdrive, and he made regular visits to the studio during the rest of the decade. In 1936 he cut 'The First Shall Be Last And The Last Shall Be First' and 'Deep Sea Love' for Decca, who mysteriously billed him on this record only as 'The

Peetie Wheatstraw on vinyl.

Peetie Wheatstraw

Peetie Wheatstraw
The picture (left) was most likely taken around 1934. Memphis Minnie's husband, Joe McCoy, was also photographed holding the same guitar.

High Sheriff from Hell'.

Popular interest in Peetie Wheatstraw's recordings may have waned in recent years, but at the time he was not only immensely popular, but also very influential on a host of performers who are still revered today – among them Robert Johnson, B.B. King, Champion Jack Dupree, Johnny Shines, Muddy Waters, and Big Joe Williams.

Our group around 1964 was called the Delta Blues Band. When we weren't doing that a guitarist and myself would go around all the local folk clubs playing 'Corinne Corinna', plus all those vulgar blues tunes, like Peetie Wheatstraw's stuff

ROBERT PLANT

The circumstances of Peetie's death are somewhat strange, and almost as confusing as his birth. There is no question that he died, along with two friends, at 11.30am on 21st December, 1941, when their car was hit by a train in East St. Louis. According to Big Joe Williams, who had been in the car with Peetie, but left to go home before the crash, they were all drunk. Less than a month before he died, Peetie's final recording session included 'Bring Me Flowers While I'm Living' and 'Hearse Man Blues' – shades of Leroy Carr's prophetic last session.

The Devil's Son-in-Law had a number of acolytes who traded on his image and his popularity. Floyd Council released a record as

WPA – THE PROJECT

In the wake of the New Deal, the Works Progress Administration (WPA) was set up to provide work for labourers as well as writers and artists. This federal relief programme attracted many thousands of out-of-work blacks and whites between 1935 and 1939.

Inevitably, given its importance to the black community, the project inspired several contemporary blues songs: 'WPA Blues' from 1936 by Big Bill Broonzy and Casey Bill Weldon; 'Project Highway' by the first Sonny Boy Williamson in 1937; and three songs by Peetie Wheatstraw, 'Working On The Project', 'New Working On The Project' and '304 Blues'.

I was working on the project,
begging the relief for shoes.
Because the rock and concrete, oooh well, well,
they's giving my feet the Blues

A perfect illustration of Peetie's style. It's very topical, and contains his trademark 'oooh well, well', which he liberally peppered throughout his recordings.

'The Devil's Daddy-in-Law'. Others appeared on record as 'Peetie Wheatstraw's Brother' or 'Peetie Wheatstraw's Buddy', and Decca used the name 'Peetie's Boy' on Robert Lee McCoy's last two releases.

The Original Kokomo Blues

In February 1936, the left-handed slide guitarist Kokomo Arnold accompanied Peetie Wheatstraw on record for the first time. But this was far from being Kokomo's first session, as he had recorded as far back as 1930 at the Memphis Auditorium for the Victor label, on the same day as Sleepy John Estes. Then 29 years old, the Georgia native was billed on his debut release as Gitfiddle Jim, a reference to his given name of James Arnold.

Arnold, who was living in Chicago and working as a bootlegger, did not cut another record for four years. Finally, back in the studio for Decca, he cut 'Old Original Kokomo Blues', from which he took his nickname. Robert Johnson later reworked the song as 'Sweet Home Chicago'. Arnold himself had based the song on 'Kokomo Blues', a 1928 recording by that other bootlegging guitarist, Scrapper Blackwell. On the flip side was 'Milk Cow Blues', which would later be reworked by many others, including Bob Wills and Elvis Presley.

Kokomo's excellent slide playing was what solidified his reputation, rather than the breadth and variety of his material. An in-demand session player, he worked with Roosevelt Sykes and the former Mrs. Lonnie Johnson, Mary Johnson, as well as Peetie. His short, but prolific career ended in 1938 after some kind of argument with Mayo Williams, who by this time was at Decca. Kokomo never recorded again, but enjoyed a brief revival in the 1960s until his death in 1968. And for his influence on the man around

James 'Kokomo' Arnold
Is he drinking his own bootleg liquor?

Kokomo: The Legend Lives On

Kokomo, a popular brand of 1920s coffee, has played a strange role in the annals of pop music. In 1961, pianist Jimmy Wisner called himself Kokomo and took 'Asia Minor', based on Greig's 'Piano Concerto', into the US Top 10, and No. 35 in Britain. Then, in 1975, a band named Kokomo enjoyed brief success on the rock circuit. Finally, in 1988, 24 years after their first US chart-topper, the Beach Boys scored their last US No. 1. It was written by Mike Love from the Beach Boys, John Phillips from the Mamas & Papas, Scott McKenzie, who had a huge hit with 'San Francisco (Be Sure To Wear Some Flowers In Your Hair)', and Terry Melcher, producer of Taj Mahal's first band, the Rising Sons.

'The Robins, a black doo-wop group in LA, cut 'Smokey Joe's Café', written by Lieber & Stoller. It influenced me a heck of a lot when I went to write 'Kokomo''

Mike Love of the Beach Boys

whom the legend of the crossroads was created – Robert Johnson – his place in the sun is guaranteed. And there was another musician associated with Peetie Wheatstraw who caused his own small controversy.

THE MYSTERY OF THE DISAPPEARING WILLS

Will Weldon, a native of Pine Bluff, Arkansas, was still a teenager when he made his first solo record for Victor in Atlanta, in autumn 1927. The 18-year-old was already well versed in the technique, having cut a number of sides with the Memphis Jug Band. His final recordings with the MJB were in early 1928. Then, rather surprisingly, nothing more was heard of Will until, it has been claimed, he recorded some solo sides, and others with Peetie Wheatstraw, in Chicago in early spring 1935. Blues historians have stated that Will married Memphis Minnie sometime in the 1920s, when they were living and working in Memphis. An excellent book by Paul and Beth Garon entitled *Woman With Guitar – Memphis Minnie's Blues* questions this theory.

While we have no evidence, we would side with the Garons; it was not Will Weldon but Casey Bill Weldon who recorded with Peetie Wheatstraw in 1935 – not least because 'Casey' (a corruption of KC or Kansas City) indicates that this Bill Weldon probably came from Kansas and not Arkansas. In any case, Casey Bill used a Hawaiian-style lap guitar, and had a more urban sound than Will's strongly country style.

Throughout 1935 to '37 Casey Bill was a busy man, recording numerous sides for both Vocalion and Bluebird, often accompanied by Wheatstraw, Big Bill Broonzy, Charlie McCoy, and pianist Black Bob. In 1937 Casey Bill hit the right note with 'Sold My Soul To The Devil'. As an accompanist he was just as busy: in addition to Peetie he sat in with Bumble Bee Slim, the Washboard Rhythm Kings (including Tampa Red and Washboard Sam), The State Street Swingers, Teddy Darby, and Memphis Minnie.

Casey Bill's last recordings were made 10 days before Christmas 1938. The four sides he cut for Bluebird were his first in over a year. Thereafter, nothing was heard of him again. In some reports he moved to California and was working on film soundtracks; in others he was living in 1960s Detroit. Whatever the truth, it's hard to believe that such a talented and well-recorded artist could just disappear.

MEMPHIS MINNIE
She possibly married Will Weldon – but was her husband the Bill Weldon who recorded with Peetie Wheatstraw?

The Best Thing Goin' In The Woman Line

Whether or not Will or Casey Bill was ever married to Memphis Minnie is conjecture, what is irrefutable is the fact that Casey Bill recorded with Minnie. On the same day that he cut his first Bluebird sides in October 1935, he backed Minnie on four numbers. Unlike her accompanist, Memphis Minnie's subsequent career is far from mysterious. She not only recorded across four decades, but Minnies's was practically the sole female voice in the increasingly male-dominated 1930s urban blues scene.

Guitar Giants

❛ Despite Lonnie Johnson's talent and popularity he was affected by the Depression. He moved to Cleveland and took a job outside of music, playing in local clubs just to keep his hand in. By 1937 he was back recording for Decca and later Bluebird; once again as popular as ever. On Friday 6th November, 1964, Brian Jones, Scott Ross (a New York DJ), and myself went to Greenwich Village to see Dizzy Gillespie. Unfortunately we were too late to catch his show but we did see John Hammond Jr. perform. One of the reasons that we were late was that we bumped into Lonnie Johnson, who had just finished playing a gig in the Village. He was amazed we recognised him, and we chatted for about twenty minutes, telling him that we knew and liked his music. Four days later we were in the Sherman House Hotel in Chicago and I bumped into Les Paul in the lobby; he was playing shows at the hotel. Ian Stewart and I went to see his show, which was very interesting. He had a little black box attached to his guitar which enabled him to play something and then double track it, and go on multi-track from there. After the show we went back to his room and chatted for several hours ❜

Bill Wyman

Her style was rooted in the country but flowered in the vibrant Chicago music scene, which is where she recorded the majority of over one hundred pre-war releases. As a testament to her talent, she worked with a host of excellent blues performers, and she is even rumoured to have beaten Big Bill Broonzy in a musical contest. Amongst those who recorded with her were Joe McCoy (her husband from the late 1920s), the Jed Devenport Jug Band, Georgia Tom, Tampa Red, Black Bob, Blind John Davis, and Little Son Joe. She also sat in with Little Son, Bumble Bee Slim, and the Memphis Jug Band, and appeared live with Big Bill, Sunnyland Slim, and Roosevelt Sykes. By 1935 Minnie and Joe McCoy had split up, and she subsequently married Little Son Joe in the late 1930s.

Minnie was an early convert to the electric guitar, which she used to good effect in her biggest hit, 'Me And My Chauffeur Blues', recorded in 1941 with 'Little Son'. The song, which utilised the same tune as 'Good Morning Little Schoolgirl', left its mark on many musicians. Koko Taylor said, "It was the first blues record I ever heard". Lightnin' Hopkins even 'answered' Minnie with his 1960 song, 'Automobile Blues'. Chuck Berry based his 'I Want To Be Your Driver' on 'Chauffeur', while Jefferson Airplane adapted it as 'Chauffeur Blues' on their 1966 debut album. Unfortunately the group neglected to acknowledge Minnie's recording and as a result she received no royalties from their version.

The breadth of her subject matter matched the longevity of Minnie's career. Many of her songs, like 'Bumble Bee', 'Dirty Mother For You' and 'Butcher Man', were openly sexual, all delivered in her confident way. Others, like 'Ma Rainey' and 'He's In The Ring (Doing That Same Old Thing)', were inspired by celebrities. 'Ma Rainey' was recorded just six months after the blues diva's death, while the latter song was a 1935 tribute to the legendary boxer Joe Louis. Among the other subjects Minnie covered were crime, voodoo, trains, health, and the perennial topic of chickens! Minnie was constantly touring, playing jukes and fish

Jo Ann Kelly

Jo Ann Kelly, the British blues singer who recorded in the late 1960s and 1970s, always claimed Memphis Minnie as an inspiration. She and her brother raised money for Minnie at a British blues club benefit and arranged for a Memphis blues fan to deliver it to her in the nursing home.

fries, which helped to maintain her popularity. She stayed in touch with her audience, singing about what they both knew, and understood.

The lady who was at the forefront of transforming the Blues into pop music continued to record up until 1954. By then Minnie's health was failing, and she and Little Son Joe retired to live in Memphis. Little Son died in 1961 and soon afterwards Minnie, remembered by many of her musical contemporaries from Chicago as "a hard drinking woman", suffered a stroke.

For a while, she was looked after by her sister, and then she moved into a nursing home. Despite her huge popularity and considerable record sales Minnie had little or no money, but after various magazines printed appeals, fans began sending her donations. Minnie, described by Bukka White as "the best thing goin' in the woman line", finally died on 6th August, 1973.

LES PAUL
An early picture of the electric guitar pioneer, who made his recording debut on a side by blues singer Georgia White.

THREE WOMEN BLUES

None of the other blues women who recorded during the 1930s ever matched Memphis Minnie's popularity, regardless of their stature. Amongst the most prolific was Georgia White who first recorded in 1930 but did not launch a serious career until spring 1935. Among her best recordings are 'Trouble in Mind', which became her signature tune, and the exuberant 'The Blues Ain't Nothin' But'. 'Trouble In Mind' featured the 20-year-old Les Paul playing some neat guitar, at what was probably his first recording session. Georgia formed an all-girl band in the late 1940s before fading from the scene in the 1950s.

Georgia White

Lil Green

In 1937 a 25-year-old from Mississippi named Merline Johnson burst onto the scene. For the next four years the girl with the sensual, jazz-tinged style was one of the busiest recording artists around. From her first record with ARC she was known as 'The Yas Yas Girl'.

Another performer still very active at this time was the tough-singing, salacious Lucille Bogan. She cut many of her best records between 1933 and 1935, often under the name of Bessie Jackson.

And then there was Lil Green, who recorded her first Bluebird sides in 1940. Just 20 when she first recorded, she came from Mississippi and offered an altogether more sophisticated view of the Blues.

Performers such as Peggy Lee and Billie Holiday covered her records and their renditions overshadowed Lil's own excellent versions. She died in relative obscurity from pneumonia in 1954, aged 35 – one of the great lost singers in blues history.

Baby Please Don't Go

Few blues songs have been covered as frequently as 'Baby Please Don't Go' – or changed as much in the process. The original copyrighted version was recorded by Joe Williams on Thursday 31st October, 1935, in Chicago, but the song is undoubtedly much older than that. Not that Williams was the only person to copyright it, as there are numerous versions with different writing credits, including one by McKinley Morganfield (alias Muddy Waters).

Joe Williams

The 1935 original was released on Bluebird by Joe Williams' Washboard Blues Singers. This riotous dance version featured Joe on vocals and guitar along with Dad Tracy on one-string fiddle and Kokomo Collins on washboard. Joe recorded it again for Bluebird in 1941 and Columbia in 1947, both times with Sonny Boy Williamson No. 1 on harmonica. The 1947 version also featured Ransom Knowling on bass and Judge Riley on drums, which provided the 'feel' that inspired most of the subsequent versions.

Muddy Waters

Muddy's 1960 version was recorded on 3rd July at the Newport Jazz Festival and included on the album *Muddy Waters At Newport*. Lyrically it was similar to Big Joe's version, but Muddy dropped the reference to ice cream! Just before James Cotton's harmonica solo, he says, "Look out Sonny Boy".

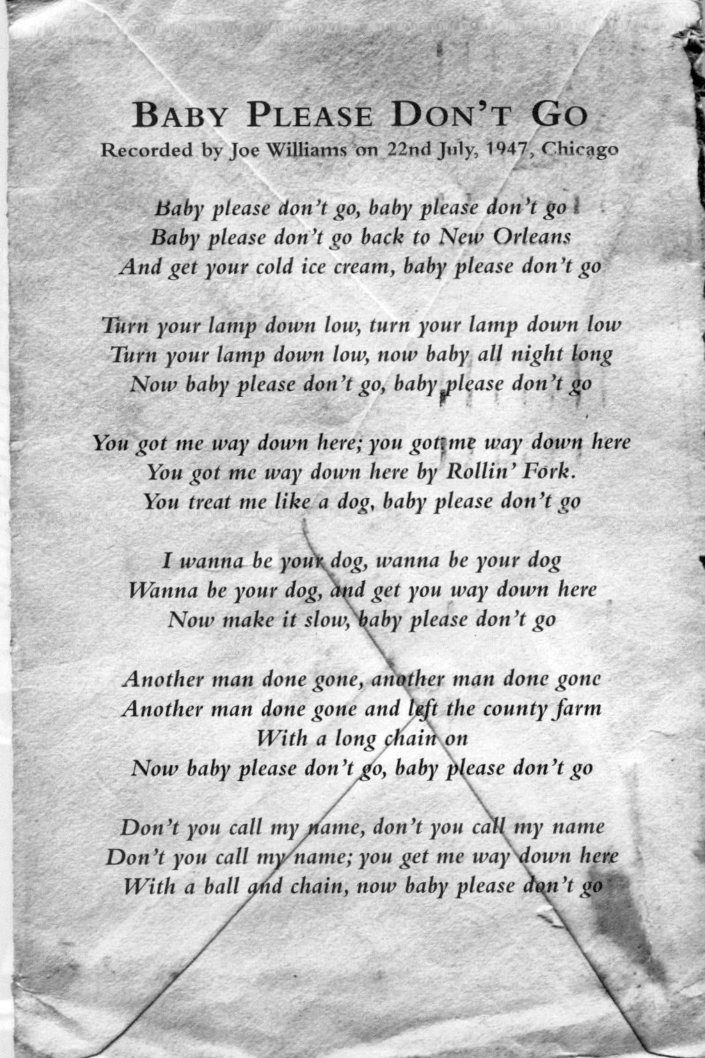

Baby Please Don't Go

Recorded by Joe Williams on 22nd July, 1947, Chicago

Baby please don't go, baby please don't go
Baby please don't go back to New Orleans
And get your cold ice cream, baby please don't go

Turn your lamp down low, turn your lamp down low
Turn your lamp down low, now baby all night long
Now baby please don't go, baby please don't go

You got me way down here; you got me way down here
You got me way down here by Rollin' Fork.
You treat me like a dog, baby please don't go

I wanna be your dog, wanna be your dog
Wanna be your dog, and get you way down here
Now make it slow, baby please don't go

Another man done gone, another man done gone
Another man done gone and left the county farm
With a long chain on
Now baby please don't go, baby please don't go

Don't you call my name, don't you call my name
Don't you call my name; you get me way down here
With a ball and chain, now baby please don't go

Van, Peter, and Jimmy

When Van Morrison went into Decca's studio in the autumn of 1964 to record 'Baby Please Don't Go', he did so without Them. Decca had decided that as the group's debut single had flopped, they didn't want the rest of the group to play on their new single. Instead, they brought in Peter Bardens to play organ and Jimmy Page on guitar. It was a wise move, as the single reached the UK Top 10 early in 1965. Van had learned the song from a 1959 John Lee Hooker album, explaining later: "It struck me as being something really unique and different, with a lot of soul".

Mose Alive

The version by Paul Revere and the Raiders undoubtedly took its lead from Them, while Georgie Fame must have been listening to Mose Allison's version on *Mose Alive*. We're still working out how Gary Glitter came to record it!

Selected Versions

- 1936 Tampa Kid
- Sam Montgomery
- 1948 Lightnin' Hopkins
- 1949 John Lee Hooker
- 1952 Big Bill Broonzy
- 1959 Sonny Terry & Brownie McGhee
- 1960 Muddy Waters
- 1964 Them
- 1965 John Hammond
- 1966 Paul Revere & The Raiders
- Mose Allison
- 1967 The Amboy Dukes
- 1968 Georgie Fame
- 1970 Al Kooper
- 1972 Gary Glitter
- 1983 Thin Lizzy
- 1989 Beausoleil
- 1994 Willie & The Poor Boys
- 1997 John Mooney

NEW YORK CITY BLUES

JOSH WHITE
Jac Holzman, the founder of Elektra Records, first listened to Josh White and Lead Belly when he was in college around 1949/50. "My own upbringing and sentiments were liberal," he recalled. "Signing Josh gave me an artist with a broad reputation who might actually sell some records." Every year between 1955 and 1962 Elektra Records released a Josh White album. The first, The Story Of John Henry, *sold 20,000 copies, helping to secure the future of this influential label. In 1965 Holzman repaid another personal debt when Elektra released a triple album of Lead Belly's Library of Congress recordings.*

ON HER FINAL RECORDINGS in 1935, Lucille Bogan was accompanied by 21-year-old Josh White. Josh was no stranger to recording, having first entered the studio when he was 14 years old. In 1928 he played second guitar to Blind Joe Taggart, a singer who could never quite make up his mind whether to follow the Devil or Jesus. Josh, who left school almost before he joined, spent his early years leading different blind singers around the streets of his hometown, Greenville, South Carolina. A year after his debut he recorded 'Wang Wang Harmonica Blues' with the Carver Boys, a white 'old time' group. After this initial taste of recording he went back to school, and sometime around 1930 he moved to New York, where he lived for the rest of his life.

Soon after arriving in New York in 1932 Josh was broadcasting on radio and cutting his first solo sides – it was the start of a prolific career. He walked a thin line between the secular and the religious, recording his blues sides as Pinewood Tom and religious titles such as 'There's A Man Goin' Around Taking Names' as Joshua White, The Singing Christian.

Some historians have been disparaging about White, an excellent guitar player in the Piedmont tradition, with a melodious voice. The revisionists see him as somebody who sold out. There is certainly no doubt that he became popular among white audiences in New York. He performed for President Roosevelt, acted on stage and in films, recorded for the Library of Congress, and toured Mexico for the US State Department. White also held left-wing views and took a stand against social injustice – he rallied against racial prejudice and the FBI even had a 473-page dossier on him. That some would prefer his name omitted from the 'official' history of the Blues, is mystifying.

While White was neither a true original nor an innovator, he brought the Blues to a white audience and through his work with

JOSH WHITE
He gave many white Americans their first taste of the Blues.

Pete Seeger, helped to 'spread the word'. White let people into the Blues tent, enabling them to discover all sorts of performers who perhaps, in the eyes of the experts, offer a purer undiluted blues. The man who gave many young white liberal Americans their first taste of the Blues died in New York in 1969.

Nobody In The World Is Better Than Us

Like Josh White, Lead Belly has aroused prejudice in certain quarters. After he had been re-discovered by the Lomaxes in Angola Prison, his musical career strayed from pure blues, and his material and singing put him firmly in the songster tradition. Lead Belly was in his mid-forties when he first recorded, and his repertoire reflected this.

Lead Belly settled in New York in the mid-1930s and first recorded commercially in 1935 for the Arc label (all his earlier recordings had been for the Library of Congress). Like White, he befriended Pete Seeger and Woody Guthrie, and became a darling of the liberal left. There is no question that Lead Belly was more popular with white audiences, and it was whites not blacks who bought the majority of his records. He was even more influential than Josh White in allowing young white Americans and Europeans access to the Blues and the folk traditions of black America. His influence has spread far beyond the folk arena, and everyone from Lonnie Donegan to The Beach Boys, and Led Zeppelin to Little Richard, has covered his songs.

When Lead Belly died he was virtually penniless, which is a sad indictment of those who had sought to befriend him to further their own ambitions. How amazed he would have been to discover that long after his death, his songs would still top the charts, and his influence and legend would be acknowledged by so many…but then again, maybe he wouldn't have been. He was a proud man who was not above a bit of self-promotion, and who had no shortage of self-belief. If you can sing your way out of prison, then topping the charts must seem pretty ordinary.

Lead Belly

His life was as remarkable as his musical influence was deep.

Take This Hammer

Lead Belly's influence spread far beyond folk and blues. Many of his songs became the staple diet of British skiffle musicians of the 1950s, including the teenagers who later called themselves The Beatles.

Lead Belly Goes Disco

In 1977 Ram Jam made the charts with 'Black Betty'. This was one of the more curious covers of a Lead Belly song, since Ram Jam turned it into a disco record! Then again, Lead Belly played music for people to dance to at parties, so perhaps Ram Jam were not so far from the mark.

FROM SPIRITUALS TO SWING

'AN EVENING OF AMERICAN NEGRO MUSIC'

John Hammond, producer of From Spirituals To Swing.

Sometime in 1938, the jazz critic and part-time recording scout, John Hammond, hit upon the idea of arranging a concert at New York's Carnegie Hall to celebrate black music from its earliest days to the latest jazz sounds. Today this sounds like an ambitious and exciting concept, but in 1938 it was an audacious idea. It proved to be the first major concert (and at such a prestigious venue) to feature black artists performing for an integrated audience. Hammond faced opinions ranging from antipathy to out-and-out hostility, which made finding a sponsor very difficult. Finally, having tried almost everyone, he persuaded the journal of the US Communist Party, *New Masses*, to put up the money.

Two days before Christmas 1938 Hammond walked on stage to introduce this landmark concert. It was sold out, and those lucky enough to be at this 'socially significant event' witnessed legendary performers at 'a musical milestone'.

In 1959 Hammond, with less than perfect recall, wrote about the concerts, saying that Big Bill Broonzy had left his Arkansas farm and mule to come to New York.

> *'William 'Big Bill' Broonzy bought a new pair of shoes and got on a bus in Arkansas to make his first trip to New York'*

wrote John Sebastian, in a review that appeared in *New Masses*. His first trip? Only if you ignore his eight days of recording at three separate sessions in 1930 and 1932!

Hammond also talked about having signed Robert Johnson, who supposedly failed to show up because he had died after a bar-room brawl (this inadvertently provided further fuel for the Johnson legend). The concert was dedicated to the memory of Bessie Smith, who had died 15 months earlier; her niece Ruby, accompanied by James P Johnson, sang her songs at the event.

Probably the star turns of the concert were the pianists Albert Ammons, Pete Johnson, and Meade Lux Lewis. Their appearance proved to be sensational and New York

Meade Lux Lewis

From Spirituals To Swing

Left: The front cover of the concert programme featuring Bessie Smith to whose memory the concert was dedicated. Right: A Columbia Phonograph Company ad in the programme promotes an album of Bessie Smith songs, and Robert Johnson's new release of 'Walking Blues', plus recordings by Mitchell's Christian Singers and Big Bill Broonzy.

society went wild for these charismatic performers. The Count Basie Orchestra, originally signed by Hammond to MCA in 1936, was also on the bill. Mitchell's Christian Singers and Sister Rosetta Tharpe represented the gospel tradition, while Sonny Terry, Joe Turner, Jimmy Rushing and Helen Humes played the Blues.

On Christmas Eve the following year there was another concert. Many of the same stars were on parade, as well as the Golden Gate Quartet, The Benny Goodman Sextet, featuring Charlie Christian, and Ida Cox, who had cut her first blues sides way back in 1923. White middle-class America was only just catching up with the Blues.

On Record

John Hammond had the foresight to record the concerts, and an album from the 1938 event was released in 1959. In 1999 Vanguard released a three-CD boxed set of both concerts – providing a memorable tribute to John Hammond's achievement and a feast of great music.

"Just over 25 years later, on 20th June, 1964, I stood on the stage of Carnegie Hall along with the rest of the Stones. We played two shows, the final dates on our first American tour. On the bill with us were The Counts, Kathy Carr, and Jay & The Americans. Disc jockey Murray the K introduced us individually to the packed audience at the matinee before we played our first number, 'Route 66'. By the time we had finished fans were already climbing on the stage. Mayhem broke out and we only managed to play a few songs, none of which could be heard, before we were surrounded by police and marched off the stage. During the interval the management and police met us in our dressing room, and tried to persuade us to cancel the evening show. We refused, but compromised and agreed to go on earlier, allowing Jay & The Americans to close the show. This time we managed to finish and afterwards we were herded off stage and across the street to the Park Sheraton Hotel. We just managed to make it to the elevators, chased by a shrieking mob. As one reporter wrote, "They turned Carnegie Hall into a teenville heaven."

Bill Wyman

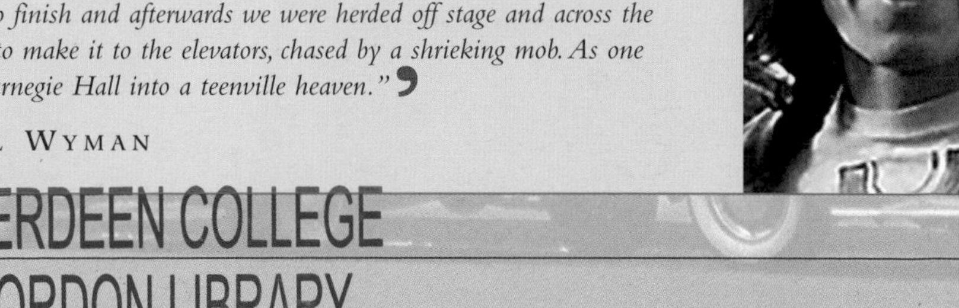

FOUR BLIND BOYS – BUT ONE COULD REALLY SEE

Sonny Terry and Brownie McGhee were part of the same New York music scene as Lead Belly and Josh White. Sonny had come to prominence via *From Spirituals to Swing*, while Brownie first recorded in 1940 having been discovered by JB Long, a talent scout. The duo formed one of the longest-running partnerships in the history of the Blues, which endured for more than forty years. They met in New York and through Lead Belly they found work in the city, playing coffeehouses, clubs and parties.

McGhee came from Knoxville, Tennessee, and while still a teenager he joined the Golden Voices Gospel Quartet, before taking to a life on the road. Sanford Terrell grew up in North Carolina and played the harmonica. While he was still a young boy he was blinded in both eyes, in separate accidents. The link between the two men was Blind Boy Fuller. Sonny met the blind guitarist in Durham, and they first recorded in September 1937, which is around the time that Sonny moved to New York. They continued to work together until Fuller died in 1941. Like Brownie, Fuller had been

SONNY TERRY AND BROWNIE MCGHEE

For several decades after their spectacular debut at From Spirituals To Swing, *Sonny & Brownie were one of the most popular attractions on the blues circuit - particularly in Britain and the rest of Europe.*

managed by JB Long, and after his death Brownie even made records as Blind Boy Fuller No. 2.

While Brownie was not actually blind, he had contracted poliomyelitis when he was four, which resulted in a shortened right leg. Whatever their condition, many handicapped men were offered a lifeline by the Blues. It allowed them to earn a living in a society ill-equipped to look after those who were afflicted. Back then, the family was the main source of support, and in an era when families were often large, and in such dire straits, supporting an infirm member could be a heavy burden.

The original Blind Boy Fuller was born in Wadesboro, North Carolina, in 1908, and his real name was Fulton Allen. He became partially blind in 1926 and fully blind two years later – some sources attributing this to disease, others to lye water being thrown in his face (or indeed a combination of the two factors). He became well-known throughout the area for playing at dances and parties, and also worked the front of the Bull Durham tobacco factory for tips. Fuller and his wife settled in Durham in 1935, which is where he met JB Long. Besides scouting for record companies Long managed the local United Dollar Store, much like his Mississippi contemporary HC Speir. Long and Fuller went to New York for his first recording session for the ARC label in July 1935. Over four days Fuller, whom Long described as 'a little bitty feller', recorded 13 sides, including a wonderful version of the traditional tune 'Rag Mama Rag' and 'I'm A Rattlesnakin' Daddy'. Released as his debut, these songs did much to establish Fuller's reputation. Guitarist Blind Gary Davis, and the wonderfully named washboard player, Bull City Red (George Washington), supported him on many of these initial 13 songs.

The eclectic Fuller was head to head with Big Bill Broonzy in the popularity stakes throughout the second half of the 1930s, as the two men became the foremost figures in the urban country blues scene.

Fuller remained truer to his country (or folk) roots, and his output was prodigious, totalling some 135 sides, as he often recorded eight or ten songs in a single day. Indeed, on 29th October, 1938, he cut 12 titles in Columbia, South Carolina, including the enigmatically entitled 'What's That Smells Like Fish' and 'Get Your Yas Yas Out'.

In his book *Crying For The Carolines*, Bruce Bastin offers the hypothesis that Fuller was in fact a copyist, someone who adapted songs he heard from friends as well as the records that

JB LONG

The talent scout and store manager is pictured around 1934 in front of a consignment of records.

❛ On 27th and 28th November, 1969, we recorded a live album at Madison Square Garden with Glyn Johns co-producing and engineering the recording. Glyn was the first producer we ever worked with back in early 1963. It may well have been on this tour that we were first introduced as "the Greatest Rock'n'Roll Band in the World"… and it certainly stuck! We called the album Get Yer Ya-Ya's Out *❜*

BILL WYMAN

'GET YER YA-YA'S OUT!'
The Rolling Stones in concert

JOHN HAMMOND ORGANISES FROM SPIRITUALS TO SWING

When John Hammond needed country blues performers for his concert, he went to Elon, near Durham, where JB Long lived. Hammond was looking for Blind Boy Fuller and Mitchell's Christian Singers, both discovered by Long. Hammond and Long visited Fuller's house in Durham only to find he was in jail, for shooting his wife in the leg! Fuller missed out on the concert, and instead Hammond booked Sonny Terry, whom he considered 'a far superior performer'. Fuller reminisced about his spell in jail in the song 'Big House Bound', recorded in 1938:

❛ I never will forget the day they transferred me to the county jail. I had shot the women I love, ain't got no one to come and go my bail. ❜

Fuller's incarceration was, as you would expect, a mistake. A blind man accused of shooting his wife? I don't think so!

JB Long says he bought. Bastin also expresses the view that this in no way diminishes Fuller's reputation. Fuller was a good guitar player with a great voice who made excellent records. Like many of his contemporaries, from Big Bill to Robert Johnson, he adapted and moulded lyrical ideas and melodies. Fuller, like the greats from any era, stamped his personality and style on material that would be ordinary in the hands of others.

Eighteen months after recording 'Get Your Yas Yas Out', Fuller cut one of his best records, 'Step It Up And Go'. That day he cut just five sides, as he did on each of the next two days. This reduced output was perhaps the first sign of the illness that tragically claimed Blind Boy Fuller at the age of 32. By the time of his last session, three months later in June 1940, his kidney problems were becoming acute. Soon after he entered hospital for an operation, contracted blood poisoning and died at his home in Durham on the eve of Valentine's Day, in February 1941.

One of Fuller's accompanists, Blind Gary Davis, was also one of his influences. Born in Laurens, South Carolina, in 1896, Davis was without doubt one of the most talented guitarists of his generation. No one is sure whether he was blind from birth, as Davis would never confirm the details of his affliction. By the late 1920s Davis had moved to Durham and was working the streets for change. Sometime in the early 1930s he found God, and in 1933 he was ordained a Baptist minister, although he did not use the title on his pre-war recordings. Davis cut 15 solo sides in July 1935, almost all of them religious songs, but none sold in any great quantity. He found no difficulty in combining the secular and spiritual sides of music, recording as Fuller's second guitarist on his 1935 blues sides. Davis moved to New York in the late 1930s where he met up and worked with McGhee and Terry. From the 1940s onwards he recorded, sang, and preached in Harlem, and like McGhee, Terry, and many others, he will re-enter our story as the 1960s folk blues revival takes off.

BLIND BOY FULLER
Died aged 32 in 1941

BLIND GARY DAVIS
In September 1962 at Ida Noyez Hall, Chicago.

The Delta's Last Stand

Bukka White
Christened Booker T Washington White, he recorded spiritual material under the name of Washington White.

Bo Carter and Bukka White were both recording at the start of the Depression, although Carter recorded well before White got his chance at the microphone. Bo Carter was born Armenter Chatmon at Dr Dupree's plantation in March 1893, and his background shaped his career from the outset – the Chatmons were well known across the Delta as a musical family. His first session, as Bo Chatmon for Brunswick in late 1928, yielded four sides including 'Corrine Corrina', giving him the distinction of being the first to record this staple of practically every folk blues artist before or since. It was recorded not only by blues artists, but became very popular amongst Western swing bands like Cliff Bruner and his Texas Wanderers, as well as performers as diverse as Dean Martin, Tampa Red, Joe Turner, Piano Red, the Rising Sons, Chet Atkins, Count Basie, and Jerry Lee Lewis. Bo did not record again until 1930 when he cut six sides for OKeh, the first of which was 'I'm An Old Bumble Bee'. This set the pattern for Bo Carter's (as he was now calling himself) career.

'I'm an old bumble bee,
A stinger just as long as my arm.
I stings every good-lookin' woman,
Now, everywhere I goes along
I'm an old bumble bee'

'I'm an Old Bumble Bee'

Bo became the 'King of the Double Entendre', proving that anything the raunchy blues women thought they could do, he could at least match. He built a career around songs that left little to the imagination. 'My Pencil Won't Write No More', 'Banana In Your Fruit Basket' and 'Please Warm My Weiner' were some of the more obvious titles, while the words were just as risqué:

> *I met a hot mama, I wanted to love her so bad I lost all the lead, in the pencil I had Cause the lead's all gone – the pencil won't write no more*
>
> 'MY PENCIL WON'T WRITE NO MORE'

PLEASE WARM MY WEINER
One of the many blues album covers illustrated by the inimitable Robert Crumb in the 1970s. A big blues fan, Crumb was inspired by the risqué double entendres of blues titles of the 1930s and 1940s.

However, it would be unfair to consider Bo Carter just a dirty blues singer. He was a skilled musician with an original guitar style that enabled him to play in five different tunings. He no doubt saw the risqué side of his repertoire as offering good earning potential, and who can blame him? By the time of his final session in 1940 Bo had cut around 75 sides. His life thereafter went steadily downwards: living in poverty, he died in 1964 after a series of strokes.

Bo Carter was one of a large family of Chatmons who played locally in the Delta, and later recorded as the Mississippi Sheiks. They came from Bolton, Mississippi, and their fiddle-playing father had been what they called a 'musicianer' in slavery times. The nine Chatmon bothers all played various instruments; for instance, Bo played clarinet as well as guitar. By the time the Mississippi Sheiks recorded in 1930, the group consisted of Lonnie, Sam, and Bo, along with Walter Vinson. Later Charlie McCoy played with them, while both Sam and Bo became occasional members. The Sheiks' best known song 'Sitting On Top of the World', was eventually covered by a whole host of artists, including Howlin' Wolf and later Cream. Like Bo, the Sheiks dabbled in double entendre, but they were essentially a dance band, and that is how they made their money, playing jukes and dances in Memphis and the Delta.

After the band ceased recording in 1935, Sam and Lonnie played together as the Chatmon Brothers. But Bo, Lonnie, and Sam all eventually left the world of music to go back to farm life. Sam did record again in the 1960s, and proved that he was still a deft guitar player. Sam always claimed that he composed 'Cross Cut Saw', which Tommy

> *When The Stones played San Francisco's Winterland on 8th June, 1972, Bukka White and John Lee Hooker came backstage to see us. Bukka wanted to play dice with us. Nearly thirty years later, when we filmed the TV series, I talked with BB King about Bukka:*
>
> *"Well the record company spelled it Bukka but I knew him as Booker. He was my second cousin, my mother's first cousin. I loved to hear him play, but he was not my idol as a guitarist, but as a person I was crazy about him. He was a good timer, loved to have fun, and loved his drinks and so on. I liked him because when I was a small boy he used to come visit my mom and he'd always bring us candy or something. He was a good talker, he always had something nice to tell you and he'd make us laugh. When I first started to get into the music he used to tell me, you always dress as if you're going to the bank to borrow money. That's why I started, a long time ago, to try to be like the old blues singers: most of them dressed pretty nice."*
>
> BILL WYMAN

McClennan and Albert King successfully covered. In 1935, brother Harry released four records as Harry Carter. The brief duration of his career was indicative of his limited success, but not his ability.

From Pitcher to Parchman

While the Chatmons, in their various guises, were prolific recording artists, Bukka White was the total opposite. But his lack of records was more than compensated for by the quality of his music. He first recorded in 1930 and between then and his final session in 1940, he released just nine records. Christened Booker T. Washington White, he cut 14 sides for Victor in May 1930, only two of which were released, one a blues and the other a religious record under the name of Washington White.

Booker was born in 1909, the son of a railroad worker, and rather appropriately his first record was 'The New Frisco Train', coupled with 'The Panama Limited', reflecting the passion many blues artists shared for trains. White's guitar playing on both these sides was excellent, capturing the rhythm of a moving train to perfection. Booker was a musical veteran by the time he first recorded: he had left home when he was just thirteen, moving to Chicago to play religious songs on the streets with a blind guitarist – an early life reminiscent of Josh White. By the late 1920s he had returned to the Delta, and inspired by Charley Patton he was back to the Blues. The two religious sides from his first session featured a certain Miss Minnie, and as Memphis Minnie recorded the same day it seems likely that the two women were one and the same.

As neither side sold very well, Victor did not bother to release any more of the 1930 session. White went back to living as an itinerant musician, as well as spells as a baseball pitcher and as a boxer. But seven years later Booker travelled to Chicago and cut 'Pinebluff Arkansas' and 'Shake 'Em On Down' for Vocalion. The latter is one of his best tunes, and it was soon covered by Bo Carter, Tommy McClennan, and Big Bill Broonzy. Unfortunately it was not success that soon came banging at his door, but the police. He had apparently shot a man, sometime before the recording session, so he was sent to the Mississippi State Penitentiary at Parchman Farm. In 1939, while he was in Parchman, John Lomax recorded two songs with White, noting him on the recording sheets as Washington (Barrelhouse) White.

By late '39 White was out of prison and able to record, but he was past his sell-by date. The Bluebird Beat, as Victor's subsidiary label's material has been dubbed, was all the rage, and it was a long way from Bukka's Delta blues. In an effort to 'modernise' White's sound, Washboard Sam was drafted in. Over two days in spring 1940, Washington and Washboard recorded 12 wonderful sides. 'Bukka's Jitterbug Swing', 'Parchman Farm Blues', and 'Special Streamline Special' are diamonds amongst pearls.

Despite this output, Booker T Washington White retreated back into obscurity, only to be rediscovered in the 1960s when he received the adulation he could never have imagined back in 1939, while he was in Parchman Farm.

Parchman Farm
Officially known as Mississippi State Penitentiary, it passed into local legend and the history of the Blues as Parchman Farm.

> *Never will forget that day*
> *when they had me in Parchman Jail.*
> *Would no one even come and go my bail.*
> *I wonder how long before I can change*
> *my clothes*
>
> 'When Can I Change My Clothes

ROBERT JOHNSON

FACT FILE

BORN: *8th May, 1911 Hazlehurst, Mississippi*

DIED: *16th August, 1938 Three Forks, Greenwood, Mississippi*

INSTRUMENT: *Guitar, harmonica*

FIRST RECORDED: *1936*

ACCOLADES: *Inducted into the Blues Hall of Fame, 1980*

INFLUENCES: *Lonnie Johnson, Charley Patton, Son House, Willie Brown*

INFLUENCED: *Just about everyone who has played the Blues since 1937*

Robert Plant of Led Zeppelin chose 'Walkin' Blues' as the first record he would take as a castaway on the BBC Radio show, Desert Island Discs.

HIS LIFE AND LEGEND HAVE FASCINATED people for 40 years or more, and his records have been an inspiration to almost every rock guitar legend. During his short career he made just 29 recordings, and each one has been studied and dissected to extract every last nuance. There is an insatiable demand for information about his life, and a desire to understand not just his playing but also his motivations and influences. One thing is certain: Robert Johnson is the King of the Blues.

The facts of Robert Johnson's life are somewhat sketchy. But in their own way, these meagre details have contributed to his legend.

Robert's mother, Julia, had ten children with her husband Charles Dodds before Robert was born. But Robert was born illegitimately when Julia was probably around 40 years old; his father was a plantation worker called Noah Johnson. Dodds had already moved to Memphis to escape some problems he was having with prominent Hazlehurst landowners. Robert was sent to live with him when he was around three or four years old, joining the rest of Charles' children.

Robert grew up in Memphis and first learned the basics of the guitar from his brother. Then, aged around eight or nine, Robert moved back to the Delta to live with his mother and her new husband, Dusty Willis. He now became known as Little Robert Dusty. By all accounts, Robert was more interested in music than he was in working in the fields, which put him at odds with his stepfather.

By the time he was nineteen Robert had married a girl of sixteen, but she died shortly afterwards while giving birth. Around this time, in 1930, Son House moved to live in Robinsonville.

Son House recalled many years later that "he blew a harmonica and he was pretty good with that, but he wanted to play guitar". It was from House and Willie Brown that Robert learned. He would watch them play and when they took a break he would use one of their guitars. According to House he was not good at all, "Such a racket you never heard!... get that guitar away from that boy, people would say, he's running people crazy with it."

By 1931 Robert had married again and started to travel, improving his guitar skills and playing at Delta juke joints and picnics. A year or so later Johnson played for Son and Willie; they were staggered by his improvement: "He was so good. When he finished, all our mouths were standing open."

Robert resumed his Delta wanderings, his reputation growing as he played. He also travelled further afield, visiting Chicago, New York, Detroit, and St Louis. All the while he developed his 'audience technique', which also added to his reputation as a womaniser. He often concentrated his performance on just one woman in the audience, which led him to form relationships of varying duration with many different women. Robert travelled and played with Johnny Shines, who later recalled that Robert was always neat and tidy, despite days spent travelling dusty Delta highways. Johnny also recalled that Robert was just as likely to perform others' songs, as he was his own. He covered everyone from Bing Crosby to Blind Willie McTell, and Jimmie Rodgers to Lonnie Johnson. Like many others, in fact, he simply performed the songs that would earn him money, and that his audiences requested.

ROBERT JOHNSON
The second of only two confirmed photographs of the enigmatic blues legend.

When Robert was in his mid-20s, he wanted to make records the way that his influences and contemporaries had done, so he went to HC Speir's store in Jackson, Mississippi. Speir contacted the ARC label and by late November 1936 Robert was in San Antonio to record the first of his twenty-nine sides. On Monday November 23 he cut 'Kind Hearted Woman Blues', the first of thirteen takes of eight different songs recorded that day. Three days later he was back to cut '32-20 Blues', and then the following day he cut nine more takes of seven different songs. He then took a train back to Mississippi and his life as an itinerant musician. He was temporarily richer, having pocketed money from his recording session, although it is doubtful whether it was more than $100.

Robert's first release was 'Terraplane Blues' coupled with 'Kind Hearted Woman Blues'. It would be his only record to sell in any great quantity at the time. His next release, '32-20 Blues' coupled with 'Last Fair Deal Gone Down', was followed by 'I'll Believe I'll Dust My Broom' and 'Dead Shrimp Blues'. Sales were not fantastic but were clearly good enough for Robert to be summoned back for more recording. This time he went to Dallas and recorded three more sides on 19th June, 1937. Then the following day he cut 13 more takes of 10 more songs.

After these sessions Robert went 'touring' in Texas with Johnny Shines. They played jukes, parties, and dances, as they did in the Delta, before heading back to Mississippi via Arkansas. Precise details of the last year of his life are somewhat imprecise, although it is known that Robert spent some time in Memphis and Helena, Arkansas. Gayle Dean Wardlow, a Mississippi journalist, went in search of Robert Johnson's death certificate, eventually finding it in 1968. It confirmed that Robert had died in Greenwood on 16th August, 1938, aged 27.

> *His supreme sense of time, which permitted him to break tempos and to sing, over implied rather than stated rhythms*
>
> ALEXIS KORNER

> *Robert Johnson is one of the great mysteries of the Blues. The first album of his that I bought was* King Of The Delta Blues Singers. *I learned a lot from Peter Guralnick's book,* Searching For Robert Johnson. *There is also an excellent documentary by John Hammond Jr. called* The Search for Robert Johnson
>
> BILL WYMAN

ESSENTIAL RECORDINGS

CLASSIC SONGS

'I Believe I'll Dust My Broom' 1936
'Sweet Home Chicago' 1936
'Cross Road Blues' 1936
'Terraplane Blues' 1936

CLASSIC ALBUMS

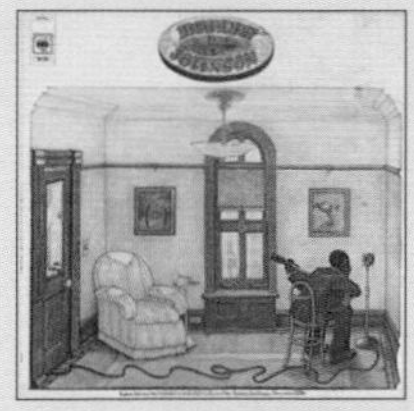

King Of The Delta Blues Singers Sony

THE SOURCE

Robert Johnson: The Complete Recordings
Sony

THE NAME GAME

Robert Lee McCoy recorded six of his own songs at Williamson's first session, with Sonny Boy playing harp on three of them. Robert, who was six years older than Sonny Boy, came from Helena, Arkansas and like Sonny Boy he played harmonica, having learned it before he took to the guitar. He began by playing harmonica in support of his guitarist cousin, Houston Stackhouse. The two men played weekend jukes and parties while they worked on a Delta farm during the week.

McCoy and Sonny even supported the white country singer, Jimmie Rodgers, at a Jackson, Mississippi, hotel sometime in the early 1930s. Rodgers, already a star, literally picked them off the street to accompany him. At the end of the night the hat was passed around and Rodgers let the two younger men keep the $12 in tips.

McCoy was actually born McCullum but changed his name when he moved to St Louis around 1935. Some problem with the police and a gun seemed to have sparked this name change. He had a third identity when he recorded as Ramblin' Bob in 1938, before recording for Decca as Peetie's Boy, to trade on The Devil's Son-in-Law's legacy. And the name game didn't end there. In the early 1940s, perhaps inspired by his own recording of 'Prowling Night Hawk', he became Robert Nighthawk and went on to have a very successful career in post-war Chicago.

The man who was probably responsible for bringing McCoy and Sonny Boy to Bluebird was Big Joe Williams. He cut four sides that same day, having already recorded twice before for the label. At a session in 1935 he cut the classic 'Baby Please Don't Go', which has probably been played by as many artists as 'Good Morning Little Schoolgirl'. The man described as the "quintessential itinerant Bluesman" hailed from Crawford in the Delta and began a lifetime of hoboing in his early teens.

Joe's unique contribution to the blues, and to guitar technology, was the nine-string guitar, a testimony to the 'necessity being the mother of invention' theory. He was known to be a little rough on his guitars, and during yet another piece of reconstructive surgery on a favourite instrument, he chanced upon the nine-string effect, which created a sound like nothing else. He may well have recorded in the 1920s with Jed Davenport, which would mean his recording career covered six decades. Big Joe was no small talent, and we shall pick up with him and the other two architects of the post-war Chicago Blues sound later.

LA SALLE STREET, CHICAGO
Chicago acted as a magnet for Delta blues players. What must they have thought when they got there?

THE YAZOO CITY ALL STARS

Tommy McClennan, a small man with a remarkably big talent, was born in the Delta in 1908, near Yazoo City. In common with so many others, few facts are known about his early life. He played house parties and jukes throughout the Delta during the late 1920s and 1930s. From early on he worked with Robert Petway who came from the same area, becoming so close musically that it is difficult to tell them apart. Big Bill Broonzy claimed the credit for introducing Tommy to Lester Melrose, while others say Melrose went in search of artists on a scouting trip to the Delta.

Whatever the truth Tommy was in Chicago by late 1939, recording the first of his forty sides. At this session he covered 'Shake 'Em On Down', recorded 'Bottle It Up And Go', which was his signature tune and also 'Baby Don't You Want To Go', his adaptation of 'Sweet Home Chicago'. 'Bottle It Up And Go' highlights the widening gap between city and rural black communities, and not just in their choice of music. Broonzy recounts, in his autobiography, how he was in the studio when

BIG JOE WILLIAMS
His career stretched six decades.

BLUES GAZETTEER AND RAILWAYS

THE IDEA OF USING PLACE NAMES in blues songs began with the classic blues singers of the 1920s, and was just as keenly followed by Depression era performers. By the 1930s, the train had emerged as a feature of the Blues, although it first made its entrance when WC Handy came across his 'loose-jointed Negro' at Tutwiler, and heard him sing of "goin' where the Southern cross' the dog".

DENVER
'Denver Blues'
TAMPA RED
(1934)

KANSAS

'Chicago Blues'
MISSISSIPPI MOANER *(1935)*
'I'll Believe I'll Make Chicago'
HARLEM HAMFATS *(1938)*
'Sweet Home Chicago'
ROBERT JOHNSON *(1936)*

UNION PACIFIC

ILL

'Illinois Blues'
SKIP JAMES *(1931)*

ST LOUIS
'East St Louis Blues'
BLIND WILLIE MCTELL *(1933)*

MISSOURI
'South East Missouri Blues'
WALTER DAVIS *(1931)*

'Going Back To Arkansas'
BIG BILL BROONZY *(1938)*

MEMPHIS BLUES SONGS OF THE 30S

'Going Back To Memphis' MEMPHIS MINNIE	*(1930)*
'Heart of Memphis' YANK RACHEL	*(1934)*
'Memphis Blues' NITE OWLS	*(1938)*
'Memphis Shakedown' MEMPHIS JUG BAND	*(1934)*
'Memphis Town' LEROY CARR	*(1930)*
'Memphis Yodel' CLIFF CARLISLE	*(1930)*
'North Memphis Blues' MEMPHIS MINNIE	*(1930)*
'Beale Street Breakdown' JED DAVENPORT	*(1930)*

ARKANSAS

Brownsvill
MEMPHIS

'West Helena Blues'
JAMES HALL *(1938)*
W Helena

Pine Bluff
'Pinebluff, Arkansas'
BUKKA WHITE *(1937)*

Clarksdale
'Clarksdale M
SON HOUS
(1930)

DALLAS
Fort Worth
Frost
'Fort Worth And Dallas Blues'
LEAD BELLY *(1935)*

'Louisiana'
BIG BOY TEDDY EDWARDS
(1936)

Jackson
Vicksburg
'Vicksburg Blues'
LITTLE BROTHER
MONTGOMERY *(1930)*

'Frost Texas Tornado Blues'
TEXAS ALEXANDER *(1934)*

TEXAS

'Texas Got The Blues'
TEXAS ALEXANDER *(1934)*
'Texas Tommy'
YANK RACHEL *(1938)*
'My Texas Blues'
GEORGIA TOM DORSEY *(1930)*
'T For Texas'
JIMMIE RODGERS *(1927)*

LOUISIANA
Baton Rouge
'Baton Rouge Rag'
KITTY GRAY & HER
WAMPUS CATS
(1937)

NEW ORLEANS
'New Orleans'
WALTER DAVIS
(1939)

RAILROAD-INSPIRED SONGS OF THE 1930S

'B & O Blues'	PETE JOHNSON (1939)
'B & O Blues No.2'	BUDDY MOSS (1933)
'C & A Train Blues'	PEETIE WHEATSTRAW (1934)
'CWA Blues'	JOE PULLUM (1934)
'L & N Blues'	BILL GAITHER (1936)
'M & O Blues'	RAILROAD BILL (Thomas A. Dorsey) (1932)
'New Frisco Train'	BUKKA WHITE (1930)
'Rock Island Line'	LEAD BELLY (1937)
'Santa Fe Blues'	PEETIE WHEETSTRAW (1936)
'Southern Railroad Blues'	KOKOMO ARNOLD (1935)
'Southern Whistle Blues'	CHARLEY PATTON (1934)
'Streamline Train'	CRIPPLE CLARENCE LOFTON (1939)
'Streamline Train'	RED NELSON (1936)
'T P Window Blues'	JACK RANGER (1930)
'T.P.N. Moaner (Down On The Sante Fe)'	MACK RHINEHART & BROWNIE STUBBLEFIELD (1936)
'The Panama Limited'	BUKKA WHITE (1930)
'Wabash Blues'	MEMPHIS JUG BAND (1934)
'Midnight Special'	LEAD BELLY (1935)

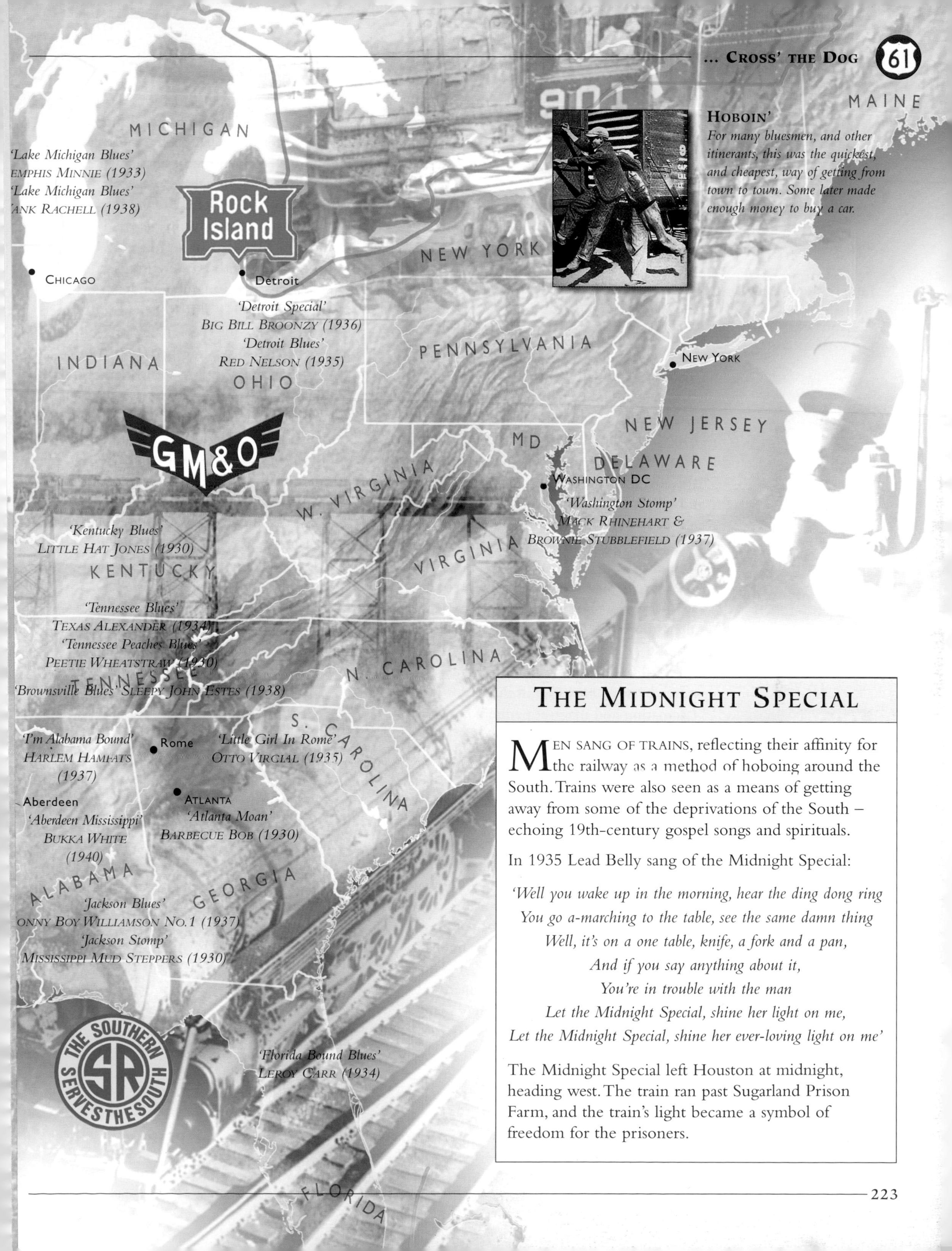

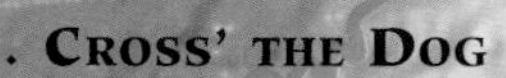

MAINE

Hoboin'
For many bluesmen, and other itinerants, this was the quickest, and cheapest, way of getting from town to town. Some later made enough money to buy a car.

MICHIGAN

'Lake Michigan Blues'
Emphis Minnie (1933)
'Lake Michigan Blues'
Ank Rachell (1938)

Rock Island

NEW YORK

Chicago

Detroit

'Detroit Special'
Big Bill Broonzy (1936)
'Detroit Blues'
Red Nelson (1935)

INDIANA

OHIO

PENNSYLVANIA

New York

NEW JERSEY

GM&O

MD

DELAWARE

W. VIRGINIA

Washington DC

'Washington Stomp'
Mack Rhinehart & Brownie Stubblefield (1937)

'Kentucky Blues'
Little Hat Jones (1930)

KENTUCKY

VIRGINIA

'Tennessee Blues'
Texas Alexander (1934)
'Tennessee Peaches Blues'
Peetie Wheatstraw (1930)

TENNESSEE

'Brownsville Blues' Sleepy John Estes (1938)

N. CAROLINA

S. CAROLINA

'I'm Alabama Bound'
Harlem Hamfats (1937)

Rome

'Little Girl In Rome'
Otto Virgial (1935)

Aberdeen

'Aberdeen Mississippi'
Bukka White (1940)

Atlanta

'Atlanta Moan'
Barbecue Bob (1930)

ALABAMA

GEORGIA

'Jackson Blues'
Onny Boy Williamson No.1 (1937)
'Jackson Stomp'
Mississippi Mud Steppers (1930)

The Southern Serves the South
SR

'Florida Bound Blues'
Leroy Carr (1934)

FLORIDA

The Midnight Special

Men sang of trains, reflecting their affinity for the railway as a method of hoboing around the South. Trains were also seen as a means of getting away from some of the deprivations of the South – echoing 19th-century gospel songs and spirituals.

In 1935 Lead Belly sang of the Midnight Special:

'Well you wake up in the morning, hear the ding dong ring
You go a-marching to the table, see the same damn thing
Well, it's on a one table, knife, a fork and a pan,
And if you say anything about it,
You're in trouble with the man
Let the Midnight Special, shine her light on me,
Let the Midnight Special, shine her ever-loving light on me'

The Midnight Special left Houston at midnight, heading west. The train ran past Sugarland Prison Farm, and the train's light became a symbol of freedom for the prisoners.

9

Big Bands, Strikes & Mr Hitler

Wartime Blues

Yesterday, 7th December, 1941 – a date which will live in infamy – the United States of America was suddenly and deliberately attacked by naval and air forces of the Empire of Japan

President Franklin Delano Roosevelt:
His War Message to Congress
after the Attack on Pearl Harbor

By the end of 1941 World War II, which had been raging in Europe for over two years, finally, and officially, involved the American people. Ironically, the onset of war allowed the American people to escape from the persistent grip of the Depression, generating an economic boom that sparked significant change at just about every level of society. As industry expanded in the North, as well as in the West, there was a rapid upturn in the fortunes of poor black and white people alike. The expansion of industrial output required people and a new migration began, a migration not to an uncertain future, but to the guarantee of work. These changes meant that black Americans began to experience accelerated progress towards a more equal society, although the situation was still a long way from where it needed to be.

The war also marked a sea-change in the music industry. Entertainment had to give precedence to the nation's need for machinery, raw materials and military manpower. But music and entertainment did not stop, and records continued to be manufactured and to sell.

As if to prove that the war was not going to get in the way of the music business, the music trade magazine *Billboard* launched its first chart, exclusively catering for black music. Called the 'The Harlem Hit Parade', it was based on the sales of records at six New York record stores, which included Harlem De Luxe Music Store and Frank's Melody Music. The first song to top

The News is Out
Although World War II never reached the American mainland, the shadow of the conflict crept over every layer of US society from prominent politicians to the ghetto between 1941 and 1945.

> *When I was looking for songs to record for my fourth Rhythm Kings album,* Double Bill, *released in spring 2001, I remembered a song by Les Paul and Mary Ford called 'Bye Bye Blues'. When I started to look into the background of the song, I found that it was the theme tune of the Bert Lown Orchestra and had first been recorded in 1930. Bert Lown and three members of his band wrote the song while he was the resident bandleader at New York's Biltmore Hotel, from where they also broadcast on radio. Cab Calloway recorded the song in 1941, and then Les and Mary scored a Top 5 hit with it in early 1953*
>
> Bill Wyman

Glenn Miller

Bluebird's biggest star of the wartime era was a swing bandleader who met a mysterious death.

the chart, of just ten records, was 'Take It And Git' by Andy Kirk and his Clouds of Joy. Kirk, a 44-year-old Kentuckian, and his twelve-piece swing band from Kansas City had been playing together, in one form or another, since 1929, and by 1935 Mary Lou Williams, a gifted pianist, was a featured artist. Like many other swing bands they had blues influences within their sound, as well as boogie woogie. In 1942 Kirk issued 'Boogie Woogie Cocktail', a showcase for Mary Lou's swinging left hand.

Andy Kirk

His record 'Take It And Git' was the first single to top the Harlem Hit Parade.

Big Band Swing

Looking back at the period immediately before World War II the tendency is to think of little else but the big bands, an era when swing was the thing. Just weeks before Pearl Harbor, Glenn Miller and his Orchestra had become the first artist to be awarded a 'Certified Gold Record', when 'Chattanooga Choo Choo' sold over a million copies. Miller and his Orchestra, like many of the most popular blues artists of the pre-war period, recorded for the Bluebird label.

From the second half of the 1930s big bands were all the rage in America and Britain. One of the first big hits of the big band era, and a million seller, was 'Boogie Woogie' by Tommy Dorsey and his Orchestra. 'Boogie Woogie' was actually 'Pinetop's Boogie Woogie', first recorded in 1928 by Clarence 'Pinetop' Smith. Tommy Dorsey was quick off the mark to capitalise on the craze for boogie woogie. It was sweeping the nation in the wake of the *From Spirituals To Swing* concerts, which was boosted by the success of the Boogie pianists at New York's Cafe Society. Dorsey's recording had staying power, as it was reissued in 1943, '44 and '45 and sold well each time. Boogie woogie was not entirely confined to big bands, either, as one of the best-selling records of 1941 was the Andrews Sisters' 'Boogie Woogie Bugle Boy'.

Neither was it just boogie

woogie that had struck a chord with the big bands. Many of them, along with their singers, recorded blues songs, or in some cases pseudo-blues material. In earlier years, the word 'rag' had been inserted into the title of a song to make it fashionable; now the same thing happened with the Blues. As early as 1935 the Boswell Sisters recorded 'St Louis Blues' (a year earlier, the Boswells recorded the first ever song called 'Rock And Roll', even if it actually did neither). 'St Louis Blues' was very much a big-band favourite, as Cab Calloway recorded it in 1930, The Mills Brothers in '32, Benny Goodman in '36, and Guy Lombardo in '39. Earl Hines, who accompanied a number of blues singers in the 1920s, covered all the bases by recording 'Boogie Woogie On St Louis Blues'.

Other artists followed the same formula. They included Artie Shaw's 'The Blues' in 1938, Count Basie's 'Goin' To Chicago Blues' in 1941, Harry James' 'Feet Draggin' Blues' in 1939, and Woody Herman's 'Bishops Blues' and 'Blues In The Night' in 1941. In fact, 'Blues in the Night' was one of the biggest sellers of that year. The song came from a film of the same name and was written by Johnny Mercer (words) and Harold Arlen (music). Mercer and Arlen were both white, but managed a fairly faithful rendition of the Blues. Dinah Shore enjoyed a big hit with the song, and Artie Shaw, Cab Calloway, Benny Goodman, Harry James, and Jimmie Lunceford also cut it around the same time, with many other artists to follow.

The Boswell Sisters

Recorded the first ever song called 'Rock And Roll', and also applied their harmonies to 'St Louis Blues'.

Woody Herman

The wartime bandleader recorded both 'Bishops Blues' and 'Blues In The Night' in 1941.

The point is that the Blues, even if it was only in name in some cases, had moved out of the 'race label only' market and edged its way into popular white American music. Doubtless many who heard 'the Blues' as performed by big bands and singers like Bing Crosby, had no idea of its heritage. Racial segregation still affected every aspect of daily life, and musical taste was no exception. Record releases were effectively segregated through the 'race' labels, but also through the radio. But there was nothing to prevent a white kid listening to a black station, other than in-built prejudices and habit. Eventually, white kids, in the spirit and tradition of rebellious teens, did exactly what they thought their parents would find abhorrent. This would bring about some remarkable results for the music industry and American society as a whole.

Lady Day Sings the Blues

Make no bones about it, Billie Holiday was not a blues singer, but she certainly had them, sang them, and lived them. Because of films like *Lady Sings The Blues* and her own assertion in her biography of the same name, many people today think of Billie as a blues singer. She certainly came in a direct line of descent from Bessie Smith, Ma Rainey, and the other classic blues singers. At the time some record companies, booking agents, and fans categorised her as a blues singer.

Billie's father Clarence (a guitarist with Fletcher Henderson's Orchestra) and her mother Sadie Fagen probably never married; in any event, they soon split up. Billie moved to New York around 1929, when she was about 15. She was discovered in 1933 by the legendary Columbia Records talent scout John Hammond, himself only 22 at the time, when he reviewed her performance at the 133rd Street Club and began to champion her cause. Her two earliest influences were Bessie Smith and Louis Armstrong; she listened to records that belonged to a brothel madame for whom Billie ran errands. It was through Hammond that Billie got the opportunity to record with Benny Goodman. Her first two sides were a disappointment, but within a few months she was back in the studio and this time there was no disguising her talent. Teddy Wilson directed the accompaniment, and the relaxed, almost 'jam-session' feel of 'Miss Brown To You' and 'I Wished On The Moon' suited her perfectly.

From then on, Lady Day, as Lester Young had nicknamed her, was on her way. She was soon singing with Count Basie and later the Artie Shaw band. In early 1939 she opened at

‘I ain’t good looking, and my hair ain’t curled,
But my mother she give me something,
It’s goin’ to carry me through this world’

'Billie's Blues'
Billie Holiday, 1936

T-BONE WALKER

FACT FILE

BORN: *28th May, 1910*
Linden (Cass Co.), Texas

DIED: *16th March, 1975*
Los Angeles, California

INSTRUMENT: *Guitar, Organ, Piano*

FIRST RECORDED: *1929*

ACCOLADES: *Inducted into the Blues Hall of Fame, 1980*

INFLUENCES: *Leroy Carr, Lonnie Johnson, Blind Lemon Jefferson*

INFLUENCED: *BB King, Buddy Guy, Eric Clapton, Otis Rush, Chuck Berry... everyone!*

AARON THIBEAUX WALKER'S PARENTS were both musicians, while his grandmother was a Cherokee Indian. His family moved to Dallas when he was two years old. Walker had sung in church, and in his late teens he was often to be found leading Blind Lemon Jefferson along Central Avenue in Dallas. He was self-taught on the guitar and began playing local parties from around 1923, later touring in medicine shows with Ida Cox. In 1929 he made his first recordings in Dallas as Oak Cliff T-Bone, for the Columbia label. Soon afterwards Walker went to Oklahoma City, where he learned to single-pick notes on his guitar from a man named Chuck Richardson. Walker's boyhood friend Charlie Christian accompanied him; Christian became one of the top jazz guitarists of the early 40s, as much an inspiration to jazz as Walker was to the Blues.

In the early 30s, Walker toured Texas with various bands before moving to California in 1934. He also frequently worked at Los Angeles clubs like the Little Harlem. Around 1940, he joined the Les Hite Orchestra, recording 'T-Bone Blues' with them. Two years later, he was working as the featured guitarist with the Freddie Slack Orchestra, besides recording in his own right.

All the time, starting around 1936, Walker had been experimenting with the potential of the electric guitar, a musical adventure that was to have an enormous influence. In the early 40s he also developed his stage act, incorporating gimmicks that became part of the rock'n'roll tradition. He would do the splits while playing the guitar behind his head or between his legs, moves that were later copied by the likes of Jimi Hendrix and Chuck Berry. But it was not all flash; there was a huge amount of substance to the way he played. His intricate jazz chords, coupled with his superb tone and sense of dynamics, made Walker

'Finally I heard 'Stormy Monday', my guy called T-Bone Walker and I went crazy for the guitar and then crazy in every sense. I'd never heard anything sound like that guitar to me'

BB KING

"I believe it all comes originally from T-Bone Walker"

Freddie King

an inspiration for almost every guitarist who followed. He had a sense of 'oneness' with the guitar that no one has since been able to match.

By 1946 Walker was back in California, having spent a lot of time in New York and Chicago, where he signed to the Black & White label; enjoying his first R&B hit in 1947 with 'Bobby Sox Blues'. The next year it was followed by 'Call It Stormy Monday (But Tuesday Is Just As Bad)', better known as 'Stormy Monday Blues'. Over the next two years Walker scored seven more R&B hits including 'T-Bone Shuffle'. In 1950 he joined the Imperial label, where he recorded 52 sides. This remarkably consistent body of work demonstrates the wonderful liaison between his voice and guitar, and it is the very embodiment of sophisticated post-war blues.

A switch to Atlantic in 1955 produced the last of his great recordings, notably the 1959 album, *T-Bone Blues*. During his time with the label he recorded with Junior Wells and modern jazz guitarist Barney Kessel. In the late 50s, however, his over-indulgence in alcohol and a recurring ulcer began to take their toll. He was now touring with pick-up bands rather than a regular group, but 35 years into his career his guitar playing was still top-notch.

In 1962 Walker appeared in Europe for the first time as part of the *American Folk Blues Festivals*, and he returned a number of times over the next decade, the last time in 1962. But his performances in the US became less frequent as the 60s progressed, and he now only recorded sporadically. In 1970 he won a Grammy for the album *Good Feelin'*, but his ulcer was getting no better and he couldn't give up the drink. In 1974 he suffered a stroke and by the following spring the man who was called 'the bluesman with a jazz soul' was dead from bronchial pneumonia.

Essential Recordings

Classic Songs

'T-Bone Blues'
'Call It Stormy Monday (But Tuesday Is Just As Bad)'
'Strollin' With Bone'
'Vida Lee'

Classic Albums

T-Bone Blues 1959 Atlantic

The Source

The Complete Imperial Recordings
EMI

activities. In actual fact there was a rapid fall-off in blues records released in the first half of 1942. While Sonny Boy Williamson No. 1 had cut six sides just four days after the attack on Pearl Harbor, he was one of just a few artists who recorded. Others included Tampa Red, Lonnie Johnson, Rosetta Tharpe, Roosevelt Sykes, and Joe Turner – in essence the big names, established artists, and those likely to sell.

In actual fact Lead Belly and Josh White were two of just a very few blues artists who made records during the post-1943 period up until the end of the war. White was particularly active for the Asch label, which at the same time recorded Gary Davis, Sonny Terry, and Brownie McGhee. Lead Belly even went to Hollywood and recorded a few sides for Capitol, making him one of the first bluesmen to record on the West Coast.

In 1942 Capitol signed T-Bone Walker, and he became the featured guitarist with Freddie Slack and his Orchestra. Slack, an excellent boogie woogie pianist and veteran of Jimmy Dorsey's band, was white, and his band was of mixed race. They actually helped to establish the fledgling Capitol label when 'Cow Cow Boogie', featuring the excellent singer Ella Mae Morse, made the charts in late 1942. Two of the sides T-Bone cut with Freddie, 'I Got a Break, Baby' and 'Mean Old World', did much to establish T-Bone's standing with those that were to follow. These seminal recordings of what we now call the West Coast blues sound feature T- Bone's mellow

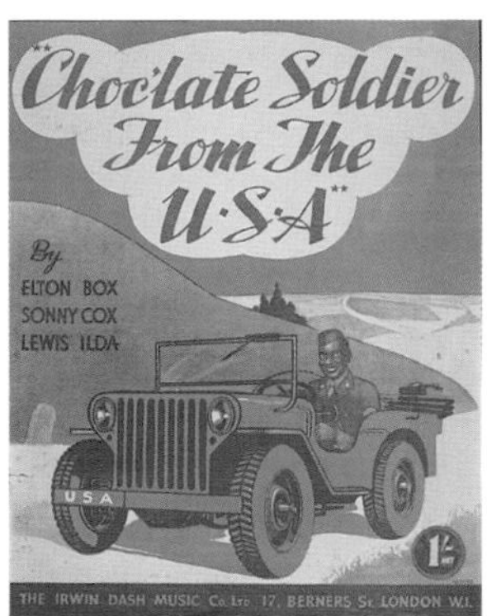

'Chocolate Soldier From The USA'

A patriotic song designed to make black soldiers feel part of the war effort, despite the hardships they faced at home.

Ella Mae Morse

Morse's recording of 'Cow Cow Boogie' gave new label Capitol one of its first hit records.

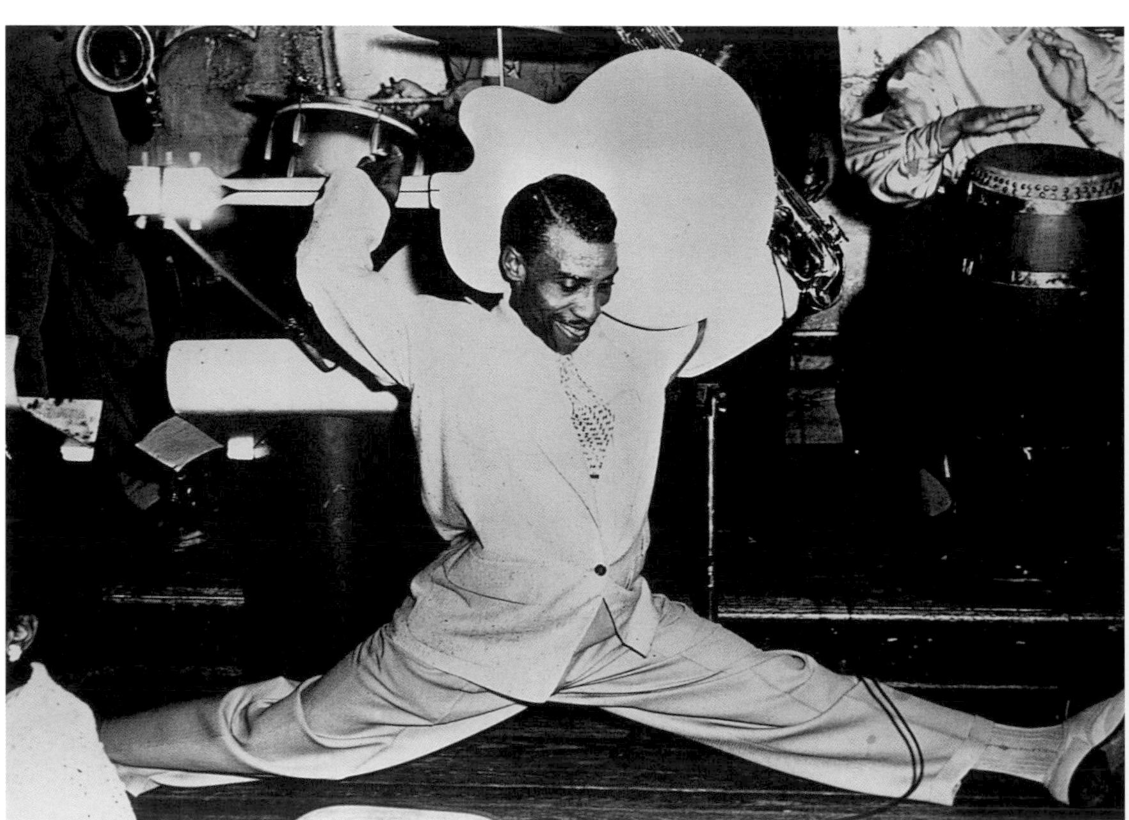

T-Bone Walker

T-Bone was the featured guitarist with Freddie Slack and his Orchestra, striking theatrical poses more than 25 years before Jimi Hendrix.

GOOD MORNING, SCHOOL GIRL

THE SONG THAT WE ALL THINK OF TODAY as 'Good Morning Little Schoolgirl' was first released as 'Good Morning School Girl'. The original version was cut at Sonny Boy Williamson's first recording session for Bluebird on 5th May, 1937, accompanied by Big Joe Williams and Robert Lee McCoy on guitars. The confusion surrounding the title is equalled by the uncertainty about the identity of the composer: many later versions have erroneously credited the second Sonny Boy Williamson (Rice Miller) as the writer of the song.

STAPLE DIET

'Good Morning Little School Girl' became part of the staple diet for both Chicago bluesmen and British blues bands in the 50s and 60s. It has even been called 'the first rock'n'roll record' (but then again, so have many others). Whether or not that's strictly true, 'Good Morning Little School Girl' can certainly claim to have been at the birth.

FRED MCDOWELL

In September 1959 Alan Lomax was travelling through the South with a reel-to-reel recorder, much as he had done with his father two decades earlier. Lomax had been directed to Fred McDowell's house in Como, Mississippi, as Fred was well known in the area from playing at weekend fish fries and parties. Lomax recorded 14 tracks with Fred, including 'Good Morning Little Schoolgirl', and most fans consider these seminal recordings to be among the best by a musician who was soon 'discovered' during the early 60s folk revival.

GOOD MORNING, SCHOOL GIRL

Recorded by Sonny Boy Williamson on Wednesday 5th May, 1937 at the Leland Hotel, Aurora, Illinois.

Hello little schoolgirl, good mornin' little schoolgirl
Can I go home with, can I go home later with you?
Now you can tell your mother and your father
That Sonny Boy is a little schoolboy too

I woke up a-this mornin', I woke up a-this mornin'
Lord, and I couldn't make no, Lord, I couldn't make no time
Well, that I didn't have no blues, woman,
But I was all messed up in mind

Now, you be my baby, come on and be my baby.
I'll buy you a diamond; I'll buy you a diamond ring.
Well if you don't be my little woman
And I won't buy you a doggone thing

I'm gonna buy me a airplane, I'm gonna buy me a airplane
I'm gonna fly all over this man's,
I'm gonna fly all over this man's town
Don't find the woman that I'm lovin',
Then I ain't goin' to let my airplane down

I don't hardly know, I don't know hardly,
Baby, what in this world to, baby, what in this world to do.
Well, that I don't want to never hurt your feelin'
Or either get mad with you

ROD AND THE YARDBIRDS

The song actually made the British charts, although it has never been a hit in the US. A version recorded by The Yardbirds in October 1964 made No.44 in November. Their version, with a writer's credit to Demarias, has lyrical similarities with the original but is in fact melodically different. It was recorded when The Yardbirds' original line-up was still in place, with Eric Clapton on lead guitar and Keith Relf on vocals. A more faithful version became the A-side of 19-year-old Rod Stewart's Decca debut. After busking in Europe Stewart returned to the UK and joined Jimmy Powell and The Five Dimensions. He then moved to London becoming the harp player with Long John Baldry's Hoochie Coochie Men, before recording his first single for Decca. It is unclear whether it was The Yardbirds or Rod Stewart who recorded the song first.

MUDDY WATERS

Muddy's version of 'Good Morning Schoolgirl' appears on the excellent *Muddy Waters Folksinger* album released in 1964.

SELECTED VERSIONS

- 1947 Smokey Hogg
- 1958 Big Joe Williams
- 1959 John Lee Hooker, Mississippi Fred McDowell
- 1961 Lightnin' Hopkins
- 1963 Muddy Waters
- 1964 Rod Stewart, The Yardbirds
- 1965 Paul Butterfield Blues Band, Junior Wells
- 1967 Grateful Dead
- 1968 Steppenwolf
- 1969 Taj Mahal, Ten Years After, Johnny Winter
- 1994 Van Morrison
- 1997 Jonny Lang

and polished riffs, the epitome of laid-back style. While the sound was neither as definitive nor as successful as the Chicago sound, it has an important place in the story of the blues, as well as rock and pop music. For it was during the immediate post-war period that the 'West Coast Sound' was preparing the ground for rock'n'roll.

Further along the California coast from Los Angeles, many black people from Texas and Louisiana went to work in the San Francisco shipyards of Oakland, Richmond, Vallejo, and Hunter's Point. Bandleader Johnny Otis recalled hearing boogie and barrelhouse piano players while growing up in Berkeley. The area's first blues hit came when bandleader Saunders King's 'SK Blues' was recorded by Joe Turner in 1945.

Like its competitors, the Bluebird label suffered a distinct slowdown in its recording activity after July 1942. Bluebird releases were confined to more mainstream activities for the next two years. The label had moderate hits with artists like The Four Vagabonds, The King Sisters, country singer Carson Robison, and Alvino Ray and his Orchestra. However, on Thursday and Friday 14th–15th December, 1944, the label rediscovered the Blues, and not surprisingly they turned to their major stars. Over the two days Roosevelt Sykes, Tampa Red, Lonnie Johnson, and Sonny Boy Williamson No. 1 were among those who recorded. Sonny Boy even cut 'Win The War Blues' in a rare show of recorded wartime patriotism from a blues singer. One of the sides that Roosevelt Sykes cut on 15th December was 'I Wonder', which became the second No. 1 record on *Billboard*'s new black music chart. The 'Juke Box Race Records' listing, as it was now called, was launched in February 1945.

On 15th December, 1944, while the busy blues session in Chicago was in full swing, Glenn Miller, Bluebird's biggest star, was flying across the English Channel. Miller, who had enlisted in the US Air Force in 1942, was on his way to perform for the

Mr Hitler

Just six weeks after Pearl Harbor, Lead Belly made a broadcast on WNYC Radio from City College in New York City. In his set he included two songs about President Roosevelt and another entitled 'Mr Hitler':

"When Hitler started out
He took the Jews
From their home
That's one thing
Mr Hitler, you know
You done wrong.

You ain't no iron,
You ain't no solid rock
(No, you ain't)
But we American
People say
Mister Hitler,
You ain't got no stuff"

Because of the AFM strike and the record company cutbacks, this proved to be one of the few blues recordings that related directly to the war.

Richmond Shipyards

Black workers from Texas and Louisiana came west to California to boost the war effort.

African American Troops, 1942

The 41st Corps of Engineers, an African American army battalion, stand to attention at Fort Bragg, North Carolina. African American soldiers still fought in segragated units in World War II.

Black US Troops

Segregation in war time was little different to peace time.

troops who were engaged on the post D-Day push to Berlin. Something happened to his aircraft, but no one ever found out what because the wreckage was never discovered. The fate of the most popular of the big band leaders is still a mystery. Between July 1935 and his disappearance, Miller had 128 hit records. Some would argue that he was not the best of the big-band leaders, but no one has come close to matching his enduring popular appeal.

In the summer of 1945, two weeks before America tested the A-bomb at Los Alamos in the New Mexico desert on 16th July, the Bluebird regulars were back in the studio. Sonny Boy recorded 'We Got To Win' on 2nd July, but it was not released at the time as events overtook both Bluebird and Sonny Boy. A month later on August 6, Hiroshima was destroyed by an atomic bomb, with Nagasaki suffering a similar fate three days later, and the Japanese surrendered on 14th August, 1945.

With the war over, things began to get back to normal – although identifying what was 'normal' for the Blues was not easy. The evolution from country blues to urban blues that had started back in the 1930s was about to become a revolution – and its effects would be felt all over the world.

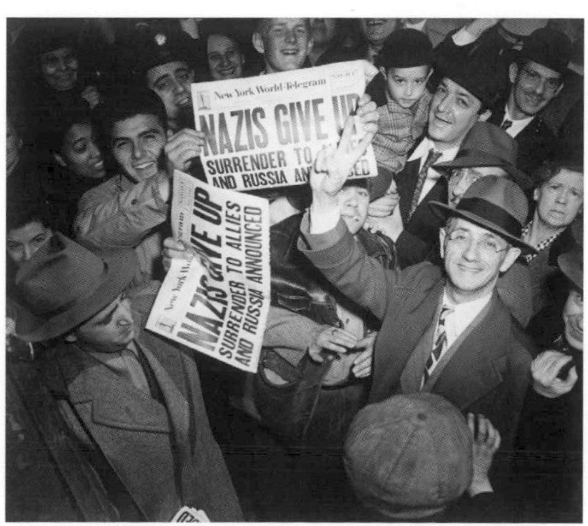

'Nazis Give Up' – VE Day, 1945

In The mood

Bandleader Glenn Miller, Bluebird's biggest star, continued to have hits throughout the war, after his first big record, 'Moonlight Serenade', in 1939. 'In The Mood', probably his best-known song, became his biggest hit as 1939 became 1940.

0020

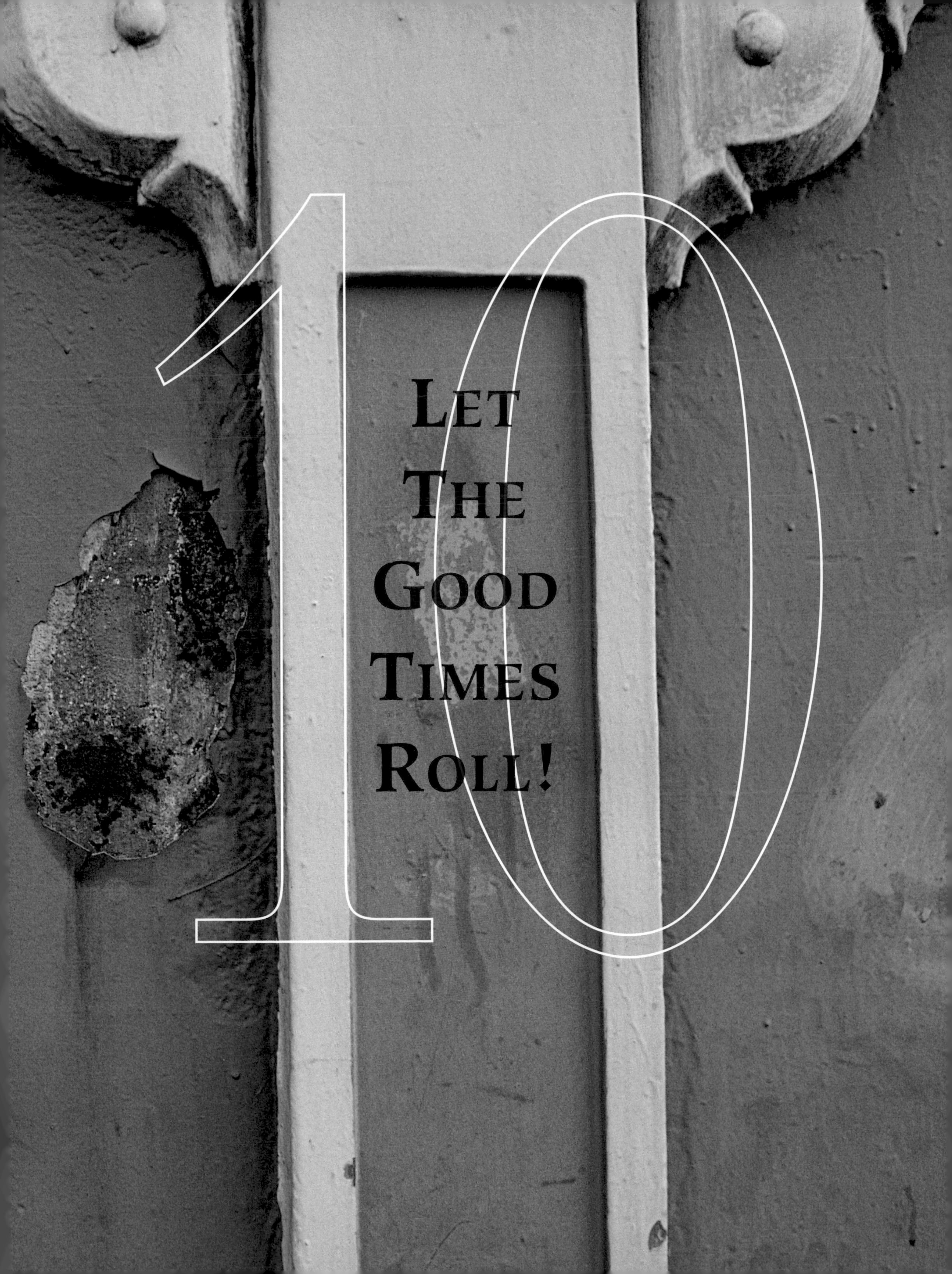

10

Let The Good Times Roll!

WAR IS OVER – THINGS HAVE CHANGED

'The nation's security depends not only on its military strength, but also the physical, spiritual, religious, and moral fibre of its young men'

PRESIDENT HARRY S TRUMAN
RADIO BROADCAST, 21ST DECEMBER, 1946

Harry S Truman

IN APRIL 1945, just a few weeks before the fall of Berlin, Franklin D. Roosevelt died, suddenly elevating Vice President Harry S. Truman to the Oval Office. Truman's early tenure was a difficult one, not least because he was the one who had to give the order to drop the atomic bomb, a project about which he knew nothing until he became President. He was dubbed 'The Accidental President', and initially little was expected of his term in office. But the man who had once joked, 'My choice was either to be a piano player in a whorehouse or a politician, and to tell the truth there's hardly any difference', proved to be very effective. This was especially true until in his second (but first elected) term in office he became bogged down in the Korean War. However, hindsight has shown him to be a solid leader, which was vitally important at the dawn of the 'Cold War'. Winston Churchill told Truman in 1950: "You, more than any other man, have saved Western civilisation."

Truman had to oversee a period that was fraught with potential difficulties. Returning ex-servicemen had strong expectations of work, and of prosperity; after all, wasn't that what they had been fighting for? Many shunned their homelands, and looked to set up a new life in the areas that had benefited from war work. The cities of the North attracted many black ex-military personnel. In some cases, in fact, their families had already moved North in search of war work. Meanwhile, around half a million blacks had left the South to seek their fortunes out on the California coast between 1940 and 1945.

This shift in the blues audience from the South to the North, and especially to the West, also inspired musical change. Migration created new markets, and this in turn altered the way in which records were made and sold. Independent record companies, which had begun to emerge in the early 1940s, were soon springing up all over America. But despite their impact, it was a major label that produced the artist who had the most significant impact on the black music scene. This same artist emphasised, more than any other, the way in which music was changing – Louis Jordan.

Before the war, urban blues always seemed like an offshoot or an extension of country blues, but in the hands of Jordan, and others like him, it sounded entirely new, and a whole lot more exciting. Jordan's music has been described as 'chic blues', for although urban blues was definitely tinged with sophistication, Jordan's music simply overflowed with it... and he was very funny, too.

ACTING AGAINST DISCRIMINATION

On 26th July, 1948, Truman signed an order ending racial discrimination in the military. In World War II, almost one million blacks had served in segregated units, often enduring the worst quarters, inferior supplies, and most arduous duties.

KING OF THE JUKEBOXES

"With my little band I did everything they did with a big band. I made the Blues jump"

LOUIS JORDAN

"A great musician, and way ahead of his time"

BB KING

LOUIS SCORED HIS FIRST R&B hit, 'I'm Gonna Leave You On The Outskirts of Town', back in October 1942. His hits continued throughout the war years, with songs like 'Five Guys Named Moe', 'Is You Is Or Is You Ain't My Baby?', 'GI Jive', and 'Caldonia'. Born in 1908, Louis hailed from Arkansas and followed his father into the famed Rabbit Foot Minstrels, playing saxophone. He later worked with band leader Chick Webb until his death, before forming his Tympany Five (although there were usually eight or nine members in the band!), and signing to Decca in 1939.

Jordan's brand of the Blues was christened jump blues - a fusion of jazz and blues. In fact, jump blues represented the last period of really close interplay between these two dominant black musical forms. Jordan took on board the sounds of the big bands and boogie woogie, as well as Louis Armstrong's Hot Fives and Hot Sevens, creating and amazing sound that has been dubbed "honking and shouting". This referred to the honking of the saxophone and the shouting of the singers – the latter a necessity if they wanted to be heard over the full-throttle, driving sound of the band. The singers who came to the fore in this period thus became known as shouters, even the women!

HONKING AND SHOUTING
Louis Jordan pioneered the style that became known as jump blues – a rowdy blend of jazz and blues.

BLACK STAR RISING

It was in mid-1945 that Louis Jordan started his greatest run of R&B hits, which made him the biggest black star of his day. 'Caldonia', backed by 'Somebody Done Changed The Lock On My Door' (actually written by Casey Bill Weldon), made No. 1 on the newly constituted JukeBox Race Records chart.

In August 1946, Jordan's 'Choo Choo Ch'Boogie' spent 18 weeks on top of the R&B chart, placing it alongside Joe Liggins' 'The Honeydripper' as the most successful No. 1 record of all time. For the whole of 1946 and 1947 Louis had multiple records on the R&B chart, with songs like 'Ain't Nobody Here But Us Chickens', 'Boogie Woogie Blue Plate' and (most famous of all as far as many blues fans are concerned), 'Let The Good Times Roll'.

Despite appearances in films like *Meet Miss Bobby Socks* and *Swing Parade Of 1946*, Jordan's appeal rested mainly with the black market. Only his double-sided recording 'GI Jive' and 'Is You Is Or Is You Ain't My Baby?' from the film *Follow The Boys* proved to be a significant hit with white audiences.

THE R&B CHART

FROM OCTOBER 1942 until February 1945, the US black-music chart was called the Harlem Hit Parade. From 1945 until June 1949 there was a chart known as the Juke Box Race Records. From May 1948 there was a concurrent chart known as the Best Sellers Race Records Chart. From June 1949 these two charts continued to run in tandem, but instead of being called 'race' records they were known as 'rhythm and blues' records. To avoid confusion, we will refer to all these as the 'R&B charts' throughout the remainder of this book. All references to the *Billboard* Hot 100 are to the pop charts, which officially began in 1955.

FIVE GUYS NAMED MOE

In 1990 Clarke Peters, an American living in London, wrote and produced a musical based on the music of Louis Jordan. Clarke also presented the TV documentary of Bill Wyman's Blues Odyssey.

'Today there are few people who are unaware of Louis's achievements. He had a total of 57 hits on the R&B charts, making him one of the most successful artists ever on that chart. I wanted to write a show that celebrated the persona of the man. He went from tent shows to television and influenced everyone from Chuck Berry to James Brown'

BEWARE! LOUIS JORDAN

The band leader in his prime.

LET THE GOOD TIMES ROLL

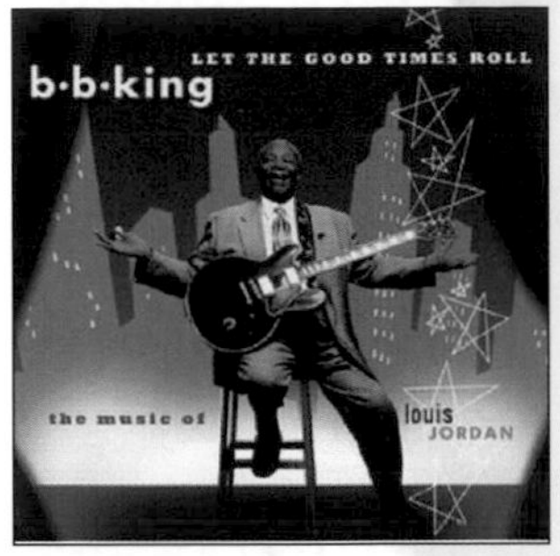

BB's album of Jordan songs.

AT THE END OF BB King's 1980 biography by Charles Sawyer, BB revealed that one of his ambitions was to record an album of Louis Jordan songs. Nineteen years later that album was finally recorded and released, both acknowledging BB's debt to Louis and celebrating the string of great hit records by the man known as the 'King of the Jukeboxes'. Appropriately, the album's title was *Let The Good Times Roll.*

LOUIS & B.B.

BB King first saw Jordan when he came to play Jones' Night Spot in Indianola, King's hometown, probably in 1943 or '44. Louis didn't record 'Let The Good Times Roll' until 26th June, 1946, in New York City, so it is unlikely that the teenage Blues Boy would actually have seen him perform the song. Decca released Jordan's original version in late 1946 on a massive double-sided jukebox hit with 'Ain't Nobody Here But Us Chickens'. The song was credited to Fleecie Moore and Sam Theard, but as Fleecie was Louis's second wife, it seems likely that it was actually Louis who wrote it. Theard, from Alabama, had recorded a couple of sides with Cow Cow Davenport back in 1929.

Moore and Theard's song should not be confused with 'Let The Good Times Roll', a late 50s R&B hit for the husband-and-wife duo, Shirley & Lee; or Sam Cooke's 'Good Times', which uses the same phrase as its hookline.

LET THE GOOD TIMES ROLL

Written by Fleecie Moore & Sam Theard. Bobby Bland & BB King's single from the album *Together For The First Time... Live* reached No. 20 on the R&B chart

Hey everybody, let's have some fun
You only live for once and when you're dead you're done
So let the good times roll, let the good times roll
And live a long, long time
I don't care if you are young or old, no, no,
Get together and let the good times roll

Don't stand there moaning, talking trash
If you wanna have some fun
You'd better go out and spend some cash
And let the good times roll, let the good times roll
I don't care if you young or old,
Get together and let the good times roll

Hey, mister landlord, lock up all the doors
When the police comes around
Tell them Johnny's coming down
Let the good times roll, let the good times roll
And Lord I don't care if you young or old,
That's good enough to let the good times roll

Hey everybody! Tell everybody!
That B.B. and Bobby's in town
I got a dollar and a quarter
And I'm just raring to clown
Don't let nobody play me cheap
I got fifty cents to know that I'm gonna keep
Let the good times roll, I don't care if you young or old
Let's get together and let the good times roll

Q'S JOOK JOINT

In 1995 Quincy Jones made an album called *Q's Jook Joint* which includes 'Let The Good Times Roll'. 'This is based on my 1958 version for which I received my first Grammy,' said Quincy. On the updated version Ray Charles once again took the vocal, but this time he was joined by Stevie Wonder and Bono of U2.

> *When I started touring with my group the Rhythm Kings, we were looking for an opening number and somehow 'Let The Good Times Roll' seemed perfect. I know BB King has been using it for the last 25 years or so to open his live shows, so it has to be a good choice! What we play is a mixture of Quincy Jones' arrangement for Ray Charles and Louis' original version. Georgie Fame, Gary Brooker, and Beverley Skeete share the vocal*
>
> BILL WYMAN

SELECTED VERSIONS

- 1946 Louis Jordan
- 1959 Ray Charles
- 1965 Animals
- 1966 Alexis Korner
- 1971 Pee Wee Crayton
- 1973 Clarence Gatemouth Brown
- 1974 Freddie King
- 1975 Muddy Waters
- 1976 Bobby Bland & BB King
- 1978 Koko Taylor
- 1995 Quincy Jones
- 1998 Bill Wyman's Rhythm Kings
- 1999 BB King

The Independent Record Labels

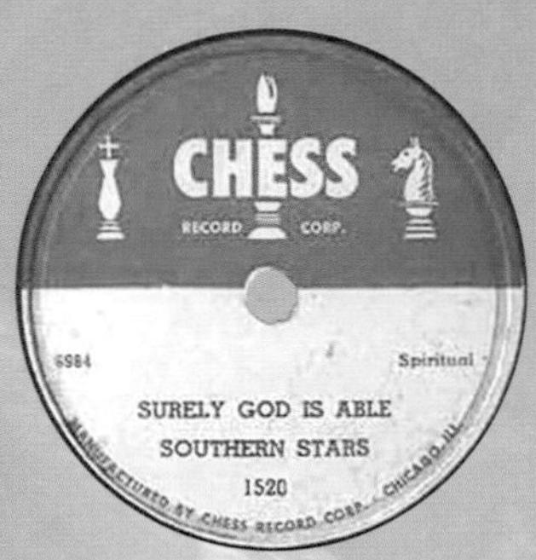

The Harlem Hit Parade listing the most popular black records was first published in 1942, and gave way to the Juke Box Race Records chart in 1945. It was another four years before it became known as the Rhythm & Blues Chart. The best-selling records in the first five years that these charts were compiled were mostly releases by major labels. Decca was the most successful of these, largely thanks to the efforts of Louis Jordan.

Of the 57 records that topped the charts between October 1942 and the end of 1947, 31 (54%) were Decca releases. Of the rest, nine came from Capitol and nine more from Victor/Bluebird. Just six independent releases topped the chart during this period. However, all that quickly changed in 1948 and '49. Of the 31 records that topped the chart in those years, Decca, Victor, and Capitol could only muster five between them. The independents had well and truly arrived.

In the pre-war period, Bluebird had reigned supreme, only challenged by other major labels. The switch to small independent labels during and after the war was, in part, a result of the majors failing to understand the market. With urban audiences increasing in size, as immigration swelled the cities, the economics of the record industry changed. Individual cities became big enough to support their own local labels. A company could make money without having a national hit, and as artists grew in popularity they created their own local and regional hype. The music and record industry became a relatively self-contained business within definite regional areas, occasionally breaking out with nationwide best-sellers.

Savoy

The first successful independent of the 40s was Savoy, which scored a No. 1 on the Harlem Hit Parade with Bonnie Davis and 'Don't Stop Now' in March 1943. Founded in 1942 by Herman Lubinsky in Newark, New Jersey, Savoy started life as a jazz label. But Lubinsky and Fred Mendelssohn were monitoring the changes in musical tastes and began to sign R&B, Blues and vocal harmony artists. Like many of the other top independents, Savoy also branched out into Gospel. By the end of the 40s the label had reaped success with Big Jay McNeeley's Blue Jays, Paul Williams and his Hucklebuckers, and the Hal Singer Sextette. They would later sign Little Esther Phillips, Johnny Otis, Nappy Brown, and the Robins.

Excelsior & Specialty

The first independent to set up on the West Coast was Excelsior, which the Rene Brothers, Leon and Otis, launched around the same time as Savoy. They scored a big hit with 'The Honeydripper' by Joe Liggins after they changed the label's name to Exclusive.

Two years later, Art Rupe, a native of Pittsburgh and a UCLA graduate, founded Jukebox Records. He had already failed with Atlas Records, which went bankrupt within

a year. Jukebox's first release was 'Boogie No. 1' by the Sepia Tones, which secured the label's short-term future when it sold 70,000 copies. By 1946 Jukebox had become Specialty, and an even brighter future was assured when Roy Milton and His Solid Senders had a big hit with 'RM Blues'. This was the first of around 20 R&B hits that the band and label registered over the next seven years. Specialty later signed Jimmy Liggins & His Drops of Joy, Jimmy's brother Joe, and Percy Mayfield. In the 50s their roster would include Lloyd Price, Guitar Slim, Sam Cooke, and Little Richard.

Aladdin and Modern

Los Angeles, with a population swelled by former service personnel and immigrants, became home to a number of other independents, including Bronze, Four Star, Super Disc, Imperial, Gilt Edge, Aladdin, and Modern. Aladdin was originally called Philco and formed in 1944, assuming its new name by 1946. Launched by Eddie and Leo Mesner, the label set about signing some of the best Jump Blues artists in Southern California, including Amos Milburn and Charles Brown.

Modern was started a few months later by the Bihari Brothers, Jules, Joe, and Saul. The Biharis had a penchant for guitar Blues, and in particular looked for talent outside California. Amongst Modern's early signings were PeeWee Crayton and Johnny Guitar Watson. They also distributed records from even smaller labels, and this made them pivotal in the early success of BB King and Elmore James on their subsidiary labels, RPM and Flair.

Miracle and Vee-Jay

Miracle Records was one of the first independents to surface in the windy city, Chicago. Miracle was less Delta blues-based than the giant of Chicago blues labels, Aristocrat/Chess (the subject of its own feature on pages 260–261). Launched in August 1946 by Lee Egalnick, Miracle's office at 107 East 47th Street was in the main business area of Chicago's South Side. Most of its artists were jazz or ballad singers, but the label did sign Memphis Slim. He gave Miracle a No. 1 with 'Messin' Around' in 1948, and the label enjoyed two other smashes that year with Sonny Thompson and his Sharps and Flats.

Vee-Jay was the other Chicago giant. It began trading in 1952 and was unusual in that it was a black-owned label, while almost all of its competitors were Jewish-owned. Vee-Jay, also based on East 47th Street, became the most successful Black-owned label in America until Motown came along in the 60s. Founded by Vivian Carter (the "Vee") and her husband, Jimmy Bracken (the "Jay"), the label boasted Jimmy Reed, John Lee Hooker, and Billy Boy Arnold among its blues acts. Vivian's brother, Calvin Carter, was the company's A&R head and the musical mainstay behind the label. Vee-Jay's first release was 'Roll And Rumba' by Jimmy Reed, released in July 1953.

Vee-Jay and The Beatles

Under license from EMI in Britain, Vee-Jay issued the first Beatles records in America. 'Please Please Me' backed by 'Ask Me Why' (Vee-Jay 498) was followed later in 1963 by 'From Me To You' coupled with 'Thank You Girl'. The Beatles later signed with EMI subsidiary, Capitol Records.

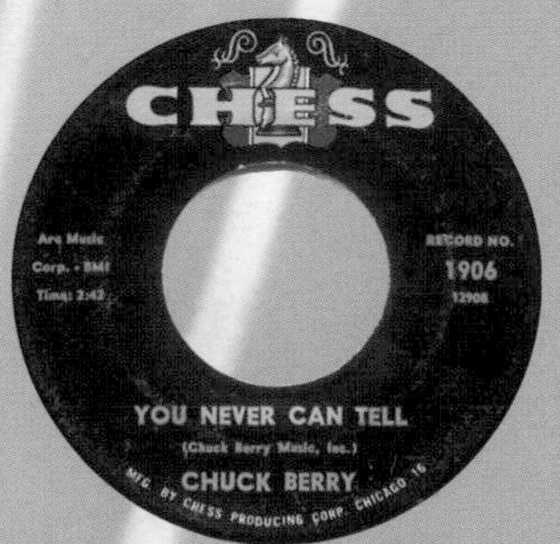

HOME TOWNS OF THE INDIES

THE POST-WAR RISE in independent record companies changed the face of popular music forever. While Sam Phillips' Sun Records is arguably the most famous indie label, it was just one among many, many labels that served as nurseries for some of the biggest names in the Blues and rock'n'roll. With their knowledge of local talent and their ability to attract would be stars, the indie labels were usually the first to record future music legends.

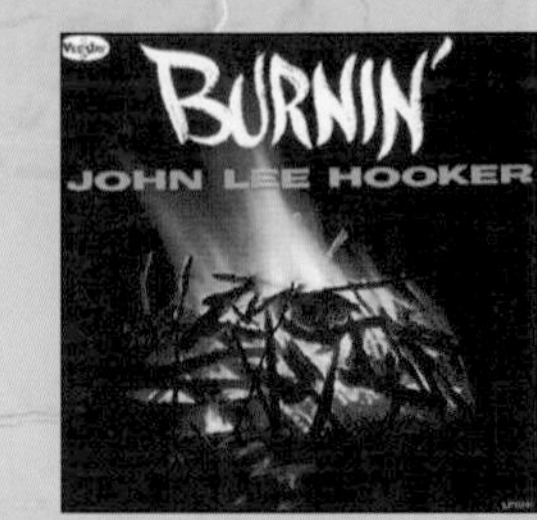

VEE JAY
John Lee Hooker recorded his Burnin' *album on Vee-Jay.*

Oakland
PACIFIC *1946*
BIG TOWN/ DOWNBEAT *1946*

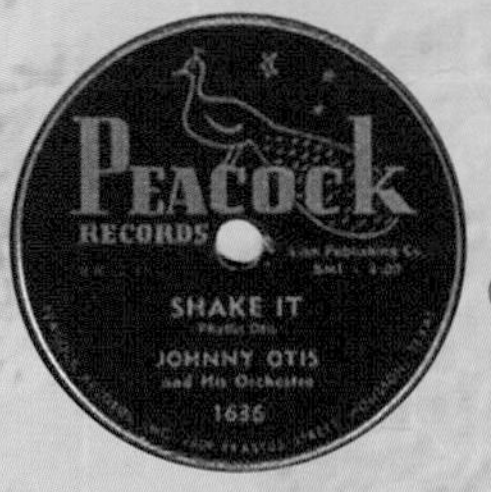

PEACOCK RECORDS
One of the few black-owned labels, it was started by Don Robey to record Clarence 'Gatemouth' Brown after Robey rejected Aladdin's contractual terms. In 1952 Robey bought Duke Records and would later release sides by Bobby Bland and Big Mama Thornton.

LOS ANGELES

LOS ANGELES

EXCELSIOR	*1942 (became Exclusive in 1944)*
JUKEBOX	*1944 (became Specialty in 1946)*
GILT EDGE	*1944*
PHILCO	*1944 (became Aladdin in 1946)*
MODERN	*1945*
BRONZE	*1945*
FOUR STAR	*1945*
SUPER DISC	*1945*
IMPERIAL	*1949*
CLASS	*1951*
METEOR	*1952*

HOUSTON
GULF-GOLD STAR *1944*
FREEDOM *1949*
MACY'S *1949*
PEACOCK *1949*

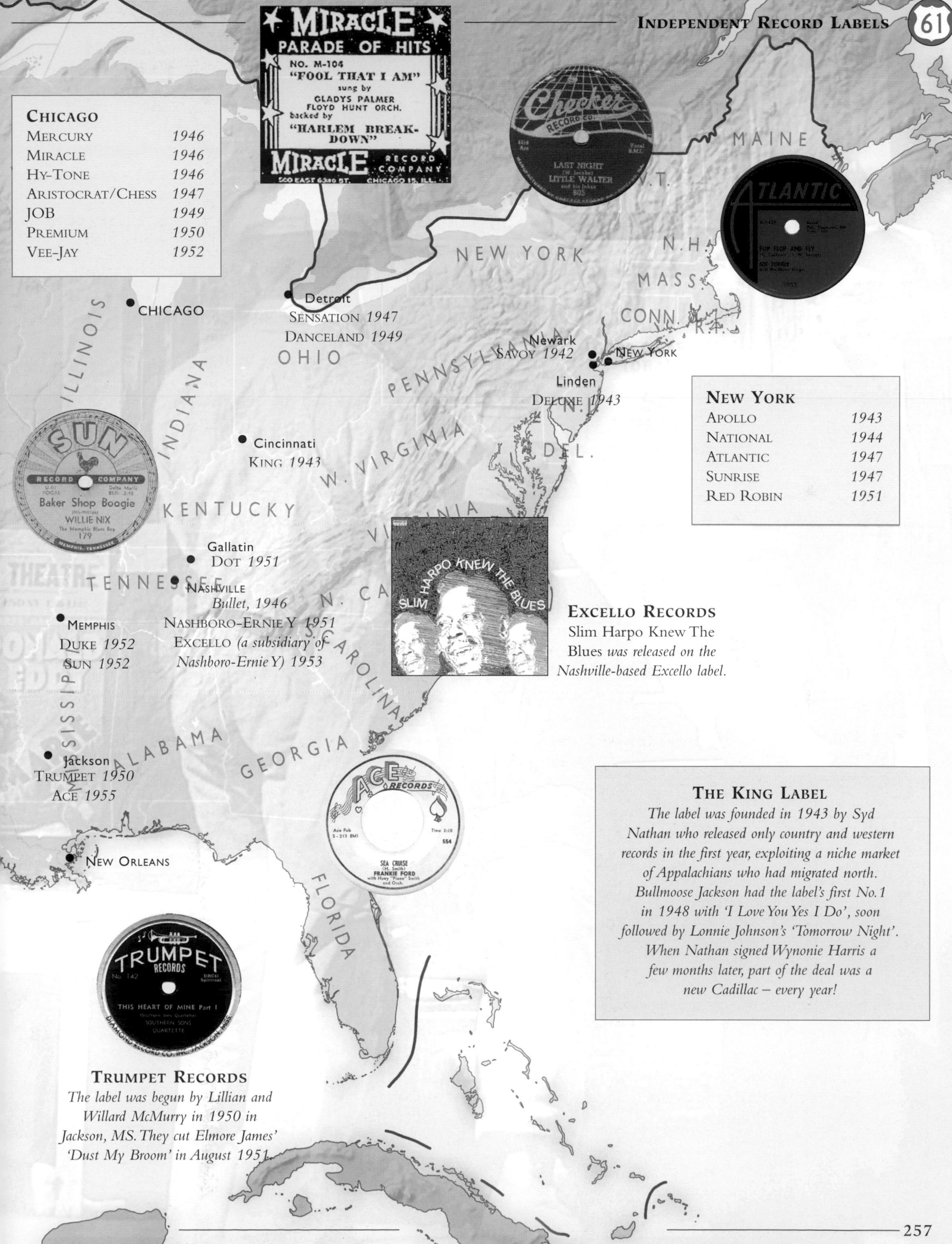

CHICAGO

MERCURY	1946
MIRACLE	1946
HY-TONE	1946
ARISTOCRAT/CHESS	1947
JOB	1949
PREMIUM	1950
VEE-JAY	1952

NEW YORK

APOLLO	1943
NATIONAL	1944
ATLANTIC	1947
SUNRISE	1947
RED ROBIN	1951

EXCELLO RECORDS

Slim Harpo Knew The Blues *was released on the Nashville-based Excello label.*

THE KING LABEL

The label was founded in 1943 by Syd Nathan who released only country and western records in the first year, exploiting a niche market of Appalachians who had migrated north. Bullmoose Jackson had the label's first No. 1 in 1948 with 'I Love You Yes I Do', soon followed by Lonnie Johnson's 'Tomorrow Night'. When Nathan signed Wynonie Harris a few months later, part of the deal was a new Cadillac – every year!

TRUMPET RECORDS

The label was begun by Lillian and Willard McMurry in 1950 in Jackson, MS. They cut Elmore James' 'Dust My Broom' in August 1951.

AT LAST... THE 1948 SHOW

JULIA LEE
Julia Lee was a Kansas City legend, who worked in the city for nearly four decades.

PERHAPS BECAUSE OF the AFM strike, no single artist held sway over the charts in 1948 the way that Louis Jordan had done in the previous two years. The launch of the Best Sellers R&B listing meant there was greater diversity in the charts. Twenty different records, by 16 different artists, topped either the Jukebox or Best Sellers chart during 1948. They included Julia Lee & Her Boyfriends with 'King Size Papa' and 'Snatch And Grab It' (those girls still loved a little double entendre) and Dinah Washington's 'Am I Asking Too Much'. Then there was Lonnie Johnson's 'Tomorrow Night', which Elvis would cover in September 1954 for Sun. Other artists with a more traditional feel did well, such as pianist Sonny Thompson who with his group the Sharps and Flats, made No. 1 with the boogie blues instrumental 'Long Gone (Parts 1 and 2)'.

Late in the year Amos Milburn entered the charts with his infectious 'Chicken Shack Boogie'. Those chickens keep coming back to the Blues! It went to No. 1, the first in a run of 19 hits for Amos on the Aladdin label from 1948 to 1954. Amos, who was just 21 years old when he had his first chart success, had served in the navy from 1942 to 1945, having lied about his age. He signed to Aladdin in 1946 after his demob, and the label was very patient with him, allowing him to release a number of records before he hit it big – among them the excellent 'Down The Road Apiece'.

In keeping with the spirit of the time, when people were looking for fun, and the relaxed, easy-going Californian lifestyle, Amos built a career on records about booze. From 1950 onwards he had hits with 'Bad Bad Whiskey', 'Thinking And Drinking', 'Let Me Go Home Whiskey', 'One Scotch, One Bourbon, One Beer', and 'Good Good Whiskey'. After his relationship with Aladdin

34 WEEKS ON THE CHARTS

IN MARCH 1949 Jimmy Witherspoon entered the R&B charts with his version of the Bessie Smith classic, 'Ain't Nobody's Business'. It stayed on the R&B chart for 34 weeks, longer than any record had charted up to that point - in fact, most tended to stick around for relatively short periods. It was the start of a highly successful year for the former merchant seaman from Arkansas, who had been the featured vocalist with his back-up musicians on this release, the Jay McShann Band. He charted with three further songs, including the old Leroy Carr song, 'In The Evening (When The Sun Goes Down)'. His career was overtaken by rock'n'roll but he made a successful switch to jazz, performing at the Newport Festival in 1959 and from then on working with some of the best jazz players. In 1954 he recorded at Chess and cut an excellent single written by Willie Dixon, 'When The Lights Go Out', which proved that the Blues lost an excellent singer when Jimmy switched styles.

finished, so did his hits. He continued working through the 1950s and 1960s, but his reputation was all he had left to get his bookings. He suffered a series of strokes in the 1970s and died in 1980.

THE BROWNS SING THE BLUES

The writer of 'Good Rockin' Tonight', Roy Brown, charted the song in 1948, but it fared less well than Wynonie's version, only reaching No. 11 on the R&B chart. Brown, who wrote the song on a brown paper bag, originally offered it to Wynonie, who at first refused it. After Roy scored a local hit in New Orleans, Wynonie changed his mind, and must have been glad he did.

While Brown did not rock as hard as Harris, he influenced many artists and can lay claim to be one of the founding fathers of rock'n'roll. In fact, it was Brown's version rather than Harris's that Elvis followed more closely when he covered the song in September 1954. In 1949, Brown had seven songs on the R&B charts, including 'Long About Midnight', which got to No. 1. The following year, 'Hard Luck Blues' also topped the chart, while three others made the Top 10. After 1951, Brown's star faded, as like Harris, he somehow could not make it in straight-ahead rock'n'roll. He continued to record throughout the remainder of the 1950s and into the 1960s for a mass of different labels, only managing a couple of small hits in 1957. Brown died from a heart attack in 1981, the same year he was inducted into the Blues Hall of Fame.

Amos Milburn

Roy Brown

❛Amos Milburn's was not the original version of 'Down The Road Apiece'; he was covering Will Bradley's 1940 version, featuring Ray McKinley. Along the way he definitely made the song his own, giving it a rockin' rhythm that not even Chuck Berry could match when he covered it in 1960. It was surprising that Amos never had a hit with it. Given that it was released in early 1946 he may have been a little ahead of the boogie revival that started later in the year. We covered 'Down The Road Apiece', cutting it at Chess Studios in Chicago on 11th June, 1964. In the middle of us playing the song, Chuck walked in – you can imagine our surprise. Keith, who idolised Chuck, was probably the most surprised of all of us, and it certainly inspired him to a great solo on the record. After we finished Chuck stayed around for a while and chatted with us❜

BILL WYMAN

CHESS RECORDS

‘The Blues is at the heart of popular music and Chess Records are at the heart of the Blues’

BUDDY GUY, 1998

IN THE EARLY 40S, two Polish-born brothers, Leonard and Philip Chess (whose real name was Chez), owned a number of Chicago nightclubs, including the Macomba Lounge on the city's South Side. These establishments acted as their stepping-stone to owning what is arguably the most famous record label in the whole history of the Blues. As a result of their contacts on the club circuit, they were able to ‘buy into’ the established Aristocrat label in 1947, which concentrated on jazz and jump blues. The brothers’, and the label’s, first major success was Muddy Waters’ ‘I Can't Be Satisfied’. Nearly two years later, Leonard and Phil bought out their original partner and renamed their label Chess.

Leonard Chess

With the change of name came a rash of new signings, including Jimmy Rogers, (a key man in Muddy’s band), Eddie Boyd & His Chess Men, Willie Mabon, Memphis Slim, and Howlin’ Wolf. They even cut records with John Lee Hooker as early as 1950, although it would be unfair to say they signed Hooker, given his penchant for giving ‘exclusive’ contracts to several labels at the same time.

Following their initial success they decided

Phil Chess

Background photo: L to R: Eddie Boyd, Buddy Guy, and Fred Below at Chess.

CHESS & CHECKER R&B NO.1’S

THE LABEL’S TWO BIGGEST blues stars, Howlin’ Wolf and Muddy Waters never did manage to top the R&B chart. The Wolf’s biggest hit was ‘How Many More Years’, which made No. 4 in early 1952; the best for Muddy was a No. 3 hit in 1954 with ‘I’m Your Hoochie Coochie Man’.

Chess 1458	Jackie Brenston	‘Rocket 88’	1951
Checker 758	Little Walter	‘Juke’	1952
Chess 1531	Willie Mabon	‘I Don’t Know’	1952
Chess 1538	Willie Mabon	‘I’m Mad’	1953
Checker 811	Little Walter	‘My Babe’	1955
Checker 814	Bo Diddley	‘Bo Diddley’	1955
Chess 1604	Chuck Berry	‘Maybelline’	1955
Chess 1653	Chuck Berry	‘School Days’	1957
Chess 1683	Chuck Berry	‘Sweet Little Sixteen’	1958
Checker 1105	Little Milton	‘We’re Gonna Make It’	1965

to form a subsidiary label in 1952 called Checker. Among the artists on this new label were Elmore James, Little Walter, Memphis Minnie, and Sonny Boy Williamson. Later, in 1954, Lowell Fulson had a big hit on Checker with 'Reconsider Baby'. By 1955 Chess had expanded further still, as well as crossing over into the white rock'n'roll market with Chuck Berry and Bo Diddley. This success brought a new breed of bluesman into the fold, led by Otis Rush and Buddy Guy.

❛ *On the Rhythm Kings album* Struttin' Our Stuff, *we covered Willie Mabon's 'I'm Mad'. Geraint Watkins played organ and sang the song in his own inimitable style:*

'I'm mad and you have the nerve to try to be glad'

... Wonderful lyrics! ❜

BILL WYMAN

Much of the label's success can be attributed to the crucial work of Chess A&R man, composer, performer, and general Mr Fix-it, Willie Dixon. Dixon's bass playing, coupled with Fred Below's peerless drumming, was pivotal to the Chess sound. They were brilliant at creating that tight yet loose feel that epitomises Chess's output during the 50s, always leaving just the right amount of room for the vocals. Little Walter's 'My Babe', written by Dixon and recorded in 1955, sums up their approach perfectly. The guitarist on this session was another of the brothers' early signings, Robert Jr Lockwood.

Another vital key to Chess's success was its ability to 'pick up' records originally recorded by other labels, often in other US cities – including, most famously, Sam Phillips' Sun Records in Memphis. That was how Chess first became involved with Howlin' Wolf. It also leased Jackie Brenston's 'Rocket 88' from Phillips, cited by many as the 'first rock'n'roll' record. While that debate is still going on, the record was brilliant – and it made Chess a lot of money when it spent five weeks at the top of the R&B charts in early summer 1951.

MAKING NOISE WITH ETTA

The 60s were not as productive for the label, as its sound was being surpassed by the younger white rock bands, who used much of the Chess template to achieve their own success. But Chess did make some noise with Etta James, whose records were issued on a new subsidiary label, Argo. Both 'All I Could Do Was Cry' and the stunning 'At Last' reached No. 2 on the R&B chart.

Many of the label's best records were produced by Ralph Bass or by Leonard Chess. Leonard died in 1969 and the label was then sold, eventually ending up in the hands of MCA Records. Today it is owned by Universal, which has concentrated on selective reissues of this classic catalogue of the Blues. Phil Chess went on to run radio station WVON in the 70s, while Leonard's son Marshall ran Rolling Stones Records.

Chess 1571: Muddy Waters' 'Just Make Love To Me'

MUDDY'S BEST

Appropriately enough, given the pioneering stature of Muddy Waters, the Chess label's first album release was The Best of Muddy Waters *in 1957.*

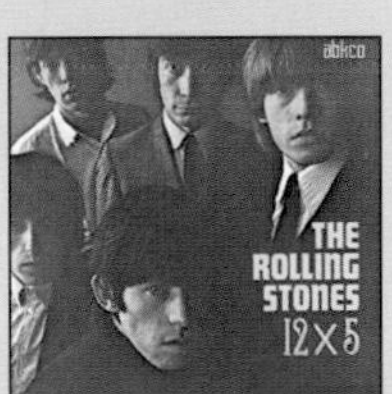

2120 SOUTH MICHIGAN AVENUE

❛ *This was the address of Chess Studios in Chicago and the title of a Stones track that appeared on our UK EP* Five By Five *and the US album* 12 x 5. *We cut it and a number of other tracks at the studio on 10th and 11th June, 1964, with engineer Ron Malo, who had worked with most of our idols. Amongst the numbers we did there were Chuck Berry's 'Around And Around' and 'Confessin' The Blues', and Muddy's 'I Can't Be Satisfied' and 'Look What You've Done'. Over the two days we cut 15 tracks. Probably the highlight was the Womack's 'It's All Over Now', which became our first British No. 1 later in the summer. On the first day Buddy Guy dropped by the studio with Willie Dixon, who tried to sell us a few of his songs! The next day Muddy Waters helped us unload some of our gear from our van... we were stunned and near speechless* ❜

BILL WYMAN

COLLEGE BLUES

In early 1949, the middle-class, university-educated Texan Charles Brown cut 'Get Yourself Another Fool' for Aladdin and made No. 4 on the R&B chart. There followed a string of hits that lasted until 1952. During these three years Charles made No. 1 twice, with 'Trouble Blues' and 'Black Night'. 'Trouble Blues' was a massive hit, spending 15 weeks at No. 1 on the R&B chart in 1949. Of his 12 hits, 10 made the Top 10, including a cover of Leroy Carr's 'In the Evening (When The Sun Goes Down)'. Charles' sound was very definitely West Coast, and its patina of urban sophistication meant that it was dubbed 'night club blues'. While these records were hits under his own name, Charles Brown was no stranger to the charts. As the pianist and vocalist with Johnny Moore's Three Blazers, Charles had already enjoyed a long run of hits from the end of 1945 until he left the group in 1948 to pursue a solo career. These included 'Drifting Blues', which got to No. 2 in 1946 and was voted R&B song of the year, and 'Merry Christmas Baby', which was released for Christmas 1947 and remained one of the most popular seasonal records for over three decades. While Brown's chart career went on the wane after 1952, he continued recording and working live for the next five decades. He was still recording in the 1990s, and opened for Bonnie Raitt on her 1990 tour.

CHARLES BROWN
A huge influence on the young Chuck Berry, Ray Charles, and Elvis Presley.

Clarence 'Gatemouth' Brown

THE GATEMOUTH OPENS

Although he grew up in Texas, the third blues-singing Brown was actually born in Louisiana. Clarence Brown served in the army during World War II and on his discharge he settled in Houston. In 1947 he found work in a Houston nightclub, impressing its owner, Don Robey, who secured a contract for the man nicknamed 'Gatemouth' with the Aladdin label in Los Angeles. His Aladdin debut, 'Gatemouth Boogie', opened with the line: 'My name's Gatemouth and I've just got in your town'; but both it and a follow-up failed to score.

Robey then decided to start his own label called Peacock, and immediately signed Brown. His first hit, in 1949, was 'Mary Is Fine,' which made No. 8 on the R&B charts, while records such as 'Okie Dokie Stomp' and 'Dirty Work At The Crossroads' became regional hits.

Brown was a big influence on the Texas bluesmen who followed him. He finally left the Peacock label in 1960 and moved to Nashville. After playing in a house band on a television show, and working on some country sessions, he was 'rediscovered' in the 70s by European audiences. Brown, who played both guitar and fiddle, showed the clear influences of Western swing in his music.

WEST COAST GUITAR SLINGERS

THE 'WEST COAST SOUND', best portrayed by T-Bone Walker, soon found other exponents, who were keen to exploit the public's interest in the guitarist as a front man. Pee Wee Crayton's 'Blues After Hours' topped the R&B chart in November 1948. The Texan had moved to the West Coast in 1935 and recorded with Ivory Joe Hunter in the mid-1940s. He signed to Modern Records, and his debut hit was the start of a long, long career as a solo artist. His follow-ups on Modern included 'Texas Hop' and 'I Love You So', which both reached the R&B charts in 1949. While he continued to record throughout the 1950s and 1960s for a variety of labels, however, Crayton could never match his success at Modern.

If you had only three minutes and wanted to know what the West Coast blues sound was like, then T-Bone Walker's 'They Call It Stormy Monday (But Tuesday's Twice As Bad)' would solve the problem. T-Bone, who had taken up the electric guitar in 1939, recorded 'Stormy Monday', as it has become known, in mid-1947 in Hollywood for the Black & White label.

Released just before Christmas, it climbed to No. 5 in the R&B charts in early 1948. In actual fact it is one of those songs that has had a much greater impact than its original chart position suggests. Its importance was acknowledged in 1991 with a Grammy Hall of Fame award.

T-Bone's rendition, with its laconic vocals, great brass arrangement, and his deft touch (alternating between delicacy and attack) on the electric guitar, has become the definitive version. T-Bone recorded the song a number of times during his career, but he was not the first to record it. Earl Hines had charted with the song in 1942, with Billy Eckstine handling the vocals.

Other fine versions include Bobby Bland's 1962 chart hit, Muddy Waters', and the Allman Brothers' from their *Live At The Fillmore East* album in 1971. A few months after recording 'Stormy Monday', T-Bone cut 'T-Bone Shuffle', which has become an essential piece for every aspiring blues guitarist to learn.

Walker left Black & White in 1950, switching to the Imperial label to record more than 50 wonderful sides. While none of these could match his earlier chart success, he

'I believe it all comes originally from T-Bone Walker. BB King and I were talking about that not long ago and he thinks so, too'

FREDDIE KING,
MELODY MAKER, 8TH MARCH, 1971

T-BONE WALKER
His recording career spanned 45 years and he made the Rock & Roll Hall of Fame in 1987.

SONNY BOY WILLIAMSON

FACT FILE

BORN: *4th December, 1899 Glendora, Mississippi*

DIED: *25th May, 1965, Helena, Arkansas*

INSTRUMENT: *Harmonica, Guitar, Drums*

FIRST RECORDED: *1951*

ACCOLADES: *Inducted into the Blues Hall of Fame, 1980*

INFLUENCED: *James Cotton, BB King, Junior Wells, Muddy Waters*

LIKE THE MAN WHOSE NAME he took, the second Sonny Boy Williamson did much to establish the harmonica's place in the story of the blues. He was born Aleck Ford, the illegitimate son of Millie Ford, but later took his stepfather's name, and became known as Rice Miller. He began playing when he was just five years old and quickly developed into an accomplished harmonica player. From a young age Sonny Boy earned tips on street corners and at dances and house rent parties.

Throughout his life he was a master of misinformation and so the details of his life are both sketchy and confusing. An inveterate liar, he even maintained that he (and not John Lee Williamson) was the original Sonny Boy Williamson, who had recorded in the 1930s. But his liberal attitude to the truth, and his desire to confuse and confound, should not be allowed to detract from his talent. He was a giant, not just of the harmonica, but also as a composer and performer. Sonny Boy commanded attention on stage, with a presence even larger than his wiry 6ft frame. Quite simply he was one of the most charismatic performers in the whole history of the Blues.

Sonny Boy married Mary Burnett, Howlin' Wolf's half-sister, in the 1930s, and taught the young man to play the harmonica. He worked throughout the Delta, and Homesick James said: "We used to call him Little Boy Blue. He had a belt round his waist for all his harmonicas." Sonny Boy learned his trade well, and when he and Robert Lockwood Jr began performing daily on KFFA in 1941, he was already a 'star' of the Delta blues scene. Like all his public appearances, his performances on the 15-minute radio show, *King Biscuit Time*, showed him as part-musician, part-raconteur, and part-showman.

'Just before we do this next number, ladies and gentlemen, tonight's a big night in Greenwood, Mississippi, yes sir... Meet me there, beat me there'

SONNY BOY PROMOTING HIS OWN GIG DURING A 1965 RECORDING OF *KING BISCUIT TIME*

Sonny Boy used the radio to promote his evening performances, which earned him better money from club owners, as well as generally advancing his career.

He worked on *King Biscuit Time* until 1948 (his face was even printed on the bags of cornmeal to help sell the product), and continued to broadcast into the 1950s. Sonny made his recording debut for the Trumpet label in Jackson, Mississippi on 12th March, 1951. His first release was the classic, 'Eyesight For The Blind', which featured Willie Love on piano, Henry Reed on bass, and Joe Dison on drums. More Trumpet sessions followed between 1951 and 1954, producing sides like 'Nine Below Zero', while he also played harmonica on Elmore James' classic 'Dust My Broom'. Sonny Boy later re-recorded many of his early, self-composed recordings, but these early sides capture the feel of his raw, juke joint blues to perfection.

By 1955 Sonny Boy's contract had been 'sold on' to the Chess subsidiary label, Checker. For some time he had been playing in the bars of Detroit, where he worked with Baby Boy Warren, and Chicago. His first sides for Checker were recorded in Chicago, and they featured Muddy Waters, Otis Spann, Jimmy Rogers, and Fred Below. 'Don't Start Me Talkin' was a great debut for the label, which made No. 3 on the R&B chart. Subsequent Checker sides reunited him with Robert Lockwood Jr, and Robert's playing perfectly complemented Sonny Boy's rhythmic sense. Living and working in Chicago did not stop him from returning periodically to Arkansas and taking up further residencies on *King Biscuit Time*.

His travelling ways continued in 1963 when he was included in the second American Folk Blues Festival tour of Europe. Sonny Boy loved Europe and Europe loved him, and he chose to stay behind in Britain after the tour ended, recording with both The Yardbirds and The Animals, and playing club dates with both bands across the country. He travelled throughout Europe and even played behind the Iron Curtain in Poland. He appeared with the festival again the following year, delighting audiences with his funny stories, casual asides and all-round showmanship.

By 1965 Sonny Boy had returned to Helena and another spell on *King Biscuit Flour Time*. He also met the future members of the Band, who came to pay their respects. He talked about returning to Europe, but it was not to be. He died in his sleep in May 1965.

SONNY BOY CORN MEAL
Sonny Boy's face was printed on bags of cornmeal to help sell the product.

SHE'S GOT THE POWER TO HEAL YOU, NEVER FEAR
With songs like 'Eyesight To The Blind' (which Pete Townshend used in The Who's Tommy*), and this side cut for Trumpet Records, it seems that Sonny Boy held a strong belief in women's healing powers.*

> *'He was, in fact, one of the most genuinely creative, persuasive, strikingly individualistic performers the Blues has ever seen'*
>
> PETE WELDING'S SLEEVE NOTES FOR THE CHESS ALBUM *ONE WAY OUT*

ESSENTIAL RECORDINGS

CLASSIC SONGS

'Eyesight To The Blind' 1951
'Don't Start Me Talkin' ' 1955
'Nine Below Zero' 1961
'Bring It on Home' 1963

CLASSIC ALBUMS

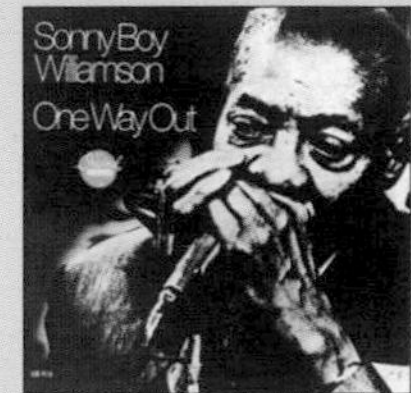

One Way Out 1968

THE SOURCE

His Best Chess/Universal

THE ALLMAN BROTHERS
Their Live At The Fillmore *album not only featured a superb version of 'Stormy Monday', but also staked their claim to being one of the great blues-rock bands of all time – thanks in no small part to Duane Allman's lead guitar work.*

continued to be an inspiration for every guitar wannabe. By 1955 he had switched to Atlantic Records and released the album *T-Bone Blues*, an acknowledged classic. Increasing health problems, coupled with sporadic success, saw Walker in steady decline during the 60s, and he died in 1975, having suffered a stroke the previous year. Everyone on the blues scene now acknowledges a debt to T-Bone Walker, however, and a casual dip into his extensive catalogue of recordings will prove what a consistent performer he was at every stage of his career.

THREE O'CLOCK BLUES

Another apostle of the West Coast guitar sound, Lowell Fulson, was born in Tulsa in 1921. His father was a Cherokee Indian and his mother Mammie played the guitar and sang. Having learned the guitar, Lowell took up with Texas Alexander.

The pair played dances and parties in Texas from around 1940 until 1943, when Lowell was drafted into the Navy. He was posted to Oakland, near San Francisco, and met label owner Bob Geddins, for whom he began recording in 1946. Geddins owned Big Town Records and Down Beat, who released Lowell's early records.

Initially Lowell could find only local success, but then in late 1948 he reached No. 6 on the R&B chart with 'Three O'Clock Blues' on the Down Town label, which featured his brother Martin on acoustic rhythm guitar. His follow-ups included 'Everyday I Have The Blues', a reworking of Memphis Slim's 'Nobody Loves Me', and 'Blue Shadows', which topped the R&B chart in the summer of 1950.

In the early 50s Lowell's 10-piece travelling band featured Ray Charles on piano and Stanley Turrentine on tenor sax. In 1954 Lowell made No. 3 on the R&B charts with the brilliant 'Reconsider Baby' (later covered by Elvis), on the Checker label. His career slowed down after that, despite a string of fine Checker singles like 'Do Me Right', featuring some excellent piano from Lloyd Glenn.

> *'My first hit record was Lowell Fulson's 'Three O'Clock Blues'. I idolised Lowell... I liked his singing better than his playing'*
>
> BB KING

T-Bone Walker

By 1964 he had switched to Kent Records, which seemed to revive his career. He recorded 'Black Nights', which put him back into the R&B charts at No. 11, following it with 'Tramp' in 1967, written by Lowell and Jimmy McCracklin. This single, which was much closer to mainstream soul than any of his earlier work, reached both the R&B chart and the *Billboard* Hot 100 before becoming an even bigger hit for Otis Redding and Carla Thomas.

While Lowell Fulson continued to record during the 1970s, 80s, and even into the 90s, he was regrettably past his best. He toured throughout Europe and America in the final decades of the 20th century, and in doing so gave many people their only opportunity to see a living link to pre-war country blues. Lowell Fulson died in 1999.

LE COMMANDER OF ARTS & LETTERS

WHILE ALL THE ARTISTS we have mentioned flourished after World War II, the slowdown in recording during the conflict affected even those artists with established pre-war careers. With few exceptions, most of the survivors saw their careers falter during the 1940s. Some veterans had no choice, like Sonny Boy Williamson No. 1, who was murdered in 1948, or Lead Belly, who died a year later. But a lucky minority of those who recorded before the war went on to have far greater success afterwards. One of them was John Len Chatman, who first recorded in 1940 as Peter Chatman – but is better known as Memphis Slim.

Memphis Slim really did come from Memphis, having been born in Shelby County in 1915. A pianist in the style of Roosevelt Sykes and Speckled Red, he got his break when he moved to Chicago in 1939, becoming Big Bill Broonzy's regular accompanist the following year. After early releases on OKeh he switched to Bluebird, cutting around 20 sides, the last at a session three days before Pearl Harbor. It was another three years before Slim recorded again, and when he did it was for one of the new independents, Chicago's Hy-Tone Records. This was the start of a post-war career that spanned the next five decades.

Memphis Slim and his seven-piece House Rockers cut the influential 'Nobody Loves Me' in early 1948 for the Miracle label. A few months later he reached No. 1 in the R&B chart with 'Messin' Around'. More hits followed for labels across the US. Besides his 1940s Miracle sides, he cut records that decade for King in Cincinnati and Peacock in Houston. During the 1950s he recorded for Premium, Chess, United, Mercury, and Vee-Jay in Chicago, and Folkways and Verve in New York. In 1961 Slim moved to Paris, continuing to record and tour extensively. He was a popular fixture at Les Trois Maillets Club on the Left Bank, often showing up in a Rolls Royce. Slim died of kidney failure in February 1988, but not before the US Senate made him an Ambassador-at-Large of Good Will. More bizarrely the French government gave him the title of Commander of Arts & Letters – odd, simply because Slim was neither one of the best nor the most successful bluesman.

MEMPHIS SLIM
Ambassador-At-Large of Good Will and Commander of Arts & Letters to the French government.

THE KILLER

In 1949 Sticks McGhee and his Buddies had a No. 2 R&B hit with 'Drinkin' Wine Spo-Dee-O-Dee' on the Atlantic label. Sticks, whose real name was Granville, was the brother of Brownie McGhee. Big Chief Ellis played the piano, and his work proved to be inspirational for the 14-year-old Jerry Lee Lewis. The teenager played the record over and over again, learning the piano and vocal parts, and then performing the song at the opening of a Ford dealership in Ferriday, Mississippi. Jerry Lee, who would later be nicknamed 'The Killer', cut the song at Sun in the 50s, and then took a drunken version, cut in London in 1973, into the Hot 100 later that year.

RADIO WAVES

DURING THE DEPRESSION, radio became a popular means of entertainment, showcasing jubilee singers like the Golden Gate Quartet. Then in the post-war period radio began to erode the boundaries between black and white. While you could enforce physical segregation, it was impossible to police what people listened to. If cotton was the anvil of slavery, music and radio became the sledgehammer for change.

WDIA, Memphis, Tennessee

THE GOODWILL STATION

WDIA, or the 'Goodwill Station' as it became known, started broadcasting in Memphis in 1948 on 730 AM. Rufus Thomas began his career as a DJ on WDIA and he was still broadcasting in 2000.

'Growing up in the early 50s, in the same neighbourhood, Elvis and I listened to WDIA. R&B was becoming popular, quite a contrast to what our parents listened to - shows like the Hit Parade, and records like 'How Much Is That Doggie In The Window?' At night we'd tune in and catch 'You Ain't Nothing But A Hound Dog' by Big Mama Thornton. DJs like Dewey Phillips on WHBQ helped create this underground music with its teenage following. In 50s Memphis there was a dichotomy. Very segregated in certain aspects, but then we got this music that we love... It went right over that boundary. It was a really exciting time'

JERRY SCHILLING

KFFA in Helena, Arkansas, went on air in November 1941, and two weeks later, Sonny Boy Williamson and Robert Jr Lockwood broadcast live on the *King Biscuit Time* show.

'They called Sonny Boy one of the King Biscuit boys. When we came out of the fields to the house for lunch, or dinner as we called it, we'd get a chance to hear Sonny Boy, 15 minutes daily from 12.15 to 12.30'

BB KING

Right up to his death in 1965, Sonny Boy was a regular on the show, and other artists continued to play live in the KFFA studio until 1969.

'When I left Indianola I heard that Sonny Boy was now in West Memphis just across the river from Memphis, Tennessee. So I went over there, I felt I knew him because I'd been listening to him all the time. So I begged him to let me sing a song on his show. So he made me audition for him, he liked it and he put me on. Soon after I went to Memphis. Two partners, Mr Ferguson and John Pepper, opened a new radio station, the first all-black operated station. They hired me and I went on from 5.30 to 5.40, just me and the guitar. We advertised a new tonic, called Peptikon, which was competitive to Sonny Boy's Hadacol.

Peptikon sold more because it was 12% alcohol! One of the disc jockeys left, and they trained me. They never did learn me a proper way to talk though, my diction is still horrible but I got quite popular as a disc jockey

BB KING

WDIA, or the 'Goodwill Station' as it became known, started broadcasting in Memphis in 1948 on 730 AM. Rufus Thomas began his career as a WDIA DJ (he was still broadcasting in 2000) and artists such as Bobby Bland, Johnny Ace, and Rosco Gordon cut records in its studios.

CHAMPIONS OF BLACK MUSIC

WDIA wasn't the only station with prominent black DJs. Fifty miles south in Clarksdale, Mississippi, Early Wright was one of the first black disc jockeys in the Southern USA. He began working on WROX in 1947, and was still working on the station throughout the 90s. Shelley 'The Playboy' Stewart began broadcasting in summer 1949 on the white-owned WEDR in Birmingham, Alabama. In Nashville, meanwhile, WLAC broadcast their 50,000-watt signal across the whole of the east and south of the US from the late 40s; the station's DJs were white but sounded black! Chicago also had two very prominent stations, WOPA and WVON. During the 50s and 60s, crossover hits from R&B to pop stations helped introduce young whites to black music, creating a platform for the whole new generation of blues-influenced artists that surfaced around 1964.

ALAN FREED
A champion of black music on white radio.

R&B radio was not just based in the South. In 1942, 21-year-old Alan Freed took a job as a sports presenter on a station in Akron, Ohio. Freed is credited by many as 'inventing' the term rock'n'roll, but whether he did or didn't is not the point: either way, he was a champion of black music on white radio, and the argument sometimes overshadows his true importance. By 1949 Freed had moved to WXEL-TV in Cleveland, where a local record storeowner convinced him to present an R&B programme on WJW radio. Calling himself 'Moondog', Freed went on the air in July 1951. Such was his popularity that at his *Moondog Coronation Ball* at the 10,000-capacity Cleveland Arena in March 1952, up to 20,000 fans, almost all black, showed up, causing the dance to be cancelled. This is now considered to have been the first 'rock' concert.

Freed was now attracting an increasing number of white listeners, and by late 1954 he was working on WINS radio in New York. Among the artists who the *New York Times* reported he was playing were Muddy Waters, Guitar Slim, and Little Walter. Freed also presented stage shows at the Brooklyn and New York Paramount Theatres, as well as broadcasting on CBS national radio.

In 1957 he was given his own nationally televised rock'n'roll show – on which Frankie Lymon, the first black teenage idol, danced with a white girl. This so enraged ABC's Southern affiliate stations that the series was cancelled.

From the late 1940s to the early 1960s, radio changed the musical preferences of the nation. But if at first radio brought about cohesion and similarity in teenage taste, later it would fragment it forever. Was that what Queen meant when they sang about 'Radio Ga Ga'?

WDIA was a prominent leader in bringing all people – both black and white – closer together

BB KING

WABG, near Greenwood, Mississippi

JOHN LEE HOOKER

FOUR-TIME GRAMMY WINNER, John Lee Hooker is a true original. He is the last living link to the pre-war Delta blues tradition and remains a giant of the Blues. Recognition in the rock music field was confirmed by his induction into the Rock & Roll Hall of Fame in 1990. John Lee Hooker has lived long enough to reap rewards greater than any of his contemporaries could have imagined. As he told a *Newsweek* reporter in 1995: "I got chauffeurs. I got a long stretch black limousine. Bar in it. VCRs, telephone, everything. I got a suit for every day of the week." It's a long, long way from Clarksdale.

FACT FILE

BORN: *22nd August, 1918 Clarksdale, Mississippi*

INSTRUMENT: *Guitar*

FIRST RECORDED: *1948*

AKA: *Texas Slim, Delta John, Birmingham Sam, John Lee Booker, Little Pork Chops*

ACCOLADES: *Inducted into the Blues Hall of Fame, 1980, and the Rock & Roll Hall of Fame, 1990*

INFLUENCES: *Blind Lemon Jefferson, Blind Blake, Charley Patton, Tommy McClennan,*

INFLUENCED: *Canned Heat, The Yardbirds, The Animals, Buddy Guy*

John Lee was his mother Minnie's fourth child. His grandfather taught him guitar in his early teens, and he grew up on a farm where his stepfather, Will Moore, taught him his unusual foot stamping, guitar-playing technique. He sang gospel music, but the blues soon took hold. Aged 14, Hooker enlisted and spent three months with the army in Detroit. When they discovered how young he was, they sent him home. Unsuited to a life on the farm, he took to the road.

Hooker's first stop was Memphis, where he tried to start up his musical career while working as an usher in the Beale Street Theater. Whether the competition was too tough, he was too young, or there were simply too many blues players, he was unsuccesful. So he left Memphis for Cincinnati, working in a variety of day jobs and at night playing juke joints and house-rent parties. He also sang gospel with The Fairfield Four and The Big Six. In 1943, with well paid war work available, he returned to Detroit. With a burgeoning music scene on Hastings Street, Hooker was soon a big draw; he was spotted playing the Monte Carlo club.

In 1948 Hooker teamed up with businessman, Bernie Besman, who helped him cut his first record. 'Sally Mae' was to be the A-side, but the B-side 'Boogie Chillen' quickly took hold. It was released by Los Angeles-based Modern Records, which soon had a number one R&B record on its hands. Hooker, or The Boogie Man as he had been christened, had three more big hits in 1949, 'Hobo Blues', 'Hoogie Boogie', and 'Crawling King Snake'. In 1951 he was at the top of the charts again with 'I'm In The Mood', co-written with Jules Taub. Hooker over-dubbed his vocal three times, adding an even more powerful resonance to the song.

"It was in 1963 that I bought my first proper blues album and it was one by John Lee Hooker. On 3 March 1969 I went to see him at the Rhodes Centre in Bishop Stortford, Essex. He was amazing, stamping his foot and playing... He looked like a God"

BILL WYMAN

THE YOUNG JOHN LEE
An early publicity photo of John Lee issued by Modern Records in 1949.

Hooker was probably the busiest blues-recording artist of all. Despite being under contract to a number of labels, he also cut records for a variety of independents. "I cannot accurately recollect how many times I have cut records. I think that I've made discs for about 30 different labels," he admitted in the summer of 1964. During this period he was also touring Britain with John Mayall's Bluesbreakers and at No. 23 on the UK singles chart with 'Dimples'. By 1955 he had signed to the Vee-Jay label and this partnership yielded

HEATED
Hooker 'n' Heat, *the album John Lee Hooker made with Canned Heat in 1970.*

'Boom Boom' in 1962.

In 1962 Hooker visited Europe for the First American Folk Blues Festival where he impressed many of Britain's young musicians. He left Vee-Jay in 1964, recording for various labels, including Chess and Verve – Folkways. In 1965 there was an unsuccessful collaboration with British blues band, The Groundhogs, followed by his acclaimed 1970 recording *Hooker 'n' Heat*, with Canned Heat, which became his best-selling album in years.

During the lean blues years of the 70s and early 80s Hooker recorded and toured, making a cameo appearance in the 1980 *Blues Brothers* movie. He produced nothing of note until 1989, when he recorded *The Healer* with guests including Bonnie Raitt, Keith Richards, and Carlos Santana. 1991's *Mr. Lucky* reached No. 3, making John Lee the oldest artist to reach that high on the UK album chart. In 1992 Levi Jeans used 'Boom Boom' for a commercial; it then made No. 16 in the UK.

Today he still records and enjoys spending time at his home in California.

> *'It is the most erotic thing I ever heard'*
>
> BONNIE RAITT ON HOOKER'S GUITAR PLAYING

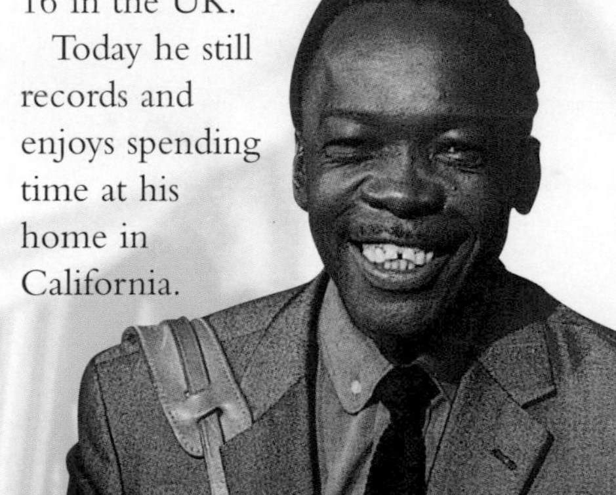

ESSENTIAL RECORDINGS

CLASSIC SONGS

'Boogie Chillen' 1948
'I'm In The Mood' 1951
'Dimples' 1956
'Boom Boom' 1962

CLASSIC ALBUMS

House Of The Blues 1959

I'm John Lee Hooker 1960

Concert At Newport 1964

THE SOURCE

The John Lee Hooker Collection: A Mess 'A Blues Deuce 1996

> *'My grandfather taught me to pick out harmony on strips of inner tube nailed in different tensions to the barn door'*
>
> JOHN LEE HOOKER

Left: On Ready Steady Go! *in 1964*

MUDDY WATERS

MUDDY WATERS – band leader, writer, guitarist, singer, song interpreter and the prime mover of the Chicago electric blues scene – hailed from the Mississippi Delta. When he was about three years old McKinley Morganfield's mother died so he was sent to the Stovall Plantation to stay with his grandmother. Throughout the 1920s and 30s he grew up and worked on the plantation, at the same time teaching himself harmonica and guitar. He began playing in juke joints and at parties and dances in and around the Clarksdale area from about 1935 onwards.

FACT FILE

BORN: *4th April, 1915*
Rolling Fork, Mississippi

DIED: *30th April, 1983*
Chicago, Illinois

INSTRUMENTS: *Guitar and harmonica*

FIRST RECORDED: *1941*

ACCOLADES: *Inducted into the Blues Hall of Fame, 1980*

INFLUENCES: *Robert Johnson, Son House, Charley Patton*

INFLUENCED: *The Rolling Stones, Johnny Winter, Stevie Ray Vaughan, Mike Bloomfield, Paul Butterfield*

‘Muddy, one of the first guys to drive a tractor at our plantation, wasn't the most contented tractor driver in the world and he couldn't wait to get out of farming and into a life as an entertainer’

HOWARD STOVALL

In mid-summer 1941 Alan Lomax recorded Muddy at Stovall's for the Library of Congress; Muddy sang ‘Country Blues’ and ‘Burr Clover Country Blues’.

In 1943 Muddy, who got his nickname from his grandmother because he played in a nearby creek, moved north to live in Chicago. Big Bill Broonzy helped the country boy break into the urban scene and he got his first opportunity playing guitar behind Sonny Boy Williamson No.1. Muddy's recording career began in 1947 playing guitar for Sunnyland Slim. Waters and bass player Big Crawford recorded two other songs but Leonard Chess was unimpressed and so they went unreleased. However, the following year Muddy and Crawford were back and cut ‘I Can't Be Satisfied’ and ‘Feel Like Going Home’, which Leonard Chess released on Checker. It sold out in less than a day, going on to make No.11 on the R&B charts. Chess was anxious not to upset a winning formula, and so even though Muddy had his own band he continued to record Muddy in a duo, or with Leroy Foster on guitar. By 1951 the Muddy Waters Blues Band was recording as an entity. It was the epitome of the hard-edged, driving electric blues band of Chicago, the very fountainhead of what we call rock music today.

Among those who played with the Muddy Waters Blues Band were guitarists Jimmy Rogers, Luther Tucker, and Earl Hooker; harmonica players Little Walter, Junior Wells, Big Walter Horton, and James Cotton;

‘I knew Muddy well, and played with him in the 1970s. He was very dignified, a man that you would easily respect, just from the way he carried himself. He was funny, and he was always so charming and sweet and always had plenty of time to listen to other people talking’

BILL WYMAN

Willie Dixon on bass; pianists were Memphis Slim, Otis Spann, and Pinetop Perkins, along with drummer Fred Below. In the 1950s Muddy put 15 records on the R&B charts including 'I'm Your Hoochie Coochie Man', 'Just Make Love To Me', and 'Mannish Boy'. It was not just singles that worked for Muddy; his albums began to attract attention as the new format found favour with record buyers. A tribute to his mentor, Big Bill Broonzy, *Muddy Waters Sings Big Bill*, cut in 1959 a year after Bill Broonzy's death, shows the similarity in style between the two singers. 'I Feel So Good' from the album exemplifies Muddy's approach – brilliant interpretation and vocal delivery that is underpinned by tight ensemble playing. Otis Spann on piano, James Cotton's harmonica, and Pat Hare's guitar are near perfect. The following year at the Newport Folk Festival, Muddy performed the song and captured it on his album *Muddy Waters At Newport*. As the band powers through the song the crowd can be heard responding to their brilliance with spontaneous shouts. Not that this one song was any different from many that Muddy performed; he injected everything he did with style and class.

Muddy and Otis Spann

Muddy meets some young blues fans at the Palladium, New York, in 1977.

As the 60s continued, Chess released the *Muddy Waters Folk Singer* album, still anxious to capture those who saw the blues as a rural rather than urban form of music. As the Blues languished in the late 60s, then so did Muddy's career. In the 1970s he toured constantly and by 1977 he had signed with CBS Records. Collaborating with Johnny Winter, Muddy's career took an upturn with the release of the album *Hard Again* in 1977, winning him a Grammy. A second album, *I'm Ready*, was followed by a tour of the US including a performance at the White House for President Jimmy Carter.

> *Muddy can really sing the blues… hollering, shouting, crying, getting mad – that's the Blues*
>
> BIG BILL BROONZY

Muddy worked live in the early 80s with Johnny Winter before succumbing to a heart attack in his sleep, aged 68 in 1983.

ESSENTIAL RECORDINGS

CLASSIC SONGS

'I'm Your Hoochie Coochie Man' 1954
'Mannish Boy' 1955
'I Feel So Good' 1960
'My Home Is In The Delta' 1964

CLASSIC ALBUMS

Muddy Waters At Newport 1960

Muddy Waters Folk Singer 1964

Hard Again 1977

THE SOURCE

His Best 1947–1955 (Universal/Chess)
His Best 1956–1964 (Universal/Chess)

THE RIDDLE OF THE HONEY DRIPPERS

Joe Liggins and His Honeydrippers, 1945

AFTER HIS HIT with 'I Wonder', the man who had become known as the Honey Dripper made a return to the charts in late 1945 with what else but 'The Honeydripper'. But Roosevelt Sykes was not remaking his 1936 recording; he was actually covering a song of the same name by Joe Liggins. Shortly afterwards, his recording of 'Sunny Road' got to No. 2 in the R&B Chart. The single was credited to Roosevelt Sykes and his Original Honeydrippers, making the point that it was Roosevelt who was the old pro, rather than Liggins, the young pretender to his title.

Joe Liggins, an Oklahoma native, had written his song called 'The Honeydripper' back in 1942. He finally recorded it under the name of Joe Liggins and His Honeydrippers. When he performed the song live it lasted around 15 minutes, which was one reason for splitting it over two sides on the original 78rpm release in November 1945. Liggins recorded for Leon Rene's Exclusive label, and given the difficulties that this small independent label had in distributing the record, it is a wonder it was ever a hit at all. In fact, the record was more successful on the Jukebox chart than it ever was from sales. Rene found out that an East Coast operation was bootlegging his record, from which he of course earned nothing. It is alleged that when he confronted the bootleggers they confronted him in turn with a machine gun! Joe's original was soon overtaken by a Jimmie Lunceford version on Decca – no problems in distribution for them! Other covers by Cab Calloway and Sammy Franklin, Joe's old bandleader boss, further undermined his sales. All in all, it was a typical tale of the Blues.

JOE LIGGINS
The man who wrote the second blues song called 'The Honeydripper', was inspired by the original tune penned by Roosevelt Sykes.

EXCLUSIVE RIGHTS

Liggins had a string of hits on Exclusive, including the excellent 'Got A Right To Cry'. Eventually Exclusive folded, and Liggins signed for Specialty Records in 1949. The label's owner, Art Rupe, re-recorded 'The Honeydripper' after he was unable to buy the original masters from Exclusive's creditors. While the record failed to chart again, it remained in the catalogue for many years and this is the version that is still often heard. But Joe did manage another R&B chart topper with Specialty, when 'Pink Champagne' stayed on top for 13 weeks in 1950. After a couple more hits, however, his popularity began to wane, along with the rest of the jump blues specialists. Liggins left Specialty in late 1954 and label-hopped throughout the remainder of the decade. Continuing to play live on the West Coast as late as the mid-1980s, he died in 1987.

Even if you look very hard you will fail to see the join – the moment, that is, when jump blues metamorphosed into R&B. Meanwhile, traditional blues was going through its own changes, which proved to be as fundamental as the influence of jump blues on rock'n'roll. Late 1940s Chicago was the breeding ground for a whole new mess of blues. Country blues got plugged in and turned on, becoming the hard core of what we now call rock.

THAT'S ALL RIGHT

ON 6TH SEPTEMBER, 1946, above a pawnshop, three men initiated a remarkable chain of events that would change the face of 20th century music. Drummer Judge Riley, bass player Ransom Knowling, and singer/guitarist Arthur 'Big Boy' Crudup, cut five songs that day, among them Arthur's composition 'That's All Right'.

'Well, that's all right now, Mama, That's all right for you'

'THAT'S ALL RIGHT'

LESTER MELROSE owned the publishing and the copyright on all of the sides Arthur cut for Victor, a fact that Arthur would come to regret. Arthur made a few hundred dollars for each of his recordings and in between he went back to farming in Mississippi. By the time 'That's All Right' was released, 40-year-old Arthur had chalked up three R&B hits, but his latest release failed to add to his tally.

THE BATTLE OF THE SPEEDS

Two years later, on Friday 28th June, 1948, Columbia Records held a press conference at New York's Waldorf-Astoria Hotel to launch the 33 1/3rpm long-playing microgroove record. Columbia had high hopes for its new format, but could scarcely imagine just how far-reaching the effect would be. Columbia had asked RCA Victor to join in the launch, but Victor declined, having nearly gone bust in the 30s trying to develop its own long-playing concept. Instead, Victor had a secret plan to develop a 45rpm, seven-inch single to rival the 78rpm.

A key player in RCA Victor's plan was to be Arthur Crudup, for 'That's All Right' became the first 45rpm single in Victor's R&B series. Some dynamic marketing executive had the idea of colour-coding the RCA releases. 'That's All Right' came out on orange vinyl, popular music on blue, and country records, rather appropriately, were green. 'That's All Right' did get some airplay on black radio stations, but again failed to chart. That would have been the end of the story, but for a certain Mr Elvis Aaron Presley.

Arthur 'Big Boy' Crudup

THE BIRTH OF A LEGEND

Elvis, Scotty Moore, and Bill Black found themselves hard at work in Sun Studios in Memphis on the evening of Monday 5th July, 1954. Having run through various numbers without much success, it was already after midnight. Then Elvis started messing around on an old song, Scotty and Bill took up the rhythm, and Sam Phillips told them to stop and start over again. The three men conjured up a chemical reaction that was irresistible. Excited by what he heard, Sam took an acetate of 'That's All Right' to local DJ Dewey Phillips. 'Hey Man, this is a hit', said Dewey and proceeded to play it seven times on his show that night.

While 'That's All Right' didn't reach the national charts, this 1 minute 55 seconds of magic set Elvis on his way.

'The worst thing I could have done was to come out and cut a conventional ballad. I don't care how good it was, or how well we put it together, that would have been the wrong thing to do'

SAM PHILLIPS

11

The Fabulous Fifties

TIMES HAS MADE A CHANGE

TV was all the rage

IN 1950 THE POPULATION OF the United States was a little over 150 million people; in 1850 it had been just 23 million. Unemployment dropped from 5.3% in 1950 to 2.9% in 1952, reflecting a wave of optimism that had been felt with the dawning of the new decade. The increasing affluence of the 50s is perhaps best demonstrated through the ownership of television sets. In 1950 there were just 10.5 million sets in America, but by 1957 this had grown to over 47 million. TV was a catalyst for change, radically influencing how people both heard and saw music. It has to be said, though, that the Blues was affected less than other styles, as segregation was a factor on TV just as it was in real life. Radio would continue to be the driving force behind the Blues, and its stepchild, rock'n'roll. Men like disc jockey Alan Freed who championed black music, often to white kids, created a revolution in sound. During the decade the number of radio stations in the US grew from less than 3,000 to nearly 4,000, offering listeners greater choice. And the boom in car ownership meant more people listened to the radio, especially the young.

Alan Freed

There were signs that things were finally changing for the black population. In 1952 the University of Tennessee admitted its first black student. That same year, the US Supreme Court upheld a decision to ban segregation on trains, which was particularly significant as rail accounted for almost half of American domestic travel. Meanwhile, the Supreme Court heard a number of cases relating to school segregation, a widely accepted practice that was required by law in most Southern states. Two years later, the court unanimously decided that segregation was unconstitutional. However, segregation was still a major factor in everyday life, and it would be some time before things would reach anything like a level playing field. Indeed, it would take the efforts of one of the greatest leaders of the modern world, Martin Luther King Jr, to facilitate that change. Not that America was the only 'developed' country with outmoded ideas. In Switzerland, for example, men voted to refuse women the right to vote in 1950, and just to make sure, they voted that way again in 1959.

It was the era of the McCarthy communist witch-hunts, which did much to damage the reputations of people in the film and other entertainment industries. At the other end of the spectrum, JD Salinger's fictional hero, Holden Caulfield, spoke to the young through the liberating tones of *Catcher In The Rye*. The national dichotomy was just as marked when it came to sex. In 1952 the top-rated show *I Love Lucy* acknowledged pregnancy (a first for TV), but television still refused to show married people sharing the same bed. But before we tackle the decade that gave us frozen peas, *Playboy* magazine, the hydrogen bomb, and fast food, we need to revisit the 1940s and check on those Delta blues.

'Growing up in LA, white kids weren't listening to white radio, we were listening to KGFJ, an AM station. During the day it was a 1,000-watt radio station for the black community. We kind of caught it after school and as it got dark it went down to 250 watts, kind of like the way you'd have to strain to listen to Radio Luxembourg in England'

BRUCE JOHNSTON
THE BEACH BOYS

LIKE MYSTICAL GODS

IN 1952 THE LONG-PLAYING album was still a very new concept, one that a young discographer, artist, and historian named Harry Smith decided he could usefully exploit. He convinced Moses Asch, the owner of the Folkways label, to allow him to compile an *Anthology Of American Folk Music*, it eventually ran to 84 songs concentrated onto 6 LPs. For many listeners in the 50s and ever since, this set represented the Holy Grail of America's musical heritage. It contains many of the best of the pre-war blues artists, as well as country, hillbilly music, old-time songs, and sermons. Carefully annotated by Harry Smith, the *Anthology* became a starting point for historians of early music.

ANTHOLOGY OF AMERICAN FOLK MUSIC
Included performances by 'mystical gods'.

The *Anthology* introduced the American public at large to men like Dick Justice, a white coalminer from West Virginia, who had come under the influence of the Blues, as well as better-known performers like the Carter Family and the Rev JM Gates. Amongst the blues artists it included were Blind Lemon Jefferson, Sleepy John Estes and Yank Rachell, the Memphis Jug Band, Henry Thomas, Charley Patton (listed on the record as The Masked Marvel; Smith was unaware that it was really Patton), Furry Lewis, and Mississippi John Hurt. In its own way this set is as important as the work undertaken by the Lomaxes. At a time when the US was at the dawning of the modern, consumer-driven age, Harry Smith made a decisive statement about the value of the nation's artistic heritage.

The *Anthology* became a passport to a lost world of rare and unusual recordings. It helped some listeners to rediscover pre-war blues and was one of the major influences on the birth of the 60s folk blues revival. John Cohen of the New Lost City Ramblers said that the *Anthology* introduced him and many others to performers 'who became like mystical gods to us'. Folksinger Dave Van Ronk said the anthology became 'our bible'… 'we all knew the words to every song on it, even the ones we hated.'

In 2000, the *Anthology Of American Folk Music* was reissued on a boxed set of 3 CDs by Smithsonian Folkways Recordings. Every (American) home should have one.

> *The* Anthology *became our bible… we all knew the words to every song on it, even the ones we hated*
>
> DAVE VAN RONK

Dave Van Ronk

> *The rock'n'roll school in general concentrated on a minimum of melodic line and a maximum of rhythmic noise, deliberately competing with the artistic ideals of the jungle itself*
>
> ENCYCLOPAEDIA BRITANNICA, 1955

ROCK THAT BOOGIE

‘I know why the best blues artists come from Mississippi, because it’s the worst state. You have the Blues all right if you’re down in Mississippi’

JOHN LEE HOOKER, 1964

JOHN LEE HOOKER WAS RIGHT. Many post-war bluesmen came from Mississippi, with the accent on ‘came from’, as they got out as fast as they could. Hooker and the others who went North to Memphis, Chicago, and Detroit in the 40s and 50s were attracted to a new world of opportunities.

Some historians feel that there is clear (blue!) water between styles like urban, country, or jump blues. Others see the music as segmented by time periods, creating the impression that particular artists or styles developed in a vacuum. None of this, of course, is true. What we now refer to as ‘Chicago electric blues’ did not just happen. The burgeoning urban blues scene did not just consist of the jump blues of the R&B set or the updated and adapted blues of the pre-war scene. What happened was that in the late 40s, the country moved to the city. It took a little time to adapt to its new surroundings, but once it had, it changed not with a bang but with a boogie. On a September day in 1948 in a Detroit studio, John Lee Hooker cut ‘Boogie Chillen’, a record that would help to change the face of modern music.

HOOGIE BOOGIE, IT’S THE MAN

When John Lee Hooker arrived in Detroit in 1943 he was no stranger to city life. He was soon supplementing his day job by playing in clubs like Sporty Reed’s Show Bar, and the more upmarket Lee’s Sensation. Hooker acquired a manager, Elmer Barbee, in 1948 and Barbee engineered an introduction to Bernard Besman, the Ukrainian-born owner of Detroit’s Sensation label. Besman decided to record and produce Hooker, but interestingly he decided to lease his first two sides to Modern Records, to make use of their better distribution system. It was a shrewd move

John Lee Hooker

BOOGIE CHILLEN

OR IS IT 'CHILLUN'? You will see the word spelt both ways, but as 'chillen' means 'children', this seems the most logical. The song is credited to John Lee Hooker and Bernard Besman, who produced Hooker's original session. The most obvious comment to make about the song is that it is not a boogie!

HASTINGS STREET

Perhaps it all has something to do with a 1928 recording by Blind Blake and Charlie Spand. They cut a song called 'Hastings Street', which was a boogie, and in it Blake says to Spand: "On Hastings Street they do the boogie, they do it very woogie". It's not clear whether this has any connection with John Lee's song, but the lyrical similarities are intriguing, to say the least. The recording of Hooker performing the song in 1949 at a party shows his ability to absorb material and make it his own in a totally unique way.

> *In 1986 I had a band called Willie and the Poor Boys with Andy Fairweather-Low and Gary Brooker. It was a forerunner of what I'm doing now, with the Rhythm Kings. We did a song called 'Poor Boy Boogie' that was inspired by 'Feelin' Good' and 'Boogie Chillen'*
>
> BILL WYMAN

BOOGIE CHILLEN

Written by John Lee Hooker & Bernard Besman
Recorded in Detroit, September 1948.

Well my mama she didn't 'low me,
Just to stay out all night long, oh Lord
Well my mama didn't 'low me,
Just to stay out all night long
I didn't care what she didn't 'low,
I would boogie-woogie anyhow
When I first came to town people,
I was walkin' down Hastings Street
Everybody was talkin' about, the Henry Swing Club
I decided I drop in there that night
When I got there, I say, "Yes, people"
They was really havin' a ball!
Yes, I know
Boogie Chillen!

One night I was layin' down,
I heard mama 'n papa talkin'
I heard papa tell mama, let that boy boogie-woogie,
it's in him, and it got to come out
And I felt so good,
Went on boogie woogie'n just the same

BOOGIE WITH ZEPPELIN

On 1st April, 1971 Led Zeppelin performed in concert for a BBC radio show. They featured 'Whole Lotta Love' in a medley that included Arthur Crudup's 'That's All Right' and 'Boogie Chillen'.

FEELIN' GOOD

At the end of May 1953, Little Junior Parker's Blues Flames cut 'Feelin' Good' for Sun Records in Memphis. The song was clearly based on 'Boogie Chillen'. 'Feelin' Good' rose to No. 5 that October and has inspired more covers than 'Boogie Chillen' itself.

CHILLEN' AGAIN

In 1950 John Lee Hooker recorded 'Boogie Chillen 2' for the Sensation label. When he worked for Vee-Jay in the late 50s, he re-cut many of his older sides including 'Boogie Chillun', as it was listed on the label, in January 1959. In 1962 he recorded the song live in San Francisco, and in keeping with the folk-blues era this version had a more 'unplugged' feel than his others. On the album *Hooker'n'Heat* which he cut in 1970 with Canned Heat, the song was recorded again as 'Boogie Chillen No.2'.

SELECTED VERSIONS

- 1948 John Lee Hooker
- 1962 Big Joe Williams
- 1966 Magic Sam
- 1981 Buddy Guy & Junior Wells
- 1982 George Thorogood & The Destroyers
- 1996 RL Burnside
- 1998 Beau Jocque & Zydeco H-Rollers

THE UNKNOWN JOHN LEE HOOKER
This CD was released in 2000, with recordings made at a private house in Detroit in 1949.

in retrospect, as 'Boogie Chillen' (coupled with 'Sally Mae', originally planned as the A-side) went to No. 1 on the R&B chart in January 1949.

Hooker's career took off with three more Top 10 hits in 1949, including the excellent 'Hoogie Boogie'. Then in 1951 he again topped the chart with the classic, 'I'm In The Mood'. Hooker recorded at a prodigious rate, and tracking his recordings is tricky as he, like many other bluesmen, recorded under numerous pseudonyms for a variety of different labels. In the three years following his first recordings, he cut records as Texas Slim, Little Pork Chops, John Lee Cooker, Delta John, Birmingham Sam, Johnny Williams, The Boogie Man, John Lee Booker, John L Hooker, and (of course) John Lee Hooker.

JOHN LEE'S ROOTS

In early 2000 a CD was released that featured John Lee Hooker, recorded in a Detroit house in 1949. Gene Deitch, a keen music fan, heard Hooker play in a club and invited him over for dinner. He then recorded him singing and playing acoustic guitar. It is remarkable that the tape even survived, but better still it demonstrates the influences that Hooker had already taken on board in developing his unique 'electric blues' sound. He performed 'Catfish Blues', which he would cut many times in his career, as well as standards like 'Trouble In Mind', 'How Long Blues', and 'In The Evenin' (When The Sun Goes Down)'. The tape also included spirituals like 'Moses Smoke The Water' and the folk standard 'John Henry', for which Hooker created his own melody.

Hooker's career throughout the 50s was a tale of label-hopping and little in the way of chart success. After 'I'm In The Mood', he did not return to the R&B charts until 1958. Amongst the labels he recorded for during this decade were Chess, Modern, DeLuxe, Specialty, and Vee Jay. But the 60s found Hooker back in favour, another remarkable change of fortune in what was to be a long and amazing career.

REAL GONE

‘In 1997 I was looking for songs for my album Anyway The Wind Blows. *I'd liked Nellie Lutcher for years, and collected her old 78 records, so I decided to cover 'He's A Real Gone Guy'. Recorded for Capitol when she was 34, it got to No. 2 on the R&B chart in 1947, just like her first hit, 'Hurry On Down'. Interestingly for an R&B record at the time, it also crossed over to the pop charts. On my 2001 album,* Double Bill, *we recorded another Nellie Lutcher song, 'Do You Or Don't You'. When I heard John Lee Hooker's 'home' recordings, I was amazed to hear him sing 'He's Real Gone', an adaptation of Nellie Lutcher' s song. This would have been around 18 months after Nellie's record was such a big hit. Blues artists were quick to incorporate other performers' material into their own repertoire. Just like Robert Johnson, Lead Belly and many others before, they earned their living from being what amounted to a human jukebox’*

BILL WYMAN

ETTA JAMES

FACT FILE

BORN: *25th January, 1938 Los Angeles, California*

FIRST RECORDED: *1954*

ACCOLADES: *Inducted into the Blues Hall of Fame, 2001*

INFLUENCES: *Dinah Washington, Billie Holiday, Ray Charles, Guitar Slim*

INFLUENCED: *Christine Perfect (later McVie of Fleetwood Mac), Billy Fury*

BORN JAMESETTA HAWKINS, Etta moved to San Francisco when she was young, learning to sing in church choirs.

She was drawn to the world of R&B in her teens, and won her first recording deal after auditioning backstage for Johnny Otis. Her first single, 'The Wallflower', was an answer song to Hank Ballard's 'Work With Me, Annie'. Cut on Thanksgiving Day 1954, it became an R&B No. 1 in 1955. Barely 17, Etta's life was soon a constant round of touring and recording that took its toll later in her career. Despite a follow-up hit in 1955, her career didn't really take off until Harvey Fuqua of the Moonglows took her to the Chess subsidiary, Argo, in 1960. She sang backing vocals for Chuck Berry before her first single for the label, 'All I Could Do Is Cry', made No. 2 and established her as a regular on the R&B charts and, to a lesser extent, the Hot 100. Early in the 60s she succumbed to heroin addiction, but her health problems did not prevent her from recording some brilliant records. 'At Last', a cover of a Glenn Miller hit from 1942, was not a blues song, but her delivery was blues personified, while her cover of Mildred Bailey's 1937 hit 'Trust In Me' was also a classic.

If the blues is about love and loss, then Etta James recorded the soundtrack.

Her stormy personal life was another complication and by late 1963 her career had begun to stall. In 1967 Chess sent her to Muscle Shoals to record, which proved to be the right move. She was soon back in the higher reaches of the R&B charts, with 'Tell Mama' becoming her biggest hit in five years. She also recorded 'I'd Rather Go Blind', which by her own account she also wrote, in spite of the credits on the record. The early and mid-70s were lean years for Etta, as she struggled to come to terms with a market that had been overwhelmed by disco. But by 1978 she had overcome her drug dependency and was able to tour as the opening act for The Rolling Stones, repeating the performance in 1980.

Billy Fury, 1960

When I was looking for songs for my album Double Bill, *I remembered an old Etta James song. Beverley Skeete, our female vocalist, and I love Etta's singing, so we decided to record 'Trust In Me'. Bev's singing is brilliant. If there's a better ballad, I must have missed it*

BILL WYMAN

Billy Fury used to do things by Etta James and stuff like that; he was well into blues things

GEORGIE FAME

ESSENTIAL RECORDINGS

CLASSIC SONGS

'All I Could Do Is Cry' 1960
'At Last' 1960
'Trust in Me' 1960
'I'd Rather Go Blind' 1967

THE SOURCE

Etta James: Her Best
Chess Records

THE BLUEST MAN IN THIS WHOLE CHICAGO TOWN

'He'd always been kind to his family, he never got to a place where he thought he was better. He was always a humble person'

PASTOR WILLIE MORGANFIELD, MUDDY WATERS' COUSIN

MCKINLEY MORGANFIELD
The inimitable Muddy Waters.

MUDDY WATERS' BLUES BAND
Chicago, 1950's: Muddy, (guitar), Otis Spann (piano), James Cotton (harmonica), and Pat Hare (guitar).

AROUND THE SAME TIME that John Lee Hooker was establishing himself in Detroit, 28-year-old McKinley Morganfield (alias Muddy Waters) decided to leave Stovall's Plantation near Clarksdale, Mississippi, and try his luck in Chicago. Like many before him, he took the train to Chicago's Illinois Central Station, initially finding work in a paper factory. Muddy began playing for tips on Maxwell Street soon after arriving in the city, and it was Big Bill Broonzy who helped him break into the more established blues scene. He started working in clubs, playing with Eddie Boyd, as well as backing Sonny Boy Williamson No. 1 at the Plantation Club.

A switch from acoustic to electric guitar in 1944 galvanised Muddy's career. He continued to play traditional Delta bottleneck but the electric guitar transformed his sound and helped to 'invent' post-war Chicago blues. But his 1946 recordings for Columbia, made with the pre-war godfather of Chicago blues, Lester Melrose, went unreleased. It was not until the following year that Muddy would be heard playing on record, in the role of backing guitarist to Sunnyland Slim. Finally in 1948, Leonard Chess felt able to release a Muddy Waters record, 'I Feel Like Going Home' coupled

with 'I Can't Be Satisfied'. The latter was a reworking of 'I Be's Troubled', a song Muddy recorded for Lomax in 1941 and often played live. 'I Feel Like Going Home', meanwhile, was a reworking of Son House's 'Walking Blues', another song that he must have been playing for years, as Muddy had huge respect for House. The record caused a sensation, and sold out on its day of release in Chicago. Muddy later recalled that even he had trouble buying a copy!

Muddy's late 40s band included Leroy Foster on guitar or drums, Big Crawford on bass, and Jimmy Rogers on guitar and harmonica; and not long afterwards Little Walter Jacobs was added as the featured harmonica player. Muddy was only in his early 30s but he became the patriarch of the Chicago blues scene. With the pick of the city's musicians at his disposal in the 50s, it was really a question of who didn't play in Muddy Waters' band.

After 'I Feel Like Going Home' made the R&B charts in September 1948, Muddy did not reach the charts again until 1951. Then 'Louisiana Blues' became the second in his run of sixteen chart hits, which included classics like 'I'm Your Hoochie Coochie Man', 'Just Make Love To Me', 'Mannish Boy', and 'Forty Days And Nights'. The man born in Rolling Fork also cut 'Rollin' And Tumblin'', 'Rollin' Stone', and 'They Call Me Muddy Waters', in which he sang: 'I'm the most bluest man in this whole Chicago town'. Few could disagree. Each and every one of these recordings captures the very essence of 50s Chicago blues.

In 1959 Muddy released *Muddy Sings Big Bill*, a tribute album to his former mentor. Muddy considered Big Bill Broonzy to be 'the daddy of the country blues singers', so it must have been amazing for the younger man to find such a star taking an interest in him. On the album Muddy was accompanied by his band of the period: James Cotton on harp, Pat Hare on guitar, and the brilliant Otis Spann on piano.

'Muddy, he can really sing the Blues. I mean the country, wide-open blues. He ain't like those pretty boy singers who dress up the Blues so you don't know what it is... Muddy's a real singer of the Blues'

BIG BILL BROONZY

On the album Muddy sings 'Just A Dream', a perfect testimony to both men, because while Muddy makes the song his own, Big Bill's spirit comes shining through. Within a year, the whole blues scene was changing and Muddy was right there – but that's a subject we will return to later.

FROM SIDEMAN TO FRONTMAN

Among the crowd of Muddy's sidemen who found fame in their own right were two of his original band, guitarist Jimmy Rogers and harmonica player Little Walter. Rogers hailed from Ruleville in the Delta, and after moving to St Louis with Sunnyland Slim he ended up in Chicago in 1941. He cut 'Louisiana Blues' with Muddy in 1950, the start of a very fruitful relationship. Rogers' more relaxed playing style was the perfect foil to Muddy's gutsier Delta approach.

Besides playing on many of Muddy's biggest hits, Rogers had a solo career of his own. His first 'local' hit for Chess was 'That's All Right', recorded with Little Walter a few months before 'Louisiana Blues'. Rogers' contract with Chess lasted throughout the decade, but he had only one minor chart hit, 'Walking By Myself', with another excellent harmonica player, Big Walter Horton. An adaptation of a T-Bone Walker tune, it

Muddy Sings Big Bill

'I'M YOUR HOOCHIE COOCHIE MAN'
One of Muddy's best known songs but oddly, not a hit for Chess Records. (Note the odd spelling of 'coochie'.)

SMITTY'S CORNER
The club on South Indiana Avenue, Chicago, where Muddy Waters and his band often performed.

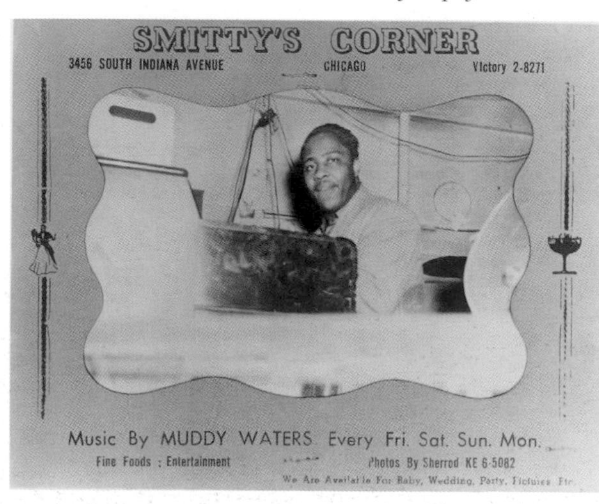

Jimmy Rogers

made No. 14 on the R&B chart in 1957. Rogers also worked as a sideman for both Howlin' Wolf and Sonny Boy Williamson before he temporarily 'retired' from the music business in 1960 to run a clothing store. He went back to recording and playing live in 1971, continuing to perform throughout the 70s, 80s and 90s, until he died in 1997. Today he is perhaps less well regarded than his contemporaries, which is unfortunate as he made excellent records throughout his Chess career.

A BOY NAMED MARION

Marion Walter Jacobs, better known as Little Walter, cut his first solo side for Chess in 1952, two years after Jimmy Rogers, and it was a killer. 'Juke' made No. 1 on the R&B charts and stayed there for eight weeks. The 22-year-old from Marksville, Louisiana, charted another 14 records by the end of the decade.

Amongst Little Walter's classics were 'Blues With A Feeling' (No. 2 in '53), 'My Babe' (No. 1 in '55) and 'Key To The Highway' (No. 6 in '58). Although Walter stopped playing live with Muddy, they sometimes recorded together and the two came to dominate the sound and success of Chess blues in the 50s. During the 60s, Walter's career went into decline and he went back to playing Chicago clubs, where his hard drinking and fiery temper got him into some serious fights. In 1968 he had a particularly vicious street brawl and he died from coronary thrombosis. It was a sad end for a man who did more than most to shape the sound of post-war blues harmonica. A stylist and an energetic live performer, his brilliant playing has been described as 'sonic sculptures'. Little Walter left a blues legacy of lasting proportions.

'Little Walter was number one. He was the greatest harmonica player that ever lived. There will never be another'

LAZY LESTER

'I have always been a big fan of Little Walter; he always added such tasteful melodic lines when he was accompanying others. My favourite Little Walter recording is the cover of Big Bill Broonzy's 'Key To The Highway', which Little Walter cut along with Otis Spann on piano and Muddy on slide. On 8th November, 1964, we cut 'Key To The Highway' at Chess Studios in Chicago. Six years later Eric Clapton covered it on his album, Layla And Other Assorted Love Songs... *and did a pretty nice job, too'*

BILL WYMAN

Ballad of a Teenage Stone

When I was about eight or nine, around the time war ended, I went with my mum's younger sister to the Orchid Ballroom in Purley, South London. There were lots of American servicemen there and they danced the jitterbug. I thought I should like to be in a band, but knew you had to be a qualified musician. In September 1948 I started clarinet lessons at school, which lasted for two years. I never really enjoyed them and my ambition appeared to be a non-starter.

In 1952 I saw Johnnie Ray on my grandmother's television with its six-inch screen. He was on the *London Palladium* show, having his trousers shredded by girls in the audience. At Easter 1953, I got a job as a junior clerk in a London betting office. I desperately wanted a record player so I decided that I would sell my stamp collection, and I got about £4 for it. I bought a wind-up gramophone and a tin of needles from a junk shop, and had enough money left over to buy two 78s – one of which was Les Paul and Mary Ford's 'The World Is Waiting For The Sunrise'.

In January 1955 my 'call up' papers arrived, and aged 18 I was conscripted into the Royal Air Force. After basic training I was sent to northern Germany. Here I listened to the American Forces Network radio, waking up to country music on *The Stick Buddy Jamboree*. I also began to listen to Elvis Presley, Bill Haley, Fats Domino, and Little Richard, long before most people in Britain had heard of them.

Private Wyman

In 1955 my 'call up' papers arrived and I was on my way to Germany.

In Germany some of the boys had record players, so around March 1956 I heard skiffle for the first time – Chris Barber's Band, featuring Lonnie Donegan. In June 1956 I saw the Stan Kenton Band perform in Bremen. I loved the 'Peanut Vendor' and 'Artistry In Rhythm', as his horn players got up and down in sequence, playing all those great discords.

Then in August I bought myself a cheap acoustic guitar, learning to play it tuned to a chord. Home on leave in February 1957, I went to the Regal Cinema, Beckenham, and saw Chuck Berry perform 'You Can't Catch Me' in *Rock, Rock, Rock!* This was it! This was definitely it; Chuck Berry was *the* man. I wrote to a record shop in Chicago and ordered Chuck Berry's album *One Dozen Berrys*. Back in Germany, in November 1957, I started a skiffle group with Casey Jones from Liverpool (Eric Clapton later played with Casey Jones & The Engineers for two weeks, in October 1963)

After I left the RAF in 1958, I saw a Lonnie Donegan concert, and got so excited, I danced in the aisles. I'd never done that before, or since! But what I really wanted was to be in a group…

One Dozen Berrys

The great Chuck Berry, star of Alan Freed's movie Rock, Rock, Rock! *who inspired legions of British schoolboys in the late 50s and early 60s.*

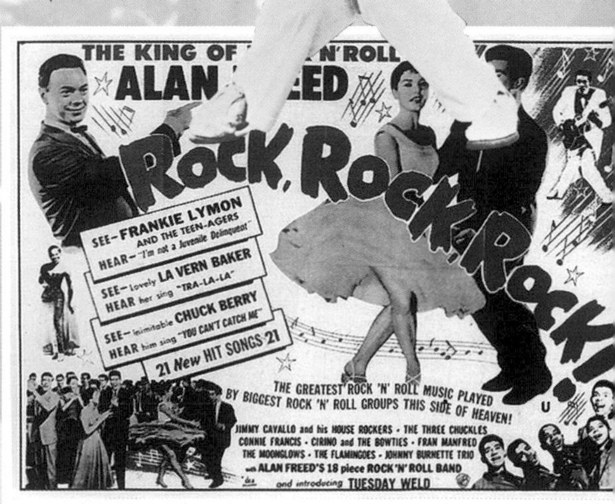

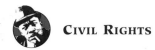

THE DREAM OF A NATION

I have a dream that one day this nation will rise up and live out the true meaning of its creed: We hold these truths to be self-evident: that all men are created equal

DR MARTIN LUTHER KING JR

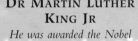

THE CIVIL RIGHTS STRUGGLE did not, as many people imagine, begin in the 60s. It was in the 50s that a man came to prominence who would act as a fulcrum for the movement. Martin Luther King Jr was born on 15th January, 1929, in Atlanta, Georgia, the second child of the Reverend Martin Luther King Sr, and his wife Alberta; the boy's grandparents were sharecroppers.

ROSA PARKS
Miss Parks refused to give up her seat to a white man on an Alabama bus.

DR MARTIN LUTHER KING JR
He was awarded the Nobel Peace prize in 1964.

Martin Luther King Jr was married in 1953 and awarded a PhD in 1955. He had become a minister in 1948, aged 19, and after gaining his doctorate he became pastor of a church in Montgomery, Alabama. In 1959 he moved to Atlanta to direct the activities of the Southern Christian Leadership Conference. During his career Dr King Jr was arrested 30 times for his participation in civil rights activities.

While he had many supporters, some of them took a more prominent place in the struggle for equality. In 1955 Rosa Parks, a 43-year-old black seamstress, refused to give up her seat to a white man on a Montgomery, Alabama, bus, and she was arrested. The next night, black community leaders met at Dr King Jr's church. The result was the Montgomery Bus Boycott, which lasted 381 days and cost the bus line 65% of its revenue. Eight months later the Supreme Court ruled that bus segregation was illegal.

The struggle was felt at all levels in the black community. In 1956 members of a white supremacist group attacked Nat 'King' Cole on stage, and that same year Dr King's home was bombed. After blacks began a voter registration drive in 1957, the Alabama Legislature re-drew its boundaries to exclude all black neighbourhoods. But in 1958 the US Civil Rights Commission began its investigation of the issue, and very gradually the political situation changed.

Much of Dr King's success was based around the power of his oratory. He could motivate both blacks and whites to see the indignity of the prevailing situation of institutionalised discrimination. He became the conscience of a nation, offering black people a vital sense of their own self-worth. When this was coupled with his theory of non-violent direct action, it produced an irresistible philosophy. On 17th May, 1957, Dr King offered an eloquent solution at a Prayer Pilgrimage to Washington DC:

Give us the ballot and we will no longer have to worry the federal government about our basic rights.

Give us the ballot and we will no longer plead to the federal government for passage of an anti-lynching law. We will by the power of our vote write the law on the statute books of the Southern states and bring an end to the dastardly acts of the hooded perpetrators of violence.

Give us the ballot and we will transform the salient misdeeds of bloodthirsty mobs into the calculated good deeds of orderly citizens.

Give us the ballot and we will fill our legislative halls with men of good will, and send to the sacred halls of Congress men who will not sign a Southern manifesto, because of their devotion to the manifesto of justice.

Give us the ballot and we will place judges on the benches of the South who will 'do justly and love mercy', and we will place at the head of the Southern states governors who have felt not only the tang of the human, but the glow of the divine

I HAVE A DREAM

Almost six years later, on 28th August, 1963, Dr King was back in Washington DC delivering perhaps his most famous speech. Standing on the steps of the Lincoln Memorial he began:

Five score years ago, a great American, in whose symbolic shadow we stand, signed the Emancipation Proclamation. This momentous decree came as a great beacon light of hope to millions of Negro slaves who had been seared in the flames of withering injustice. It came as a joyous daybreak to end the long night of captivity.

But one hundred years later, we must face the tragic fact that the Negro is still not free. One hundred years later, the life of the Negro is still sadly crippled by the manacles of segregation and the chains of discrimination

He continued:

I say to you today, my friends, that in spite of the difficulties and frustrations of the moment, I still have a dream. It is a dream deeply rooted in the American dream.

I have a dream that one day this nation will rise up and live out the true meaning of its creed: We hold these truths to be self-evident: that all men are created equal

AMERICA'S MARTYR

On 28th March, 1968, Dr King led a march through Memphis, Tennessee, which was intended to be peaceful. However, some incited other elements of the crowd to violence, and the march disintegrated in chaos. Dr King vowed to return for a peaceful march. On 3rd April he kept his word, taking a room at the Lorraine Motel. At 6.01pm on 4th April, 1968, he left his room on the first floor, to go to dinner. He leaned over the balustrade to speak to his chauffeur, and was hit by a single rifle bullet. He fell, mortally wounded.

The day before he had delivered yet another brilliant, yet prophetic, speech:

Well, I don't know what will happen now. We've got some difficult days ahead. But it doesn't matter with me now. Because I've been to the mountain top. And I don't mind. Like anybody, I would like to live a long life. Longevity has its place. But I'm not concerned about that now. I just want to do God's will. And He's allowed me to go up to the mountain. And I've looked over. And I've seen the Promised Land. I may not get there with you. But I want you to know tonight, that we, as a people, will get to the Promised Land. And I'm happy, tonight. I'm not worried about anything. I'm not fearing any man. Mine eyes have seen the glory of the coming of the Lord

Amazing!

Few have demonstrated such commitment, shown greater courage, and been as wise, all the while offering millions powerful and positive leadership. If ever you need reassurance of the art of the possible, just read his speeches. One man can make a difference.

James Earl Ray was arrested in England on the charge of shooting Dr King, and was returned to Memphis, Tennessee, to stand trial. On March 9, 1969, he pleaded guilty and was sentenced to 99 years in the Tennessee State Penitentiary. Ray subsequently died in 1998.

MARCH TO HONOUR DR KING

In death his leadership carried on.

JAMES EARL RAY

James Earl Ray was arrested in England and returned to Memphis where he was tried and sentenced to 99 years.

The Piano Men

Big-voiced, piano-thumping Sunnyland Slim had one of the longest careers in the Blues, stretching right back to the 20s. It is estimated that he played on well over 200 records, either as a sideman or featured artist. But he never achieved real solo success, and it is as a sideman that he is best remembered. The son of a Delta preacher, he was born Albert Luandrew in 1907, and first worked in Delta jukes and later on Beale Street. He moved to Chicago in the 40s, recording some tracks for Aristocrat that were followed by solo sides for more than a dozen labels during the 40s and 50s. He toured Europe in 1964 as part of the American Folk Blues Festival, the same year that he recorded for Swedish radio in Chicago with a 20-year-old white blues guitarist, Mike Bloomfield. Besides his longevity, and undoubted talent, his place in the story will be assured as the man who got Muddy the gig. In 1995 Slim slipped and fell on ice on his way home from a Chicago club and died from kidney failure not long afterwards. He had been playing for more than 70 years.

Sunnyland Slim
One of the leaders of the Chicago piano school.

Born just a year before Sunnyland Slim, Eurreal Wilford Montgomery came from Louisiana and acquired the handle 'Little Brother' as a boy. He was one of the last of the barrelhouse pianists, a veteran of house rent parties, clubs, dances, brothels, and even a concert at Carnegie Hall with Kid Ory's Jazz Band in 1948. Having left home aged eleven and slipped into the life of an itinerant player, he had plenty of opportunity to learn about life and the blues. His first session was in 1930 for Paramount, when he cut 'No Special Rider' and 'Vicksburg Blues', which became a blues standard. In 1935 and '36 he recorded extensively for Bluebird, before settling in Chicago in the early 40s. Another 'feature pianist' on the Chicago scene, he recorded solo and accompanied Otis Rush, Magic Sam, JB Lenoir, and Buddy Guy – who cut a stunning version of Montgomery's 'First Time I Met The Blues' at his debut session for Chess in 1960, with the man himself playing piano. Little Brother Montgomery last recorded in 1982 and died three years later.

The Biggest Thing Since Colossus

Little Brother, Sunnyland and Roosevelt Sykes, the godfathers of Chicago blues piano, had a godson – and his name was Otis Spann. Born in 1930 in Jackson, Mississippi, he arrived on the Chicago scene in 1951 after serving in the army. He was soon playing clubs and by 1953 he had become a member of Muddy Waters' band. His playing was a fantastic mix of boogie rhythms and deep blues feeling,

Little Brother Montgomery

Champion Jack Dupree

making him both a perfect accompanist as well as an excellent solo artist. His first solo sides, cut in 1954, featured BB King and Robert Jr Lockwood on guitar. Along with Lafayette Leake, Otis was a Chess 'house pianist', recording with Howlin' Wolf, Little Walter and Buddy Guy amongst others. He visited Britain in 1958 on Muddy's groundbreaking tour, and returned a number of times in the 60s with the American Folk Blues Festivals.

Tragically in early 1970, Otis Spann was diagnosed with terminal cancer. On 2nd, 3rd, and 4th April, he played shows with his wife Lucille at the *Boston Tea Party*. He had been released from hospital a couple of days before and he died less than three weeks later on 24 April 1970. Tapes of the shows, at which Otis played to fewer than 50 people, have recently been discovered, and a CD taken from them has been released. *Last Call* is a fitting epitaph to this blues master.

'I've heard from people who witnessed his recording sessions that everyone deferred to Spann: 'Spann, how do you think it should go right here', and so on. Paul Oscher, Muddy's late 60s harmonica player, is sure that Spann conceived some of Muddy's more sophisticated arrangements, like 'I Just Want To Make Love To You'. I lived with Spann and his wife for much of his final year and found that he holds a unique place in the hearts of many. Album titles like Otis Spann Is The Blues *and* The Biggest Thing Since Colossus *were far from marketing ploys: they simply reflect the quiet greatness, the Sweet Giant of the Blues that was Otis Spann'*

PETER MALICK
GUITARIST WITH OTIS SPANN
AT HIS LAST SHOW

CHEROKEE BLUES

The only known bluesman who can claim descent from French as well as Cherokee Indian blood, and who once lived in Yorkshire, was born William Thomas Dupree in New Orleans around 1910. Soon orphaned, the child became known as Champion Jack Dupree, on account of his boxing career (over 100 fights), and like Montgomery and Slim he learned his musical trade in the barrelhouses. He was perhaps a less accomplished pianist than his contemporaries, but whatever he lacked in piano skills he more than made up for with his blend of bawdy, raconteur-styled Blues.

Dupree's first sessions were for OKeh in Chicago during the summer of 1940. After wartime service in the Navy he stayed in

BIG TROUSERS

On 4th May, 1964 Otis Spann cut a single at Decca Studios in London with producer Mike Vernon. On 'Pretty Girls Everywhere' and 'Stirs Me Up', Otis was accompanied by Muddy Waters on rhythm guitar and Eric Clapton on lead. Some years later, Eric recalled: 'They were both very friendly, and they had beautiful shiny silk suits, with big trousers!'

OTIS SPANN
The 'godson' of Chicago blues piano.

New York, working clubs and recording for a variety of labels. He recorded prolifically, especially for the King label in the early 50s, scoring his only hit, 'Walking The Blues', in 1955. By 1958 he had switched to Atlantic and recorded an excellent album, *Blues From The Gutter*, recording for the label again the following year in London. He liked Europe and citing the lack of prejudice he found there, he moved to Switzerland in 1960 (he either overlooked or was unaware of their voting restrictions for women!). He remained in Europe, moving to Copenhagen in the mid-60s and then to Halifax, Yorkshire, when he married an Englishwoman in 1971 (he had twice before been widowed). He later lived in Paris, Sweden, and finally Germany, where he died in 1992. Throughout his European sojourn he recorded regularly, becoming a familiar face on the local blues scene. This may have detracted somewhat from his reputation, which is a pity, as he was a last link with the pre-war barrelhouses. Sam Charters described him as 'one of the great entertainers of the blues', which is no bad epitaph.

WILLIE MABON
An ex-marine who hailed from Mississippi, Mabon was a sophisticated performer.

Willie Mabon, who cut his first sides for the Apollo label in 1949, had the distinction of seeing his first two hits make No. 1 on the R&B charts in 1953. 'I Don't Know', a remake of a Cripple Clarence Lofton number from 1938, and 'I'm Mad' both emphasise Mabon's humorous lyrics and delivery. He never lived up to his initial success, with only 'Poison Ivy' of his subsequent releases making the charts in 1954. (The song is not the same one recorded by the Coasters later in the decade, although ironically Mabon was a big influence on their early releases.) These early sides were all cut for Chess, and after he left the label in 1956 his recording career went steadily downhill, despite the fact he was able to work for many different labels. In the 70s he began touring Europe, where he maintained a good following until he died in Paris in 1985.

Chess had a strong contingent of pianists who supported its various artists on recordings throughout the 50s. For example, Lloyd Glenn cut some excellent records with Lowell Fulson. On many of the Willie Dixon sessions, Lafayette Leake provided accompaniment, also playing on several Chuck Berry singles. But Berry's main pianist was Johnnie Johnson, who played with Eric Clapton in 1990 at London's Royal Albert Hall.

WILLIE MABON
Sharp, slick, and witty too.

A BOY NAMED ALLISON

Mabon's influence was felt in the UK when Georgie Fame recorded 'Seventh Son', a Willie Dixon song that Mabon had cut in 1955. Not that it was a direct influence; Fame heard the song from Mose Allison, who had originally taken his inspiration from Mabon. Allison was a rarity, a white bluesman from the Delta; he was born in Tippo, Mississippi. He travelled a road somewhere between jazz and blues, but besides his excellent rendition of 'Seventh Son' he also wrote 'Parchman Farm' and 'Young Man's Blues', two of the best blues songs written by a white man

After spells at the University of Mississippi and then in the army, Allison returned to college in Louisiana. From 1954 until 1956 he worked across the South-East, before

MOSE ALLISON

Mose Allison is a consistant performer today, and appears regularly in London at Ronnie Scott's and the Jazz Café.

settling in New York. On 7th March, 1957, he cut *Back Country Suite* for Prestige Records, the first of many albums for the label. Despite recording more than 20 LPs between 1957 and 1980, however, Mose was never able to achieve anything more than cult status, a situation which has stayed the same ever since.

DOO-WOP 'TIL YOU DROP

There is no finer instrument than the human voice, and it is the voice that is the essential ingredient in doo-wop. This musical style evolved out of gospel, blues, and jazz, with an extra dash of swing.

Groups like the Ink Spots and the Mills Brothers pioneered the form but their style was fundamentally 'white'. Classic doo-wop was a wholly black style, when groups like the Ravens and the Orioles appeared in the late 40s and early 50s. It was not long before they started figuring on the charts. The first doo-wop No. 1 was 'It's Too Soon To Know' by the Orioles, but that record definitely belonged to the earlier era. By the time the Crows released their brilliant song 'Gee' in June 1953, however, things were heading in a very different direction. 'Gee' made No. 2 on the R&B chart in 1954, and crossed over to the national pop chart, indicating that this music had broad appeal. The Orioles topped the R&B chart with 'Crying In The Chapel' in late 1953 (Elvis was to make No. 3 in the *Billboard* chart in 1965 with his version).

Records like 'Money Honey' by Clyde McPhatter & the Drifters (1953), '(I'll Remember) In The Still Of The Night' by the Five Satins (1956), 'Come Go With Me' by the Dell Vikings (1956), and 'Get A Job' by the Silhouettes (1957) provide the definitive doo-wop soundtrack to the 1950s. *The Doo-Wop Box,* released by Rhino Records, is a four-CD tour de force spanning the golden age of rock'n'roll.

DOO-WOP

'In The Still of The Night' by The Five Satins.

YOUNG MAN BLUES

An influence on Georgie Fame, Mose Allison was also an inspiration to Pete Townshend of The Who. The band performed Allison's 'Young Man Blues' on their album Live At Leeds, *recorded on 14th February, 1970, and it became a regular on their live set list during the 70s.*

"I already owned some of Mose's albums, so I went to see him on 26th January, 1966, at Annie's Room in London; he was there for a three-week residency. His playing knocked me out, and after performing he joined me at my table and we chatted for an hour or more. Recently I bought a copy of Back Country Suite on CD. I had bought it on LP just after seeing Mose live. My mate Georgie Fame told me it had been re-released… it's a brilliant album"

BILL WYMAN

SUN ARISE

SAM PHILLIPS
Memphis, Tennessee, 2000

SAMUEL CORNELIUS PHILLIPS, a radio engineer from Florence, Alabama, had a vision.

"As a young man I got a job on radio station WREC in Memphis, Tennessee. With a secure job you would think, 'Well goodness, what did I want to do fooling around with something that I was gonna get criticised for'. But the elements of the Blues, and the associations that I had with black and white people... of the South, made me understand that what I heard, the world should hear"

SAM PHILLIPS

Sam established his Memphis Recording Studios at 706 Union Avenue in January 1950 to record 'anything, anytime, anywhere'. Sam would take his equipment in his car to tape weddings, parties, or business meetings. At the same time he began to record local artists, and sell the results to established labels like 4 Star Records, Modern Records, and their subsidiary RPM. Sam also established a relationship with Chess Records in 1951. Amongst the blues artists he recorded were Lost John Hunter and Joe Hill Louis. In early 1951 he cut BB King's first sides for RPM and Walter Horton's audition acetates for Modern.

Sam's masterstroke was not to over-produce but to allow his performers to cut through on record, a triumph of spontaneity over technical expertise. Sam's first hit was Jackie Brenston's 'Rocket 88' for Chess. Brenston was a member of Ike Turner's Kings of Rhythm band and, as Ike attested in 2000, "It was my record, they just didn't put my name on it". During the rest of 1951 Sam recorded Ike Turner, Billy Love, Rosco Gordon, Doctor Ross, and others for Chess. He also cut Howlin' Wolf's first sides, amongst them the menacing 'Highway Man'

"Well Howlin' Wolf was one of the most interesting people that I worked with. He had probably the most God-awful voice you ever heard. It was so distinctive, so pronounced, that whatever you heard come out of his mouth, it had that magic charm of 'I believe this, I just believe it'. The Wolf would get in there and go into a trance"

SAM PHILLIPS

SAM STRIKES OUT

By 1952 the endless contractual wrangling with the Bihari brothers (owners of Modern/RPM) and Chess prompted Phillips to set up his own label (he had already made one abortive attempt in 1950 with the Phillips label). In April 1952 he released Johnny London's 'Drivin' Slow', the first Sun

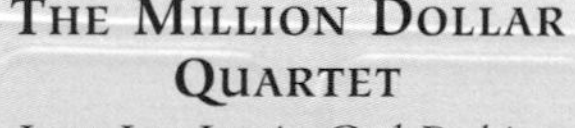

THE MILLION DOLLAR QUARTET
Jerry Lee Lewis, Carl Perkins, Johnny Cash, and Elvis Presley at Sun Studios, 1955.

"When I was in the RAF in North Germany I was very near the American bases. I heard my first Elvis Presley records on a juke box at the local bar - 'I'm Left, You're Right, She's Gone' and 'That's All Right', the very early Sun records. They blew me away, so I went straight round to the American base and bought the new 45rpm singles"

BILL WYMAN

X MARKS THE SPOT

Elvis' usual recording spot is marked by an X on the floor.

record. Sam was still making records for Chess, including sessions by Rufus Thomas, the Wolf, Sleepy John Estes, Willie Nix, David 'Honeyboy' Edwards, and Walter Horton. There was probably more money to be made from leasing sides to other labels at this stage, and so it was not until 1953 that Sam really got into his stride with Sun Records.

Early Sun releases included sides by Walter Horton, Rufus Thomas, and Big Memphis Ma Rainey. Sun's first hit came in April 1953 with 'Bear Cat' by Rufus Thomas, followed by Little Junior's Blue Flames, a group led by Herman 'Little Junior' Parker, with 'Feelin' Good' (R&B No. 5) in October. Soon Ike Turner renewed his relationship with Sam, bringing Little Milton to the label. Before the year was out Mose Vinson, Earl Hooker, James Cotton and Johnny O'Neill had all come to 706 Union. 1954 started the way that '53 ended, with sessions from Billy Love, Kenneth Banks, Little Milton, Junior Parker, and Pat Hare (later a member of Muddy Waters' band). But soon Sun was switching horses and hitching its wagon to white, country-style artists.

A NEW SUN RISES

On 5th July, 1954 Elvis Presley first stepped up to the microphone at Sun Studios and sang a Bing Crosby hit from 1950 called 'Harbor Lights.' Sometime after midnight he cut 'That's All Right'. For the remainder of 1954 and 1955 blues sessions took a back seat at Sun, eventually drying up altogether. In November 1955 Phillips sold Elvis's contract to RCA, but not before the two men had cut some other brilliant blues-inspired sides including 'Good Rockin' Tonight', 'Milkcow Blues Boogie', 'Mystery Train', and 'Baby Let's Play House'.

From then on, it was rockabilly (as the new blend of white country artists and black R&B rhythms was called) all the way. 'Blue Suede Shoes' by Carl Perkins and Johnny Cash's 'I Walk The Line' in 1956, and Jerry Lee Lewis with 'Whole Lot Of Shakin' Goin' On' in 1957, heralded the golden era of Sun Records.

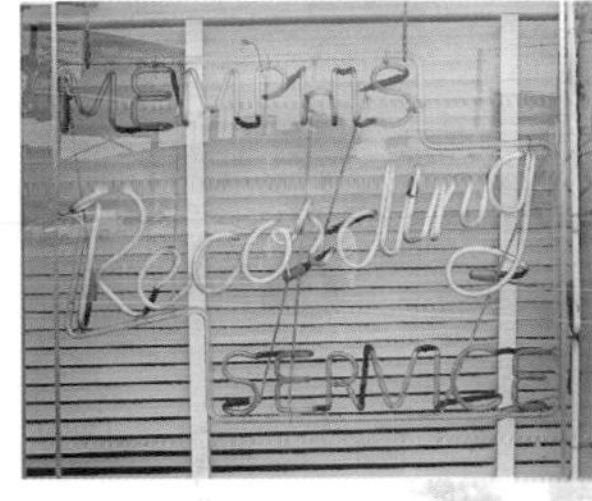

MEMPHIS RECORDING SERVICES

The somewhat modest front door to the studios.

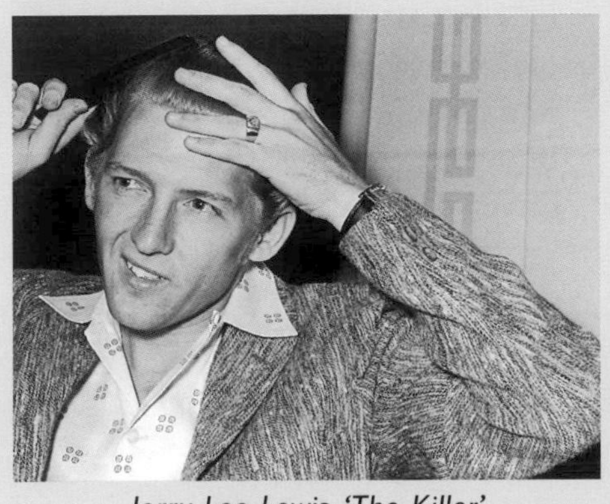

Jerry Lee Lewis, 'The Killer'

❛ *On Sunday 25th May, 1958, the* People *newspaper called on British teenagers to boycott Jerry Lee Lewis's concerts, and 'show that even rock'n'roll hasn't entirely robbed them of their sanity'. Well I obviously ignored them as I went to see Jerry Lee the next night at the Granada cinema in Tooting. He had just had a hit with 'Breathless' and I thought he was brilliant. Next day the tour was cancelled and he returned to America* ❜

BILL WYMAN

'BREATHLESS'

By Jerry Lee Lewis, Sun 288

HOWLIN' WOLF

BORN CHESTER BURNETT in the heart of the Delta in 1910, Wolf grew up to be a powerful man well over six feet tall and weighing in somewhere close to 300 lbs. He acquired his nickname when a boy – he was apparently not the best-behaved of children. As a youngster he learned to play the guitar by watching Charley Patton, from whom he also picked up some of his onstage antics.

FACT FILE

BORN: *10th June, 1910 West Point, Mississippi*

DIED: *10th January, 1976, Hines, Illinois*

INSTRUMENT: *Guitar and harmonica*

FIRST RECORDED: *1951*

ACCOLADES: *Inducted into the Blues Hall of Fame, 1980*

INFLUENCES: *Charley Patton, Tommy Johnson, Sonny Boy Williamson (Rice Miller), Jimmie Rodgers*

INFLUENCED: *The Rolling Stones, Cream, The Yardbirds, Captain Beefheart*

> *'It was he (Charley Patton) who started me off to playing. He took a liking to me, and I asked him would he learn me'*
>
> HOWLIN' WOLF

Sonny Boy Williamson (Rice Miller) taught him the harmonica, so he certainly came with an excellent pedigree. But it was Wolf's singing rather than his playing skills that commanded attention.

When he first recorded at Sun Studios, the Wolf was already over 40. Up to that point he had been dividing his life between farming and performing, not necessarily in equal measure. Perhaps that is why he was such a powerful performer, in the purest Delta tradition: he more than most Delta bluesmen felt the Delta dirt. After serving in the army during the war, he moved to West Memphis at the end of the 40s to make a career out of music. Putting a band together that included both Little Junior Parker and James Cotton, he got a job on a local radio station, performing songs and promoting his own live shows.

He got his recording break in 1951 through Ike Turner, Sun's part-time scout. He cut 'Moanin' At Midnight' and 'How Many More Years' for Sam Phillips, which became his first single when Phillips sold the sides to Chess (R&B Chart No. 4). He was soon recording for Modern as well, but after some contractual wranglings Wolf ended up with Chess. Soon afterwards he moved to Chicago where he began his prolific and successful recording career with the label. Amongst his best recordings were 'Smokestack Lightning', 'Spoonful', 'Saddle My Pony' (Charley Patton's song), 'Little Red Rooster', 'Evil', 'Back Door Man', and 'Killing Floor'. After his debut, though, he only charted three more songs during the 50s, of which 'Smokestack Lightning' was the most successful. In Chicago, Wolf began an association with the brilliant guitarist Hubert Sumlin, who remained his instrumental foil for the rest of his career. Along with Muddy Waters,

> *'He wasn't just a blues singer. I mean he was a commander of your soul and he got hold of you with the Blues. The Wolf was a hypnotiser, he hypnotised himself when he opened that mouth and let it loose'*
>
> SAM PHILLIPS

Wolf cut the most influential set of recordings of any post-war Chicago bluesman, but the two men were also highly competitive.

By the 60s Wolf's chart career was over but he continued to exert a powerful influence through his recordings and his live work. Albums like *Moanin At Midnight*, *Howlin' Wolf*, and *The Real Folk Blues* were keenly studied by younger musicians, especially white blues players. In 1964 he visited Europe for the first time with the American Folk Blues Festival, and proved to be as charismatic on stage as on his recordings. The following year he appeared at the request of the Rolling Stones on the *Shindig* TV show. He then played the Newport Folk Festival in 1966. In 1970, the Wolf recorded *The London Howlin' Wolf Sessions* with Eric Clapton, Charlie Watts, Stevie

Winwood, Ian Stewart, and Bill Wyman. By then he had suffered a heart attack and there is evidence of his failing health on the recording.

A car accident in 1971 caused irreparable damage to his kidneys, and an inevitable slowdown in live work followed. He continued to record, but his once-powerful voice was showing increasing signs of wear. Wolf's last performance was to be in Chicago just a few months later, with BB King. Two months after the concert the Wolf died of kidney failure.

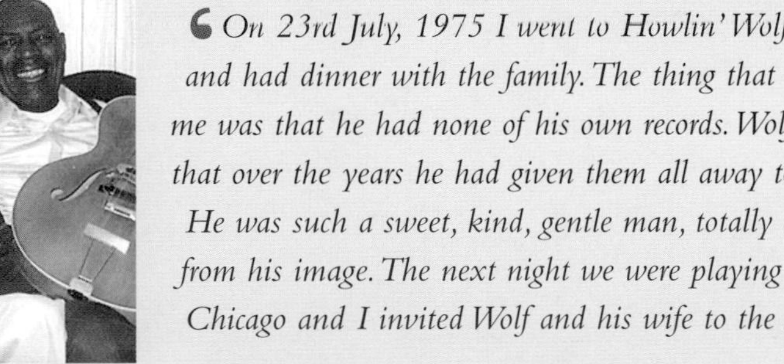

On 23rd July, 1975 I went to Howlin' Wolf's home and had dinner with the family. The thing that amazed me was that he had none of his own records. Wolf told me that over the years he had given them all away to friends. He was such a sweet, kind, gentle man, totally different from his image. The next night we were playing a gig in Chicago and I invited Wolf and his wife to the show

BILL WYMAN

You should have seen the Wolf. It was wonderful. We went to the concert, and Bill Wyman must have arranged something, because when the Wolf walked into the stadium a spotlight went on him and the whole place stood up and cheered. It was so good for him. I watched that from the side of the stage and I was so proud

LILLIE BURNETT, WOLF'S WIFE

ESSENTIAL RECORDINGS

CLASSIC SONGS

'Smokestack Lightning' 1956
'Spoonful' 1960
'Little Red Rooster' 1961
'Killing Floor' 1964

CLASSIC ALBUMS

Howlin' Wolf 1959

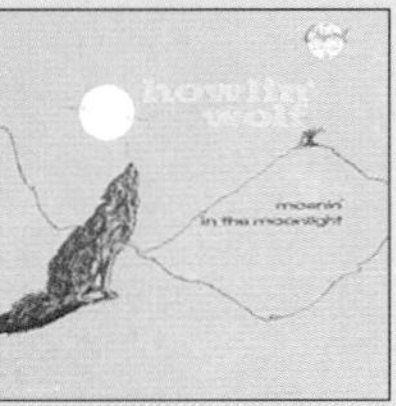

Moanin' in The Moonlight 1962

THE SOURCE

His Best
Chess Anniversary Collection
Howlin' Wolf Rides Again

It's unfortunate that I didn't get to record the Wolf a lot longer, because he would have been my entirely different approach to rock'n'roll

SAM PHILLIPS

GOING TO MEMPHIS

ONE OF HOWLIN' WOLF'S main rivals around Memphis was BB King, who had moved to Memphis about a year before Wolf. His breakthrough came via Sonny Boy Williamson's radio show.

BB King: 'I got to audition for Sonny Boy, it was one of the Ivory Joe Hunter songs called 'Blues of Sunrise'. Sonny Boy had been working out a little place called the 16th Street Grill down in West Memphis. So he told the lady that he had been working for, her name was Miss Annie, 'I'm going to send him down in my place tonight'. My job was to play for the young people that didn't gamble. The 16th Street Grill had a gambling place in the back, but if a guy came and brought his girlfriend or his wife that didn't gamble, my job was to keep them happy by playing music for them to dance. They seemed to enjoy me playing, so Miss Annie said, 'if you can get a job on the radio like Sonny Boy, I'll give you this job and I'll pay you $12 and a half a night. And I'll give you six days of work, room and board'. Man I couldn't believe it.'

Soon after Riley B King, as he was christened, was given his own radio show on WDIA. King's radio career helped him to become very popular and he and the Wolf were often rivals for the better-paying jobs around Memphis. A few years later they went head to head once again.

> *We were in Memphis at the Auditorium. Elvis was there. Watching and performing were Bobby Bland, Little Milton, Little Junior Parker, Howlin' Wolf, and myself. Everybody had been on stage. Bobby Bland is a stage mover, man, he can move the people. Little Milton and myself, you know, we do what we do but we couldn't move the crowd quickly like Bobby Bland. We had been on and now Howlin' Wolf is up and the people are going crazy, man. Milton says, "Something is going on out there". Junior Parker says, "Let's check it out". So Wolf is doing 'Spoonful', now we go out there and he's on his knees crawling round on the floor. Yes, he's on his knees and the people just going crazy. So finally we figured out what it was and the seat of his pants was busted! And all of his business is hanging out!*
>
> BB KING

Memphis must have been a wonderful place to be around this time. Vibrant and brash, it boasted a musical scene that only Chicago could rival.

> *When I was a disc jockey, they use to bill me as Blues Boy, the boy from Beale Street. People would write me and instead of saying the Blues Boy, they'd just abbreviate it to BB*
>
> BB KING

MYSTERY TRAIN

MYSTERY TRAIN WAS recorded in either September or October 1953 by a band led by Herman Parker. Herman became known as 'Little Junior' when he was growing up in Clarksdale, Mississippi, during the 30s. After working with Howlin' Wolf's band he formed his own group, the Blue Flames, in 1952, and 'Mystery Train' was the follow-up to 'Feelin' Good', his debut for Sun records.

When I first heard 'Mystery Train', Little Junior Parker hadn't quite worked it out. Back then it wasn't aeroplanes so much as trains, and when you went and put somebody on a train, it was like 'Oh man, I may never see them again'. We just messed round and it just fell into that groove, it is a perfect groove

SAM PHILLIPS

ELVIS, THIS IS IT

Elvis cut 'Mystery Train' on 11th July, 1955, just a few days over a year after his first session at 706 Union Avenue. You can hear Elvis laugh at the end as he didn't think it was a take.

Elvis cut it in one take. You heard this one-take stuff before, but it was, and I said 'Elvis, this is it'

SAM PHILLIPS

MYSTERY TRAIN

Written by Herman Parker & Sam Phillips
Recorded by Little Junior's Blue Flames,
Sun 192, did not chart

Train I ride sixteen coaches long
Train I ride sixteen coaches long
Well, that long black train carry my baby from home

Train, train, comin' on round the bend
Train, train, comin' on round the bend
Well, it took my baby; it's goin' do it again

Train, train, comin' on down the line
Train, train, comin' on down the line
Well, it's bringing my baby, 'cos she's mine all mine

The lyrical inspiration for 'Mystery Train' came from a song that both black and white people throughout the South knew very well. First recorded by the Carter Family in 1930 as 'Worried Man Blues', it included the lines:

'The train I ride is sixteen coaches long
The train I ride is sixteen coaches long
The girl I love is on that train and gone'

When Elvis came in I found out that 'Mystery Train' was so embedded in Elvis's mind that when he started to sing it, it was as natural as breathing. If it's natural it's awfully hard to beat, like you're just rolling off of a log. That's the feeling you get with 'Mystery Train'

SAM PHILLIPS

'Mystery Train'/'I Forgot To Remember to Forget' became Presley's last Sun single but failed to make either the pop or R&B charts. It did, however, make No. 11 on the country chart in September 1955.

HOW MANY COACHES WAS THAT?

On a 1944 recording Woody Guthrie added five coaches to the song. Then in October 1955, a few weeks after Elvis' 'Mystery Train' charted in America, Lonnie Donegan recorded 'Worried Man Blues'; he decided that 21 was the right amount for him too. It is doubtful that Lonnie could have heard 'Mystery Train' before he recorded 'Worried Man Blues'. The Grateful Dead performed the song just once, at a live concert in 1970. For some reason, best known to themselves, they reduced the number of carriages to 15.

Mystery Train' has always been one of my favourite songs. I recorded it live with my band, Willie and The Poor Boys, in 1992. Once we went on the road as the Rhythm Kings we all agreed that it was a great number to do live. It was a natural number for Albert Lee's country guitar picking, along with Nick Payn's harmonica and Georgie Fame and Gary Brooker on vocals. I just love the groove, it's a bass player's delight

BILL WYMAN

SELECTED VERSIONS

- 1953 Little Junior Parker
- 1955 Elvis Presley
- 1965 Paul Butterfield Blues Band
- 1968 Junior Wells
- 1970 Grateful Dead
- 1973 Flying Burrito Brothers
- 1974 Alvin Lee
- 1978 The Band
- 1980 UFO
- 1981 The Nighthawks
- 1990 The Stray Cats
- 1992 Willie & The Poor Boys
- Pat Travers
- 1995 Neville Brothers
- 1998 Bill Wyman's Rhythm Kings

SWEET HOME CHICAGO

Eddie Boyd

SNOOKY PRIOR
At the WC Handy Awards, 2000

CHUCK & BO
And the winner is…

WHILE MEMPHIS HAD GOLDEN blues years, Chicago had a golden decade. Throughout the 50s great records came out of the Windy City, the high degree of competition helping to fuel this creative fire. There was also a sense of camaraderie between many of the players, and within the goldmine bluesmen both taught and motivated each other. Besides those we have already featured, there were other musicians who played a vital part in this period.

A 36-year-old pianist from the Delta named Eddie Boyd cut the blues standard, 'Five Long Years', for the JOB label in 1952. Reaching No. 1 on the R&B charts, it became one of the city's earliest major hits. Eddie was born on Stovall's plantation and so he knew Muddy Waters while he was growing up. He actually moved to Chicago before Muddy and so it was natural that the two men should work together once Muddy arrived in the city. After 'Five Long Years', Eddie switched to Chess and had two sizeable hits in 1953 with '24 Hours' and 'Third Degree'; both got to No. 3. After his recording success waned, Eddie switched to a number of smaller labels. He first toured Europe in 1965, as part of the American Folk Blues Festival, before moving across the Atlantic permanently in the late 60s. He recorded with John Mayall, one of the leaders of the 60s British blues scene, and built a long and successful career in Europe.

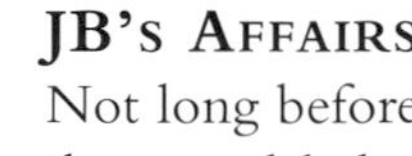

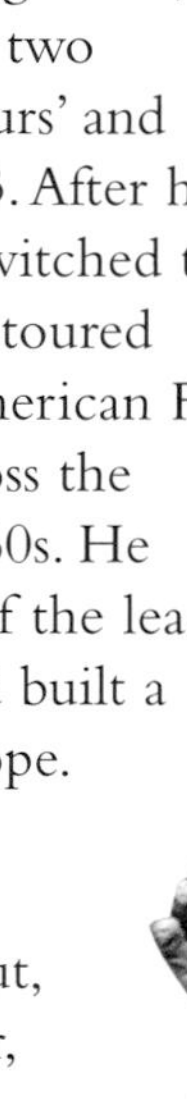

JB'S AFFAIRS

Not long before Boyd's JOB debut, the same label recorded JB Lenoir, another resettled Delta player. Unusually, JB was Lenoir's full name; he had no first names, just meaningless initials. He was 23 years old when he cut 'People Are Meddlin' In Our Affairs', the recording that set the tone for much of his output. While many bluesmen concentrated on loss and love, JB had a penchant for political themes. His first record for Chess was 'Deep In Debt Blues', while later for the Parrot label he cut 'Eisenhower Blues' and 'I'm In Korea'. Besides his politics JB liked to boogie too, and it is probably his boogie-based blues for which he will be best remembered. Bill and the Rhythm Kings cut 'Mojo Boogie', which was originally recorded in 1953, on the album *Anyway The Wind Blows*. JB toured Europe on the same show as Eddie Boyd in 1965, but two years later he was in a car crash, suffered a heart attack, and died aged 38.

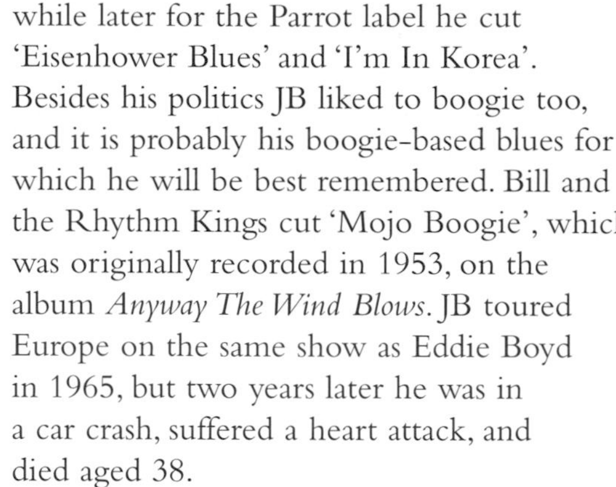

Other musicians recording in Chicago during the first half of the 50s included Billy Boy Arnold, Johnny Shines, Snooky Prior, JB Hutto, Robert Jr Lockwood, Eddie Taylor, and Albert King, who cut his first records for Parrot in 1953.

In early 1955 two 'stylists' appeared on the Chicago scene. If the foundations of rock'n'roll, as well as rock music, lay in the jump blues of the 1940s then Chuck and Bo were the ones who raised the roof.

According to Muddy Waters, in 1963: 'Chuck and Bo had a cutting contest judged by applause. According to Bo, he won!'

J.B. Lenoir

Bo Diddley

FACT FILE

Born: *30th December, 1928 McComb, Mississippi.*

Instrument: *Guitar, Harmonica.*

First recorded: *1955.*

Accolades: *Inducted into the Rock & Roll Hall of Fame, 1987*

Influences: *Louis Jordan, John Lee Hooker.*

Influenced: *The Rolling Stones, The Animals, The Yardbirds, and a host of less well-known British bands*

The man who was billed later in his career as 'The 500% Man' developed his signature guitar sound and his 'Bo Diddley beat' ('Shave 'n' a haircut, two bits') early in his career. He was born Otha Elias Bates McDaniels on a Delta farm, but after he was adopted by his mother's cousin, he was brought up in Chicago. As a child, his main interest was boxing, which is where he got his nickname. Like most black children of his era he was well versed in gospel music, but unlike most he took violin lessons and studied classical music.

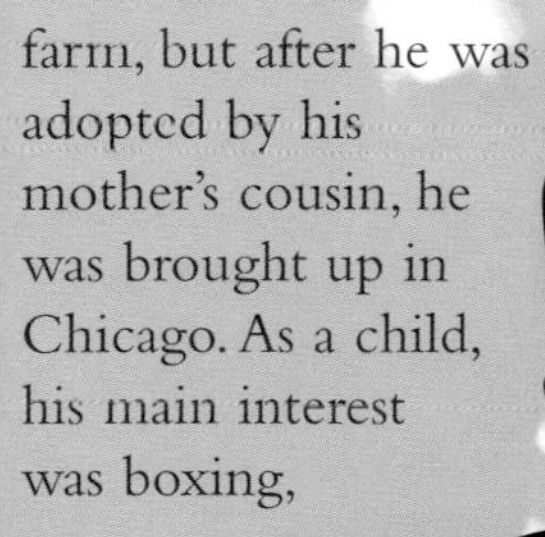

Around 1941, Diddley formed a band that included Earl Hooker. In the late 40s he assembled a trio with percussionist Jerome Green to play at parties and on street corners. By the early 50s he was playing in Chicago clubs and around this time harmonica player Billy Boy Arnold joined the group.

In 1955 Diddley signed to the Chess subsidiary, Checker Records, cutting his first record on 2nd March. Besides Arnold and Green, the session also featured Otis Spann on piano. The single of 'Bo Diddley', backed by 'I'm A Man', topped the R&B charts, establishing his reputation. Diddley stayed with Checker for the rest of the 50s and early 60s and scored a string of R&B hits. He recorded many other 'classic' sides during this period, including 'Who Do You Love' (1956), 'Hey Bo Diddley' (1957), and 'Mona (I Need You Baby)' (1957). In 1959 'Say Man' crossed over to the pop market and climbed to No. 20 in the US Hot 100, while in 1962 his version of Willie Dixon's 'You Can't Judge A Book By Its Cover' reached No. 48 in the Hot 100.

In 1958 Diddley moved to Washington and started touring with rock'n'roll package tours. Like his Chess stablemate Chuck Berry, his music was a potent mix of blues, rock and R&B. His appeal in America was on the wane after 1962, but in Britain he had hits with 'Pretty Thing' in 1963 (the inspiration for the name of the South London band) and 'Hey Good Lookin'' in 1965. Throughout the 1970s and 80s Bo was playing the oldies circuit. Time will serve his reputation better.

"At the first ever Stones recording session on 11th March, 1963, we recorded for three hours with a very young producer, Glyn Johns, at IBC Studios in London. We cut five songs, including Bo Diddley's 'Road Runner' and 'Diddley Daddy', Muddy Waters' 'I Want To Be Loved', and Jimmy Reed's 'Honey What's Wrong'… we had five minutes left, so we did a first take on Jimmy's 'Bright Lights Big City"

Bill Wyman

Essential Recordings

Classic Songs

'I'm A Man' 1955
'Who Do You Love' 1956
'Hey Bo Diddley' 1957

Classic Albums

Have Guitar Will Travel *1960*
Checker

The Source

Bo Diddley: His Best
Chess/Universal

CHUCK BERRY

FACT FILE

BORN: *15th January, 1926 San Jose (Santa Clara Co.), California*

INSTRUMENT: *Guitar, Piano, Saxophone*

FIRST RECORDED: *1955*

ACCOLADES: *Inducted into the Blues Hall of Fame, 1985*

INFLUENCES: *Louis Jordan (and guitarist Carl Hogan), Aaron 'T-Bone' Walker, Wynonie Harris, Muddy Waters*

INFLUENCED: *Everyone!*

DESPITE WHAT Charles Edward Anderson Berry says in his autobiography, he was not born in St Louis, although he moved there when he was very young. He learned the guitar in the late 30s and was soon playing at parties and school dances.

Berry worked with Ray Band's Orchestra in St Louis, but his musical apprenticeship was cut short in 1944 when he was sentenced to three years in a reform centre. After his release he formed the Chuck Berry Combo. Following his move to Chicago, he met Muddy Waters, who introduced him to Chess Records. Shortly after, on 21st May, 1955, he cut his first record, a country blues tune called 'Ida Red' that Berry renamed 'Maybellene'. The record, which featured Willie Dixon on bass and Johnny Johnson on piano, went to No. 1 on the R&B charts for 11 weeks and reached No. 5 on the Hot 100. It may not have been the actual birth of rock'n'roll, but it was a defining moment in the history of the genre.

From then until the start of the 60s, Berry was a constant presence on the R&B and Hot 100 charts. Among his biggest records were 'Roll Over Beethoven' (1956), 'School Days' (1957), 'Sweet Little Sixteen' (1958), and 'Johnny B Goode' (1958). While Berry was clearly not an outright blues player. his records were full of blues licks and influences, and on his biggest hits he was accompanied by the cream of the Chess session players.

> *Home, from Germany, on leave from the Air Force in February 1957, I went to the cinema and saw the film* Rock, Rock, Rock! *It wasn't that special until Chuck Berry appeared in a white suit, singing 'You Can't Catch Me'. As he started doing his leg movements, the audience started laughing, thinking it was a comedy number. The hair stood up on the back of my neck… I got cold shivers all over me. I'd never had a feeling like that before, or since*
>
> BILL WYMAN

HERE COME OLD FLAT TOP

The Beatles ('Roll Over Beethoven'), The Beach Boys ('Rock And Roll Music'), and The Stones ('Come On', their first single, and many more songs after that) have all paid their respects to 'Old Flat Top'.

Throughout the 1960s Berry was a major influence on both American and British bands, who were derivative of him in the same way as he had leaned on the late 40s proto-rock'n'roll of Louis Jordan, Joe Turner, and Wynonie Harris. Throughout the 1970s, 80s, and 90s, Berry continued to perform, mostly with pick-up bands – hardly a problem, given his influence on every rock and pop wannabe of the last six decades.

ESSENTIAL RECORDINGS

CLASSIC SONGS

'Maybellene' 1955
'Roll Over Beethoven' 1956
'School Days' 1957
'Sweet Little Sixteen' 1958
'Johnny B Goode' 1958

CLASSIC ALBUMS

One Dozen Berrys 1958

THE SOURCE

Anthology Chess/Universal

YOUNG MAN'S BLUES

❛I had been buying Chuck Berry records since I saw him at the cinema in 1957. A few years later, Mick, who was living in Dartford, began collecting both Chuck Berry, and Bo Diddley records. Before Charlie and I joined the Stones they cut three songs on 27th October, 1962, and amongst them was Bo's 'You Can't Judge A Book By Its Cover'. A couple of months later, at the first session with Charlie and me, we cut 'Diddley Daddy' and 'Roadrunner'❜

BILL WYMAN

THE SUCCESS OF CHUCK AND BO must have made the Chess brothers rich. They had 23 R&B hits, most of which crossed over to the US pop charts. This had the effect of tempering the Chess brothers' interest in signing some of the new artists appearing on the Chicago blues scene. And that in turn may have had some bearing on their ever-present A&R man, Willie Dixon, switching to the Cobra label in 1956.

Dixon immediately recorded the excellent 22-year-old Delta guitarist Otis Rush. The label's first record was 'I Can't Quit You Baby', a Willie Dixon composition... or at least it is according to the label copy.

❛He came by the club that I was working and he asked me would I record? I was happy to. Well, he wrote a song for me, actually he and I wrote the song 'I Can't Quit You Baby'. He has got the credit for it❜

OTIS RUSH

Given that Led Zeppelin would later record 'I Can't Quit You Baby', it was unfortunate for Rush that things worked out the way they did. Rush also worked with another brilliant guitarist, who had first recorded when he was 20, in his hometown of Baton Rouge. His name was Buddy Guy.

❛My mother had a stroke and I left Baton Rouge, Louisiana, 25th September, 1957. And I went to Chicago. I actually was looking for just a regular job to help my mum, but I ran into a bad situation. I couldn't get work, nobody would hire me. I played on the street first, one day this man grabbed me by the hand and walked me in this club. It was Otis playing. The guy told Otis to call me up and I played 'Things I Used To Do', and someone called Muddy on the phone. I was pretty hungry 'cos it was the third day without food❜

BUDDY GUY

Buddy found out, like many others before him, that help would come from his fellow musicians. At Buddy's first Chicago session for Artistic, both Willie Dixon and Otis Rush played. Chess did not sign Buddy Guy until 1960... but we're getting ahead of our story!

OTIS RUSH
An inspiration to many from Clapton to Mike Bloomfield.

Buddy Guy

WILLIE DIXON

FACT FILE

BORN: *1st July, 1915 Vicksburg (Warren Co), Mississippi*

DIED: *29th January, 1992 Burbank, California*

INSTRUMENT: *Bass*

FIRST RECORDED: *1940*

ACCOLADES: *Inducted into the Blues Hall of Fame, 1980*

INFLUENCES: *Little Brother Montgomery*

INFLUENCED: *Led Zeppelin, Otis Rush*

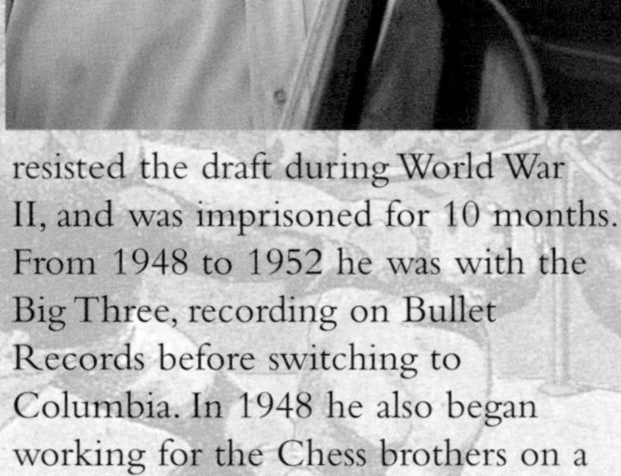

FIXER, ARRANGER, talent scout, boxer, performer, and writer, Willie Dixon was all of these and more. In fact, he did more to shape the sound of post-war Chicago blues than any other person. He was born in Vicksburg, Mississippi, and his mother wrote and recited poetry, which imbued Dixon with an acute sense of rhythm and rhyme from an early age. He sang with the Union Jubilee Singers before becoming a boxer.

WILLIE, MUDDY AND BUDDY
Willie Dixon in the studio at Chess Records with Muddy Waters (centre) and Buddy Guy (right).

He hoboed to Chicago in 1936, and by 1939 he was playing bass and formed the Five Breezes, who recorded for Bluebird in 1940. Dixon resisted the draft during World War II, and was imprisoned for 10 months. From 1948 to 1952 he was with the Big Three, recording on Bullet Records before switching to Columbia. In 1948 he also began working for the Chess brothers on a part-time basis, having met them while he was jamming with Muddy Waters at the club the brothers owned. By 1953 Eddie Boyd and Dixon himself had begun to record some of his original compositions.

> *'Pretty Thing', 'Little Red Rooster', 'You Can't Judge A Book By Its Cover', and 'I Want To Be Loved' were just some of Willie's songs covered by The Stones*
>
> BILL WYMAN

1954 was Dixon's breakthrough year, when Muddy Waters recorded his 'Hoochie Coochie Man' and Howlin Wolf cut 'Evil'. At the same time Dixon was playing bass with the Chess house band, recording with virtually every name artist in Chicago, and crossing over to rock'n'roll to play on some of Chuck Berry's hits. After falling out with Chess, Dixon decamped to the newly formed Cobra label, where he had a hit with Otis Rush's first single, 'I Can't Quit You Baby'. He returned to Chess in the early 60s, staying for the rest of the decade. He was pivotal in organising the American Folk Blues Festival tours of Europe, and also formed the Chicago Blues All-Stars, a flexible line-up that both toured and recorded.

Dixon left Chess in 1971, becoming an itinerant recording artist. In 1982, the man who had become one of the Blues' most respected ambassadors formed the Blues Heaven Foundation, which put his songwriting royalties to good use. In 1988 he recorded a critically acclaimed album, and in 1989 he published his autobiography, *I Am The Blues*. He died of a heart ailment in Burbank, California, in 1992, aged 77.

ESSENTIAL RECORDINGS

CLASSIC SONGS

'Hoochie Coochie Man' 1954
'I Can't Quit You Baby' 1956
'Spoonful' 1960
'Back Door Man' 1960
'Bring It On Home' 1963

THE SOURCE

Willie Dixon: The Chess Box
Universal

CHICAGO SERENADE

In 1961 I managed to buy an old secondhand bass guitar for £8, and set about re-shaping it. I took out all the frets, and made what was probably the first fretless bass guitar. It was a perfect instrument for playing blues, as it had more of an upright bass sound. I wanted that sound because all those records we covered, like Muddy Waters and Chuck Berry, had an upright bass played by Willie Dixon

BILL WYMAN

BILL AND THAT FRETLESS BASS
Sticky Fingers restaurant in London.

AFTER STARTING HIS CAREER in 1951 in Jackson, Mississippi, for the Trumpet label, Elmore James had worked all over the country, recording wherever he could get a deal. He first recorded in Chicago in 1952 and after that he regularly visited the city for extended periods, both to record and play. Despite his health problems (he suffered a heart attack in 1958), Elmore was back in Chicago in 1959 playing a club. Bobby Robinson, the owner of the Harlem-based Fire Records, searched him out, and signed him to a contract. In November 1959 Elmore cut a new version of his trademark song 'Dust My Broom', the version that is closest to all the renditions by the young white blues bands who idolised his slippery slide. At the same session he recorded the brilliant 'The Sky Is Crying'. Released under the name of Elmo James and his Broomdusters, it made No. 15 on the R&B chart.

Roscoe Gordon

In December 1961, Brian Jones heard his first Elmore James record at the house of Alexis Korner. Brian said: 'I discovered Elmore James, and the earth seemed to shudder on its axis'. When I joined the band in December 1962, Brian was calling himself Elmo Lewis

BILL WYMAN

ROSCOE'S RHYTHM

Other musicians working in Chicago around this time included Junior Wells, who cut the excellent 'Little By Little', which has great guitar playing by Earl Hooker. Roscoe Gordon was now living in the city, having spent much of his early recording career in Memphis. In 1959 he cut 'Just A Little Bit' for the Vee Jay label. It became his last R&B hit when it made No.2 in February 1960. He had topped the charts in 1952 with 'Booted', and almost repeated the feat with 'No More Doggin' a few months later. Roscoe had been a feature of the Memphis blues scene for most of the late 40s and 50s, and his migration North perfectly illustrates the decline of the Memphis scene. Roscoe played what became known as 'Roscoe's Rhythm': as much a shuffle as it was a boogie, it had elements of Jamaican bluebeat about it.

Vee Jay's biggest star was a man born and raised in Mississippi. He definitely had the Blues, but they were very much his 'own brand', and his name was Jimmy Reed.

Junior Wells

The sky is crying, look at the tears roll down the street

ELMORE JAMES

JIMMY REED

FACT FILE

BORN: *6th September, 1925 Leland, Mississippi*

DIED: *29th August, 1976 Oakland, California*

INSTRUMENT: *Guitar, harmonica*

FIRST RECORDED: *1953*

ACCOLADES: *Inducted into the Blues Hall of Fame, 1981*

INFLUENCED: *The Rolling Stones, Bob Dylan, The Grateful Dead*

ONE OF SHARECROPPERS Joseph and Virginia Reed's 10 children, Jimmy was born Mathis James Reed. He learned to play guitar from his boyhood pal, bluesman Eddie Taylor, and sang with the Pilgrim Rest Baptist Choir from 1940 to 1943. He moved to Chicago in '43, but was soon drafted into the US Navy, where he served until the end of the war. He then rejoined Taylor in Chicago and by 1949 they were playing clubs together. Having built his reputation, Jimmy signed to the newly formed Vee-Jay label in 1953. Husband and wife Vivian Carter and Jimmy Bracken had started the label out of their store, Vivian's Record Shop. By 1955 Reed was registering hits on the R&B chart, beginning with 'You Don't Have To Go', while he made the Hot 100 in 1957 with 'Honest I Do' (No. 32).

From 1958 to 1963, always accompanied by Eddie Taylor on second guitar, he appeared in the US singles chart a further ten times, also making the UK Top 50 with 'Shame Shame Shame' in September 1964, which peaked at No. 45. Apart from BB King, Reed was now the biggest-selling blues artist in America. At many of his sessions Jimmy's wife, Mama Reed, whispered the lyrics which Jimmy then sang; it was Mama who actually wrote the words.

Reed influenced many artists, as his easy and relaxed style of playing was very accessible to white audiences. The Stones covered Reed's 'Honest I Do' on their first album, while both The Pretty Things and Elvis Presley recorded his 'Big Boss Man'; The Animals and Them did versions of 'Bright Lights, Big City', and Little Richard tackled 'Baby What You Want Me To Do'.

A diagnosis of epilepsy in 1957 did not suppress Jimmy's enthusiasm for performing, and he kept touring constantly. During the late 60s illness curtailed his roadwork, but he continued to play during the first half of the 70s, although mainly around Chicago. In 1976 he died when he suffered an attack of epilepsy while he was asleep. Sadly this came just when he had overcome a long-term drink problem and was again appearing regularly on the Blues circuit.

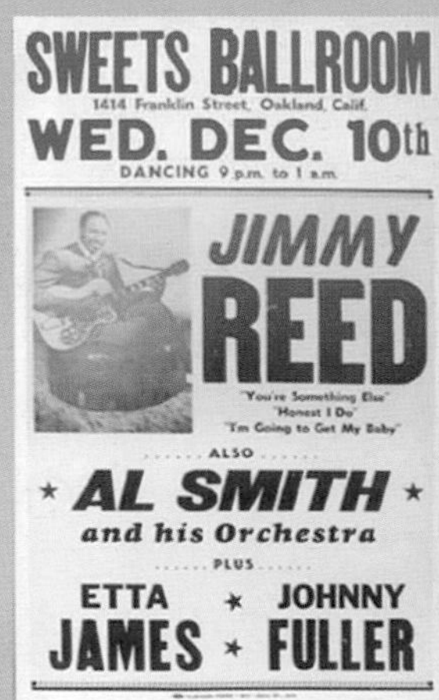

Headlining an Oakland gig with Etta James and Johnny Fuller

ESSENTIAL RECORDINGS

CLASSIC SONGS

'Bright Lights Big City' 1961
'Big Boss Man' 1961
'Shame Shame Shame' 1963

CLASSIC ALBUMS

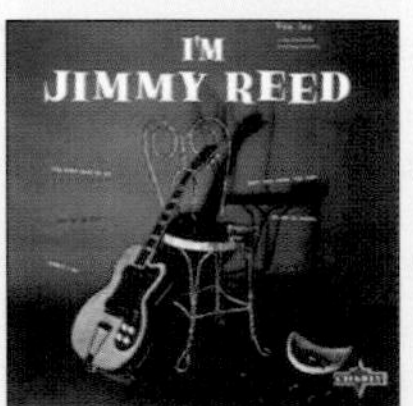

I'm Jimmy Reed 1959

The Legend, The Man 1965

THE SOURCE

The Masters Eagle Records

Down South

Lightnin' Hopkins

We shouldn't give the impression that Chicago was the only source of blues action during the 50s. Way down Texas way they had a blues scene that was entirely their own. Back in 1947 the sound of post-war Texas blues was already being recorded - not in Texas but in Los Angeles.

Lightnin' Hopkins was a man steeped in an earlier tradition. He has been described as the 'greatest folk poet of our time', and while this may be an exaggeration, there is no doubt that he recorded more than any other bluesman during the twenty years after World War II. Most of his recording took place in Houston, his adopted hometown, during the 50s. There was a lull in his activities during the mid-50s, but by 1959 he was back and recording prolifically, in the forefront of the folk blues revival.

While Hopkins' fame spread far and wide, Hop Wilson was barely a star in his own hometown of Houston. But his lap style slide playing was brilliant and he cut some wonderful sides for the Goldband label in Lake Charles, Louisiana. His debut in 1958 was 'Chicken Stuff', on which the wonderfully named Ice Water played bass. Traditional in subject matter, 'Chicken Stuff' really did deserve better, but Goldband were unable to launch Hop into the Hot 100 and he faded into obscurity after cutting around 30 sides. That's sad, because he was a true original.

The Fat Man

Just over the Texas border in Louisiana was a music scene that was not like any other. In New Orleans, Antoine 'Fats' Domino had skipped school in his early teens to play piano in New Orleans nightclubs, which is where bandleader Dave Bartholomew discovered him in 1949. Bartholomew took him to Lew Chudd's Imperial label and within a few months they had their first hit when 'The Fat Man' got to No. 2 on the R&B chart. After that, Fats was rarely out of the R&B chart during the 50s, scoring an incredible run of hits. His R&B No. 1 in 1955, 'Ain't It A Shame', crossed over to the pop charts, introducing him to an international audience. Fats Domino was one of the rock'n'roll names of the 50s, second only to Elvis. Fats, who has lived almost all his life in New Orleans, was influenced by both Albert Ammons and Fats Waller; and he in turn has been an inspiration for many others, in New Orleans and beyond. In 1986 he was one of the initial inductees into the Rock & Roll Hall of Fame.

Fats Domino, the Fat Man

LIGHTNIN' HOPKINS

FACT FILE

BORN: *15th March, 1912, Centerville, Texas*

DIED: *30th January, 1982, Houston, Texas*

INSTRUMENT: *Guitar, Organ, Piano*

FIRST RECORDED: *1946*

ACCOLADES: *Inducted into the Blues Hall of Fame, 1980*

INFLUENCES: *Blind Lemon Jefferson, Texas Alexander, Lonnie Johnson*

INFLUENCED: *Lightnin' Slim, JB Lenoir*

HE WAS BORN SAM HOPKINS, the son of a musician who died when Sam was very young. The family moved to Leona in Texas, which is where he grew up. As a child, Sam made a 'cigar box' guitar, which his older brother Joel taught him to play. In 1920 he played with Blind Lemon Jefferson at a picnic, and soon afterwards Hopkins dropped out of school and started to play picnics and dances across Texas. By the late 20s he had formed a duo with his cousin, Texas Alexander, to play on street corners for tips. Their partnership continued until the mid-30s, when Hopkins was sent to Houston County Prison Farm for an unknown offence. After his release he rejoined Alexander for another round of picnics, parties, and juke joints, though he had to hold down non-musical jobs as well, to make ends meet.

> *His blues are poetic, personal recollections and observations, and he delivers them with a sense of humour and sincerity*
>
> CHRIS ALBERTSON

In 1946 Hopkins and Alexander were offered a recording contract by Aladdin Records, but inexplicably it was Hopkins alone who recorded for them in Los Angeles on 4th November, 1946. He cut 'Katie Mae Blues' with pianist Wilson 'Thunder' Smith, and the pair were billed as Thunder and Lightnin'. The song was a hit in the southwest, so Aladdin took him back into the studio a year later. Alongside his recording work for Aladdin, Hopkins also cut records for Goldstar in Houston, sometimes doubling up the same songs. In total, he eventually recorded for more than twenty different labels. He first reached the R&B charts in 1949 with 'Tim Moore's Farm', and by 1952 he had scored four more hits, the biggest of which was 'Shotgun Express', which made No. 5.

Hopkins vanished from the recording scene after 1954, when electric blues had come to the fore and his acoustic style seemed old-fashioned. But in 1959 he was 'rediscovered' and Sam Charters recorded him for the Folkways label. Throughout the 60s his prolific output appeared on a variety of labels. Hopkins' preferred method of recording was to get the money up front – he reckoned royalty payments were far too insecure a way of earning a living – and he usually did only one take of each song! As his popularity soared during the folk-blues revival, he also began to play more prestigious venues, such as Carnegie Hall and the Newport Folk Festival, besides touring Europe with the American Folk Blues Festival in 1964.

Hopkins was still recording and touring in the 70s, although as the 80s began he came to realise that interest in his unique brand of Texas country blues was on the wane. Hopkins died of cancer in 1982.

ESSENTIAL RECORDINGS

CLASSIC SONGS

'Short Haired Woman' 1947
'Penitentiary Blues' 1959
'Mojo Hand' 1960

CLASSIC ALBUMS

Lightnin' Hopkins 1959
Smithsonian/Folkways

THE SOURCE

Mojo Hand: The Anthology
Rhino Records

SWAMP BLUES

LOUISIANA HAD AN instantly recognisable blues sound. Dubbed 'swamp blues', one of its leading exponents was Slim Harpo. Born James Moore in Baton Rouge in 1924, he was 31 when he cut his first record, as Lightnin' Slim's harmonica player. Lightnin' was the mainman of Baton Rouge blues, having moved to Louisiana from St Louis in the early 30s. Harpo backed Lightnin' Slim on 'Lightnin' Blues' and 'I Can't Be Successful' for the Excello label in Crowley, Louisiana in 1955. Just under two years later, Harpo cut 'I Got Love If You Want It' and 'I'm A King Bee', which was a local hit but little more than that. It would be four years before Harpo made the national charts and when he did, it was not with a blues song, but with a more straightforward pop song. 'Rainin' In My Heart' made No. 17 on the R&B chart and No. 34 on the pop chart. Harpo scored several more hits in the 60s, including 'Baby Scratch My Back' which topped the R&B chart and reached No. 16 on the pop chart. It is surprising that he did not have more success, given the infectious nature of his music, but he did influence an impressive list of artists. Slim Harpo died aged 46 in 1970 from a heart attack.

Lightnin' Slim (real name Otis Hicks) was born in 1913 on a farm near St Louis, Missouri. Moving to Louisiana when he was young, he learned to play the guitar in the 30s. By the late 40s he was playing in Baton Rouge bars, later working with his brother-in-law Slim Harpo. Lightnin' began making records for Excello in 1954, and after leaving

Lightnin' Slim

INSPIRING SLIM

THE INSPIRATION for Slim Harpo to write 'I'm A King Bee' came when he was on his way to a gig in West Virginia. From the car he saw some beehives, and started singing, 'I'm a king bee, baby, buzzin' around your hive...'

'*We recorded the song at IBC Studios in London in the spring of 1964. Mick really got hold of the song, making it very clear what he was singing about. Seven years later we cut 'Shake Your Hips' at Keith's rented villa for the* Exile On Main Street *album. We even named our 1965 live EP* Got Live If You Want It. *I have always enjoyed Slim Harpo's records. He should have got more attention*'

BILL WYMAN

SLIM HARPO'S LEGACY

'I'm A King Bee'
THE ROLLING STONES, 1964

'I Got Love If You Want It'
THE KINKS, 1964

'Don't Start Crying Now'
THEM, 1964

'Rainin' In My Heart'
THE PRETTY THINGS, 1965

'Scratch My Back'
OTIS REDDING, 1966

'Shake Your Hips'
LOVE SCULPTURE, 1968

'Rainin' In My Heart'
HANK WILLIAMS JR, 1970

'Shake Your Hips'
THE ROLLING STONES, 1971

'Rainin' In My Heart'
THE FABULOUS THUNDERBIRDS, 1989

Lazy Lester & Robert Johnson's (Almost) Relative

“The Handy Awards. First and only time I went there was to pick up a 'Keeping the Blues Alive' award because I did this Robert Johnson play. I guess the Blues needs heroes even if it's me. I stepped out on the stage, Robert Cray handed me the award and the late Johnny Copeland was in the the audience, so was Robert Jr Lockwood. I mean that's Robert Johnson's stepson, almost. I said my thank you and took my award. Later that night I was in the auditorium and there is Lockwood standing at the top of the aisle, and he is waving at me. I thought, Oh my God, if he accepts me I'm in the Blues Mafia. I'd no longer have to explain that I wasn't born down South, that I'm a New York City boy. So I put this real humble expression and walked up the aisle. When I got up to him, he put his arm round my shoulder and he said, 'Son, do you know where the bathroom is?'”

Lazy Lester

Harpo he recorded with Lazy Lester, another harmonica player, in 1957.

“My mother played harmonica. There was a lot of us in the family – nine kids. She knew how to keep us happy. I picked up the old guitar and started learning to play. I was about 18 years old [circa 1941] when I started to play the harmonica. Soon I started playing dances, high school proms, nightclubs, and parties, mostly playing covers”

Lazy Lester

While Lightnin' Slim did not achieve great fame, he was important in the development of the Blues in south Louisiana. Slim toured England in 1972 with the American Folk Blues Festival, and later that year he played at the Montreux Jazz Festival in Switzerland. In 1974 he died of cancer at the age of 61. Like Slim Harpo, Lazy Lester found some fame when others covered his recordings (which were mostly written by JD Miller, the Excello producer). Having covered Harpo, The Kinks must really have liked swamp blues as they cut 'I'm A Lover Not A Fighter', Lester's first 'local' hit, in late 1964. Lester left music but returned in the 80s to tour, and made something of a name for himself as one of the 'old school'. His self-deprecating humour and engaging personality created a renewed interest in his short career of the 50s and 60s.

A Period Of Transition

The closing years of the fabulous 50s were a period of transition. The change that artists such as Chuck Berry and Bo Diddley, along with the likes of Elvis, Jerry Lee, Carl Perkins, and the rest, brought to the music scene around the world was staggering. So fundamental were these changes that it was unclear where the Blues were headed.

In 1958 Chuck Berry had appeared at the Newport Jazz Festival. Along with Gerry Mulligan, Dinah Washington, Mahalia Jackson, and Thelonious Monk, Chuck appeared in the documentary film, of the concert entitled *Jazz On A Summer's Day*. It was released in England in 1959, and it

“In May 1970, the day after we recorded with Howlin' Wolf, Eric Clapton came and spent the day at my house in Suffolk. He was amazed that I was such a Lazy Lester fan. A few months previously Ian Stewart and I had gone to a record shop, which I think was in Baton Rouge. We just bought as many Excello singles as we could lay our hands on, mostly Lazy Lester and Slim Harpo. Eric shares my love of the Louisiana blues”

Bill Wyman

allowed the teenage Michael Philip Jagger to see Chuck Berry duckwalking to 'Sweet Little Sixteen'. Mick, like Bill a few years earlier, was amazed by what he saw, and he too started to write to record shops in Chicago to buy Chuck Berry albums. In an interview he gave in England in 1963 Muddy Waters remarked: 'Films really made Chuck.'

Appropriately, it was Muddy Waters who effectively closed the decade and heralded a new era with his legendary performance at the 1960 Newport Festival. Captured on album as *Muddy Waters At Newport*, this performance – made to a predominantly white audience – was stunning... confirming Muddy as the once and future King of the Chicago blues.

MUDDY WATERS
King of the Chicago Blues.

BLUES + SOUL + R&B + COUNTRY = RAY CHARLES

BORN IN GEORGIA in 1930 and raised in Florida, the man often referred to as the Father of Soul music has had one of the longest and most successful of all musical careers. Blind from the age of seven, he moved to Seattle in 1948 and formed a band. At this stage of his career he was heavily influenced by Nat 'King' Cole and Charles Brown, very much the soft West Coast blues sound.

Ray first recorded in 1949 when 'Confessin' Blues' made No. 2 on the R&B chart, the first of more than 80 hits. In the early 50s he worked with both Lowell Fulson and Guitar Slim, arranging the latter's 'The Things That I Used to Do'. Among his own long run of hits, 'One Mint Julep', 'I Can't Stop Loving You', 'What'd I Say', 'Hit The Road Jack', and 'Unchain My Heart' all made the top of the R&B charts. His influence on black music has been profound, and many white performers have seen Ray Charles as both an inspiration and an icon.

Like many other blues performers, Ray Charles has always had a great affinity with country. In 1963 he cut 'Take These Chains From My Heart', a country hit for Hank Williams, and also had a No. 1 with another country tune, Jimmie Davis's 'You Are My Sunshine'. Both these songs came from his legendary 1962 album, *Modern Sounds In Country & Western Music.*

> *'Genius, composer, first soul brother, arranger, pianist, the father of soul... he is Ray Charles, the only artist I have ever seen reduce an entire audience to tears'*
>
> BILL WYMAN

XF

B.C. 9

12

By The Time We Got To Woodstock

A Neon Rainbow

Smash the records you possess which present a pagan culture and a pagan concept of life. Check beforehand the records which will be played at a house party or school dance. Switch your radio dial when you hear a suggestive song

From a 1958 issue of *Contacts*
The Catholic Youth Center's Newspaper

Appreciating the Blues
In the late 1940s the Jazz Appreciation Society persuaded British label Brunswick to release some blues recordings, including 'Drop Down Mama' and 'Married Woman Blues' by Sleepy John Estes.

Those who had considered the 1950s to be a little risqué were in for something of a shock in the 1960s!

The economic growth in 1950s America had been phenomenal, and the situation was echoed in Britain, although there the process was much more gradual. "You've never had it so good", was the Democratic Party's election slogan in 1952. Five years later, the British Prime Minister, Harold Macmillan, echoed the phrase: 'Let us be frank about it, most of our people have never had it so good.'

Prime Minister Harold Macmillan

As the 50s became the 60s, America was in transition, as popular culture was becoming 'youth culture'. For the first time, American teenagers were not expected to get a job as soon as they legally could, to help support the family; in fact, they even had disposable income of their own. The situation in Britain wasn't quite so favourable, however, as wartime rationing only ended in 1954, long after America's release from the strictures of war.

Given the pace of communications, Britain was slower than America to grasp rock'n'roll – not least because the records were released in Britain some time later than in America.

What hastened the change in Britain was the experience of servicemen like Bill Wyman, who were based in Germany. Exposed to the music played on American Forces Radio, these servicemen brought the sounds of young America to British cities. America was glamorous, exciting, vibrant, and fun. While America was lit by neon, Britain seemed to be illuminated by a single light bulb; but it was all about to change.

Is it Blues, Is it Jazz, or Is it Skiffle?

The music known as skiffle which emerged in the mid-1950s, became an important catalyst for change. For the first time, British teenagers had their own music, not just a rehash of what their parents liked and approved of. Skiffle was also a homegrown style, nurtured by the 'jazz crowd', the very people who had first championed the Blues in Britain.

The London Jazz Club
Proudly Present a Recital
Blues • Folk Songs • Ballads
By the famous American singer
'Big' Bill Broonzy

The poster advertising the first London concert (following some in Paris) by the

It's Over!
Nine years after the end of the war rationing finally ceased.

legendary blues singer, on Sunday 22nd September, 1951, clearly positioned the Blues as part of jazz. Interest had begun to grow in the 1940s via men like Paul Oliver, the noted British blues scholar. He was the first person to write about the 'rhythm clubs', meetings of blues and jazz collectors, which were being held in rented schoolrooms in the North London suburbs of South Harrow and Watford.

In the 1950s, Alan Lomax and Max Jones gave occasional talks on BBC radio about American folksongs or work songs. On Friday evenings a programme called *Harry Parry's Radio Rhythm Club* sometimes played blues records, such as Josh White's 'House Of The Rising Sun'. Slowly the Blues began to capture the imagination of a small minority of British youth. Thought these early blues fans had a somewhat romantic notion about the music and its origins, the important thing is they were listening at all, and that they were championing black music in Britain.

A little over a year before Broonzy's visit, Josh White had appeared in Britain, singing his 'easy' blend of the blues. Then a year after Big Bill, Lonnie Johnson made a short trip to Britain. Interestingly all three men represented the more sophisticated end of the Blues. In early summer 1952, Britain's foremost music paper, *Melody Maker*, reviewed recordings by Muddy Waters and John Lee Hooker, as well as Sonny Boy Williamson No. 1, and Leroy Carr (whose records were receiving belated British release). *Melody Maker* was essentially a jazz paper, and took itself very seriously, which confirmed that it regarded the blues as more serious music than pop. As the decade wore on, a transatlantic trickle of artists appeared in Britain: Billie Holiday visited in early 1954, followed a couple of years later by Jimmy Rushing, and Joe Williams. There were return visits by Broonzy, accompanied by Brother John Sellers, as well as the white folk blues player, Ramblin' Jack Elliott.

Barber's Blues

Jazz band leader Chris Barber was a key figure in popularising the blues in Britain. In April 1958, "America's foremost folk blues singers" accompanied Barber on a nationwide UK tour. Sonny Terry and Brownie McGhee played London's Royal Festival Hall to an excellent response, from an audience who were probably more appreciative than an American one would have been during that period. A few months later, Barber arranged for Muddy Waters, along with Otis Spann, to play at the Leeds Festival, followed by a week-long UK tour. Ironically some audiences asked Muddy to turn the amplifier of his electric guitar down; as far as they were concerned, blues music was an acoustic style, as played by Muddy's mentor, Big Bill Broonzy.

Just before Muddy's visit, back in the USA, Chuck Berry played the Newport Jazz Festival. Newspapers accused him of being 'disgraceful', while in Britain the *New Musical Express* (*NME*) wrote, 'Berry is part of the context of the Blues as they are now'. Berry's 'Sweet Little Sixteen' had just spent five weeks on the UK singles chart.

This should be placed in the context of Barber's popularity. In 1958 he came second in the 'small groups' category of the *NME* poll… and the winner was Lonnie Donegan.

Skiffle Galaxy
A skiffle song book from 1957 including songs recorded by Lonnie Donegan, The Vipers, Chris Barber and Johnny Duncan.

Josh White
A flyer for a 1951 concert at Belle Vue, Manchester starring Josh White in 'a programme of Negro spirituals, work songs and blues'.

> *Club promoters would take the acts because Chris Barber was a saleable commodity. So Chris's love of the Blues was able to bring in those people and the promoters never argued*
>
> Mike Vernon, Founder of the Blue Horizon label

Chris Barber

BIG BILL BROONZY

FACT FILE

BORN: *26th June, 1893 Scott (Bolivar Co), Mississippi*

DIED: *15th August, 1958 Chicago, Illinois*

INSTRUMENT: *Guitar/Mandolin/Fiddle*

FIRST RECORDED: *1927*

ACCOLADES: *Inducted into the Blues Hall of Fame, 1980 and the Rock & Roll Hall of Fame, 1990*

INFLUENCES: *Papa Charlie Jackson, Blind Lemon Jefferson, Lonnie Johnson, Peetie Wheatstraw*

INFLUENCED: *JB Lenoir, Brownie McGhee, Memphis Slim, Jimmy Witherspoon, Keith Richards*

WILLIAM LEE CONLEY BROONZY was one of 17 children, whose parents had been born into slavery. He grew up in Pine Bluffs, Arkansas, and taking an interest in music from a young age, he learned to play the fiddle. From his mid-teens he played at country parties while still working as a farmhand. By the time he was 19 years old he was working as an itinerant preacher, before he served in the army for two years. In 1920, he moved to Chicago and played part-time with Papa Charlie Jackson, while still holding down a day job. By the mid-1920s he had learned to play the guitar and was regularly accompanying various singers.

He first recorded in his own right in November 1927 for the Paramount label; his first side was 'House Rent Stomp' under the name of Big Bill and Thomps. He recorded several more sides under that name, but by 1930 he was recording for the Perfect label as Sammy Sampson. Throughout the 1930s he was a prolific recording artist, indeed perhaps the most prolific of them all. He recorded on a variety of labels as Big Bill Johnson, Big Bill Broomsley, Big Bill and his Jug Busters, Big Bill and his Orchestra, Big Bill and The Memphis Five and just plain Big Bill.

In 1938 and 1939 he appeared on the stage of Carnegie Hall in New York in John Hammond's *From Spirituals to Swing* concert, together with many other major blues artists; he was introduced as being a Mississippi plough hand. Besides recording in his own right he accompanied artists such as Memphis Minnie, Tampa Red, John Lee (Sonny Boy) Williamson, Lonnie Johnson, Washboard Sam and Jazz Gillum. He was also a member of the Famous Hokum Boys, whose songs were both very suggestive, and very popular in the late 1920s and into the early 1930s.

Broonzy was the link between country blues and the more sophisticated urban sounds of the pre-war Chicago blues scene. But with the arrival of post-war electric blues and artists like Muddy Waters, Broonzy simply reinvented himself. He became what is best described as a folk blues artist, demonstrating how closely the two forms are linked. In 1951, he toured the UK and Europe and was perhaps the artist most responsible for boosting interest in the Blues across the Atlantic. In 1952 the pianist Blind John Davis accompanied him when he toured Europe once again.

Part of Broonzy's attraction for the blacks who had migrated to the cities was the fact that he sang about subjects that were close to their hearts, and which resonated with their experiences. He was able to give country themes an urban tinge.

For European audiences, his clear diction and abilities as a raconteur

made him the perfect ambassador for the Blues. But despite his fame, Broonzy, like almost all of his contemporaries, still needed to work outside music to support himself. He was a janitor in the early 1950s at Iowa State University, which is where he was finally taught to write by some of the students. This new skill allowed him to collaborate in the writing of his biography, *Big Bill's Blues*, with Yannick Bruynoghe, which further enhanced his reputation.

In 1956 he was diagnosed with throat cancer, which often made performing very painful. But it did not stop him, and on 12th July, 1957, he went into the studio to record a unique 'last will and testament' – a five-record boxed set that was released on Verve. Entitled *The Big Bill Broonzy Story,* this was Broonzy at his best, telling the stories behind the songs, providing vignettes from his life and taking an extensive saunter through his vast repertoire. He was second only to Lead Belly in the number of songs that he knew.

Broonzy died on 15th August, 1958, and mourners at the funeral included Tampa Red, Muddy Waters, Mahalia Jackson, Sunnyland Slim and JB Lenoir. Perhaps obscurity serves a reputation better as his legend has waned somewhat since his death.

> *'When I was about 10 years old, I made a fiddle out of a cigar box, a guitar out of goods boxes for my buddy Louis Carter, and we would play for the white people's picnics'*
>
> BIG BILL BROONZY

> *'Big Bill has been an inspiration to many and his influences are still felt today. He was a mentor, a great performer and an ambassador for the Blues'*
>
> BILL WYMAN

ESSENTIAL RECORDINGS

CLASSIC SONGS

'Good Boy' 1937
'Key To The Highway' 1941
'Southbound Train' 1957

CLASSIC ALBUMS

The Big Bill Broonzy Story 1957

THE SOURCE

10 CDs of his complete works on Document Records.
Where The Blues Began Snapper Records
Big Bill's Blues Portrait Records

BIG BILL BROONZY SINGS COUNTRY BLUES
Long out-of-print, the Big Bill Broonzy Sings Country Blues *album, released in 1957 on the Folkways label, included standards such as 'Frankie and Johnny' and 'Diggin' My Potatoes'.*

Skiffle or Piffle?

The King of Skiffle
Lonnie Donegan performs on BBC Television's 6.5 Special, *1956.*

So ran the headline of a 1956 *Melody Maker* article, written by Alexis Korner, which described the British skiffle craze: "In 1952, shortly after Ken Colyer's return from New Orleans, the first regular British skiffle group was formed to play in the intervals at the Bryanston Street Club. This group consisted of Ken Colyer, Lonnie Donegan and I playing guitars, Bill Colyer on washboard, and Chris Barber or Jim Bray playing string bass." Korner went on to criticise skiffle for introducing a vocal element, saying it was "a commercial success, but musically it rarely exceeds the mediocre".

Whatever Korner's opinion, there is no doubt about skiffle's influence on (British) music or the success of skiffle's superstar, Lonnie Donegan. Between 1956 and 1962 Lonnie had thirty British hit singles, topping the charts three times, with fourteen other singles making the top 10. His first hit, 'Rock Island Line', made the US Top 10 in 1956, a rare achievement for a British record. Many of Glasgow-born Donegan's records were remakes of blues or folk songs, including Lead Belly's 'Rock Island Line', 'Bring A Little Water Sylvie', and 'Pick A Bale Of Cotton', as well as Woody Guthrie's 'Gamblin' Man' and 'Dead Or Alive'.

Donegan, backed on some dates by the Johnny Burnette Trio, toured America in 1956, appearing on Perry Como's TV show as well as performing with Chuck Berry. Although Donegan enjoyed the first skiffle hit, it was not the first skiffle release. In mid-1955 trombonist Ken Colyer's group, with Alexis Korner on guitar, had tackled Lead Belly's 'Take This Hammer'.

Donegan's success in 1956 was surpassed the following year when 'Cumberland Gap' and 'Gamblin' Man' both made No. 1. But by the end of the year skiffle was on the wane. For groups like Chas McDevitt's Skiffle Group featuring Nancy Whisky, the Vipers skiffle group, and Tennessee-born Johnny Duncan and his Blue Grass Boys, the moment of glory was over.

This do-it-yourself musical craze, which was effectively a homemade version of rock'n'roll, may have had a short shelf-life, but it was an inspiration. Skiffle made it possible for thousands of young Brits to dream of emulating their heroes…anyone could be a pop star.

One day in late spring or early summer 1958, five young men recorded a 78rpm record at an electrical shop in Liverpool. This skiffle group called themselves The Quarry Men; three of the group members were John Lennon, George Harrison, and Paul McCartney.

‘Skiffle became enormous and everybody in the 60s rock bands, like The Who, Led Zeppelin, The Stones, and The Beatles, started off by playing skiffle’

Bill Wyman

‘John was singing 'Down, down, down to the penitentiary'. He was filling in with blues lines, I thought that was good’

Paul McCartney recalling seeing John Lennon with the Quarry Men on 6th July, 1957, before he joined the band.

Blues Incorporated

Skiffle was effectively finished by early 1958. Although Donegan continued to have hits for several more years, Britain was firmly in the grip of rock'n'roll. Elvis Presley, Jerry Lee Lewis, Buddy Holly and The Crickets, and the Everly Brothers all scored British hits in 1958 and 1959.

In the closing years of the 1950s, the UK charts were a mix of American rock'n'rollers, more traditional artists like Frank Sinatra and Perry Como, along with a new phenomenon. British copycat rock'n'rollers, such as Tommy Steele, Marty Wilde, Cliff Richard, and Adam Faith, were covering American hits, as well as performing homegrown material. Steele, the first 'beat balladeer', had his debut hit in 1956. He offered a tenuous blues connection the following year, when his version of 'Singing The Blues' made No. 1; soon afterwards, he also charted with 'Knee Deep In The Blues'.

But the real blues seemed set to remain the preserve of the jazz aficionados. Disciples such as Paul Oliver still championed the cause, while Chris Barber and others continued to arrange infrequent short tours by a handful of bluesmen. Champion Jack Dupree visited Britain in 1959, and the following year Memphis Slim, Roosevelt Sykes, James Cotton, Little Brother Montgomery, and Jesse Fuller made the trip.

Most visiting Americans played at a club started, in the wake of the skiffle, by Alexis Korner and Cyril Davies. With Korner on guitar and Davies on harmonica, they performed their own brand of country blues at the London Blues & Barrelhouse Club (in a pub). They also worked with Chris Barber's Band, playing a blues segment with Ottilie Patterson (Barber and Patterson were married in 1959). Barber continued to champion the Blues in his recordings, releasing an album in 1960 entitled *Chris Barber's Blues Book*, which featured blues tunes like Jim Jackson's 'Kansas City Blues' and Leroy Carr's 'Blues Before Sunrise'.

In 1961 Korner (who was half-Greek and half-Austrian) and Davies formed Blues Incorporated. With its harder-edged blues sound and residency at the Ealing Rhythm & Blues Club, the group became a nursery for those keen to play the Blues, many miles from its Delta home.

In late 1961 Brian Jones saw Korner playing with Chris Barber's Band at Cheltenham Town Hall. Then on 17th March, 1962, Brian hitchhiked to Ealing to see Blues Incorporated. Besides Korner and Davies, Dave Stevens played piano, Dick Heckstall-Smith was on tenor sax, Andy Hoogenboom on bass, and Charlie Watts on drums. It was to change Brian's life and the musical map of the world.

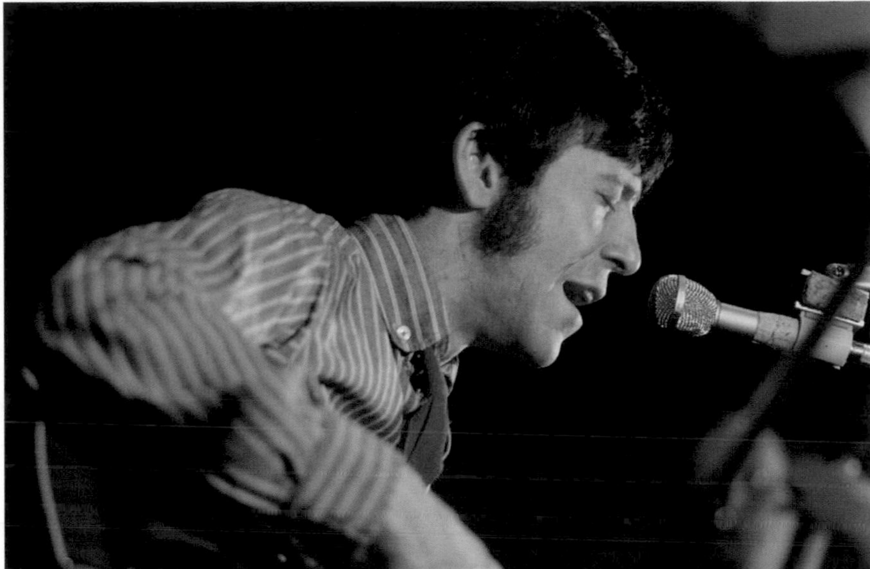

Alexis Korner

Tommy Steele
Singing his blues on the cover of Picture Post*, 1957*

Cyril Davies and Alexis Korner

Blues Incorporated live at the Marquee Club

FROM A CLIFTON TO A STONE

BY FEBRUARY 1958 I was out of the Air Force and looking for a job. At home, listening to the wireless was great because Elvis was at No. 1 with 'Jailhouse Rock'; musically, things were looking up in Britain. Soon I found a job in London Docks working for a meat packing company. I travelled to work by bus and train, but I soon began cycling the 26-mile round trip as I was only earning £6 a week.

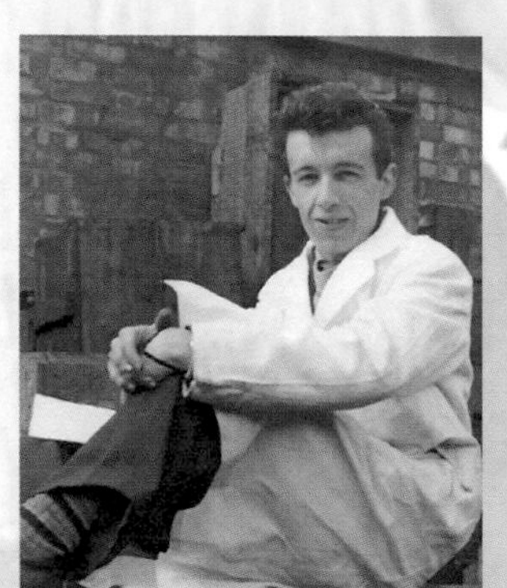

1958, I'm a storekeeper in Streatham Hill

Come September, I decided that meatpacking was not for me. I got a job at an engineering company in Streatham Hill; things were on the up, they paid me £11 per week. A year later I got married and moved to a tiny flat in Penge. Musically my interests were still those of a fan, as I had no thoughts of a career in music. In 1958 I went to see Jerry Lee Lewis and Lonnie Donegan, but live shows were few and far between. In 1960 I went to Wallington Public Hall, about six miles from Penge, and saw Nero and The Gladiators; they played on stage wearing togas! By October 1960, I had got a new job at a department store in Penge. The money was less, but so were my travelling costs. I worked with a guy called Steve Carroll who played guitar, and I introduced him to my Chuck Berry records, from which he learned the solos off by heart. We decided to form a group and got some others together to rehearse. Before long we were playing local weddings and parties. Soon we recruited a new drummer, Tony Chapman, and began calling ourselves The Cliftons.

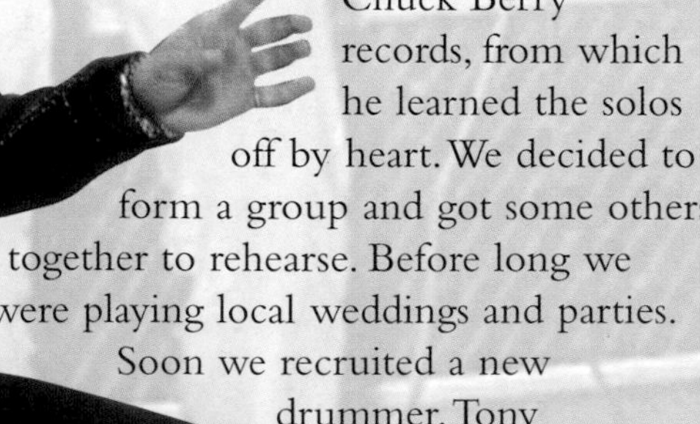

ELVIS AT NO.1

1958, I was out of the Air Force and Elvis at No.1. Things were looking up.

EVERYBODY PAYS THEIR DUES

On 29th July, 1961, my wife and I went to stay with my sister Anne in Aylesbury, Buckinghamshire. We went to a dance, in a converted cinema, and saw The Barron Knights. It was an evening that changed my life. They had an electric bass, and its big sound hit me in the right spot. I decided that what The Cliftons needed was an electric bass, and I was the one to play it; trouble was, they were expensive. Fender had introduced the electric bass in 1951; by 1961 a new one cost around £200, and we got only £6 or £10 a night for playing. One day Tony Chapman said he knew a man with an old bass guitar to sell: all he wanted was £8. It was a battered old thing, but we clubbed together and bought it.

I'd seen pictures of Little Richard's band and liked the look of the bass guitar. I drew a small guitar shape on the back of the bass and cut off what I decided it didn't need. I rubbed it down and painted and polished it until it was just right. I put all the electrics back, and found a Baldwin pick-up, which gave me two pick-ups. I bought very soft strings, but the frets rattled, so I pulled them off in preparation for putting in new ones. But when I played it, it sounded like an upright bass… it was perfect!

The Cliftons, helped by our new bass sound, were getting better. We were just like lots of aspiring bands in the early 1960s; we played in a church youth club in Lower Sydenham and even bought matching stage clothes (jeans and black mohair jumpers). We played Jerry Lee Lewis, Chuck Berry, Fats Domino, Ray Charles, and Little Richard songs, at better venues, like Shoreditch and Greenwich Town Halls.

MANNISH BOYS

Mick, Keith, and Brian first started playing together around July 1962. Mick and Keith had seen Brian and Charlie playing at Ealing Jazz Club with Alexis Korner; Charlie was working at an advertising agency at the time.

The Cliftons, 1961, featuring Bill on bass

> *I first met Bill when I was in the Paramounts and we were both playing at Greenwich Town Hall. An old trick that the promoter played was to have a band contest with a small prize. There were six bands, loads of people came to the dance and he didn't have to pay any of us*
>
> GARY BROOKER
> PROCOL HARUM & THE RHYTHM KINGS

Under Brian's leadership, Mick, Keith, and Brian began calling themselves The Rollin' Stones, playing two or three gigs a month, with others coming and going to form an ad-hoc rhythm section. Tony Chapman from The Cliftons saw an ad in *Melody Maker* and joined them. Tony told me they needed a bass player, as their bassist (Dick Taylor, who later formed The Pretty Things) had gone back to college. Tony brought his tape recorder round to my flat to play me the type of music the Rollin' Stones played. 'What is it?' I asked. 'Oh, it's blues, very slow and easy to play,' said Tony. He played me Jimmy Reed; it was the first time I ever heard one of The Stones' favourite artists.

On 5th December, 1962, I went to the Red Lion pub in Sutton to see a band called The Presidents, led by Glyn Johns. In the interval I met Ian 'Stu' Stewart, The Stones' pianist, who said, "Why not come along to our next rehearsal". Two days later Tony Chapman and I went to the Wetherby Arms pub in Chelsea where Stu introduced me to Mick, who was friendly. I then got a shock when I saw Brian and Keith sitting at the bar. They were wearing scruffy clothes with hair down over their ears; they were far from my idea of what a pop group should look like. You were supposed to be smart! I had on a jacket and tie; coupled with my Tony Curtis quiff I looked the total opposite to these shabby, arty, bohemian types. I was as unimpressed by their manners as by their looks: they were distant and hardly bothered to talk to me. Stu said later that 'they were in one of their funny moods'.

We were mutually unimpressed by each other's looks, but they were more impressed when I unloaded my equipment from the car. Vox had introduced the AC30 in 1959, and I had two of them. I also had an echo unit, my enormous wardrobe size cabinet with the 18" speaker and the amplifier that ran it. 'Oh, that's my spare Vox AC30,' I boasted, 'you can plug one of your guitars into it.' Stu later recalled: 'There is a certain amount of truth that Bill was taken on for his equipment, but Bill was very good'.

At the rehearsal I was fine on the Chuck Berry and Jimmy Reed songs that Tony

THE ROLLING STONES
Bill, Brian, Mick, Charlie, and Keith, 1964.

Michael Philip Jagger

Born 26th July, 1943, at Livingstone Hospital, East Hill, Dartford, Kent

Mike was great fun as a boy doing his thing to the telly. He had shown early skills at impersonations, and did Cliff and Elvis. I would watch my lovely boys sitting so neat and clean watching that dreadful Cliff Richard, that awful hair and that sexy dancing

Eva Jagger, Mick's mother

I've never known a youngster with such an analytical approach to things. If he copied a song, he copied it slavishly – every note. He was able to capture the sound exactly – even when he was as young as 11 or 12

Joe Jagger, Mick's dad

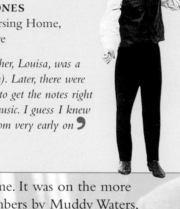

Lewis Brian Hopkin-Jones

Born 28th February, 1942, at Park Nursing Home, Cheltenham, Gloucestershire

Musically I was guided by my parents (mother, Louisa, was a piano teacher and father, Lewis, played the organ). Later, there were several piano teachers in Cheltenham. I struggled to get the notes right at first, but eventually I found I had a 'feel' for music. I guess I knew that I was going to be interested only in music from very early on

Brian Jones

had played me. It was on the more obscure numbers by Muddy Waters, Elmore James and Bo Diddley that I was in trouble. I said, 'This is great but it's all 12 bars and you can't play f*****g 12 bars all night, can you. It's boring!'

By the end of December I was playing with The Rollin' Stones. I think 5th January, 1963, was my 'official' joining date. We were to play a gig at Ealing Jazz Club and met up in a café prior to the gig. I had decided to do something about my quiff, so I combed my hair forward and started to grow it longer. When I walked in, the others all cheered. A few weeks later Charlie Watts joined and we played our first gig together at the Ricky Tick Club at the Star & Garter pub in Windsor, Berkshire. Pretty soon we added a 'g' and we were The Rolling Stones. We were a long way from 'The Greatest Rock & Roll Band in the World', but we were a BLUES BAND!

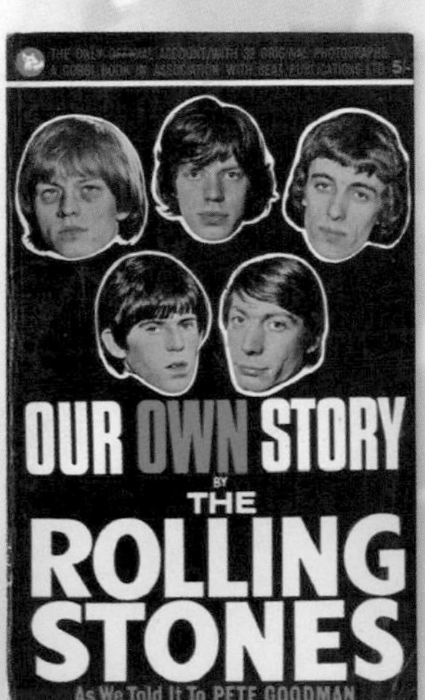

Confessin' the Blues!

Confessin' The Blues

On 27th October, 1962, not long before I joined, The Stones held a recording session at Curly Clayton's studio, near Arsenal's football ground in North London. They did three songs, Bo Diddley's 'You Can't Judge A Book By Its Cover', Muddy's 'Soon Forgotten' and Jimmy Reed's 'Close Together'. Then in February 1963 we played at the Red Lion in Sutton, along with Glyn Johns' band. Glyn was also a recording engineer and he suggested we cut a record. So on Monday 11th March, 1963 we went to IBC Studios in Portland Place, London for a three-hour session on their two-track recorder. We cut two of Bo Diddley's, 'Road Runner' and 'Diddley Daddy'; Muddy's 'I Want To Be Loved'; and two by Jimmy Reed, 'Honey What's Wrong' and 'Bright Lights Big City'. The tracks, which we thought sounded amazing, were taken to six or seven record companies. They all turned us down, saying things like, "The singer

DUST MY BROOM	
HONEY WHAT'S WRONG	ELMORE JAMES
CRAWDADDY SONG	JIMMY REED
CONFESSIN THE BLUES	BO DIDDLEY
COPS AND ROBBERS	CHUCK BERRY
BRIGHT LIGHTS BIG CITY	BO DIDDLEY
PUT A TIGER IN YOUR TANK	JIMMY REED
I'M A KINGBEE	MUDDY WATERS
PRETTY THING	SLIM HARPO
DOWN THE ROAD APIECE	BO DIDDLEY
I WANT TO BE LOVED	CHUCK BERRY
TAKE OUT SOME INSURANCE	MUDDY WATERS
YOU CAN'T JUDGE A BOOK BY THE COVER	JIMMY REED
JAGUAR AND THUNDERBIRD	BO DIDDLEY
ROAD RUNNER	CHUCK BERRY
MONA	BO DIDDLEY
OUR LITTLE RENDEZVOUS	BO DIDDLEY
	CHUCK BERRY

Typical Rolling Stones set list from early 1963

Brian Jones

Brian, a great harmonica player, was the first kid in Britain to play slide guitar. Others took it on later.

sounds too black and the band too white". The session cost about £100, which we thought was a total waste of money. After we were told our records would never sell, we became totally disheartened, because we thought they sounded fantastic. Years later, Brian said they were the Stones tracks he was most fond of. I agree: they're great.

Our live set featured 15 or 20 numbers, including Jimmy Reed, Chuck Berry, and Bo Diddley songs, along with Elmore James' 'Dust My Broom' with Brian playing slide guitar. He was the first white kid in England to play with a slide; other bands only took it on later. Mick played really good blues harmonica, while Brian played great blues harmonica. Mick used the maracas, which no one in Britain was using in those days. Our set was fine for playing the clubs, but later as we played ballrooms and theatres we couldn't do the slower blues songs, as they wanted fast stuff… three quick ones and off. So we concentrated on Bo Diddley and Chuck Berry numbers.

In July 1963, with unemployment standing at almost 900,000, its highest since the war, I gave up my job and became a professional musician, and I never did have any formal training! By October we were touring with the Everly Brothers, Little Richard, and Bo Diddley. Up until then all we had played was the Blues, pure, pure blues and loved it.

American R&B

American R&B records were released in profusion in Britain in the early 60s

Charles Robert Watts

Born 2nd June, 1941, at University College Hospital, Islington, London

"Charlie always wanted a drum set, and used to rap out tunes on the table with pieces of wood or a knife and fork"

Lillian Watts, Charlie's mother

"I'll never forget my first drumkit. It was just a collection of bits and pieces, but I got a lot of fun out of it. Any sort of jazz interested me, and I taught myself by listening to other people's records and watching drummers, and sort of picked up the technique by myself"

Charlie Watts

Keith Richards

Born 18th December, 1943, at Livingstone Hospital, East Hill, Dartford, Kent

"Gus (Keith's grandfather) had this guitar standing in the corner and he was always afraid Keith would break it when he touched it. Keith went up and strummed the strings. He loved the sound of the guitar, and positively admired Gus. Bert (Keith's dad) didn't approve of Gus because he was a bit rude"

Doris Richards, Keith's mother

"I used to pose in front of the mirror at home. I was hopeful. The only thing I was lacking was a bit of bread to buy an instrument. But I got the moves off first, and I got the guitar later"

Keith

Group Uniform

Early on the Stones dressed in a group uniform… pretty soon they didn't.

The Beat Boom

The Cavern Club
Gerry & The Pacemakers on stage, 1964.

Big City Beat

On 5th October, 1962, just a few months before The Rolling Stones formed, The Beatles released their debut, 'Love Me Do' and 'PS I Love You', recorded at Abbey Road a month earlier. Six days after Bill 'officially' joined The Rolling Stones, and two months before their first recording session, The Beatles released their second single, 'Please Please Me'.

Also in January, Blues Incorporated made their BBC-TV debut, on *The 6.25 Show*. British music was in the first flush of radical change. Before The Beatles, the 1960s' charts were much as they had been in the late 1950s, full of songs by Cliff Richard, Elvis, The Shadows, Del Shannon, Mark Wynter, and Marty Robbins. Frank Ifield did top the charts with a jaunty remake of Hank Williams' 1949 hit, 'Lovesick Blues'; but that was as blues as the early 1960s charts got.

In the wake of The Beatles, record companies set about signing any 'beat' group they could, especially if they came from Liverpool. The city had a vibrant musical scene long before The Beatles. Howie Casey and The Seniors, one of the best Liverpool bands not to make it, recorded 'The Boll Weevil Song' in 1962. They, like many Liverpool bands took their influences from American music. As a major port, it was not uncommon for returning seamen to bring back American records, a great source of material for local groups. But whereas London was the blues capital, Liverpool's penchant was for R&B. Of course it was not just Liverpool that attracted interest; Manchester, Birmingham, and Newcastle all became magnets for the A&R men.

> *"I had a friend who was a blues freak, he turned me on to the Blues. It added the real blues to my consciousness"*
>
> John Lennon

Not a Second Time!

In order to secure a record deal for The Rolling Stones, their friend, Georgio Gomelsky, had the idea of making a film of the band, for which they recorded Bo Diddley's 'Pretty Thing'. *Record Mirror* reporter Peter Jones went to see the band filming. He recalled Brian as very much the leader, with firm ideas about their mentors. "He talked about Muddy Waters, Jimmy Reed and people like that." Soon The Stones secured a manager, the ambitious Andrew Loog Oldham. It was good timing indeed, as Gomelsky had tried to interest Decca in the film and recording of 'Pretty Thing', but they were disinterested. However, within a few weeks, The Stones signed a deal with Impact Sound, the company run by Oldham and his partner Eric Easton, who in turn did a deal with Decca to release the recordings.

Matthew Street, Liverpool
Fans queue for the lunchtime session at the Cavern.

CHRIS BARBER AND HOWLIN' WOLF
The Wolf appeared with Chris Barber and his band at the Marquee, November 1964.

Following Brian's departure from Blues Incorporated and Charlie's later recruitment by The Stones, Korner and Davies added new members to their line-up. Jack Bruce, Graham Bond, Paul Jones, and Ginger Baker all became members in an ever-changing line up. The group released a live album in 1962, *R&B From The Marquee*, and soon after Davies broke away and established the Cyril Davies R&B All Stars. Jeff Beck, pianist Nicky Hopkins, and Long John Baldry all played with that band - until Davies was diagnosed with leukaemia, which killed him in 1964, aged 32. Before his death, the R&B All Stars did cut one classic single featuring his wailing harmonica, 'Country Line Special'.

REVEREND GARY DAVIS
At Studio 51, London, in 1966.

On the weekend of 10th-11th August, 1963, two weeks before Martin Luther King's 'I have a dream' speech in Washington, the National Rhythm & Blues Festival took place at Richmond in Surrey. The bill was entirely British, and included Chris Barber, the Graham Bond Quartet, Cyril Davies, George Fame – and The Rolling Stones. On the Friday before the festival, The Stones had played the California Ballroom in Dunstable, Bedfordshire. The local newspaper described them as 'five awesome apes who perpetrated fearful musical onslaughts'.

Throughout Britain, R&B clubs were being set up in pubs and halls, frequented by a young, dressing-down crowd; Brian and Keith certainly had something to answer for. In Birmingham, Spencer Davis was playing with Rhythm Unlimited; it seemed as if every city had its own version of Blues Incorporated. Fans carried blues albums around as though they were the crown jewels, with Jimmy Reed at Carnegie Hall or Muddy Waters at Newport among the favourites. The greatest concentration of blues clubs was in London, and names like the Crawdaddy, Eel Pie Island, Studio 51 and the Marquee have passed into the legend of the swinging 60s.

For many fans and musicians alike, it was a visit to Britain in October 1963 by a whole mass of genuine legends, that really helped fuel this transatlantic passion for the Blues.

'Country Line Special'

❛ Within a few days we met Dick Rowe, the Decca A&R man who was notorious for having turned down the Beatles. He came to a gig at the Crawdaddy Club, at the Station Hotel in Richmond, near London. A week later we were trying to decide what to record. None of our regular stage songs were felt to be suitable, so we narrowed it down to Chuck Berry's 'Come On', coupled with Muddy's 'I Want To Be Loved'. On 10th May, 1963, we were at the old Olympic Studios for our first recording session as Decca recording artists. The single was released on 7th June, and as Mick later said, 'I don't think 'Come On' was very good. In fact it was shit. We disliked it so much that we didn't do it at any of our gigs'. The fact is that the record was a lie: it was not what the Rolling Stones were all about, as we were a blues band. However, it did make No.20 on the NME *chart and set about establishing the Stones as rivals to The Beatles, in the eyes of the press ❜*

BILL WYMAN

THE AMERICAN FOLK BLUES FESTIVALS

THE AMERICAN FOLK BLUES FESTIVAL
Sleepy John Estes, Hammie Nixon, Willie Dixon, and Sunnyland Slim backstage in 1964.

Over in Germany two men had got the Blues in a big way. Horst Lippmann and Fritz Rau decided to mount a blues tour in the autumn of 1962, but they were unable to attract any interest from a UK-based promoter. The line-up on the 1962 tour consisted of T-Bone Walker, Memphis Slim, Sonny Terry & Brownie McGhee, John Lee Hooker, Shakey Jake, and Willie Dixon.

By 1963, British promoters realized the potential of a major blues package, and a show was booked into south London's Fairfield Halls on 18th October, 1963… and what a line-up! Those lucky enough to witness the show saw Muddy Waters, Memphis Slim, Sonny Boy Williamson, Otis Spann, Big Joe Williams, Victoria Spivey, Lonnie Johnson, Willie Dixon, and Matt Guitar Murphy. Two months later Granada Television broadcast *I Hear The Blues*, a TV show featuring the stars of the AFBF. The following year, Sonny Boy and Willie Dixon were back with Sleepy John Estes, Howlin' Wolf, Hubert Sumlin, Sunnyland Slim, Lightnin' Hopkins, and Hammie Nixon.

Many British performers and musicians went to these shows. Seeing these blues legends perform in the wood-panelled 'concert hall' atmosphere of the venues like the Fairfield Halls was a strange experience. And if the audience thought it was strange, what about the performers – more used to playing Chicago clubs or Delta juke joints. But whether it was Croydon or Chicago, it was still the Blues. They were the genuine article and these tours did more than anything to promote the Blues.

Every year after that, until 1972, the American Folk Blues Festival rolled through Europe, providing an opportunity to see some of the genuine blues greats. The 1965 tour included Mississippi Fred McDowell, Buddy Guy, and JB Lenoir. It was Willie Dixon who became the Festival's unofficial musical director, advising Lippmann who to book on the tours. But as Dixon later said, 'I wouldn't have gone over there in the first place, had I been doing all right here'.

FAIRFIELD HALL, CROYDON
MONDAY 19th OCTOBER
at 6.45 p.m. and 9.00 p.m.
"A DOCUMENTARY OF THE AUTHENTIC BLUES"
THE NATIONAL JAZZ FEDERATION
AMERICAN NEGRO BLUES FESTIVAL
LIGHTNING HOPKINS • HOWLING WOLF
SLEEPY JOHN ESTES • HUBERT SUMLIN
JOHN HENRY BARBEE • HAMMIE NIXON
SUGAR PIE DESANTO • CLIFTON JAMES
SUNNYLAND SLIM • WILLIE DIXON
SONNY BOY WILLIAMSON
TICKETS: 6/- 8/- 10/6 12/6 15/- 17/6 21/-

> *I bought the album of the 1964 Festival on 1st January, 1965.*
>
> BILL WYMAN

PAYING DUES AND CASH

The artists were paid much more than they could have expected to earn in America at the time, which of course made the tours very attractive. In 1963 Big Joe Williams asked Lippmann to save his pay from the tour until the end, just providing him with 'pocket money' for his on-the-road essentials. At the end of the tour, Lippmann handed Big Joe a couple of thousand dollars. 'Big Joe started to cry, because he never thought he'd get all this money,' said Lippmann.

A five-CD boxed set documents these 1962–65 shows. There are highlights on every CD that includes Muddy singing 'My Captain' at a soundcheck from 1963, 'Goin' Down Slow' from Otis Spann the same year, and Mississippi Fred's rendition of 'Highway 61', which takes you right there.

The Folk Blues Festival, 1965

The Stone Age – 1964

The Rolling Stones, 1964

We tried to write something for Ringo, and we came up with 'I Wanna Be Your Man' – a Bo Diddley kind of thing. I said to Mick, well, Ringo's got this track on our album, but it won't be a single and it might suit you guys. I knew Mick was into maracas, from when we'd seen them down at the Crawdaddy

John Lennon

As 1963 became 1964, The Stones were riding high on the UK singles chart with 'I Wanna Be Your Man', a song written by Lennon and McCartney. 1964 was to be the year when the Stones first topped the charts; and it was also the year when bona fide blues records by black artists made their way into the UK singles chart. Howlin Wolf's 'Smokestack Lightning' entered the chart in early June 1964 and managed to creep up to No. 42 over the next five weeks. A week later, John Lee Hooker's 'Dimples', originally cut for Vee-Jay in 1956, charted and spent the rest of the summer in the lower reaches of the Top 50. The week after Hooker charted, he supported The Stones at a gig at Magdalen College, Oxford, which must have been a thrill for the band. Four days later, Hooker and John Mayall's Bluesbreakers played with the Stones at an all-nighter at London's Alexandra Palace. The Stones were even happier when Hooker got to appear on the

While we were away touring in America and recording at 2120 South Michigan Avenue in Chicago, Britain was getting into the blues. Just after I got back from the States, Tony Chapman and Peter Frampton called to say they were playing at Wallington Public Hall. I went to see Peter and the Herd on 24th November, but imagine my surprise when I found out that Jimmy Reed was also on the bill. After I played a couple of songs with the Herd, I sat and chatted with Jimmy. His manager kept on saying that the Stones should record 'Big Boss Man'!

Bill Wyman

Little Walter
Little Walter Jacob, the man from Chicago's Ricky's Show Lounge, visited Britain in 1964. Here he is on stage at the Marquee Club.

The Animals

Eric Burdon and The Animals earned themselves a No. 1 record in 1964 with 'House Of The Rising Sun'.

SPECIAL
ALL NITE RAVE
MIDNIGHT TO 6 a.m.
CLUB NOREIK
HIGH ROAD, TOTTENHAM, N.15
PRESENTING—
SATURDAY, OCTOBER 31st
U.S.A. R & B STAR
JIMMY REED
ALSO
STEVE MARRIOTT'S MOMENTS
Tickets in advance 10/-, on night 12/6
SATURDAY, NOVEMBER 7th
JOHN LEE HOOKER
Tickets in advance 10/-, on night 12/6
Apply Club Noreik for membership
Coach parties welcomed

Jimmy Reed plays Tottenham - supported by a young Steve Marriott

TV show *Ready, Steady, Go!*, just another small step towards the Blues becoming a more prominent feature on the British music scene. In September, The Stones' hero Jimmy Reed even managed to scrape into the charts for two weeks with 'Shame Shame Shame'. Suddenly all sorts of artists were finding their inspiration in the Blues. Billy Fury cut Jimmy Reed's 'Baby What You Want Me To Do', Tommy Bruce released 'Boom Boom', and most successfully of all, The Animals got to No. 1 with 'House Of The Rising Sun'. Even the most unlikely hits turned out to have a blues influence. The Zombies 'She's Not There' reached No. 12 in late summer, yet neither the group, with Colin Blunstone's angelic vocals nor the song, were the Blues. But as Rod Argent, the group's keyboard player and the song's writer, revealed: "If you play John Lee Hooker's song "No One Told Me' from *The Big Soul Of John Lee Hooker* album, you'll hear him sing, 'No one told me it was just a feeling I had inside'. There's nothing in the melody or the chords that's the same as our record, it was just that little lyrical phrase.

The Rolling Stones registered two EPs (four-track singles with special picture sleeves) on the UK singles charts in 1964. *The Rolling Stones* was followed later in the year by *5 X 5*. All the tracks on the latter disc were recorded at Chess Studios, and they included, 'Confessin' The Blues' and 'Around and Around' from Chuck Berry's repertoire, and '2120 South Michigan Avenue', written by Nanker Phelge.

George Sherlock, a London Records promotional executive, accompanied the band on their US tour, and he inspired another Nanker Phelge composition which was

I'm The Face If You Want It

Richard Barnes, flatmate of Pete Townshend, and the man who came up with the Detours new name, The Who, recalled: "What they knew, they played, and they played them every night; just like most bands at the time". Shortly after they became The Who, Peter Meaden, their manager, persuaded them to record a number he had 'written', and also to change their name again. So for a brief time in 1964, the 'Oo became the High Numbers and released 'I'm The Face'. The song was based very firmly on Slim Harpo's 'Got Love If You Want It'.

"On 22nd December, 1963, we played a gig at St Mary's Hall in Putney, West London. Supporting us that night was a band called The Detours. They played a set similar to many other bands on the London scene at the time. It included 'Big Boss Man', 'I'm A Man', 'Spoonful' and 'Smokestack Lightnin". Soon after they changed their name to The Who. It was seeing Keith Richards swing his arm that night which inspired Pete Townshend to adopt his famous 'windmill' guitar-playing technique"

Bill Wyman

So here we are growing up in LA, listening to rhythm & blues and getting me totally excited. We listened to 'Fanny Mae' on Fire Records by Buster Brown, which went Top 10 in 1960. So down the road here comes The Stones, here come The Beach Boys. On the backside of 'Satisfaction' in summer 1965 is 'The Under Assistant West Coast Promotion Man', which is the same track as 'Fanny Mae'. And for Brian Wilson and our band, the inspiration for the track of 'Help Me Rhonda' was also 'Fanny Mae'

Bruce Johnston
The Beach Boys

Mannish Boys Play The Blues

Many British bands released blues singles in 1964. Some were covers of Chicago's finest post-war recordings, while others delved back further into the blues, and some even composed their own blues tunes. These are just some of the UK blues records from 1964, many by artists who would gain greater fame, while others just slipped quietly off the turntable of rock.

January	**Dave Berry & The Cruisers**	*'Hoochie Coochie Man'*
January	**Gerry Levene & The Avengers**	*'Doctor Feelgood'*
April	**The Sheffields**	*'I Got My Mojo Working'*
April	**The Rebounds**	*'Help Me'*
May	**John Mayall's Bluesbreakers**	*'Crawling Up The Hill'*
May	**Spencer Davis Group**	*'Dimples'*
May	**The Pretty Things**	*'Big Boss Man'*
June	**The Animals**	*'The House of The Rising Sun'*
June	**Downliners Sect**	*'Baby What's Wrong'*
June	**The Yardbirds**	*'I Wish You Would'*
June	**The Soul Agents**	*'I Just Wanna Make Love To You'*
July	**Duffy Power**	*'I Don't Care'*
July	**Billy Fury**	*'Baby What You Want Me To Do'*
August	**Them**	*'Don't Start Crying Now'*
October	**Rod Stewart**	*'Good Morning Little Schoolgirl'*
October	**Jimmy Nicol & The Shubdubs**	*'Baby Please Don't Go'*
October	**The T-Bones**	*'How Many More Times'*
November	**The Primitives**	*'Help Me'*
November	**The Rolling Stones**	*'Little Red Rooster'*
November	**Them**	*'Baby Please Don't Go'*
November	**The Blue Rondos**	*'Baby I Go For You'*
November	**The Hillsiders**	*'Cotton Fields'*
November	**Blues By Five**	*'Boom Boom'*
December	**Tommy Bruce**	*'Boom Boom'*

recorded at Chess. But he wasn't the only inspiration for the song.

1964 was also the year when Chuck Berry got out of jail, after a two-year spell for transporting a female minor across state lines. It was impeccable timing, as he was able to capitalise on the success of the British bands who, in time-honoured fashion, were using Berry's repertoire and guitar idioms to further their own careers. His British hits recorded in 1964 included 'Promised Land', 'No Particular Place To Go', and 'Nadine', the last two also charting in the US. In '64 there wasn't a band in Britain who did not include a Chuck Berry song or borrow his guitar licks in their live shows. For example, the performers appearing at the Birmingham R&B Festival in February included The Spencer Davis Rhythm & Blues Quartet, The Liverpool Roadrunners, and Long John Baldry's Hoochie Coochie Men (including one woman, Ottilie Patterson). In the audience was sixteen-year-old Robert Plant, and he would have seen all of those groups give, at the very least, a passing nod to the duck-walking dude.

Nanker Phelge was a pseudonym we used on the rare occasion that the whole group composed a song. Nanker was a face that Brian pulled, and Phelge was a guy that we knew who seemed to have an allergy to soap and to changing his clothes!

Bill Wyman

The 60s British R&B Scene

The Rolling Stones, The Beatles, and the other bands of the 'beat boom' revolutionized the British music scene. Starting out from what were often humble origins in many of Britain's biggest cities, young men, and a few young women, were inspiring a shift in transatlantic taste.

The Rolling Stones
Charlie, Bill, Brian, Keith and Mick, 1963

Ealing Jazz Club
Brian Jones met Alexis Korner and later Mick & Keith at The Jazz Club in Ealing.

Islington
Charlie Watts' birthplace.

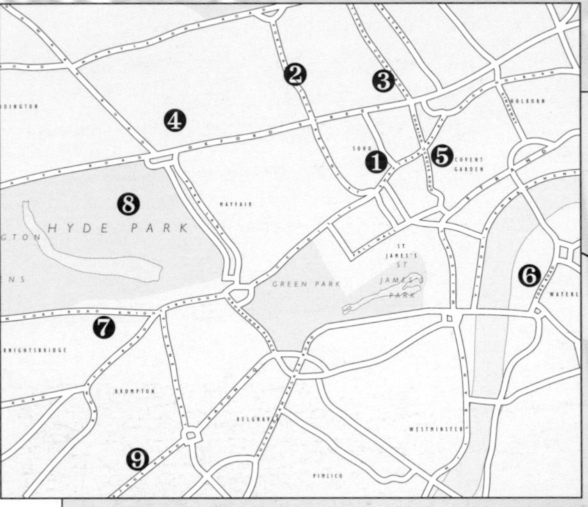

Ealing

Central London

❶ Marquee Club *Wardour Street.*

❷ IBC Studios *35 Portland Place. The venue for the first recording session after Bill joined The Stones.*

❸ London Blues and Barrelhouse Club *Tottenham Court Road, run by Cyril Davis and Alexis Korner.*

❹ Old Olympic Studios *Carton St. W1. The site of the first Stones Decca recording session when they cut 'Come On'.*

❺ Regent Sound *4 Denmark Street WC2. The Stones cut many songs at this studio, including 'Little Red Rooster'.*

❻ Royal Festival Hall *South Bank. Sonny Terry & Brownie McGhee played here in 1958.*

❼ Royal Albert Hall *London's most prestigious venue.*

❽ Hyde Park *Scene of The Stones 1969 free concert.*

❾ The Wetherby Arms *The Kings Road pub, Chelsea, where Bill first rehearsed with The Stones.*

Olympic Studios
The Stones cut 'You Can't Always Get What You Want' with Al Kooper in November 1968 at Olympic Studios, Barnes.

Fulham

Barnes

Putney

Richmond
Station Hotel
(Crawdaddy Club)

Fulham Town Hall
Bill shot a video with Charlie and Ronnie Wood as Willie and The Poor Boys at Fulham Town Hall.

Lewisham
Bill's birthplace.

Bill worked as a store-keeper and clerk at an engineering firm in Streatham Hill.

Twickenham

Eel Pie
In their early days, The Stones often played at the jazz and blues club on Eel Pie Island, Twickenham.

The Detours
The Who when they were The Detours supported The Stones at St Marys Hall, in Putney.

Streatham

Penge

Beckenham

Tooting

American Folk Blues
The first American Folk Blues Festival to play the UK did so at the Fairfield Halls, Croydon.

Jimmy Re
Bill saw Jimmy supporting The F Wallington Publi

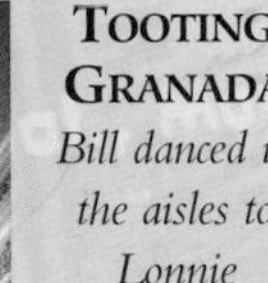

Tooting Granada
Bill danced in the aisles to Lonnie Donegan and also saw Jerry Lee Lewis on his fateful British tour.

Sutton
Bill first saw and met The Rolling Stones in Sutton.

Croydon

Wallington

Purley

Orchid Ballroom
Bill saw a big band at the Orchid Ballroom, Purley, and decided he would like to be a musician, not ever imaging he would be.

Glasgow
Lonnie Donegan's birthplace.

The South East

❶ Aylesbury *Where Bill saw The Barron Knights and knew he needed an electric bass.*
❷ Bishop Stortford *Bill saw John Lee Hooker here in 1969. "He looked like a God."*
❸ Cheltenham: *Brian Jones' birthplace.*
❹ Hartfield: *Brian Jones' house at which he died in 1969.*
❺ Knebworth, *Hertfordshire. Venue for The Rolling Stones concert in 1976.*
❻ Oxford: *John Lee Hooker supported The Stones at a gig at Oxford University.*
❼ Ripley, *Surrey. Eric Clapton's birthplace.*
❽ Windsor *The Star & Garter pub and the Windsor Jazz and Blues Festival in the 1960s.*

Newcastle-Upon-Tyne
Hometown of The Animals.

Muddy Waters and Otis Spann played the Leeds Festival in 1958.

Leeds

ock Rock
ood up on Bill's he saw Chuck k, Rock, Rock! ckenham.

Liverpool
The Beatles and the home of Merseybeat.

Manchester
John Mayall's hometown.

Bill and The Cliftons
On 17th June, 1961, The Cliftons played a private party in Penge, a week later they played a wedding in Stockwell.

Dartford

Dartford is the birthplace of both Mick Jagger and Keith Richards.

Birmingham
The Spencer Davis Group, The Moody Blues, and a young Robert Plant – who played Peetie Wheatstraw songs around the folk clubs of Birmingham.

Birmingham

Blenheim Road
Bill lived and grew up in Blenheim Road, Penge. He was working at a department store here when he first joined The Stones.

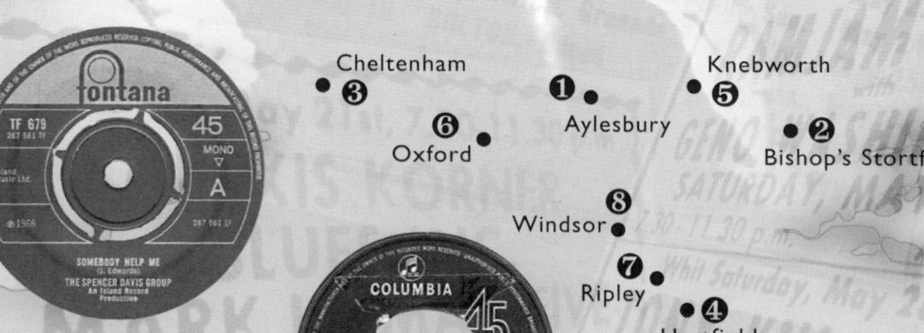

Bishopstock, near Exeter. Europe's premier annual blues festival.

Exeter

Birds & Bluesbreakers

Five Live Yardbirds
(left to right) Chris Dreja, Paul Samwell-Smith, Jim McCarty, Keith Relf and Eric Clapton.

One act on the Birmingham bill who probably did not actually cover Chuck Berry's songs were the Yardbirds, who backed Sonny Boy Williamson. After playing the Fairfield Halls with the 1963 American Folk Blues Festival, Sonny Boy met the Yardbirds at a gig. When the European tour was over the Delta blues legend returned to play with the group at Richmond's Crawdaddy club. The Yardbirds, with their teenage guitar prodigy Eric Clapton, and the hard drinking, hard living Sonny Boy must have been an impressive combination in hot sweaty clubs.

The Yardbirds' first single in June 1964 was a version of Billy Boy Arnold's 'I Wish You Would', after which their output mixed together blues and straightforward pop material. Among the blues tunes they recorded were Wolf's 'Smokestack Lightning', Eddie Boyd's 'Five Long Years' and Elmore James' 'The Sun is Shining'.

> *On December 3 1964 Glyn Johns called and asked me to go to the studio where he was producing a single for a great little band called The Cheynes. I ended up playing bass on 'Down And Out' and 'Stop Running Around'. The band's organist was Peter Bardens, who was soon to join Them, and the drummer was twenty-two-year-old Mick Fleetwood... and, oh yeah, the single bombed!*
>
> Bill Wyman

It was the release of the pop song 'For Your Love' that caused the blues-obsessed Clapton to quit the group, to be replaced by Jeff Beck on March 11,1965. Beck lasted until 1966, when after a brief spell with a twin lead guitar line-up, he was replaced by Jimmy Page. The Yardbirds have gone into rock history for producing arguably the three best British blues-rock guitarists, but more importantly the group, just like the Stones, helped to create a love of the blues amongst a large proportion of British youth.

The Yardbirds 1965
With Jeff Beck (left) and, next to him, Jimmy Page

> *Throughout 1964 we were very busy touring up and down the length of Britain as well as doing two separate tours in America. We actually played on 202 days in 1964, which was less than 1963 when we played 247 days in the year. But in 1964 we played throughout the year in bigger venues, giving two shows on 101 of those days. From our regular 1963 gigs at the Crawdaddy and Eel Pie Island, we went to the Fairfield Halls in Croydon and Usher Hall in Edinburgh. We played with many different bands, including Long John Baldry and the Hoochie Coochie Men. They supported us at the Gaumont in Bournemouth on August 30, and they had Rod Stewart singing and playing harmonica with them*
>
> Bill Wyman

I've Got The Fleetwood Mac, Chicken Shack, John Mayall, Can't Fail Blues

Adrian Henri
The Liverpool Scene

Eric Clapton quit the Yardbirds to join John Mayall's Bluesbreakers. Mayall was a somewhat unlikely 'pop star' – for a start, he was 'old'! Mayall initially learned to play the guitar, but switched to the piano, inspired by hearing Meade Lux Lewis and Albert Ammons records. At 17 he was already playing the blues with a group in Manchester. After enrolling at art school, he served with the army in Korea from 1951 to 1954. Back at art school Mayall formed the Powerhouse Four, continuing to play with them after he graduated. He soon moved to London, encouraged by Alexis Korner, to take advantage of the buzzing blues scene.

In 1963, aged thirty, he formed the Bluesbreakers, who probably went through more line-ups than anyone in the history of modern music. They were spotted by a Decca producer, Mike Vernon. Their first single, 'Crawling Up The Hill', was released in April 1964. Playing bass with Mayall then was John McVie, and by the time Clapton joined in October 1965 Hughie Flint was filling the drum stool. At Clapton's first session they cut a single for the Immediate label, which was produced by Jimmy Page. Then early the next year they cut the brilliant album, *Bluesbreakers With Eric Clapton*. While the record proved to be a musical and commercial breakthrough, it was not long before Clapton left Mayall's band, to be replaced by Peter Green. Flint had also moved on, and been replaced by Aynsley Dunbar. More excellent albums followed and by early 1967 Mayall had one of the leading blues outfits in Britain. Their repertoire consisted of Mayall originals, coupled with classic blues tunes. By mid-1967 Mick Fleetwood was playing drums with the band, but he, Green, and McVie soon departed the Bluesbreakers to form Fleetwood Mac. Within no time Mayall was back in the studio with a new guitar-slinger, Mick Taylor, and Keef Hartley on drums. Mayall kept the Bluesbreakers together while players were coming and going, including Jon Hiseman on drums and Dick Heckstall-Smith on sax.

John Mayall

John Mayall's Bluesbreakers
1967 (l to r) John Mayall, Mick Taylor, John Hiseman, Tony Reeves, Dick Heckstall-Smith, Henry (Jowther??) and Chris Mercer.

CREAM
Eric Clapton, Ginger Baker and Jack Bruce - the power trio became the archetypal blues-rock band.

To John Mayall, the individual players were less important than the unit: "If you're a bandleader, your main focus is to play your own music", he explained. He continues to tour with the Bluesbreakers to this day, but somehow never gets the credit he is due.

Clapton's departure from the Bluesbreakers culminated in his forming Cream in 1966 with Jack Bruce and Ginger Baker. Steeped as they all were in the blues, they became the archetypal blues-rock band, and the model of the powerhouse rock trio. They produced exciting reworkings of classic Delta blues songs that included 'I'm So Glad' (Skip James), 'Crossroads' (Robert Johnson), 'Spoonful' (Howlin' Wolf) and 'Outside Woman Blues' (Blind Joe Reynolds).

I owe a lot to Peter Green, you know. He wasn't so studied, but he got it

MICK FLEETWOOD

FLEETWOOD GREEN

When McVie, Fleetwood, and Green graduated from Mayall's blues academy, they could have had little or no idea of what their future would be. Green and Fleetwood left Mayall first, and were introduced by Mike Vernon to Jeremy Spencer. Fleetwood Mac, as their new group was dubbed, made their debut in August 1967, with Bob Brunning playing bass. Their first single was a cover of Elmore James' 'I Believe My Time Ain't Long'. It came out in November, by which time McVie had replaced Brunning. The band loved the blues. Green hero-worshipped B.B. King, while Spencer loved Elmore James, which made for a powerful combination.

Mac's debut album made No. 4 in the UK, and included some original songs alongside covers of Elmore James' 'Got To Move' and standards like 'Shake Your Moneymaker'. A Peter Green-composed single, 'Black Magic Woman' followed the album. In August 1968, their second album, Mr Wonderful, marked for many the pinnacle of British guitar-driven blues; the album was effectively a homage to Elmore James.

Hard on the heels of Mr Wonderful came the gentle instrumental single, 'Albatross', which topped the UK chart in January 1969, selling a million copies. Throughout 1969 the band were at their peak, with the wonderfully creative Green writing excellent singles. 'Man Of The World', released in April, made No. 2, as did 'Oh Well', which came out in September. The band's final release with Peter Green was 'The Green Manalishi (With the Two Pronged Crown)', which reached No. 10. But Green, who had experienced several harrowing LSD trips, then chose to leave the band. Fleetwood Mac soldiered on with Spencer and Danny Kirwan, who had joined in 1968.

Peter said, come on, you must join John Mayall, which was great – short-lived, but we had lot of fun. By then I was completely taken up with the Blues and that led to Fleetwood Mac. All we were about was Elmore James

MICK FLEETWOOD

Green did manage a solo album in 1970 before he disappeared to live a reclusive life in southwest London. Several attempts at a comeback over the next 25 years were more embarrassing than successful. But in the late 1990s he began to find some better form. Fleetwood Mac, on the other hand, recruited Christine Perfect from Birmingham blues band Chicken Shack, and became a rock dynasty. They left the blues behind soon after Jeremy Spencer quit the band in 1971; he went missing in California during a tour, and was later discovered to have joined the Children of God church.

Blue Horizon – Britain's Greatest Ever Blues Label

FLEETWOOD MAC's original label will forever be synonymous with the 1960s British blues scene. Mike Vernon, the Decca staff producer, also ran a fanzine, *R&B Monthly*, which was the catalyst for the Blue Horizon label. Blues was Vernon's first love: "it is the music of the people," he said, "something real, that's tangible". In the January 1965 issue of the magazine, there appeared an ad offering a limited edition single by Howlin' Wolf's guitarist, Hubert Sumlin. It quickly sold out, and this prompted Mike and his partner Neil Slavin to offer further specials.

By early 1966 the magazine had closed, because Mike and Neil no longer had the time to run it properly, but the pair continued to release various Blue Horizon special singles via their mailing list.

"I took a demo session with Fleetwood Mac and offered it to Decca to put on this new label, Blue Horizon, and they said, "Oh, we couldn't do that, it has to be on Decca. We can't give you your own label". But Peter was quite adamant: he didn't want to be part of Decca, because Mayall was already on Decca"

Mike Vernon

By the middle of 1967 Vernon had done a deal with CBS to release his Blue Horizon label; Fleetwood Mac's first single was also the new label's opening salvo. The second release featured another stalwart of the 1960s British blues scene and another Bluesbreaker refugee, Aynsley Dunbar, whose band was called Retaliation.

From the beginning of 1968 Blue Horizon began a steady release schedule featuring the best in British blues, plus recordings by visiting American artists, or material licensed from US labels like Cobra and Excello.

British Artists

- Chicken Shack: besides Christine Perfect, the band featured guitarist Stan Webb. They had two hit singles, the best of which was 'I'd Rather Go Blind in 1969.
- Duster Bennett: a one-man blues band
- Jellybread: featuring keyboard player and vocalist Pete Wingfield.
- Bacon Fat: with Rod Piazza on vocals and harmonica.
- Christine Perfect: she went solo before joining Fleetwood Mac.

American Artists

- B.B. King: re-releases of his 1950s material
- Slim Harpo
- Otis Rush
- Bukka White
- Lightnin' Slim
- Magic Sam
- Larry Johnson

The label's biggest asset was undoubtedly Fleetwood Mac, but their failure to re-sign the band's contract, which was simply an oversight, meant that they lost Mac's services to Andrew Oldham's Immediate label. Mike Vernon later recalled that their loss "gagged in my throat".

One of the most label's interesting albums was *Blues Jam In Chicago*. Fleetwood Mac were touring the US over New Year 1968/69, and Vernon asked Marshall Chess if the band could record at Chess studios in Chicago, along with some of the label's stalwarts. Some of the biggest names were not available but Willie Dixon put together an interesting bunch of artists, including Big Walter Horton, Honey Boy Edwards, Otis Spann, and Buddy Guy. Amongst the best tracks was Spann's 'Hungry Country Girl'.

By July 1972 the demand for the Blues had waned, and Blue Horizon ceased to exist. But for many years the label did a sterling job of recording original material and offering fans a chance to hear earlier material from some of the great names of the genre, which had been almost impossible to obtain in Britain.

Chicken Shack
40 Blue Fingers Freshly Packed & Ready To Serve

B.B. King
Take A Swing With Me

Lazy Lester
Made Up My Mind

Otis Spann
The Biggest Thing Since Colossus…

Elmore James

JAMES AND HIS FAMILY moved around the Delta while he was a child, finding work wherever they could by picking cotton. He taught himself the basics on a one-string, homemade guitar, and purchased his first proper instrument in 1933, a $20 National. He began his career by playing house parties and juke joints as Cleanhead or Joe Willie James, and pretty soon he was playing gigs all over the Delta, making the acquaintance of musicians like Arthur 'Big Boy' Crudup, Johnny Temple, and Luther Huff.

In 1937, Elmore moved to Greenville, Mississippi, where he met and played with Sonny Boy Williamson (Rice Miller) and Robert Junior Lockwood. It was here that he met Robert Johnson and probably first heard 'I Believe I'll Dust My Broom', the song that was to establish his reputation. It may well have been Johnson who taught James how to use a piece of metal in order to 'slide' the notes on the guitar, a talent that James would come to master. After working in a radio repair shop he served with the navy in the Pacific between 1943 and 1945. When the war was over, he reunited with both Sonny Boy and Homesick James, who both had radio shows on KFFA in Helena, Mississippi. Elmore was given airtime on these shows, allowing him to perform songs like 'Dust My Broom' to a big audience for the first time.

Poor health dogged Elmore's final years.

In 1951 Sonny Boy helped him secure a contract with Trumpet Records and in 1952, under the name Elmo James, he finally recorded 'Dust My Broom', which made No. 9 on

FACT FILE

BORN: *27th January, 1918, Richland, Mississippi*

DIED: *24th May, 1963, Chicago, Illinois*

INSTRUMENT: *Guitar*

FIRST RECORDED: *1951*

ACCOLADES: *Inducted into the Blues Hall of Fame, 1980*

INFLUENCES: *Robert Johnson, Robert Nighthawk, Sonny Boy Williamson, Charley Patton*

INFLUENCED: *Homesick James, Johnny Winter, Brian Jones, Fleetwood Mac, Duane Allman, BB King, JB Hutto*

Elmore James' grave

> *'I discovered Elmore James, and the earth seemed to shudder on its axis'*
>
> BRIAN JONES

DUST MY BROOM
Elmore's anthem was a complaint about love gone bad.

the R&B charts. By early 1953 he had scored another Top 10 hit, 'I Believe', and had settled in Chicago, where he soon assembled a new backing band, The Broomdusters. Elmore spent the rest of the 50s moving back and forth between Chicago and the Delta. In 1957 he was diagnosed with a heart condition. His poor health made him thin and his heavy spectacles gave him the look of a schoolteacher rather than a blues guitar maestro. Elmore continued to perform, but his lack of real success forced him to get a job as a DJ in Mississippi, though he still recorded regularly.

His career was revitalised in 1959 when he was signed by Fire Records, where he recorded some of his best music, including 'The Sky Is Crying', which made No. 15 on the R&B chart. He stayed with the label until 1962, when problems with the Musicians' Union forced him to stop working union jobs. Elmore began recording again the following year, but on 24th May, 1963, while he was in Chicago, preparing to go to the studio, he suffered a fatal heart attack, at the home of his cousin Homesick James. He was 45 years old. Almost two years later, James posthumously scored the last of his four chart hits, 'It Hurts Me Too'.

James' passionate vocals and soaring slide guitar became one of the most recognisable and influential sounds in post-war blues, and there is no doubt that he was one of the most important figures of the era. In particular, he had a huge impact on the sound of electric rock bands and became the inspiration to legions of would-be guitar heroes.

ESSENTIAL RECORDINGS

CLASSIC SONGS

'Dust My Broom' 1952
'The Sky Is Crying' 1960
'Shake Your Money Maker' 1961
'Done Somebody Wrong' 1961

THE SOURCE

The Classic Early Recordings
3-CD set on Ace Records

'Brian was an Elmore James devotee. His early stage name of Elmo Lewis and his bottleneck guitar work paid tribute to James'

BILL WYMAN

'Elmore James was a major, maybe even the main reason why The Stones came about… In late 1961, Brian Jones went to see the Chris Barber Band in Cheltenham; the band featured Alexis Korner in a blues segment. After the show Brian and Alexis talked and a month later Brian visited Alexis in London. This is when he heard his first Elmore James record, and he went straight out and bought an electric guitar'

BILL WYMAN

DUST MY BROOM

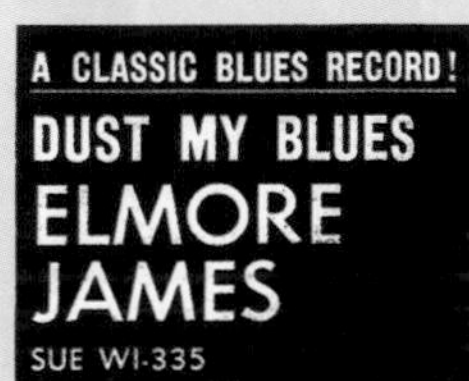

TRYING TO RECALL where you first heard the quintessential electric blues riff that opens 'Dust My Broom' is difficult. It may have been the early 1950s version by Elmore James or Fleetwood Mac's late 60s offering. Some may recall an unknown blues band at a club they visited in their youth, a few know that its true origins lie in the 1930s with Robert Johnson, or do they?

In early December 1933 Roosevelt Sykes accompanied Carl Rafferty, (a man about who we know absolutely nothing) on 'Mr Carl's Blues'. What we do know is

ELMORE JAMES' 1951 VERSION

Lillian McMurry, an independent record producer, heard Elmore and wanted to record him, but Elmore was very shy of the studio. They convinced him that he was only rehearsing and did not tell Elmore that they were recording 'Dust My Broom'. It was released on a Trumpet 146 with Elmore, billed as Elmo James, on one side and Bo Bo Thomas singing 'Catfish Blues' on the other. The record made No.9 in the R&B charts in April 1952.

LINE CHANGE

They changed the third line of the first verse to:

'I quit the best girl I'm lovin' now my friends can get my room'

James also drops West Helena and replaces it with Mississippi.

1968 FLEETWOOD MAC VERSION

The original Fleetwood Mac with Peter Green recorded their version for their 1968 album *Mr Wonderful*. It contains further lyric variations. Like many of the later versions that were both recorded and sung live they often mixed up 'Dust My Broom' with 'Dust My Blues'.

ELMORE JAMES' 1955 VERSION

James re-recorded 'Dust My Broom' as 'Dust My Blues' with minor lyrics changes and a re-arrangement of the verses. The song is credited to Johnson, arranged by Elmore James & Bihari (Bihari is one of the two brothers that owned the Modern label. James recorded for Modern's subsidiaries, Flair and Meteor).

1965 THE RISING SONS VERSION

The Rising Sons were Taj Mahal, Ry Cooder, Jesse Lee Kincaid, Gary Marker, and Kevin Kelley. They recorded a number of titles during 1965, with producer Terry Melcher (Doris Day's son). Among them was 'Dust My Broom', recorded on 3rd December, 1965. On the record it is credited to Robert Johnson, but their version is an amalgam of Elmore James' 'Dust My Broom' and 'Dust My Blues'. Two years earlier, 'Spider' John Koerner, Dave 'Snaker' Ray, and Tony 'Little Sun' Glover were probably the first white artists to record the song.

SELECTED VERSIONS

- 1936 Robert Johnson
- 1951 Elmore James with Sonny Boy Williamson
- Robert Jr Lockwood
- 1955 Elmore James ('Dust My Blues')
- 1963 Koerner, Ray & Glover
- 1965 The Rising Sons
- 1966 The Spencer Davis Group
- 1967 Canned Heat
- John Mayall's Bluesbreakers with Peter Green
- 1968 Fleetwood Mac
- Taj Mahal
- 1971 Freddie King
- 1972 Otis Rush & Johnny Shines
- 1976 Muddy Waters
- 1979 ZZ Top
- 1984 Johnny Winter
- 1987 James Cotton
- 1992 John Hammond
- 1995 Guy Davis
- 1998 Peter Green
- Earl Hooker

this session was significant in the history of the Blues. 'Mr Carl's Blues' contains the immortal lines, 'I do believe, I do believe I'll dust my broom. And after I dust my broom, anyone may have my room'. Many years later, as historians dissected Robert Johnson's songs to understand his influences, it was generally assumed that he based '(I Believe I'll) Dust My Broom' on Kokomo Arnold's 'Sagefield Woman Blues'. Although the latter has words similar to 'Mr Carl's Blues 'it was recorded some 10 months later. In truth we may never know who 'did it first', but recorded evidence points to Mr Carl Rafferty accompanied by Mr Roosevelt Sykes.

'Dust My Broom'
Several schools of thought exist as to the meaning of 'dust my broom'. It could concern cleaning a rented room before you leave – shades of the itinerant musician – or it is simply a sexual reference.

'It was an old field holler to tell everyone, except the people the hollerer didn't want to tell, that he was running away'

Son Thomas

West Helena
A town on the west bank of the Mississippi in Arkansas.

East Monroe
Monroe, Louisiana, between Shreveport and Vicksburg.

A 'Doney'
A 'no good doney' is probably a woman of low character, a slang term which is no longer in use. It is possibly derived from 'doe', an adult female deer or rabbit.

Chiney
China.

Phillipien's Island
The Philipines.

Dust My Broom

Written by Robert Johnson.
Recorded by him on Monday, 23rd November, 1936, San Antonio, Texas.

I'm gon' get up in the mornin', I believe I'll dust my broom
I'm gon' get up in the mornin', I believe I'll dust my broom
Girl friend, the black man you been lovin', girl friend, can get my room

I'm gon' write a letter, telephone every town I know
I'm gon' write a letter, telephone every town I know
If I can't find her in West Helena she must be in East Monroe, I know

I don't want to no woman wants every downtown man she meet
I don't want to no woman wants every downtown man she meet
She's a no good doney they shouldn't 'low her on the street

I believe, I believe I'll go back home
I believe, I believe I'll go back home
You can mistreat me here, babe but you can't up in the mornin'

And I'm gettin' up in the mornin', I believe I'll dust my broom
I'm gettin' up in the mornin', I believe I'll dust my broom
Girl friend, the black man you been lovin' girl friend, can get my room

I'm 'on' call up Chiney, see is my good girl over there
I'm 'on' call up Chiney, see is my good girl over there
If I can't find her on Phillipiens Island
She must be in Ethiopia somewhere

Live Dust
During the 1960's and early 70's there was probably no blues or rock band that did not include 'Dust My Broom' in their live set. Even in the early 1980s bearded Texas blues rockers ZZ Top regularly featured the song in their live shows.

Freddie King
In 1971 Freddie King played a great version of 'Dust My Broom', produced by Leon Russell, on *Getting Ready*, one of the last albums before his untimely death in 1975.

Gold Dust
In 1997 in the US a 78 rpm record of Robert Johnson's '(I Believe I'll) Dust My Broom' coupled with 'Dead Shrimp Blues' on Vocalion in what was described as 'very good condition' sold for $2,970 at auction. It ranks among the finest of the 10 to 15 known surviving copies of this record. It probably sold well under 4,000 copies at the time, which would have been considered excellent sales. Today even the least valuable of Johnson's records are estimated to be worth $3,500 each.

Guy Davis
Guy Davis' plays his version on his *Stomp Down Rider* album in the traditional Delta blues acoustic slide guitar style.

Mystical Gods – Old and New

Urban blues was flourishing at the end of the 1950s in Chicago, New York, Detroit, and Los Angeles, albeit with regional peculiarities and differences. But it seemed that country blues had simply died and gone away. There was no market, or so it seemed, for the acoustic blues music that Muddy and his fellow Delta transplants had originally played. Even Lightnin' Hopkins, the most recorded 1950s bluesman, was out of fashion. The only blues heard out in the country was played by old men, who had probably been playing guitar their whole lives. They played for their families and friends the way they always had done, on Saturday nights or at local parties.

Harry Smith's 1952 *Anthology* lit a beacon for many young whites who were eager to learn more about their musical heritage. It set some of them on a lifelong path of collecting original blues recordings, which soon supplied some amazing discoveries. Another factor in the unexpected rebirth of country blues was provided by Josh White, whose Elektra recordings sparked interest from younger people who were keen to know where some of this music came from.

It was two young men, one from England and one from New York, who did as much as anyone to revive the genre through their writing. Sam Charters published his book *The Country Blues* in autumn 1959, following extensive field research throughout the South; while Paul Oliver's first book, *Blues Fell This Morning*, came out a year later. Charters wrote about Blind Lemon Jefferson, Blind Willie McTell, Big Bill Broonzy, and all the other great names of pre-war blues. In his foreword to the first edition, he said: 'Two singers, Rabbit Brown and Robert Johnson, have been discussed at length, despite their minor roles in the story of the Blues.' Given the limited research material at his disposal, Charters' book was a remarkable introduction to country blues, which should still be read if you want to gain further insight. Many of those who read it when it was first published were encouraged to seek out old recordings by the bluesmen that Charters and Oliver mentioned. Some

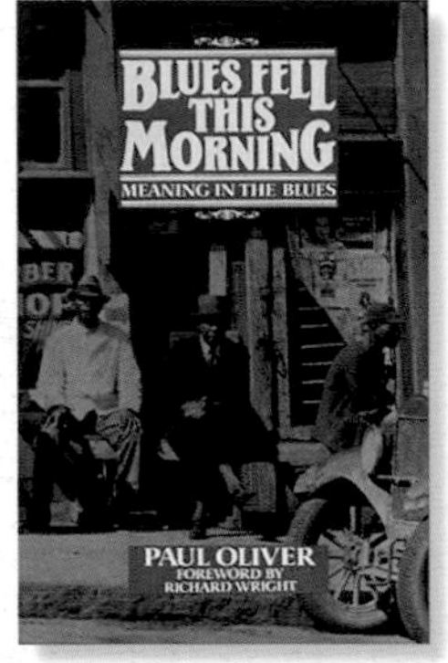

Country Revival
Blues Fell This Morning, *Paul Oliver's 1960 book, which helped generate a new interest in forgotten country blues.*

Mississippi Fred McDowell

enterprising souls went a step further, and set out on the trail of these old men. After all, it was less than 30 years since they had recorded: some of them might not even have reached retirement age!

Oliver's Army

What Charters and Oliver did was to make the names on the fading labels of 78rpm records come back to life. Back in the 1920s and 30s, no one seriously thought that this music would have a longevity beyond the year in which it was recorded. There was no serious 'music press' back then, either, which meant that little in the way of interviews ever took place. In many ways this lack of information made the collectors' pursuit of knowledge seem somehow worthier, and more serious. The result was a sudden blossoming of interest in country blues around 1961 and 1962.

Men like Chris Strachwitz, Harry Oster, Mack McCormick, and John Fahey left their homes to comb the south in search of these 'mystical Gods'. It wasn't long before these blues panhandlers began discovering hidden gems. As has been made clear throughout earlier chapters in the book, the country blues singers didn't 'give up' recording; usually it gave them up, for reasons that had little or nothing to do with their popularity or talent. Although pre-war record companies were interested in building artists' careers, the label was strictly in control. This was an era long before managers, accountants, lawyers, tour promoters, agents, and the like. It was a fickle business that often relied on whether or not your face fitted with scouts or men like Lester Melrose.

Amongst the long-forgotten country bluesmen who were 'rediscovered' in the early 60s were Skip James, Son House, Mississippi John Hurt, Furry Lewis, Bukka White, and Peg Leg Howell. Others, such as Mississippi Fred McDowell and Robert Pete Williams, had never been given the chance to record 'the first time around'. John Fahey made his discovery by writing a letter addressed to 'Bukka White, Old Blues Singer, c/o General Delivery, Aberdeen, Mississippi'. Not that Bukka lived in Aberdeen: it was just that a relative of White's was working at the post office and told Fahey that White had been living in Memphis since the 1940s… as BB King could actually have told him!

Bukka White

Rediscovered in the early 1960s, White was very much back in demand. Here he plays Chicago University, 1968.

House's Homecoming

Dick Waterman's rediscovery of Son House is a story best told in his own words: "I promoted a week of shows with John Hurt in February 1964 and then I did another show with Bukka White. In talking to Bukka White he said that he had seen Son House alive in Memphis. Son House was a Delta giant who had recorded in 1930

Furry Lewis
Back on stage in 1964. Like Skip James, Son House, Mississippi John Hurt, Bukka White, and Peg Leg Howell, Furry Lewis was rediscovered in the 60s.

for Paramount, then again for the Library of Congress in '41–'42 and then vanished. So now this is 22 years later and he was supposed to be still alive.

So I gathered up two guys and went down to Mississippi in the summer of 1964. In hindsight, that was the terrible summer when Mississippi was burning with Voter Registration and George Wallace was running for President. Looking back, we were three Jewish kids who had a yellow Volkswagen with New York plates, and we had like no sane reason to be there, but we came down and we were looking for Robert Johnson, Son House, Skip James, any of them we could find. So we pretty much ascertained that Johnson was dead, and no one had ever heard of Skip James or anyone who played like him, but we backtracked Son House. It turned out that Bukka's story of seeing him in Memphis was bogus, he had made the story up. But we had got over into the area around Robinsonville, a little north of Tunica on the old Highway 61, and we found an old man whose son had once been married to Son's stepdaughter, as Mrs House had children by her first marriage. So we found him and he said, 'Yes, I was once married to the daughter of Son and Mrs House'. Then we found her and we talked to her and she said, 'Oh, yes, they came over to Detroit a couple of years ago'. So now we are really excited and we know that Son House is alive in the 60s. So we got someone on the phone, Son didn't have a phone at that point, and he brought the man to the phone – Sunday 21st June, 1964. So we said, 'Are you the Son House that recorded with the Library of Congress and recorded for Lomax? Did you know Charley Patton? Did you know Robert Johnson? Did you used to live in Robinsonville?' And there was this long pause, and he said, 'Who is this anyway? Yes, that's me, I done all those things'. And we said, 'OK, don't go anywhere, we're on our way'. And he was in Rochester, New York. So we had come from Cambridge, Massachusetts, down to the Delta and turn around and went back up to Rochester, New York."

Shortly after finding House, Waterman introduced him to Al Wilson, who later formed Canned Heat. House was due to play the Newport Folk Festival and as Wilson played bottleneck guitar in open tuning, he was the ideal person to help Son House relearn his songs – because he hadn't played them for 16 years or more. Waterman later recalled that Wilson literally taught Son House to play Son House. His performance at the Festival set House on the road to a broader audience appeal than he could ever have imagined when he was recording in the 1930s.

Not all the artists had to be taught how to play again. Many had continued playing, so it was just a matter of picking up where they had left off. Mississippi John Hurt was one whose talents remained undiminished despite the passing years and likewise Skip James, Bukka White, and Furry Lewis were all on good form.

MISSISSIPPI JOHN HURT

FACT FILE

BORN: *3rd July, 1893*
Teoc, Mississippi

DIED: *2nd November, 1966*
Grenada, Mississippi

INSTRUMENT: *Guitar, harmonica*

FIRST RECORDED: *1928*

ACCOLADES: *Inducted into the Blues Hall of Fame, 1990*

INFLUENCES: *Jimmie Rodgers*

INFLUENCED: *Bob Dylan*

THE MAN DUBBED THE 'patriarch hippie' came from a typically large Delta family of 10 siblings. When he was very young his family moved to Avalon, Mississippi, where he learned to play the guitar in his distinctive three-finger picking style. He was soon playing and singing at parties and dances as well as pursuing the life of a full-time farmer.

On Valentine's Day 1928, Hurt was in Memphis to record for the OKeh label, who released just one record from this first session. It must have been encouraging because they took him to New York City in December that year for another two sessions. A week apart he cut a dozen sides, of which all but two were released at the time. Having got his recording out the way he was back to a life spent farming, that is until 1963 when a young fan, Tom Hoskins, used the words of 'Avalon Blues' to track Hurt down… to Avalon, a small place on a rural road between Greenwood and Grenada. The 71-year-old was not overly impressed with the whole idea of recording, but went along with it. Hurt went to Washington in March 1963 and cut an album for Piedmont, it was the beginning of a short but hugely successful renaissance. In the summer of 1963 he appeared at the Newport Festival, which launched his career on the folk blues circuit of the north east US.

Hurt's style was the antithesis of the typical Delta player; he was relaxed in voice and guitar playing, giving his songs a sweet feel. It is probably one reason why he became so popular when he was rediscovered; he showed a softer side to the Delta, more usually associated with more easterly states. There are a whole host of 60s folkies that owe Hurt a debt as their vocal teacher, in particular the lilting throwaway at the end of the line. What is so remarkable is the fact that Hurt, who was never a professional musician could perform with such consummate skill. If you know any one who feels that the Blues is hard, gruff, and heavy, give them a dose of Mississippi John… they will be converted.

A deeply religious man he retired to Grenada, Mississippi in 1966 and died at the end of the year from a heart attack.

> *'I saw him at Newport '63 and he just killed me. His voice, his face, his attitude, his gentle innocence, his real profound thoughts; I was just lost, lost into the world of John Hurt'*
>
> DICK WATERMAN

ESSENTIAL RECORDINGS

CLASSIC SONGS

'Avalon Blues' 1928
'I've Got The Blues And I Can't Be Satisfied' 1967
'Monday Morning Blues' 1967

CLASSIC ALBUMS

The Immortal Mississippi John Hurt
1967

THE SOURCE

The Greatest Songsters 1927–1929
(Mississippi John Hurt & Hambone Willie Newbern)
Document Records

Newport Folk Festival

From their inception the Newport Folk Festival featured the blues, which was a reflection of the interests of both white folk performers and their audiences. In 1959, Sonny Terry and Brownie McGhee, Reverend Gary Davis and John Lee Hooker opened the blues account at Newport, which would go on to play host to many of the performers who were rediscovered during the folk blues revival. The importance of the festival was that it introduced many young white performers and their audience to 'first hand' country blues.

Newport Folk Festival 1960
John Lee Hooker shares the stage with Joan Baez and Flatt & Scruggs.

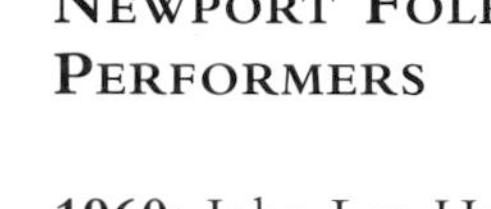

Newport Folk Festival Performers

Muddy Waters At Newport
Muddy Waters' 1960 appearance at the Newport Folk Festival was captured on this wonderful live album.

1960: John Lee Hooker, Muddy Waters.

1963: Mississippi John Hurt, Sonny Terry & Brownie McGhee.

1964: Jesse Fuller, Mississippi John Hurt, Mississippi Fred McDowell, Odetta, Muddy Waters, Otis Spann, Son House, Sleepy John Estes, Hammie Nixon, Yank Rachell, Skip James, Robert Wilkins, Robert Pete Williams.

1965: Son House, Josh White, Reverend Gary Davis, Lightnin' Hopkins, Mississippi John Hurt, Mance Lipscomb, Odetta.

1966: Son House, Skip James, Bukka White, Howlin' Wolf, Richie Havens.

Ask rock music fans about the 1965 Newport Folk Festival and they usually mutter something about Bob Dylan upsetting the folk purists by performing with an electric blues band. According to Al Kooper, nothing could be further from the truth. Kooper had played organ on Dylan's 1965 single 'Like A Rolling Stone', He had gone to the session thinking he was to play guitar, but Dylan had brought a friend from Chicago, Mike Bloomfield, to do just that. So Al Kooper had to play Hammond organ, which was far from his instrument of choice: 'I waited until the chord was played by the rest of the band, before committing myself to play the verses. I'm always an eighth note behind everyone else.'

A few months later, in the summer of 1965, Kooper was asked to go and meet Dylan at Newport. After a one-night rehearsal, Kooper along with Bloomfield, Jerome Arnold, and Sam Lay (the last two being veterans of Howlin' Wolf's band), took to the stage to back Dylan on 'Like A Rolling Stone' and 'Maggie's Farm'. Many have written about Dylan cutting short his set after being booed off the stage. In reality, according to Kooper, those two songs were all they had rehearsed together. As they came off stage, Peter Yarrow, of Peter Paul and Mary, gave Dylan his acoustic guitar, and he went back on to sing 'It's All Over Now Baby Blue'. The point of it all? The close interplay of Dylan and the other young 'folkies' who had a deep affection for the Blues. It influenced their lyrics, melodies and their entire raison d'être. To attempt any meaningful analysis of Bob Dylan would take more space than this book, so suffice it to say here that without the Blues there would be no Bob Dylan, the best white blues singer of them all… it's that simple.

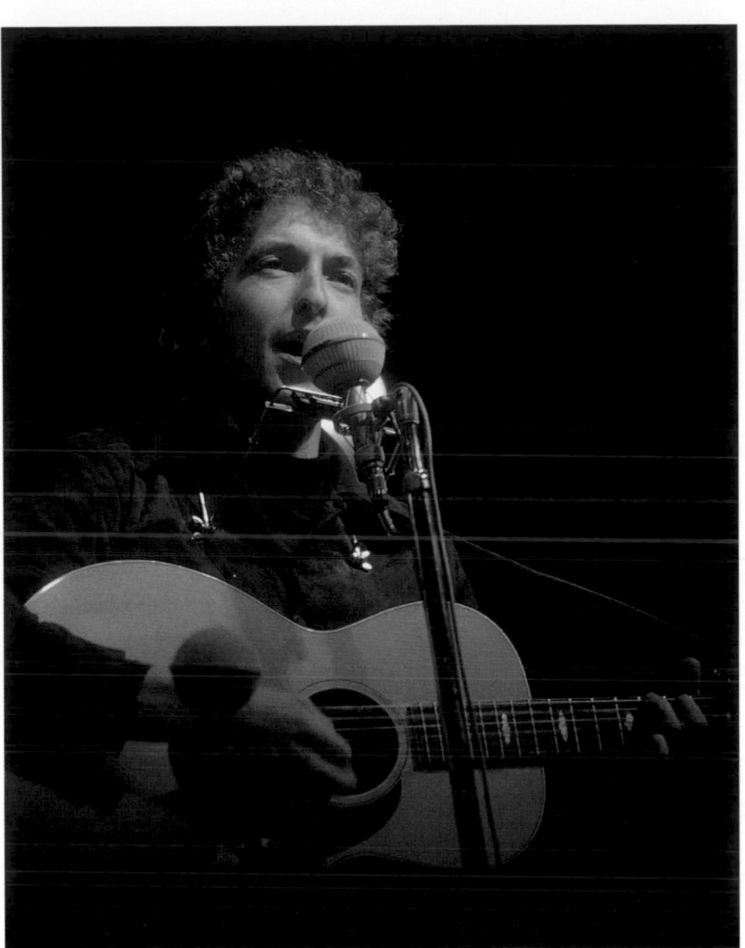

Bob Dylan at Newport 1964

The following year, Dylan caused enormous controversy at the festival by playing an electric set with members of the Paul Butterfield Blues Band.

Spider, Snaker and Little Sun

On 24th March, 1963, as The Stones were playing at Studio 51 and the Station Hotel in Richmond, three Americans in their early to mid-twenties were recording an album at the Woman's Club in Milwaukee, Wisconsin. John Koerner, Dave Ray, and Tony Glover had met at the University of Minnesota where Koerner and Ray were taking classes and Glover was hanging out in search of like-minded blues fans to play with. Unusually for the late 1950s, they were all white boys high on the Blues, whose mentors were Lead Belly, Sonny Terry, and Blind Lemon Jefferson. When they began playing together they adopted the nicknames Spider (Koerner), Snaker (Ray), and Little Sun (Glover). They met ED Nunn, the heir to the Nunn-Bush Shoe Company. Nunn had his own record label, Audiophile, whose previous biggest seller was an album featuring a whole side devoted to a thunderstorm.

> *Over the years music people would tell me about records that had influenced their lives, and Koerner, Ray and Glover always come up*
>
> Jac Holzman
> Founder of Electra Records

The album that Koerner, Ray, and Glover cut included Lead Belly's 'Hangman', Muddy's 'Down To Louisiana', and Blind Lemon's 'One Kind Favor', along with originals by the group. The album came out in June 1963; just 300 copies were pressed on translucent red vinyl. Mr Nunn would not give any of the band free copies of the album, but he did sell some to them at cost. Glover bought three copies, one of which he sent to Jac Holzman the founder of Elektra Records. Holzman loved it and flew to Minneapolis to meet the band. He signed them over dinner with Ray's parents, and purchased the master tape from Nunn. Elektra released the album in November, and the band played the Newport Folk Festival the following year.

Koerner, Ray & Glover

Their 1963 debut album Blues, Rags & Hollers *included songs by Lead Belly, Muddy Waters, and Blind Lemon Jefferson.*

THE LOVIN' SPOONFUL
John Sebastian (left) and Zal Yanovsky (bottom left) co-founded the group, whose name was inspired by a line in a blues song.

THE RETURN OF THE JUG BANDS

"Koerner, Ray, and Glover were a step along the path towards the style that the Lovin' Spoonful drew upon", recalled John Sebastian, the co-founder of the most commercially successful jug-band group of all time. The 20-year-old Sebastian and Zal Yanovsky met at 'Mama' Cass Elliot's house in New York to watch the Beatles' US TV debut on *The Ed Sullivan Show* in February 1964. John had played with Fred Neil and Tom Rush and been a member of the Even Dozen Jug Band, while Zal, who was from Canada, played with the Halifax Three. They spent the rest of 1964 playing with other members of the Greenwich Village folk scene before they formed the Lovin' Spoonful in January 1965, naming themselves after a phrase in Mississippi John Hurt's 'Coffee Blues'. They quickly synthesized into what they called 'good time music' and the press named 'folk rock', but as with many other artists in this period, their music developed from the blues. Other bands which fall into this category include the Holy Modal Rounders, whose 1964 debut album included 'Hesitation Blues', and New York's Blues Magoos.

One of the leaders of the New York folk scene was Dave Van Ronk. A native New Yorker, Van Ronk released his first album in 1959, having fallen under the spell of Harry Smith's *Anthology*. Unlike Dylan, Van Ronk stuck firmly to his purist beliefs and performed and recorded under the influence of the southeast blues style, Gary Davis in particular. He was a regular on the 1960s festival circuit and his commitment to maintaining folk and blues traditions has brought him perennial respect and a steady, if not prolific, recording career.

DAVE VAN RONK
A traditionalist in the southeast style of folk blues.

Like Father Like Son

Given his father's passion, it was inevitable that John Hammond Jr would become involved in music in some way. Born five years after his father staged the *From Spirituals To Swing* concerts, John Jr attended Antioch College in Ohio during the late 1950s and started to work coffee-houses playing guitar and harmonica. He signed a deal with Vanguard Records in 1962 and recorded his debut album at the age of just twenty. His principal influence was Robert Johnson, but he had affection for all the great Delta bluesmen.

Hammond's career has spanned five decades, in which he has done more than most to promote many of the classic blues songs. Fans seeing him perform or hearing his records often want to discover where his material comes from, so Hammond – like so many of his contemporaries – has been a conduit, a doorway into the vast blues tent.

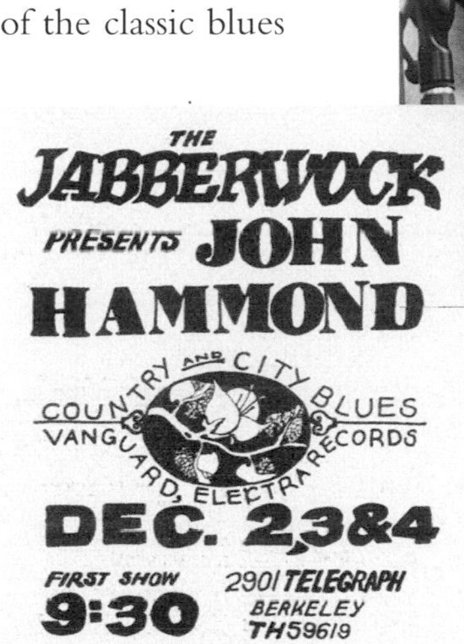

Hammond at the Jabberwock
Five months after Bill played with John Hammond, this advert appeared in San Francisco's Mojo Navigator, *the original 'rock' newspaper, for a performance in Berkeley.*

> *'On 6th November, 1964, Brian Jones and I went to the Village Gate in New York City to see Dizzy Gillespie, but we were too late and missed his show. Instead we saw John Hammond, who I thought was fantastic, just him playing his guitar and singing. After the show we got talking to him and went back to his flat, which was a huge loft. After the party John drove me back to my hotel on his motorbike. Almost two years later all the Stones went to the Albert Hall to see Bob Dylan and The Band – it was a great show and certainly showed us the way that folk-rock was heading. Three weeks later we went to New York and stayed at the Holiday Inn, the only decent hotel that would have us! The following day, 23rd June, 1966, I got a call from John Hammond saying he was recording in the studio and would I go on over and play bass. I said I would and called Brian and Stu and we all went over to Atlantic Studios. Robbie Robertson was playing guitar and we cut three tracks that evening, including 'I Can Tell' and 'I Wish You Would'. While we were recording Bob Dylan dropped by and chatted for a while and invited us back for drinks. So when we finished, it was all back to Bob's place. One thing's for sure; it's better than a proper job! However, the next morning, our 'manager' Allen Klein called me and said I must never do anything like that again, as I would have work permit and tax problems. Some people really know how to make your day!'*
>
> Bill Wyman

THE BRITISH INVASION

EXPORTING THE BEATLES
John, Paul, George and Ringo leave London for their first American tour, 1964.

DYLAN'S EVENTFUL trip to Newport followed one of the most remarkable years in American music history – one that changed forever the music that America and the rest of the world listened to. If 1964 was the year that the Blues took hold of Britain it was also the year that Britain took a musical hold on America. Dubbed the 'British Invasion' by the press on both sides of the Atlantic, it was a year in which the US charts were dominated by the sound of Britain's beat groups, and in particular The Beatles. History has a funny way of tricking us into forgetting that things were often very different from the way we remember them. For a start, The Stones were one of the less successful British bands in America in 1964!

AMERICA'S BAND

The Beach Boys, or "America's band", as they have been called, first entered the US charts in February 1962, when 'Surfin' staggered up to No. 75 on the Hot 100. The follow-up, 'Surfin Safari', made it to a healthy No. 14 and established The Beach Boys and their surf sound as a phenomenon in the late summer of 1962. Around the time that Bill Wyman was joining The Rolling Stones, Brian Wilson was recording a demo of a new song, 'Surfin' USA'. Brian's singing and piano playing on the demo were somewhat reminiscent of Chuck Berry's guitar-driven anthem to 'Sweet Little Sixteen'. In fact, the whole song was built around the chords, rhythm and structure of Chuck's song, which became very apparent when the group recorded their hit single in January 1963. Chuck's lawyers were quick to capitalise upon the situation, and later issues of the song showed a writing credit of 'C Berry and B Wilson' – one of pop music's great ironies.

By the time The Beatles first entered the Billboard chart in January 1964, The Beach Boys had charted nine songs, pre-empting a move away from the more traditional male and female vocalist hits that had become

SHARP SUITED BEACH BOYS
Carl, Dennis and Brian Wilson, Mike Love, and Al Jardine.

America's chart fodder. In fact, in this post-rock'n'roll era, white America's music scene had taken on a pretty bland flavour. Even Ray Charles had left his more traditional blues-oriented fare and scored with a remake of Jimmie Davis' pre-war hit, 'You Are My Sunshine'.

Britain Takes Over The US Charts

There is no question that the American charts in 1964 belonged to The Beatles; they had five No. 1 songs, along with five other Top 10 hits and four more in the Top 20. Multiple entries meant that The Beatles were on the US Top 20 every week of 1964, except for an eight-week period in October and November. And while The Beatles were away, Manfred Mann (formerly The Mann Hugg Blues Band) topped the chart with 'Do Wah Diddy Diddy' and The Zombies made No. 2 with 'She's Not There'. We have already established the John Lee Hooker connection to The Zombies, but The Manfreds had their own blue umbilical chord. 'Do Wah Diddy Diddy' was written by Ellie Greenwich and Jeff Barry, two writers who worked out of 1650 Broadway in New York (not the Brill Building, as is often cited). You can't help believing that they might have taken some inspiration from Bo Diddley's 1956 single 'Diddy Wah Diddy', which he co-wrote with Willie Dixon. And Willie and Bo may themselves have heard, in the distant past a 1929 recording by Blind Blake entitled 'Diddie Wa Diddie'!

It was not just The Beatles who beat The Stones for chart honours in America during 1964. The Dave Clark Five (four Top 10 singles), Gerry & The Pacemakers (two Top 10 entries), and even Billy J Kramer (two top 10 songs) did better than The Stones. Bands like The Searchers, The Kinks, and The Animals, who topped the American charts with 'The House Of The Rising Sun' in late summer, also fared at least as well as The Stones.

Manfred Mann
Formerly The Mann Hugg Blues Band, topping the UK charts in 1964 with 'Do Wah Diddy Diddy'.

Barely The Blues

'Not Fade Away', the Stones' cover of the Buddy Holly B-side of The Crickets' 'Oh Boy', made No. 48 in the US chart. The track borrows Bo Diddley's trademark rhythm, exactly as Holly's version had done. The Stones' next two singles, 'Tell Me' and 'It's All Over Now', scraped into the Top 30 before 'Time Is On My Side' got to No. 6 in December 1964. Like 'Not Fade Away', 'Tell Me', a Jagger-Richards composition, and 'It's All Over Now' were much closer to the beat boom material of the other British bands than to R&B, but there is no mistaking the Blues-R&B pedigree that pervades all The Stones' early work. 'Not Fade Away' featured Brian's harmonica riffing incessantly in the background, while 'It's All Over Now', a cover of the Valentinos' song written by their lead singer Bobby Womack, was recorded at Chess Studios in Chicago – and the Chess sound is unmistakeable, making this an altogether classier record than many of the band's British recordings. 'Time Is On My Side' was a cover of an Irma Thomas song and featured Ian Stewart's gospel-sounding organ. What is strange is the fact that London Records passed on releasing the Stones' most overt blues record, 'Little Red Rooster', as a single in America, something that angered the band at the time.

The Stones version of Bobby Womack's 'It's All Over Now'

Beatlemania
One of a series of bubblegum cards. By 1965 Beatlemania was sweeping the US.

AMERICA REDISCOVERS THE BLUES

MUDDY WATERS FOLK SINGER
Released in 1964 and featuring an acoustic Muddy, accompanied by Buddy Guy, Willie Dixon, and Clifton Jones. Was this the first 'unplugged' album?

THE STONES' INITIAL success in America owed less to the Blues than to their membership of the British Invasion. But it was not long before their pedigree began to show, particularly on their album tracks. Who better to put The Stones' importance into perspective than Muddy Waters?

> *Before The Rolling Stones, people didn't know anything about me and didn't want to know anything. I was making records that were called 'race records'. I'll tell you what the old folks would have said to kids who'd bought my records. They'd have said 'What's that?' Take off that nigger music! Then The Rolling Stones came along, playing this music, and now the kids are buying my records and listening to them*

The Rolling Stones' recording sessions at Chess were like visits to a shrine. Meeting Chuck Berry ("Swing on, gentlemen" said Chuck, "You are sounding most well"), having Muddy ("that guitar player, Brian, weren't bad") help unload their gear and Willie Dixon trying to sell them a song, made a huge impact on the band. At the time of their first visit to 2120 S. Michigan Avenue, in June 1964, Mick and Keith were still 20 years old, Brian was 22, Charlie a year older, and Bill was 27 (although press hand-outs knocked four years off his age).

Muddy Waters

Less than a year before the Stones' visit, Muddy, Buddy Guy, Willie Dixon, and drummer Clifton James recorded what is arguably the first 'unplugged' album of the rock era. Released in April 1964 as *Muddy Waters Folk Singer*, the album boasted some brilliant performances that harked back to Muddy's days in the Delta and yet presented the songs in a contemporary setting. The album showed Chess and Muddy trying to come to grips with the changing times. Some critics have criticised both label and artist for bowing to blatant commercialism – critics can be so pompous at times. Muddy's performances of 'My Home Is In The Delta', 'Feel Like Going Home', and 'Good Morning Little School Girl' demonstrated downhome blues to some of those who had come to the Blues via the folk blues revival.

> *When I first recorded without any electric you had to sit down and just play for a house of people. They danced the two-step, waltz, Charleston, black bottom, and the slow dance that's always been. But if you are a blues singer you have to be right NOW in this business*
>
> MUDDY WATERS, TOURING BRTAIN IN AUTUMN 1964

In May 1965, The Stones gained some measure of revenge over London Records for their frustration about 'Little Red Rooster'. They were on their third trip to America, and on the cusp of cracking the No. 1 spot on the Hot 100 with 'Satisfaction', when they were invited to play the *Shindig* TV show on 20th May in Hollywood. Other guests on the show were Jackie de Shannon, Adam Wade, Sonny & Cher and, at the insistence of The Stones, Howlin' Wolf. Today it is difficult to comprehend the enormity of seeing Wolf on what was very much a 'white' TV show. This was just two years after Martin Luther King's "I had a dream" speech and still three years before his assassination.

> *The producer of* Shindig *was the expatriate Englishman, Jack Good. He constantly referred to Wolf, in his very proper accent, as Mr Howling Wolf. He sang 'How Many More Years', which certainly must have been a revelation to many people watching the show. While we were rehearsing for the show, Son House and his manager, Dick Waterman, came by the studio*
>
> Bill Wyman

Magic Man

Clapton, Page, and Beck were proof of the demand among young white males for guitar heroes – something the Blues had known about for a long time. The lineage from T-Bone Walker through BB King to younger men like Otis Rush took on a head of steam as the blues-rock field took shape in the second half of the 60s. One of the best and most original black guitar players to come out of Chicago was Samuel Maghett, better known as Magic Sam. Born in the Delta, he cut his first sides for the Chief label in 1960, but mainly earned his living from playing live. His debut album, recorded for Bob Koester's Delmark label in 1967, has been described as one of the truly essential Chicago blues albums of the 1960s. Sadly, Sam was never able to capitalise on his talent, as he died of a heart attack on 1st December, 1969; he was just 32 years old. Other guitarists, such as Albert King, Albert Collins, and Freddie King (no relation to any of the other blues guitar Kings), all became revered by white rock audiences who were keen to acknowledge their heroes' mentors.

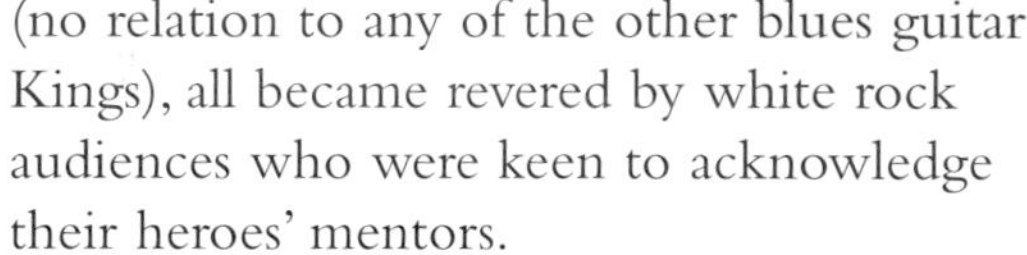

Magic Sam

Howlin' Wolf

> *Son was in California to play the UCLA Folk Festival. We talked our way in and came in through the back of the stage, walking across the stage. I knew Wolf because he had played in the Boston area and I had seen him in '64–'65, so I turned to Son and I said, 'Are you sure you're going to know him?'. He said, 'Oh man, I know him, a big old skinny bag of bones, big, skinny guy, big guy'. So I said, 'Well he may have changed a little'. So as we came across the stage and started down, Wolf was sitting alone on the aisle in a theatre seat. Wolf saw Son and recognised him and Wolf came out of that seat like an elephant coming out of a phone booth. He came up in sections and Son looked at him and says, 'Man, he has got his growth', because Wolf was about 260 lbs. Brian Jones was watching me and then came up and tapped me and said, 'Excuse me, who is the old man that Wolf thinks is so special? Wolf is in awe of that old man, who is the old man?' And so I said, 'That's Son House'. And he turned to me and said, 'Ah, the one that taught Robert Johnson'. There was a Rolls Royce on stage, Wolf and The Stones draped all over it. They sang 'I Can't Get No Satisfaction'*
>
> Dick Waterman

ALBERT KING

> *"One of the most important guitar players who ever lived"*
>
> WAYNE JACKSON OF THE MEMPHIS HORNS

FACT FILE

BORN: *25th April, 1924 Indianola (Sunflower Co), Mississippi*

DIED: *21st December, 1992*

INSTRUMENT: *Guitar, Drums*

FIRST RECORDED: *1953*

ACCOLADES: *Inducted into the Blues Hall of Fame, 1983*

INFLUENCES: *Blind Lemon Jefferson, T-Bone Walker, Lonnie Johnson*

INFLUENCED: *Jimi Hendrix, Eric Clapton, Stevie Ray Vaughan, Taj Mahal*

KING'S FATHER WAS an itinerant preacher and Albert (real name Albert Nelson) was one of thirteen children who were raised on a plantation. He sang at his local church in Areola and taught himself to play on a home-made guitar by the end of the 30s. In the late 40s he was working in Arkansas with the In The Groove Boys, besides holding down a day job, while from 1949–1951 he was in the Harmony Kings. He then moved to Indiana and by late 1951 was playing drums for Jimmy Reed.

In 1953 he recorded a single for the Parrott label, but it failed to create an impression, and King moved on to St Louis. He did not record again, or work full-time in music, until 1959, when he signed to the Bobbin label. He cut a number of sides for them and for the King label over the next three years, many of them produced by Ike Turner. These included 1962's 'Don't Throw Your Love On Me So Strong', which became his first hit making No. 14 on the R&B chart.

CLASSICAL BLUES
Albert King appears with the St Louis Symphony Orchestra, 1969.

In 1966 King signed to Stax Records in Memphis and began recording with Booker T and The MGs as his backing band. They scored five R&B hits together, including 'Born Under A Bad Sign' and 'Laundromat Blues'. In 1968 he played the opening night of the legendary San Francisco rock venue, the Fillmore East, along with Jimi Hendrix and John Mayall, while in 1969 he performed with the St Louis Symphony Orchestra.

King left Stax in 1974 just after enjoying his biggest hit, 'That's What The Blues Is All About'. Although the last of his 19 hits on the R&B chart came in 1979, he continued to tour until his death, from a heart attack, in 1992.

BORN UNDER A BAD SIGN
King's 1967 album Born Under A Bad Sign *included both the title track and 'The Hunter'. Written by Willie Dixon, 'The Hunter' was also covered by British band Free on their 1968 debut LP* Tons Of Sobs.

ESSENTIAL RECORDINGS

CLASSIC SONGS

'Born Under A Bad Sign' 1967
'The Hunter' 1967

CLASSIC ALBUMS

King of The Blues Guitar 1969 Atlantic

THE SOURCE

The Very Best Of Albert King 1999 Rhino Records

Chicago The Blues Today!

In early 1953 JOB issued a single which coupled Walter Horton's harmonica skills with the powerful singing and bottleneck playing of Johnny Shines. Shines was one of the last links to the Robert Johnson legacy, as he had travelled and played with Johnson as far afield as Canada, when he was barely out of his teens. After a spell in Memphis, Shines moved to Chicago in 1941 and began to work part-time at music. He cut some sides for OKeh in the mid-1940s, which were not released, and then in the early 1950s for Chess. Shines' material did not click with the record buyers, though there was no real rhyme or reason for that, because he cut some really good songs. In particular, 'Brutal Hearted Woman' deserved to do well.

Both Big Walter and Shines reached the attention of a broader market through Sam Charters. Having done such sterling work in pointing people in the direction of pre-war blues, setting in motion the resurgence of interest that spawned the folk blues movement, Charters turned his attention to urban blues. In fact, Charters has been somewhat scathing about the folk-blues purists who attempted to reshape the Blues in their own image. Their efforts to create a more downhome image for the music ignored what was happening in Chicago and other urban centres.

Charters, by his own admission, was finding it tough to make a living as a record producer and writer, so he made a deal with the owner of Vanguard Records (predominantly a folk label) to cut a series of albums by contemporary Chicago musicians in the winter of 1965. The result was a set of three LPs, titled *Chicago The Blues Today!* (their exclamation mark), which included many of the city's premier musicians – among them Otis Spann, Junior Wells, James Cotton, Homesick James, JB Hutto, Buddy Guy, Willie Dixon, Johnny Young, and a young white harp player, Charlie Musselwhite.

These LPs demonstrated the power of the music that was still being heard in the city's clubs, night after night, and proved influential to a number of young rock artists. There is a famous photograph of Jimi Hendrix clutching a copy of the album. Billy Gibbons of ZZ Top called it "one of those promising landmarks"; it was "a very important slice of history", according to Eric Clapton; and Bonnie Raitt said "I learned blues piano from Otis Spann's great cuts".

Without the growing interest in the Blues amongst a broader slice of the American audience, albums like *Chicago The Blues Today!* might never have been made. The record companies were astute enough to see that there was financial potential in the blues market; but more often than not in the late 1960s, it was for blues with a white face.

Chicago The Blues Today!

Johnny Shines

ALBERT COLLINS

FACT FILE

BORN: *3rd October, 1932 Leona (Leon County), Texas*

DIED: *24th November, 1993, Las Vegas*

INSTRUMENT: *Guitar*

FIRST RECORDED: *1958*

ACCOLADES: *Inducted into the Blues Hall of Fame, 1986*

INFLUENCES: *BB King, Aaron 'T-Bone' Walker, Clarence 'Gatemouth' Brown, Wes Montgomery*

INFLUENCED: *Robert Cray*

COLLINS, WHO WAS A FIRST COUSIN of Lightnin' Hopkins, was born on a farm. When he was seven years old, he moved the 125 miles to Houston's Third Ward, where he first learned to play piano and later guitar. He formed his first band in the mid-40s, and by 1948 they had evolved into The Rhythm Rockers, who were playing local clubs. From 1951–54 he toured the South with the Piney Brown Orchestra. Returning to Houston, he was forced to take a full-time job, while playing part-time with musicians such as Clarence 'Gatemouth' Brown.

In 1958, his recording debut for Houston's Kangaroo Records, 'Freeze', won him a local reputation and sold quite well. For the next few years he worked and recorded locally on the Great Scott and Hall labels. Collins' reputation was not established on a national scale until 1968, when he met Bob Hite of Canned Heat. Hite helped him secure a record deal with Canned Heat's label, Imperial Records in Los Angeles, prompting Collins to move to California.

He recorded three albums of blues-soul crossovers for Imperial in the late 60s and early 70s, before signing to Tumbleweed Records in 1971. An otherwise unsuccessful album did yield his only R&B chart hit, 'Get Your Business Straight', which reached No. 46 in March 1972. A switch to Alligator Records in 1977 put him back on the blues map. The album *Ice Pickin'* is a stunning display of his unrestrained guitar style. More Alligator albums followed, but they failed to match the power of his debut.

Collins' growing reputation was enhanced when he appeared at *Live Aid* in 1985 with George Thorogood.

> *'I tried to have my own sound. The minor tuning helped. So did the capo, which I started using after I met up with Gatemouth (Brown)'*
>
> ALBERT COLLINS

After two more Alligator albums, including the Grammy Award-winning *Showdown*, Collins switched to Point Blank Records in the early 90s. Shortly after his 1991 debut,

SHOWDOWN!
Albert Collins' 1983 album with Robert Cray and Johnny Copeland.

Iceman, he was diagnosed with liver cancer. It was a cruel blow, as Collins had been looking forward to reaping the financial rewards he deserved as an established elder statesman of the Blues, and he had recorded with Jack Bruce, David Bowie, and Gary Moore. He died in his adopted hometown of Las Vegas in 1993.

ESSENTIAL RECORDINGS

CLASSIC SONGS

'Freeze' 1958
'Don't Lose Your Cool, Man' 1962

CLASSIC ALBUMS

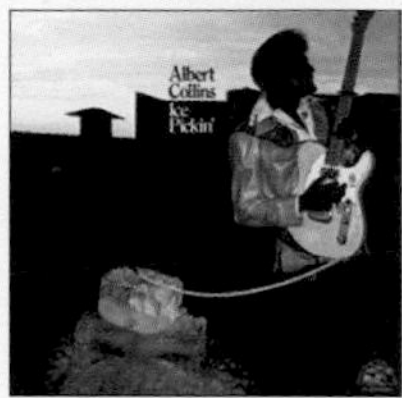

Ice Pickin' 1978

THE SOURCE

The Complete Imperial Recordings EMI

West Coast Psychedelic Blues

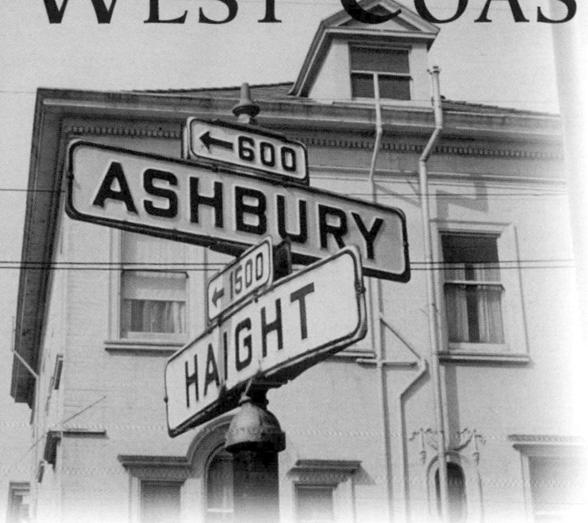

It has been said that the original soundtrack to Haight Ashbury, the epicentre of San Francisco's peaceful hippie revolution, was the Beatles' album *Rubber Soul*, released in December 1965. Of course, the Beatles inspired young musicians throughout America. But out in California, and particularly in San Francisco, musicians added a good dollop of the Blues to the Beatles' template, and emerged with 'psychedelic blues' and 'electric folk rock' – the ingredients of what became known as the 'West Coast sound'. The sound did not simply grow out of the city, however. It was greatly influenced by the young itinerants who made their way to this hippie Mecca, not knowing quite what they would find when they got there, but knowing it was "gonna be great".

Sons Arise

Los Angeles was another magnet for the young hopefuls, especially because of its heavy concentration of record labels, and its vibrant live scene. In 1964 a young man calling himself Taj Mahal left Massachusetts. Along with his friend, a 12-string guitar-playing disciple of Reverend Gary Davis, called Jesse Lee Kincaid, they headed to LA in search of Kincaid's friend Ry Cooder. Cooder had studied guitar with Jesse Lee's uncle and Jesse and Taj reckoned he would be ideal material for forming a band. They duly put together the Rising Sons and by mid-1965 they were signed to Columbia and put in the studio with the label's staff producer, Terry Melcher (Doris Day's son). Melcher's credentials were impeccable, as he had produced the Byrds' 1965 American No. 1, 'Mr Tambourine Man'. However, as Melcher later remarked, "the thing about The Byrds was, they were all going in the same direction". The Rising Sons were altogether different, torn between pop and traditional blues, and the mix really didn't work. For all that, they cut some remarkable sides, which were well ahead of their time, including Robert Johnson's 'Last Fair Deal Gone Down' (undoubtedly the first group to cover the song), 'Dust My Broom', and Charley Patton's 'By and By (Poor Me)'.

The Grateful Dead
The ultimate hippie band.

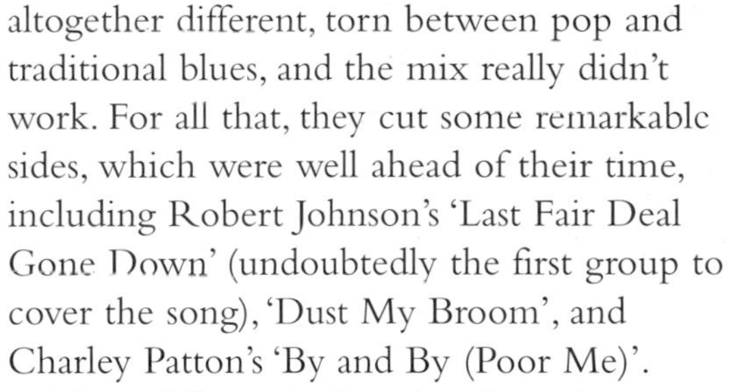

Meanwhile up in San Francisco the Warlocks, who mutated out of various Jerry Garcia-led jug bands, were in the throes of becoming the Grateful Dead. In November 1965, the Dead and Jefferson Airplane played the opening night of Bill Graham's Fillmore East in San Francisco. Five months later the Avalon Ballroom opened with a show starring the Great Society (featuring future Jefferson Airplane vocalist Grace Slick) and the Blues Project.

Taj Mahal at Jann Wenner's house, San Francisco, 1968

> *Basically we got our first gigs because we were a blues-oriented, Rolling Stones type band*
>
> Jerry Garcia

BE SURE TO PUT SOME BLUES ON YOUR ALBUM

DAN HICKS

'A band that I really like who emerged from this period were Dan Hicks and His Hot Licks. Dan was the original drummer with the Charlatans and formed the Hot licks in 1968. The Rhythm Kings and I have covered their 'Walkin' One And Only' and 'Where There's Money''

BILL WYMAN

DURING THIS PERIOD on the West Coast, the Blues were not confined to the margins, as though they were of interest to just blacks or a small segment of the white audience. Amongst the Black Blues guitar players who appeared regularly in San Francisco was Magic Sam. Others often appeared at the Fillmore or the Family Dog shows at the Avalon as support acts to local or visiting bands. Albert King supported Jimi Hendrix, while Albert Collins supported Country Joe and The Fish. It was not just the guitar players: Howlin' Wolf, Muddy Waters, Lightning Hopkins, Little Walter, James Cotton, Big Joe Williams, and John Lee Hooker all played shows featuring the new breed of rock bands. Among the bands with whom they shared the bill were The Doors, Buffalo Springfield, Big Brother & the Holding Company, The Grateful Dead, Quicksilver Messenger Service, and Dan Hicks & His Hot Licks. The Blues was a major influence on the West Coast bands.

COUNTRY JOE AND THE FISH released 'I Feel Like I'm Fixin' To Die Rag' (inspired by Bukka White) in October 1965.

CAPTAIN BEEFHEART's first single in 1966 was 'Diddy Wah Diddy'.

JEFFERSON AIRPLANE included 'Chauffeur Blues' (by Memphis Minnie) on their September 1966 debut album.

THE DOORS included 'Back Door Man' on their March 1967 debut album.

THE CHARLATANS recorded 'The Blues Ain't Nothin' in 1967 for their eponymous debut album.

MOBY GRAPE issued five singles on the same day in June 1967, including 'Mr Blues'.

BIG BROTHER AND THE HOLDING COMPANY included 'Easy Rider' (by Lead Belly) on their November 1967 debut album.

GRATEFUL DEAD included 'Sitting On Top Of The World' and Gus Cannon's 'Viola Lee Blues' on their December 1967 debut album.

Country Joe and The Fish

CHOCOLATE WATCH BAND covered 'Milk Cow Blues' on their 1967 debut album *No Way Out*.

STEPPENWOLF originally formed in Canada as Sparrow, a blues band, in 1966. They relocated to Los Angeles in 1967, changed their name, and cut 'Hoochie Coochie Man' on their May 1968 debut album.

ELECTRIC FLAG were formed in April 1967 by Mike Bloomfield. 'Killing Floor' was included on their July 1968 debut.

CANNED HEAT issued their self-titled debut album in August 1967. It was a reworking of the Delta's finest moments and included 'Rollin' and Tumblin', Henry Thomas's 'Bullfrog Blues', 'Dust My Broom', and Tommy Johnson's 'Big Road Blues'.

STEVE MILLER BAND featured 'Key To The Highway' on their September 1968 debut album.

THE SANTANA BLUES BAND

In 1966, The Santana Blues Band was formed by guitarist Carlos Santana in San Francisco. Among the other bands inspired by the Blues were: Billy Moses Blues Bag, Littlejohn Blues Band, Liquid Blues Band, Rhythm Method Blues Band, Smokestack Lightning, and the T & A Blues Band

The Blues Project – Folk Becomes Rock

The Blues Project started in early 1965, as refugees from various bands on the New York folk scene came together. Guitarist Danny Kalb had been with Dave Van Ronk's Ragtime Jug Stompers and Steve Katz with Jim Kweskin's Even Dozen Jug Band. In fact Kalb recorded Muddy's 'I'm Troubled' (along with future Lovin' Spoonful member John Sebastian) in 1964 for an Elektra album called *The Blues Project*. Others on the album included Dave Ray (backed on one track by Bob Dylan playing piano under a false name), John Koerner, and Dave Van Ronk. Kalb had been to Britain in the summer of 1964, and he had clearly come under the influence of the more rock-orientated blues scene happening across the Atlantic.

The Blues Project's other musical mainstay was Al Kooper, who joined in October 1965, fresh from his Dylan sessions. Their repertoire at the time of their Avalon show included songs such as Willie Dixon's 'Back Door Man', Mose Allison's 'Parchman Farm', Jimmy Reed's 'Bright Lights Big City', and Bo Diddley's 'Who Do You Love' (which would become a mainstay of the San Francisco rock scene). The band never achieved sales to match either their talent or their live shows, but their inspiration outlived them. Kooper left in 1967 to form Blood Sweat and Tears, and brass-rock was born!

Boogie Blues

Around the same time as The Grateful Dead were playing their jug band music in San Francisco, further south in Los Angeles 'Blind' Al Wilson (vocals & guitar) and Bob 'The Bear' Hite (vocals & harmonica) were forming their own jug band. They became Canned Heat (taking their name from a pre-war Tommy Johnson blues song) in 1966, adding guitarist Henry Vestine, Larry Taylor on bass, and drummer Frank Cook. They signed to Liberty Records after appearing at the Monterey Pop Festival in June 1967. The follow-up to their debut album, which had been released in late 1967, appeared in February 1968. Among the tracks on *Boogie With Canned Heat* was 'On The Road Again', which reached No. 16 in the UK and No. 8 in America, establishing their reputation as the Boogie Blues band.

More hits followed including 'Going Up The Country' (US No. 11/UK No. 19) and 'Let's Work Together' (US No. 26/UK No. 2), while the band endured some personnel changes and played the Woodstock Festival in 1969. Wilson died in September 1970 from a

Bob 'The Bear' Hite
Vocalist and harmonica player for Canned Heat, the band he named after a pre-war Tommy Johnson song.

> *'On 17 November 1968 we did an all-night recording session on the 8-track at Olympic Studios in Barnes, London. We cut 'You Can't Always Get What You Want' with Al Kooper playing organ. It came out the following year, on the B-side of 'Honky Tonk Women', which made No. 1 in both Britain and America'*
>
> Bill Wyman

drug overdose but the band stayed together, recording the album *Hooker'n'Heat* with John Lee Hooker in 1971.

Bloomfield and Butterfield's Blues

Mike Bloomfield was twenty-one when he backed Dylan at Newport. He grew up in Chicago, taking inspiration from Muddy Waters and the other blues greats in the city. Prior to his session with Dylan, he had already joined Paul Butterfield's Blues band, cutting an album with them in December 1964.

Butterfield was another Chicago native whose harmonica playing was so exceptional that he regularly sat in with black bands on the city's Southside. He played with everyone from Otis Rush to Howlin' Wolf and Muddy Waters. In 1963, Butterfield put a band together to play in a white club on the city's northside. The band included Jerome Arnold and Sam Lay, who played with Howlin' Wolf (and would also back Dylan at Newport), along with Elvin Bishop on guitar. This line-up secured a deal with Elektra and brought in Mark Naftalin to play keyboards. Their debut album, recorded in early 1965, is one of the best white blues albums ever to come out of America. Their covers of 'Blues With A Feeling' (Little Walter) and 'I Got My Mojo Working' sit proudly alongside the originals, and the album introduced many young white listeners to the Blues.

The band issued a follow-up in 1966 (*East West*), before Bloomfield left to form the Electric Flag with Nick Gravenites (who had composed 'Born In Chicago', the opening track on Butterfield's debut). Butterfield continued to front his own band and recorded with John Mayall and Peter Green in England. In 1969 Butterfield and Bloomfield were reunited on Muddy Waters' album *Fathers And Sons*. This project was a 'super session', a typical concept of the era, which brought together musicians such as Otis Spann, Buddy Miles (from the Electric Flag, and later to play with Jimi Hendrix), and Duck Dunn (from Booker T & the MGs).

Bloomfield's stay with the Electric Flag lasted just one album; he quit and teamed up with Al Kooper to record *Super Session*. They followed that with the *Live Adventures of Mike Bloomfield And Al Kooper*, recorded in San Francisco in September 1968. The live album featured originals and rock covers, as well as Arthur Crudup's 'That's All Right', Sonny Boy Williamson's 'No More Lonely Nights', and Albert King's 'Don't Throw Your Love on Me So Strong'.

Mike Bloomfield
His quicksilver guitar playing was lost to us when Bloomfield died from an overdose at 38.

Pepper's Lounge
Charlie Musselwhite with Mike Bloomfield and Paul Butterfield at Pepper's Lounge watching Otis Rush, December 1963.

Otis Rush

FACT FILE

Born: *29th April, 1934 Philadelphia (Neshoba County), Mississippi*

Instrument: *Guitar*

First Recorded: *1956*

Accolades: *Inducted into the Blues Hall of Fame, 1984*

Influences: *Muddy Waters, Kenny Burrel, T-Bone Walker, BB King*

Influenced: *Eric Clapton, Peter Green, Mick Taylor, Jeff Beck, Luther Allison*

Otis Rush was one of seven children born to a farming family in East Mississippi. He learned to play the guitar when he was eight years old by watching his older brothers, although being left-handed he played it upside down. Rush hated farming, so he moved to Chicago in 1948, working in the steel mills and stockyards as well as playing an occasional gig. In 1953, he formed his own group, calling himself Little Otis, and was initially recognised for his talent as a singer.

Rush continued to work a 'day job' until 1955, when Willie Dixon spotted him and took him to the Cobra label, where he was working as an A&R man. Dixon worked with Rush, polishing his style, and in the summer of 1956 they cut 'I Can't Quit You Baby', with Walter Horton on harmonica. It received strong local airplay and eventually made No. 6 on the national R&B chart. He then recorded some sides with Ike Turner's band but could not repeat his chart success. But his Cobra records have lost none of their power. They are full of dark imagery, portraying Rush as an angry young man.

By January 1960 Rush was at Chess, where he cut the excellent 'So Many Roads, So Many Trains'. Chess had passed on the chance to record Rush back in '56, because they thought he sounded too similar to Muddy Waters, and when he did finally record for the label, they never really put their promotional muscle behind him.

As the 60s progressed, Rush recorded for several labels. Mike Bloomfield produced one album which included Duane Allman and Mark Naftalin as sidemen. The 70s were lean times commercially for Rush, despite recording albums in a variety of countries, often with less than skilful accompanists. The early 80s proved to be even tougher, and it was not until the mid-90s that Rush was able to re-establish his reputation.

Covered
In 1969 Led Zeppelin covered Otis Rush's 'I Can't Quit You Baby' on their debut album Led Zeppelin I.

Essential Recordings

Classic Songs

'I Can't Quit You Baby' 1956
'Double Trouble' 1958
'So Many Roads, So Many Trains' 1960

Classic Albums

Right Place, Wrong Time

The Source

Classic Cobra Recordings 1956–1958
Uni/Fuel

"If you want to hear how Otis Rush influenced Eric Clapton just listen to them sing. Eric's vocal styling is pure Otis"
Bill Wyman

JIMI HENDRIX
Jimi listens to some Dylan and some Lenny Bruce in the flat he rented from Ringo Starr in London.

HEY JIMI

WHAT WAS HAPPENING out on the West Coast created opportunities for others, but at the same time it helped hasten the decline of the Greenwich Village folk scene. Unaware of exactly what was happening in the Village, a 23-year-old guitarist and former paratrooper blew into New York City in early 1966. Jimmy Hendrix was already a veteran of the Isley Brothers, Little Richard's backing band, and King Curtis's band when he arrived in the city. He met John Hammond Jr, who was able to get Hendrix, and the band he helped put together, some work at the Café Au Go Go. It was in New York that the ex-Animal-turned-manager, Chas Chandler, first saw Jimmy play and offered to take him to England to record (legend has it that Jimmy became Jimi on the plane). On 21st September, 1966, Chandler and Jimi arrived in London, and within three months 'Hey Joe' was at No. 6 on the UK chart.

Hendrix played many extended blues jams in his live shows; songs like 'Red House' or 'California Night' demonstrate Jimi's commitment to the Blues. In his early shows, including those in New York, he played Robert Johnson as well as Jimmy Reed. Throughout his work you can hear the influences of Muddy, BB King and Chuck Berry, and in turn Jimi's influence on Buddy Guy in particular. By the time of his astonishing debut album, *Are You Experienced*, Jimi Hendrix had become the new yardstick for guitar virtuosity. If Eric Clapton is God, as graffiti in the 1960s often claimed, where does that put James Marshall Hendrix?

> *On 2nd July, 1966, The Stones played a gig at Forest Hills Tennis Stadium in Queens, New York. At the end of the show there was considerable pandemonium as the fans broke through the police cordon while we played our finale, 'Satisfaction'. After the house lights went up we made a quick exit via helicopter, which flew us back into New York. We went to a club to see a guitarist that John Hammond was raving about; Jimi Hendrix, who was calling himself Jimmy James at this point in his career. This must have been a few weeks before Chas Chandler signed him, as it was actually Keith Richards' girlfriend, Linda Keith, who told Chas to check Jimi out*
>
> BILL WYMAN

THE BLUES ARE BACK IN TOWN

CREAM WERE AT THE heart of the resurgence of the Blues in Britain around the end of 1966. It took a little while for the record companies to catch up, but once they did there was another shift in what young British white males, in particular, were listening to.

SEPTEMBER 1966 Savoy Brown Blues Band's debut single, 'I Tried'/'I Can't Quit You Baby', appears on the Purdah label (part of Blue Horizon). The band's debut album comes out in December 1967, featuring 'Rock Me Baby' and 'Shake 'Em Down'.

DECEMBER 1966 Cream's album *Fresh Cream* makes No. 6 on the UK album chart and No. 39 in the US (in August 1968). It includes 'Spoonful', 'Rollin' and Tumblin' and 'I'm So Glad'

OCTOBER 1967 Ten Years After, and their flamboyant speedster guitarist Alvin Lee, release their eponymous debut album featuring 'Spoonful'. The album also features Al Kooper's 'I Can't Keep From Crying Sometimes' from a 1966 *Blues Project* album.

NOVEMBER 1967 Fleetwood Mac's Elmore James cover 'I Believe My Time Ain't Long' comes out on Blue Horizon.

DECEMBER 1967 Chicken Shack's first Blue Horizon single is released. Their debut album follows in June 1968, and includes Buddy Guy's 'First Time I Met The Blues'.

APRIL 1968 Taste, an Irish band featuring the brilliant former showband guitarist Rory Gallagher, release their debut single, 'Born On The Wrong Side Of Time'. A year later their debut album includes 'Catfish'.

JULY 1968 The Jeff Beck Group with Rod Stewart on vocals release their album called *Truth*, which includes 'You Shook Me'.

LED ZEPPELIN
John Paul Jones, Robert Plant, John Bonham and Jimmy Page took their name from a glib remark made by The Who's Keith Moon and John Entwistle that the group would go down like a lead Zeppelin.

SEPTEMBER 1968 Love Sculpture's second single is Willie Dixon's 'Wang Dang Doodle'; three months later their debut album *Blues Helping* is released.

NOVEMBER 1968 The Groundhogs, a band based around guitarist Tony (TS) McPhee, release their debut album, featuring original Blues songs, along with covers that include Robert Johnson's 'Walkin' Blues'.

NOVEMBER 1968 Free release their debut album, *Tons of Sobs*, covering 'Goin' Down Slow'.

SEPTEMBER 1969 The Sheffield-based Climax Chicago Blues Band release their debut single, 'Like Uncle Charlie'.

BLODWYN'S BLUES
Other bands who were part of this revitalised blues boom included Blodwyn Pig, John Dummer's Blues Band, and the Keef Hartley Band (led by a former drummer with Mayall's Bluesbreakers)

'On 22nd June, 1968, I was at Olympic Studios in London when Jimmy Page popped in for a chat. He said he had been working on some new songs and asked me to have a listen. They were very powerful, completely different in style from what he had been doing with The Yardbirds. Some of these tracks formed the basis for his new band's first album when it came out in March 1969. Led Zeppelin made their debut in October 1968 at Surrey University and their album Led Zeppelin *featured 'You Shook Me' (Willie Dixon & JB Lenoir), 'I Can't Quit You Baby' (written by Willie Dixon and performed by Otis Rush), and self-composed blues-based songs'*

BILL WYMAN

Have You Seen A Blues Band?

The Rolling Stones At Hyde Park
On 5th July, 1969, two days after the untimely death of Brian Jones, The Stones played a free concert in London's Hyde Park.

Two days after Jimi Hendrix arrived in London, The Stones played the opening night of a 12-night UK tour (23rd September, 1966). Supporting them were The Yardbirds featuring Jeff Beck and Jimmy Page, Jimmy Thomas, and Bobby John, along with Ike & Tina Turner and his Kings of Rhythm Band. The compere on what was to be the last British tour by the Stones during the 60s was Long John Baldry.

The opening night of the tour was recorded by Glyn Johns for release as a US-only album. It was not a classic, as the sound quality left a lot to be desired, but it did prove that The Stones were no longer a blues band, as their show consisted simply of their hit singles (although a studio version of Otis Redding's 'I've Been Loving You Too Long' did appear on the album). It was left to others to further the cause of the Blues. It also caused some to question the future of The Stones. Just two weeks after the end of the tour, the *New Musical Express* printed a reader's letter: "Own up Stones, your days at the top are now well and truly numbered". Could this possibly be true?

On the same day in 1966 that the letter was written, Cream's 'Wrapping Paper' entered the UK singles chart. It was Cream, more than any other band, who heralded a change in the group scene in Britain, and signalled a new blues boom. Would the Stones and other artists be able to respond?

The Soul of the Rolling Stones

On 3rd July, 1969, the man whom *Rolling Stone* magazine called the soul of The Rolling Stones was found dead at his home in Sussex. Keith Richards once said to Brian, "You'll never make 30, man", to which Brian replied, "I know". Brian was just 26 when he died following a swim in his pool, after he had been drinking and taking drugs.

The day after Brian's death, 'Honky Tonk Women', one of The Stones' finest singles, was released (their 15th UK single and 20th in America). Brian had left The Stones before he died, as Mick and Keith in particular could no longer put up with his unreliability. His replacement was twenty-one-year-old

Mick Taylor who, having been with John Mayall, had impeccable credentials. Mick joined the band while they were recording at Olympic Studios on June 1 1969; and it was a baptism by fire,. The first song he played with them was 'Honky Tonk Women'.

Two days after Brian's death, The Rolling Stones gave a free concert in London's Hyde Park. The concert had been planned for weeks and there was some question about whether it should go ahead in the wake of the tragedy. The band wanted to pay tribute to Brian and Mick Jagger decided he would read some lines by Percy Bysshe Shelley from his poem 'Adonais' before the opening number.

The Woodstock Music and Art Fair

> *Life, like a dome of many-coloured glass,*
> *Stains the white radiance of eternity,*
> *Until death tramples it to fragments – Die,*
> *If thou wouldst be that which thou dost seek!*

As Mick finished his recitation, 3,500 butterflies were released from the stage and the Stones blasted into Johnny Winter's 'I'm Yours, She's Mine'. But according to Bill, it was not one of their best concerts: "It was our first concert for 14 months, we were dragging, we were off form. Perhaps the sheer weight of the occasion got to us". The concert drew a crowd of between 250,000 and 500,000, and later many more watched on TV. The set featured many classic Stones songs including 'Jumpin' Jack Flash', 'Sympathy For The Devil', 'Satisfaction', and Robert Johnson's 'Love in Vain'. Few watching had any idea that 'Love in Vain' had first been recorded on a summer's Sunday in Dallas, Texas, thirty-two years earlier.

Maybe it's The Time of Man?

Blind Faith, a group made up of Steve Winwood (ex-Spencer Davis Group and Traffic), Rik Grech (ex-Family), Eric Clapton, and Ginger Baker from Cream, played their only ever UK show in Hyde Park a month before The Stones. Giant open-air events were now dominating the rock calendar. In America the 16th Newport Jazz Festival in July 1969 featured John Mayall, Ten Years After, Led Zeppelin, Johnny Winter, and BB King. In August the three-day Woodstock Music and Art Fair took place, and Canned Heat, Jimi Hendrix, The Who, Ten Years After, The Grateful Dead, and Country Joe & the Fish were among the many acts who appeared. But apart from Hendrix, Richie Havens was the only black performer with any real blues credentials at the festival. This was a taste of what was to come in the 1970s, as the Blues were about to be marginalized by the Woodstock generation. Rock was the thing, and its roots were becoming less well-defined. Those who worshipped The Stones and the other monster rock acts paid little heed to their heroes' influences. The Blues were about to enter the doldrums.

Blind Faith

Blind Faith's self-titled album, re-released in 2001 with a second CD of bonus tracks, includes Sam Myers' blues shouter 'Sleeping In The Ground'.

> *Brian was a pioneer, he was way ahead of his time, in his love of Elmore James, as well as being the first man to play bottleneck guitar in Britain. He was always learning new instruments, which he did very quickly. He also was the first to spot new trends, introducing the rest of the Stones to what we might have missed otherwise. For all his weaknesses, his hang-ups, his bad behaviour, and his impertinence, he was pivotal to the Rolling Stones. He helped shaped us and I think he is entitled to a free pardon. As Alexis Korner said, "I hope that people give him a better deal in death than they did in life"*
>
> Bill Wyman

13

Long Live The Blues & Rock'n'Roll Too

Lost in the Seventies

"To me the blues are just a feeling"

Venessia Young, 16-year-old graduate of Clarksdale's Delta Blues Education Programme

The 1970s was a period of divergent musical styles, which spawned prog rock, glam rock, country rock, Southern boogie rock, arena rock, disco, soul, singer-songwriters, the supergroups, heavy metal, soft rock, pop, and punk… to name just a few!

The 1970s were also predominantly a bad time for the Blues. Was it a case of art reflecting fashion or did fashion mirror art? Whatever the case, the (black) Blues left the main stage in the early 70s. The style had already been overtaken as the dominant form of black music by soul during the 1960s. The rise of Motown and Atlantic Records, along with Stax and other smaller labels, captured the imagination of both urban and rural blacks, and it also did a pretty good job of infiltrating the white community. Muddy, the Wolf, and Hooker were no longer the taste of the nation. Back then, pop stars were meant to be young; the idea of a 55-year-old blues (or rock) god was anathema to the majority of young people in America, as well as in Europe.

YES

Their prog rock albums seemed as far away from the Blues as you could get.

Tales from the Prog Rock Ocean

When Yes supported Cream at their farewell concert in 1968, it marked an important step for the music that would become known as progressive (or prog) rock. To many, this style, which took hold of the rock world in the 1970s, was about as far away from the Blues as you could get. Yes issued double albums that featured songs which lasted for the whole side of an LP; they opened their live shows with extracts from Stravinsky's 'Firebird Suite'; and throughout it all, took themselves awfully seriously. If the Blues was originally music to dance to, prog rock was music to listen to in the confines of your own home, probably while wearing very expensive headphones. But if you scratched a prog rock legend, there was usually a bluesman lurking not too far below the surface…

In 1968, Yes vocalist Jon Anderson, then calling himself Hans Christian, was a struggling solo artist for Parlophone, and released a single entitled 'The Autobiography of a Mississippi Hobo'. Yes's drummer, Bill Bruford, previously played with the Savoy Brown Blues Band. Carl

Palmer's first band was The King Bees, from which he graduated to Chris Farlowe's Thunderbirds. Pink Floyd's connection to the Blues through their name has been well documented, but they also cut 'I'm A King Bee' as an acetate in 1965, and recorded 'Jugband Blues' on their second album in June 1968. The list is potentially endless, but the point is that even this curiously British musical style had its roots firmly in the Mississippi Delta.

PINK FLOYD
Roger Waters, Rick Wright, Nick Mason, and Syd Barrett.

As its name suggests, however, the practitioners of prog rock saw themselves as progressing; and that was very much the watchword of the 1970s. The Blues, despite being very popular in some quarters, was seen by most people in that decade as a somewhat arcane, even predictable musical form.

NEVER TOO OLD FOR THE BLUES

In 1969 Muddy Waters recorded *Fathers And Sons* with white, blues-inspired musicians such as Paul Butterfield, Mike Bloomfield, and Donald 'Duck' Dunn. It proved to be a role model for others from his generation. The album, which was a qualified success, set an example for others from his generation to follow. Many of his contemporaries jumped at the idea of using young white rock players as a way to revive their own careers. Two years later, 56-year-old Muddy Waters made an album in London with Rory Gallagher, Georgie Fame, Stevie Winwood, and Mitch Mitchell, but apart from Rory's contribution the album was sadly lacking in any originality. 51-year-old John Lee Hooker recorded with Canned Heat in 1971. And the year before, in May 1970, 59-year-old Howlin' Wolf went to London.

THE LONDON HOWLIN' WOLF SESSIONS

Wolf came to London in the midst of a European tour. Playing with him on 4th May was his long-time guitarist, Hubert Sumlin, along with Ringo Starr on drums, Klaus Voormann on bass, and Stevie Winwood on piano and organ.

This line-up managed to record just one song, 'I Ain't Superstitious', before it became clear that the rhythm section were not sufficiently steeped in the Blues for Wolf's satisfaction. The next day Bill Wyman and Charlie Watts were drafted in, along with Eric Clapton and Ian Stewart, to provide a more authentic feel.

MUDDY WATERS
Muddy's Fathers And Sons *album became the model for others of his generation.*

"The first time I had ever met the Wolf was at the Shindig *TV show. Six years later at Olympic Studios in London we recorded* The London Sessions. *By then he was not a well man, but he still had the sense of presence that Sam Phillips talked about. Although most of us were playing together for the first time we all knew and loved his songs. Somehow we struggled to create the right dynamics and Wolf was on hand to keep us right. I am proud to have worked with Wolf, and thankful of getting the opportunity to work with THE man. I kept in contact with him over the last years of his life, doing what little I could to acknowledge my debt to a man who really was a LEGEND"*

BILL WYMAN

BB King

FACT FILE

Born: *16th September, 1925 Indianola, Mississippi*

Instrument: *Guitar*

First Recorded: *1949*

Accolades: *Inducted into the Blues Hall of Fame, 1980*

Influences: *Robert Johnson, Blind Lemon Jefferson, T-Bone Walker, Django Reinhardt, Sonny Boy Williamson*

Influenced: *Eric Clapton, Otis Rush, Albert Collins, Johnny Winter*

Riley B King may have come from the plantation, but it was not long before the Beale Street Blues Boy, as he became known, set out to change all that. The sharecropper's son first went to Memphis in 1946 and stayed with his cousin Bukka White, but he soon returned to Indianola to work as a tractor driver.

'My salary, which was the basic salary for us tractor drivers, twenty two dollars and a half a week, was a lot of money compared to the other people that was working there'

BB King

Inspired by Sonny Boy Williamson's radio show, young Riley moved back to Memphis in 1948 and got a job at WDIA. His popularity in the city earned him the chance to record for the Bullet label in 1949. His first sides were not too successful, but then Sam Phillips took BB into his Memphis Recording Services studio in September 1950. The Bihari brothers, who ran RPM Records, were visiting Memphis in search of talent, and they signed BB to their label, and agreed to release the sides that he had cut with Phillips. These records failed to sell, so Joe Bihari went to Memphis and recorded BB himself in a room at the YMCA on 8th January, 1951. On a subsequent visit to Memphis, Bihari recorded BB's version of Lowell Fulson's 'Three O'Clock Blues'. It entered the R&B chart on December 29, 1951 and eventually spent 5 weeks at No. 1 in early 1952. King was maybe not quite an overnight sensation, but this was the start of the most successful and enduring career in the modern history of the Blues.

Throughout his time with RPM, King churned out hit after hit, topping the R&B chart three more times, until he left the label for Kent in late 1958. His sojourn at Kent lasted until the late 1960s, and while he never again topped the R&B charts, he continued to rack up many hits. His sweet, gospel-tinged voice, coupled with his brilliant single-string guitar picking, proved to be an

'In 1969 BB toured America with The Stones, which for many would have been the first time they had seen one of the all-time greats in the flesh. We used to go on the side of the stage and watch BB play. He had a 12-piece band and they were brilliant musicians. The thing that always stunned me about his playing was the way he would hammer it out and then just go down to a whisper. I absolutely adored that. There was just silence in the place, and you could hear a pin drop. He would suddenly start to build, and it would build and it would build to a big climax. That's what I liked about his playing, the dimensions of his music'

Bill Wyman

irresistible combination. It made King one of THE all-time most successful artists on the R&B charts.

By the late 1960s BB, like his fellow blues guitar players, was discovered by the young white rock fraternity, which undoubtedly gave his career a boost. In 1970 'The Thrill is Gone' made No. 3 on the R&B chart, and it also crossed over to the Hot 100 and became his biggest pop hit, reaching No. 15. He visited Europe on the first of many visits in 1969, and was readily accepted by audiences who were already well aware of his influence on Eric Clapton and Peter Green. King's *Live At The Regal* album, recorded in 1964, had long been held in high esteem on both sides of the Atlantic, by musicians and fans alike.

> *Well BB was like a hero. You listen to the way that band swings on* Live At The Regal, *it's just like a steam roller*
>
> MICK FLEETWOOD

Much of BB's success can be attributed to his live shows. He has always been one of the hardest working live performers in any field of music, playing 250 to 300 dates a year, even in lean years. He also had a knack for keeping his bands together – an indication of his skill as a bandleader, and probably reflecting his gracious nature as a boss.

> *The guys are not only great musicians, they're loyal to me, I'm loyal to them, and we get together and have a good time. Everybody's been with me a long time. My late drummer, Sonny Freeman, was with me around 18 years and now my senior trumpeter has been with me 21 years and everybody, except one, has been with me more than 10 years*
>
> BB KING

> *Mick Jagger and Keith Richard tried to form a band in Dartford in 1962, before The Stones, and did some demos. They called themselves Boy Blue and The Blue Boys*
>
> BILL WYMAN

LUCILLE

BB has always played beautiful black, gold-plated, pearl-inlaid Gibson 335 guitars that he calls Lucille. In 2000, he was playing Lucille the 16th!

Throughout the 1970s, when others found it difficult to find decent work, King kept his career on track. He even appeared on TV, when almost no other blues artist could get a booking. His reputation with other guitarists gave him the position of elder statesman of the Blues. He has always been articulate in explaining the meaning of the Blues, and and he helped to keep the fire burning when it had all but gone out. King has been criticised as being too smooth for the Blues, but that is simply a case of sour grapes from those would have given anything to achieve a modicum of his success.

The year after he was inducted into the Rock & Roll Hall of Fame (1987), King worked with U2 on their album *Rattle & Hum*. His performance on 'When Love Comes To Town' proved he could still cut it, at 63 years old. This was not King's first excursion beyond the borders of the Blues, as earlier in his career he played with the jazz group, The Crusaders, and he has also worked with the blind singer Diane Schuur, Alexis Korner, Stevie Winwood, and Bobby Bland. In 2001, long-time friends BB King and Eric Clapton won a Grammy award for their album, *Riding With The King*. Amongst the covers the pair tackled were 'Worried Life Blues' and 'Key To The Highway', while they also revisited 'Three O'Clock Blues'.

King's great skill has been to ride out the mood swings of modern music and continue to come up with interesting albums. He, more than anyone, brought the Blues out of the margins and into the mainstream of American music – and he is deservedly known as the King of the Blues.

ESSENTIAL RECORDINGS

CLASSIC SONGS

'Three O'Clock Blues' 1951
'Sweet Little Angel' 1956
'The Thrill Is Gone' 1969

CLASSIC ALBUMS

Live At The Regal 1964 Uni/MCA

THE SOURCE

His Definitive Greatest Hits
1999 2-CD set
The RPM Hits 1951–1957
1999 Ace Records

Bonnie's Blues

Septuagenarian Chartman

In October 1992, John Lee Hooker, then 75 years old, entered the UK singles chart with 'Boom Boom', taken from his album of the same name. The following year, 'Boogie On Russian Hill', and 'Gloria' (with Van Morrison) also charted, followed by 'Chill Out (Things Gonna Change)' and 'Baby Lee' (with Robert Cray) in 1995 and 1996 respectively.

Four months after Bill worked with the Wolf, The Stones started a six-week European tour at the Tennis Hall in Malmo, Sweden. Supporting the Stones on the tour were Buddy Guy and Junior Wells, along with Bonnie Raitt. Bonnie, whose father appeared in Broadway productions, began working local gigs in 1967 when she was just eighteen. She graduated to working with John Hammond Jr, Son House, Mississippi Fred McDowell, and Robert Pete Williams.

Bonnie Raitt and John Lee Hooker

Bonnie getting up close and personal with John Lee's erotic guitar.

Shortly after the Stones tour Bonnie released her self-titled debut album, which inevitably included a Robert Johnson cover, 'Walking Blues'. Since 1970 she has been a consistent and prolific performer, recording around 20 albums. In 1989 she won six Grammies for her album, *Nick Of Time*. The record was much less blues-orientated than her previous outings, but it introduced people to her music and many of her new fans must have gone back to her older albums, with their more obvious blues influences. In 1991 Bonnie played on John Lee Hooker's remake of 'I'm In The Mood', duetting with Hooker and adding some wonderful slide guitar licks.

(West) Indian Blues

In 1973 Bonnie Raitt's album, *Takin' My Time*, featured guest appearances by Little Feat's brilliant slide guitarist Lowell George, along with Taj Mahal. Unsurprisingly, Taj Mahal is not his real name! Henry St Claire Fredericks was born in New York in 1942; his father came from St Kitts in the Caribbean and his mother from South Carolina. After his abortive efforts with the

The Rock'n'Roll Circus

'I first became aware of Taj in late 1967. I bought his debut album in New York on 14th November, or so it says in my diary! The following year Taj came over to London to appear in The Rolling Stones Rock'n'Roll Circus *which we were filming for TV. We met on 9th December at the Marie Antoinette room in the Londonderry House Hotel. Eric Clapton, Jethro Tull, Stevie Winwood, and the Who were also there. Taj rehearsed 'Leaving Trunk' and 'Corrina Corrina' the next day. The album and video finally came out in 1996 and featured Taj singing 'Ain't That A Lotta Love'*'

Bill Wyman

'I talked to Bill and found he was involved in the horticulture society, and my work had been done in agriculture before I started off as a musician, so we had something in common. So I was like, wow, you know, hip blues player guys from England, and this guy's in the national horticulture society. Bill is a very innovative bass player. I always liked his bass lines and the way the band played together, the tone, and the fact that they respected the music'

Taj Mahal

Taj Mahal

For me it's basically kind of an ancestor worship, in the sense of accessing the great things that ancestors have done

Taj Mahal

Rising Sons, Taj signed a solo deal with CBS and released his self-titled debut album, on which covers of 'Statesboro Blues' and 'Dust My Broom' were mixed in with originals.

Taj's career has continued unabated – a career in which he has constantly experimented, mixing reggae, hip-hop, and older traditions; he is also steeped in the songster tradition. The name of his backing band has changed constantly – the Intergalactic Soul Messengers and The Phantom Blues Band being just two examples. Taj has been an inspiration to other artists, recording as he did through the lean years of the 70s, and many of the new breed of solo bluesmen cite Taj as a key influence, in the same way as he was influenced by those who went before.

People such as Larry Johnson, who was a protégé of the Reverend Gary Davis, have maintained the songster or country blues tradition. Jesse Fuller was another artist in this field who proved to be very popular.

In more recent years, Guy Davis, John Mooney, Blind Mississippi Morris, RL Burnside, Eric Bibb, Robert Lockwood Jr, and John Hammond Jr have still kept their own brands of country blues alive. They all acknowledge the debt that they owe to those who have gone before, but each one of them has added his own ingredients to the sound of the Blues.

The Dukes of Southern Blues

Prog rock never caught hold with American artists, despite the fact that some of the UK bands in that style became hugely popular on tours and on record. In the US, it was the bands who stuck more closely to a blues-based formula who prospered most.

Duane Allman's appearance on Eric Clapton's *Layla* album came just a couple of months after the release of the Allman Brothers' self-titled debut album. It featured Muddy Waters' 'Trouble No More', while the band's second album included Muddy's 'I'm Your Hoochie Coochie Man'. But it was their third album, in summer 1971, that

Robert Lockwood Jr

Guy Davis

On his 1995 album Stomp Down Rider, *Davis performs Robert Johnson's 'I Believe I'll Dust My Broom' and 'If I Had Possession Over Judgement Day'.*

In the late 1960s while we were on tour, I went to the Ash Grove, a small club in Los Angeles, and saw a concert by Jesse Fuller, who by then was in his 70s. There were only about 30 people there. Fuller was a one-man-band playing guitar, with a neck brace with a harmonica and kazoo, cymbals on his elbows, and a foot pedal that played bass notes on a home-made instrument called a footdella, while he played the hi-hat with the other foot. He was wonderful in his old suit, cloth cap, and hobnailed boots. At the end of his show he put down his instruments and did an elaborate tap dance. Watching him, I couldn't help thinking that this was what it would have been like to see many performers in the early days of the Blues

Bill Wyman

introduced them to a wider audience, and also became established as one of the finest live albums of the rock era. *At The Fillmore East*, recorded in New York in March 1971, featured several band originals alongside Willie McTell's 'Statesboro Blues', Elmore James' 'Done Somebody Wrong', and T-Bone Walker's 'Stormy Monday'. The twin lead guitar work of Duane Allman and Dickey Betts became the model for just about every dual-led guitar band that has followed since.

Lynyrd Skynyrd

Four days after the album went gold, in October 1971, Duane Allman crashed his motorbike and died from his injuries. The bass player on *At The Fillmore East*, Berry Oakley, was also killed in a motorbike accident a year later, only a few hundred yards from the site of Duane's tragic crash. The band soldiered on through the 70s, with some conspicuous success, but in truth they were not a patch on their former selves. More break-ups and regroupings continued in the 80s and 90s, but the Allman Brothers were never able to recapture the magic of *At The Fillmore East*.

The Allmans proved to be the model for a whole string of Southern (blues) rock bands. 38 Special, Lynyrd Skynyrd (produced by Al Kooper), Molly Hatchett, and the Marshall Tucker Band all made a passing nod to the Blues, though that influence may well have been unconscious in some cases. Soon the whole arena-rock phenomenon took off, with artists such as REO Speedwagon, Journey, Foreigner, Styx, and Bill's old protégé, Peter Frampton, selling millions of albums and concert tickets!

But for the most part the 70s were lean times for the Blues. Aside from Taj Mahal, most artists in the field kept their hands in by touring, both at home and in Europe, but to much smaller crowds than before. Albert King was one of the few artists who managed a significant showing on the R&B charts. For most of the decade, and onwards into the 80s and 90s, the taste of the young black record buyers was moving well away from the Blues, embracing dance and more urban-based music.

The Allman Brothers

Don't Mess With Texas

Johnny Winter, an albino white blues guitarist, was hailed as America's answer to Clapton, Beck, and Page. Born in Leland, Mississippi, he grew up in Beaumont, Texas. His Imperial album, *The Progressive Blues Experiment*, was the first blues-rock album in the power-trio tradition of Cream by an American. Johnny and his brother, Edgar, started out with a band called Johnny & The Jammers in their hometown, playing little but the Blues. He visited England in early 1969 and on his return signed a management deal with a New York club-owner. Columbia signed Winter for one of the highest ever advances up to that point, and in May 1969 his debut for the label followed his Imperial album into the American Top 50 chart. *The Progressive Blues Experiment* was pure blues, featuring 'Rollin' And Tumblin', 'Broke Down Engine' and 'Tribute to Muddy'.

Over the next few years Winter continued to release albums regularly, although he strayed further from traditional blues material into a more straight-ahead rock format. After recording with some of Muddy's band in 1977, he produced Muddy's album *Hard Again*. The project reinvigorated both of their careers, earning a Grammy award. It was a fine album that saw Muddy returning to the form he had not experienced on record for almost a decade. To be accurate, it was America that abandoned Muddy, while his appeal in Europe remained as strong as ever.

Hard Again
Muddy Waters' 1977 album was produced by Johnny Winter. The album features new recordings of many of Muddy's classic songs including 'Mannish Boy' and 'I Can't Be Satisfied'. It features James Cotton on harmonica and Johnny on 'miscellaneous screams'!

Johnny Winter
A totally charismatic performer.

'By 1974 I had been living in France for three years and one day I got a call from Claude Nobs, the promoter of the Montreux Jazz Festival, to put together a rhythm section to back Buddy Guy, Junior Wells, and Muddy Waters. Dallas Taylor, who worked with Crosby Stills and Nash, and who I played with on Steve Stills' Manassas *album, was staying at my house. So Dallas played drums and my friend Terry 'Tex' Taylor came along to play slide guitar. We went to Montreux to rehearse on June 27 and the next day we performed. Playing with Buddy, Junior, and Pinetop Perkins was brilliant, and we did 'Hoodoo Man Blues', Sonny Boy's 'Checking On My Baby', and Buddy's 'Ten Years Ago' in our set. We later played a set with Muddy that included 'Hoochie Coochie Man', 'The Same Thing', 'Got My Mojo Working', and 'Mannish Boy', during which Muddy did a little dance as he sang! Interestingly, in the middle of his set Buddy gave a little speech that was quite emotional. He said: 'We get a better thrill out of playing over here than we do at home'. In July 1977 I went to the Nice Jazz Festival and saw Muddy perform. Bonnie Raitt was there too, and a week later I played with Muddy at Montreux once again'*

Bill Wyman

'In the middle of the set Muddy turned around, looked at me, pointed, and said 'S O L O'. Being told to play a slow solo by Muddy Waters was one of the most daunting moments of my musical career. But I think I managed it OK'

Terry Taylor

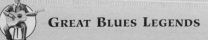

BUDDY GUY

GUITAR LEGENDS do not come any better than Buddy Guy. He is feted by his peers and loved by his fans for his remarkable ability to make the guitar both talk and cry the Blues. Over 40 years of playing the guitar have in no way diminished his power or his glory.

FACT FILE

BORN: *30th July, 1936*
Lettsworth (Pointe Coupée Parish), Louisiana

INSTRUMENT: *Guitar*

FIRST RECORDED: *1958*

ACCOLADES: *Inducted into the Blues Hall of Fame, 1985*

INFLUENCES: *John Lee Hooker, BB King, T-Bone Walker, Lightnin' Slim, Howlin' Wolf, Guitar Slim*

INFLUENCED: *Jimi Hendrix, Jeff Beck, Eric Clapton*

George 'Buddy' Guy was born on a farm and made his first guitar when he was 13 years old, teaching himself to play. By 1953 the 17-year-old was sitting in with other Louisiana musicians like Lightnin' Slim and Lazy Lester, playing at Baton Rouge clubs. "My mother had a stroke and I left Backridge, Louisiana 25th September, 1957," he recalled.

"I went to Chicago. I actually was looking for just a regular job to help my mom." At first Guy could not find work and he was getting hungry. Then one day, while he was playing on the street, a friend took him to a club where Otis Rush was playing and he sat in with him. Someone else then called Muddy Waters, who came to the club to see the 21-year-old play.

By 1958, Guy had become a regular player on the thriving Chicago club scene, and he was ready to record. His first session was for the Artistic label, where he recorded 'Sit And Cry The Blues' and 'Try To Quit You Baby' with Willie Dixon and Otis Rush. A second session later in the year produced two more tracks; this time Ike Turner played guitar on one side. But there was little attention from record buyers until Guy signed for the Chess label in 1960.

At his first session for them on 2nd March, he recorded four tracks, including the wonderful 'First Time I Met The Blues', a classic meeting of Guy's soulful vocals and his slashing guitar. Besides making his own records he was also an in-demand session player, backing Muddy Waters, Little Walter, Sonny Boy Williamson (Rice Miller), Koko Taylor, and the ever present Willie Dixon.

In 1962, his one and only hit on the R&B chart, 'Stone Crazy', which featured Otis Spann on piano, got to No.12, enabling Guy to reach a wider audience. He toured Europe as part of the American Folk Blues Festivals in 1965 and 1967, playing solo and as part of other artists' backing bands. By

Junior Wells

1967, Guy had left Chess and moved to the Vanguard label where he cut some great albums.

By now, he had also formed a strong working relationship with the harmonica player and vocalist, Junior Wells. In 1965 the duo cut an album for Delmark, entitled *Hoodoo Man Blues*, and it remains a classic. Guy's reputation was now beginning to spread among white audiences, and he and Junior Wells were regularly appearing together outside the US.

While Guy made some very good studio albums during this period, his reputation as a live artist definitely surpassed his recording reputation.

In 1970, he toured with The Rolling Stones, and by the early 1970s he was already beginning to set the tone of his concerts for the next 30 years. They were unpredictable then, and they still are!

Such is Buddy's mastery of the guitar that there is virtually no one that he cannot mimic, sometimes at the cost of his own reputation. Those who are lucky enough to catch a Buddy Guy blues-show know that they are seeing the greatest living exponent of the post-war blues guitar, without any of the meandering or time-wasting that other 'legends' have been known to deliver.

> *‘By far and without doubt the best guitar player alive’*
>
> ERIC CLAPTON

In 1974, Bill appeared with Buddy Guy and Junior Wells at the Montreux Jazz Festival, along with Bill's long-time friend Terry Taylor. In the second half of the show, they supported Muddy Waters.

In 1989, Guy opened his own blues club in Chicago, called Legends; he had come a long way from not eating for three days and living rough on the Chicago streets. By 1991, Eric Clapton took Guy to London to perform at his Royal Albert Hall concert series. It revitalized Guy's recording career and he recorded a fine album for Silvertone Records, *Damn Right I've Got The Blues*.

ESSENTIAL RECORDINGS

CLASSIC SONGS

'First Time I Met The Blues' 1960
'Stone Crazy' 1981
'Damn Right I've Got The Blues' 1991

CLASSIC ALBUMS

BUDDY GUY
Damn Right, I've Got The Blues

Damn Right I've Got The Blues
1991 Silvertone

Hoodoo Man Blues
(Junior Wells with Buddy Guy)
1965 Delmark

THE SOURCE

The Complete Chess Recording Sessions
1992 Uni/Chess

> *‘And Muddy came in and just smacked me and said, “Wait a minute, I heard about you, they done call me and got me out of bed.” He said, “You hungry?” I said, “You Muddy Waters? I'm not hungry, I'm full, I met you.”’*
>
> BUDDY GUY

Buddy Guy performing at the Newport Folk Festival, Rhode Island, 1968.

KEEPING THE FAITH

ZZ TOP
Their first album showed a great Delta influence on songs such as 'Just Got Back From Baby's'. The album also included 'Brown Sugar', but not The Stones song of the same name.

When I was in San Antonio in June 1964, two local guys took us to some bars. They all had swing doors and I was amazed because the jukeboxes were full of Sam Cooke and Jimmy Reed records

BILL WYMAN

WHILE OTHERS LOST HEART, Texas kept the faith. Beginning with ZZ Top, and on through Stevie Ray Vaughan and Double Trouble, they have always held the Blues close to their heart, in Texas. Maybe it has something to do with pick-up trucks and long highways, or maybe it's the legacy of Blind Lemon Jefferson, Lightnin' Hopkins, and the other Texas legends.

In 1970 *ZZ Top's First Album* came out; and throughout the 1970s, before they became an MTV 'show band', they were playing the Blues. Their commitment was demonstrated when they paid for a headstone for Robert Johnson at a graveyard where he is thought to be buried.

BEARDS IN TRAINING
ZZ Top's Billy Gibbons, Ron Beard, and Dusty Hill on their Texas World Tour, *1975.*

In 1983 Stevie Ray Vaughan, a 29-year-old guitarist from Dallas, Texas, released his debut album, *Texas Flood*. It catapulted Stevie Ray to a level of stardom not experienced by any other guitarist who appeared on the rock scene during the 80s. With a style that somehow managed to combine Hendrix with Hubert Sumlin and Albert King, Vaughan regularly played clubs in his adopted hometown of Austin. He and his band, Double Trouble, attracted the admiration of Buddy, Muddy, and Hooker before they were signed by Epic. *Texas Flood* deservedly won a Grammy as the best traditional blues album of 1984.

Throughout the 1980s Stevie Ray and his brother Jimmie, who worked with the Fabulous Thunderbirds, often played together, but Stevie's drink and drug habit took its toll. By 1989 he was back in the studio and sounding as good as ever. Then in 1990, after he'd jammed with Eric Clapton at Alpine Valley, Wisconsin, the helicopter that was taking Stevie Ray home crashed, and he – along with all the other passengers – was killed.

In the mid-90s, Kenny Wayne Shepherd from Shreveport, Louisiana, and Jonny Lang from Minneapolis arrived on the scene to take up, in part, where Stevie Ray had left off. While they were both clearly being groomed for music television (MTV et al), their roots are definitely in the Blues. Although they are somewhat frowned upon by more traditional blues lovers, they have introduced a younger audience to the

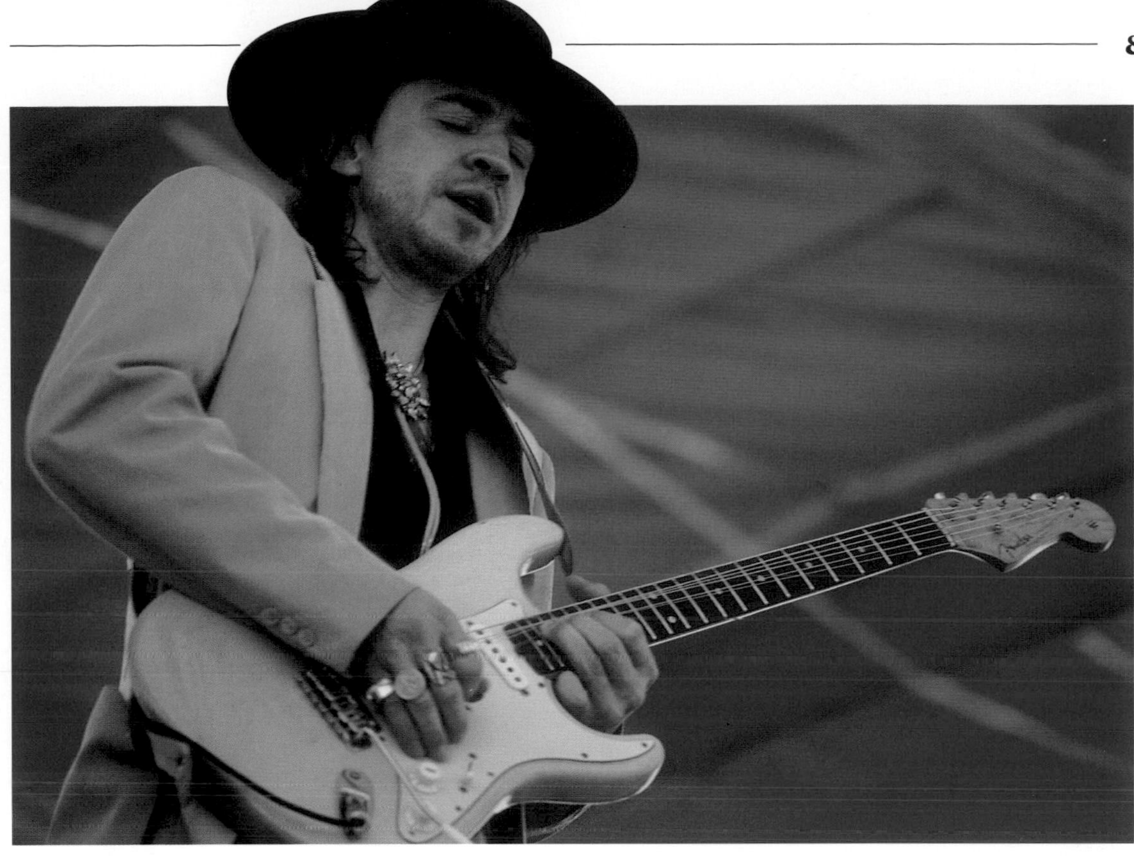

Stevie Ray Vaughan
An inspiration to young white guitar-playing wannabes.

music. Someone who heard 16-year-old Johnny Lang's version of 'Good Morning Little Schoolgirl' may have gone back to check out Sonny Boy's version, or perhaps they may have only got back as far as Muddy's 1963 version, or even the British covers by artists such as the Yardbirds and Rod Stewart. Either way, Lang has put them in touch with the tradition of the Blues.

The Greatest Rock'n'Roll né Blues Band in the World

Once the 60s ended, The Stones settled into a steady pattern of touring and recording albums that owed less and less to the Blues, but it did give Bill the opportunity to pursue his own musical interests, as well as working with some different artists.

In 1972 and '73 The Stones toured both Europe and America and at the time Mick

‘When The Stones toured with Bonnie Raitt, Buddy Guy, and Junior Wells in 1970, we rarely got to see them. They were always staying at different hotels, and had usually done their set by the time we got to the venues. We all flew from Vienna to Rome together and at the same time we landed, President Richard Nixon landed there on board Air Force One. Later we heard that Nixon was freaking because he knew, through his security people, that The Rolling Stones had landed at the same time and he was afraid to exit Air Force One! At this point, Mick took the initiative and decided to disembark first. So, Mr Nixon waited onboard Air Force One while all these Italian fans went nuts. When he finally did leave his plane, there was nobody left at the airport to greet him! It was a small triumph for music over politics’

Bill Wyman

THE J GEILS BAND

Magic Dick on harmonica and the leaping Peter Wolf, vocals.

THE KNEBWORTH SET LIST

'(I Can't Get No) Satisfaction'
'Ain't Too Proud To Beg'
'If You Can't Rock Me' / 'Get Off Of My Cloud'
'Hand Of Fate'
'Around And Around'
'Little Red Rooster'
'Stray Cat Blues'
'Hey Negrita'
'Hot Stuff'
'Fool To Cry'
'Star Star'
'Let's Spend The Night Together'
'You Gotta Move'
'You Can't Always Get What You Want'
'Dead Flowers'
'Route 66'
'Wild Horses'
'Honky Tonk Women'
'Country Honk'
'Tumbling Dice'
'Happy'
'Nothing From Nothing'
'Outta Space'
'Midnight Rambler'
'It's Only Rock'n'Roll'
'Brown Sugar'
'Rip This Joint'
'Jumping Jack Flash'
'Street Fighting Man'

Jagger told the *Daily Mirror* newspaper in London that he would quit the music business in 1976 when he was 33. The crowds were getting bigger and bigger as the Stones moved into the stadiums, filling them to capacity.

Another act who toured with The Stones in the 70s was the J Geils Band. They turned down a chance to play Woodstock, but were signed by Atlantic in 1970. Their debut single, a version of Otis Rush's 'Homework', immediately showed off their blues roots, but it was as a live band that they really shone. With former DJ Peter Wolf up front, and the harmonica playing of Magic Dick, they became favourites on the festival and college circuit. Their live album, *Full House*, features a wonderful version of Hooker's 'Serves You Right To Suffer'. But like so many others, they drifted away from the Blues as the potential for better-paying music beckoned.

By 1976 Mick Jagger had obviously changed his mind about retirement, and The Stones played at Knebworth in Hertfordshire to a crowd of 100,000. Philip Norman wrote in the *Sunday Times*:

> *The Rolling Stones' appearance four hours late at the Knebworth Festival did not result entirely from their contempt for their audience. Shortly before they were, at last, ready to play, several of their amplifier leads were found to have been cut. Suspicion, I hear, has fallen on the bands who shared subordinate billing*

Knebworth Festival 1976

By this time the band's set list had come a long way from the Blues. Besides hits such as 'Satisfaction' and 'Little Red Rooster', only 'Stray Cat Blues' made even a passing reference to the Blues. By 1981 their typical set had lost both 'Little Red Rooster' and 'Stray Cat Blues', with only 'Down the Road Apiece' being an occasional concession to

Rory Gallagher

He produced album after album of brilliant guitar blues.

Rory Gallagher

A brilliant guitar player who never deserted the Blues. He consistently made great albums such as Against The Grain, Tattoo, *and the excellent* Blueprint *(above).*

their heritage. On 1989's *Steel Wheels* tour, 'Little Red Rooster' had returned, but it was the sole blues song among a mass of the Stones' stock-in-trade rock belters.

Defender of The Faith

When Mick Taylor left the Stones, Rory Gallagher, the brilliant Irish guitarist, jammed with the band for a couple of nights in January 1975. Rory, who grew up in Derry, became interested in music at a young age when he listened to a radio station from a nearby American base that regularly played the Blues.

Eighteen-year-old Rory and his band, the Impact, started playing in Hamburg, mostly delivering Chuck Berry covers. Then in 1968 he formed Taste, before going solo in 1971. He produced album after album of brilliant guitar blues, on which his own clever compositions were mixed with thoughtful covers of Sonny Boy, Muddy, and Lead Belly. Sadly, in June 1995 Rory died from complications after a liver transplant operation. He never deserted the Blues, unlike many of his generation who only seemed to slip back into them when they sensed anything smelling like a revival. Rory had real integrity, plus a down-to-earth approach; and most of all, he loved the Blues.

> *"Near the end of our 1975 US Tour we played in Atlanta and I got the chance to go and see Piano Red play at the Atlanta Underground. He was brilliant, belting out his Dr Feelgood music on songs like 'Right String Baby But The Wrong Yo-Yo', 'Rocking with Red' and 'Red's Boogie'. All three had made the R&B Top 10 in 1951. He was a superb performer. I had first met him the year before when he played at the Montreux Festival. After he finished playing I took him backstage to watch the playback of his performance on the monitors. It was very touching, as Red had never seen himself on screen and he actually cried. The day after the Atlanta Underground show he came to my hotel room and I taped us chatting. It was wonderful to get him reminiscing about people he had seen and worked with in pre-war Atlanta. He amazed me at one point when he said, 'You may not have heard of a guy called Willie McTell, but he used to come over to my house and play on my porch.' Blind Willie had by then become one of my favourite performers and it was great to talk to someone who both knew and had worked with a blues legend"*
>
> Bill Wyman

THE SOUNDTRACK TO BILL WYMAN'S BLUES ODYSSEY

TRYING TO COME UP with a definitive list of essential blues albums is the equivalent of trying to hit a moving target while wearing a blindfold. The blues reissue market is very volatile. Releases constantly appear and disappear, often at incredible speed. Fortunately, labels such as Document Records maintain their catalogue, as do many of the major labels.

Use this list as a guide and if you find that a particular album is unavailable, then you will often find one on a different label with a very similar track listing. From the Fabulous 50s onwards, things happily tend to be somewhat more stable. In any event this is no more than a list to get you started, if you haven't already. If you have already, it might remind you of some you have missed. It's all very well writing about the Blues, but in the end it's music and music should be listened to and loved.

PRE-WAR BLUES

Blind Blake *Georgia Bound* (Catfish).

Big Bill Broonzy *The Big Bill Broonzy Story* (Vanguard). Big Bill talks about his life and plays the Blues. Unlike other spoken-word material, this will stand repeated listening.

Leroy Carr *Hurry Down Sunshine – The Essential Recordings Of Leroy Carr* (Indigo).

Bo Carter *Bo Carter's Advice* (Catfish).

Sleepy John Estes *I Ain't Gonna Be Worried No More 1929–1941* (Yazoo).

Blind Boy Fuller *East Coast Piedmont Style* (Columbia Legacy).

Blind Willie McTell *Travelling Blues* (Catfish) and *1940 Library of Congress Recordings* (Document).

Robert Johnson *King Of The Delta Blues Singers* (Sony).
"If you are starting your blues collection, be sure to make this your first purchase" Cub Koda, blues expert and member of rock band Brownsville Station.

Skip James *Skip James' Complete 1931 Recordings* (Document).

Blind Willie Johnson *Dark Was The Night* (Columbia Legacy).

Son House *Son House & The Great Delta Blues Singers* (Document)
Also includes sides by Willie Brown, Garfield Akers, and Blind Joe Reynolds (the original of 'Outside Woman Blues', which Cream covered).

Lead Belly *King Of The 12-String Guitar* (Columbia Legacy).

Memphis Minnie *The Essential Memphis Minnie* (Allegro/Document).

Tampa Red *The Essential Tampa Red* (Allegro/Document) and *The Bluebird Recordings 1936–1938* (BMG).

Lonnie Johnson *The Essential Lonnie Johnson* (Allegro/Document).

Charley Patton *Complete Recorded Works Vol 1* (Document).

Ma Rainey *Ma Rainey's Black Bottom* (Yazoo).

Blind Lemon Jefferson *Squeeze My Lemon* (Catfish).

Papa Charlie Jackson *Complete Recorded Works Vol 1* (Document).

Ethel Waters *Ethel Waters 1926–1929* (Jazz Chronological Classics).

Bessie Smith *Bessie Smith Vols 1–8* (Frog).

Various Artists *Mississippi Blues* (Catfish). This two-CD set includes Bukka White, The Mississippi Sheiks, Charley Patton, Louise Johnson, Tommy Johnson, and Robert Johnson.

Various Artists *Broke, Black, and Blue* (Proper). This is a four-CD set at a very low price, covering some of the best in pre-war blues, as well as some of the rarest. It includes Peetie Wheatstraw, Kokomo Arnold, Texas Alexander, Jim Jackson, The Memphis Jug Band, Casey Bill Weldon, and Lonnie Johnson.

Various Artists *From Spirituals To Swing* (Vanguard).

Various Artists *Anthology of American Folk Music* (Smithsonian/Folkways). Six CDs of Harry Smith's original work.

Various Artists *Good Morning Blues* (Charly). Four CDs featuring just about every important pre-war blues artist.

White Country Blues and Western Swing

Cliff Carlisle *Blues Yodeller & Steel Guitar Wizard* (Arhoolie).

Jimmie Rodgers *The Essential Jimmie Rodgers* (BMG).

Various Artists *Doughboys, Playboys, and Cowboys* (Proper). Four-CD box set at a low price, covering the best in western swing.

Various Artists *As Good As It Gets – Hillbilly*. (Disky). A two-CD set that includes Jimmie Rodgers, Hank Williams, Jimmie Davis, and Vernon Dalhart.

Let The Good Times Roll

Louis Jordan *Let The Good Times Roll* (Disky) and *Louis Jordan 1938–1950* (JSP). Five-CD set.

Wynonie Harris *Complete Recordings* (Proper). Four CDs at a very low price.

Various Artists *As Good As It Gets – Jukebox Blues* (Disky). Late 1940s jump blues, along with straight blues sides; including Lowell Fulson ('Three O'Clock Blues'), John Lee Hooker ('Boogie Chillen'), Amos Milburn, Joe Liggins, Muddy Waters, and Julia Lee performing the excellent 'King Size Papa'.

Various Artists *Juke Box Jive* (Charly). Two CDs featuring T-Bone Walker, Helen Humes, Louis Jordan, Dinah Washington, and Wynonie Harris. Also in the series, *Good Rockin' Tonight* and *Bootin' The Boogie*.

The Fabulous Fifties and Chicago Blues

Ray Charles *The Very Best Of Ray Charles – Vols 1 and 2* (Rhino).

Chuck Berry *His Best Volume 1* (Chess Records). Includes all the great early recordings.

Bo Diddley *His Best* (Chess 50th Anniversary Collection).

Lonnie Donegan *Lonnie Donegan Showcase* (Castle).

Albert Collins *Ice Pickin'* (Alligator).

Buddy Guy *The Complete Chess Studio Recordings* (Chess).

Slim Harpo *The Best Of Slim Harpo* (Ace Records).

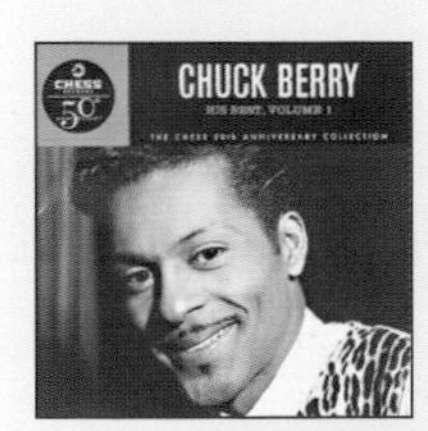

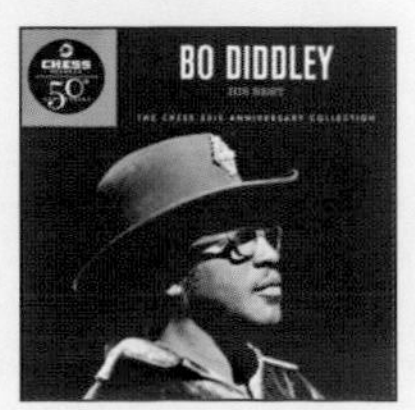

John Lee Hooker *Original Folk Blues* (Ace Records) and *The Legendary Modern Recordings* (Virgin).

Lightnin' Hopkins *Mojo Hand* (Rhino).

Albert King *King Of The Blues Guitar* (Atlantic).

BB King *The RPM Hits 1951–1957* (Ace) and *Live At The Regal* (Universal/MCA).

Clifton Chenier
Clifton Chenier Sings The Blues (Arhoolie).

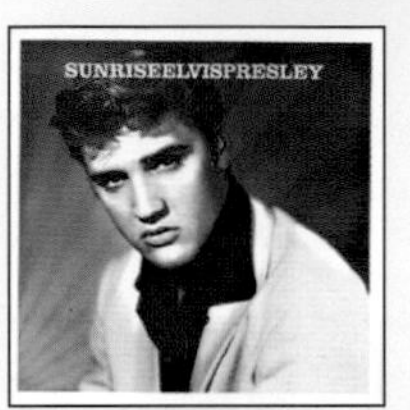

Elvis Presley *Sunrise* (BMG). All the original Sun singles, along with alternate takes. Elvis displays his roots!

Jimmy Rogers *That's All Right* (Blues Encore).

Muddy Waters *Muddy Waters At Newport/Muddy Waters Live* (BGO) and *The Folk Singer/Sings Big Bill* (BGO).

Otis Rush *Classic Cobra Recordings* (Uni/Plow).

T-Bone Walker *The Complete Imperial Recordings 1950–1954* (EMI).

Junior Wells (with Buddy Guy) *Hoodoo Man Blues* (Delmark).

Sonny Boy Williamson (Rice Miller) *King Biscuit Time* (Arhoolie).

Howlin' Wolf *Howlin' Wolf/Moanin' At Midnight* (MCA).

Elmore James *The Sky is Crying – The History of Elmore James* (Rhino).

Etta James *Her Best* (Chess 50th Anniversary Collection).

Otis Spann *Otis Spann Is The Blues* (Candid) – with Robert Lockwood Jr on guitar.

Big Joe Turner *Greatest Hits* (Atlantic).

Magic Sam *West Side Soul* (Delmark).

Little Walter *His Best* (Chess 50th Anniversary Collection).

Jimmy Reed *The Legend, The Man* (Joy).

Various Artists *The Blues Volume 2.* Includes Little Walter's 'Blues With A Feeling' and 'Key To The Highway', 'Evil' by Howlin' Wolf and 'So Many Roads' by Otis Rush. A compilation which introduced a lot of people to the Blues when it first came out in 1964.

Various Artists *The Chess Blues Rock Songbook* (Chess) A two-CD set including just about every important blues rock side from Chess, featuring Muddy, the Wolf, Chuck Berry, Bo Diddley, Willie Mabon, and Eddie Boyd.

Various Artists *Sun Records – The Blues Years 1950–1958* (Charly). Eight CDs containing everything! From Wolf's first sides to Mose Vinson, who is still playing boogie piano in Memphis today.

Willie Dixon *Willie Dixon* (Chess). Two-CD set of Dixon's songs featuring Wolf, Muddy, Jimmy Witherspoon, Little Walter, Little Milton, and Willie Dixon himself.

Various Artists *Chicago The Blues Today!* (Vanguard). Three-CD set.

Various Artists *American Folk Blues Festival* (Evidence). Five-CD set of the best years of the Festivals, from 1962–1965. Just about as good as it gets!

PIANO BLUES

Fats Domino *My Blue Heaven – The Best Of Fats Domino* (EMI).

Champion Jack Dupree *Blues From The Gutter* (Atlantic).

Fats Waller *The Very Best Of Fats Waller* (Collectors Choice Music).

Various Artists *Boogie Woogie – 40 Classic Performances* (Proper Retro). This two-CD set includes Pinetop Smith, Meade Lux Lewis, Albert Ammons, Pete Johnson, Harry James, and Count Basie.

The Folk/Blues Revival

Reverend Gary Davis *From Blues To Gospel* (Biograph).

Mississippi Fred McDowell *I Don't Play No Rock'n'Roll.* (Capitol Blues Collection).

Skip James *Devil Got My Woman* (Vanguard).

Mississippi John Hurt *The Immortal Mississippi John Hurt* (Vanguard).

Jesse Fuller *Favorites* (Funboy/Original Blues Classics).

Sonny Terry & Brownie McGhee *The Folkways Years 1944–1965* (Smithsonian/Folkways).

Koerner, Ray & Glover *Blues, Rags & Hollers* (Red House).

John Hammond Jr *I Can Tell* (Atlantic).

Taj Mahal *Taj Mahal* (Columbia Legacy).

Various Artists *Blues At Newport* (Vanguard). Three CDs from the Newport Folk Festivals, 1963–1966.

Various Artists *Rural Blues Volumes 1 & 2* (BGO). Two LPs on one CD.

Various Artists *Living Country Blues* (Evidence). Three CDs of field recordings from the early 1980s, including Othar Turner, Hammie Nixon, Son Thomas's brilliant version of 'Catfish Blues', and Guitar Slim.

White Blues Rock

Mose Allison *Mose Alive* (Atlantic).

Allman Brothers *Live At The Fillmore East* (Polydor).

Paul Butterfield Blues Band *The Paul Butterfield Blues Band* (Elektra). Their 1965 debut album.

Eric Clapton *From The Cradle* (Reprise) and **Derek & The Dominos** *Layla & Other Assorted Love Songs* (Polydor).

Fleetwood Mac *Mr Wonderful* (Sony).

Rory Gallagher *Irish Tour '74* (Capo/BMG). Caught live and at his best.

J Geils Band *The J Geils Band* (Atlantic).

John Mayall's Bluesbreakers *Bluesbreakers With Eric Clapton* (Decca).

Bonnie Raitt *Give It Up* (Warner Bros).

Ry Cooder *River Rescue – The Very Best Of Ry Cooder* (Warner Brothers).

Stevie Ray Vaughan *Texas Flood* (Epic).

"If I could take just one album and one single to that desert island? It would have to be Muddy Waters At Newport *and* Mr Howling's 'Smokestack Lightnin'*"*

Bill Wyman

ERIC CLAPTON

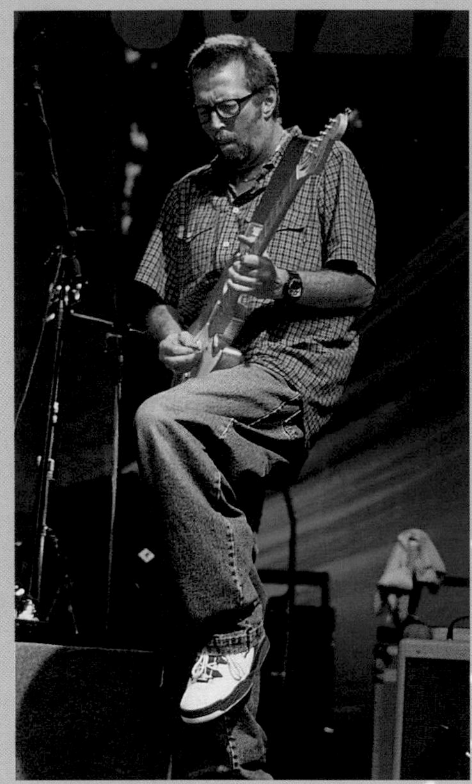

FACT FILE

BORN: *30th March, 1945 Ripley, Surrey, England*

INSTRUMENT: *Guitar*

FIRST RECORDED: *1964*

ACCOLADES: *Inducted into the Rock & Roll Hall of Fame, 2000*

INFLUENCES: *Blind Lemon Jefferson, Blind Boy Fuller, Robert Johnson, BB King*

INFLUENCED: *You – if you've ever picked up a guitar*

IN THE MID-1960S, graffiti appeared all over London, proclaiming 'Clapton is God'. It marked a staggering rise to fame, given the fact that young Eric Clapp's grandparents, who raised him, only bought him his first guitar in 1959. Eric's first band was The Roosters. He briefly joined Casey Jones and The Engineers and then joined The Yardbirds in October 1963.

The Yardbirds followed The Stones as the resident band at the Crawdaddy Club, during which time Eric acquired the nickname 'Slowhand'. For a while, Clapton was happy to do reasonably well-paid gigs in a band that played mostly blues. But as the band drifted towards more chart-orientated pop, Clapton became disillusioned and left, though not before he had toured and recorded with Sonny Boy Williamson.

John Mayall offered him a slot in The Bluesbreakers alongside John McVie and Hughie Flint in April 1965. Interrupting his career to take a trip to Greece, Eric returned to record the album *Bluesbreakers* in April 1966. It was a classic: produced by Mike Vernon, it featured Mayall originals alongside 'All Your Love' by Otis Rush, Mose Allison's 'Parchman Farm', and Little Walter's 'It Ain't Right'. Eric the God-like deity had arrived.

In early 1966 Jack Bruce played some gigs with Mayall, and a little later drummer Ginger Baker sat in. Somehow the idea of forming a band came up between Ginger and Eric and in July 1966 Cream was formed, "sort of like Buddy Guy with a rhythm section".

For two years Cream were it. The band's internal strife (Bruce and Baker apparently hated each other, but loved each other's playing) produced dynamics that have never been bettered by a powerhouse trio. Cream sold massive amounts of albums, featuring innovative band originals such as 'Sunshine Of Your Love' and 'White Room', alongside classic pre-war blues songs given a makeover. 'Spoonful', 'I'm So Glad', 'Rollin' And Tumblin', and 'Crossroads' became great studio songs, as well as giving Eric the chance to demonstrate his brilliant guitar playing at live gigs. They also covered, stunningly, Albert King's 'Born Under A Bad Sign'.

By November 1968 Eric had grown tired of Cream, and he was especially stung by criticism from *Rolling Stone* magazine, which called him "the master of the cliché". Clapton, who had become close friends with George Harrison, played the solo on The Beatles 'While My Guitar Gently Weeps', before forming Blind Faith in February 1969. Having met Delaney & Bonnie while touring in America,

'He's been a tremendous friend to me. I love the man, he's a great man. There's Eric Clapton, then you talk about the rest of the guys'

BB KING

he decided on a more organic approach to music. He went on the road as part of Delaney & Bonnie and Friends, in a line-up that also included Harrison and Dave Mason.

Throughout Eric's brief time with Blind Faith, he continued to play sessions with friends such as Leon Russell (one of the Delaney & Bonnie circle). Amongst the songs he cut with Russell were 'Sweet Home Chicago' and Russell's 'Blues Power'. He also recorded with John Lennon as part of The Plastic Ono Band, and with Dr John, The Crickets, and George Harrison.

In spring 1970, just after the Howlin' Wolf sessions and during his work on Harrison's first solo album, Eric went into Apple Studios to record as Derek and The Dominos. He used Carl Radle (bass) and Bobby Whitlock (drums and keyboards), along with Dave Mason and George Harrison on guitars. Phil Spector produced these first tracks, but they didn't work out and were soon superseded by material recorded in Miami in August and September 1970. Joining Radle and Whitlock at these sessions were Jim Gordon (drums), and Duane Allman on guitar. The music they made, eventually released as *Layla And Other Assorted Love Songs*, included 'Key To The Highway' alongside self-composed songs such as 'Bell Bottom Blues' and 'Why Does Love Got To Be So Sad'.

By now Eric's heroin habit was a real problem. He was pawning his guitars to feed his habit, and friends even feared for his life. Helped by Pete Townshend, among others, a heroin-free Eric was back on track by late 1973. His solo career took off in earnest, and multi-million-selling albums and tours carried him through the 1970s and 1980s, despite suffering an acute alcohol problem. But it must be said that during this period the Blues usually took a back seat to rock and pop material. There were notable exceptions, however, such as 'Motherless Child' on the 1974 album, *461 Ocean Boulevard*.

In 1991 Clapton played a record 24 nights at London's Royal Albert Hall, including some memorable 'blues only' shows featuring Buddy Guy, Albert Collins, Robert Cray, Jimmie Vaughan and Johnnie Johnson. In 1993 Cream were inducted into the Rock & Roll Hall Of Fame.

His 1994 album, *From The Cradle*, demonstrated Eric's love affair with the Blues. It features songs by Leroy Carr, Lowell Fulson, Muddy, Elmore James, and the ubiquitous Willie Dixon amongst others.

‘I first met Eric in the London clubs in the mid-1960s, and really got to know him better when we did a promo video of 'Jumpin' Jack Flash' (party version) at Olympic Studios, Barnes, London in the spring of 1968. He is without doubt the best blues guitarist to come out of Britain. He also loves cricket, and we played dozens of charity cricket matches together during the 80s and 90s, and shared some wonderful and hilarious times. In late 1983 Charlie Watts and I played a dozen gigs with him as part of the ARMS tour in both London and the US, where he impressed us as a true professional. When I recorded my first Rhythm Kings albums, Eric generously played on 'Melody', which Mick and Keith wrote and The Stones recorded in 1975 for the Black And Blue *album’*

BILL WYMAN

ESSENTIAL RECORDINGS

CLASSIC SONGS

'Crossroads'
from ***Wheels of Fire*** *(Cream)* 1968
'Layla' *(Derek and The Dominos)* 1971
'Malted Milk' *from* ***Unplugged*** 1992
'Motherless Child'
from ***From The Cradle*** 1994

CLASSIC ALBUMS

Bluesbreakers With Eric Clapton 1966
John Mayall's Bluesbreakers

Layla and Other Assorted Love Songs 1971
Derek and The Dominos

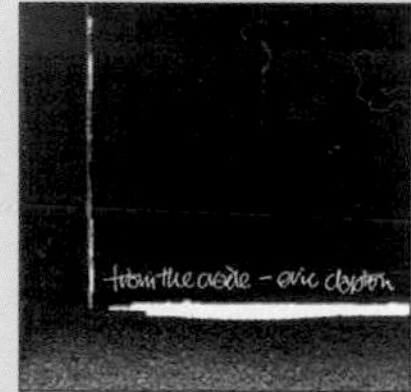

From The Cradle 1994

THE SOURCE

Strange Brew: The Very Best of Cream
1983 Polydor
Blues 1999 Polydor

JE SUIS UN ROCK STAR NO MORE

A FEW DAYS BEFORE CHRISTMAS 1979, I recorded a demo of a song I had written at my home in Vence, France. I called it '(Si Si) Je Suis Un Rock Star', and a few months later in April 1980 I recorded it. Eventually released as a single in the summer of 1981, it went to No. 14 in the UK and top 10 in many countries. It became the most successful of my solo projects away from The Stones and the most successful solo single by any of the band. I also had a hit in France in July 1974 when 'I'm Gonna Get Me A Gun' got to No. 27, taken from my first solo album *Monkey Grip*.

"I remember when I looked in my daddy's eyes through the later days, I just saw this old soul, you know, this old soldier that had been through a lot of battles and was just a little tired. At the funeral BB King came, he's such a gentleman, Bobby Bland sent flowers, and a lot of people sent stuff. But BB actually took the time to show up and that meant a whole lot to me. He was there along with Johnny Winter and a lot of the other guys"

BIG BILL MORGANFIELD

Stone Alone

Bill Wyman

Green Ice

Willie and The Poor Boys

Between touring and recording in the 70s I had time to devote to my own interests. As Charlie Watts said in the 80s, when asked what it meant to be in The Stones: "Five years of working, 20 years of hanging about".

Besides my other early solo albums like *Stone Alone* in 1976 and *Bill Wyman* (now there's a catchy title) in 1982, I did the music for the soundtrack to a film called *Green Ice*. I also played some interesting gigs. In 1983, along with Ian Stewart and Charlie, I played a gig at the Marquee Club with Alexis Korner and Georgie Fame. We rehearsed for two days at the Half Moon in Putney and then on 18th and 29th April we did two shows. The following day Muddy died, which was a sad day indeed for the Blues. I recently met Muddy's son, Big Bill Morganfield, who is himself a performer (he won a WC Handy Award in 2000 as Best Newcomer), and we talked about his dad:

Me and Alexis at the Marquee, 1983

Sadly, Alexis Korner died on New Year's Day 1984. Six weeks later, I presented a posthumous award to him at BBC TV's *Rock Awards Show*. Few men did more for the Blues in Britain than Alexis. Another who did, but received far less praise for his efforts, also died, just under two years later. On 12th December, 1985, my friend, and fellow Stone, Ian Stewart died from a heart attack in a doctor's waiting room. Ian and I shared many great times together, often going in search of blues records when we were touring in the US and Europe. Ian also gave me many compilation tapes of old blues songs, and I still play them today.

It was in the mid-1980s that my own solo career took another turn when I formed Willie and The Poor Boys. Charlie and Ronnie Wood played on some of my new band's recordings, as well as a video we made at Fulham Town Hall in March 1985. In

IAN STEWART
"C'mon my little three-chord wonders"

many respects this was the prototype for The Rhythm Kings.

When I decided to leave The Stones I thought I would do some more of my own musical projects. The TV series and this book were on my list, but I also wanted to play the sort of music that I love. My first Rhythm Kings album came out in 1997 and set the pattern for what followed. My mate Terry Taylor helped write some of the songs, played great guitar, and co-produced the album. Eric Clapton, Peter Frampton and two great British vocalists, Geraint Watkins and Mike Sanchez, guested on the album. By April 2001 we had released our fourth album, *Double Bill* (yes, it's a double album!). Guests included Chris Rea, who is a fantastic slide player, Andy Fairweather Low (who was in Willie and The Poor Boys), and George Harrison. With great singers like Beverley Skeete, Gary Brooker, Georgie Fame, and Albert Lee, we are never short of a vocalist. Martin Taylor, probably the best jazz guitarist in Britain, is a perfect foil for Albert's wonderful country-inspired picking. Graham Broad on drums, Frank Mead and Nick Payn on horns along with Janice Hoyte on backing vocals make up the rest of the band.

Playing live with a 12-piece band, and at small gigs, means we don't make much money. So everybody in the band does it for the same reasons as I do: to have a good time and send the crowd home with smiles on their faces. For the first time in many years, I really feel close to the audience; the kind of venues that we play give you that. It's the same thing with our albums. It's real music, played on real instruments, by real people… which seems to me to hark back to what many of the bluesmen I admire did. We toured for over four months in 2001 taking in the UK, Europe, and America. I'm 65 in October 2001, so I wonder what we'll do in 2002. Maybe nothing… no, somehow I don't think so!

ANDY FAIRWEATHER LOW
A great guitarist.

DOUBLE BILL
2001's double album where we cover Fats Waller, Louis Jordan, Nellie lutcher, Etta James, and Ethel Waters to name just a few.

The Rhythm Kings, from left to right, back row: Georgie Fame, Graham Broad, Gary Brooker, Terry Taylor, Martin Taylor, Albert Lee. Front row: Nick Payn, Janice Hoyte, Bill Wyman, Beverley Skeete, Frank Mead.

THE BLUES FIRE STILL BURNS

National Blues

GIVEN THE FACT THAT MANY of the great bluesman have died in recent years, you could be forgiven for wondering how interest in the Blues was kept alive during the last two decades of the 20th century. With more and more corporate involvement in the world of music, the Blues have continued to rely on the dedication, enthusiasm, and efforts of individuals, along with the small independent record labels. But sometimes this has come from the least obvious of quarters.

ADVERTISING

One somewhat surprising outlet for the Blues, and a real opportunity to gain converts, has been advertising, especially TV ads. Muddy Waters' music was used on ads for Busch Beer, while Albert Collins was used by Seagrams and BB King worked for both Kentucky Fried Chicken and Northwest Airlines.

Interestingly Northwest not only used BB King in advertising; he also played live shows, having been identified as the right type of artist to appeal to their frequent flyers. Other blues artists who the airline have used include Dr John, Ruth Brown, Keb Mo, The Neville Brothers, and Magic Slim and The Teardrops.

THE REISSUE MARKET

When all is said and done, the music has to speak for itself. The long-playing vinyl record offered a fantastic opportunity for reissuing old blues material. LPs were an easier-to-listen-to format than 78 or 45rpm singles. In 1966, CBS issued *King Of The Delta Blues Singers* by Robert Johnson, a collection of his finest sides. This was not the first reissue album of pre-war blues material, but it was without doubt one of the most successful and significant blues LPs of all time. It further encouraged other, often very small, labels to reissue recordings that were 30 or more years old.

The advent of the CD in the 1980s gave the whole reissue process a new lease of life. Thanks to labels like Charly, Ace, Flyright, Arhoolie, Yazoo, Rhino, and most importantly Document Records, which was started by an Austrian, Johnny Parth, there are virtually no pre-war blues recordings which have not been re-released. There are some who argue that owning a CD reissue of a blues classic robs the listener of the true experience of listening to a 78 with its big sound, but while this may be true, it is somewhat churlish. While it would be wonderful to own a

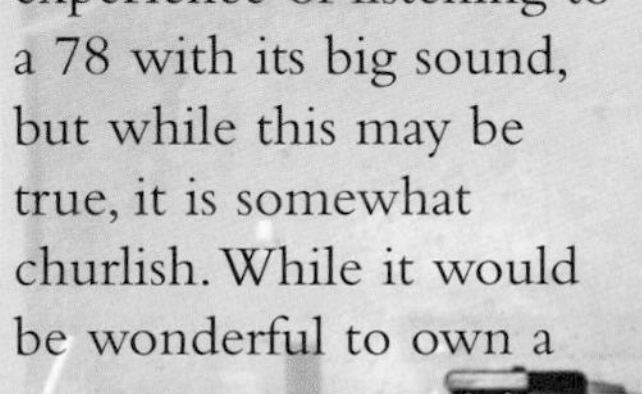

A Clarksdale juke joint

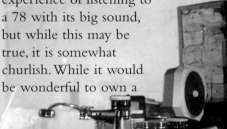

complete set of Robert Johnson or Charley Patton 78s, that ambition would be almost impossible to achieve.

In 1990 a box set of Robert Johnson's complete recordings was issued by Sony, and by 1992 it had sold a staggering half-million copies. There is no questioning the power of Johnson's recordings, but this story shows what can happen when a major label gets behind a release and uses its marketing muscle.

Fortunately many collectors make available their (often priceless) 78s to the specialist reissue labels. These originals are 'cleaned' for reissue, offering modern-day listeners the opportunity to hear as close an approximation as possible to the original 78s.

THE WRITTEN WORD

The insatiable appetite amongst aficionados for all things to do with the Blues has stimulated the market for specialist magazines (as well as articles in more general music magazines like the excellent *Mojo*). The first true blues magazine was either Britain's *Blues Unlimited*, started by Mike Leadbitter in 1964, or *Jefferson*, a Swedish magazine started around the same time; no one is quite sure which came first. Since then numerous others have followed. *Living Blues*, which started in America in 1970, and *Blues Access* are both excellent magazines. In Britain two more recent contenders are *Juke Blues* (started in 1987) and *Blues & Rhythm* (1984). There is also the eclectic *78 Quarterly* – which is far from quarterly, more like annually! Each one offers its own slant on the subject, anything from detailed research into the lives of obscure bluesmen to concert and album reviews.

THE BLUES WEB

The internet has been a godsend for the Blues, and for that matter every other non-mainstream musical genre. You can find almost anything you want about the Blues on the net, although as ever selectivity is key. Whether it is blues lyrics, general information or just the opportunity to buy blues CDs, the web is the place. Many small labels offer direct sales and major retailers such as CDNOW and Amazon carry a far better selection of blues CDs than any retail outlet. There are also specialist companies such as Red Lick in Wales, who offer an online service as well as a mail order catalogue. "Blues people use Red Lick the way rural Americans used Sears Roebuck", is how Tony Russell, a writer and broadcaster described them. They are knowledgeable, enthusiastic and straightforward – and they tell the blues the way it is.

BLUES FESTIVALS

One positive aspect of the renewed interest in blues during the 1980s and 1990s has been the upsurge in festivals around the world. They offer fans, both casual and serious, the opportunity to see a whole cache of blues players on one bill, usually at an affordable price. They also provide older, established artists and younger players the chance to travel and play, spreading the word as they go.

In 2001, for example, the 5th annual Bishopstock Blues Festival in England offered Ray Charles, Johnny Winter, Taj Mahal, Robert Lockwood, Homesick James, Honeyboy Edwards, Buddy Guy, and Lazy Lester, amongst almost thirty artists spread over three days. This is one of Europe's most prestigious festivals but there are others. A wide spectrum of artists can be seen in Burnley (13 years and going strong), Notodden in Norway and Blues Estafette in Utrecht. In America there is the Beale Street Music Festival and the WC Handy

HAVE BLUES, WILL TRAVEL
A Bluesmobile in Chicago.

THE BLUES FOUNDATION
If you love the Blues you should join!

Blues Award weekend, while in Chicago there is a blues festival every June – among the acts in 2001 were James Cotton, Taj Mahal, and Guy Davis. And those are just three of more than 200 festivals which take place each year in America.

THE BLUES FOUNDATION

Founded in 1980, the Blues Foundation's mission is to preserve blues history, celebrate blues excellence and support blues education. It promotes the appreciation of the Blues through its Blues Hall of Fame induction, which seeks to honour the music's pioneers. Through its annual WC Handy Blues Awards and International Challenge, the Foundation also celebrates the best in current blues. What's more, through its Blues Kids competition and development of programmes, it explores ways in which the Blues can take its rightful place in a school's curriculum.

The current Executive Director of the Blues Foundation is Howard Stovall, who maintains his family's link with the Blues. This is his verdict on the evolution of the Blues and where it might all be going:

'Musicians are musicians, regardless of genres. They will take the best of what they hear around them. With the incredible communication in the world today, blues artists are getting bombarded by influences that you wouldn't have found in Mississippi in the 1920s, 30s or 40s. So the music continues to evolve and any attempt to draw a line in the sand and say whatever is on the other side of this line is no longer blues is just killing a real dynamic and evolving art form. You can't put it under a bell jar and say this is blues and everything else isn't. The fact that the Blues has had an identity separate from other genres for as long as it has, is a testament to the fact that it is an art form that you can't dilute or compromise, no matter how many influences come into it'

HOWARD STOVALL

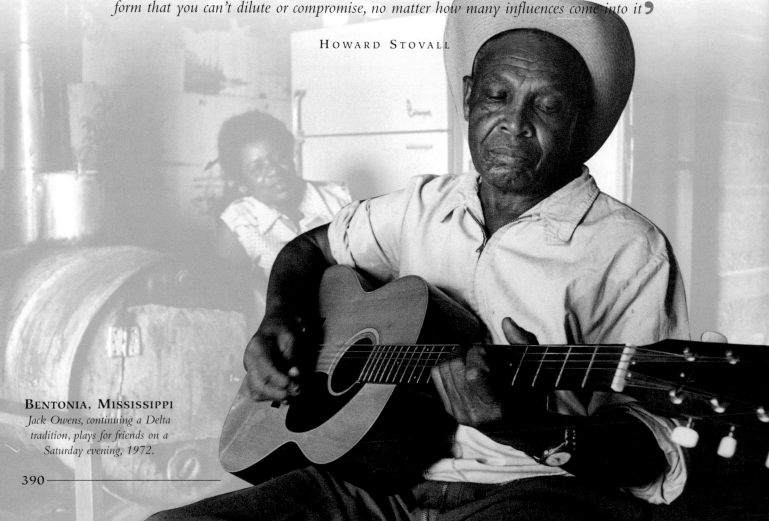

BENTONIA, MISSISSIPPI
Jack Owens, continuing a Delta tradition, plays for friends on a Saturday evening, 1972.

DAMN RIGHT WE GOT THE BLUES

'Blues is really America's finest art form and the most dominant art form of the 20th century'

GEORGIE FAME

MOST OF THE PEOPLE who lay in the mud at the Bath Festival of Progressive Music in June 1970, listening to Pink Floyd, Led Zeppelin, and the other bands, or saw Hendrix, Santana, or Canned Heat at Woodstock a year earlier, are now in their fifties. They have proper jobs, families, and commitments. But for many of them, their passion for music is undiminished. They still buy CDs and go to concerts, sometimes with their kids.

Damn right we got the Blues, as the song says: they are so ingrained on our minds that we are often unconscious of them. Without them there would have been no Rolling Stones, Eric Clapton, Led Zeppelin, Allman Brothers, or any other rock band. Don't let anyone tell you differently. Today, as we face far greater change than ever before in the history of mankind, at a faster rate than most of us could ever have envisaged, the Blues have an even greater value. We all feel the need to check out our roots and establish a sense of where we came from. That is why the Blues are so important, both in musical terms as well as in social terms.

So did God give us rock'n'roll or is it man's creation? Nowadays there is increasing evidence to suggest that music, whether it be rock, the Blues, or just about anything else, is given to us by the BIG corporations, and that's not just the record companies. Some of the biggest corporations are the artists themselves. It's all a very long way from a Saturday night at Dockery Farm, deep in the Delta, where Charley Patton was putting on one of his shows. Playing the guitar behind his head, between his legs, singing:

'Some people tell me that
Them overseas blues ain't bad
It must not have been
Them overseas blues I had'

Then he would pass around a tin cup to collect a few bucks. What would he have made of it all if he were alive today?

While filming the pilot for the TV series, Bill was asked if white men could play the Blues. He paused, smiled, and said: "If they try hard enough". The truth is that Bill, Muddy, Buddy, Eric, BB, Jimmie Rodgers, the Wolf, Hooker, John Hammond, and many, many more all play the Blues, and are all passionate about the power of the music. Some play the Blues because they lived them; others just love them. Either way, a wonderful gift has been bestowed upon us – a blessing born from the harsh and often cruel history of a beleaguered people.

'The Blues can chill you out, level you off, bring you up, make you laugh, make you cry. The Blues are perfect, however you feel. They have been a part of my life now for forty or more years, and I really hope that more people listen to the Blues, and make them a part of their lives. They have helped make me what I am today, and what I will be tomorrow... So let the Odyssey continue!'

BILL WYMAN

Keepin' the Blues alive today

INDEX

Bold type refers to feature page numbers and *italics* refer to illustration page numbers.

PHOTOGRAPHY & ILLUSTRATION

Dorling Kindersley would like to thank the following for their kind permission to reproduce their photographs and illustrations:

Abbreviations key: tl = top left, t = top, tr = top right, ac = above centre, c = centre, bc = below centre, cl = left of centre, cr = right of centre, l = left, r = right, bl = bottom left, br = bottom right, bgd = background

Every effort has been made to trace the copyright holders. Dorling Kindersley apologizes for any unintentional ommissions, and would be pleased, if any such case should arise, to add an appropriate acknowledgment in future editions.

Bridgeman Art Library: New York Historical Society, New York 20t.

Jane Rule Burdine: 43cr, 50/51bgd, 50cl, 50bl, 51tr, 51cr, 51br, 51bl, 135, 145, 335bgd'

Center for Southern Folklore: 43bgd, 92br, 129c, 130, 137br, 141bl.

Chansley Entertainment Archives: 92c, 132c, 139br, 253bgd, 260c, 260bl, 264bl, 271(Modern Records), 272tl, 285br, 286tl, 286br, 292c, 342, 343tr, 352bc; Peter Amft 351bl; Don Bronstein 304bl; Frank Driggs Collection 5bl, 6cr, 6br, 7br, 13tl, 33t, 65t, 66t, 72tl, 76bl, 78tl, 80r, 88br, 96tl, 97t, 100l, 101c, 103bgd, 103bc, 108t, 111tl, 114, 120tl, 132tl, 133t, 160tl, 161tr, 165br, 179cr, 180tr, 180bl, 181t, 181c, 182tl, 184 bgd, 184tr, 185, 189tl, 192t, 193tr, 197bc, 199bl, 200, 202tl, 202tr, 202b, 205tr, 206tl, 210t, 219, 221, 224br, 236/237bgd, 259l, 259r, 262tl, 274tl, 275c, 286 crb, 296 tl, 317br, Joe Alper 211; Henry Delorral 159t; Ray Flerlage 80/81bgd, 146/147bgd, 150, 151bgd, 170, 210br, 226, 290cl, 290br, 291br, 303br, 308tl, 340br, 341, 350bl, 351tr, 353b, 358bl, 358tr, 359bgd, 367cr; James Fraher 354bgd; Wayne Knight Collection 7tl, 7cl, 81r, 138cr, 153tr, 187b, 190tl, 191tl, 228, 236tl, 266tr, 269c, 274bl, 280br, 282bl, 299tr, 332cr, 352tl, 361t, 370br, Brian Smith 260/261bgd, 374/375bgd.

Corbis: 4/5bgd, 66b, 68, 86bgd, 107bgd, 128bgd, 136bgd, 143bgd, 156bc, 161bgd, 166t, 171, 173b, 188bgd, 196, 198br, 232, 233tr, 235, 241bgd, 242tr, 281bgd, 288bl, 316/317bgd, 336/337bgd; Lucien Aigner 206/207bgd; Jeff Albertson 296/297bgd; Paul Almasy 307bgd; Bettmann 63tl, 63b, 65bgd, 72/73bgd, 80l, 129r, 153bgd, 156l, 164l, 164r, 165bgd, 174tl, 189tr, 191b, 193bgd, 204, 220, 229tr, 233br, 234tr, 234bl, 239r, 243bc, 247t, 248br, 254/255bgd, 272/273bgd, 278r, 280l, 287bgd, 288t, 289br, 302bgd, 311bl, 338/339bgd; Horace Bristol 182b; CRDPHOTO 167tl, 178c; Terry Cryer 167br, 208, 267, 273bl, 291tl, Sandy Felsenthal 389br; Kevin Fleming 152b; Lowell Georgia 91bgd; Todd Gipstein 169 bgd; © E O Hoppe 69t, 70t, 120bgd; Hulton-Deutsch Collection 63bgd, 90, 243t; Lake County Museum 178bl; George Lepp 158bl; © The Mariners' Museum 70/71bgd, 246bgd; Minnesota Historical Society 48bgd, 79bgd, 113bgd; Mosaic Images 206br; Museum of the City of New York 128c; PEMCO – Webster & Stevens Collection; Museum of History & Industry, Seattle 83b; Arthur Rothstein 283bgd; Flip Schulke 289tr; Underwood & Underwood 100/101bgd, 186..

Mary Evans Picture Library: 10, 18/19b, 19tr, 19br, 21b, 22b, 23cr, 24br, 25br, 28c, 30b, 38, 47br, 108bgd, 304bgd.

Richard Evans: both endpapers, 1, 3, 16/17, 23bgd, 26/27bgd, 26l, 34/35, 40tl, 44bgd, 44tl, 45tr, 47t, 54c, 57cr, 58/59, 69br, 74/75, 98/99, 109, 112l, 118trbgrd, 118acbgrd, 118crbgrd, 118blbgrd, 126/127, 134cl, 138tlbgd, 138trbgd, 138bcr, 138blbgd, 139 trbgd, 139brbgd, 140tl, 142, 143c, 143bl, 143br, 148, 154/155, 176blbgd, 176br, 177 tlbgd, 177blbgd, 194/195, 214/215bgd, 216/217bgd, 216br, 217t, 217cr, 217bl, 225bgd, 227tr, 227c, 230/231, 239bl, 244/245, 269br, 275bgd, 276/277, 283c, 294/295bgd, 294tl, 295tl, 295tr, 299bgd, 300cl, 305tr, 308bgd, 312/313, 323tr, 323br, 324cl, 364/365.

Dorling Kindersley: 4, 116, 146l, 146r, 147r.

Don Grant: 20b.

Richard Havers: 42bgd, 72br, 84bgd, 84c, 149, 199r, 213, 248tl, 278cl, 336bl.

Hulton Archive: 32bl, 33bgd, 33bl, 36b, 37b, 39t, 40tr, 42ac, 43tl, 43bl, 49tr, 52bl, 53tl, 55c, 60, 71t, 78bgd, 95, 96b, 97b, 105c, 134br, 166b, 203bgd, 233tl, 239tl, 242b, 246cl, 247br, 288/289bgd, 295bl, 299cl, 307br, 314cr, 319cr, 332tl, 348tl; Beat Publications, Ealing 318bc; Frank Driggs Collection 15, 62tl, 67tr, 76b, 77, 83tr, 85b, 87br, 93tl, 93cr, 94, 106l, 115br, 122tr, 122bl, 268/269bgd, 294b, 300tl, 301bl, 302bl, 320bl; Walker Evans 123bgd, 256/257bgd; Terry Fincher 314bl; Bernard Gotfryd 343bgd; Bert Hardy 318tl; John Hammer Collection 261cr, 268c; Sheldon Hine 158tl; Hirz 104bgd, 104bl; Fred G Korth 88/89bgd; Russell Lee 176brbgd; Gene Lester 250bl; Clive Limpkin 329tl; Metronome 238t, 252, 258tl; George Pickow 249bgd; Marion Post Wolcott 174/175bgd, 176tlbgd, 176trbgd, P.L. Sperr 93tr;

Hipgnosis: 378b.

Impact Photos: Giles Moberley 27tl; David Reed 27tr.

Courtesy of the late JB Long, via Bruce Bastin: 209tr.

Mainspring Press: 89br, 105cr.

Chris McCourt: 293tr.

Susan Montgomery/The Greenwood Commonwealth: 216cl.

Peter Newark's American Pictures: 5tl, 11, 12, 18tl, 20c, 21cr, 22tl, 23br, 24tr, 25t, 28tl, 28bl, 29t, 30t, 31t, 32br, 37t, 39b, 40bgd, 41t, 44c, 45br, 45l, 46br, 46t, 49tl, 49b, 53bl, 55r, 56t, 61br, 62b, 64tl, 64b, 65cr, 67c, 79tr, 82, 92tr, 102t, 106tr, 115tr, 124/125, 128cl, 157tl, 157br (Fitzpatrick), 162tl, 162br, 198tr, 240tl, 352bgd; Walker Evans 223tr.

Sylvia Pitcher Photo Library: 325tl, 325bl, 326bgd, 327br, Brian Smith 326tl, The Weston Collection 326br.

Redferns: Richard Aaron 370tr, 372cl; Cyrus Andrews 328tl; Glenn A Baker Archives 264/265 bgd, 324tl, 337tl; Colin Beard 357; Fin Costello 376bl, Deltahaze Corporation 6tr, 214tl, 215cl; James Dittiger 2; Frank Driggs Collection 86tl; Dave Ellis 378t; Jeremy Fletcher 327t, 349tr; Gems 336cr; Herb Greene 355tr; Harry Goodwin 334bl; Max Jones Files 5cl, 33bc, 190bgd, 281tr; K&K Studios 324br; Bob King 323tl; Ivan Keeman 334tl; Robert Knight 371tr; Elliott Landy 270/271bgd, 356tr, 363bgd, 375bc; Andrew Lepley 293tl; Marc Marnie 310tl; Steve Morley 372br; Leon Morris 388tl, 388br, 391r, Petra Niemeier 360r, 360bl; Michael Ochs Archives 48t, 107tr, 113tl, 240tr, 240b, 251, 258br, 262b, 279br, 283tr, 284tl, 298, 300br, 303cr, 305c, 306tl, 307tl, 309tr, 309br,328br, 346tl, 346br, 354tl, 355tl, 356tl, 361bgd, 366cl, 368tl; Andrew Putler 379tl; RB 333cr; David Redfern 132bgd, 151tl, 172r, 237tr, 263, 304t, 305br, 306bgd, 311t, 315br, 319tr, 319bl, 348br, 377t; S&G Press Agency 322/323bgd, 330tr; Peter Sanders 362; Gerrit Schilp 316bl; Gai Terrell 345tl.

Retna: David Atlas 371tl; Jay Blakesburg 370tl; Flusin 359tl, Gary Gershoff 273ac, G. Hanekroot/Sunshine 384/385bgd, Jim McCarthy 347tr, 375tl; Michael Putland 333b, 369ac, 373tl; Luciano Viti 7bl, 384tl; Baron Woman 355bl, 367t.

Rex Features: 329br; Dezo Hoffman 321br, 322tl, 322c, 323cl, 323bc, 363bl.

The Collection of Duncan Schiedt: 102br, 117cr, 119ac.

Oscar Schmidt: 147tl.

Brian Smith: 315tr, 315c, 318bl, 331ac.

The Center for Popular Music, Middle Tennessee State University, John W. Work III Field Collection: 175tl.

Val Wilmer: 138c, 253bl, 271bc, 297bl, 301bgd, 366r, 368/369bgd, 374tl, 390b; Archive 163, 284.

Bill Wyman's Archive: 8, 27bc, 46lc, 57b, 73bl, 140bl, 160cl, 168b, 183bl, 192b, 198tl, 201, 207br, 212br, 215bl, 216tl, 218bgd, 218tl, 218cl, 218c, 218bl, 227br, 229br, 265tl, 270tl, 270bl, 272bl, 287cl, 287br, 293bl, 297bl, 306tr, 310bl, 320bgd, 320tl, 321tl, 330bgd, 331cr, 331bl, 332bl, 336tl, 337bl, 359br, 361br, 363tl (artist: Arnold Skolnick), 367bl, 368br, 371bl, 373b, 377b, 383br, 385cl, 386bgd, 386c, 387tl, 387tr, 387b, Terry O'Neill 238bl.

Jacket: Corbis: front c; **Chansley Entertainment Archives:** Frank Driggs Collection back tr; Wayne Knight Collection front tbgd; **Richard Evans:** front b, front flap, back t, back b; **Peter Newark's American Pictures:** back br; **Bill Wyman's Archive:** front tr, back flap; **Redferns:** Gerrit Schilp back bl.

Acknowledgements

Writing this book has been made all the more enjoyable and interesting because of the people that have helped us in so many different ways.

Those we have interviewed and talked to have added their own unique perspectives and insights, this book would have been the poorer without their contributions. Blind Mississippi Morris, Gary Brooker, Eddie Cusic, Guy Davis, Georgie Fame, Mick Fleetwood, Clarence Fountain and The Five Blind Boys of Alabama, Buddy Guy, Bruce Johnston, Kevin Kane, BB King, Lazy Lester, Albert Lee, Mike Love, Peter Mallick, Big Bill Morganfield, Pastor Willie Morganfield, Rosetta Patton, Sam Phillips, Wilson Pickett, Otis Rush, Jerry Schilling, Mrs. Nancy Stovall, Howard and Gil Stovall, Taj Mahal. Pat Thomas, Ike Turner, Othar Turner, Mike Vernon, Mose Vinson, Dick Waterman, Brad Webb and Venessia Young.

In America and particularly in Memphis and Mississippi, people showed us extraordinary kindness. Regena Bearden, David Nicholson, Valerie Parker and Denise Dubois Taylor from the Memphis Convention and Visitors Bureau were brilliant, as was Steve Martin from the State of Mississippi Tourism Office. The Clarksdale Chamber of Commerce and the Tourism Office in Oxford, Mississippi guided us. James Butler and Bill Talbot at the Hopson Preservation Company were hospitality itself. The Blues Foundation, Judy Peiser, Larry Nager, Sherman Cooper, Scott Barretta, Craig Braasch at Northwest Airlines, Lisa Chaffey at Continental Airlines, Wendy McDarris, Robert Birdsong and Billy Johnson in Leland all helped in various ways. Jane Rule Burdine has been with the project for a long time, her local knowledge and her brilliant photography have helped make this a better book.

In the music industry there have been many generous people who have added to the creation of this book, not least those record labels that do such brilliant work in keeping the Blues alive. In particular Russell Beecher at Catfish, Edward Chmelewski at Blind Pig Records, John O'Toole at Charly, David French at Frog and most of all Gary Atkinson and everyone at Document Records. Amongst the larger labels we have had help from Larry Cohen at Sony Music, Andy McKaie at Chess/Universal, and our old friend Klaus Schmalenbach at BMG in Germany. Ken Smith at Red Lick Records has been great, as has Maggie Woodward, Donal Gallagher, Paul Swinton and Bruce Bastin.

We must offer thanks to the hundreds of blues archivists and writers who have done such sterling work over the last 40 years or more in researching, annotating and analysing the Blues. Their work has helped us to write this book and some in particular must be mentioned. Tony Russell, Mick Brown, Paul Oliver and Peter Guralnick are all very different writers and all very good. The discographies published by Paul Pelletier at Record Information Services have proved very useful. Messrs Dixon, Goodrich and Rye and their publication *Blues and Gospel Records 1890-1943* has been referred to many thousands of times, it is a work of staggering proportions.

At Ripple, Karen Kearne-Moxey, Penny Thompson, Sally Ann Kenneally, Bruce Clarke, Mike and Julie Haugh and Stephen Wyman have all gone that extra mile. Howard Siegal in New York and Tony Panico in London have also done their bit. Terry Taylor has been a constant source of encouragement, help and back up when we have flagged.

At Dorling Kindersley our editorial team headed by Anna Kruger and Lee Griffiths have been wonderfully supportive, long suffering and always there. Richard Evans is a brilliant designer and all his team have done a fantastic job in setting new standards for music books. Peter Doggett's editorial skills have been stretched, while Jake Woodward, Mike Evans, Emily Hedges, Mike Edwards, Lynne O'Neill and Fiona Allen have all been such a great help. A big thank you to Simon Jollands and Christopher Davis who have been there from the start and stayed with us. Special thanks also to Russell Jarman Price (we couldn't have done it without you).

Finally Bill's wife, Suzanne and children, Matilda Mae, Jessica Rose and Katherine Noel and Richard's partner Christine Firth have all been long suffering... we love you and we couldn't have done it without you.

Bill Wyman and Richard Havers,
London and the Scottish Borders,
August 2001.

101
102